D1097953

A MAN OF INFLUENCE

Also by J.L. Granatstein

The Politics of Survival: The Conservative Party of Canada 1939-45
Peacekeeping: International Challenge and Canadian Response
Conscription in the Second World War
Marlborough Marathon: One Street Against a Developer
Forum: Canadian Life and Letters 1920-70. Selections from the Canadian
*   Forum*
Canada Since 1867: A Bibliographical Guide
Canadian-American Relations in Wartime: From Great War to Cold War
Canada's War: The Politics of the Mackenzie King Government 1939-45
Mackenzie King: His Life and World
Broken Promises: A History of Conscription in Canada
American Dollars/Canadian Prosperity: Canadian-American Economic Rela-
*   tions 1945-50*

A
MAN
OF
INFLUENCE

Norman A. Robertson
and Canadian Statecraft
1929-68

J.L. Granatstein

DENEAU
PUBLISHERS

This book has been published with the help of a grant from the Social Science Federation of Canada using funds provided by the Social Sciences and Humanities Research Council of Canada.

Canadian Cataloguing in Publication Data
Granatstein, J.L., 1939–
A man of influence

Bibliography: p.
Includes index.
ISBN 0-88879-046-5

1. Robertson, Norman A., 1904–1968.
2. Civil service – Canada – Biography. I. Title.

FC621.R62G72   971.064'3'0924   C81-090044-0
F1034.3.R62G72

©Deneau Publishers & Company Ltd. 1981

For Percy and Harriet Hitchcock

Contents

Preface

NORMAN ROBERTSON WAS one of that exceptional group of civil servants who provided the ideas and advice that turned Canada into a modern nation. From the 1930s on, Robertson and his colleagues, a group that included O. D. Skelton, Clifford Clark, Graham Towers, W.A. Mackintosh, Hume Wrong, Lester Pearson, Robert Bryce and a dozen or so others, collectively brought to a civil service, which had previously been noted only for devotion to patronage, a discriminating and progressive understanding of economics, a strong Canadian nationalism, and a desire to have Canada assume its fit place in the world. The heyday of the mandarins largely coincided with the Liberal hegemony that lasted under Mackenzie King and Louis St. Laurent from 1935 to 1957, and their period of peak influence unquestionably came during and immediately after the Second World War.

So too with Norman Robertson. He had the most extraordinary career of any Canadian civil servant, filling the highest positions in the public service for twenty-five years. He worked closely with five Prime Ministers, offering advice and preparing policy for Mackenzie King, R.B. Bennett, Louis St. Laurent, John Diefenbaker and Lester Pearson, and accompanied Sir Robert Borden when that Prime Minister of the Great War period went to the League of Nations in 1930. In 1941, at the age of thirty-seven, he became Under-Secretary of State for External Affairs, the senior permanent position in the Department of External Affairs; following this, he was High Commissioner to Great Britain twice, Secretary to the Cabinet and Clerk of the Privy Council, Ambassador to the United States, and Under-Secretary once more during the Diefenbaker years and through the whole of the crisis over nuclear arms that eventually destroyed the Conservative government in 1963.

Such powerful positions in succession gave Robertson enormous and continuing influence throughout the government. During the 1930s he had been the aide closest to Dr. Skelton, "deputy prime minister" to both Bennett and Mackenzie King. On Skelton's death in 1941, Robertson became King's closest adviser, exercising influence on the entire range of Canadian war policy, domestic and external. After 1945, he played a major role in adapting his country to the new era and in developing the policies that created the prosperity that marked the booming postwar years in Canada.

In many ways, Robertson was the model civil servant. He wanted influence and sought constantly to exercise it, but he had no craving for power and none for the limelight. His role was to advise, and he performed that task superbly, offering his political masters the benefits of his well-stocked brain and his deep learning. His forte was the calm and well-considered judgment of policy, and his reputation in Ottawa—and in London and Washington—was enormous and unmatched by that of any other Canadian civil servant.

Yet despite his renown in the East Block, Robertson remained completely unknown to the general public and in some ways to his colleagues as well. He was a man of a scholarly bent, but he failed to complete the work for his doctorate and, for the last twenty-five years of his life, seldom wrote anything, not even memoranda or telegrams. He was noted for his indolence, particularly in his youth, but in a real sense worked himself to death. He supported close ties with Britain and the Commonwealth and strong economic links with the United States, and yet he was a confident and firm Canadian nationalist, untroubled by shibboleths and unafraid of taboos. He was by conviction a civil libertarian and a humanist, and yet was unafraid to bring the full power of the state to bear on those suspected of subversion. He was a man of contradictions, a gentle man who operated in the world of power and was comfortable in it, and yet one who remained somehow aloof from it.

Norman Robertson was first and foremost a civil servant. That profession today is routinely scorned, and bureaucrats are labelled as slothful featherbedders. But that was not how he saw it or lived it. To him, the public service was the highest of callings; to serve the nation, by offering the best advice he could to the government of the day, was his duty and his pleasure. Norman Robertson was proud of his calling and his colleagues, and felt it was a joy to have found a role where he could at once serve his country, use his intellect to the fullest, and be fulfilled in his work. He lived for his work and he did it supremely well.

This book is neither a full-scale biography of Norman Robertson nor a comprehensive history of Canadian policy during the years he served in the Department of External Affairs. The range of issues in which he involved himself was very broad indeed and by ro means confined to foreign policy, so I have had to be extremely selective in choosing which questions to treat here. Moreover, unlike some of his colleagues, Norman Robertson was not concerned with the way posterity treated him, and, as a result, his personal papers are very scanty. Indeed, after the 1920s he wrote few personal letters and kept copies of almost none. There are substantial collections of files in Departmental records, of course, but very often Robertson's views tend to disappear beneath the weight of telegrams, minutes and memoranda. Nonetheless, the bulk of the material on which this study is based is to be found in governmental records, on the papers left by Robertson's political masters, colleagues and friends, and from many interviews. Full details of sources are provided in the reference notes and bibliography of primary sources (pp. 387-476).

If I have been forced to study Norman Robertson largely through the material by him or concerning him in the papers of others, similarly I have been obliged to present relatively little detail on his private life. For the most part, this is a consequence of the difficulties with sources described above. But it was also Mrs. Norman Robertson's wish, and one that I have honoured. Both Robertson and his wife were private people, and I respect her desire to maintain that privacy. Norman Robertson deserves to be remembered for his deeds, and *they* are the focus of this book.

The subject-matter of this study was suggested to me by the Department of External Affairs, through the Director and Deputy Director of Historical Division, A.E. Hart and Dr. Don Page. The Department managed to secure my release from teaching duties at York University for one year, paid the costs of research, and forbore from trying to influence my work. Mr. Hart, his successor H.H. Carter, Dr. Page, and the officers of the Division assisted in myriad ways, not least in securing permission for me to sit in at a Round Table discussion on Norman Robertson arranged by the Governor-General, the late Rt. Hon. Jules Léger, and held at Government House in February 1978. Saul Gray, late of the Canadian High Commission in London, was also most helpful, as were a number of other officers of the Department.

I have been greatly assisted in my work by a very large number of men and women who granted me interviews and access to material they control. Those I interviewed are noted in the bibliography; those who granted access to papers were Mrs. N.A. Robertson, Mrs. C.H.A. Armstrong, Mrs. June Wrong Rogers, Louis Rasminsky, Dr. C.J. Mackenzie, Hon. J.W. Pickersgill, G.A.H. Pearson, H.B. Robinson, R.B. Bryce, Hon. Paul Martin, Hon. H.C. Green, Henry Borden, Douglas Le Pan, Mrs. A.D.P. Heeney, Professor Brian Heeney, Escott Reid, Mrs. A.F.W. Plumptre, Mme. Pauline Vanier, Mrs. J.J. Deutsch, William Herridge, Professor Claude Bissell, Professor George Glazebrook, Mrs. Watson Sellar, Galt MacDermot, the late Professor R.A. MacKay, Professor H.F. Angus, Floyd Chalmers, the Warden of Rhodes House, Oxford, the Librarian of Balliol College, Oxford, and the Brookings Institute, Washington. I also wish to acknowledge the permission of Her Majesty the Queen to examine some material in the Royal Archives, Windsor.

In addition, I was given access to a number of collections of records left by government departments and agencies. The Department of External Affairs opened all its files to me, except those relating to security and intelligence questions, and also gave me access to files retained at the Canadian Embassy in Washington. Michael Pitfield and the Privy Council Office allowed me to use records from the period when Robertson was Clerk of the Privy Council. The Bank of Canada, through its able archivist, Ms. Jane Witty, allowed me to use its papers, those of the Foreign Exchange Control Board, and those left by Graham Towers. I am most grateful for this unusual access, without which this book could not have been written.

In consequence, however, this study has been subjected to "vetting" on security grounds. The Department of External Affairs asked that two or three minor alterations be made, and I have accepted these.

A number of colleagues and friends, regrettably far too many for me to list completely, helped by sharing documents or reading sections of the work in progress. I must, however, thank Susan Houston, Ramsay Cook, Robert Bothwell, Blair Neatby, Norman Hillmer, Bill Young and Tilly Crawley. Mrs. Ardith Francis, Stanley Pollin, Terry Popowich, and Peter McGovern helped with research. Assistance was also given by Hon. J.W. Pickersgill, R.B. Bryce, H.B. Robinson, R.G. Robertson, D.V. Le Pan, G.A.H. Pearson and John Holmes, who read all or parts of the manuscript. Excellent editing was provided by Ramsay Derry and Jonathan Williams. They gave a sow's ear of a manuscript some of the refinements of a silk purse.

My wife, Elaine, and my children, Carole and Michael, as always have tolerated my lengthy absences doing research and my surliness when writing; Michael has even become an aide.

Finally I must express my gratitude to Mrs. N. A. Robertson for her continuing assistance throughout. Her pride in her husband and in his career is understandable, and much of interest and value in these pages is present because Mrs. Robertson uncovered material, suggested sources, or told it to me in a lengthy series of interviews that stretched over two years. I am very grateful to her.

One thing only remains to be said. The views expressed in this study of Norman Robertson are my own, as are any and all errors that remained after the warnings of my friends and colleagues.

J. L. Granatstein

Toronto. Summer 1980.

First Years

N ORMAN ROBERTSON'S FIRST trip overseas came in September 1923 when he went to England, at age nineteen, to take up his Rhodes Scholarship at Balliol College, Oxford. The passage across the Atlantic had been uncommonly rough, but Robertson had recovered in London, falling in love instantly with the great city. "Everything is wonderful," he wrote his parents in Vancouver, "and even I have trouble finding enough words to attempt to tell what it's like."[1] But there was one difficulty. Aboard ship, Robertson had loaned a friend £8 to allow him to take a cabin and then had bought some clothes and books in London. The result was that Robertson lacked the railway fare to get to Oxford and so had decided to walk.

Postcards home told the tale. "Left London in forenoon," he wrote on 8 October from Uxbridge, "& tramped hours through monotonous suburbs. You will be able to locate [Uxbridge] better than I. For I have neither guide book nor chart nor have I seen a map of England. . . ." The next day he was "25 miles from Oxford with 8s 6d capital. If careful will make it O.K. Glorious weather but have to buck stiff wind. Coat is heavy & chafes so am not making good time." On the 10th he left Stokenchurch—"a vile place"—at 9 a.m. "and reached Oxford 18 miles distant at 1:30 p.m. exactly four miles an hour which was not bad in the pouring rain that drenched and weighed down my coat." He had arrived at Balliol College with 1s 3d, "exactly 30 cents to my name,"[2] and must have been the first Rhodes Scholar to walk to the University.

I

Norman Robertson was born in Vancouver, British Columbia on 4

March 1904.[3] His parents, Lemuel and Floretta Robertson, were both Prince Edward Island Scots who separately had made their way west before the turn of the century.[4]

Lemuel Robertson had first left the Island to study Classics at McGill University under Sir William Peterson. He had proven himself a first-rate student in the class of 1899, and had left Montreal for the Pacific Coast to begin a career teaching high school. Vancouver had a tight little community of Prince Edward Islanders, and Robertson was quick to notice among them Floretta Macleod, a gay, very bright and attractive young woman with long dark hair and deep-set blue eyes. The Macleods had abandoned Orwell, PEI for Vancouver in 1890, and were established figures there, almost old-timers. Floretta was a good catch for the young teacher.

In 1901, Robertson became a Classics teacher at Vancouver College, a curious institution with both secondary school and university departments and, since 1899, affiliated with McGill University, which exercised a supervisory role and set the examinations.[5] In 1904, he took up the offer of a one-year lectureship from Principal Peterson at his alma mater, an offer that provided the chance to complete his Master of Arts degree. The difficulties of a trip across the country with a new baby must have seemed small in comparison to the benefits, and certainly Robertson settled in quickly. As the history of McGill University records, Lemuel Robertson "inspired the Principal with the idea of using McGill's resources and prestige to establish a McGill College beyond the Rockies." Robertson argued that the West was virgin territory for education, one that should be moulded by the universities of the East and by McGill in particular.[6] By November 1905, his idea had won the support of the McGill authorities, and in February 1906 the British Columbia legislature approved the necessary enabling legislation. Lemmy, as he was soon to be universally known to generations of British Columbia university students, became the first registrar of McGill University College of British Columbia, and Professor of Greek and Lecturer in Latin.[7] When the University of British Columbia was subsequently created from the McGill-sponsored college, Lemmy Robertson carried on there.

He soon established a reputation for being both a splendid teacher and something of a campus character. In some ways the classic absent-minded professor, apt to appear before classes in mismatched stockings,[8] he was nonetheless a university politician of some skill and an able administrator. He took his politics seriously, too. Robertson was a fierce Liberal partisan, never without a red tie to display his Grit leanings and, unlike many

English-speaking Liberals, remained loyal to Sir Wilfrid Laurier in the conscription election of 1917.[9] Despite his politics, Robertson managed to stay on good terms with provincial Tory administrations, and through his connections with the examining board, became a major figure in education on the coast. His circle of friends and acquaintances was very wide and many of his friends' sons later worked with Norman Robertson in Ottawa. Arnold Heeney, Hugh Keenleyside, Howard Green and Alfred Rive, to name only four men with whom Robertson worked, were all family friends from McGill or Vancouver.[10]

Thus, Norman Robertson's home was that of an established middle-class scholar and teacher. If a professor's pittance was tiny, there were always books, much good talk and continuous dinner-table discussion of politics and affairs. The Robertson household in short was almost an ideal one for a future civil servant. It was a happy family. In 1906, a sister, Mary, was born, followed by another, Barbara, three years later.

Norman was something of a prodigy. One story, handed down in family lore, illustrates this. In 1908 or 1909, Lemuel and his son went on one of their regular browsing trips to the downtown bookstores. The boy, fed on his mother's strong devotion to her ancestral homeland, fell in love with the illustrations in A.R. Hope-Moncrieff's *The Heart of Scotland* and desperately wanted his father to buy him the book. But the price was $3, a substantial sum to the Robertsons and a high price for a book in those days. Norman got his way, however, when he told his father that it was "just six 50¢ pieces."[11]

Floretta Robertson, a good Presbyterian, often tough in laying down the law to the children, was the dominant figure in the house, and Norman was closest to her. His mother had a mystical streak, sometimes thinking she was gifted with "second sight," but little of that or of her attachment to Scottish and Prince Edward Island ways passed down to Norman. His father had a sentimental attachment to heroes—Laurier, for one—and, in consequence, Norman found himself forced to the conclusion over time that he could never have serious discussions with him. But that was later, much later. As a boy, Norman admired his father, almost certainly picking up his scepticism about organized religion from Lemuel's quiet agnosticism. The message seemed to be: you had to attend church on Sunday and you had to be polite to the minister when he paid a call, but you didn't have to believe it all. Norman never did, and by his teens had already abandoned any formal beliefs, substituting for them a tough-minded rationalist perspective. He never felt any need for the crutch and comforts of religion, although the phenomenon of religious beliefs interested him because of the hold it had on people. On him, it had none at all.

That was still in the future, however, and Robertson's future did not seem particularly promising in his first years. The child was ill much of the time, and an early bout with infection left him almost completely deaf in one ear. In 1911-12 his father returned to Montreal and McGill for another year as a visiting professor, and there Norman nearly died of "scarlatina" or scarlet fever. Lemuel Robertson, duly thankful, wrote to friends at the College in Vancouver that the disease had cleared up, the period of quarantine was almost complete, and there were "no complications or ill effects of any sort . . . our boy is a bug catcher, but this time he seems to have relented some."[12] The illness, however, left Norman in weak condition, and when the family returned to Vancouver in the spring, Lemuel borrowed the money to buy a cottage on the North Arm of Burrard Inlet, a place where his son could recover his strength. "Sunshine", as the cottage was called, became an idyllic part of each year with swimming, rowing, canoeing, climbing and the teasing of his sisters as Norman's recreations.[13] His earliest extant letter, written to his mother when he was eleven, tells in good prose of typical times at "Sunshine":

Here's my diary to date. On Friday morning after dad went, Mary, Nelly and I rowed up to Broom Point. I landed and got some broom. I went all over the point while Mary and Nelly rowed around waiting for me. I found besides broom fox-glove and species of lily like a hyacinth but the flower came only on one side. . . .

I went down to the store to get some butter and eggs and when we came home I went in swimming. The water was cold and I only swam from one foot to the other. . . .

. . . Then Mary, Nelly and I rowed up to Brighton to get some apples to make apple sauce. There was [a] crowd of rough young men up there and the girls were scared and wouldn't land. I got a few apples but Mary and Nelly almost cried and were scared they'd be roasted on a fire up there so we decided to row up further and come back when they had gone. . . .[14]

Norman's early education was in the Vancouver public schools and then, for the usual three years, at King Edward High School. The boy's precocity was quickly spotted, and in his second year he was streamed into an advanced class that offered special instruction.[15] In his final year, 1918-19, he led his class of twenty-five in the fall term, standing first in Composition, English Literature, History and Greek, and scoring high 90s in Algebra and Geometry.[16] Unfortunately, he came down with diphtheria at the time of his finals and had to write the exams at home.[17] Nonetheless, he was ready for university at fifteen years of age.

The University of British Columbia that Norman Robertson entered in September 1919 was a small institution. Approximately thirty faculty taught a thousand or so students at the campus,[18] located not at the present and splendid Point Grey site but in the area of Vancouver bounded by 10th and 12th and Laurel and Heather Streets. The buildings were largely temporary (they were known as "the Fairview shacks"), and throughout the last year or so of Robertson's attendance at UBC the students waged a continuing campaign for the University to move to Point Grey.

Robertson was a tall, rather awkward boy, with a curious loping gait. He had a full head of dark hair, deep-set eyes like his mother, and a full, almost sensuous mouth. Although he looked even younger than his age, something that was particularly noticeable in a class with a substantial number of war veterans in its ranks, he was certainly a good-looking, even handsome, figure. Those of his classmates who had come with him from King Edward were all delighted that at last he had got rid of the knickers and long woollen stockings he had worn in his last year there.[19]

But if he was just out of his knickers, there was no doubt of the maturity of his mind or his firm convictions. Robertson had grown up through the unrest and turmoil of the Great War in Vancouver, and had watched the developments in Russia and Europe as Communism spread with amazing rapidity among the ruins. Not unnaturally, his views had been affected, and the young man already considered himself a socialist, itself a mark of maturity among colleagues, some of whom were probably almost unaware that such a doctrine existed. The Robertson family, however, was sympathetic and liberal: Mary was taken to radical meetings by her brother, and his maternal grandmother had even voted socialist in a provincial election, "for Norman's sake".[20]

Still he was probably socially immature.[21] Certainly, he was tone deaf and "couldn't dance worth sour apples," or so his sister Mary recollected,[22] and his occasional dates were not always great successes.[23] But he enjoyed parties, and could talk brilliantly, something that attracted toward him a group of male and female friends, including Alfred Rive, Harry Cassidy and J.V. Clyne. He was very precise in his speech, with a reserved manner that seemed never to allow him to open up except to those with whom he was close. His friends never doubted his first-class abilities and were in some awe at the speed and thoroughness with which he read his way through the library shelves[24] and still managed to take an active part in class activities. [25]

Nor was Robertson narrow in his interests. Before he left UBC, he was heavily involved in the Men's Literary Society, the Student Parliament, the Letters Club, the Historical Society, the Classics Club, the Economics Discussion Club, the Social Science Club, the Student Council, the Literary and Scientific Department, and the Student Socialist Society.[26] Undoubtedly he was best known for his politics. On 2 December 1920, the *Ubyssey*, the student newspaper, reported on the establishment of the Student Socialist Society—under the headline "Come on, Reds." Robertson had been elected vice-president, it was decided "that any ladies interested in socialism would be permitted to become members," and J.S. Woodsworth, a new Labour Member of Parliament, was invited to address the Society. Woodsworth did come and, according to legend, lost his dentures in the middle of his remarks, but picked them up and missed not a word.

The next year, the Opposition in UBC's Mock Parliament was led by Harry Cassidy, later a distinguished social scientist and an unsuccessful candidate for the leadership of the Ontario Liberal Party. Robertson acted as his chief lieutenant,[27] and also participated in a "heated discussion" on Ireland at the Historical Society.[28] He even won great success at debating, something that might astonish those who recollect Robertson's later agonizing about the speeches which his duties forced him to deliver. The *Ubyssey* reported on 9 February 1922 that Cassidy and Robertson had defeated the senior class' debaters, arguing the affirmative side of the question, "Resolved that the railways of Canada should be nationalized,"* and a year later the same duo won again, arguing against the resolution "that the French were justified in the occupation of the Ruhr valley."[29] Political questions fascinated him, and there seemed justification for the descriptive doggerel in the 1921 yearbook:

---

* The *Seventh Annual of the U.B.C.* (1922) reported on this debate in the traditional and obscure style of yearbooks, (p.35): "Ex-King Harry and 'Red' Robertson did defeat the traditional enemies of the Tribe of Twenty-three in a battle of tongues concerning the tribal ownership of the Iron Trails. 'Red' of the tribe of the Bolshevike [*sic*] is also the King of the Social Sciencers and a singer of the chant called 'Hallelujah, I'm a bum, bum'".

In the discussion on the Literary and Scientific Department (p.104), it was noted that Robertson always sat at the end of the table. "One of the most remarkable features of the conference is that motions are sometimes made by others despite severe competition experienced from this quarter. We believe that even the Versailles Conference had its Robertson."

The soul of Norman doth aspire
To dreams of high desire.
Tis not on marks his hopes are laid,
Nor yet sweet charms of a maid,
The passion which his soul has swayed,
The cause of all his youthful fire—
Protection and Free Trade![30]

Norman Robertson was not moved only by political debate. In the fall of 1921 he was elected to membership in the Letters Club, a select group of ten male and ten female undergraduates, selected by faculty members from among many applicants. The Club was the leading intellectual group on campus, devoted to the pursuit of literature through the presentation of learned papers and discussion. As an "astounding early phenomenon," he was a natural selection for the Letters Club.[31]

Robertson gave a paper on H.G. Wells to the Club in November 1921.[32] More than thirty pages long, it was based on a thorough reading of Wells's already vast *oeuvre*, was well-written and argued, and all the more remarkable for being done on an extra-curricular basis. In it, critically but fairly, Robertson looked at Wells's attitudes, his protests at convention and society, his rejection of absolute values and, in the process, at his own state of mind at the age of seventeen. Conservatism, Robertson wrote in a paragraph that closely followed Wells, was the "residuary legatee of all anti-intellectual movements," that

unintelligent, uncritical adherence to things as they are simply because they are— they exist. It is not at first start apparent how the bare fact of an object's existence, endows it with an odor of sanctity, renders it immune from criticism. We make a fetish of the absolute, of what exists; because an institution has somehow or other come to exist, men attach to it a particular significance. Such significance is not dependent on the merits or demerits of the object. Its latent potentialities for service or disservice are apparently irrelevant. The fact that it is, that it exists is alone of significance. . . .

A confident and unreasoning belief that this is the best of all possible worlds, that somehow or other, our traditional institutions and habits of thought will always and in all circumstances carry us through . . . is the slovenly creed of the herd mind.

Toward the end of his paper, Robertson reminded his listeners that, however harsh his criticism of the writer, "When one remembers that

Wells's real concern is for the future of humanity, for social betterment, such criticism . . . seems petty, carping and ignoble. He suffers more than the rest of us do," he continued in a flash of self-appraisal, "because he has the constructive imagination which can place along side our present social disorder a vision of rational order." And finally to this peroration: "There are no absolute values in anything; just in so far as anything has a collective significance, just in so far does it signify to H.G. Wells."

This paper was an extraordinary performance for a youth still in his middle teens. It was based on a vast acquaintance with political writing, psychology and literature, and Robertson had marshalled the evidence and presented his arguments in a fashion that would have done credit to many a doctoral candidate.

There must have been an air of inevitability, therefore, when at the end of his third year Robertson was elected president of the Literary and Scientific Department, the umbrella body governing all student cultural activities. "Mr. Robertson is well qualified for the post he is to hold," *Ubyssey* said on 30 March 1922. "He is an effective debater, and is famous for his argumentative abilities. He has been the moving spirit in the formation of a number of clubs and societies. . . . This is evidence of the fact that he is always doing something."* He was a powerful figure in his class, and H.F. Angus, his professor in government and economics, was probably correct, if a bit tart, in saying that Robertson's fellow students "have a very great, probably an exaggerated respect for his ability and for his debating power which gives him a good deal of influence with them."[33]

Still, he was at the university to get an education, and here too he succeeded. By his own choice, Robertson took a pass course, preferring the freedom to range—to choose those courses that interested him. In his first year, his least successful at UBC, he studied English, History, Greek, Latin, Algebra, Geometry, Trigonometry and Physics (in which he took a bare pass). The next year he took Economics, Geology, English, Greek and Latin. In his final two years, Economics, Philosophy and Government dominated his timetable, as he took first-class honours and tied for first place in the pass course.[34]

His UBC career had been a brilliant one, and his Rhodes Scholarship,

---

* The *Eighth Annual of the U.B.C.* (1922-23) noted (p.83) that Robertson had conducted the Literary and Scientific Department's affairs "on strictly soviet principles, with a very dictatorial proletarian in the chair. What has been lost in deliberation has been made up in disputes."

announced in the *Ubyssey* on 23 November 1922, merely put the cap on it. His letters of recommendation had been impressive. Stuart Schofield, his Geology professor, said that Robertson's work was of such high order "that I had hoped he would follow geology as his life work. . . ." Angus noted that his intellectual capacity was high and he was "capable of doing very fine work in any sphere which can command his whole-hearted interest." T.H. Boggs, Professor of Economics, called Robertson brilliant and assessed his "mental and moral qualities" as being such as to "guide him to esteem the performance of public service as his highest aim," an assessment that was directly on target. Boggs admitted that Robertson was not "proficient in athletics,"[35] the sole area at UBC in which he had not shone.* But he seemed the natural winner of the Scholarship, and although some of his fellows rather resented his carrying off the fellowship at eighteen, there was nonetheless an element of tribute behind the joshing, when his classmates presented him with a bouquet of vegetables at a class party just after the award's announcement.[36] He had earned his laurels—and cabbages and carrots.

He had probably also earned Jack Clyne's ribbing tribute in the biographical sketch that appeared in the Class of '23 Yearbook:

Norm. is our ultra-radical prodigy—a brilliant student, a successful debater and an indefatigable talker. The Rhodes scholar for 1923 is President of the L.S.D. and injects some pep into the proceedings, we hear. The interests of the 'hoi-polloi' are very near his great, big, bursting heart. We hear that there is a young Freshette who really has taken over some of the masses' share. Norm. is at frequent intervals overcome by the fair sex's interest in him. He is doing the 'social stint' in a brilliant manner this year and often drops his studies even for the men of his class.[37]

By March 1923, Robertson had learned that he had been elected to Balliol College, his and his father's choice. This had been arranged, in part at least, because of the efforts of Professor W.N. Sage of UBC.[38] Moreover, with his Bachelor of Arts degree already in hand, Robertson had been given "senior standing," which entitled him to begin in Oxford's second year.[39] What course he would follow—Greats, perhaps, with its

---

* J.V. Clyne, who had also sought the Rhodes Scholarship, had told Robertson that he needed more sports to get the award (as Robertson had told him he needed more academic work) and persuaded him to turn out for inter-class rugger. Within the first few minutes of the game, Clyne said, Robertson had broken his arm in a scrum. (Clyne interview, 30 April 1978). Presumably such participatory zeal must not have hurt with the selection committee.

requirement of Greek and Latin, or Modern Greats with its emphasis on Philosophy, Politics and Economics—was still unclear.

Robertson set off for Oxford in mid-September. The initial stage was a train journey from Vancouver eastwards, a trip of some days marked by breaks in Winnipeg, Toronto and Montreal, and visits to family friends. "Had a wonderful day in Winnipeg," Norman wrote from the train, "dinner all over the town, exhibited to all Islanders. . . ."[40] In Montreal he visited his father's old McGill friend, Andrew McMaster, then Liberal MP for Brome. McMaster gave him letters of introduction to John W. Dafoe of the *Winnipeg Free Press* and to Dr. O.D. Skelton, the Queen's University professor, both of whom were en route to the Imperial Conference with Prime Minister Mackenzie King and travelling on the *Montcalm*, the ship that was also to carry Robertson to England. McMaster wrote to the Robertsons in Vancouver that their boy "is so young and eager. . . . I do not know whether I ever met anyone who was so utterly free from self consciousness and could make himself at home so readily without at the same time possessing the slightest forwardness or too great self possession."[41] Robertson also wrote glowingly of his reception by McMaster, adding that his host's politics were almost "straight labour," that he "does not admire King enormously," and that he believed "our imperial policy is to be dictated by Wall Street and Imperial oil."[42]

The crossing on the *Montcalm* was terrible, with storms pitching and tossing the ship. Robertson suffered greatly and in his last letter home from aboard ship said: "It is certain beyond possibility of doubt that I am never coming home again."[43] A later and longer letter, written from Balliol, filled in the detail. He had gone to see Dr. Skelton, he wrote, and found him "extremely dull and if he isn't saturated clean through with dullness then he was also rather discourteous." Dafoe, however, was "extremely pleasant agreeable & talkative." Unfortunately, he failed to meet the Prime Minister.

But I did hear him speak very volubly for a good half hour in between two parts of a concert program. He orated on the perils of the deep (the concert was in aid of Sailors' orphans and dependents). We called it the 'Widow in every port' Fund. He was very eloquent and all inclusive. He does not apparently know that there is such a thing as selection. For he left nothing out. When he made some complimentary reference to members of the ship's passenger list he scrupulously strove to avoid any invidious distinction by going through the whole ship's list—omitting no group, profession or interest therein represented & referring to each in cumbrous circumlocutions that he invented with real agility.

If you want to understand King you should spend a little while pondering over the diagrams at the back of 'Industry & Humanity'. In my judgment they afford a genuine clue to his mind or more accurately soul. For he is very pious & thinks like a theosophist. Very decent, kindly democratic—hopelessly undistinguished. . . . For King really has a wonderful vocabulary plus a peculiar knack of infusing a real but pathetic emotion into such phrases as Brotherhood of man, humanity, fellowship, etc. His mind seems to travel in the Harding groove but with infinitely greater facility and speed than that worthy ever possessed.

I'm told he makes a wonderful impression over the radio. Shorn of his seediness he might go far.[44]

Dull and seedy perhaps. But King and Skelton were to become the two dominant figures in Robertson's life, the men with whom he worked most closely in the Department of External Affairs and to whom he owed his rapid advance in the Department and in influence. Still, his comments on Mackenzie King's book and the way it revealed King's soul were extraordinarily accurate. Could any other nineteen-year-old Canadian have made them?

II

Oxford at the beginning of the 1920s was smack in the middle of a period of decay. Professor Vincent Bladen remembers being told in 1918 by a distinguished economist who came to Oxford to tutor the few students interested in the subject "that the examiners might not have read Marshall so that I must be careful in criticizing Mill." "What a sad light," Bladen adds, "this throws on the state of economics at Oxford."[45] And Sir John Hicks, the Nobel laureate in Economics, remembered that philosophy too was blighted, the ancients holding sway and the modernists nowhere to be found.[46] Other memoirs of the period comment critically on the paucity of required academic work. Peter Quennell, the writer who was a classmate of Robertson's at Balliol (along with Graham Greene and Anthony Powell), wrote that "my academic tasks were confined to the preparation of a weekly essay."[47] Evelyn Waugh, another contemporary, estimated that "At least half of the undergraduates were sent to Oxford simply as a place to grow up in."[48]

Nor were conditions good. Quennell found his Balliol rooms meagrely furnished and painted "a dark, depressing brown"; the Dean of the College was a notorious homosexual, and too much drinking was one of the curses of the institution.[49] Above all, perhaps, was the pervasive class feeling. It was not as bad as it had been before the war, when J.M. Macdonnell, a Canadian Rhodes Scholar and later a cabinet minister, wrote of Balliol that the Eton boys had separate tables in the dining hall and felt superior to all. "They look on me," Macdonnell quoted one public school graduate from an unfashionable institution, "just like a workman out on the street."[50] That class prejudice had moderated by 1923, but it was still strong enough to shake any graduate of a Canadian university.

All this awaited Robertson as he walked through the rain into Oxford on 10 October 1923. He was, perhaps, not quite what Wilfred Sheed would later describe as "a quintessential Rhodes scholar: absolutely average in looks, mind, and bodily hygiene";[51] he was possibly closer to fitting Robertson Davies's remark that "Education in England spoils so many Canadians—except Rhodes Scholars who come back and get Government jobs right away."[52] Certainly he did not fit Sheed's "average" model in looks—his powerful chest and shoulders gave him an almost lopsided look when contrasted with his thin legs. And certainly, as we have seen, there was nothing average about his mind. As for his bodily hygiene, no records survive.

Robertson arrived at Balliol tired but still game, turning immediately to attempting "to make my rooms look as if they might have been lived in." His first meetings with Oxford men left him "still sanguine of keeping my end up in competition of any sort."[53] Two days later he wrote his sister that, after meeting other Canadian Rhodes Scholars, "I've come to the conclusion that I would sooner have gone to UBC than any place in Canada...." He also offered some off-the-cuff and instant assessments of certain fellow students, who, because of his career in the Department of External Affairs, would turn into friends. George Glazebrook "is from Toronto—over on his own & quite anglicized but amiable." David Johnson "is from MacGill [sic]...Gov. General's medalist with all the earmarks. A very good head but strictly limited interests."[54]

Another letter home on 15 October (at this stage of his life, if no other, Robertson was a prolific letter writer) gave the news:

This P.M. went to Chapel... my latest problem in Conduct. How shall I hit a happy medium between discourtesy as refusal to take part in service would be— and downright hypocrisy as a semblance of genuine participation in it would be as assuredly?

Have seen my tutor & decided on Mod. Greats with Italian for language on tutor's advice. Very nearly lapsed into Greats at last minute. They told me that I'd have no trouble & little work to clean up in it but that Mod. Greats would entail a vastly greater volume of reading plus a wider field to prepare for examinations. I nearly succumbed but held on. . . ."[55]

A few days later, Robertson observed shrewdly that "Oxford economics seems rather academic, detached, unreal," adding that "I've got to be careful all the time over here to ward off the contagion of sleeping sickness that does seem to hang over Oxford. Balliol has a reputation of comparative immunity. But such a rep. is a frightful commentary on other colleges."[56] And there was a touch of nationalism: "Threw consternation into ranks of the natives by declining to join Colonial Club here. I have neither time nor particular desire but rather shocked them by explaining that as a Canadian I was ineligible. . . . Despite all guff to the contrary," he appended, "English freshers . . . much like Canadians of same age. As yet have developed no inferiority complex."[57] That, at least, was more than obvious from his letters. He was also appraising Oxford. "This tacit acceptance of 'good form'," he wrote his father, "of compliance in a delightful but unreal convention seems to me the worst thing about Oxford . . . the polite fiction that 'taste' is the ultimate arbiter in social and political life. . . ."[58]

But critical as Robertson's spirit was, that first Oxford term was highly enjoyable. He was rowing "Torpids", the aptly named second-string boats that were "clinker-built eight-oar monsters . . . with fixed seats and rowlocks, which were supposed to be mandatory training for manning a racing, sliding-seat eight without putting a foot through the bottom." The Torpids, J.M. Minifie, a 1923 Oriel College Rhodes Scholar from Saskatchewan, later remembered, were "murderous brutes. . . . They had to be thrashed along with a quick stroke, which was detrimental to sliding seat style, tending to make novices bucket forward in a rhythm which neutralized the drive of their oars."[59] The one benefit of Robertson's rowing career was that he got better food at the training table than most of his peers received at theirs. Still the rowing was a strain: "I felt very rotten at close—quite ill in fact but exercised my usual self control & came through"—but clearly he was proud of it.[60] There was even some work: "had to settle down immediately after dinner to write an essay on Spinoza for Monday morning. . . . Worked frantically until midnight when couldn't see paper any longer. I was a bit nervous about the result but tutor seemed well pleased."[61] That tutor was John Macmurray, the Jowett lecturer in Philosophy, who with C.R. Morris, a Classicist, was responsible for Robertson.[62]

For his first "vac," Robertson went off to Paris to hole up in a small hotel in the *6e arrondissement*. It was his first visit and he revelled in walking around the city, browsing in the bookshops (at Sylvia Beach's he bought a copy of Joyce's *Ulysses*),[63] and in trying, vainly, to improve his spoken French. He could read tolerably, he said, but "can no more think French than fly.... Today [shopping] I got dates, ammoniated quinine (my supreme achievement), aspirin, cough drops and two meals. Not bad, but what a sweat."[64] On another occasion, as his Balliol friend Denis Brogan later wrote, Robertson was "sitting having a drink outside the Renault plant.... As the men came out on their bicycles, he shouted, 'Workers of the world unite. You have nothing to lose but your chains.' This frivolous quotation of the sacred text was not well received by the *proletaires*."[65]

His letters home continued, offering his family his developing views on Oxford, education and his future. One from Paris noted that he had just read Bertrand Russell's *ABC of Atoms*, the beginning of a life-long admiration for Russell's work. He was attracted to Russell, he said, but without chemistry and mathematics how could he properly tackle philosophy? "The more I read the more I think that mathematical logic is the proper method for dealing with the problems of philosophy. And alas the more I work at mathematical logic the more conscious I am that I...can never know enough mathematics to be a useful philosopher. This, of course," he could not forbear from adding, "makes no difference at Oxford where they pride themselves on their humanism which seems to be a polite name for loose and inaccurate thinking." Then he turned to his future:

You needn't worry about my staying in [England]. I shall clear out as soon as I decently can. If I was a free agent I would come back to Vancouver to live.... The odd things that were irritating at home and that I thought I'd dodge by running away to Europe have turned out not [to] be local irritants after all. They have little here that cannot be got in America and the people I've met are neither keener nor more alert.... The truth is that among other things I'm a bit disappointed in the work. So far it seems pointless and the Dons have no more notion of that preamble to Mod. Greats in the Oxford Calendar meaning anything, than fly [*sic*].... I want sometime or other to work with men like Russell. If I can't work with him over here I shall come back to America and plough ahead on my own.[66]

In the same reflective mood, he wrote from Paris to his Vancouver friend Alfred Rive, who was planning to come to England for a year of study. Where should he do Economics? Rive had asked. Certainly not Oxford,

Robertson advised. Better go to London or Cambridge, he said, offering chapter and verse for his views. As for himself,

... if as seems not unlikely I shall go into Economic work at home, it is not with matters like these [the fields practised by the "scientific Liberals of the Cambridge Economics school"] that I shall bestir myself. It is not just a question of preference and interest. Useful work in economics needs a capacity for rigorous and sustained hard thinking that I do not believe I have. I have got heaps of sympathy and enthusiasm and little besides.... However, I still think that the difficulties of labor in industry, the interlocking problems of hours of work, living standards, adequate leisure can only be tackled from an angle far removed from the Cambridge approach.

That was what he wanted to work at, Robertson said, suddenly slipping into a critical self-analysis of his motives that was usually foreign to him:

Perhaps a misguided & prejudiced romanticism has numbed any capacity for judgment I ever had. A man has no right to go into a science like economics who feels quite irrationally that whatever the particular circumstances may be, 'the workers are always right.' I'm not a worker. If I'm lucky I never shall be. I've no vested interest in persecution or oppression per se and I can't adduce a single moral principle in support of my opinions. But the bias is there. I feel that however badly the workers may be led, whatever tactical blunders they or their leaders may commit, still in the long run the Lord is on their side. This is the only question in the world about which I ever cared.... This queer absorption in a rather remote and intellectual problem has warped and twisted everything I think or do.... It is not difficult to trace the prejudices that have made me a realist or better a Russellite in Philosophy to the odd passion that's made me a radical....

What complicates matters and makes me essentially ineffectual is that I am a thoroughgoing sceptic. People used to tease me about being young and cynical. I couldn't help it. It has meant a deal of denial to me. I've not been able to share in most of the things of life that people call good because I had the unhappy capacity of looking at myself and the things I did from the outside.... In every part of living I'm a cynic.... It's a chronic condition that stultifies most decent ordinary animal herd instincts. And it will someday or other include the labor movement within its sphere of influence.... I don't know how I'll end up but I have a vague fear that sometime my radicalism will vanish. Already I know I can't be a revolutionary. It is a physical impossibility for me to believe absolutely in any side on any issue. And yet one must take sides.... This I know well to be wrong. But I swear I shan't sit on the fence.[67]

This was a most perceptive letter, one that rigorously analyzed Robertson's ideas and that foreshadowed his gradual shift toward the political centre. That scepticism of which he was aware, that inability to accept any revealed truth as fixed or final, were traits he displayed all his life.

With his vacation finished, Robertson returned to Oxford for his second term, bringing with him two bags filled with the books he had purchased in Paris.[68] His first chore on his return was an examination on the History of Philosophy, followed by extensive reading on Ethics and Economics. "I have to do an essay on Trade Unions' legal aspects prior to 1875," he wrote his sister, " . . . and another essay on Naturalistic Ethics. . . ."[69] That did not seem too heavy a load, but he was voluntarily sitting in on fifteen lectures a week and rowing each afternoon. The lectures were dreadful—"dull and uninspiring," he said of a course in Modern Realism, " . . . for ten days now the lecturer has never been within striking distance of his subject."[70] That, in fact, was becoming his general view of Oxford. His Economics tutor did nothing but correct grammar and his Ethics tutor was ignorant and quarrelsome. "From the point of view of work & dons the Rhodes is a bust. I wouldn't cross the street to listen to any of these men."

He clearly did not cotton on to his tutors, nor they to him,[71] something that was readily apparent when Robertson received his first "hand-shaking" or report on his work. He had been rated as solid and satisfactory, rather heavy and ponderous, too serious, and told that he would likely earn only a good second. The road to a first, he was told, was work and play, a judgment that to Robertson seemed "uncommonly obtuse."[72] It was in fact directly on target. Still, the second term was a difficult one, and in desperation over the course of his work, he determined to list Economics as his major for the "schools" or degree examinations. Considering his views on the state of the dismal science at Oxford, his desperation must have been very great indeed.

The one triumph of that first year came in rowing, when Robertson's Torpids crew "bumped" or defeated the Balliol first boat, "something which has never been done before."[73] The best education came in Florence during the spring vacation, when he had the chance to see Fascism in action and to watch the brutality with which Mussolini ran an election while simultaneously showing the "consummate effrontery" of appealing "to the Spirit of Mazzini."[74] And there were his friends at Oxford, men such as Arnold Heeney, the son of his father's McGill friend, Bertal Heeney. Arnold was "quite the most prosperous looking Rhodes scholar in Oxford."[75] There was Dave Johnson, now "my best friend from Canada,"[76] Graham Spry, like Heeney a Manitoba Rhodes Scholar, and Denis Brogan, "quite a terrific talker, without exception the best read person I've come across in Balliol ... a wonderful gift of explicit reference."[77] And closest of all was John Hicks, a future Nobel prizewinner in Economics, and one who shared Robertson's views on the dons, economics and Oxford.[78]

The summer of 1924 Robertson passed largely in London, and the second year at Oxford began with "collections", a series of examinations on which he did well. There was even a chance to meet the great anarchist leader Emma Goldman, to breakfast with her, and to help smuggle her aboard the Balliol barge on which a red flag was then hoisted.[79] There were ruminations on his Canadian colleagues:

... fear I'll never be a successful Anglo-Canadian. ... Can't think any domestic revolution during the next five terms can make me share their opinions on a single controversial question. ... Really the 'Oxford manner' is the special prerogative of anglicized Canadians—it isn't anything they pick up at Oxford. Not at all—it's more or less conscious pose that they assume when they get back to Canada. Over here I'm quite a rabid imperialist & anglophile compared with most Canadians—but when they get home they'll begin to ape English externals—in voice and clothes and opinions with the usual disastrous effects.[80]

Neither Robertson nor his close Canadian friends would choose that course.

In March 1925 he moved out of College and into "digs". He was now cramming for "schools", a series of ten or a dozen examinations over two weeks. This was a difficult chore at any time, but one that in his disillusioned frame of mind Robertson found particularly trying. A complication was the impending visit of his parents, scheduled to arrive right in the middle of schools in June 1925.[81] Then there was the whole question of staying or not for a third year. He was "very much fed up with the actual work ... with myself & most Englishmen."[82]

The schools did not go well. One examiner on his *viva* told him: "You don't seem to have much natural piety, Mr. Robertson,"[83] a remark calculated to send him off shaking his head. Brogan wrote that Robertson's second-class result "annoyed him and continued to annoy him. It annoyed a good many other people, too, for the examiners ... that year ... were thought by the bright young men with whom I associated to be a lot less bright than the people they were examining."[84] Hicks also got only a second. There was almost certainly something to these complaints, but Robertson deserved some of the blame for his result. The report from Rhodes House, Oxford to the British Columbia Rhodes Scholarship selection committee noted Robertson's vigour and ability. But it also quoted a Balliol report that Robertson was a "little irresponsible".[85] Sir Francis Wylie, the Warden of Rhodes House, wrote confidentially—and accurately—that Robertson was a "very capable fellow, who should have done even better than he did. Did not perhaps quite settle down here— & remained a little too critical to get just the best out of the place."[86]

Nevertheless, Robertson reluctantly decided to remain for his third year, still angry about his second and determined to put off seeing his tutors as long as possible. He was reading on the history of the Canadian tariff, but he was "just waiting around until the boat goes."[87] He shared his rooms with Arnold Heeney and lived next door to his friend Dave Johnson and a New Zealander, W.P. Morrell, a congenial group of neighbours.[88]

The highlight of that last, wasted year was the great General Strike of 1926. "I was only in [London] two days," Robertson wrote to Vancouver, "escaped arrest and got back to Oxford." The strike was an error, he believed, "but once it was on it was war when one couldn't be neutral. So I did what I could. . . ."[89] What he had done, apparently, was to work in London in the offices of the *Daily Worker*, the Communist newspaper, or so Arnold Heeney, who was on the other side of the lines, recollected.[90]

The strike ended just before Robertson returned to Canada after three years abroad. He had changed and matured; the man of twenty-two was not the same boy of nineteen who had crossed the Atlantic in 1923. He had been unhappy with the training he had received at Oxford, but the university had nonetheless shaped and polished him. Oxford had confirmed the eclectic quality of his mind and had strengthened his humanism; it had also given him that special assuredness that only Balliol men seemed to possess, and he had made a number of friends and many contacts that later were to be of value to him. In addition, his time at Balliol had forced him to make up his mind on a wide range of questions on morals, religion, politics, and the Empire. He was no fanatic—what cynic and sceptic could be?—and he had shaped his own responses to every question. His friend Hicks recalled more than fifty years later that he had learned about intellectual courage from Robertson, a fine epitaph for anyone.[91] Clearly if Robertson had learned much, he had taught something too, perhaps enough to justify historian Denis Brogan's judgment that "Norman was the most remarkable of the group of Rhodes scholars I knew at Balliol in my time. . . ."[92]

III

But what was Robertson to do back in North America? In his time at Oxford he had become interested in Jacob Viner's work on international trade and Canada's foreign indebtedness—"although I did detect a slip in his figures that has thrown out a great many of his results"[93]—and he now thought he knew what he wanted to do: "to find out the history and result of the Canadian protective tariff and pick up a Ph.D. in the process."[94] He decided to seek a University of Chicago fellowship, but he also put out feelers to Harvard and Stanford as well and became interested in the new Brookings graduate school in Washington, D.C., where his UBC debating partner, Harry Cassidy, was finishing a doctorate.

The Robert Brookings Graduate School of Economics and Government had been functioning in Washington since 1924, training a small number of selected students for public service. Cassidy had strongly recommended Robertson to Walton Hamilton, the school's leading faculty member, and the application forms had been duly forwarded to Oxford.[95] Robertson in turn returned the forms in March 1926, listing his undergraduate courses in Economics in UBC, his studies at Oxford, his gainful occupations as "office boy, farm hand, and casual labourer," and his intended research:

I want to write the history of the Canadian Customs Tariff starting with the position of the several provinces under the British Trade and Navigation Acts— i.e., from 1763-1867. The second and most important period from 1878 includes the development of the "New National Policy" of Protection. The third phase (contemporary) is the present revolt of the Prairie Farmers against the established and generally accepted policy. My interest is first of all in the economic problems that the Canadian Tariff has created and only indirectly in the political history of our customs system.

That was a good subject. But what infuriated Professor Hamilton was Robertson's flip response to the question, "What are the shortcomings which you have perceived in your scholarly efforts so far?" "Chiefly indolence."[96]

"Frankly," Hamilton wrote on 31 March, "we think much better of you than we do of your application. From the testimony of persons who know you well, I am quite persuaded of your interest, your qualities, and your promise, but the application strikes me as a rather off-hand and ill-considered performance...."[97] Academics were more forthright in those days. Somewhat chastened, Robertson replied that his application "was apparently an unfortunate botch." He could not resist, however, saying that this was because he had been "asked what I thought were silly questions to which I probably gave rather casual answers. If it struck you as an off-hand performance I am very sorry . . . but somehow could not take questions about my 'Life Work' very seriously." In the circumstances, "I think I had better withdraw my application. . . ."[98]

But as well as Cassidy's enthusiastic advocacy, Hamilton had received a number of letters of recommendation which impressed him. A.D. Lindsay, the philosopher who was Master of Balliol, sang Robertson's praises, while S. Mack Eastman, an old British Columbia history professor then at the League of Nations, called him "much more intelligent than the great majority of post-graduate students. In many respects he is brilliant." Eastman, however, added shrewdly that "He appears something of a dilettante and I fancy it might mean quite an effort for him to get right down to some piece of grinding research work."[99] Those letters, as well as Robertson's explanation of and semi-apology for his application, did the trick, and a jubilant telegram from Cassidy conveyed the offer of a $750 fellowship. That was better than Chicago's offer of a $500 fellowship, and Robertson was quick to accept.[100]

But it was not to be. A greatly embarrassed Robertson wrote to Brookings on 14 June, just after his landing at Quebec, that personal reasons, most notably his mother's ill health and his three-year absence from home, had forced him to accept a one-year teaching position at UBC. "My family asked me to accept—so I am doing so." Brookings, he added, had already had more than enough to do "with the likes of me," but "if it would not be impudent to apply for a fellowship for the year 1927-1928 I would like to do so."[101] A man with the patience of Job, Hamilton made courteous reply and indicated that the application would be considered the following year.[102]

Robertson was appointed a Sessional Lecturer in Economics at UBC from 15 September 1926 to 15 May 1927, as a substitute for Professor Boggs, who was on leave. The salary was $200 a month, a respectable university pay at that time.[103] In Vancouver, Robertson met some new people, young instructors such as Fred Soward, and renewed acquaintance with former professors, including H.F. Angus. He was not, Professor Angus remembers, a marked success as a lecturer, but Robertson probably could have had a permanent appointment if that had been his choice.[104] In this year, he also joined the Canadian League, a small but, for a brief time, influential nationalist organization dedicated to fostering Canadian pride and countering sectionalism.[105]

Robertson's interest in the tariff survived the year's teaching, and he arranged a summer job with the Advisory Board on Tariffs in Ottawa, an appointment that did not preclude his accepting the fellowship that Brookings once again offered him. [106]

Ottawa was splendid. He quickly found Oxford friends such as Graham Spry, and friends of friends: Norman Rogers of Queen's University, temporarily working for Prime Minister King; John Stevenson, the *Times* of London correspondent and "the first friend I made in Ottawa"; [107] Russell Smart, an Ottawa lawyer and father of Elizabeth Smart, the novelist; and "a very intelligent and likeable man Col. something or other with whom I'm having dinner on Wednesday." [108] That turned out to be Colonel O.M. Biggar, a powerful lawyer and Smart's partner, the wartime Judge Advocate General and Canada's Chief Electoral Officer since 1920.

The friends were all pleasant and potentially helpful, but the truth was that the job had fallen through. " . . . I have been rather badly sold about this summer's work. They now offer clerical work—compiling figures at a clerical salary—rock-breaking as unemployment relief. I was very sore— but silent," he wrote, "so that business is over and done with." [109]

But luck was with him. Those connections made in his first days in Ottawa were good ones. A job was quickly found for him as a Temporary Principal Clerk in the Dominion Bureau of Statistics, then and for many more years under the leadership of Dr. R.H. Coats, one of the few intellectuals and genuinely able men in the public service at that stage. [110] Robertson's assigned task was to write a study of the Canadian textile industry, a pleasant enough chore and one that allowed his social life to flourish. "It is the pace that kills," he wrote to his sister Mary, "and I am driving the old machine at a giddy pace these days." [111] The nabobs of Ottawa were astonishingly accessible to the young Robertson, and he met Mackenzie King's Under-Secretary of State for External Affairs, O.D. Skelton, the first time since the *Montcalm* in 1923, at Coats's home one weekend. " . . . I must say that I've changed my mind about him," Robertson said. "Not as easy and casual as Coats and Biggar but a very good sort indeed." [112]

Clearly Robertson had impressed those he met. He had the proper credentials in his Oxford degree, but there was something about his mind and character that drew people to him, even much older men. That those men were in a position to assist him, to find him a summer's work at the Dominion Bureau of Statistics or to help him in his career, was a pleasant bonus, and Robertson was willing to sit and listen and to consider any opportunities that were presented to him. In a letter written from Washington a few days after his work had ended in Ottawa, Robertson said that Biggar, Stevenson and Mr. Justice Lyman Duff of the Supreme Court of Canada "have been taking thought together about my future and concur that my proper calling is the law. This isn't entirely an academic question since B[iggar] invited me to join him if ever I decided against University work."[113] It was a flattering offer—Biggar's firm was prosperous and there was no junior partner—but for the moment Robertson still thought of teaching as his career.

The Brookings Graduate School that Robertson entered in September 1927 was a tiny institution operating out of three houses on I Street. There were only half-a-dozen resident staff members,* but Associates included the likes of Isadore Lubin and Edwin Nourse and occasional lecturers such as Harold Laski, Charles Beard, Bronislaw Malinowski and Carl Becker. The students, too, were few. In 1926-27, the year before Robertson arrived, there were forty-three, a number that included some who would do well, such as Max Lerner and J.U. Nef.[114] The School's avowed purpose was to offer unusual opportunities for professional and cultural training in studies which had to do with the "control of a developing industrial society . . . to turn out craftsmen who can make contributions toward an intelligent direction of social change. . . ." Professor Hamilton was the leading permanent staff member, and his idea was that "The School should prefer the 'brilliant' lad, even though he is erratic, to the youth who is almost certain to do 'good' work. It should play for high stakes, even if this means a considerable increase in the 'hazards'."[115] Robertson answered that description to a tee.

His proposed written work at the School was to include his study of the tariff, as well as work on the "concept of productivity" and a "critique of the specific productivity theory of wages,"[116] and his intention was to emerge from Brookings with a doctorate. In addition to the writing, there were to be regular conferences with the faculty, directed reading and seminars, and a social life with a group of lively minds "just waiting for the New Deal."[117]

It was this that struck him instantly. His room was small, the food was

---

*How high the quality was was in some doubt. An investigation by Abraham Flexner in the summer of 1927 reported that the staff "of three men and a girl was hopelessly weak." The students' mock heroic song differed: " . . . The common man will humbly come/ To gaze on bended knee/ On that peer of intellectuals/ The Brookings Ph.D." (Brookings Inst. Records, R.G. Moulton, "The History of the Organization . . . ," mss. 1928, p. 21 and last page.)

good, and the "company I think first rate. Americans all very matey and chummy—me a bit distant I'm afraid but enjoying it. So all I have to do is sit down and write my book—what about God only knows.[118] That concern persisted but, except for a few residual (and surprising) twinges of affection for Oxford and England,[119] there was no doubt that he was having a fine time:

I'm rather tired this afternoon.... I've been doing some odd jobs for the Canadian Press and going about a good deal.... Yesterday I covered the armistice show in the morning and went out to Arlington for the unveiling of the monument in the afternoon [commemorating the war service of Americans with the Canadian forces]. It was a glorious day in a beautiful country and our troops and pipers cut a great figure before a big crowd. Ralston [Minister of National Defence in King's government] spoke well ... and I liked the cut of his jib. Last night I had tickets, complimentary, for the Military Ball in the Willard Hotel. It was a very curious show; very gay and brilliant but neither food nor drink—not even a prohibition punch bowl.... The orchestra broke off for breath twice: once to give the pipers the floor and once for prayers....

This morning I was down at the White House when Coolidge received the Canadian soldiers in the gardens. As an English journalist remarked at the time the last occasion on which British Troops entered the White House the President did not wait to receive them.[120]

Robertson's occasional jobs for the Canadian Press continued into the spring of 1928. "There is not much money in it nor is there much work either; but the practice is good and the connections useful." There were Canadian contacts as well. " ... I have to run along and get my old suit from the cleaners," he wrote in May 1928, "and trot up to see [Vincent] Massey [the Minister to the United States] this morning. Don't like him and can't stand Hume Wrong but the rest of the Legation outfit are very nice."[121] One of those opinions later changed radically.

And then there was Jetty, the girl Robertson had taken to the "very curious" military ball in November 1927:

To repair some errors of omission [he wrote home in February 1928]: Henriette Welling—Jetty—is a Hollander 24 years old, 5'7" or 8" in height—weighing I should guess about 130 lbs.—and generally sound in wind and limb—she is of the notorious moneyless middleclasses and hails from the Hague—and for the rest it is a long time since your errant son looked twice at a homely girl.[122]

Jetty lived at the Brookings residence but was not a student of the School. Instead she was in the United States on a Laura Spelman

Rockefeller scholarship in Economics, one that permitted and encouraged travel and study in various American centres; she planned to go to New York and Chicago before returning to the Netherlands in the summer of 1928. Robertson was not the only suitor for the hand of the "fascinating and flashy"[123] Miss Welling, and their relationship remained unresolved in June. "Jetty to whom I am not at the moment engaged left yesterday," Robertson wrote on 14 June. "...I would have been proud to marry [her]. However I have been reading a novel of André Gide's recently in which the writer is asked 'pourquoi un celibataire?' and gives the entirely adequate answer 'Oh... pour plus de la simplification.' "[124] By fall, however, matters had been arranged between the two, presumably after many letters and after "Jetty had the honour and notoriety of receiving the first direct telephone message from America to Holland...."[125] The marriage was scheduled for December 1928.

But first Robertson had to complete his Brookings' work, and on 12 May he sat his oral examination. A mimeographed list of forty-two questions covering six pages survives from this thorough grilling by a four-member faculty board. The questions ranged over economic theory, the Canadian tariff, monetary theory, philosophy, Marxism, and more general areas.[126] There is no record of how he handled the questions, but certainly he passed, and Hamilton felt able to write Lemuel Robertson in Vancouver "a word of appreciation of our having Norman as a member of our community this year."[127]

But in one area at least, Robertson's time at Brookings was a failure. His study of the tariff had not proceeded very far nor would it ever, and he never received his Brookings doctorate. Difficulty in settling down to write was perennial for him, and here he disappointed his instructors and probably himself.

IV

While at Brookings, Robertson was concerned about his employment prospects for the coming year. There were possibilities for him at Yale and at Princeton, and then Harvard soon came through with an offer, "the same salary for vastly different work [than Princeton]... more leisure and a better library with less responsible work."[128] The proposal was that he become an instructor in Economics and tutor in the Division of History, Government and Economics,[129] and Robertson accepted it.

But in May 1928 a wholly new opportunity arose. "I had a letter from

Skelton last week," he wrote home on 21 May, "advising me that there were two posts vacant in the department of external affairs—first and third secretaryships— and suggesting that I might apply."[130] Skelton was looking for bright young men and he must have remembered Robertson from the previous summer. "The type of man we would like to get," he had written a university friend, "would be one who would be suitable for appointment as an Assistant or Associate Professor."[131]

Robertson faced a difficult decision:

I have been in a double dilemma ever since; should I apply at all and if I did which job should I stand for? Applications have to be in this coming Friday so I must make up my mind by tomorrow at the latest. I hope I can hear from Biggar and Norman Rogers before I am compelled to decide.... I could probably get the junior post without much trouble but I am afraid it would mean the regular diplomatic service with long spells abroad and if that is the case I would not give up teaching to take it. The other post would be very attractive, but I am afraid I was not born in time to be a serious candidate. Still it is an open competitive exam for which I think I have the paper qualifications at least and there is no age limit specified so I may have a fling at it.[132]

The positions had been advertised by the Civil Service Commission at the end of April 1928, offering $3,840 for the "First Secretary (Male)" and $2,520 for the "Third Secretary (Male)". The qualifications demanded for the first post were: "Education equivalent to graduation from a University of recognized standing; specialization and post-graduate training in political economy, political science, or international law ... exceptional knowledge of international relations, economics or law, of diplomatic methods and procedure and of the phrasing and construction of diplomatic documents; preferably ability in at least one modern language, in addition to English or French ... undoubted integrity; tact; astuteness; keen perception; good judgment, and good address."[133] Only a saint could have fulfilled all those conditions.

But Robertson was as confident of his own abilities as ever, and he determined to write the First Secretary examinations. His application, filed on 24 May, listed as references Colonel Biggar, Stevenson, and Professor Thorlief Larsen of UBC.[134] After a futile attempt to secure permission to write in Washington, Robertson learned that he had to travel to Montreal. A comedy of errors, one that ranked with his trek to Oxford, ensued.

... I was inclined to drop the whole business for I had counted on writing in

Washington. . . . However I thought it over a bit, saw Beaudry the chargé d'affaires in Massey's absence and was urged to go by him. So I mustered my resources, bought a return ticket, took ten dollars cash and left Washington Tuesday night. At Albany where we had to change trains I was hustled on board a Montreal express waiting in the Station and only discovered half an hour later that I was on the D. & H.—when I should have been aboard the Raltand or B. M. I thought I had to be in Montreal Thurs. morning at all costs so I paid my way from Albany: it cost $8.88—all told I had $8.93—so I arrived in Montreal with five American coppers at ten o'clock at night. I didn't relish a park bench the night before an exam; Dave Johnson lived a long way out in Lachine so I went to the Queen's Hotel, took a room and waited for something to turn up.

What turned up was more confusion. When he arrived at the appointed place to write the examination, he "found the good father in charge of exams weeding in his backyard. He hadn't received the exam papers—and thought they might be held sometime next week! For this I'd come to Montreal." It took a trip to Ottawa to sort out matters, and there, presumably, Robertson wrote his exams.[135]

They involved an essay, questions on international affairs, a choice of two from a list of questions on political economy, political science, international law and modern history, and the writing of a précis.[136] He did well, scoring 77.4 per cent, enough to qualify him for the position of First Secretary. Ahead of him ranked one Lester Pearson with 86.5 per cent, Kenneth Kirkwood with 84.3 and, because of the preference accorded veterans, two candidates who had scored substantially lower.[137] Another candidate, Hugh Keenleyside (whom Robertson had known from his UBC days), "ranked first on the papers written but was prevented from writing on one paper."[138]

Robertson had done very well, considering his youth, against candidates of much greater experience. But he had not done well enough to win one of the first appointments, despite some political influence exerted from Vancouver by his father.[139] The winners of the competition were Pearson and Keenleyside as First and Third Secretary respectively,[140] with Kirkwood next in line and Robertson after him—subject only to the preference for veterans. "If any returned man fulfills the minimum qualifications," Skelton said, "even the tenth on the list, he would under the present arrangements be entitled to the appointment."[141] This immediately affected Robertson, for one qualified veteran was seriously seeking a position. Massey in Washington thought this man unsatisfactory but, said Skelton, "he will have to be given an appointment of some kind before we can consider Robertson. . . ."[142]

Still in Washington in August, Robertson was bitterly disappointed. "Nevertheless," he wrote his mother, "I am on the eligible list. . . . There is nothing to do but go to Harvard and let Skelton clear it up. . . . I may be too hopeful in believing that something will turn up—still I think Skelton will do what he can."[143] In the meantime, Robertson was off to Cambridge, Massachusetts.

His only contact at Harvard University was Professor W.S. Ferguson, a distant relative, who took Robertson under his wing, showed him around Boston, and settled him into an office in Holyoke House, next door to a Canadian historian, Arthur R.M. Lower, who was tutoring in history. Robertson's responsibilities required him to teach sixteen or eighteen hours a week—"not back breaking by any means—but quite enough for one's first whack at this sort of job."[144] His students were sophomores and juniors and, curiously, his specialty was listed as money and banking;[145] but whatever his expertise, Robertson could not have harmed his charges. Under Harvard's system, sophomores, juniors and seniors saw tutors individually and their work for them was ungraded and independent of course work. The tutor was a friend, not a taskmaster.[146]

In such circumstances Harvard was fun, full of good people, good talk, long walks, political meetings and theatre. Paul Martin was at the law school, as were Wishart Spence and Angus L. Macdonald—a good trio that, consisting of a future long-time Liberal cabinet minister, a Justice of the Supreme Court, and a very successful Premier of Nova Scotia—and Robertson met Martin at a reception for Canadian students organized by an expatriate faculty member.[147] William Yandell Elliott was an Assistant Professor of Government, and the future mentor of Henry Kissinger had much influence on Robertson. And although he and Lower were not close, they were friendly; Lower in 1978 could still remember Robertson's epigrammatic phrase that "to a free enterpriser, [Herbert] Hoover [the Republican presidential candidate in 1928] seems like the word made flesh."[148] Certainly Hoover did not impress him. If he had a vote, he wrote his grandfather, it would be for a Socialist candidate, but nonetheless he was supporting Al Smith, the Democratic and Catholic candidate. "I think I fear the Catholic Church as much as you do," he said, "but in the United States the Methodists are a much more serious menace . . . a thoroughly corrupt and unscrupulous machine that could teach the Tammany Tiger tricks."[149]

Without doubt, however, the most important event of 1928 was his marriage to Jetty Welling in Halifax on the day before Christmas. Why Halifax? Because, under the American immigration regulations, Jetty was unable to return to the United States. But once married to a Canadian employed in the United States, she could then re-enter the holy land. Robertson had tried to sort out this mess with Immigration officials in Boston, but had got nowhere, despite his suggestion that he was willing for the marriage to take place in a bonded warehouse if that would facilitate matters.[150] Jetty too had been talking with US Immigration officers in the Netherlands to no further avail. But the Americans did tell her that if she applied for entry to Canada on the grounds that she was to marry a Canadian, she would be refused entry. The solution was to write to the Robertsons in Vancouver and ask them to invite her to Canada as a visitor. Although she came with her trousseau in many boxes, fortunately no one in Halifax questioned the story, and the couple met again at the dock.[151]

The marriage took place at the home of an old family friend, Professor McIntosh of Dalhousie University's Chemistry department, with Rev. Dr. Clark officiating and a phonograph playing 'The Wedding March', or so McIntosh wrote Vancouver. Mrs. McIntosh also wrote to add that the ceremony caused such "a pleasant flutter in our house," a most charitable comment considering that it was the day before Christmas. She said "I fell very hard for Norman, who had a most exhilarating &, I am afraid, rather bad effect on me for I behaved more giddily than I have for years. . . . As to Mrs. Robertson, Jr.," she went on for the benefit of the family, who had yet to meet their daughter-in-law, "she is a lovely girl, not pretty exactly, but at times, far more than that."[152]

That comment probably short-changed Jetty Welling Robertson, who was a woman of character, great intelligence, and much courage, as well as substantial attractiveness. She had married knowing that Robertson had little money and that his future was as yet uncertain, and she was fully aware of the difficulties that lay ahead. "Things will not be easy," she had written to the Robertsons in Vancouver just before she left for Canada, "but I'll do my honest best and I shall help Norman in all I can— through the meagre years and if the plentiful years come—through them too."[153] That she did, but the first few days of the marriage verged on farce, as always seemed to be the case when Robertson travelled. "You know we had a wild time with the U.S. immigration authorities" in Halifax, Robertson wrote, "spent days scurrying back and forth across Halifax." And when those problems were finally unravelled, "a minor misunderstanding made us miss the Boston boat—so we waited for the next boat. . . . I settled my hotel bill . . . and left orders to be called at six o'clock. When we awoke the sun was pouring in the window. . . . We raised particular cain to no particular purpose—and finally had to take the all rail route the next day."[154] There was worse to come, for both Robertsons caught 'flu on their arrival in Boston, and since their flat was not yet ready, they had to be housed and attended by the Fergusons. Soon all was well, and Jetty "was scrubbing for dear life with no after effects whatever."[155] It was a chaotic beginning to a marriage and life together of singular happiness.

The couple had scarcely settled into their quarters before a letter from Skelton arrived "asking me if I was in a position to accept an appointment with the new Legation to Tokyo 'in the near future'." He had replied, Robertson told his parents, that he could be available when his Harvard contract had been met. Since then,

... the new minister has been named, a fact which complicates the case in two ways. In the first place, it means an almost immediate departure—in the second ... the minister is H.M. Marler. I've never met him but ... I've heard some unattractive anecdotes. He is a member of our slim and select silk hat brigade; of Massey's stamp but perhaps not even Massey's calibre—these millionaire amis du peuple affect an acquired elegance that rubs me the wrong way. The last vestige of my meagre Oxford manner falls from me when I meet them. I start looking around for the spittoon or make shift with the coal scuttle; forgive this vulgarity but remember it's my reaction to piped vests and white spats.

There was also the simple fact that he was no longer a free agent. "If I weren't married I think I'd pull up stakes and go like a shot, for two or three years in the Orient in that capacity would or should be fascinating."[156] In February, still undecided, Robertson went to New York City for an interview with Marler[157] and, as might have been expected, failed to hit it off with the new Minister, who seemed most concerned with the applicant's drinking and church-going habits.[158] A note on the file indicated that Marler "rejects Robertson," but, given Marler's peculiar obtuseness, that should not have been surprising. Certainly Robertson was lucky to escape.[159]

Still, everything was in limbo. By this time Robertson had received a feeler from the University of Toronto and an offer of a job from the University of Western Ontario,[160] and he was trying to delay decisions there until the External Affairs situation had been resolved. In April there was some movement: "my desultory correspondence with Ottawa has taken another fillip—hope renewed under these circumstances is worse than ditto deferred. . . . I've believed the business dead and buried half a dozen times in the last twelve months," he wrote his sister, "now another letter from Skelton has lugged it out of its charnel case—and once again I'm led to believe that a week will decide things. So I've put off [Western] Ontario," and with characteristic wryness, "am once more prepared to answer my country's call to any place but Tokyo."[161] He vacillated uneasily until May, with the civil service formalities delaying matters,[162] but at the end of the month finally joined the Department of External Affairs, reporting to the Legation in Washington for his first period of training.[163]

Even so, the appointment was not a permanent one. As confounded as his new recruit by the Civil Service Commission's pettifogging regulations, Skelton told Massey that "we have been thinking of providing for the temporary appointment of Norman Robertson as Third Secretary on the Washington vote for two months, and utilizing him here until the permanent appointment can be made in July or August."[164] Again it would take longer to sort out the paperwork. As early as June, Skelton (who curiously seemed to believe that Robertson had received a Harvard doctorate) was convinced that all had been arranged,[165] but his letter to the Civil Service Commission on the appointment was not written until 23 September. A Commission memorandum two days later observed that "Mr. Robertson passed the examination for First Secretary and is next in line for appointment as such. However, he is willing to accept appointment as Third Secretary. . . ."[166] After signing a waiver of his right to the senior appointment, Robertson's transformation into a diplomat was all but complete. On 2 October 1929 a "Notification to the Department" appointed Norman Robertson Third Secretary at $2,520 a year with effect from 23 September.[167] The period of preparation was completed; at age twenty-five Robertson had found his life's work.

CHAPTER II

Becoming a Civil Servant

"**B**EFORE ROBERTSON GOES to Ottawa," Hume Wrong wrote to Dr. Skelton in September 1929 from the Legation in Washington, "I should like you to have in your hands my estimate of his capacity." Wrong, highly intelligent and able, was a cool appraiser of his colleagues in the Department of External Affairs:

I think I can say, without qualification, that you are certain to find him a really useful member of your staff. Though at first he may strike one as being slightly uncouth, my appreciation both of his personality and of his ability, has steadily increased since he came to Washington. His work has been sound, he has a gift for rapidly grasping the essentials of a problem, and he shows a considerable resource in his methods of obtaining information. [1]

That was a perceptive appraisal of the young Robertson, but it left no doubt that he was still a student, a learner of the ways in which diplomacy was conducted and the ways it was practised by Canada's fledgling Department of External Affairs. That was true enough, and as Robertson dealt with a bewildering array of duties, major and minor, over the next half-dozen years or so, he was slowly mastering the tools of his craft, learning how to be both diplomat and bureaucrat.

I

The Department of External Affairs was a tiny one. Dr. Skelton, the Under-Secretary, supervised a bare handful of officers that included Counsellor Laurent Beaudry, Legal Adviser John Read, First Secretary Lester Pearson, Second Secretary J. Scott Macdonald, and at the bottom of the totem pole, Third Secretary Norman Robertson. There were clerks and messengers, numbering about fifty, but except for Agnes McCloskey, who largely handled the Department's administration, and Edouard Handy, a stenographer who eventually became the recorder of Mackenzie King's diary, none of these played roles on the national stage.[2] Robertson, taken on the strength of the Ottawa establishment on 23 September 1929, was much the most junior member of the officer staff, but, even so, he had his own areas of responsibility. One memorandum detailing the Department's work in 1930 noted that: "The Third Secretary devotes about half his time to League of Nations matters ... and assists in any question requiring investigation."[3] League questions were important, but not vital—an ideal way to break in a new officer. The roving commission that made up the other half of his duties was by chance something that fitted perfectly both Robertson's interests and the Department's. From Skelton's point of view, Robertson could be used as a jack of all trades, or rather he could be once he was trained. From Robertson's, his wide mandate was ideal for one with such breadth and range of interests, and the League of Nations work suited him for its idealism. It seemed a good arrangement and so it proved.

The first task was to learn how the Department did things: how to read the telegrams from London and Paris, how to draft replies so they could be read and understood by Skelton, and by the Prime Minister and Secretary of State for External Affairs, Mackenzie King. There were new colleagues to meet: Beaudry, a courteous, gentlemanly *Québécois*; Read, older, wiser and a good law professor; Macdonald, a near contemporary and soon a close friend; "Mike" Pearson, funny, hard-working and a good man with whom to talk and work;[4] and his old UBC friend Alfred Rive, who joined External Affairs in 1930. It was a congenial group.*

---

* Except in one peculiarly Canadian area, the relations between French- and English-Canadians. "There is bitterness and jockeying," a British official at the High Commission reported, "as well as one case, at least, of flat refusal on the part of an English Canadian to serve under a French Canadian, which bodes ill for the future of this Service. Perhaps in course of time this acrimonious feeling may be toned down; otherwise we shall have Paris more or less stocked with French Canadians, London with English Canadians, and Washington, probably, with those belonging to the nationality of each minister appointed. A house cleaning and a thorough revision of the present system, both of appointments and service in the Department of External Affairs, are undoubtedly needed; but I fear none will come, and this is a subject on which Dr. Skelton, in particular, will brook no outside advice." (Public Record Office, Dominions Office Records, D.O. 35/68/D6765, extract, Hadow to Whiskard, 30 Apr. 29. Cf. *Le Devoir*, 12 Apr. 29 on French Canadians in External Affairs; and Mrs. C.H.A. Armstrong Papers (Toronto), Hume Wrong to Marga Wrong, 29 Mar [1928?].)

Above all, there was Dr. Skelton. Oscar Skelton had come to the Department of External Affairs from Queen's University in 1924 and the next year Mackenzie King had made him the Under-Secretary. Quickly the political economy professor and biographer of Sir Wilfrid Laurier became a trusted adviser to the Prime Minister, one who offered his wisdom over the whole range of government business and one who generally shared King's responses to the problems that Canada faced. Certainly this was true in areas of imperial and foreign policy. Skelton was a nationalist, convinced since his youth that Canada's destiny was to be an independent nation within a British Commonwealth, free to choose its own course, free to make its own mistakes. That was his goal and, if it was not always certain that it was Mackenzie King's as well, Skelton was there to remind the Prime Minister of his dreams and duties.

But if Canada was to achieve independence, it needed its own foreign service. Skelton set out to recruit like-minded men, and in general he did very well, attracting to the government service an extraordinary crew of well-educated and well-trained young officers. To them he passed along his ethos, his nationalism, his unpretentiousness. Skelton was a rumpled man, casual in his dress, casual in his administrative habits. He disliked the high-falutin style adopted by some diplomatic representatives, he scorned the court dress and formality that British protocol required, and he practised a genuine Canadian democracy in his department and in his own life. There was, literally, a side of beef hanging in the back-kitchen of his home from which the Doctor sliced off the Sunday joint![5]

Skelton got on well with Mackenzie King, but could he and his department flourish— or survive—under R.B. Bennett and the Conservatives, who came to power in the election of 1930? Bennett might have been forgiven if he viewed the Doctor as a Liberal, as one too close to the outgoing Prime Minister to be trusted at the heart of a new régime. That thought had occurred to Skelton, of course, and he determined not to resign but to wait to be fired. Absorbed in creating his administration, Bennett found himself, much to his surprise, increasingly reliant on the Under-Secretary for advice on a myriad of questions. Thus, if Skelton had been intended for the axe, the Prime Minister failed to swing it, and Skelton and his department served the new master exactly as they had served the old.[6] The non-political character of the Department of External Affairs had been confirmed, a matter of substantial importance for the civil service, for Skelton, and for Norman Robertson.

Certainly the immediate result of the elections had its impact on Robertson's career. On 9 August, just after the new government had taken office, the Prime Minister, concerned that Canada be given "competent and prestigious representation,"[7] asked Sir Robert Borden to lead the Canadian delegation to the League of Nations meetings in Geneva. Borden accepted,[8] and the next ten days were a flurry of activity and briefings for the old wartime leader. They were busy days for Robertson too, who had been given the task of ensuring that the necessary papers were prepared.[9] They became busier still when a day or so before Borden was to sail on the *Empress of Scotland*, Skelton asked the young Third Secretary to accompany Borden as his adviser.

On Saturday [Robertson wrote to his parents] Skelton raised the question as purely hypothetical. Could I get away if I were wanted? We argued it over and Jetty said yes so I told him I could go. . . .But it all turned on Bennett who is properly worried about the financial situation and thought of lopping a thousand dollars off the million dollar deficit by sending Sir Robert . . . alone. However, Skelton and Borden talked him into sending me—told me at three o'clock yesterday to get this morning's 6.30 train and if possible the boat at Quebec.[10]

That kind of last-minute rush, perhaps caused this time more by the election results than by inefficiency in the department, was not untypical throughout the rest of the 1930s.

Robertson had met Sir Robert for the first time the day before they sailed from Quebec but, he said, "if first impressions are worth anything he is going to be about the nicest man I've ever worked with."[11] First impressions were important, and Borden's initial reactions to his aide, formed during the voyage and in London, Paris and Geneva, are also worth noting. They are also very funny.

22 August 1930 [at sea]: Mr. Robertson came in afternoon. We discussed proposed amendments to Covenant. They seem to me very badly drafted.

23 August [at sea]: Sent for Robertson at 9 a.m. He arrived at 12.40, sat on my bed (although there were two chairs) and munched my grapes.

31 August [Paris]: Désy [from the Paris legation] and Robertson stupidly left small luggage at Station and it arrived so late that I could not accompany Roy [Canadian Minister in Paris] to Comedie Francaise for which he had got tickets.

3 September [Paris]: Roused Robertson at 9.

8 September [Geneva]: Robertson came to my door at 7.30 a.m. terribly penitent that he had not turned up at all yesterday. After I had arisen I told him frankly

that he was the most casual & elusive person of whom I ever had experience. I then lectured him in the same strain & finally said we wd regard the incident as closed.[12]

To his great credit, Borden did consider the incident closed and there were no further problems. Indeed, as we shall see, the tone of his comments altered markedly as the mission proceeded.

But what had been wrong with Robertson that he behaved in so casual a fashion to a man for whom he had great respect? Why did he neglect his duties? Any answer must be based on surmise, but it might be assumed that Robertson took advantage of his government-paid grand tour of Europe to enjoy himself in a fashion that had been impossible when he was a relatively impecunious Oxford undergraduate. Further, the trip probably marked the end of Robertson's youth and his realization that he had to give his full attention to his work if it were to be properly done. There had been a broad strain of off-hand indolence in his Oxford years[13] and some in his Brookings work. The doctoral thesis, for example, remained incomplete. The rocket from Borden on 8 September seems to have been almost the last one ever directed at Robertson, whose work thereafter was marked by diligence and great thoroughness, if not always by speed. Clearly Sir Robert had scored a direct hit.[14]

Once the unpleasantness was out of the way, Robertson settled down to his task at Geneva, attending League sessions and committees with Borden, and assisting in the preparation of his speeches. "I worked at my speech yesterday," Borden wrote on 11 September, " . . . and had useful suggestions from [Georges] Vanier [a military adviser to the delegation] and Robertson."[15] That was the first word of approbation for Robertson. Borden's speech was well received as "a model of literary form, striking imagery and sincere emotion," or so Mack Eastman wrote in his *Canada at Geneva*. Eastman, however, also noted that the Canadian's remarks were "strangely immune to European realities," delivered as they were at a time of rapidly expanding armaments, Nazi electoral successes in Germany, and economic depression.[16] Still, it was a success for Borden and some of the credit went to Robertson.

Nonetheless, Borden was finding his role a strain. A note to Skelton pronounced "Our staff . . . quite inadequate for the work in which we are engaged. . . .Mr. Robertson is working very hard and has his hands more than full."[17] A few days later, Borden wrote the Prime Minister that, while his mission was interesting, the noise, duties and parties were fatiguing.[18] So they were, and Borden soon departed for a holiday in Oberammergau, leaving Robertson in Geneva.

Those were happy days wandering around Geneva, into the bookstores and to the parties. Here Robertson met Louis Rasminsky, a young Canadian just hired by the League,[19] and either this year or the next he again met Tommy Balogh, a British economist and a friend from Harvard days, who remembered him as a progressive thinker on economic questions, well aware of the damage reparations payments had done to the world economy.[20] There were also the Vaniers, Pauline and Georges, who became close friends. To Mme Vanier he was a "bear" with a marvellous sense of humour, one who made parties "bubble". When Vanier was absent, Robertson escorted his wife to a Geneva ball, and Mme Vanier still remembers his caustic but not inapt comment on Philippe Roy, the Canadian Minister to France: "he was a bag of sawdust—if pricked it would all come out."[21] By 3 October, it was all over in Geneva, and Borden and Robertson set out for home by way of London. On the tenth they sailed for Canada.[22]

By this time the two men had become friendly and the tart note was entirely gone from Borden's diary. On 9 November, back in Ottawa, "N.A. and Mrs. Robertson... for tea. I discussed with Robertson my speech." The next day Robertson was there again "and after tea gave me suggestions as to my speech." And next month, most glowing of all, "Robertson (N.A.) came for luncheon. A very able young man."[23] Thus Borden's initial impressions had come full circle; surely Robertson's work had also improved.[24]

II

Geneva had been pleasant, but it was just an interlude, a respite from Robertson's regular and more mundane duties. Those were myriad. He served on committees and handled some of the initial work for the League's Preparatory Commission for the Disarmament Conference.[25] He worked with Pearson in preparing the Canadian response to the League's equally futile Draft General Convention to Improve the Means of Preventing War[26] and there was even work on calendar reform[27] and a radio talk on disarmament:

A couple of weeks ago [Robertson wrote home on 26 February 1931] I made my debut on the air... but alas my station just covered Quebec and Ontario—so you couldn't have heard my edifying little homily on the draft disarmament convention. I was very nervous... but after the first half minute it wasn't a very

terrifying experience. Perhaps you will have heard me at one remove already—
for tomorrow I'm writing a speech for Bennett to deliver on Sunday next over a
national hook-up. He probably won't use it—but if anything subversive seems to
have slipped in—you will know whom to blame.[28]

Robertson was also assisting Skelton, in 1931 the President of the
Canadian Political Science Association, by handling the membership
correspondence.[29] And occasionally, as in a long memorandum on "Some
Phases of the Present Economic Depression," he was even able to use his
academic training.

This memorandum, probably prepared early in 1931, is a skilful
examination of prices but not, as Robertson admitted at the beginning,
any attempt "to plot the behaviour of business in Canada on the pattern
of cyclical theory" nor "any general hypothesis of the origin or evolution
of cyclical fluctuations in business." The key factors in Canada's
Depression, he observed, were her export markets—"basic industries rely
on foreign markets to absorb the bulk of their production." And, worse
luck, "The world markets of the principal raw materials have shown signs
of satiation for some years past. . . .Canada has, therefore been adversely
affected—both absolutely and relatively by the general glut or over-
production of raw materials that characterized the first phase of the
present world depression."[30] Those comments were not original but they
were not unsound, and certainly there was no other officer in the
department in 1931 who could have produced them. Striking too is that
there was no evidence in this memo of Robertson's once strong socialism.
In part, this was because a department memorandum ordinarily did not
permit the expression of personal views; but equally there seems little
doubt that Robertson's politics had moderated, that he had become more
aware of the complexities of government, and that like others in Ottawa
he had gradually become inured to or unaware of the human costs of the
Great Depression.

Perhaps Robertson's memorandum on the Depression and staples had
been prompted by his growing involvement with wheat questions, a
subject that he continued to deal with for much of the rest of his career.
"I've been busier than ever before these past three months," he wrote his
mother in the spring of 1931. "My regular assignment the League of N.
has been stretched to include three wheat conferences—in Paris, Rome
and, tomorrow, in London. There are more congenial jobs than writing
instructions for the egregious G. Howard [Ferguson, Canadian High
Commissioner in London]. But no one needs them more—so perhaps it's a
patriotic duty."[31] That was typically tart but undoubtedly true. More

important, Robertson was beginning to find his ideas on policy taken seriously by Skelton and Bennett. To Robertson, the problem with wheat, much as he had said in his Depression study, was "over-production and consequent low prices." How could this be resolved? A direct limitation of production was impractical in Canada, but perhaps some international agreement to limit exports (similar to that recently reached for sugar) might be sought. The idea caught Bennett's imagination, as C.F. Wilson noted in a recent study of wheat policy, "for he was still in the early stages of fulfilling the mandate he had sought and won to negotiate for markets abroad, and it was an inexpensive sort of external activity by which the government's interest on behalf of the Canadian wheat farmer could be demonstrated."[32] It was a long time before much came of Robertson's idea, but it seems clear that his first major intervention on a question of policy brought him favourably to the attention of his masters.

Robertson was soon en route to Geneva again, this time as the adviser to the 1931 delegation headed by Hon. Hugh Guthrie, Bennett's Minister of Justice. Again he had prepared the briefing papers, but now, after his experience the year before, he was full of suggestions. There should be a private car for the delegation and a French stenographer for Senator C.P. Beaubien, one of the delegates. Despite the fact that these ideas were pooh-poohed by Dr. W.A. Riddell, the permanent Canadian representative at Geneva,[33] it was a pleasant trip. "Robertson arrived back yesterday from Geneva," his colleague Scott Macdonald wrote to Norman Rogers at Queen's University on 10 November 1931, "where he had been acting as technical adviser....He was present...during the sessions of the Council dealing with the Manchurian question. It begins to look as though Canada might be called upon to give serious consideration to a foreign policy...."[34]

Macdonald's remarks suggested that Canada had no foreign policy, a view that would have been applauded by some members of the new foreign service. Pearson "has been for a year at Ottawa in the Dept. of External Affairs," Hume Wrong had written to his sister in June 1930, "& he & I spend most of our spare time reforming our elementary and rather absurd diplomatic service."[35]* But Norman Robertson did not seem to have reacted that way. "I have an extraordinarily interesting and

---

* According to Hugh Keenleyside, Wrong later joked bitterly about Canada being represented abroad by the deaf, the dumb and the blind. Minister Roy in Paris was deaf, Minister Bruce in Tokyo was blind, and Minister Marler in Washington was, well, Marler. (Keenleyside interview, 4 May 78.)

satisfying work," he wrote his father in March 1932. "I can't think of a post I'd trade it for anywhere. League affairs as a routine responsibility with a roving commission in other fields. It has its shortcomings but on balance it is a job that has to be done and that I enjoy doing."[36] He said similar things to H.F. Angus, adding that he was being paid to work at matters he would have wanted to work at on his own. External Affairs offered him an intellectual career without teaching, and that was what he wanted.[37] Certainly his satisfaction was in marked contrast to the boredom and unhappiness of Wrong and Pearson.[38]

Robertson was aware of the problems, of course; his letter to his father had mentioned "shortcomings," but had glossed over them. Probably Robertson—and Wrong and Pearson—could have agreed with the confidential analysis prepared by Burgon Bickersteth, the Warden of Hart House at the University of Toronto, who wrote to friends in the British government in May 1932 to say that: "It would not be an exaggeration . . . that the most crying need in Canadian public life today is a Civil Service of the English type—a Service which would attract the best brains of the country, which would be entirely independent of all party consideration, and would enjoy an altogether higher status."[39] Bickersteth saw many matters through Anglo-coloured spectacles, but in this instance he was correct.

Surely Robertson believed that higher pay was necessary. In early 1932 the Bennett government froze promotions and cut civil service salaries by ten per cent as a depression economy measure.[40] That hurt, and Robertson told his parents that "salary cuts—including (1) suspension of normal annual increase (2) 10 p.c. off present salary and (3) at least another year's postponement of a promotion promised twelve months ago—will taken together leave me about $800 less next year than we reasonably anticipated."[41] That pinched the Robertsons' budget, even though deflation had increased the real worth of a salaried income, primarily because Jetty had been safely delivered of a daughter on 8 March 1931. The child, named Flora Johanna (but later known to almost everyone except her mother as Alix), altered the Robertsons' style of life, as all children are wont to do. There was less money for clothes and entertainment, more needed for doctor bills and housing. Robertson's suits, always more serviceable than elegant, were now worn after the serge began to get shiny, and his black coat and hat in winter looked well used. So too did Robertson. By this time, his hair had largely fallen out, and he was left with only a fringe on the sides and back. The great bald dome rising above his already high forehead made him look intellectual and much older than his years, something that added to the natural gravity that he could bring to his pronouncements. But above all he was happy, happy with his family and delighted with his work.

Despite his pleasure, Robertson occasionally allowed thoughts of other employment to cross his mind. In January 1932 W.Y. Elliott from Harvard University came to Ottawa to scout the terrain and to see politicians about his research interests.[42] One of his ideas was that Robertson should return to teaching at Harvard. "Might go for a year if leave of absence could be secured," Robertson noted, "but not likely anything will be done. If I went it would be in Government not Economics."[43] That possibility resurfaced later.

But for the moment it was work and more work. "I've been rushed at the office all month and anticipate no let up in the immediate future," Robertson told his mother in one of his increasingly infrequent letters. "When arrears are out of the way, the [parliamentary] Session will be upon us and at last we are at work on the preparations for the Imperial Conference." That conference, to be held in Ottawa in the summer of 1932, was to bring together all the Dominions, many of the colonies, and Britain to discuss how best to deal with the effects of the Depression on trade. There seemed little doubt that the proposed remedy was going to be higher tariffs against non-Empire countries. "Skelton, Coats [from the Dominion Bureau of Statistics], MacDonald [sic] and I are the committee coordinating plans," Robertson noted, "—all free traders! Isn't it a farce?"[44]

Technically, Robertson was not a member of the General Preparatory Committee for the Ottawa Conference. But presumably his duties remained flexible enough for him to work where and how Skelton wanted, since during this period Skelton was coming to rely on Robertson all the more. His major task was as Secretary of the General Economic Committee, one of the key Conference planning bodies and one charged with the preparation of a host of memoranda for the Canadian delegation and, where possible, for the information of all the Empire delegations.[45] Robertson himself was to prepare seven memoranda on subjects such as the "Movement for European Union" and the "Relation of Commonwealth Countries to the Gold Standard."[46]

This was interesting work, but Robertson was not sanguine about the results the Conference would produce.

What it can bring forth the Lord only knows. An empire that can survive Ferguson and Thomas [the British Dominions Secretary], Bennett and de Valera [Irish Free State Premier] must be indestructible. If it can weather this summer's meeting I think we can say that the Commonwealth has come thro' its most critical stage. I am not sure it will but prospects are more propitious than some months ago. . . . Bennett to do him justice is as ready to bully the C[anadian]. M[anufacturers]. A[ssociation]. as any other organization—and has already read them the riot act. They have not taken his orders with a very good grace but have at least abandoned their first . . . impertinence of asking for further all round increases on the British Preference as a preparatory 'bargaining measure' for the coming Conference. The export industries—notably lumber and mining— have organized their own influential lobbies and are busy looking for concessions on manufactured goods to be offered in return for preferences in the British market.

As Robertson noted, the subject of the Conference was trade and tariffs, a topic that always heated up the political climate and exposed cabinet ministers to the flat-out threats of their constituents and financial supporters. Bennett, as Robertson knew, was sometimes a bully and often indiscriminate in whom he bullied. But the Prime Minister, whatever his flaws, seemed a more able man than the Leader of the Opposition.

Of Bennett I see next to nothing [he wrote his father] but Skelton finds him a satisfactory man to do business with. I think he is a man of great industry, honest and with rather an ingenuous faith in his own star. He has the gift of mastering a brief quickly, a retentive memory and an ex cathedra manner of speech that taken together enable him to dominate the house. King is increasingly a liability to his party . . . and I can't believe [he] has sufficient strength in the country to outweigh his incapacity in Parliament. (Charlie Murphy's [a former Liberal Minister and bitter enemy of King] new nickname for his late leader is 'Willy of the Valley'.) . . . The Cabinet is very weak, weaker than King's Cabinet which was not strong.[47]

Willy of the Valley clearly impressed Robertson no more than he had in 1923 on board the *Montcalm*.

Before long, Robertson was completely caught up in the increasingly frantic preparatory work for the Imperial Economic Conference. The final agenda reached participating governments only two weeks before the Conference opened, and the delays, the leading historian of the Ottawa Conference wrote, "resulted entirely from the incompetence of the Canadian bureaucracy, as supervised by O.D. Skelton . . . and from the vacillations and obsessions of R.B. Bennett. . . ."[48] Perhaps that was so, but Robertson was going all-out. In a letter to Vancouver in July, he wrote that the "last month has been the busiest I've ever spent. It's been 'morn to midnight' every day but the back of the work is broken. The

preparatory work started late and on a very ambitious scale is practically finished. I'm busy editing and proof-reading, but the end is in sight."
His conference work was, however, just beginning.

> Tomorrow ... I start again on a new job. Macdonald and I are the joint secretaries of the Canadian Delegation appointed two days ago, months after every other delegation had been constituted. We move into the Parliament Buildings tomorrow afternoon or Tuesday to have everything in working order there by Thursday. Between an ill-informed and inexperienced Cabinet delegation and a horde of scattered 'expert advisers' we shall have our hands full.

Nor had Robertson's expectations risen since the winter.

> It is altogether an absurd and rather tragic situation. I've never been much of an imperialist but do believe that what's left of the Empire is well worth keeping. How it can be kept I simply cannot imagine.
>   By the time you get this letter the fat will probably be in the fire for the P.M. anticipating deadlock in the tariff negotiations has his own red herring to serve the Conference. They are all ready to launch a general attack on the U.K. for continuing to trade with Russia—will ask for a general embargo on Soviet products—and if that is refused will feel on strong ground in refusing further preferential concessions. It's a palpable bluff but one that nobody dare call. I've been bombarding them via Skelton with memos until I've acquired a fellow feeling for Sergeant Leopold [an RCMP undercover agent of some notoriety]. However, you'll probably hear Bennett on the radio ... Thursday—and if he mentions Russia you'll know I've been overruled. [49]

Robertson was overruled, and Bennett and the Canadian delegation played the Soviet card to the limit. [50]
    Once the Conference began, Robertson was caught up in the whirl, serving on committees and sub-committees, and pushing paper for the Canadian delegation. He served on a shipping committee and on the procedures sub-committee of the Committee on Methods of Economic Cooperation. [51] One British delegation member, Sir Geoffrey Whiskard of the Dominions Office, wrote to his chief that Bennett "regards advisers merely as a nuisance," but he did note that "The Canadian representative on the Sub-Committee—Robertson of the Ministry of External Affairs— seems to me an extremely able fellow but he is evidently under orders to hang back a bit." [52]
    The decisive event of the Conference, the bargaining between the Canadian and British delegations, was being carried on in secret. One British politician watching from the sidelines wrote to Stanley Baldwin: "I

think there is a very real danger that the British delegation is driving too hard a bargain all round."[53] Another official, from a vantage point at Government House, later said that Bennett, shouting in the negotiations and playing a game of bluff, "was behaving in a manner that must have seemed to all of you remarkable (to put it mildly)."[54] Both opinions were likely correct, complicated further by the unpreparedness of the two sides and the simple fact that, as Ian Drummond has noted, the "Ottawa Conference, in fact, was a muddle, and its Agreements were the results of *ad hoc* concessions and desperate last-minute bargaining."[55]

So it was, and Robertson apparently had some substantial part in securing a British-Canadian agreement on trade. According to the historian of the Department of Trade and Commerce, Bennett turned for a way out of the negotiating impasse to three civil servants: Hector McKinnon, the Commissioner of Tariff, Dana Wilgress, just named as head of Trade and Commerce's Commercial Intelligence Service, and Robertson. With H.H. Stevens, the Minister of Trade and Commerce, the three civil servants had to formulate a list of tariff concessions that the British might accept, and that chore kept them steadily working over a weekend. "Literally at the last moment, with the British delegation threatening to pack up and go home," the Trade and Commerce history says, "an acceptable agreement was reached."[56] The results, not made public until the fall of 1932, altered the tariff on 225 items and gave the British concessions for their iron and steel products, drugs, textiles, leather, glass and some other commodities, in a deliberate attempt to switch Canadian imports from the United States to the United Kingdom. In return, and far more significantly, the Canadians received larger preferences in the British market on a wide variety of raw materials, rubber goods, chemicals and canned fish. The Canadians had given Britain perhaps $15 million in new trade, while the preferences received had guaranteed Canada's markets in England.[57] This negotiating team of McKinnon, Wilgress and Robertson, here combined for the first time, worked together happily and effectively throughout the decade.

With the Ottawa Conference concluded, Robertson's tasks reverted to routine. He continued his work on disarmament questions, and also served as secretary at Bennett's Dominion-Provincial Conference of January 1933, a meeting that ineffectually considered how to deal with unemployment, then reaching its peak.[58] He maintained his watch over League of Nations questions and became peripherally involved in the "Cahan incident," when C.H. Cahan, the Secretary of State and the Canadian representative to the League Assembly, in an address at

Geneva on 7 December 1932, went against his instructions and supported
Japan's "civilizing" mission in Manchuria. Cahan later tried to justify the
unjustifiable by saying that his instructions, ordering him to withhold
support from Japan, "were prepared up in a room in the East Block, that
Dr. Skelton was too busy to give them his careful consideration, and that
the Prime Minister with his multitude of duties could only have glanced at
them...."[59] All that was true, but no excuse. Almost certainly Robertson
had drafted the instructions, and there can be no doubt that his own
views on the League and the Manchurian question went well beyond the
instructions. He was a believer in collective security as a counterweight to
aggression, and wanted the League to play an active role in mobilizing
peaceful countries against Japan and any other assailant.[60] Canadian
policy in 1932 could not stretch that far, however, but Robertson must
have been appalled by Cahan's repudiation of his government's
instructions.

All the more curious then was Robertson's encounter with W. Arnold-
Forster, a veteran of the British peace movement, who came to Ottawa to
lecture to the League of Nations Society in March 1933 on "Disarmament To Date." Robertson was one of a party that dined at the Rideau
Club with the visitor, and Sir Robert Borden noted in his diary that there
had been a "Brilliant encounter between him & Norman Robertson as to
applying economic sanctions against Japan."[61] Presumably Robertson
argued against sanctions, the official Canadian position, although not one
that he personally supported. There was a debater's ability in Robertson
to marshal arguments with great force on any side of a question, a useful
tool for a civil servant who often had to supply his minister with
arguments explaining the inexplicable. He was also developing a cold-
blooded willingness to argue any question on a straight and hard national
interest line—another useful approach, particularly when dealing with
outsiders.[62]

Skelton had that knack too, and Robertson had patterned himself on
his mentor. Indeed, on occasion he sounded as nationalistic as the Under-
Secretary of State for External Affairs, particularly on questions of
Imperial policy, where there was something approximating a master-
student relationship between the two men.[63] That became evident when
Robertson went to London in the summer of 1933 as one of Bennett's
advisers at the World Monetary and Economic Conference (the others
were Clifford Clark, the new Deputy Minister of Finance, and Dana
Wilgress).[64] Robertson arrived in London on 10 June and accompanied
the Prime Minister to the Conference's opening, "where I shared the

distinction with the delegates of the Kingdom of Saudi Arabia of being the only man on the floor not in morning coat—and they were in burnooses."⁶⁵ Canada was a member of the Bureau, the Conference steering committee, and Robertson suddenly found himself briefly at the centre of events when Ramsay MacDonald, the British Prime Minister and Conference host and chairman,

... in presenting for the approval of the Conference a list of countries to constitute the Bureau, read it out in alphabetical order, from Allemagne to U.S.S.R., and then said: 'and a representative of the British Dominions,—in this case Canada.' With some difficulty I secured Mr. Bennett's authorization to object to this new style of nomenclature, had the offending phrase deleted, and Canada installed sans phrase in its proper alphabetical position in the list.⁶⁶

That was how Robertson described the incident to Skelton, back in Ottawa. To his father, he was a bit franker about the British effort to forget about the Statute of Westminster of 1931: "I objected on good constitutional grounds and after ten minutes pretty heated argument with R.B. [Bennett] got authorization to carry the fight a stage further. It was a small constitutional point—one that Bennett was loath to recognize and one that MacDonald is prone to override—but I got the record put straight ... and now the ghost of John S. Ewart [the Canadian constitutional expert] can rest." Robertson added that "R.B. is a little subdued, I think, whispered the speeches he'd have liked to make into my deaf ear. Which isn't a bad beginning. I won't advise him to make a speech," he concluded rather too grandly, "unless I can be sure he'll make the right speech—and he is incalculable."⁶⁷

The Conference itself was a hopeless mess. As Hume Wrong wrote from Washington shortly after the opening: "Mr. Hull [the US Secretary of State] is evangelizing in London for all the doctrines which Mr. Roosevelt is repudiating in Washington ... the U.S. will be the wrecker. ..."⁶⁸ That was good prophecy, for the world drifted helplessly onto the shoals of economic disaster and the Conference went nowhere. Robertson wrote to Vancouver on 18 July:

... one can't be sure whether it is wiser to accept defeat and adjourn or press for continuance in the hope that circumstances may soon prove more propitious. Roosevelt's tone & tactics have made matters difficult, though fundamentally I think he's right. ...

The wrangling over procedure has been transferred from the Committee to the Bureau which I attend with R.B.B.—the discussions have been prolonged and ill concealed bitterness underlies them. Hull is decent, kindly, well meaning—but not very keen and treated abominably by his President. . . .R.B.'s support has been helpful, though a bit heavy handed. [69]

More productive were the simultaneous discussions on wheat, held in London, where Robertson worked closely with Bennett and High Commissioner Ferguson and served as Canadian representative on the technical and drafting committees. The United States sought agreement on acreage reduction, a position that Canada received sympathetically, qualified, as Robertson's report noted, "by frank recognition that the methods of reduction contemplated by the United States could not, on financial and economic grounds, be applied in Canada. . . ."[70] The wheat talks deliberately were kept outside the ambit of the World Economic Conference, Robertson wrote to Geneva, since the exporting countries preferred to "keep their conversations . . . secret and informal."[71] Those discussions produced an agreement, signed 30 June 1933, to establish a system of export quotas for Canada, the United States, Australia and Argentina and for acreage reductions "to the extent of 15 %." The four major wheat exporters then attempted to sell their agreement to the rest of the world at a conference held at Canada House, London, a meeting organized by Robertson.[72] That conference ultimately produced an International Wheat Agreement, but one so riddled with reservations that its effect was largely vitiated.[73]

The London talks marked Robertson's last Departmental duties for almost a year, however, for he had managed, with great difficulty, to win the Civil Service Commission's approval to go to Harvard for an academic year as a visiting lecturer in Government.[74] The offer had come through W.Y. Elliott, now Chairman of the Government Department.[75] But in fact, as Robertson admitted frankly, "I don't much like lecturing and am not a very good lecturer, so I don't really wish to stay in University work, pleasant though this year promises to be. Its usefulness is largely tactical, at least I hope a grateful government draws the proper moral and offers me some sort of suitable salary. I shall go back anyway," he added, "whatever the salary but would like some tangible rewards sometime."[76] In fact, as Jetty Robertson remembers it, Skelton had told Robertson to accept the Harvard offer so he, Skelton, could use it as a lever to overcome the freeze and get Robertson promoted. "We will lose this bright young man to Harvard," Skelton could say to Bennett in arguing Robertson's case.[77] Still, the Department was so short-staffed that Skelton soon came to regret his decision to let Robertson go. As he told W.D. Herridge, the Minister in Washington: "we have been swamped here, particularly since we quixotically allowed Robertson to take leave."[78]

But for Robertson it was a good year. He gave a course of lectures at Harvard and at Radcliffe College on problems of international government and, in the second semester, on "new factors in international relations."[79] He also served as a tutor for sixteen students, much as he had done in 1928-29, and his colleagues were a distinguished group that included Elliott in Government, Herring and Schumpeter in Economics, and Brinton, Langer, Morison and Merk in History.[80] There was an active social life (although "formal entertaining palls quickly and isn't easily repaid")[81] and, thanks to Mike Pearson's brother Duke, the vice-president of Armour Leather Co., there was access to the St. Botolph Club in Boston for six months. There, he said, "I can earn an honest penny at bridge now and then."[82] (Robertson had been playing bridge since his early teens; he had honed his skills at Oxford, and by the early 1930s was a very good player indeed.) Over the Christmas holidays there were visitors from home, his sister Barbara, and from Washington his and Jetty's Brookings friend, Eleanor Bontecou. It was pleasant and cheerful, and when in a cold snap the water pipes froze in their house at 998 Memorial Drive, all the Robertsons, their guests and their live-in mother's helper went off to Adams House, the building in which Robertson's office was located, to wash.[83]

Nonetheless, the Robertsons were very glad to return to Ottawa in the spring of 1934. As promised, Skelton was doing his best to get that promotion. A Civil Service Commission memorandum in July 1934 accepted the "reclassification" of Robertson's position "in view of the special circumstances connected with [his] employment," noting that he had been chosen for "certain special assignments in connection with which his work has been highly satisfactory." As a result, the Treasury Board agreed to change the Departmental organization by creating a new Second Secretary's post with effect from 1 April 1934. Robertson's promotion was effective that date but his salary was not raised to $3,120 until 1 June.[84]

Skelton presumably was pleased that he had succeeded in getting his protégé promoted. But at this point, apparently for the only time in the 1930s, there was some thought of posting him. "Robertson (Second Secretary) to Washington if Wrong leaves," one of the Doctor's memos said, adding that Robertson was "doing valuable work." Or, perhaps, he might be "loaned for a year or so, if satisfactorily replaced at Ottawa."[85] But Wrong stayed in Washington and Robertson, to his pleasure, remained in Ottawa. "I am an unadventurous soul," he later wrote to a Departmental colleague, "and quite happy to stay here."[86]

Robertson was in the East Block for the duration, and a little more than a year after his promotion to Second Secretary, was promoted once more, replacing Pearson, who had been posted to London. This time he was made First Secretary, the rank for which he had qualified when he wrote the examinations in 1927, and as of 1 October 1935, was paid an annual salary of $3,840, subject to the civil service's ten per cent salary deduction. As he wrote home, "we have been able to balance the books and even think of a new suit."[87]

III

At some point in 1935, Robertson's duties in the Department were altered. League of Nations questions, soon to become matters of first importance because of the Italian-Ethiopian War, were shifted elsewhere, and Robertson was assigned to "United Kingdom and United States Commercial relations" and "General economic and financial questions."[88] Certainly those new areas fitted his inclinations, and since the Bennett government was trying—and had been since 1933 with increasing desperation—to strike a trade agreement with the United States, Robertson was at the centre stage.[89]

Trade between the two North American nations had been severely hit by the Depression, to be sure, but the tariffs that each country had put in place against the other had worsened matters. In 1930, the United States had enacted the Hawley-Smoot tariff, which subjected imports from Canada to high and often prohibitory duties. Canada had retaliated in 1930 under the King government, and Bennett's régime had raised the walls higher still. Worse yet, in American eyes: the British preferential system, put in place at Ottawa in 1932, seemed a deliberate challenge. To the Roosevelt administration and particularly to Secretary of State Cordell Hull, lower tariffs and increased trade were articles of faith, the way out of the Depression and the road to peace. Considering that trade between Canada and the United States had fallen by 1933 to the lowest level since 1910 and to less than one-third of the 1928 level, there was ample room to manoeuvre for both countries.[90]*

---

* In 1928, Canadian exports to the United States were $502,690,000; in 1933, $172,955,000. Imports from the United States in 1928 were $825,652,000 and in 1933, $217,291,000. (M.C. Urquhart and K.A. Buckley, *Historical Statistics of Canada* (Toronto, 1965), p.183.)

The first efforts to improve matters took place in 1933 when Bennett met President Roosevelt and agreed with him "to begin a search for means to increase the exchange of commodities between our two countries. . . ."[91] From this date, preparations and studies were underway in Ottawa, but for a variety of reasons, most notably delays in the passage of a Trade Agreements Act, which gave the American government power to negotiate trade agreements without the necessity of Senate ratification, the Americans were not in a position to begin negotiations.[92] The Act was finally passed on 12 June 1934, and W.D. Herridge, the Canadian Minister in Washington, began to press the Canadian case.

By February 1935, Herridge could report that: "The Committees set up to prepare the American side of the picture are working night and day,"[93] and no one had any doubt what the American tack would be. The thrust of their case was that: "The United States is the only important country whose exports to Canada are dutiable under the 'General,' or highest, tariff rates . . . the effect is direct discrimination. . . . Canadian products, however, enter the United States without discrimination." The aim would be to win "most favoured nation" treatment, a rate no worse than that accorded the foreign (or non-Commonwealth) country most favoured by Canadian tariffs.[94]

But it was not until 25 August 1935 that the two sides met to begin negotiations. The Canadian team of Robertson, Dana Wilgress and Hector McKinnon, reunited again after their success at the Ottawa Conference, had come to Washington in secrecy,[95] ready to begin the horse-trading. The American negotiators were led by Jack Hickerson, an amiable Texan who had served in the Ottawa legation; his team took a tough position, so strong that the commercial attaché in Ottawa remarked that "the concessions offered to the Dominion are somewhat short when balanced against concessions required."[96] What the Americans wanted was straightforward:

Relief from the application of the present system of arbitrary valuations for duty purposes.
General application of the most favoured (foreign) nation treatment.
Reductions in duty below the most favoured nation rate on a limited number of items.
Assurance that products of any third countries might be shipped through United States ports without disability.

In return, the United States offered Canada most favoured nation treatment, the binding (or guaranteeing) of newsprint, wood pulp, shingles and shell fish on the free list, and substantial reductions in duty on a number of items, including cattle, cheese, apples, whiskey and certain hydro-metallurgical products. The Americans refused concessions on codfish, milk or cream, potatoes and some other agricultural products. This was highly disappointing to Robertson's team, and there was some discussion in Ottawa about the futility of proceeding. The decision was made, however, as Robertson put it, "that negotiations should be steadily pursued in the hope that some modification of the United States position, particularly on these 'key commodities' might be achieved."[97] The brief but intensive negotiating sessions nonetheless ended on 26 August, both sides licking their wounds and contemplating their positions.

Efforts to get back to the bargaining table before the election on 14 October 1935 came to naught, and the government of Mackenzie King, swept into power with a huge majority, was handed the opportunity to strike a deal with the Americans. There seemed little doubt that the new Prime Minister wanted to proceed, and Dr. Skelton told the American Minister in Ottawa so even before King had taken office.[98] King himself soon reiterated his willingness to the Minister, adding that he was prepared to go to Washington to see President Roosevelt about the matter.[99] On 31 October King and the cabinet ministers concerned met Skelton and Robertson and his colleagues and "canvassed the situation until nearly one o'clock, during which time," King wrote, "I got the impression that it was going to be possible for us to effect an agreement."[100] At that meeting it was determined that Robertson, Wilgress and McKinnon would be sent back to Washington on 2 November "to get underway with their negotiations on Monday or Tuesday."[101]

The negotiators did their work, according to Jack Hickerson, at a "terrific pace,"[102] and by 8 November everything hinged on President Roosevelt. On that day, just before Roosevelt met Mackenzie King, William Phillips of the State Department saw his chief:

. . . I had nearly ten minutes to give him a background picture of the importance of the agreement [Phillips wrote in his diary]. I reminded him of Mackenzie King's sentimentality, his belief in the development of trade north and south between the two countries, that his party had been ousted because of the Hawley-Smoot tariff, that the Conservatives had come into power on a retaliatory basis against us and that if the present Liberal government could not go along with us in improved trade relations, they would have to tie up again ... with the British Empire ... the President was favorably disposed toward the new schedules and in going over them he became more and more enthusiastic. [103]

That at least the negotiators had accomplished. What they had begun, Mackenzie King largely completed, securing in his talk with the President some advance on the key questions of lumber, cattle, cream and potatoes. [104]

The treaty had been made now, except for the final drafting, and Skelton and Robertson remained in Washington to complete this. [105] By 11 November, almost all the details had been ironed out, the Canadian and American cabinets had accepted the terms, and all was in readiness for the signatures on 15 November. [106]

The agreement was a major advance—the first trade agreement between Canada and the United States since 1854. [107] The two nations exchanged most favoured nation status, the Americans excepting Cuba, and Canada excepting the British preferential rates. In addition, the United States reduced its tariff rates by 20 to 50 per cent on 63 items, including lumber, cattle, fish, cheese, cream and apples, and undertook to keep 21 items on the free list. In return, Canada extended its entire intermediate tariff to American products, a reduction of 2.5 to 5 per cent on most items, and agreed to amend the Customs Act to eliminate arbitrary valuations. In sum, the agreement rolled back the clock to 1929, before the higher tariffs of the 1930s; [108] it also marked Canada's turn toward the south and away from Britain.

The agreement drew somewhat mixed reviews in Canada, but on the whole was well received. Robertson's final connection with the 1935 agreement came in February 1936 when it was debated in the House of Commons.

Yesterday [he wrote his parents] I had my first experience on the floor of the House of Commons—in Committee of Ways and Means had to sit at a little table in front of King & Dunning [the Minister of Finance] opposite R.B. ready to brief the former in rebuttal of the latter's criticism of the Trade Agreement. Felt very nervous and unprepared but searching questions are seldom put in Parliament so survived the ordeal all right. ... I had an uneasy feeling in Parliament that I shone from the crown of my head to the seat of my pants and unfortunately could not say as much of my shoes. [109]

IV

By this stage in his career, after more than six years in Ottawa, Robertson had established a reputation. He had been trusted by Bennett. He had become indispensable to Skelton, as his preferential treatment on leaves of absence and promotions at a time of a civil service freeze indicates. And by his performance in the negotiations with the United States, he had gone some distance to winning Mackenzie King's regard. In a small civil service, one with relatively few men of talent and ability, Robertson stood out, and his friends were the movers and shakers.[110]

Robertson and his friends met at lunchtime in the cafeteria of the Chateau Laurier, convenient to the East Block and other government offices and with tables arranged so that friends could sit in groups and talk.[111] A good deal of business was done informally there, issues were canvassed, and Robertson could even find jobs for men such as his Oxford colleague Dave Johnson—"acting legal adviser to the Finance Dept. My one successful bit of log rolling."[112] He could also occasionally cause his friends problems. Paul Martin, whom Robertson had met at Harvard in 1927, was elected to the House of Commons as a Liberal in 1935. At the first session in 1936, Martin, one of the few Members interested in and knowledgeable about foreign policy and anxious to make a mark quickly, asked Robertson over lunch one day for the government's view on the recent assassination of a Japanese minister by army officers. Perhaps mischievously, Robertson urged Martin to ask the Prime Minister if he drew significance from this event. Martin did, thus violating the rule that new members should know their place, and for his pains he was rebuked by the Government Whip and by an Opposition friend. Nonetheless, later Martin was named to the Canadian delegation to Geneva, something he attributed in part at least to Robertson's efforts on his behalf.[113]

Robertson had even acquired some reputation with diplomats stationed in Ottawa. The British High Commissioner, Sir Francis Floud, was perhaps not the ablest representative who ever served in Canada nor the most charitable toward his temporary home,* but he had developed a

---

*Floud's views on Canada were one long complaint: " . . . I have never known a place where colds and rheumatism are so prevalent . . . it is folly to attempt to do as much as one has been accustomed to do in England. The absence of outdoor exercise in winter is also very trying . . . there is practically no spring in the English sense. . . . June is made almost unbearable in the country by the mosquitoes. . . . I can't say we find Canadians in the mass

high regard for Robertson. In a letter to the Dominions Office in January 1936, Floud said that "Most of our business is ... done with the Department of External Affairs, and though Skelton is not a very easy man to get on terms with he has been very kind and friendly. He is not a good administrator and his office is badly organized, but some of the men on his staff, particularly Loring Christie [who had rejoined External Affairs in 1935 after a decade in private business] and Norman Robertson, are exceptionally able and always very helpful." [114] A year and a half later, after close contact with Robertson on trade matters, Floud told Mackenzie King that "he regarded Robertson as the ablest brain he had met with in Canada," a remark that triggered an idea in the Prime Minister's mind. [115]

For a month, King had been concerned by the difficulties of staffing his office. His aides, H.R.L. Henry, the nominal Private Secretary, and E.A. Pickering, the Assistant Private Secretary and the real workhorse, had not grown into the work, he believed, [116] and he desperately wanted a Skelton-like figure to take hold of the office and make it hum. Now Floud's praise for Robertson had suggested just the man. "Skelton is equally appreciative of Robertson's judgment in these large matters," King wrote, adding:

I spoke to Robertson in conversation ... and am having him come more immediately into association with my office to take a position there corresponding, in some respects, with that which Skelton, himself, has with regard to External Affairs. Skelton has tried to keep both roles in one, and broken down in consequence.

The next day, King visited Skelton, recuperating from heart strain at home, to complete arrangements:

... I could see he did not like losing him, and would have preferred my taking [Scott] Macdonald, he nevertheless said that Robertson had the better brain, and would be more useful man for the Prime Minister's Office. He agreed that as Prime Minister, I should have the call on any man in the service. He also agreed that the present situation was nothing short of ludicrous. [117]

---

an attractive lot. Most of them are mid-Victorian, conventional, snobbish, touchy and suspicious of English people. ... Everyone, and particularly the women, talk with the rapidity and persistence of a machine-gun, and in most cases their voices are a perpetual torment. At cocktail parties, which are the favourite form of entertainment, the note of screaming becomes higher and higher as the time goes on, and it becomes almost impossible to make oneself heard at all ... we feel sometimes that we shall explode unless we let off steam." (Churchill College, Cambridge, P.J. Grigg Papers, PJGG 2/7, Floud to Batterbee, 16 Jan. 36 and *ibid.*, Floud to Grigg, 19 Jan. 36.)

On 1 November, the Prime Minister informed his staff of Robertson's appointment to their number. He noted in his diary that, while it would be "hard on [Skelton] and his staff to rob them of Robertson . . . I cannot hold out as things are."[118]

No one had asked Robertson his views, and he was horrified at the prospect of working directly under the Prime Minister. His early views on King had not altered very much, and he had seen enough of the Prime Minister's capriciousness and regularly inconsiderate treatment of his staff to know that a post in his Office was no bed of roses. J.W. Pickersgill later recollected that Robertson "wasn't in great sympathy with [King] at that time. . . .I think he regarded the Prime Minister's Office as very second rate in 1937."[119] All that was true. Worse, Robertson, although never a careerist, could not help worrying about the effect of service in the Office on his long-term prospects. In addition, he feared that the existing PMO staff, Henry, Pickering, and Walter Turnbull, might resent his being parachuted in over their heads, and there were widespread stories in the bureaucracy about the tendency of the PMO officers to throw spokes in the wheels of newcomers.[120] The future did not look very bright, and Pickersgill still remembers a solemn and mournful dinner with the Robertsons the day that Mackenzie King snatched Robertson away from his Department.[121]

The only saving grace was that Robertson kept charge of his existing duties in the Department, but even this caused him problems and forced him into "leading [a] double life shuttling back & forth between his office and my own which I continue to occupy for half of each day. It is not a satisfactory arrangement," Robertson told his parents in Vancouver, " & will not, I think, last after Skelton's return."[122] That in fact was so. In December Skelton had recovered sufficiently to go south with Mackenzie King for a rest; while there, he apparently persuaded the Prime Minister to release Robertson from his servitude in the Prime Minister's Office on the grounds that he was too valuable as a trade negotiator to be spared. King reluctantly agreed on the one condition that he receive further assistance, a condition that was satisfied by seconding Pickersgill to the Office before the end of 1937. Pickersgill had found his niche and never returned to Departmental duties; Robertson had escaped from durance vile and remained happily in the service of External Affairs.[123]

Robertson's time in the Department since 1929 had seen him concentrating primarily on League of Nations questions, on a variety of special chores for Skelton, and, increasingly from 1935, on trade policy. He had turned into the workhorse of the Department and into a genuine expert on tariffs and trade. He had tackled the art of negotiation, and had clearly impressed his chief, Dr. Skelton, with his good judgment and his expertise.

As important, Robertson himself had changed greatly. The radical socialist of Vancouver and Oxford had disappeared forever; the man who had sat on Sir Robert Borden's cabin bed and munched grapes was no more. In his place was a rather cautious and somewhat conservative bureaucrat, who knew how the government worked and who was quite capable of holding his own in discussions with a cabinet minister or in negotiations with a foreign diplomat. Robertson could still write frank letters to his parents or to close friends in the Department, but most of his writing now was in the form of memoranda, often designed to conceal his own views as much as to explicate them. Robertson had changed and matured. He had become a civil servant.

CHAPTER III

Trade Negotiator

B Y THE BEGINNING of 1936, Norman Robertson was in effective charge of his Department's share of trade and tariff questions and negotiations with Britain and the United States. This was important work, much the most critical that he had undertaken for the Department, for most of Canada's trade was with the two great powers. It was also detailed work, hard to grasp, complicated in its interrelationships, and excruciatingly political. Robertson's ability to master it was spectacular. His technical skills, his powers of concentration and application over an extended period, and the ultimate success of the negotiations established his reputation in the Department and with Mackenzie King. This chapter presents a detailed analysis of these negotiations, which occupied Robertson from 1936 until the eve of the Second World War.

I

Norman Robertson spent most of 1936 labouring on questions of trade with Britain. In March he worked on ways to maintain the export of oats,[1] and on 12 June he sailed for England, accompanied by Wilgress, McKinnon and Hugh Scully, the Commissioner of Customs, with a view to renegotiating the trade agreement produced by those hectic days of bargaining during the Imperial Economic Conference at Ottawa. "They will discuss the British negotiations with Mr. Massey & you when they arrive," Dr. Skelton wrote to L.B. Pearson at the High Commission in a slightly testy mood. "[P]ossibly by that time Cabinet here will have found time to frame a definite line of policy."[2] But in fact nothing had been accomplished by the time the team left for Britain. The difficulty was that, because of the Ottawa agreements of 1932, seen at the time as a victory for Canada, the Dominion had lost substantial freedom to revise her own tariff rates. "The Canadian officials believe," the author of a Board of Trade memorandum wrote, that the United Kingdom is likely "to oppose the reduction of duties under the Intermediate tariff" in items such as diesel engines, silk and glass. "Failure on the part of Canada to reduce or to have authority to reduce, the Intermediate rates, will, in their judgment, make it difficult to negotiate with" other nations.[3]

On 24 June, the cabinet took up a long memorandum, drafted and left behind by Robertson, that the Prime Minister called "one of the most valuable External Affairs has thus far produced."[4] Robertson's report analyzed clearly and fully the Canadian desires and the likely British responses, concluding rather bleakly that revision of the preferential system is "not likely to meet with the sympathetic response it would have received in 1932, and that, unless negotiations with Canada are recognized as inaugurating a new and decisive departure from the narrowly conceived policies followed by the United Kingdom from 1932 to 1936, it will be extremely difficult to reach a mutually satisfactory agreement." Too true.

The difficulties were many,[5] and for almost two months Robertson and his colleagues in London engaged in a prolonged series of negotiations.[6] The stakes were substantial, for Canadian exports to Britain were worth £56 million and British exports to Canada £21 million in 1935 (a considerable increase over the 1932 figures, which were £43 million and £16 million respectively).[7] According to Wilgress's later recollection, Robertson "felt very deeply about the bad way we had treated the British in '32 and he wanted to make it good without it appearing to be a one-sided deal, so it was largely a question of talking over with the British the Canadian tariff side of the Agreement."[8] That was probably true, and an additional goal was to expand even further trade between the two countries. The Canadians, flying in the face of a British policy of restricting and controlling food imports,[9] won an expansion of meat sales, assurances of reduced duties on some commodities, and guaranteed margins of preference on items such as wheat, butter, apples and copper. They also earned a marginally freer hand to negotiate with other countries than had previously been the case, since fixed margins of preference were eliminated in a number of cases.[10] For their part, the British secured lower tariffs on 179 items, including textiles, glass, steel and iron, boots and shoes, and guarantees that there would be no upward revision of the existing preferential rates on a substantial range of items.[11] The negotiators initialled the draft agreement on 20 August.

Both governments had to haggle directly, however, before they could accept the work of their negotiators.[12] In December 1936, four months after the conclusion of the draft agreement, Robertson became directly involved in the final stages of the negotiation. King appreciated the worth of his experts, but he could still "feel that the official mind does not grasp the political" when he was confronted with a memorandum that objected to the line he was trying on the British. Considering that the Prime Minister was staging an elaborate bluff to win concessions at the last minute, that was probably so. Nonetheless, the final Canadian position was prepared by King and Skelton with "Robertson and McKinnon . . . on hand with memos and suggestions."[13] By 11 January 1937 the cabinet had essentially accepted the agreement, "a very large transaction," just as King called it.[14]

For Robertson it was all anticlimactic. As he wrote to his mother early in 1937: "We've been pretty busy all winter, rather short-handed in the Department, so I'm kept fairly stretched by a number of interesting jobs. You will have seen from the Speech from the Throne that the U.K. agreement has been concluded—practically identical with the draft we brought back from London last August. So that all our squirming . . . came to nothing at all."[15] In his view, the agreement simply retained and stabilized for a further period the conditions established in 1932.[16]

II

In 1937 and 1938, the major item on Robertson's agenda was the negotiation of a new and expanded trade agreement with the United States, a negotiation that involved Canada in simultaneous bargaining with Britain. Robertson prepared the basic memorandum on the American problem. The 1935 agreement, he said, "was described in its preamble as a *first step* toward the lowering of the barriers impeding trade between the countries." Its scope was limited by the margins of preference bound in favour of Empire countries and by the fact that under the United States Trade Agreement Act, the President could not authorize a reduction of more than fifty percent in the United States Tariff," He added: "Political conditions in the United States . . . prevented . . . any concession on certain important products, notably grains and

fresh codfish." Much had been gained in 1935, therefore, but there was
still more to be won, and Robertson laid out the case:

In offering to negotiate a new agreement with the United States at the same time
that we prepared to forego, in substantial part, certain margins of preference
currently enjoyed by Canadian products in the United Kingdom, Canada is in a
position to ask for the maximum reduction possible under the United States
Trade Agreements Act on every dutiable article entering the United States of
which this country is, has been or may be 'the principal supplier' of United States
import requirements. In the rush and pressure of the 1935 negotiations, when
both governments were anxious to bring discussions once initiated to a speedy
conclusion, a good many products in which trade was small or had been stopped
altogether by United States tariffs were left out of consideration in view of the
necessity of concentrating our efforts on securing the best possible terms for the
entry of such major exports as lumber, cattle and fish into the American market.
This year, there will be, therefore, a good deal of mopping up to do.

What precisely was a margin of preference? Robertson offered an
example:

Our own tariff on American cheese is 7 cents a pound and we are obligated to
maintain a margin of preference in favour of Australia of 6 cents a pound over
foreign cheese so that we could only reduce the duty on American cheese to 6
cents a pound, and then on condition that Australian and New Zealand cheese
entered free.

Thus, the process was interlocking, complex and highly political. To
reduce the duty on cheese angered domestic producers in Ontario and
Quebec; to try to keep it up angered the Australians and Americans, who
might then retaliate by refusing to lower their tariffs on another product
of interest to the Maritimes or British Columbia. To negotiate on tariffs
was to try the soul, to play a balancing game, and never wholly to satisfy
anyone.

Certainly Norman Robertson was well aware of the complications
after his experience of the last two years. He also understood the political
necessities that obliged President Roosevelt to try to get American
agricultural products into the protected United Kingdom market, and he
knew that "It is beyond question ... that the United States negotiators
will press primarily for reductions in duties on *natural products, chiefly
agricultural*, normally exported to this country." He also expected that the
Americans would want Canada to secure release from bound margins of

preference with Britain and other Empire countries on a number of agricultural products. [17]

Robertson had laid out the trade predicament in this model memorandum. Canada was caught in a situation where the interests of the United States and the United Kingdom were paramount and where Canadian concerns, on balance, had little weight. But if those Canadian requirements were small internationally, domestically they had substantial weight, and to suggest, as some soon did, that Canada should make sacrifices to help achieve Anglo-American harmony, smacked of political madness. It was a touchy matter, made more so by the prospect of a new German war, a possibility that made the economic arrangements of the North Atlantic triangle all the more crucial. Robertson was at the centre of one of the great issues of the day. [18]

The first shot in the war of words that was to occupy almost two years took place on 17 January 1937 when the State Department told the British that the Canada-United Kingdom trade agreement (not formally signed until 23 February) "raises the question of whether the cumulative effect of such policy is not to obstruct and impede the broad program for economic disarmament that is underway. . . ." In Ottawa, Mackenzie King could scarcely have agreed that Canada was obstructing "economic disarmament," but he was concerned that "the British are playing the old game and stating to the States that they cannot lower duties because of the opposition of Canada." That was false, King firmly, if not quite accurately, believed—"we meant what we said about our liberal policy." [19]

Nonetheless, the Americans were genuinely concerned about the implications of the Canada-United Kingdom agreement. On 3 March Robertson set out the reasoning. Secretary of State Hull believed that the agreement could hamper the Congressional renewal of the Trade Agreements Act, that it might interfere with the negotiation of the American agreement with Britain, and that it might hinder his long-term objective of freer trade. The first fear was no more, Robertson said, because the Senate had done its duty and renewed the Trade Act the same day the Canada-UK agreement had been tabled in Ottawa. The other points were harder. On the second, Robertson wrote, "the only question is how far does Schedule III [of the Canada-UK Agreement] obligating the United Kingdom to maintain margins of preference in favour of Canada on some twenty commodities, prevent the United Kingdom from making adequate tariff concessions in favour of the United States."

That was the question all right, and Robertson answered it by noting that on sixteen commodities the British were bound by agreements with the Dominions to maintain margins of preference; that the margins were moderate, scarcely formidable obstacles to international commerce; that American exports to Britain of the goods in question were small, less than one-tenth of American exports to Britain before 1932; that Canada was relatively more dependent on foreign markets and on the British market in particular than the United States was; and finally that most British duties were "autonomous"—the British could raise or lower them at will "without asking by your leave of any Dominion." As for Hull's final point, Robertson pointed out that every tariff alteration in the Canada-UK agreement was "a downward revision of existing rates"; that the number of fixed margins of preference on the Canadian side had been reduced from 215 to 91; and that, of those remaining, "the height of a good many has been reduced."[20] That was effective advocacy, and presumably Mackenzie King carried Robertson's memorandum with him when he went to Washington a few days later to see Hull and President Roosevelt.[21]

Those talks with the American leaders were long, as Roosevelt attempted to get King to mediate between Britain and the United States on trade.[22] What the Americans wanted, Robertson said later, was "Canadian help in modifying the system of Imperial preference in so far as it stands as an obstacle in the way of freer world trade, and therefore, the argument runs, in the way of peace."

Was this a fair assessment of the British preferences set in place in Ottawa in 1932? Writing in guarded bureaucratic prose, Robertson said that many "responsible persons in different countries" agreed with the Americans:

On the economic plane, it is contended that discriminatory preferences not only tend, as do national tariffs, to restrict the volume of world trade, but by affecting its diversion into uneconomic channels, further limit the contribution to national wealth that might result from effective geographical specialization. . . .

Politically, the case against Imperial preferences from the point of view of the United States Secretary of State . . . can be summed up as follows: . . . they make effective political cooperation between the United States and the Commonwealth countries more difficult; . . . their existence . . . is a repudiation of the principle of commercial equality on which a good many people believe any permanent revival of international trade must be based. . . .

Then Robertson pointed out that Secretary Hull was undoubtedly looking to the Imperial Conference, scheduled to follow the coronation of

George VI in May. Hull, he argued, "thinks that we might carry our initiative [in trying to lower tariffs bilaterally, as in the agreement with the British] a little further and try and get the Commonwealth countries, as a whole, to consider as a question of high policy whether or not, on balance, our true interests are really best served in the long run by the perpetuation of a system of customs discrimination." If the British Commonwealth, Robertson went on, setting out Hull's views and almost certainly his own, "would accept in the economic field the implications of the idea of equality on which they insist in their political relations . . . it would give an enormous impetus to the movement toward freer trade. . . ."[23] But as a realist, Robertson recognized that such a move at the Imperial Conference would occur only if Canada and Mackenzie King took the initiative; and that, he knew, was exceedingly unlikely.

King in fact did little to advance the cause of "economic appeasement" at the Conference. The agenda, to which he agreed, did not stress economic questions, and the Prime Minister's remarks to his fellows gave only one brief bow in the direction of American economic aspirations.[24] So much for that. It was almost as if the coronation and the panoply of Empire had dragged Mackenzie King away from his North American attitudes.

Robertson's work in London had to do with trade, where he was the only official for economic and financial discussions. In a memo prepared on 10 May, he looked at Canada's difficulties, caught between two bigger, stronger, richer powers. An Anglo-American trade agreement, he wrote,

is to be desired on both political and economic grounds. The question is how could Canada facilitate it. It will clearly be more difficult now that our agreement with the U.K. has been revised and confirmed for a fixed period of years, to waive guaranteed margins of preference that stand in the way of the U.K.-U.S. agreement, than it would have been this time last year when the situation was fluid. It would not be politically feasible to relinquish any present preferences in the U.K. market if the only quid pro quo Canada got was a certificate of contribution to the general political appeasement of the world.

A certificate of good conduct would not be enough. But what would prepare the Canadian public for a triangular trade deal? Robertson summarized the points to be borne in mind:

1.   For all practical purposes Canadian goods already enjoy free entry into the U.K.

market, so that there is no opportunity or need for upsetting the waiver of preferences by tariff concessions.

2. The bacon and cattle provisions of the Canada-U.K. Agreement . . . need not be re-opened.
3. . . . the U.K. could be asked to surrender the right reserved under both the 1932 and 1937 Agreements to impose duties on Canadian dairy and poultry produce . . . [this] would undoubtedly be regarded in Canada as a very important improvement. . . .
4. Some compensatory modifications of the bound margins of preference in favour of the U.K. . . . might reasonably be asked for in return for the modification of bound margins of preference in favour of Canada. [If this were done on some products such as iron and steel] . . . Canada would be in a position to make more advantageous trade arrangements with the U.S., Belgium and the Netherlands.

Robertson pointed out that Canada as a most favoured nation automatically received the benefit of any reductions in tariffs that the British negotiated in the American market. And there might be other opportunities for indirect compensation to Canada. Direct concessions, however, could be made only in a new Canadian-American agreement, and that possibility, he urged, should be considered. "In such a revision we should seek, among other things, the maximum reduction on cattle, potatoes and fish."[25]

Robertson's direct discussions with the British began on 1 June when he and Pearson met with a British official team headed by A.E. Overton of the Board of Trade.[26] Overton went over the familiar ground, and then indicated that Canada was the first of the Dominions to be approached about the forthcoming Anglo-American trade talks because Britain recognized that the question was important for Canada. As to compensation for the abandonment of any preferences, "the United Kingdom has already requested the United States to consider the possibility of making such compensation directly to Canada in the way of tariff reductions." Robertson knew there was little chance of that, but he must have been more interested in Overton's suggestion that, in return for Canadian cooperation in waiving preferences, the United Kingdom "would undoubtedly adopt a most sympathetic attitude toward any future Canadian requests . . . to waive fixed margins of preference if these margins stood in the way of Canadian trade negotiations with foreign countries." That was potentially important to Canada, as Robertson realized, but he gave nothing away initially, simply saying that it was a question "of immediate and tangible disadvantages vs. deferred and intangible advantages." Jam tomorrow was scant substitute for jam today. The British offer nonetheless seemed to get lost, and it later became a bone of contention between Ottawa, Washington and London.[27]

Matters proceeded no further before the Canadians returned home. On 11 June, however, Mackenzie King had met his accompanying colleagues and told them that Canada had to begin trade talks with the Americans, "this being the only method of approach to enable us to meet the British Ministers in giving up some things."[28] One of Robertson's ideas had been accepted.

By mid-July, Robertson was back in Canada after an absence of three months from his family. The trade negotiations that Mackenzie King had expected to be concluded in time for the next session of Parliament[29] were to go on for almost a year and a half more.

Part of the problem was mutual incomprehension. For example, Pierrepont Moffat, a senior official in the Department of State at Washington, was annoyed with the British for asking Washington to pay for modifying the Ottawa preferences, despite American refusals to do so.[30] The British were blaming the Canadians and claiming that their talks with Washington were stalled because Ottawa could not decide what to do.[31] Much of the difficulty hinged on the Robertson-Overton meeting of 1 June, and the Americans tried very diligently to sort out what had occurred, pressing their investigations in Ottawa and Washington,[32] and ultimately concluding, as Moffat wrote on 6 August, that the British were at fault. "They claimed to have mentioned the matter once in general terms to Norman Robertson, but the terms seem to have been so general that the latter (despite his keen mind) had not gathered the import. They had not spoken to Skelton or Mackenzie King and had apparently sent no communications to Canada since the end of the Imperial Conference." It was not a pretty episode, Moffat concluded, and one indicative of the British lack of seriousness.[33]

That question resolved, and blame appropriately apportioned by the Americans, at least, matters then began to proceed. The British and the Americans both agreed on the usefulness of talks with the Canadians,[34] and on 7 August Mackenzie King told the American Minister that he was prepared for "exploratory conversations between officials . . . with a view to ascertaining how far it might serve the interests of both Governments to proceed with negotiations."[35] A few days later, Armour was instructed to accept King's suggestion and told to ask that "Doctor Skelton . . . and Mr. Norman Robertson . . . be designated . . . to take part in these discussions, rather than technical experts prepared to discuss individual commodities, because of our view that the conversations must necessarily be of a very general character."[36] The Americans were also interested in speed, an indication of their view that the talks were less to discuss trade than to clarify matters so that the Anglo-American discussions could proceed in earnest.[37]

In fact, the visit to Washington was made by Skelton alone in dark secrecy.[38] Well-briefed by Robertson,[39] the Under-Secretary had discussions with Cordell Hull and heard that free trade enthusiast denounce Imperial preferences. Hickerson told him of the Americans' need for an agreement with an important industrial country, one that would bring advantage to US agricultural producers. The American problem was one of timing, and Hickerson was frank when he told his old friend that "they did not see what advantage there would be in giving detailed consideration to negotiations for a Canada-United States treaty if in the end they were still to come up against this blank wall."[40]

The result was an impasse. Skelton argued that Canada could not give up preferences to make an Anglo-American agreement possible unless there were simultaneous negotiations in which Canada participated. To the Americans this was impossible. But both agreed that further confidential and informal discussions could be held,[41] and Hickerson a few days later suggested that Wilgress and McKinnon were "so well-known as the ace negotiators of trade agreements for Canada, that their presence here might give rise to embarrassing speculation ... for the immediate future it would be preferable for Norman Robertson to come here alone."[42] Presumably Robertson was not yet known as an "ace". In any case, Mackenzie King had his cabinet authorize Robertson and his two trade colleagues to begin to explore "what we want" and "what we can give."[43] At the same time, the British were beginning to suggest that the "proposed Canadian-American negotiations" had shifted the initiative for the Anglo-American talks to the United States, a suggestion that angered the Americans, who were also told it was their responsibility to make Canada relinquish its right to preferences.[44]

At this stage, Dr. Skelton fell ill with what was shortly to be diagnosed as heart strain. The Under-Secretary did not disappear from the picture entirely, since he could deal with memoranda from his home and he even went to the office for brief periods, but far more of the work of the Department and particularly of the work on trade questions fell on Robertson.[45]

Certainly Mackenzie King now began to call Robertson directly for information on the state of preparations for the talks with the United States. In a conversation on 30 September, the Prime Minister told

Robertson he could not go to Washington alone, as Hickerson had suggested. "There were several Departments concerned in the conduct of commercial negotiations and if we took too much initiative in the matter they would resent it. He said," Robertson informed Dr. Skelton, "he was willing to have Wilgress, McKinnon and me go to Washington. . . ." The First Secretary had told the Prime Minister that the work of preparation was well in hand, that Canada's agreements with Commonwealth countries had been studied, and that the British could help persuade those countries to give up their preferences in Canada that stood in the way of an agreement with the United States. "I said I still thought that the biggest contribution we could make, at the least cost, to the general settlement would be the giving up of the margin of preference on wheat." King knew that was sure to cause him trouble with his Western ministers, but he asked Robertson to prepare a detailed memorandum for cabinet.[46]

This long paper, characterized by Skelton on his sickbed as "admirable,"[47] laid out the situation and demonstrated clearly that concessions helpful to the United States could be made by the British without harm to Canadian interests. That was some reassurance for the ministers, but Robertson's detailed exposition once again pointed to the problems—the American concern for timing, the Canadian concern for compensation. He also pointed out the broader implications:

The main line of Canadian commercial policy . . . is a determination to liberalize the system of imperial preference by insisting that freer trade within the Empire shall be a stride toward and not a flight from freer trade with the world. . . .

Our stake in world trade and the peculiar degree of dependence of our industries on export markets have identified Canada's real national interest with the revival and liberation of international trade. At this particular juncture of affairs, the most effective single agency operating in the direction in which we want to go is the United States Trade Agreement policy. . . . We have, therefore, every interest in the maintenance of what are now the main lines of American commercial policy. . . . We cannot take the continuation of this policy on the part of the United States for granted. . . . It is probably true to say that the success or failure of this new direction of American policy depends on the successful conclusion within the next few months of a trade agreement with the United Kingdom. . . .

It is true that there are a number of important local and sectional interests which in the short run, and perhaps in the longer run, stand to lose rather than to gain from the adjustments in tariffs and preferential margins which our collaboration in new agreements with the United Kingdom and the United States would involve. These are the inevitable consequences of protectionist policy and follow as surely from a lessening of protection in markets abroad as from a reduction of tariffs in markets at home. Some conflict of interest of this sort is inescapable. All that is submitted, is that this country's general national interest is, for better or worse, bound up with the prospects of freer international trade and that this paramount interest should outweigh special ai d local interests which may be deriving exceptional advantages from an uneconomic policy. . . .[48]

This was an important memorandum by Robertson, one that set out the guidelines of Canadian policy for the next generation, and one that stated his own long-held beliefs on the virtues of freer trade. It was also a shrewd paper, in that it took Mackenzie King's own beliefs and put them into concrete form. When the cabinet discussed Robertson's work on 8 October, with the Prime Minister leading his colleagues paragraph by paragraph through the text, the wisdom of Robertson's approach was apparent. "At each stage Minister would balk," King scribbled in his diary. "Dunning has habit of objecting, and of deliberately misconstruing or seeking to see some objection never stated. Euler [Minister of Trade and Commerce] & Gardiner [Minister of Agriculture] kept interposing objections to each immediate change suggested—forgetting continually the larger considerations." But, King added, sounding not unlike Robertson, "It is a difficult task—our sacrifice is of the vicarious variety which is always difficult in politics." Nonetheless, the Prime Minister prevailed, as he almost invariably did when his mind was firm, and won acceptance for the basis of negotiation suggested by Robertson.[49]

King's instructions to Robertson were for the officials to proceed immediately with a survey of the possibilities for an agreement with the United States and to have this ready for cabinet by 13 October. If the prospects were favourable, "the officials should be ready to go to Washington for preliminary and exploratory conversations at the end of the week with a view to ascertaining whether the United States would be ready to make such concessions on Canadian goods as would bring into play our contingent willingness to give up certain margins of preference." If there was some hope there, the Prime Minister said, the British could be advised of the modifications Canada would accept on preferences in the United Kingdom—and of the compensatory adjustments affecting British margins in Canada "and the opportunities for selling Canadian goods in the United Kingdom market which we would expect in return."[50] The Prime Minister still was determined to get a price for his concessions.

By 14 October, King had arranged to have Robertson, Wilgress and McKinnon go to Washington.[51] Upon their arrival there on 18 October, the Canadians discovered, somewhat to their surprise, that, despite all the preliminary palavering, the Americans were unprepared to consider a new agreement to supersede the 1935 one. They had been thinking only of a supplementary agreement, they said, and were concerned that any announcement of intent to negotiate a new agreement would cause difficulties. The Americans, Robertson reported, had again raised the question of timing, but they had eventually agreed that this question could not be considered in the abstract and without reference to the scope and character of a new agreement with Canada. The Americans also consented to examine sympathetically the Canadian proposals, although Robertson warned that that meant a delay of at least three or four weeks.[52]

On 17 November, finally, the United States informed London that it was ready to begin negotiations. At the same time the United States told Ottawa that it was prepared to announce within two weeks that negotiations for a new or supplementary agreement with Canada would commence shortly.[53] This was a substantial shift in American policy, an indication of willingness to negotiate simultaneously with Britain and Canada. Mackenzie King was delighted, but for his own domestic political reasons he wanted the announcement of negotiations with Canada to be made at the same time as that with Britain, and further, he wanted reference in the American announcement to the fact that talks had been underway since August. This was no simple matter, and Robertson protested. "Just here," King wrote on 17 November,

one saw the difference between the political and the Civil Service type of mind, Robertson viewing the situation from the point of view of the caution and care necessary to phrasing announcements, etc., was much of the view that the matter could not be hastened in the manner in which I felt it must be. He was fearful of embarrassing the diplomats, etc., etc. I let him see that large political considerations were more important than any matter of etiquette or feelings at this stage, and that neither of the latter need be lost sight of in pressing a just demand which is bound to be as helpful to others as to ourselves. Robertson was inclined to sympathize with the Americans' desire to have their farmers have a fortnight to see the possible advantage of the possible British Agreement. I felt strongly from the start that this might be of advantage to them, would all be of disadvantage to us, and, in the end, confusion would be avoided by getting everything as close together as possible.[54]

King was probably correct, and got his way.[55]

For the next several months, matters dragged on slowly, thanks to the convoluted and cumbersome American procedures required because of the provisions of the Trade Agreements Act. Finally, on 14 March 1938, just a week before he and his colleagues left Ottawa for Washington and the negotiations, Robertson prepared yet another paper for cabinet. He pointed out that the American requests required the modification of certain margins of preference that Canada had guaranteed to other parts of the Empire,[56] and while Canada had learned unofficially what some of the products in question were, there was as yet no word on the extent of the desired concessions, a factor that made consultation impossible as yet. Furthermore, US requests of Britain, almost as an afterthought, had included the Colonial Empire and represented an American attempt to secure an "open door" in the Colonies. On balance, Robertson indicated, if Canada could secure a relaxation of American preferences in Cuba in return for an easing of Canadian preferences with the Colonies, this would be advantageous. There were bound to be difficulties in completing such a complicated trade-off quickly, however. That memo was read by King to cabinet on 14 March and was approved.[57]

Thus, by the last week in March, Robertson, Wilgress and McKinnon were settled in Washington for the duration. The complexity of the task was staggering, and Robertson was able to return home only once or twice until November and the signature of the agreement. This was a long time to be away from his family, but in those days the Department of External Affairs was remarkably unconcerned about the personal lives of its officers, and if Robertson missed his wife and daughter, that was unfortunate but secondary to his work.

But was he lonely or bored? Probably not, for so long as he had congenial colleagues—and he did in Dana Wilgress, Hector McKinnon, Jack Hickerson, and some members of the British delegation, to say nothing of friends made in his Brookings days—and one or two good bookstores, Robertson was happy. There were also the Washington Senators' baseball games once the season began, and on one occasion Hickerson hauled his friend down and away from a dangerous lined foul ball.[58] It was hard, complicated work, but it was never unpleasant, and for Robertson, a man who lived for his job, the eight months in the American capital were absorbing.

For the first six weeks, however, the pace was anything but hectic. The Americans had not yet progressed to the stage where they were ready to negotiate formally with Canada, and much of the detail of the US-UK negotiations remained confidential. Wilgress and McKinnon were directly concerned with working out the position on, respectively, the concessions to be sought from the Americans and the concessions to be offered to them.[59] As in 1935, Robertson's mandate was more general, and he was charged with holding a watching brief on the whole range of the negotiations and, not least important, with keeping Skelton and the Prime Minister informed on progress.*

Sometimes this meant educating Ottawa on the difficulties in sorting out the ways in which the Anglo-American negotiations overlapped with the Canadian-American and Anglo-Canadian positions. Just how complex this was could be seen from a long report Robertson made to Skelton on 10 May. The objective of a simultaneous signing of agreements still existed, he wrote, although, since the Anglo-American talks were further advanced, they might have to be slowed "so we can overtake the head start they gained. . . ." More important to satisfy the United States was the necessity of reducing the bound preferences accorded some Canadian goods in the British market. That was a *sine qua non* of an Anglo-American pact, but since Canadian approval was required and "Since the measure of Canadian concurrence will depend in part at least upon the terms of the new Agreement that can be worked out between Canada and the United States," the sets of negotiations were interlocked. Moreover, the American requests of Canada required the acquiescence of a number of Commonwealth countries in the modification of preferences, and without such ratification, only "some sort" of agreement could be concluded.[60] How long would this tangle take to resolve? In Robertson's view, based on talks with the British and American teams, there was only a fifty-fifty chance that the agreements could be wound up by mid-June, a date of importance to the Canadian government's forthcoming budget. At least no one was now blaming Canada for the delay, Robertson said. In fact, the American list of concessions to and requests of Canada had neither been formally approved nor given to the Canadian team.[61]

The proposed concessions were finally delivered only on 25 May. "It was given to us," Robertson reported, "with the explanation that it should not be regarded as necessarily a final offer, although it represented the limit that their economic and political advisers thought the United States Government could do in the way of tariff reductions on agricultural and

---

* More than three years later, Robertson told the American Minister in Ottawa that "The Canadian negotiations up to the final phase had been carried on by personal correspondence between Robertson and Skelton, and Skelton and the Prime Minister. The rest of the Cabinet were not brought into the picture until a balanced whole could be presented. If Cabinet Ministers once get their hands on a first list of demands each one automatically vetoes concessions where he is interested and the result is invariably no agreement." (Harvard University, Pierrepont Moffat Papers, Memorandum of Conversation, 25 Sep. 41.)

primary products. ..." The team's examination of the lists was not yet complete, he added, but while it did have much of value on a number of items, "it falls a long way short of the objective, set out for us in our instructions, of a comprehensive and definitive trade agreement. ..." The Americans offered concessions on cattle, cream, cheddar cheese, potatoes and fish but, he pointed out, the offer

is not big enough as it stands to swing the modifications of our overseas preferences which we will be forced to face as part of the simultaneous conclusion of an agreement between the United States and the United Kingdom. For that matter neither does it represent the trading counterpart of the tariff concessions the United States will seek and that for reasons of general policy we assume that the Government will be inclined to grant. We have insisted as strongly as we could that a comprehensive trade agreement was the condition of Canadian consent to modification of margins of preference—and we are meeting the United States negotiators daily with a view to securing a major expansion of their offer before proceeding to any examination of their requests.[62]

The waiting was over and the battle had begun.

In a detailed report a few days later, Robertson said that the draft schedule of American concessions proposed no reduction on wheat and flour. "We have pointed out," Robertson told Ottawa on 30 May, "that our Government's willingness to relinquish the guaranteed margin of two shillings per quarter on wheat in the United Kingdom was contingent on the conclusion of otherwise satisfactory arrangements," which meant the maximum possible reduction under the Trade Agreements Act. The difficulty was that, although the US was usually a large wheat exporter and in ordinary years there was no wheat imported from Canada, Hickerson's team feared the public reaction to a concession on that item. When the Canadians in turn served notice "that this attitude on their part would compel our Government to reconsider its position in respect of the margin of preference on wheat in the United Kingdom," Hickerson then indicated that it might be possible to offer reductions instead on bran and other feeds, all of which were imported into the United States, and during the last year to the tune of $7 million. That sounded helpful, but not "as any kind of political makeweight to balance our waiver of the United Kingdom's duty on foreign wheat." In Robertson's view, the situation was that Canada had to pay too much for any concession on wheat from the Americans. "We did not therefore think it advisable to press them further ... and told them that we would sooner take the whole wheat position under advisement and ... secure further instructions. ..."

Robertson did not hesitate to suggest what those instructions should be: " ... we are inclined to think that we should forget about the United States duties on such products of which we are both exporters and try to get in return for the waiver of the wheat preference ... an undertaking that the United States would not bonus the export of wheat to world markets. ..." By this Robertson meant that both Americans and Canadians could agree not to offer export subsidies to their producers, a device of benefit to Canada, given the larger size of the American wheat belt. That was a fair trade for the British wheat preference.[63]

After a brief visit to Ottawa in mid-June,[64] the Canadians began a long series of discussions with Hickerson's team, "who have been outlining their requests for tariff concessions from Canada. For better or worse," Robertson said, "they have taken our Government's wish for a 'broad and comprehensive Agreement' pretty literally and are going through the Canadian Customs Tariff from beginning to end, seeking reduction of duty, in addition to the removal of the 3 percent special excise tax, on most of the important commodities of which the United States is the principal foreign supplier of Canadian requirements." In his view, the American aim was the complete restoration of the *status quo ante* Bennett. In addition, they were seeking improvement in those areas where they had earned no "betterment in their position" in 1935, although they did recognize that "substantial industries have been developed and expanded under the protection of the higher tariffs that have been in force against American goods for the last seven or eight years. In most such cases," he added, "while some trimming of rates is unavoidable and probably desirable, we are hopeful that, in the course of the negotiations, they can be persuaded to accept tariff reductions substantially more moderate than those they are now seeking."[65]

A few weeks later, after more hard slogging, Robertson wrote again to Skelton, seeking "some indication of the Government's wishes, sufficiently explicit to enable us to proceed with the negotiations now in hand." To what extent, he asked, was the government "prepared to use a new Agreement with the United States as an instrument for effecting major tariff changes intended to implement Government policy....?" As he and his colleagues understood the position,

we feel that a new Agreement with the United States would be expected to contain not only such purely bargaining concessions as might be required to secure the compensatory concessions we seek from the United States, but should also contain everything that would have been included in a comprehensive tariff budget, if the Government had been in a position to undertake unilateral action in tariff matters this year. Proceeding on this assumption, we have had in mind a schedule of Canadian tariff concessions which would constitute a thoroughgoing and comprehensive downward revision of the Canadian customs tariff. . . .

On a good many items the tariff reductions which we could offer the United States would be almost identical with those that McKinnon would have recommended to his Minister had they been preparing a tariff budget this Spring. There are, however, a number of important producers goods on which, by and large, the existing tariff protection is relatively low but on which, for reasons of general policy, the Government may feel obligated to make further cuts in duties. . . . In the ordinary course, my own feeling would be that it would be wiser to proceed gradually, lopping off excrescences, getting rid of anomalous rates and classifications, and lowering duties that are obviously in excess of the mean or average protection accorded secondary industries in Canada, hoping in this way that the advantages and economies of freer trade could be achieved with a minimum dislocation of existing industrial establishments, and with the smallest adverse effect on employment and payrolls.

There were in addition, Robertson said, a few items, such as farm implements, cream separators and fertilizers, on which the current rates were low. Should entry of such goods be made free? And what was the Prime Minister's view on the removal of the 1¢ a gallon duty on gasoline, "perhaps the most important single 'consumer's item' in the tariff"? [66]

The Prime Minister's reply was conveyed by Skelton on 14 July. "Mr. King said his own view coincided . . . that, as a general rule, it would be wiser to proceed gradually. . . ." But King did not favour anything more than cuts in the rates on farm implements and cream separators although, as Skelton wrote, "He would see no insuperable objection to their being made free. . . ." On the other items he was prepared to go along with Robertson's suggestions but, Skelton warned, "he was indicating his own first reactions, not his final judgment. He has not discussed it with his colleagues". [67]

Just what those cautious, qualified instructions meant or could mean to the negotiators remained unclear. King's "on the one hand" was as usual balanced by his "on the other hand," and Robertson was more than a little piqued and frustrated in a letter he sent to Pearson in London. "I've always been on the Ottawa end of the wire up to now, but these four months (approaching five) that I've been in Washington has put the boot on the other leg and I'm now ready to rail against External with the rest of you—except that I know & you should remember that extracting instructions from what are sometimes referred to as 'the Competent Departments of Government' is a completely impossible task." On the broad subject of the negotiations, however, Robertson remained hopeful.

We're plugging away here in hot muggy weather—with rather more prospect of success than you might gather from the Press. At least I've kept a Micawberish faith that somehow we can pull off something worthwhile. Triangular trade negotiations—with Australia, S[outh] A[frica] & the Colonial Empire each off at its own peculiar tangent are dreadfully difficult & rather discouraging. I was the last Imperialist in the Dept.—and now I've gone too. You may never have had the 'language difficulty' but I can get on with the Americans a damn sight more easily than with the English & Australians.... Our direct negotiations with the U.S. are the least of our worries right now. We can cope with them but not with God's Englishmen and the inescapable moral ascendancy over us lesser breeds. [68]

Those closing comments were most uncharacteristic of Robertson, who had been disposed to be more considerate of and more sympathetic to the English than many of the more nationalistic Canadians in Skelton's Department. But he was frustrated now by British stubbornness and obtuseness, for, interspersed with the transactions with the Americans, had been numerous meetings with the British negotiating team. Those meetings had been heated, [69] and only with difficulty had an acceptable trade-off been reached. The Canadians agreed to give up their preferences on apples and pears in the British market, and in return the United Kingdom gave up its preferences on tin plate, steel and automobiles in Canada. [70]

The Australians, already singled out by Robertson as the equal of the British in bloody-mindedness, [71] continued to cause difficulties. According to Skelton, they had made "the rather naive request that we should postpone the completion of the Canada-United States Trade Agreement until such time as the Australians would be able to effect their Agreement with the United States." The Prime Minister, of course, had "said any such arrangement would be absolutely out of the question." [72] But when Robertson met Sir Earle Page, the Australian representative, he was astonished to learn that Euler, the Minister of Trade and Commerce in Ottawa, had told Page that such a delay would be sensible. Mr. King's right hand obviously did not know what his left hand was up to, but that slip caused difficulties. So too did Page's charges that Canada had sold the pass to the Yankees on preferences, that Canada and Britain had cold-shouldered Australia, and so on. Robertson said that he had replied with equal force, but he was not unsympathetic to the Australian position: "the United Kingdom ... have tried for a variety of reasons, some sound and some selfish, to block immediate Australian-United States negotiations. The Australians are quite ready to believe everything of us that they simply dare not suspect of the United Kingdom." [73]

Of course, there were still problems with the Americans too. The Anglo-American negotiations had begun to bog down and both sides were beginning to threaten to break off the talks.[74] That worried Ottawa, and Skelton wrote about his fears that Canada might be caught in a "squeeze play": "There is a possibility that we may be 'pilloried' if we do not make wide last moment concessions. My own feeling is that the time is coming when we will have to tell the United States that we must have some substantial concessions. . . . It is time that somebody else besides ourselves should show a little readiness to make concessions for the good of the world."[75] That fear was reinforced in September, just at the time President Roosevelt was giving final approval to the list of concessions that could be made to Canada.[76] With the Czechoslovak crisis bringing the world close to war, Mackenzie King had learned from London that Sir Ronald Lindsay, the British Ambassador in Washington, looked for "a last moment effort . . . to have Canada make further concessions in order to save the negotiations between England and the United States." The Prime Minister's response was sharp: "I told Skelton to send word immediately to Robertson to tell both the United States and the British negotiators that I would not allow our Government to be pressed in this manner at the eleventh hour." There had to be time for discussion, and the Czech situation could not be used to justify everything Britain wanted.[77] Skelton, always the careful shepherd of his officials (and this was one reason that Robertson loved his chief), was concerned that, in the face of a potential collapse of the negotiations, "someone would be sure to try to hold the Canadian delegation rather than the Cabinet responsible. . . ."[78]

That eventuality (and war) was averted, and the Canadian negotiators returned to Ottawa in the last week of September to explain the proposed agreement with the United States to the key cabinet members concerned. Mackenzie King met his team on 26 September and was near ecstasy at the result:

I confess the agreement is even better than I thought it would be possible to have it, with the possible exception of a 5% reduction on furniture and boots and shoes which would be disliked by Euler and [Ernest] Lapointe [Minister of Justice] because of the number of factories in their individual constituencies. There is little else about the agreement which I believe would not be generally acceptable to the Cabinet with the possible exception of some further question of bituminous coal. It seems to me that the negotiators with the guidance they have had, have weighed with extreme care all arguments pro and con and have reached what is obviously the best agreement that can be made in existing circumstances. Personally I would be prepared to accept it as it stands without a word. It comes to us now in the form of a firm offer from the U.S., the President having approved it as it stands. This would make it very difficult to reopen any part without prejudicing the whole. . . .

The only thing that might seem to necessitate Parliament's approval in advance is what we forego in the way of margins in the British market. . . .

I was immensely proud and pleased at the way in which Robertson, Wilgress and McKinnon presented the case; the most intricate and involved and complicated matter presented with great calm and perfect clearness. They have been invaluable servants of the administration. [79]

The next day, while Robertson returned to Washington to make sure that nothing came unstuck there, Wilgress and McKinnon appeared at a full meeting of cabinet where the American and Canadian concessions were explained. There were a few cavils, but King wrote in his diary that "The matter . . . is now virtually settled, as whatever changes can or cannot be made are practically left in the hands of the negotiators." [80]

King's praise for his negotiators was undoubtedly heartfelt, and when he indicated that the final alterations in the draft would be left to them, he was simply reflecting the reality. Indeed, in Robertson's own view, that had been the case throughout. "I am back in Washington again," he wrote on 29 September, "after a strenuous but not unsuccessful week in Ottawa where I managed to get retroactive sanction for the instructions I've had to invent all summer. So that I am now clear again—which is rather a relief." Robertson was concerned about the boiling crisis over Czechoslovakia, but he was wrapped up in his own work, and his only comment on the crisis in a letter to his mother was that, "We're working against time now for I do not know what war would mean—even for the job in hand." [81]

In fact, the tentative agreement between Canada and the United States remained in the background in Washington for another month as the British and Americans fought with increasing bitterness over their agreement. This was the subject of a long letter from Robertson to Skelton, written just after his return to the United States.

The United Kingdom and United States Delegations are not much nearer agreement than they were three weeks ago. . . . There is . . . little evidence of disposition in either camp to settle things quickly. They blame each other for the delay and each is waiting for the other to give ground.

For Robertson, there was no doubt as to where the blame should be put:

... I must admit I cannot understand the British attitude in the present circumstances. Why they should feel that their self respect compels them to take so much firmer a line in negotiating with the United States than they have ever shown in their discussions with Germany or Italy, or even with Poland or Hungary, is beyond me. It may quite well be that under pressure of the development of events in Europe in the last month the conduct of the negotiations with the United States has been pigeon-holed and left to departmental decisions dictated by the Board of Trade's concept of British commercial interests. ... If this was the explanation of the impasse it may be that Chamberlain, by whose earnest desire for a settlement with the United States I was very much impressed at the 1937 [Imperial] Conference, may take the situation in hand at the first lull in the European situation. But there may not be a lull and the opportunity may not come.

Perhaps, Robertson suggested, the Prime Minister should intervene with London. He could point out the concessions Canada had made to facilitate an Anglo-American agreement; he could indicate that "at some political risk" the government had based its whole fiscal policy on the premise that a satisfactory arrangement would be worked out between London and Washington, and possibly he could even stress the fundamental importance to Canada of Anglo-American economic cooperation. Those were good suggestions, and while King did not find it possible to act on them in detail, he did telegraph Chamberlain to urge the necessity of an early conclusion of the agreements.[82]

Nonetheless, the Anglo-American discussions remained immobile, paralyzed by the approaching American mid-term elections and not eased at all by the "resolution" of the Czech crisis at Munich. Some had looked to a British-American agreement as the harbinger of political cooperation in a dangerous world; but the lengthy and bitter talks had tended to produce the opposite effect. Lindsay, the British Ambassador in Washington, was sore: "The protracted negotiations ... have brought me personally to that state of bitterness and exasperation which usually results from dealing with the United States Government."[83] And then, suddenly, the British final position, presented on 25 October, became the basis for an agreement on 5 November.

Robertson, summoned by King, proceeded to New York to meet the Prime Minister and Skelton.[84] The three Canadians went over the agreements on 6 November, a Sunday morning, at the Harvard Club:

We sat in the large reading hall, and listened to Robertson go over details of recent negotiations. ...
   I was glad to be able to ask that a further effort be made to reconsider duties on

boots and shoes. Apart from that, everything else seems to have been worked out in a most satisfactory manner.[85]

By the 8th, the Prime Minister was back in Ottawa meeting his cabinet, with Wilgress and McKinnon present, while Robertson stayed in Washington. The negotiators had managed to meet the wishes of some members of Council on specific items but, as King wrote later, "The British ... had been absolutely opposed [to] allowing us to reduce our duties on anthracite coal. (This shows how wrong this system of bargaining is. Keep our poor people in winters paying more for coal. Just to help the British miners in Wales.)"[86] The negotiators had failed to block the lowered duties on shoes, and had struck a compromise on wooden furniture that, after some difficulty over the telephone with the Minister of Trade and Commerce, was accepted. " ... I made the remark," King wrote, 'then there is unanimity with respect to the agreement. That is a great achievement.' I think it is an amazing achievement, and too much credit cannot be given to the skillful negotiations of Robertson, Wilgress and MacKinnon [sic]."[87] The Canadian-American and Anglo-American agreements were signed in Washington on 17 November.[88]*

For Canada, the agreements saw the abandonment of preferences in Britain on wheat, pears, honey, salmon, preserved apples and patent leather; the British gave up their preferences in Canada on a range of manufactured products. With the United States, Canada bettered everything it had gained in 1935, with 129 new reductions in duties. Where there were quotas in the 1935 accord, the new agreement either removed or substantially increased them. Reductions in the Canadian tariff were extensive for American products.[89]

The agreement Robertson and his colleagues had negotiated did not win unanimous approval in Canada. R.B. Bennett, no longer Conservative leader, complained to Robertson, "in an exclusive interview" on the

---

* According to Pierrepont Moffat, Sir Herbert Marler, the Canadian Minister in the US, caused enormous difficulties over the protocol for greeting Mackenzie King on his arrival for the signature: "as he did not like his position in Car 2, he announced that he would go home from the station in his own car in order to greet the Prime Minister on his arrival. By this time Summerlin [the State Department official responsible] was so fed up that he did not tell him that with the motorcycle police escort the Prime Minister would arrive well ahead of him. This amused Jack Hickerson's sense of humor. He therefore telephoned Summerlin pretending to be Sir Herbert Marler, and said that [he] had a new idea which was that he, the Minister, instead of going straight home from the station might kill two birds with one stone by riding one of the motorcycles that headed the procession. It was not until this final proposition that Summerlin discovered that it was not, in fact, Marler speaking." (Houghton Library, Harvard University, Moffat Papers, Diary, 17 Nov. 38.)

steps of the Parliament Buildings, that the treaty was "a complete sell-out to the Americans." According to a memo Skelton prepared, Robertson had replied that "he hoped he would read the Agreement carefully, and felt he would come to the conclusion that no Canadian industries were seriously affected and that the Canadian market in the United Kingdom was well preserved—in fact, much more secure than it had been before because ... the preferences were now much more likely to be secure."[90] The Canadian Manufacturers' Association objected vehemently,[91] and every special interest that had lost protection protested too.[92] Still, the British High Commission in Canada could report that the agreement "has met with a reception on the part of the press and public opinion in Canada which probably exceeds in its warmth anything that the Government had expected."[93]

The response of the public and industry might have been anticipated. What Robertson and his colleagues might not have looked for was the praise that Mackenzie King gave them in the House of Commons on 14 February 1939. King told the Commons that Canada was fortunate to have had such "loyal, able, efficient and highly skilled service" from its negotiators. "I do not think it is possible to commend these services too highly."[94] Without doubt, Robertson had established his worth with Mackenzie King. And deservedly so.

CHAPTER IV
To War 1939-41

ECAUSE OF HIS work on trade questions, Norman Robertson had not played much part in the crisis in the Department of External Affairs as war neared in the late 1930s. Dr. Skelton and several of his officers were essentially neutralists, men who believed that Canada should stay aloof from a war that was, they believed, as much a result of British bungling as Hitlerian aggression. Others, such as Hume Wrong and (after much soul-searching) Lester Pearson, had become convinced that Canada had to go to war.

Norman Robertson shared that latter view, no doubt of that. Canada had to join in the struggle against Hitler and Nazism. However bad the behaviour of Britain and France, however inept their policy and its practitioners through the dark years of the 1930s, a war against Germany was still a war for freedom, a just war.

But as late as 24 July 1939, Robertson still hoped against hope that war might be averted. His wife and daughter were in the Netherlands, visiting Jetty's parents, and he was hoping to get away in August to visit Vancouver. "Even Skelton has been nagging me to take some holidays," he wrote his parents, "but I've been nurturing the idea of my indispensability for such a long time now that I'm its prisoner myself.* I've a good many irons in the fire—some of them hot and I don't like to leave them for a month—or to be quite so far away from Ottawa at a time like

---

* That notion of indispensability was not Robertson's alone. In a long, handwritten, and very critical letter from Canada to Vincent Massey in London, L.B. Pearson bemoaned the "mess" of External Affairs and Skelton's condition as a "tired saint." He added, "I'm worried about Robertson—they are working him to death and at the present rate he'll be burnt out in 6 months. The Doctor also is an unwell man ... with those two away I shudder to think what External would be like." (Massey College, Toronto, Vincent Massey Papers, unboxed material, Pearson to Massey, 16 Jul. 39.)

this."¹ A few weeks later, Robertson wrote on 19 August to say that he had had to cancel his holiday plans. "I don't much like the look of things this week-end—not enough to run out on them for a holiday." What worried him too was that Jetty and Alix were not scheduled to sail from Holland until 30 August,² and a few days later he informed his worried parents that he had asked the Legation in The Hague to contact them and urge an earlier sailing. (Fortunately that was arranged, and the family returned to Canada just before the war's outbreak.) Robertson added, his despair obvious, "As you can imagine, I'm in pretty deep. . . . It is all pretty hideous."³ The Nazis invaded Poland on 1 September, Britain and France declared war on the 3rd, and Canada followed suit on the 10th. The horror had begun.

I

The question of shaping government policy on subversives and enemy aliens was the first problem to engage Robertson at the onset of the war. Indeed his concern with that matter dated back to 1936, when Skelton named him as Departmental representative at a Royal Canadian Mounted Police meeting on 23 March "to discuss a number of questions arising out of the activities of Fascist and Nazi agencies in Canada."⁴ Probably Robertson simply happened to be free to attend; certainly Skelton trusted his colleague's judgment and knew that Robertson was as firm a believer in civil liberties as he himself and as firm an opponent of anti-semitism.⁵ Whatever the reason, Robertson became External Affairs' man on this question, one that forced on him the unpleasant chore of reading imported propaganda from Germany and Italy and equally noxious domestic varieties.⁶ For the most part, he simply held a watching brief, gathering information from domestic sources and reports from Canadian posts abroad.⁷

The Canadian government had not been disposed to take any action against foreign or domestic Fascism in the late 1930s. But there was a desultory process of planning underway from the spring of 1938, after the cabinet ordered the establishment of a Committee on the Treatment of Aliens and Alien Property. At the time Robertson was tied up with the trade negotiations, and John Read was External Affairs' representative. The Committee's report, not printed and circulated for a year, suggested that an effort be made to consider on its merits the case of each individual enemy alien, a sound position indeed. In the case of a war with Japan, however, the report said: "It might be necessary . . . to recommend the internment of nearly all the enemy nationals, since it is recognized that public feeling . . . might render this course necessary, not alone to avoid danger of espionage and sabotage, but also for the protection of persons and property of enemy aliens." That suggested course, realistic as it may have been, was scarcely progressive, and the policy eventually adopted in 1942 against Japanese Canadians caused one of Robertson's thorniest wartime problems. [8]

By the spring of 1939, after Munich and after the Nazis had seized all that remained of Czechoslovakia, there was a belated effort by the Canadian government to grapple with the propaganda distributed in the country from German and Italian consulates. In part this was a response to a growing public protest;[9] in part it was one aspect of Canada's preparation for the war that almost all feared was drawing nearer. Robertson himself, agonizing over the approaching war, saw his role in this anti-Fascist effort as one of mixed pleasure and pain. He had not the slightest sympathy with the racism and hate being preached by the consuls and few qualms about using the power of the state to frustrate their efforts. But he was sensitive to the difficulties such efforts caused the ordinary German and Italian Canadian, and in a tough memorandum he prepared in May 1939 this was made clear.

First, he suggested the full use of the law to block the import of "seditious, disloyal or scurrilous" propaganda and limitation of consular privileges to bring in films, records, printed matter and the like. He urged strongly that the government "Refrain from any sort of administrative encouragement—however indirect—of Nazi and Fascist activities in Canada" by stopping advertising in newspapers published by such groups, by blocking government employment for "notorious Fascists," and by giving no official acknowledgment or recognition to suspect organizations (as had come the year before when the Governor General's office sent a telegram to Fascist leader Adrien Arcand). "The lower middle class attitudes and origins of Fascist and Nazi groups make them particularly susceptible to this sort of social ostracism," Robertson analyzed, like the good social democrat he had been, adding that the Fascists should be sent "to Coventry with the Communists." There were a host of other suggestions, including tax audits, the refusal of immigrant entry to propagandists, RCMP investigation, "in the same way that the Police now check the records of persons believed to be of radical or communist sympathies," of applicants for naturalization from Italy or Germany, and possibly the revocation of naturalization of those whose membership in such organizations as the *Fascio* was "incompatible with a

loyal fulfillment of the oath of allegiance they have taken on naturalization."[10]

Suggestions of that sort troubled the liberal in Robertson, but he had
little hesitation in offering such advice. In his view, it was the duty of the
state to defend itself with all means against those who would destroy it,
from within no less than from without, and as a servant of the state
Robertson was never slow to act when he considered that security
required it. Still, he was well aware that the government had never
worked to integrate immigrants into Canadian life, and this concerned
him. In a more positive, handwritten memo, possibly a draft of the
memorandum written in May, he had set forth a series of steps to help
correct the situation. These encompassed English classes "under
Canadian auspices—night schools & adult education associations—
possible to give preferred employment to refugees"; social work among
immigrant groups—"we've lacked a Jane Addams—no Hull House or
Henry Street Settlement—nor any University Settlement work worth
mentioning—responsibility of churches & university groups—middle
classes generally—Canadians quite conscious of problem in 1910-16 but
it has since receded into background." There were other measures, such as
legal aid, social medicine for the poor, the use of the CBC and National
Film Board, the incorporation of individuals into political parties, and the
enlistment of churches and such groups as the YMCA into the process of
Canadianization. That was his goal, a "positive affirmation of concept of
Canadian Citizenship based on loyalty & domicile [and a] repudiation of
'blood & soil'."[11]

Robertson's hardline memo* had more impact than his positive one,
however, and through the summer of 1939 committees continued to meet
to consider these questions.[12] But in fact the coming war was outpacing
the committee work, and the Royal Canadian Mounted Police were
getting nervous. On 28 August, Robertson told Dr. Skelton that the
RCMP had gone to the Justice Department with its programme for
"suppressing subversive activities" at the outbreak of hostilities. The
RCMP proposed to outlaw immediately all Nazi, Fascist and Communist
organizations, all foreign language political organizations of Fascist or

---

* In a letter to his parents on 24 July 1939, Robertson wrote that "I've wandered into a
new line of country as a one man Cheka or Gestapo which is quite a lot of work but
congenial," a curious word to describe his duties. "I never expected to find myself one day
as civilian commissar with the R.C.M.P.. . . ." (Mrs. N.A. Robertson Papers (Ottawa),
Robertson to mother, 24 Jul. 39.)

Communist affiliation or complexion, the suppression of the English-language Communist press and of the Nazi, Fascist and Communist foreign press, the seizure of the assets of all such organizations, and of their records, "including those which might be found to be kept in Consular archives." Robertson told his chief that "I was appalled by the programme contemplated. . . ."

that it involved a great deal of bitter inter-racial resentment and the prospect of endless labour troubles throughout industrial and mining areas, as well as the alienation of the sympathy and support of great blocs of opinion which, if properly handled, could be led to support any efforts the Government was making rather than to oppose them. I thought the Police should concentrate on their plans for the immediate arrest of persons suspected of treasonable activity, and that they would be ill advised to destroy organizations about which they now know a good deal and with whose personnel they are familiar. It would drive them underground, which would greatly increase the Police problems in this country in war time. I thought, further, that as regards the whole question of the status of the Communists, we should not take any precipitate action, but should wait and see how they adapt themselves to new international alignments; that the wind had been taken out of their sails by the events of recent days [the Nazi-Soviet pact], and they had been badly compromised. . . . I would be surprised if the Police found them abetting Nazi or Fascist activities in this country or very actively prosecuting their own propagandist activities.

Robertson had initially put those views to J.F. MacNeill of the Department of Justice, who was as horrified by the RCMP plans as Robertson. MacNeill had asked if External Affairs was willing to remain associated with his Department "in deciding questions of policy in respect of the handling of subversive activities in war time. I said that in the circumstances I thought that you felt about these matters much the way I did," he told Skelton, "and that you would probably approve of our continuing in war time the contacts with the Police in this sphere that we had built up in recent years, and in that case I would probably continue to be our Department's representative. . . ." [13]

Skelton would and did, and three days later Robertson found himself chairing a meeting at the Justice Department "to discuss treatment of enemy aliens and persons suspected of treasonable or seditious purposes." The RCMP representative, Superintendent E.W. Bavin, wore that force's usual red-coloured spectacles and told the committee of the RCMP view "that the Communists are of far more importance than either the Italians or Germans, in the event of war." [14] Although the Minister of Justice had instructed his representative, MacNeill, that the RCMP "should be the guiding light . . . closer to the facts than we are," the meeting decided not to act against the Communists for the time being. What it did do was to go over the lists of persons to be arrested. There were initially 641 names on the list, 90 percent of them landed immigrants and only 65 Canadian citizens. Robertson successfully cautioned against precipitate action against Italians so as not to disturb Italian neutrality, and added:

I am confident that, in the Italian community, if we could get the leaders then the rest could go their way, performing their ordinary work. I think you will find— especially among the Italian societies—that many have hooked up with these organizations as a social obligation; with an eye to business; to be in with the crowd, as far as persons of their own nationality are concerned; or for some such reason. You must remember that tremendous pressure has been brought to bear from Rome. In other words a large majority of these persons are 'sheep', and if we could segregate the leaders the remainder would tend to be loyal Canadians. . . . We don't want to tie up too much money and too many persons in guarding these people and keeping them on relief in concentration camps when they could be out doing a useful job.

That was a typical Robertson view—hard-headed, compassionate and sensible, and one based on substantial knowledge of his subject. The RCMP view, predictably, was that every man, woman and child should be swept up. Again Robertson countered this successfully by reminding the committee that its task was to go over the lists of potential enemies and check the files, "thus making sure that there is a good and sufficient reason for internment." There were reasons in many cases, and the committee quickly agreed to the arrest of all Nazi party members and all members of the *Arbeitsfront*, the "junior" Nazi group. For the next two days the committee went over the files, and J.W. Pickersgill, who shared Robertson's house that summer while Jetty and Alix were in the Netherlands, remembers seeing Robertson and MacNeill poring over the lists on Robertson's dining-room table.[15]*

---

* Robertson knew a good deal about the German and Italian communities and about propaganda and recruiting attempts made by the German and Italian consuls in Canada. One source for his information was Fred Rose, a Communist Party member who later in the war was elected to Parliament and who, in 1946, was seriously implicated in the Gouzenko spy revelations. In 1939 and after, as Robertson later told Pearson, Rose sent him a number of letters with "information from Communist Party sources about Fascist and Nazi activities in Canada. . . . I told Fred Rose that I would be glad to receive any information he could furnish me about Fascist and Nazi activities, and passed on to Bavin, who was then in charge of R.C.M.P. Intelligence, information of this kind which was unlikely to reach the R.C.M.P. direct." (PAC, L.B. Pearson Papers, N1, vol. 13, Robertson to Pearson, 29 Oct. 46.)

Again and again Robertson demonstrated his concern for the facts of each case, as well as his desire to be certain that the government's actions, its necessary actions, would be understood by the Canadian people. "We must be sure to include in our report," he said as the committee broke up, "statements to the effect that this is not a mass round-up but a discriminating list of individuals who are dangerous. . . . What we want to show is the number of German nationals in Canada and the number of German nationals recommended for arrest. . . ."[16] The committee reported to the Minister of Justice on 3 September, the day Britain declared war on Germany. Its recommendation was that 325 persons be arrested, 265 German nationals and 60 naturalized Canadians. The report pointed out, as Robertson had suggested, that the 1931 census had shown 35,809 persons of nominal German allegiance.[17] Arrests began that night under the authority of the Defence of Canada Regulations, put into force that day (one week before the Canadian declaration of war against Germany) under the broad authority of the War Measures Act. The Regulations gave the government vast powers to control freedom of expression through censorship, control and suppression of the press; they gave power to punish any criticism of the government "likely to prejudice . . . recruiting," a phrase broad enough to encompass just about anything; and they gave the Minister of Justice the authority to intern "any particular person" who might be "acting in any manner prejudicial to the public safety or the safety of the State. . . ."[18]

To advise the Minister of Justice, Ernest Lapointe, on the internment provisions of the Regulations, the government established two committees of officials. One, the successor to that Robertson had chaired, continued its work with the same membership and advised on questions concerning Nazi and Fascist sympathizers; the other, headed by a Justice Department official, advised on Communists, radical trade union leaders, Jehovah's Witnesses and other allegedly troublesome individuals.[19] Those arrangements lasted until June 1941. On the outbreak of war, the government also established an Advisory Committee on Orders of Restriction and Retention, charged with assessing the fairness or otherwise of internment orders.[20]

Within that structure, Robertson operated, spending substantial amounts of his time in dealing with the cases of "interned aliens, people that he had never heard of and had no personal interest in, and judged the evidence as it came out. . . ." The time and care he devoted, remembered his colleague, George Glazebrook, "indicated his approach to the belief in the importance of human rights."[21]

Robertson made every effort to interpret the provisions of the Defence of Canada Regulations as liberally as possible. In a letter to Walter Tucker, the Liberal MP for Rosthern, Saskatchewan, a constituency with a high percentage of German immigrants in its population, Robertson remarked that "Too many naturalized Canadians of German origin have put themselves in an awkward and embarrassing position by their active participation, in peacetime, in Nazi and Nazi-controlled political and social organizations. I quite realize that a good many persons of German origin or birth may have joined ... in good faith without appreciating the strain which other people might think such membership put on their loyalty to Canada."[22] He at least could recognize that simple membership did not automatically equate with disloyalty. On the other hand, however, when his old friend, J.S. Woodsworth, wrote him about the case of one internee and cited information that the man had been arrested for some casual remarks in a Saskatchewan blacksmith's shop, Robertson replied that "I happen to know [the internment] ... was on the strength of information previously received about his activities as an organizer and officer of the Bund [one of the Nazi organizations] and as a recipient and distributor of Nazi and anti-Semitic propaganda."[23]

But there was no doubt in Robertson's mind that the state had to provide hard evidence before he would recommend internment. MacNeill expressed both men's views when he said to Robertson that "you share responsibility with me for the evil situation in which some of these poor devils find themselves."[24] So he did, and he was fully aware of the iniquitous nature of his work on occasion and sensitive to the wider ramifications of it.

In one case, for example, a native-born American citizen of German origin was arrested and interned for three months in circumstances that provoked the interest and natural concern of the American Legation in Ottawa. Robertson agreed that the man "is in a position (if at liberty) to act in a manner prejudicial to the State," but nonetheless he was prepared to recommend release from internment because "we would lose more than we could gain by refusal to release a natural born American citizen whom we could not hope to convict in any court of law on any count of espionage, attempted or intended."[25] In this case, as in many others, the RCMP strenuously objected to Robertson's recommendation.

Not only the RCMP wanted stronger action. Ernest Lapointe, for one, was very firm in his view that the government had to act vigorously against Nazi and Communist organizations. The Prime Minister was reluctant to agree, telling Lapointe in cabinet that "I did not trust the judgment of the Mounted Police on these matters."[26] Neither did Skelton, who wrote to the Prime Minister in December 1939 to urge that care be taken to avoid drafting errors in regulations that could permit action to be directed against "the C.C.F. or any other radical or liberal organization. . . ." Skelton also pointed out that "Sedition is one thing, criticism is entirely another. A good many people in Canada are prone to think that anyone who differs from their convictions or prejudices should be suppressed."[27] Robertson shared his chief's view.[28] Nonetheless, King finally acceded in early January 1940 to the Minister of Justice's desires for stronger action.[29]

To his credit, Robertson continued to resist the paranoia endemic in wartime Canada. One small example: when one internee was released and ordered to report regularly to the RCMP, Robertson was insistent that "reporting" meant more than simply turning up once a month at Police headquarters. " . . . I think the Police should know whether he has settled back with his family, whether he has a job and, if so, what kind of job and at what salary. It seems to me," he went on, "that the best security we can get that people . . . are not going to turn dangerous . . . would be the fact that they have been actually absorbed back into the civilian community and are not simply turned out of Petawawa [the internment camp] as stragglers, dependent on casual employment and therefore susceptible to offers which mischief makers might make to them."[30] There was similar, enlightened good sense in the action of the government's key Economic Advisory Committee in September 1940, action that was without doubt attributable to Robertson, in stressing that relief agencies must "specifically guard against discrimination against aliens since these, if they are denied employment and prohibited from getting relief, will be driven into subversive activity." The committee pointed out that since relief was being given to the dependents of interned aliens, it was inconsistent to deny it to the uninterned.[31]

Through the first sixteen months of war, therefore, Robertson's involvement with the RCMP increased until Skelton could refer to him as "our Departmental secret service operative."[32] The relationship did not give him a uniformly high opinion of the force's skills in the sensitive work in which his committee had been involved. For example, when Skelton asked his views on a proposal to have liaison officers exchanged between the RCMP and the FBI, Robertson replied that "My own feeling is that if the R.C.M.P. had any one man who could do a useful job as general liaison officer with the F.B.I. he would be an invaluable aid and reinforcement to the present Intelligence Division."[33] The implication was clear. On another, later occasion, Robertson told the Prime Minister after a Cabinet War Committee meeting in which the Minister of Munitions and Supply, C.D. Howe, and others pressed for action against labour unions, "that he thought Ministers were being influenced by reports of the Mounted Police."[34] Again, there can be no doubt what he meant.

But there were other departments of government with problems. This was clearly revealed by the Bortolotti case of 1939-40. Bortolotti was an Italian anarchist and anti-Fascist who had been arrested early in September 1939 by the RCMP and the Toronto City Police "Red Squad". A series of spurious charges were laid and promptly tossed out of court, at which point the Immigration Branch of the Department of Mines and Resources moved to deport Bortolotti, despite the certainty that Mussolini's government would treat him harshly. The case became a civil libertarian *cause célèbre*.[35]

Robertson's initial involvement came in October. The Crown Attorney handling the case did not believe that he had enough evidence to secure a conviction and suggested that Ottawa simply use the Regulations to intern the anarchist. To its great credit, Robertson's committee refused.[36] In March 1940, the Director of the Immigration Branch, F.C. Blair, wrote to Skelton about Bortolotti and asked the Department of External Affairs to secure his FBI file. Blair pointed out that Bortolotti had once worked for the Ford Motor Company in Detroit and had been discharged "on account of arrest by the Detroit Police for the distribution of subversive literature . . . on the second anniversary of the execution of one, Sacco Van Zetti [*sic*]. . . ."[37] Robertson, who had been at Harvard during some of the Sacco and Vanzetti furore, replied:

What you say about Bortolotti's participation in memorial services for Sacco and Vanzetti [NAR's forbearance here was superhuman] while in the United States fortifies our fears of what might happen to him if he were deported to Italy. Sacco and Vanzetti were, you will remember, two Italian anarchists who were executed in Massachusetts in 1927 or 1928 after a long drawn out prosecution which profoundly shocked a great many Americans. . . . The fact that Bortolotti was actively identified with [the protest] and fell foul of the municipal police authorities on this score is not, I think, very much to his discredit.

Robertson added that historically, both in Canada and the United States, immigration authorities had been reluctant to deport persons likely to suffer for their political ideas. "This policy, I think, was not only a just and humane one, but I am satisfied that it was the only politically expedient course. Now we are at war it is perhaps more important than ever to maintain these principles."[38] Skelton was quick to support Robertson,[39] and at the end of April, after ministerial consideration, Blair finally agreed that Bortolotti could remain in Canada. As Blair wrote to the anarchist's lawyer, "it has long been our practice to avoid deportation whenever possible, when, if carried out, it would return a person to a country where his life would be in danger."[40]

Robertson's liberalism, as we have seen, had encompassed his efforts to press the government to do more to integrate immigrants into Canadian life, and in April 1940 he returned to this theme. He had been struck, he wrote Skelton, by the number of interned Germans who had argued that they had joined Nazi organizations in good faith. "Naturalized Canadians of German origin were told that there was no official objection to their belonging to the Bund, in fact, its membership was, by its Constitution, confined to naturalized Canadians." In Robertson's view, a number of internees were genuinely surprised by their arrest. "It had never been put to them clearly and unequivocally, at the time of their naturalization or afterwards, that continued membership in organizations under foreign political control was incompatible with the loyalty they had promised to Canada and its institutions. I feel that we have been, in part at least, responsible for allowing this confusion to continue in the minds of what are, for the most part, simple and not very well educated people."[41]

Robertson demonstrated similar concern when, after the catastrophic Allied defeats in France and Flanders, Lapointe and the RCMP pressed for still stronger action against "alien enemies."[42] The Prime Minister tried to resist,[43] but soon gave in and, on 4 June, the Communist Party and several of its front organizations were proscribed.[44] Robertson's committee, fortunately for him, had no part in this decision, but, as he told the Prime Minister later, the proscription of the Communists was a policy "that I have been personally a good deal worried about." That policy presumably led him to seek release from his alien duties, but Skelton kept him on the job.[45]

Despite the pressures of public opinion, Robertson's approach to the difficult cases that came before him never altered. Without firm evidence, internment could not be justified.[46] And indeed, the numbers interned were never very large. By January 1941, 763 Germans had been arrested and 127 released; 586 Italians arrested and 105 released; 87 Communists arrested and 5 released; and 28 members of the National Unity Party, a domestic Fascist variant, had also been interned.[47] In June 1941, finally, after his committee had sunk into inactivity, the internment advisory committee structure was recast and L.B. Pearson became the Departmental representative in place of Robertson, by then the acting Under-Secretary.[48] Robertson's involvement in a direct and continuing way had ended, although when Canada declared war on Hungary, Romania and Finland in December 1941, he was successful in persuading the Cabinet War Committee to exempt immigrants of those countries from the draconian provisions of the Defence of Canada Regulations.[49] His role throughout had reflected only credit upon him.

II

In the midst of his hours of going through the files of those who were subject to internment in the first days of the war, Robertson somehow found the time to participate in the hasty planning for Canadian war organization. On 15 September, he was named as a member of the Foreign Exchange Control Board [FECB], the body charged with the regulation of all foreign exchange transactions between Canadian residents and the world outside.

Planning for the FECB had been underway since January 1939[50] and had been speeded up from August. Late in that month the general managers of the chartered banks met Graham Towers, the Governor of the Bank of Canada, and agreed to convene a meeting of exchange experts in Montreal on Labour Day. A further meeting followed in Ottawa on 15 September, where Towers announced to a captive audience of every exchange expert in the country that controls would take effect the next day. In a major feat of organization (and duplication) the requisite forms were ready for distribution.[51] Towers's planning was based on the assumption of a major war lasting two or three years. "I came reluctantly to the conclusion that the abandonment of our traditional policy of allowing free movement of capital between Canada and other countries is less prejudicial to the country," he wrote to the Minister of Finance and the cabinet, "than an attempt to struggle through the war with a laissez-faire policy." If controls on exchange had to be imposed, he added, the time to do it was now while the markets were disturbed.[52]

The FECB members were Towers, Clark, Fortier, the Chief Inspector of the Post Office, Robertson, Scully and Wilgress, and the Board's first meeting took place on 16 September.[53] There were five further sessions in September and regular meetings were held thereafter throughout the war and into the Cold War. Robertson attended with great regularity,[54] and although he was no economic theorist, he was a member of the Board because his knowledge of economics was respected and recognized by Towers and Clark, the two leading economic figures in the government. Robertson, as his friend Louis Rasminsky recalled, could perceive the interrelationships between questions instantly, was consistently concerned with the long view, and anxious to ensure that posterity not be jeopardized for a short-term gain. [55]

Robertson also found the chance for a conversation with Donald Gordon, the Deputy Governor of the Bank of Canada, a talk that produced a long list of matters to be considered, such as the need for adequate statistics, production and food control, and war finance. [56] Discussions with Skelton, and probably with Clifford Clark, the Deputy Minister of Finance, had led by 1 September 1939 to what Robertson would call an "Economic Defence Advisory Committee" of civil servants. [57]

This body, formally entitled the Advisory Committee on Economic Policy, but usually known as the Economic Advisory Committee [EAC], was first proposed to the Prime Minister by Skelton on 9 September. It might be helpful, Skelton said in a one-paragraph memorandum, "if a small economic advisory committee could be set up. It might consist say of Towers, Clark, Wilgress, Robertson and one or two others . . . it would be of material help for primary surveys to make sure that all necessary points are being examined and measures coordinated." [58] A draft order-in-council gave fuller details, listing the EAC's duties as facilitating the work of cabinet committees in the fields of supply and war finance, avoiding duplication, and ensuring effective coordination of economic and financial policy. The draft order listed the members as Skelton, Clark, Towers, Scully [Commissioner of Customs], Hector McKinnon [just named to head the Wartime Prices and Trade Board], Wilgress, Coats [Dominion Statistician], Maclachlan [the Associate Deputy Minister of National Defence], and Robertson. Provision was made for other representatives to be named from various boards and committees. [59]

The proposal came to the cabinet on 12 September where it ran into some difficulty. The Minister of Finance, Colonel J.L. Ralston, said he had never heard of the proposal, although his deputy, Clark, had helped to draft it. That provoked the Prime Minister, who grumbled that this was "one of the mistakes our bureaucracy continually makes, taking for granted Ministers will simply follow what they suggest." King was also worried that "we have far too many committees already," [60] but in the end he agreed to the EAC. [61] The organization of the Committee was modified, however, and now included Clark, Towers, Scully, McKinnon, Wilgress,

Coats, Barton, the Deputy Minister of Agriculture, Camsell, the Deputy Minister of Mines and Resources, Desrosiers, another Associate Deputy Minister of National Defence, and Robertson. Desrosiers was present because someone had belatedly realized it would be a mistake to create such a powerful committee without a francophone member. Robertson, the most junior member in both rank and age, was there because he was trusted by Skelton, liked by Clark, and because he was the natural member of his Department on any such economic committee. [62]

Junior or not, his role on the Economic Advisory Committee was important. The committee had a wide mandate, one that permitted it to examine questions on its own or at the behest of the cabinet or any Minister, and from its first meeting on 18 September, the committee's role was crucial. Initially, it dealt with various trade problems as Canada struggled to adjust its exports and imports to the disruption brought about by the war. Policy had to be thrashed out for exports to Britain in the light both of the United Kingdom's war needs (which at that point seemed very small to the Canadians) [63] and its desire to conserve dollars and cut non-essential imports. That caused problems for some Canadian producers. [64] There was also the need to conclude a wheat sale to Britain, a matter complicated, as always, by questions of price.

In the EAC on 7 October, Robertson argued strenuously that the Grain Exchange, the free market for wheat in Winnipeg, should be closed, since its continued functioning suggested that Canada was seeking the highest possible price. Wheat sales were sluggish, he argued, this was certain to be reflected in the price Canada could get, and what was really wanted was to make a big bulk sale at as good a price as possible, even though that could only be a salvage price. The British were reluctant to buy from Canada on the open market, he went on, so the desirable course was to close the Exchange. The committee rejected Robertson's advice and decided to take advantage of any bullish tendencies that might result from the war. [65] The result was that a large wheat sale was not concluded until May 1940, after much bitterness. [66]

That episode is important. Robertson had never sought power for himself, but he had most definitely sought influence. To help to shape the flow of events was all he had ever wanted, [67] and his role on the EAC illustrates that. The wheat episode, where his views were overruled, was scarcely a convincing example of his skill, but what was striking was that Robertson had no hesitation in putting forward views that he knew were unpopular. He was not afraid to argue with his superiors, the most powerful civil servants in the government, and they were not offended when he did so. Such a thing could not happen in Ottawa fifteen years later.

Robertson was also very much involved in the EAC's discussions on bacon exports, copper sales and the sugar situation.[68] He served on sub-committees on economic warfare and exchange conservation,[69] and he was influential on all questions involving exports of strategic materiel to "aggressor" or "aggressive" nations, a group that in the fall of 1939 included Japan and the Soviet Union. Robertson had no desire to help strengthen existing enemies, but he remained fully aware of what other countries were doing. In October, for example, he had argued that nickel exports to Japan should be continued because "it would be difficult to explain a discriminatory embargo on exports to one neutral nation while allowing shipments to other neutrals to go forward," and particularly while both Britain and the United States continued to trade freely with Japan.[70] Nonetheless, the export of nickel was severely restricted.

Robertson was soon in Washington, this time accompanied by Graham Towers, for conversations about planned budget decisions and their effect on Canadian-American trade. They arrived on 11 June, deeply concerned by the disaster in France and by the resulting problems with foreign exchange. "The volume of essential imports from the United States was increasing," they told American officials, "and was bound to increase further in the next few months with the acceleration of the war supply programme and the necessity Canada was now under of obtaining from the United States goods which, up to the last few weeks, it had been expected to obtain from the United Kingdom." After Dunkirk, Canada could no longer count on securing machinery and war materiel from Britain. "Our normal export trade to the United States was unlikely to expand," Towers and Robertson continued, "and the prospects of our securing the large credit from tourist expenditures which our balance of payments required, had become extremely uncertain." In the circum-stances, drastic action was required, and Robertson explained that the government had decided to apply a ten percent War Exchange Tax on all imports except those from the sterling area. The Americans recognized Canada's right to act and were surprisingly accommodating, but they made clear that such action would cause difficulties for them with Congress.[71]

The simple fact, however, was that even this measure was not sufficient. On 18 September,* Robertson told Pierrepont Moffat, the American

---

* About this time there was a proposal to send Robertson to England with a food mission.
(Cont'd)

Minister to Canada, that, while in the first six months of 1940, Canadian exports to the United States had increased from $166 million to $221 million, imports from the US had risen from $240 million to $395 million.[72] In consequence, the Economic Advisory Committee had been considering further ways of coping with the growing exchange crisis.[73] Word of this soon found its way to Moffat,[74] and early in November 1940 he met Skelton and Robertson to discuss the situation.

The Americans recognized both the seriousness of the Canadian exchange disparity and the Canadian government's right to act to meet the situation, Moffat said, but felt "very strongly that a system of excluding or rationing a selected list would create so much resentment and so much bitterness that the drawbacks would be greater than the immediate advantages." Robertson reminded the Minister that Canada was almost alone in not resorting to licensing imports, but Moffat countered by arguing toughly that the United States "was almost the only market left to which Canada could send her exports freely and it would be a shame if restriction begetting restriction we ended up with the loss of our Trade Agreement and an embitterment of feeling. . . ." At that tense moment Towers and Clark arrived at Skelton's office for a meeting, and Moffat, repeating his complaints and fears yet again, informed Towers that he had learned that the Department of Agriculture had been working for weeks on a plan to ration American fruits and vegetables. Towers "remarked that I knew more than he did," Moffat recorded, "but Norman Robertson said that was unimportant, inasmuch as I had drawn perfectly normal deductions from scraps of information. . . ." The meeting ended inconclusively but Moffat urged his Canadian friends not "under any circumstances" to confront the United States with a *fait accompli.*[75] In Washington, the State Department took the first opportunity to make similar representations to the Legation.[76]

By 8 November, those pressures had begun to have their effect, and Robertson told Moffat that he was almost certain to be sent to Washington for conversations in the near future. But, as Robertson told

---

"I strongly opposed the idea of Robertson . . . going," King wrote, "though S[kelton]. would rather have him go, I think, with a view to keeping E[xternal]. A[ffairs]. hand on everything than have him stay and save his own strength." (PAC, W.L.M. King Diary, 19 Sep. 40.) Had he gone, Robertson would have found London changed greatly because of the blitz. Pearson wrote from there to say "that a lot of [Robertson's] old haunts have disappeared; I do not mean the churches and hospitals, but some of the better known pubs and restaurants." (PAC, L.B. Pearson Papers, N1, vol. 8, Pearson to A. McCloskey, 17 Oct. 40.)

the increasingly angry Minister, "he did not wish to go to Washington until the Cabinet had at least reached a decision in principle as to the method to follow. I told him," Moffat wrote, "that this was the one thing we were anxious to avoid. If a decision were reached, there was no point in his going. Furthermore," he added, cognizant of the importance of the United States to Canadian policy in every field, "it was hard to see how a decision could be properly reached unless the Cabinet knew exactly what the repercussions of a given policy would be in the United States." Robertson indicated that not even the experts knew how to handle the exchange difficulty, "but that the pressure was becoming so formidable" that time was running out. A very tough man indeed, Moffat "reminded" Robertson that "last June he had come to Washington asking our comments and then promptly ignored them on the ground that the decision in principle had already been taken. This we were particularly anxious to avoid. Norman Robertson said he saw the point but would feel happier if he had a little more by way of guidance from the Cabinet."

Moffat remained upset and sceptical, recording his "distinct impression" that Robertson "was not being entirely frank with me," that his own probing had interrupted the Canadian schemes before they had come to maturity, and that the time had come to have Jack Hickerson, still the key man on policy toward Canada in the State Department, intervene directly with Robertson from Washington.[77] Hickerson agreed and called Robertson the next day. "Mr. Robertson said," Hickerson noted, "that he had not fully understood our idea of timing, and that he agreed that [prior to a cabinet decision] would be the most suitable time for Canada to send someone to Washington."[78]

The Americans had made their point. As Moffat later said, he knew that Canada would have to step on some American toes to deal with the exchange problem; from his point of view, the important point was "to avoid her stepping on any of our toes which had a corn."[79] But as he had learned that the Canadian desire was to save $20 million in exchange each month, a "terrific" amount,[80] it would be very difficult to avoid the tender parts of the American anatomy.

Robertson, accompanied this time by Clifford Clark, went to Washington for the discussions in late November. He explained to the Americans that the balance of payments was running against Canada "even more radically than the public suspected" and probably to the tune of $300 million a year. Because Canada could no longer convert her sterling surplus in London into dollars (the prewar method of covering the perennial Canadian deficit with the United States), there were few options open, and the only feasible one was to block American exports to Canada. Four lists had been prepared, therefore, giving items to be completely prohibited; articles whose import was to be subject to license; articles the manufacture of which were to be largely prohibited through confiscatory excise taxes; and articles from the sterling area on which tariffs were to be suspended for the war's duration. The plan was intended to save, not the $20 million monthly Moffat had heard, but $8 million a month.

The heart of the matter for the Americans was the proposed inclusion in the prohibited list of fruit and vegetables, "almost everything except oranges, lemons and grapefruit juice. The Department [of State] told Robertson and Clark in no uncertain terms that an embargo on these items would imperil the Trade Agreement. Canada had a legal right under the War Escape Clause. . . . But for her to select the items for which we had paid heavily through admitting at a lower rate Canadian cattle, potatoes and fish would not seem in harmony with the spirit of the agreement." To the Americans, perhaps ignoring the fact that Canada was in a war, it seemed more a device to protect Canadian farmers than a way of conserving exchange, and the State Department convinced itself that fruit and vegetable exports to Canada had been "saved."[81] For their part, the Canadians came away impressed with the importance that the Americans attached to absolute secrecy. The United States would be put in an "intolerable" position if critics could charge that it had agreed to alterations in the 1938 agreement to meet the Canadian dollar shortage. On 27 November, Robertson and Clark reported their conclusions to the Cabinet War Committee,[82] Robertson's first attendance at the committee, and the cabinet accepted them. When the War Exchange Conservation Act was put through Parliament, it omitted measures to check the import of American fruit and vegetables, and the Minister of Finance, J.L. Ilsley, was uncommonly frank when he explained why this was done: "we had to weigh . . . the inevitable public reaction there would be in many of the agricultural districts of the United States, the embarrassment this restriction would cause . . . and the danger which would ensue not only to our own trade relations with the United States . . . but to the whole trade agreement policy of the United States."[83]

Robertson, as the draftsman of the 1938 trade agreement, knew the implications of interfering with American agricultural exports to Canada. But he could not have liked the way that Canada had been big-sticked by Moffat, Hickerson and their colleagues. The concessions to the United States, he later said to the Prime Minister, "were hard to take, difficult to defend, and only justified by the importance the Canadian Government attached to the long range considerations governing Canadian-American trade relations."[84]

At the same time as the discussions on import restrictions were underway, Robertson was handling External Affairs' side of Canada's export control policy.[85] In February 1940, the authority of the War Measures Act had been invoked to prohibit the export of certain specified minerals and metals except under license. No shipments of nickel to Japan had been permitted since February 1940, and even before that change in policy, only 2,435 tons had been exported there since the beginning of the war.[86] The Japanese had protested about the restrictive Canadian policy and had been answered that Canada's own wartime needs were the cause of it.[87] As Skelton and Robertson explained it to Pierrepont Moffat in October 1940: "Had Canada not suspended the publication of trade statistics it would have been impossible to maintain this position." In other metals and minerals, the situation varied. Aluminum exports to Japan had stopped with the war;[88] zinc, scrap iron and scrap steel exports had ceased with hostilities; asbestos of secondary grades only had been exported;[89] lead had been freely exported to Japan because demand elsewhere was low, production was high, and Canada needed foreign exchange;[90] and copper, too, was being exported in small quantities to Japan, Canada supplying about ten percent of Japanese needs and the United States some sixty percent.[91] Licenses to export copper, however, were to be refused in future. The Canadians told Moffat that the question of metal and mineral exports showed "the great difficulty arising from the fact that the United States and Canada were not pursuing entirely parallel courses."[92]

This was the situation in December 1940 when Robertson became directly involved in a most unpleasant affair with Dr. Robert McClure, then a Canadian missionary doctor serving in China with the International Red Cross. McClure told the Toronto press on 4 December that Canadian nickel was still being shipped to Japan, that some had left as recently as the week before, and all because "Canadian merchants want the profit.... For three years," he said, "I have been digging Canadian scrap iron out of Chinese bodies and I expect someone soon will be digging it out of British bodies...."[93]

McClure's charges were raised in Parliament the next day, where they met a flat and absolute denial from the Prime Minister. "Let me say at once that no nickel has been shipped to Japan ... since the beginning of this year," King stated. He added that no permits for scrap iron shipments to Japan had been issued since the autumn of 1939.[94] The Prime Minister also wired McClure, asking him to provide evidence for his charges, a request that McClure answered by citing "a Canadian official 'friendly with the Prime Minister' " and "the American Committee for Non-Participation in Japanese Aggression." McClure stated that he could apologize for his charges only if the Prime Minister proved that no Canadian nickel had been trans-shipped to Japan.[95] This too was raised in Parliament and King assured the House that "we have taken far-reaching precautions to see that nickel exported from Canada to another country is not re-exported in primary or fabricated form to any destination for which we would not grant an export permit for nickel in the first place."[96]

On 7 December, at McClure's request, the missionary met in Ottawa with Dr. Skelton and with the official in charge of the export control policy, Robertson. McClure's account of this meeting, apparently based on memory alone, was published 37 years later. According to this version, McClure had been summoned to Ottawa for a meeting with Skelton, who was affable but who soon withdrew, leaving McClure alone with Robertson. The two men apparently had met on several occasions in the past, but this meeting was not a friendly one. Heatedly, Robertson denied McClure's allegations, and then ushered him in to see the Prime Minister. King, contrary to the statements he had made in the House and to the position taken by Robertson, not only did not deny that exports had gone to Japan but admitted that the amounts were ten times that stated by McClure. The Prime Minister then offered the missionary a choice of jail or recantation. "The meeting with the Prime Minister was over," McClure's biographer wrote. "It had been of such little importance to Mr. King that he made no reference to it in his diary." That at least was so.

But the account in McClure's biography then goes on to defame Norman Robertson in an extraordinary way:

The meeting with Norman Robertson continued. Bob could hardly bring himself to speak to him. King was at least a politician working at the politician's trade but Robertson, as a senior civil servant, was supposed to be above the muck of the moment. But here he was acting as a political 'yes-man' to Mackenzie King. Worse. He had denied what King had admitted. McClure went into a slow burn that remained with him. . . . 'I was disgusted to see a man of Norman Robertson's achievements prostitute himself in doing a lackey job for Mackenzie King. I was really disgusted, nauseated. I'm afraid it's one of the things I don't excuse, a gutless, gutless political lackey'.[97]

These are very serious charges indeed, as serious as any ever made against

Norman Robertson in a career that spanned almost forty years in the public service. They deserve close examination, if only because of Dr. McClure's distinguished career as a missionary surgeon and later as Moderator of the United Church of Canada. The evidence suggests very strongly that the charges are inaccurate.

First, as McClure's biographer, Munroe Scott, notes, there is no record of a meeting between the Prime Minister and McClure. Students of the King diary will find that puzzling, for King was a faithful diarist, one who would not have omitted his description of the incredible scene McClure described. They will be puzzled as well by what seems to be flat-out lies told by the Prime Minister in the House and then admitted in conversation with McClure. We have now been conditioned to believe almost anything of Mackenzie King, and his cunning was legendary; but if he had lied in Parliament (and this is doubtful, since what he said was consistent with the policy that Robertson had been working out since the war began), King would certainly never have admitted doing so to McClure. That could only have put a loaded gun into the hand of a man who might do irreparable damage to the Prime Minister and his government. Scott makes no mention of King's statements in the House.

Most important, perhaps, as a piece of evidence is the memorandum prepared by Skelton of his meeting with McClure, an account that the missionary's biographer did not discover. This memorandum, dated 7 December, was sent to King in the afternoon, after Skelton and McClure had talked. It makes clear by inference that McClure did not see the Prime Minister and thus adds support to the negative evidence of the King diary. The Under-Secretary told the Prime Minister that McClure was "rather aggressive and evasive and I had to talk with him pretty frankly as to the irresponsibility and recklessness of his charges. . . . He was informed again that anyone, whoever it was, who had made any statement to the effect that Canadian nickel is being shipped to Japan was not only telling an untruth but was doing so without having made the faintest effort to find out what was the truth. . . ." There was no excuse for a man in McClure's position making such charges, Skelton said.

He tried to say [Skelton continued] that the United States Committee probably meant shipments of scrap nickel. I told him that it was probable neither he nor the Committee had ever heard of scrap nickel until it had been mentioned by the Prime Minister that not an ounce of scrap nickel had left Canada . . . we had gone out of our way to see that there was as watertight control over nickel as any country had over any commodity. . . .

Finally he agreed to make a brief statement to the press to the general effect that he had been informed of the facts . . . and wished to withdraw the statement he had made. I turned him over to Robertson to assist in drafting a brief statement.[98]

McClure's apology was complete, admitting that the government was making every effort to prevent Canadian nickel reaching Japan and regretting "the reflection which my statement may have cast on the Dominion Government."[99]

It seems, therefore, that McClure's discussions were primarily with Skelton and not with Robertson. Why McClure in his recollections so roundly assails the innocent Robertson, and why with such vehemence, is unclear.

There is one final piece of evidence to point up the errors in McClure's recollection of the events of 7 December 1940. Everyone familiar with his career might have expected him to choose jail—and a subsequent public uproar that could only have been beneficial to his genuine aim of helping China—over the ignominy of a public apology when faced with King's alleged choice of recantation or prison. That he did not is additional evidence that the choice was never offered, and never offered because the two men did not meet that day. The account in McClure's biography is not only insulting and defamatory to both Robertson and Mackenzie King, it also seems to be untrue.[100]

III

The strain of war and the shock of a succession of uninterrupted defeats weighed heavily on Canadians at the beginning of 1941. In the Department of External Affairs, the senior officers were all tired, overworked and serving on far too many committees. Dr. Skelton, despite his general ill-health, continued to work terrifically long hours, "a hurt, tired look in his eyes."[101] His officers tried to protect him as best they could from drains on his time and energy, but they could not deflect his willingness to tackle all the problems of government for the Prime Minister. In January, he had been active in the planning and execution of the Dominion-Provincial Conference, there were the daily duties of the Department, and there was the heavy strain of attending the Cabinet War Committee. On 27 January, he had spent four hours in the War Committee,[102] and the next morning had had a discussion with Hume Wrong, at this stage (as so often in those days) in an obstreperous frame of mind* because of the unimportant work he had been given to do since the war effectively shut down his post at the League of Nations.[103] On his way home for lunch, driving his own car, Dr. Skelton had suffered a severe heart attack, his car then colliding with a streetcar in downtown Ottawa. By the time the tram driver had reached Skelton's automobile, Canada's "greatest civil servant,"[104] the "irreplaceable"[105] O.D. Skelton was dead at sixty-two.

But irreplaceable or not, someone had to fill Skelton's role within the Department of External Affairs. Clearly it would take time before anyone could replace him in the confidence of Mackenzie King and in the councils of the nation, but in war the Department could not be left unattended.

Thanks to Skelton's successful recruiting over fifteen years, there were a number of credible candidates within the Department and, of course, there was nothing to prevent the Prime Minister from going outside for a successor if he chose. Within the Department, there was Laurent Beaudry, the senior French-speaking officer in Ottawa, affable and charming; Hume Wrong, extremely able and competent, a skilled diplomatic technician and a highly intelligent man, but one who was increasingly bitter about the way he believed he had been treated by the Prime Minister and the Department; L.B. Pearson, very bright, able and popular, but posted in London, an ocean away from the scene; John Read, the Department's Legal Adviser, one of the most senior of the officials and possibly the wisest, but not a man who hitherto had had much interest in the political and economic sides of foreign policy; Loring Christie, the Minister in Washington, able and experienced, but in ill-health and under attack at the moment, ostensibly for his public relations failures in Washington but really because he was viewed in some quarters as an anti-British isolationist;[106] Hugh Keenleyside, a British Columbian of substantial ability, a man of principle and a certain rigidity, but the organizer of the triumphal 1939 Royal tour, a feat that had brought him favourably to the Prime Minister's attention; and, finally, Norman Robertson, the youngest of the contenders and the most junior in service.

Any one of these officials could have succeeded Skelton and done a creditable job — the highest of tributes that could be paid to the late

---

* "Please don't write," Skelton had said in 1938, " . . . as if you were a desolate and forgotten orphan, and one who was born with a chip on your shoulder. I value so highly your judgment and initiative and the quality of your despatches, which I won't compare with certain others, that I have not said anything about the revival of your fondness for sharp sayings and remarks about resigning." (PAC, Civil Service Commission, Historical Personnel Records, vol. 359, Wrong file, Skelton to Wrong, 28 Feb. 38.)

Under-Secretary who had built the Department from nothing. But of this group it was Norman Robertson who was selected by the Prime Minister, and with great speed. Why Robertson?

From Mackenzie King's point of view, the others all suffered from liabilities that prevented their selection. Pearson was in England, away from the scene. Beaudry had drawn himself forcibly and unfavourably to King's attention by demanding, while he was acting in Skelton's place in 1937, that all correspondence from the Department should be in French, a position that led King to see him as "nervous" and unstable.[107] Wrong was unpopular with the Prime Minister because he had caused difficulties over postings, refusing offer after offer, and because he made no effort to hide his opinion that King had an intellect inferior to his own.[108] Keenleyside had fallen into difficulty, as King later wrote in his diary, by creating "so strong a feeling against him in the H[ouse]. of C[ommons]. arising out of reports that he had made regarding the Japanese" in British Columbia in late 1940,[109] that his appointment was certain to cause political troubles in that province. Read did not seem a real possibility. Christie was, but his health had broken, and King told Pierrepont Moffat that if he had been well, "he would have brought him back and put him in Skelton's place, but agreed that under present circumstances it would kill him."[110] That left Norman Robertson.

Robertson had favourably impressed the Prime Minister since 1935 with his skill in trade negotiations, with his knack for keeping out of trouble, and with his intelligence. Also, and somewhat inexplicably perhaps, King felt comfortable with Robertson, or at least more comfortable than with other possible candidates.[111] He had been, as well, highly regarded by Skelton, and while it overstated matters to suggest that the Doctor had viewed Robertson as his potential successor—it was too revolutionary to think of a thirty-seven-year old as the heir apparent[112]*—there was little doubt that Robertson had been closest to Skelton of all the officers in the East Block. And, some think, Robertson was strongly recommended to the Prime Minister in the hours after Skelton's death by Arnold Heeney, the Secretary to the Cabinet and Robertson's long-time friend, and by L.W. Brockington, an assistant to the Prime Minister.[113]

---

* Almost certainly, as J.W. Pickersgill remembers, the Prime Minister did not fully realize how young Robertson was. Pickersgill told King once that Robertson was only eighteen months older than himself, a revelation that the Prime Minister greeted by saying, "Impossible, Pickersgill." (J.W. Pickersgill interview, 13 Oct. 78.) Brooke Claxton, MP, wrote Robertson to say that the only obstacle to his appointment being made permanent
(Cont'd)

Whatever the advice and whatever his reasoning, Mackenzie King moved decisively to fill the vacuum. The Prime Minister had learned of Skelton's death about 3 p.m. on 28 January and had gone immediately to the Skelton house, accompanied only by Hugh Keenleyside,[114] and then to the hospital to see the body. He had then gone to a Cabinet War Committee meeting at 4:30 p.m. where he told his colleagues that he intended to have Robertson "assume, immediately, the responsibilities of Deputy Minister of the department."[115] The meeting ended later than 7 p.m. and it was after 8 p.m. before King left his office. Then as King's diary has it, "Phoned Robertson to take on the duties of acting Deputy."[116] The next day, Arnold Heeney prepared a note for Beaudry, the nominal second-in-command under Skelton, that "Last evening the Prime Minister instructed me to prepare an Order-in-Council, to be passed today, appointing Norman Robertson. . . . He also telephoned Mr. Robertson," Heeney went on, perhaps attempting to forestall Beaudry from moving into Skelton's office and causing an incident, "and asked him to move into the Under-Secretary's office, and take over, immediately."[117]

So it was to be Robertson as Under-Secretary *pro tem.* He had never contemplated the possibility and the thought simply stunned him. Max Wershof, a junior colleague, remembers seeing Robertson late on 28 January and finding him almost traumatized by having to sit at Skelton's massive desk. It was as if he had been hit over the head.[118] The shock showed in a letter written to his parents in Vancouver on 30 January:

. . . we have had a pretty terrible week. Skelton had more of the qualities of greatness than anybody I've ever known and his death has left us all pretty badly shaken up. The request to try & carry on in his shoes came therefore as rather staggering & frightening. How things will work out it is impossible to say. The present arrangement is temporary & probationary—as everything should be in war time. . . .

The job is a big one & calls for a number of qualities I simply have not got. . . . My senior colleagues without exception will be helpful—the P.M. is encouraging—but I dislike very much assuming so much responsibility in unfamiliar fields—and my inability to organize my own work is an ominous note for a

---

was "your positively childish age of 37. I am having someone remind the P.M. that he was 26 when he was appointed deputy minister." (Department of External Affairs, John Starnes Papers, Claxton to Robertson, 6 Feb. 41.) Skelton had promoted Robertson to Counsellor, the then-highest rank below his own, in May 1940. (External Affairs Records, vol. 836, file 54, Memo, 15 Dec. 39 and Revision of Classification, 20 May 40.)

department desperately in need of organization. Policy is not such a worry as personnel and the two questions are unfortunately not separable as matters stand.

He also added that "technically I suppose I have made a good promotion but feel pretty bleak & miserable about it."[119]

Robertson also sent a personal, handwritten note the same day to Mike Pearson in London. Skelton's death "has just flattened out everybody. It's only when you start taking an inventory that you realize what a range of responsibilities he took—and how we all lived & worked secure in the shadow of a great rock . . . we unloaded—ultimately—almost every worry on him." Then Robertson got to the heart of his message to his friend and colleague:

. . . I did not really write to praise or bury Caesar, but to say you have been on my conscience for the last year—and now worse than ever—for if you had come back with the other visiting firemen you would undoubtedly have been asked to carry on in O.D.'s place rather than I. You were a lot on his mind in these last months. I thought we might usefully have swopped jobs . . . [but] we have to swing for it, for a while anyway.[120]

Robertson went on to suggest that, if Pearson wanted, he could have a new Latin American legation of his own (although "there is no shadow of doubt . . . that your London job is bigger and more important" than a South American legation), and to bemoan his difficulties with Wrong. "I've got the P.M. to agree to Hume carrying on in the Dept. on the same sort of emergency 'acting' basis as I am, but he is still inclined to fuss about definition of function and official style. Having fought his fight with O.D. for the last year and a half I was a little discouraged this morning."[121]

As that letter to Pearson hints, there were some hard feelings in the Department over Robertson's rise. He was, after all, junior in years of service and age, if not in rank, to Wrong, Pearson, Read, Christie, Keenleyside and Beaudry, and that clearly mattered. Wrong was initially unperturbed, telling his sister that Robertson was "a great friend of mine and a very enjoyable fellow," who had "in his hands more of the threads which passed through Skelton's office than anyone else, and his choice is intelligent as a temporary move."[122] The operative word in that sentence was "temporary," and by the next month Wrong was complaining to Grant Dexter of the *Winnipeg Free Press* that he had been passed over and that it would have been better if Pearson had got the job.[123] His wife, too, was upset.[124] Hugh Keenleyside was similarly annoyed, writing in his diary that Robertson had been "pushed up" over many others, including himself, that he had high qualifications but no organizational ability, and could not delegate work. [125] There was some truth in those complaints.

Another who was upset was Pearson. Affable and charming as he was, Pearson ordinarily hid his substantial ambition. But not in this instance. He believed that he was entitled to the Under-Secretaryship rather than Robertson, and although he was not one to blame Robertson for his good fortune, there are some suggestions that his wife, Maryon, then in Ottawa, was less charitable. [126] Some of the upset was perhaps caused inadvertently by Robertson's letter of 30 January, not for its contents, but because it failed to reach Britain until 27 February. [127] More of Pearson's annoyance resulted from a telegram from the Prime Minister that reached London on 29 March 1941. Because of the shortage of senior officers in Ottawa— Skelton was dead, Wrong was going to Washington as number two to Leighton McCarthy, the ill Christie's replacement—Pearson was to be brought back to Ottawa, "probably as an additional Assistant Under-Secretary." This, King said, was the only way of meeting the "absolute necessity . . . of obtaining best possible assistance for Robertson. . . ." [128]

While he was probably pleased at the prospect of rejoining his family, Pearson hated to leave London at that time, unless the work he was going to was more important than that he was relinquishing. "Of course," he added in his sporadically kept diary, "I don't like the idea really of going back to Department, except as Under-Secretary, and I am not quite sure what this post of Joint Assistant Under-Secretary means. My own view," he said, "is that it means that Mr. King wants Norman Robertson as a sort of super personal assistant and is going to give him the rank of Under-Secretary for that reason, while I am to be brought back to do the work . . . without being given the rank." [129]

Pearson set out immediately to seek clarification of his position, and Vincent Massey, the High Commissioner, sent King a message on 2 April that implicitly suggested that Pearson should still be made Under-Secretary. [130] Pearson himself wired personally to Robertson, indicating his concerns that as Assistant Under-Secretary he "would have less responsibility for the direction of the Department than I have now for the work of Canada House. In this sense, I am not much enamoured of the proposal, especially if I am right in interpreting the telegram as meaning that the Under-Secretaryship is closed." [131] Robertson replied the next day, explaining Pearson's position as one of three Assistant Under-Secretaries, his duties and his salary. "As regards question of Under-Secretaryship," Robertson added with complete honesty, "I can only say that I have had no word with the Prime Minister about duration of present arrangement which should I suppose be regarded as emergency measure." That did not mollify Pearson (although he did say that "At least Norman has been frank"), who calculated that the transfer would reduce his income by more than half, thanks to the loss of his overseas allowances. [132]

In the end, Pearson had no choice. He returned to Canada in mid-May, fully intending to press his claims to the Under-Secretary's post. In an interview with the Prime Minister, however, his efforts were balked:

I saw the Prime Minister the Monday after I arrived. . . . Even then I didn't see him alone as Robertson was present. I had about 15 minutes, 5 of which were taken up by a panegyric on Norman, much to his embarrassment, 5 by a panegyric on me—much to my embarrassment and 5 by a moving discourse on the spirit and soul of Britain. About my duties and position not a word except that, on leaving, he indicated that Robertson and I would be able to share the work and agree on some arrangement for that purpose. I was quite defeated in my intentions to force any issue along these lines. My own view—and it is Robertson's too—is that the Prime Minister is quite happy with the present arrangements and that no permanent appointment may be made for a considerable time. It's hard on Robertson, who is bearing a terrific load, and not satisfactory, I should think to anyone else. [133]

King's version was that Pearson was "Very modest, unassuming. He is going to be valuable to Robertson." [134] Indeed he was, and to his credit, Pearson soon went out of his way to squelch the stories that he resented being passed over. "I want it known right now," he told a luncheon meeting of the Ottawa Canadian Club shortly after his return, "that I think Norman Robertson's appointment was an excellent one and that I will be glad to work with him. If anyone can take Dr. Skelton's place, he is the man." [135] That was a gracious gesture, but the hurt did not dissipate so easily, and although Pearson and Robertson worked closely together for a quarter-century more, they were rivals in a subtle way ever after. Pearson forgave Robertson, but he did not forget.

Robertson's appointment, of course, was still temporary, and on occasion he had difficulties with Mackenzie King that must have made him wonder if he wanted his position to be made permanent. On 5 April 1941, for example, there was a sharp dispute about the contents of an innocuous statement on Canadian-Polish friendship. "I was really amazed," an angry Mackenzie King wrote, "at how tenacious he seemed to be in the matter of holding to his own view. However, when he saw I was determined, he gave in." That experience led King to bemoan the "idea which has been growing up in E.A. that these advisers are the men who are to settle everything and Ministers or P.M.'s only to be second. Robertson is much worse in that regard than S[kelton]. was. S. knew when to yield but R. hangs on too tenaciously." If that were not bad enough, that same day the Prime Minister heard from his close friend Joan Patteson a nasty piece of malicious gossip about Jetty Robertson. It was, King noted, "indeed a serious matter and if it became known generally, would make it impossible for Robertson to be appointed head of the Department."[136] The tale was nonsensical, and King presumably soon discovered so, for nothing more was said of it.

But it was not until 24 June that King finally acted to confirm Robertson's appointment. "I recommended Robertson for Under-Secretary at $10,000, to date his salary back to time of S.'s death." At the same time, at the request of Leighton McCarthy, Wrong was appointed Minister-Counsellor in Washington, and Pearson and Keenleyside made Assistant Under-Secretaries. "Salary of last three to remain what they are at," King added.[137] At one swoop, Robertson's salary increased by $4,000, a raise that, because of war conditions and taxes and because of his and Jetty's unusually frugal style of life, made not the slightest difference to their standard of living.[138] The one difference was that Robertson was now so loaded with work that he was home even less than when Skelton was alive.

There was a flood of congratulations from friends, politicians, deputy ministers and diplomats,[139] and substantial newspaper comment. The *Globe and Mail* called Robertson a man of "first-class calibre ... [his] intellectual powers are rated of the highest order, his capacity for work is immense and his range of experience ... very wide." The *Winnipeg Tribune* said Robertson's appointment was "inevitable" because of his "sheer ability," and *The Financial Post* headlined its story, "Able Skelton Successor."[140] Skelton's widow also wrote warmly. "You have evidently made a fine beginning," she said. "But that was what I expected, because I know with what confidence and love my husband always warmed to you: 'Norman is so unselfish & has such good judgment.' "[141] The Prime Minister added his mite by wishing Robertson "a long and successful tenure of the important office to which our great friend, your predecessor Dr. Skelton, gave such high distinction."[142] But of all the letters, the one that must have produced the most hilarity was that from the Warden of Rhodes House, Oxford, congratulating Robertson on his appointment to the cabinet.[143] Oxford never could get anything right.

CHAPTER V

Problems of Alliance Warfare

A s UNDER-SECRETARY OF State for External Affairs, Norman
Robertson had the good fortune to be situated at the very
heart of Canada's war effort from January 1941 on. It was a
frightening, dangerous, yet exciting time, a period in which he
exercised very great influence on the Prime Minister, the cabinet and the
government, and indeed on the course of the war. The nation's business
brought him into contact with the leading actors and the great events,
and although he suffered from occasional doubts about his ability to
administer the Department of External Affairs, he revelled in his work.

As Under-Secretary, Robertson had to deal with a vast array of
responsibilities, decisions and crises. First and most essential, he had to
learn to work closely and directly with Mackenzie King, as always a
difficult taskmaster and one who expected to get his own way. Then he
had to handle the problems of his Department and its able, ambitious
officers, and to preside over successive reorganizations so that External
Affairs could deal with the wartime expansion in its workload. Finally, he
had to shape the Department's policy on the great issues of the day. How
could Canada get on with the new world power to its south and with the
battered mother country across the Atlantic? What role could Canada
secure for itself in the organizations set up to coordinate the Allied war
effort? What new world assembly should be established to ensure the
preservation of peace? And what did Canada want in such an
organization? Other issues, as difficult to resolve if less cosmic in
importance, also occupied him, and there were problems with Japanese
Canadians and Soviet spying in Canada that posed excruciating
dilemmas. Norman Robertson's plate was always full with the hardest of
problems, and he struggled with them until he was close to exhaustion.

I

To work with Mackenzie King, as Robertson already knew, was a difficult, exasperating chore at the best of times. In 1941, the Prime Minister turned sixty-seven years old, and he was querulous, crotchety, suspicious and quick to take offence. That he was also wise and shrewd, sensitive to the public mood, and a skilled political operator did little to compensate those who had to work closely with him. King's telephone calls could come at any hour, his complaints and his demands for assistance were unending, and he expected all who worked for him to be as dedicated and devoted to his service as he was to the country's and party's. Astonishingly, they were, and although King often griped about Robertson, Arnold Heeney, the Secretary to the Cabinet, and Jack Pickersgill, the key staff member in the Prime Minister's Office, he was unfailingly well served by his three closest collaborators, and he knew it.

The Cabinet War Committee was, as Robertson said later, "the real policy-making component of the Cabinet,"[1] and here Robertson played his most important role and exercised his greatest influence on affairs. The meetings were irregularly scheduled, and during crises they could occur four or five times a week. On 19 December 1941, for example, Robertson told the American minister that he was on his way to the fourth War Committee of the week. "They sat four hours at a stretch and the conversation wanders all over the field. Arnold Heeney tries his best to keep a fixed agenda but with little success."[2] Of course, in those situations there were occasional opportunities for someone like Robertson. "I then frequently found it easier and quicker to get decisions on policy questions from the Prime Minister in the War Committee ... than from him in his Ministerial capacity," Robertson told Escott Reid after the war. "Frequently the War Committee discussion was perfunctory because the Prime Minister's special and rather exclusive prerogative in matters of foreign and Commonwealth affairs was very strongly entrenched."[3] And after a few lost battles, Robertson was too shrewd ever to overplay his hand with King and his colleagues. "The important thing," he said, "is never to use a word that a Cabinet Minister won't understand or a word which will lead him to believe that you are trying to be superior."[4]

His tact and wisdom were ordinarily supreme, and as a result Robertson acquired a place and role in the War Committee that was unprecedented for a civil servant in Canada. The Auditor-General, Watson Sellar, came before the Committee in November 1943, for the first time since the opening weeks of the war, and was astonished. "A change is that a Privy Council secretary is present to take notes. Norman Robertson appears to be present as a right. He comes and goes and joins in the discussion."[5] He did indeed, essentially representing the bureaucracy, reporting on interdepartmental committee recommendations, and occasionally offering the views of departments with no minister on the War Committee. Of course, the presentation of recommendations on foreign policy was his task in cabinet, and during the war there were very few questions that did not in some way impinge on external affairs.

The War Committee was one of Robertson's major tasks; another was the duty he shared with Malcolm MacDonald, the British High Commissioner in Ottawa after the spring of 1941, of acting as a buffer between King and Winston Churchill. The two Prime Ministers, in their very different ways, were difficult, prickly, and suspicious of each other, temperamentally ill-fitted for cooperation. But that was not the case with Robertson and MacDonald, who got on like a house on fire, quickly becoming good friends. "We kept nothing back from each other," MacDonald said.[6] Nowhere was this more necessary than when the two had to interpose themselves between their masters. Occasionally, on Robertson's advice, the High Commissioner would withhold a telegram from Churchill and simply convey the message in his own, milder words; sometimes King's drafts were undiplomatic and MacDonald, with Robertson's aid, would suggest a phrasing likely to be more soothing to Churchill's ear.[7] There was nothing disloyal in this at all, but someone with less confidence in himself than Norman Robertson, and someone without so clear an understanding of Mackenzie King, would probably not have dared to act in this way.

He could work similarly with American friends as well. Robertson's relationship with Pierrepont Moffat (which lasted until Moffat's death in January 1943) was close and warm and much to the advantage of relations between the two countries. And at their fairly frequent meetings, he could talk frankly with his old friend Jack Hickerson.

The relationship was closer yet with his friends in the Ottawa mandarinate, men such as Clifford Clark, the Deputy Minister of Finance, Robert Bryce, his ablest aide, W.A. Mackintosh, Clark's old friend from Queen's University and his wartime Special Assistant, and Graham Towers, the Governor of the Bank of Canada.* These men often sought

---

* These same men were also often present at the Five Lakes Fishing Club, a Gatineau retreat that had been discovered by Clark in the spring of 1940 and, after some difficulty, bought by a group of thirty or so, mostly civil servants, for $12,500. The lodge was rustic

(Cont'd)

Robertson's advice on a vast range of questions, and he was fertile in suggesting strategy. On committees with these and others, he operated with "sweet reason" and skill, opening the discussion on contentious questions with anodyne statements and then somehow manipulating the discussion, sometimes with only a great sigh and always through clouds of cigarette smoke, so that the consensus represented the desired position.[8] Above all there was his tact. There was little point in insulting a dullard who might be on a committee. "I have to work with this man for many years," Escott Reid remembered Robertson telling him of one such roadblock to progress, "and I can't afford to annoy him."[9]*

The chief pressure on Robertson was overwork. In August 1942, Mackenzie King told Athlone, the Governor General, that Robertson "has not had a vacation since the war began" and had been forced to take a rest.[10] Forced was the operative word, and Hume Wrong wrote him that "you are not to consider returning until you have had three clear weeks," adding jocularly that, "You will judge from all this how easily dispensable you are."[11] Robertson's rest on this enforced holiday was occasionally interrupted by a baby's crying, however, for in April 1942 he and Jetty had had another daughter, Judith. Robertson's relaxation was complete, however (aided by his deaf ear which helped insulate him from household noise), so long as he had something to read, and somehow he made the time on holiday or at work to read omnivorously. His Oxford friend, Denis Brogan, gave him a copy of his *The Development of Modern France*, which Robertson liked and pronounced first-class in a letter to his fellow Balliol man—except for three obscure slips in the text which he proceeded to point out.[12]

---

and there were few amenities (then or later), but it served as a vital safety-valve for men working under great pressure. Robertson attended whenever he could, as he did at the Dining Club, another exclusive Ottawa group, many of whom were friends from Robertson's 1927 summer in Ottawa. The Club met the first Tuesday of each month at the Country Club for good food, good talk, and good gossip, under the nominal leadership of Chief Justice Lyman Duff. (Queen's University, W.A. Mackintosh Papers, Box 8, file 203, Mackintosh to Professor G. Wilson, 27 May 40; PAC, N.A. Robertson Papers, vol. 2, G. Maclaren to NAR, 20 Jun. 40; A.O. Gibbons interview, 31 Jul. 78; David Mansur interview, 6 Oct. 78; Queen's University, John Stevenson Papers, docs. on vol. 1, file 4, Robertson Papers, vol. 2, Personal Correspondence, Dining Club members; C.J. Mackenzie Papers (Ottawa), Diary, 25 Mar. 41, 28 Nov., 5 Dec. 44.)

* Robertson's tact could not prevent External Affairs from being disliked by many civil servants for its Oxbridge manner, its old boy networks, its tea and sherry atmosphere. One temporary External Affairs officer remembers a colleague saying the Department was stuffed with "bloody colonials," but more damning still was Watson Sellar's dismissive comment that External Affairs was stuffed with "intellectuals". (J.M.S. Careless interview, 4 Oct. 78; PAC, Watson Sellar Diary, 25 Jun. 42.)

Hume Wrong, on whom Robertson came to rely totally, helped to ease the strains of work. In May 1942 Robertson had brought Wrong back to Ottawa from Washington, sending Lester Pearson there in his place, and Wrong became, in Robertson's description of him to Mackenzie King, "the ablest man in the Service."[13] A slender man of an academic turn of mind and an intellect every bit the equal of Robertson's, Wrong was organized and polished, as Robertson was not; the two worked together, in Max Wershof's happy phrase, "like twins."[14] Their partnership was probably unique in the Department's annals, and was all the more remarkable because Wrong, the unhappiest of men in the Department until his return to the East Block, waxed in the arrangement. Occasionally some officers thought they detected a tension between the two, an effort on Wrong's part to show that he and Robertson were coequals rather than subordinate and superior;[15] and Wrong certainly worked more efficiently than Robertson, something that provoked him to occasional bouts of exasperation with his friend.[16] Nonetheless, the two got on famously, much to the success of Canadian diplomacy, and Wrong's long experience of Washington, where he had served for a decade before the war, was of the greatest importance in making Canadian policy.

II

Relations with the United States were perhaps the most crucial ones for Robertson, his Department, and the government. The links extended from the military sphere through to the economic and the political, and in every area there were complications and difficulties enough to upset an ordinarily harmonious relationship.

As Under-Secretary, Robertson had to be concerned with the whole range of Canadian-American dealings. Certainly the scope of the problems he and Pierrepont Moffat faced together was enormous. In their first three months of direct contact after Robertson became Under-Secretary, Robertson and Moffat discussed, among other subjects: the Canadian regulation of auto imports; the St. Lawrence waterway; Canadian diplomatic relations with Chile; problems in personnel at the Canadian legation in Washington; foreign exchange difficulties; an entrance permit to Canada for a movie salesman; problems in the Canadian-American trade agreement of 1938; timber; export control; the 1938 agreement's cattle quota; the request of a former Congressman that a client be allowed to salvage hulks in Halifax harbour; and a visit to

Washington by Clifford Clark, the Deputy Minister of Finance. On these disparate subjects, amazingly enough, Robertson seemed to be aware of the detailed ins and outs, and if he could not provide ready answers to Moffat's queries, he got them quickly or explained why decisions were delayed.[17] It was an impressive performance by a new boy, and all the more so for the difficulties Robertson was facing in working himself into Dr. Skelton's shoes across the whole range of government policy.

One of the first major questions to concern Robertson was Canada's growing exchange problems with the United States. The country was caught in a cruel dilemma: the more it exerted itself to help Britain in the war, the greater the difficulties with Washington. The issue arose primarily because Canada had to import more machine parts, more raw materials, and more components from the south to fill the war orders for Britain, and since London had blocked the convertibility of sterling, the problem could not be eased (as before the war) by using the surplus in London to cover the deficit in trade with the United States. Complicating matters was the Lend-Lease programme, which threatened Canadian industry with its offer of "free" goods to Britain, in contrast to the largely cash basis of sales from Canada.[18]

The way out seemed to be some scheme that let the required war material that Canada imported from the south for export to Britain be covered under lend-lease on the British account. The problem, as Robertson reported to the Prime Minister on 12 March 1941, was that "it was unlikely that the United States would grant aid to Canada under Lease-Lend until this country had taken similar steps [to those the USA was forcing on Britain] to realize its United States investments." That concerned the Canadian government, which certainly did not want to be forced into a sell-off of such investments as Canadians had in the south— "going through the wringer,"[19] Robertson called it—and there were genuine concerns about the implications for Canadian sovereignty of taking lend-lease from so big and powerful a neighbour. But in principle, Robertson said, "it would be reasonable to ask the United States to supply materials to Canada for processing for United Kingdom use under the same conditions as it will itself be supplying similar finished goods. . . ."[20]

The advantage of such a plan was the effect it might have on the deteriorating trade balance. "Our merchandise exports to the United States are keeping up quite satisfactorily," Robertson wrote to the Prime Minister in a memorandum that King carried with him to his meeting with President Roosevelt at Hyde Park, New York, in April 1941, "but they do not come close to paying for the great expansion of imports from the United States required by our war industries." Robertson was the Department's, and the government's, expert on trade relations with the United States, and he was fully aware of the implications of this trend. "Under pressure of circumstances we have had to execute a series of tactical retreats away from the goal of closer and freer trade relations toward which both our countries were working through their similar trade agreement policies." Then Robertson detailed all the measures Canada had taken—pegging the dollar at 90¢ US, the War Exchange Tax, the War Exchange Conservation Act—and, while admitting that these were temporary moves, nonetheless "it must be recognized objectively that such measures taken to meet an immediate and critical wartime situation are bound to have continuing consequences which it will be very hard to eradicate. The longer they remain in force," he said, "the firmer will be the moulds within which Canadian industry has had to adapt itself." These problems, Robertson added, referring to the suggestion of joint economic committees that Canada had made to Washington,[21] would be harder to resolve after the war.

It seems to me that we should study how far our two Governments could go to relieve the fundamental strains on our war economies which compel us to maintain and introduce trade and exchange restrictions, rather than plan to put poultices on those strains which might for a time conceal their fundamental significance. For instance, immediate exchange difficulties might be lessened and the post war problem of economic adjustment partly solved if a way could be found to increase Canadian exports to the United States. . . .

. . . A second constructive approach . . . would be to have the Canadian-American trade position kept continuously in mind in planning United States Government production and purchasing programmes. An example of what might be done in this direction is afforded by the negotiations now under way for the purchase by United States Government agencies of part of their additional aluminum requirements from the output of a new producing unit which it is planned to erect in Canada. In this case consideration of cost and speed in delivery both, I am told, argue in favour of expanding Canadian capacity to produce a commodity which Canada can economically supply, instead of adding to what might easily become surplus capacity in the United States.

Robertson also suggested what amounted to a new trade agreement with Washington, and, while that was too ambitious, his suggestions on increased American purchases in Canada (and particularly on aluminum) found their way into the Hyde Park agreement that King and Roosevelt produced after their "grand Sunday" at the President's estate.[22] Robertson had had an impact on events.

As his memorandum had demonstrated, Robertson was still deeply concerned with trade matters, but new difficulties soon arose. The Atlantic Charter, as proclaimed by Roosevelt and Churchill in August 1941, was one such, for its point on freeing trade had a reservation—"with due respect for existing obligations"—that to Robertson seemed likely to preserve intact the whole structure of Imperial preferences. "This must weaken the force and scope of the promise of free access for all countries to markets and materials," Robertson noted, "and makes it difficult to say much about the free trade implications of the Declaration."[23] A conversation with Moffat the next month, after Robertson had returned from a trip to England, touched on Robertson's assessment of British trade attitudes. Both men feared that the British were heading toward a policy of "straight bilateralism" after the war, something that Canada and the United States found hard to swallow. In Robertson's view, this trend was caused by what he initially saw as the "virtually complete abdication" of the Foreign Office from commercial policy and "the strong entrenchment" of the bilateralists in the Treasury.[24] Moffat later noted that if only Robertson "could get away he would love to spend a few days in Washington talking over problems with the people he had worked with in years past."[25] Robertson's heart was still in trade policy; clearly he remained a free trader, too.

Nonetheless, when Washington began to press the United Kingdom for the "consideration" it was to receive in return for lend-lease, Robertson became very upset. In Article VII of the draft Anglo-American agreement covering "mutual aid," the Americans asked that the two nations "provide against discrimination in either country against importation of any produce originating in the other country." In his view, the United States was pressing to be paid for lend-lease "not at the expense of the United Kingdom but at the expense of the other parts of the Empire which enjoyed a preferred position in the British market. We spent months in Washington in 1938," Robertson complained to the Prime Minister, "convincing the United States Government that, when the United Kingdom reduced its duties on United States wheat, apples and lumber, it was not the United Kingdom but Canada that was really making an economic concession. . . ."[26]

Robertson's anger showed through when he met Moffat on 8 October. "His mind was filled with worries," Moffat wrote, "over what he called our 'assault on the preferential system.' He was so exercised over this that he talked about it for fifty minutes." Robertson gave the Minister a lesson in the theory of preferences, and then said it was not really the American attempt to modify the Ottawa 1932 system which he resented. "What he did object to was our assumption that this was purely an Anglo-American problem." Some in Britain desired a closed Imperial system, he admitted, but Canada could never live in such a world. Further, it was not enough to talk only of discrimination. "Discriminations were one side of a picture, of which the other side was the absolute height of tariffs. He did not feel that we could solve the problem unless we faced both phases simultaneously. The worst possible thing for Canada," the exercised Under-Secretary continued, "would be cut-throat competition between two self-sufficient economies,—British and American. Canada could not afford to join either one of them, and she was not strong enough to play the game independently." Above all, he urged, the United States must not leave Canada on the sidelines when discussing with Britain issues vital to Canada's economic and financial future. "In the sixteen months I have worked closely with Mr. Robertson," Moffat reported, "I have never seen him as perturbed as he was today."[27]

The Americans set out to calm down Robertson. Jack Hickerson in the Department of State sent a soothing message, pointing out that American aims were much the same as Canada's, that the goal was a new and open economic order with reduced tariffs all over the world. "Implicit in the very draft that Norman criticised," Hickerson said, "is an obligation on the part of the United States to cooperate with the United Kingdom Government toward this objective. . . ." And, he added, Washington "of course" realized that Canada had an interest in this. "It makes me very unhappy that Norman did not know all this."[28] Robertson told Moffat that he accepted Hickerson's word "implicitly, but that no matter how many times he read the draft he would never have been able to find our ideas implicit in the text. The only mention of cooperation is found in the preamble and he had worked long enough with documents to attach very minor importance to preambles, which are without binding force." The problem, Moffat opined, was that he "still cannot reconcile himself to the fact that the United States and the United Kingdom should have gotten as far as exchanging draft and counter-draft on a matter so closely affecting Canada without consulting her."[29] It was not the only instance of that during the war years.

Undoubtedly that was in Robertson's mind when he sent an important paper, surveying Canadian-American relations, to Mackenzie King on 22 December 1941, just two weeks after the Americans had come into the war. "In recent years," he began, "Canadians have tended to take it for granted that the United States will continue to follow a friendly, cooperative and unassuming policy toward Canada." That was still the general case, he said, but there "have been a number of warning developments in the last year or so ... which suggest that we should not be too cavalier in our confidence that the United States will always regard Canadian interests as a close second to their own and appreciably ahead of those of any third country." What had changed? Robertson believed that the Americans' "acceptance of leadership of the democratic cause" inevitably meant that Roosevelt had to deal more and more with the Great Powers and could afford little time on the "specifically Canadian aspects of American international relations. Canada naturally loomed much larger in the American scheme of things when the President and both political parties in the United States were thinking primarily in terms of continental and hemispheric defence."[30] But now that the war was a world-wide one, "the United States is, not unnaturally, inclined to take Canadian concurrence and support entirely for granted." The result of this and of the American tendency to view Canada in "a more modest and more nearly domestic perspective" was that changes in Canadian-American relations had proceeded quickly and "not too tactfully" in recent months. Part of this was caused by alterations in the American government, as agencies grew and as the State Department slipped in status. Part of it was the Americans' new consciousness of their strength and confidence and a "turning everywhere to more direct and forceful methods of exerting ... influence." It was, Robertson said, "a new sense of their 'manifest destiny' and a corresponding disposition to take decisions and accept responsibilities." On one level, that was a healthy sign; on another, it could be dangerous.

As evidence, Robertson cited a number of instances where the United States had acted with scant consideration for Canada. There was the Atlantic Charter, negotiated without a word to Ottawa; there was the Article VII affair in the mutual aid agreement, in an area in which "Canada had taken a much greater initiative than any other part of the British Commonwealth"; there was the way the Americans had handled negotiations with Japan, failing to keep Canada informed—a result of their "tendency to regard their special relationship with Canada as an internal domestic relationship rather than an international one"; and there was the way the United States had gradually assumed "hegemony" in Newfoundland.* All these and more problems[31] indicated the way relations had dramatically altered.

---

* Canadian concerns over Newfoundland arose from the way the US had secured bases there through negotiation with the UK alone. Later, Roosevelt had sent coastal defence
(Cont'd)

The controversy over Article VII fitted directly into the picture Robertson had painted. Through a long series of meetings with Moffat, Robertson continued to express his irritation at the way the United States was tying lend-lease to trade policy, and in another long paper for the Prime Minister on 30 December 1941, he reviewed the whole question.

"What the United States wants," he said, "is an undertaking now that the United Kingdom will cooperate ... in pursuing a liberal international economic policy after the war. The United States regards the abolition of import discriminations as an essential objective. ...The United Kingdom is reluctant to accept this objective ... because it feels that it implies the ultimate abandonment of the right of Empire countries to grant each other exclusive trade preferences." There were a host of reasons for and against Article VII, Robertson said, not least the effect of a British refusal to accept it on American opinion so soon after the United States had at last come into the war. The situation was special for Canada because it had not taken lend-lease. "We have a certain interest in perpetuating whatever preferred marketing positions we can hope to maintain after the war. At the same time, I think we have a greater interest in supporting the main objectives of American international economic policy." That was true and had been for some years. But, Robertson said, "We have been worried about the disposition on the part of the United States to determine, by bilateral negotiations with the United Kingdom, questions of policy intimately affecting us. Under present circumstances, however, I do not think we would be justified in pressing our objections on this score

---

guns to St. John's without consulting Ottawa, and this left a conviction "that the United States did not in fact take Canadian interests in Newfoundland as seriously as Canada felt they ought to be taken," or so Robertson said. (Harvard Univ., Moffat Papers, Memo, 12 May 41.) At the same time, Robertson indicated that he viewed confederation as one alternative for Newfoundland and, above all, he added, "the situation deserved better handling and franker interchange than it was getting at present." (*Ibid.*) Moffat and Robertson talked about Newfoundland again on 8 July 1941, when the Under-Secretary admitted that Canada had difficulties in dealing with Newfoundland, but again said that "in the ... very long run, he assumed that Canada and Newfoundland would have to face the problem of confederation." In the past such problems had broken down over money, but the war was making the island prosperous, something that would make union acceptable to Canada and make it more difficult for Newfoundlanders who still held to the "vain hope of regaining Dominion status." (*Ibid.*, 8 Jul. 41.) Robertson had learned a good deal about Newfoundland, Moffat noted, and he recorded that he was reading on the early history of Canada-Newfoundland relations. (*Ibid.*, 23 Jun. 41.) That was a typical method of Robertson's. One difficulty was that few in Ottawa were interested in the island. In 1946, Robertson reportedly called a meeting to discuss matters and began by saying, "There are collected here just about everyone in Ottawa who is interested in Newfoundland"—all four of them. (Richard Gwyn, *Smallwood the Unlikely Revolutionary* (Toronto, 1968), p.76.)

to the point of imperilling the direct negotiations between the United Kingdom and the United States. . . .All things considered, including the practical impossibility of putting any kind of price on the value of particular post-war preferences, I am inclined to think we should let the United Kingdom and the United States know that we are glad to see them trying to work out new arrangements governing international trade which would be of so broad a character as to make the continuance of Imperial preferences unnecessary to protect the commercial interests of the Commonwealth."[32] That was good advice, and a few days later Robertson told Moffat and the British High Commissioner of the Canadian position.[33]

The British and Americans thus signed their mutual aid agreement on 23 February 1942.[34] Article VII still talked of eliminating discriminations in trade, but in the final version this was put into the context of expanding production and employment and the exchange and consumption of goods, a far broader approach than that initially advanced by the Americans.[35]

The Article VII dispute was only a skirmish, but the whole question of relations with the United States remained unsettled and troubled, much as Robertson had foreseen in his December 1941 paper; concern was widespread throughout his Department. One of the wartime special assistants, R.G. Riddell, wrote to a friend at the University of Toronto in February 1943 that: "One is interested in the way our Canadian nationalists are now looking southward with all the terror they previously reserved for their eastward glances . . . we are letting the Americans get away with things that would have broken the Commonwealth in little pieces if London had tried them."[36] That was probably true, although war conditions excused much. Nonetheless, in the Canadian north, matters were slipping quickly out of control.

Canada had willingly accepted an American presence in the north in the period when the Japanese armies were advancing on every front and seemed to pose a threat to Alaska. In August 1941, Robertson himself told an American group that included Representative Warren Magnuson, Chairman of the Alaskan International Highway Commission, "from the Canadian point of view there was only one prevailing consideration, namely that of national defence. If it could be shown that the armed services of the two countries gave the [Alaska Highway] project a high priority rating Canada would be able to agree with the United States on the terms of construction in a very few days."[37] That was proper, and on 13 February 1942, two months after the war with Japan had begun,

Moffat told Robertson that the War and Navy Departments had reached the conclusion that it was "imperative" for a land route to Alaska to be built as soon as possible.[38] Canadian concurrence followed quickly— approval of some aspects was given Moffat by Robertson that day—and the Americans soon had units of army engineers working in the north. Other requests followed for weather stations, airfields, and the development of the oil fields at Norman Wells, NWT, all of which were readily granted as a gesture to the combined war effort.[39]

But by 1943 the Americans had 33,000 servicemen and civilians in Canada, and there were several incidents where the US Army seemed to feel that it was operating on territory where the writ of the Canadian government was not recognized and even where access to parts of the north was forbidden to Canadians. Surprisingly, the first serious consideration of this state of affairs did not come until Malcolm MacDonald, the British High Commissioner, talked to Robertson on his return from a trip to the Northwest Territories at the end of March 1943.

As the Under-Secretary informed King, MacDonald "has come back very concerned about the completeness of the American penetration and the absence of any apparent Canadian representation in the vast new territories which have been opened up since the war. I gathered," Robertson continued, "that for most practical purposes, the Canadian Government's representative in local contacts with the American forces in the Northwest is the Secretary of the Alberta Chamber of Commerce and Mines. . . ." There was a dangerous situation there, and Robertson was quick to see it. "I am afraid that the diplomatic precautions and safeguards that we could take from Ottawa to make sure that American operations in this area are purely for war purposes and terminable at the close of hostilities will not amount to much if there is not an adequate local assertion of Canadian interests in the development of this part of Canada." Robertson suggested a survey of the situation and possibly the appointment of "some kind of commissioner for the Northwest Territories whose business it would be to see that Canada was kept fully informed of all developments . . . likely to have a post war implication. . . ."[40] That was the course followed, and on 19 May a Special Commissioner was appointed to ensure that "the natural resources of the area shall be utilized to provide the maximum benefit for the Canadian people and to ensure that no commitments are to be made and no situation allowed to develop as a result of which the full Canadian control of the area would be in any way prejudiced or endangered."[41] The situation was soon in hand.

Robertson's direct involvement increased when he participated in discussions with American officials on the future of the Canol development at Norman Wells, NWT. This development, an oil field and pipelines, had become a contentious issue in Congress as well as a complicated question involving two governments and a private oil company. What is of interest here is Robertson's attitude to American efforts to have the agreements on the Norman Wells fields renegotiated to safeguard US interests and to secure postwar rights. At the first meeting in December 1943, Robertson pointedly set out the overriding Canadian consideration: "Canadian public opinion was worried about possible implications of the extent of United States participation in joint defence projects in Canada . . . a feeling that the United States had been allowed to construct a good many defence facilities in Canada that this country could have built if its war effort had not been fully extended in other directions. This," he added, "is the background against which we have to consider revision of any of the defence arrangements."[42]

But could the oil not be considered as a North American strategic reserve? Robertson dealt with this at the next meeting on 31 January 1944. The government had considered the idea, he said, and "If there was oil in ample quantity, it was reasonable to think that the requirements of continental defence should be the first charge. Canada was mindful of the important and essential way in which she has received oil from the United States throughout the war and of the manner in which the United States have shared their coal production." But, he went on, with a toughness that surprised the Americans, "we would prefer to see the Canadian Government, rather than a private company, taking the responsibility for making a resource available for continental defence." Nor could Canada permit a situation to develop in which the United States could veto developments in the Canadian Northwest, for that, as he put it with exquisite tact, "might place them in a difficult and invidious political position." Canada had to be able to decide the rate and kind of development on its territory.[43]

All that was eminently sensible, and at a War Committee meeting on 17 February, Robertson added that the United States was now trying to extend its interests in the Middle East by arguing that during the war it had depleted its resources in the common interest. Such a tactic had not been used over the Norman Wells field, but it would be "unfortunate" if it was.[44] Indeed. On 22 February, the War Committee agreed to assert Canadian control and to facilitate the "early withdrawal" of the Americans from the oil fields.[45] The facilities there ultimately became the subject of a settlement between the two countries, on terms that effectively protected Canadian interest and sovereignty.[46] Other American facilities in Canada were also paid for in full, and the fears that Malcolm MacDonald fortunately had aroused were temporarily set at rest.[47]

Other issues also pointed to increasing difficulties in Canadian-American relations. When the invasion of Sicily took place in July 1943, Mackenzie King and Robertson had to struggle ferociously to have Canada, which had provided one-third of the initial landing force, mentioned in the communiqués.[48] At the Quebec Conference of 1943, the Dominion was shut out of everything except the photographs. General Maurice Pope wrote in his diary that he had had a long talk with "Robertson down at the Chateau [Frontenac]. It is some consolation to learn that in respect of political affairs my civilian colleagues are quite as much in the dark as I am myself...."[49] And there was no longer Pierrepont Moffat to abuse for the sins of his countrymen; he had died suddenly on 24 January 1943 and his passing left a gap that was not filled by the appointment of the less able Ray Atherton as his successor. Atherton was a career officer but a man of a different stripe than Moffat, and King and Robertson agreed that "He is a curiously detached type, enigmatic in manner and in movements. 'Not at all like Moffat', Robertson says."[50]

Postwar commercial matters with Britain and the United States continued to worry Robertson, and this was one area that he personally directed. In April 1943 he had warmly supported a United Kingdom proposal for an early approach to Washington and a prior Commonwealth discussion on postwar trade policy as "one which it is strongly in Canada's interest to encourage and support. Their approach, on the basis of a multilateral Convention of Commerce providing for tariff reductions and the removal of other barriers to the exchange of goods, is the only really sound and comprehensive method of securing satisfactory conditions of trade and perhaps, in the long run, of political security." Canada, Robertson said, had very little left to gain by further bilateral negotiations "and must look to a multilateral convention ... if we are to secure ready access to the United States and to world markets. We should, therefore, I think, throw our whole weight behind the British proposal." Mackenzie King wrote "I agree" beside that paragraph. Robertson went on to add that some compromise had to be found between equal and proportional reductions in tariffs, and stressed that any programme had to be adopted as a whole. If Imperial preferences were to go, so too must discriminatory preferences, such as those arranged between Cuba and the

United States.[51] The Prime Minister accepted it all, a salutary result for the Under-Secretary as teacher.

The Commonwealth trade conversations took place in Britain in June 1943 and looked at the whole range of commercial policy questions and even at specific tariff rates.[52] Robertson explained the results to Lewis Clark, the chargé d'affaires at the American legation, and told him that "bold, or even heroic, action" was needed to implement the freer trade sentiments of Article VII. He was convinced "that the best time to negotiate basic tariff reductions is during the depths of a depression when the inefficient industries have been driven to the wall and eliminated, or at a time, like the present, when because of the exigencies of war normal trade has been disrupted and directed into new channels....If we do not strike now," Robertson said, "we will drift back into the old pre-war methods. . . ." What was heroic action? Clark asked. Robertson was clear: "the possibility of concluding a broad multilateral agreement under which each nation would agree to a progressive reduction in all tariffs or in certain categories of tariffs to a maximum reduction of, say, 70%. Such a multilateral agreement could . . . be supplemented by bilateral agreements between countries. . . ." Robertson added that the key to the ending of Imperial preferences was the lowering of the American tariff. And he was not backward in assuming that he could carry the government with him. "Mr. Robertson says that he is fundamentally in favour of liberal trade policies and low tariffs, and he is confident that he can negotiate on the bold lines he suggests." But the fly in the ointment, Robertson knew, was Washington. "If the United States will realize that it must buy in order to sell," he said, "then Canada . . . can do likewise."[53]

For Robertson, the trade discussions for the postwar future had to take place in a broad forum, one where all the great trading states could meet, and not in two-country haggling sessions, as had been the usual procedure in the past. In December 1943, therefore, Robertson was pleased to report to the Prime Minister that the United States had proposed "confidential exploratory conversations" between the two countries on the ways to implement the principles of Article VII. "This is a most important invitation," Robertson said. "I feel, very strongly, that what we do, or leave undone, in these next few months may determine the whole course of international economic relations. In this particular field Canada is in a key position because of the volume of our trading relationship with the United States and with the United Kingdom. The latter countries are working toward a programme of multilateral action to free world trade. It is a very ambitious and wide-ranging programme. . . ." Robertson added that he believed "there may be a chance, right now, of securing a comprehensive and thoroughgoing trade agreement with the United States, which could be the first major instalment of the multilateral programme which nearly everybody recognizes as the desirable goal. The American invitation for general talks on economic policy is an opportunity to find out whether they would be ready to go along with us right now in something pretty big." Robertson was excited by the prospect, so excited that he apologized to the Prime Minister for his "incoherent" note.[54] Unfortunately, the reality was less exciting.

When the Canadian and American teams met for "informal economic discussions" at the State Department on 4 January 1944, Robertson's enthusiasm was still high. There was quick agreement that a convention should be negotiated by the United States, the Commonwealth countries, the Soviet Union and a few other states, and that, while adherence might be offered to other nations, the terms could not be altered to suit them. If they refused to join, such countries would be denied the benefits of the commercial convention.[55]

For the next three days the discussion ranged over the full sweep of commercial issues. There were dangers from state trading, Robertson agreed, but if in Canada the CCF became much stronger, the government might have to continue it. This was not necessarily a disaster, he said, for state trading could increase volume in some products. There was discussion about quantitative restrictions on imports, on subsidies, and on a proposed international trade organization. Here Robertson had strong views. Canada, he said, had reluctantly accepted "the four-power pact as the nucleus in the political sphere. This is not necessary in other branches of international organization; in fact in the economic and financial field there is no merit in arrangements limited to a few powers, since the problems of representation in economic bodies are very different from those in political bodies." In other words, Canada was entitled to a full share in any international commercial body.

On Imperial preferences, Robertson said that "Canada would be willing to wipe out the preferences in many cases and in some cases to make the rate free to all. The underlying necessity," he stated, hitting the heart of the postwar problem, "is for the United States and Canada to increase their imports from Europe and the rest of the world. In fact, in view of the world economic situation, the United States should correct [its] tariff unilaterally regardless of Empire preferences."[56] Later that same day, Robertson added that a multilateral agreement should state that "it is contrary to the policy of the convention to agree not to reduce the duty to any country. This," he maintained, "would result in returning to the pre-1932 legal position and would eliminate the bound Ottawa preferences, thereby weakening the whole preferential structure."[57] Again the free trader in Norman Robertson had surfaced; in his view, by 1944 Imperial preferences were almost a dead letter.

The result of the meetings and of two further days of conversations in New York City on 12 and 13 February was a "Summary Statement," the draft of which Robertson had extensively revised.[58] The statement covered the whole field of the talks, setting out the two countries' positions, often going into surprising detail for such informal and non-binding conversations. The road to a multilateral trading world had been mapped out and that was in the Canadian interest. There was no hint of any new Canadian-American trade agreement.

But the idea was not out of Robertson's mind. In March, after renewed Commonwealth discussions in London, he thought he detected apparent signs of British backsliding in their commitment to multilateralism and a renewed desire to preserve the preferential system.[59] That concerned him, and he wrote Graham Towers, the Governor of the Bank of Canada, to say that "In general, objectives seem to be shrinking and receding. It seems to me that, as the multilateral programme becomes more modest and more remote, we shall have to look more seriously and more quickly at the specific problem of Canadian-American trade relations. I had envisaged a bilateral agreement with the United States, supplementing a general multilateral tariff reduction," he went on, "but if effective multilateral action is to be indefinitely deferred and, when achieved, prove modest, then I think we may have to look at the question again from the continental viewpoint."[60] That stayed in his mind for some time, and he kept on top of the situation in London during the Prime Ministers' meeting in April-May 1944 and with a one-day trip to Washington in October.[61]

In fact, Robertson learned in February 1945 that the British and Americans had moved ahead and had reached a considerable measure of agreement on a draft multilateral convention.[62] But the pace was still too slow and the aims too modest for him, and it was not until July 1945 that he led a Canadian delegation to Washington for a new round of discussions with the Americans. Those talks centred on the ways to achieve tariff reduction—selectively or by straight horizontal cuts that affected all tariffs. The Americans, headed by Assistant Secretary of State for Economic Affairs Will Clayton, were cool to horizontal cuts, stating that their renewed Trade Agreements Act did not contemplate such action, that Congress's reaction was certain to be critical, and that there would be serious difficulties in bringing the other trading nations along. In the American view, the goal should be to work out "a multilateral plan under which tariff reduction could be carried out selectively," possibly by a multilateral-bilateral approach that saw each country introduce a trade agreements programme and negotiate bilateral agreements with its principal suppliers. The Canadians were surprised by this because—in an astonishing failure on the part of the Washington Embassy—they "had not until that moment realized that there were commitments in connection with the renewal of the Trade Agreements Act which would be an obstacle to the adoption of a plan for horizontal tariff reduction by the United States." All saw this as a blow to world trade liberalization, and feared that the American selective tariff cut plan would force them to make a "complete reappraisal".[63]

The talks resumed in Ottawa on 14 and 15 July when Robertson opened the discussion with one last effort to reverse the American position. Any selective cut method was "hopelessly inadequate" to the needs of world trade. Further, three great advantages would be sacrificed. The timing could never be better than the present, for the whole world trade structure was in flux. A horizontal cut substantially eliminated the preferences problem and made it possible to compel outsiders to come along by threatening to withhold tariff benefits. But as one American reported to Washington, "We spent all morning and part of the afternoon explaining the impracticality of this plan from the standpoint of the United States."

If that was a non-starter, so in the Canadian view was the American plan for an international trade conference early in 1946 to seek to resolve all trade barrier problems except those of the tariff, "the agreement to be conditioned upon consummation thereafter of mutually satisfactory and substantial tariff cuts." Timing made this impractical, Robertson said, as well as the complications in negotiating tariffs under such circumstances. In his view, the conference should be scrapped and replaced by a series of bilateral negotiations among the leading trading states. The Americans countered by proposing "immediate negotiations among a nuclear group consisting of the leading trading nations, looking to the consummation of a series of coordinated bilateral trading agreements." Then a general international conference could be held, its prospects for success enhanced by clear indications of the extent of tariff cuts and of the widespread agreement on non-tariff matters among the leading traders. That seemed more likely to work, or so Robertson and his colleagues thought.[64]

But it was a discouraged Norman Robertson who contemplated the ruin of his hopes for postwar trade. He had been confident at the end of 1943, but the discussions with the United States and others had pointed out all the difficulties in the way of liberalizing the existing tariff structure, however battered the war had made it.

There were scant grounds for optimism as the plans suggested by the Americans in July began to collapse. In January 1946 an American team visited Ottawa to discuss the timetable for the preliminary gathering and the full-scale conference to follow. It expected a draft charter of an International Trade Organization to be produced by the preliminary meeting, as well as a protocol and tariff schedules.[65] But in April the Americans unilaterally postponed the preliminary meeting,[66] and it was October 1946 before it took place. As Robertson wrote to the Prime Minister: "My feeling has been that we had a real opportunity immediately after the end of the war and during the first phase of reconversion for drastic and relatively painless tariff revision. The longer this operation is postponed, the more difficult it will be to carry out. . . ."[67] He was right then and he had been right since 1943. The chances for immediate and major changes in trade policy had diminished mightily.

III

If Norman Robertson had difficulties in dealing with the powerful Americans, his task was no easier in handling the British. During the late 1930s, he had described himself as the last imperialist in the Department of External Affairs, and perhaps he had even been that for a time. But the trade negotiations of 1937-38 had eliminated much of his sentimentality for the Empire and all traces of it were gone by the war. Now he was a nationalist, favouring Canadian involvement in the world and supporting his country's continued membership in the Commonwealth. But that Commonwealth had to be linked not by pacts, treaties or Committees of Imperial Defence, but by interests and shared origins, nothing more. He was against centralization, as much so as Mackenzie King, but he took the sensible view that Canada and Britain had much to gain from each other. That attitude led him to support Canadian gifts to Britain during the war and to favour a loan for the postwar transition years, something that might help Britain recover while it kept Canadians working and preserved markets in the United Kingdom for Canadian goods. Norman Robertson was a pragmatist.

The most difficult question in relations with Britain was to resist the persistent efforts of Churchill and his colleagues to speak for the Commonwealth as a whole. It was an attitude that infuriated Canadians. For example, in the fall of 1942, London had ordered the shackling of German POWs in retaliation for the alleged chaining of Canadians captured after the abortive Dieppe raid in August. There had been no consultation with Ottawa at all, although this was a matter that directly concerned Canada. Was there an explanation? Pierrepont Moffat asked. The British had expressed regrets, Robertson said, "coupled with promises not to do it again, but had then justified their stand on the ground that if retaliatory measures were to have had any effect at all they had to be announced immediately....It was merely a repetition on a smaller scale of Churchill's methods exhibited at the time of Chanak in 1922. Mr. Robertson suggested that I re-read the fifth volume of the World Crisis, as Mr. Churchill therein sets forth his policy in such matters. He has always run true to form ever since."[68]

This Churchillian style led a cautious Mackenzie King and an equally careful Norman Robertson to resist London's suggestions for an Imperial War Cabinet on the model of that of the Great War. In July 1941, for example, Robertson had advised King that "If there is likely to be need in the next few months for closer co-ordination of war policies, it will not necessarily be closer collaboration between the Commonwealth countries per se but between the Commonwealth countries and the United States...."[69]

Nonetheless, in August Robertson accompanied King on a visit to the United Kingdom. It was their first flight, and a stripped-down and cold bomber was perhaps not the most comfortable way to cross the North Atlantic.[70] For Robertson, with his deaf ear, the trip must have been particularly uncomfortable, but like every Canadian he was anxious to see London in the war. Still, the visit was a bit of a disappointment. It was too rushed, Robertson told Moffat on his return, with too many calls on the troops (who had booed King on one occasion), too many audiences with royalty and treks to the Prime Minister's old haunts, and too little time with the British ministers.[71]

In one sense that was not unfortunate. King was a nationalist in Ottawa, but in London tended to become a sentimental colonial again. The attentions of the monarch, the flattery of dukes and duchesses, and the solicitudes of Churchill all took his edge off. And as the Prime Minister simply failed to trust either the good sense or Canadianism of Vincent

Massey, the High Commissioner in Britain, this meant that Robertson's relationship with the British High Commissioner in Ottawa was decisive.[72]

Fortunately once Malcolm MacDonald became High Commissioner in the spring of 1941, that relationship was close and confidential. MacDonald understood King and came to know and like Canada and Canadians. His position in Ottawa allowed him easy access to high officials, and he grasped the Canadian system quickly. That Canada was so generous to Britain during the war was not attributable only to MacDonald's own judgment and efforts, but there could be no doubt that he had helped. And there was no Canadian with whom he was closer or whom he met more frequently than Robertson.

Like other British officials and ministers, MacDonald believed that Britain had to lead the Commonwealth in concert if she was to hold a place in the postwar world as the equal of the Americans and Russians. But unlike many of his colleagues, MacDonald believed that this could be achieved only by "treating [the Dominions] as true partners . . . and paying due heed to their opinion." In his view, expressed in a despatch home that was printed and circulated, that meant accepting the Canadian case for greater representation. MacDonald went on to suggest that "We have under-rated Canada's quality in the past. We, in Britain, felt reasonably confident before the war that the Dominion would be with us if we got into trouble. But I doubt whether any of us expected that Canada's contribution in war would have the magnificent power and generosity which it now displays . . . the vast Commonwealth Air Training Plan, her varied munitions production, and her two 'billion dollar gifts'. . . ." The High Commissioner also noted the great talents of "a group of high officials who are still comparatively young . . . and whose influence over Canadian policy is and will continue to be at least as important as that of Ministers. . . .They are the heads of Government Departments and other official bodies. They are able, enlightened and forceful. If we do not discourage them, but on the contrary encourage them . . . to be our colleagues in affairs, we shall find them good allies."[73] That was excellent advice and, although Whitehall talked about it, Churchill's policy was sometimes very different in action.[74]

Robertson set out his concerns for the Prime Minister in October:

Mr. Churchill's insistence on the 'family character' of the [civil aviation] discussions [in October 1943], his reiterated use of his new phrase 'Commonwealth and Empire' and its pendant 'The Dominions and India' are significant. . . .Recent developments . . . are, I am afraid, going to force us to look pretty seriously at the implications for Canada of the prevailing trend toward Imperial centralization. . . .My own feeling has been that we were maintaining a pretty satisfactory working relationship with the countries of the Commonwealth and with the other members of the United Nations outside it. I see no good reason for attempting to tip the present balance one way or another, but I am rather afraid that efforts in other quarters to strengthen and tighten the Imperial connection at the expense of our relationship with other countries may not only have some bad effects on our relations with those other countries, but may reopen domestic political differences about our relationship to the Commonwealth and to the international community in general.[75]

There were other signs, too, even on unofficial levels. The Royal Institute of International Affairs, late in 1943, was organizing a conference on Commonwealth Relations and, as Edgar Tarr, the guiding light of the Canadian Institute of International Affairs and a strong nationalist, pointed out to his friends in Ottawa (a group that included Robertson and almost every other mandarin in town), the draft agenda was "wholly unsatisfactory". In the first place, Tarr wrote, "by implication it seems to assume that the greatest degree of group action and group organization which is possible, is desirable."[76] In other words, the aim of a centralized Commonwealth was being pressed even in unofficial quarters.

What really set the cat among the pigeons was the speech made by Lord Halifax, the British Ambassador in Washington and a member of Churchill's War Cabinet, in Toronto in January 1944. Halifax told a Board of Trade gathering, graced by the presence of Premier George Drew of Ontario and national Progressive Conservative leader John Bracken, that the goal was unity for the Empire so that Britain could be on equal footing in the postwar world with the Russians, the Americans and the Chinese.[77]

Halifax's remarks were not all that different from those of MacDonald in February 1943 or those by other British, Australian or South African public men. But his speech was a bombshell because it was made before a Toronto audience, a forum that gave it a partisan cast, and because it was a direct challenge to the policies that had been adopted for at least two years by the Canadian government. For the British Ambassador to speak as he did in Canada, without first clearing his text with the Canadian government, was utterly stupid.

The Prime Minister was "simply dumbfounded" and Robertson, King noted in his diary, was "appallingly depressed."[78] Now the fight would have to be waged in the open, and the first instalment was the Prime Minister's speech in Parliament on 31 January, a firm but low-key rejoinder that rejected a common policy.[79] The second instalment was delivered at the Prime Ministers' meeting in London.

The Conference opened on 1 May. "Both [Mackenzie King] and Mr. Robertson," noted a Canadian Press despatch, "wore striped trousers, dark sack coats and black homburgs" to the opening. That report provoked great hilarity back in Ottawa, where Robertson's usual garb included a floppy black hat that made him look like the man on the Sandeman sherry label, and a shapeless overcoat or buffalo robe. "You should treasure" the story, Wrong wrote, "as I doubt if there will be any other occasion on which your sartorial perfection will be commended in the public prints."[80]

There was not much more about the Conference to inspire laughter. Churchill clung tenaciously to his desire for a regionally coordinated postwar organization, something Canada—and Churchill's own Foreign Office—rejected. With Robertson's arguments in hand, Mackenzie King struck down the idea. There was some talk of a Commonwealth secretariat, but under Robertson's prodding, King killed that.[81] There was discussion of the need for postwar Commonwealth defence arrangements. "It would be unrealistic," Robertson advised the Prime Minister, "to consider defence arrangements between Commonwealth countries as in any way an alternative or substitute for a strong world security organization to which each of us will have to make our appropriate and proportionate contribution."[82] And as always there was the watchfulness until the last moment to ensure that the British did not slip references to a common Empire policy into the communiqué. Robertson found one example of this in the draft on 15 May and had to insist that the document be altered.[83] Finally, King's formal address to the meeting on 11 May, drafted by John Holmes and revised by Robertson, effectively set out the case against a common policy for the Commonwealth.[84] There were other struggles, but the Conference was a triumph for Canadian policy. The centralized Empire in truth had been dead for years, but the corpse could never again be resuscitated.

It had been hard, gruelling work, and the trip home had its frightening moments as well. As King wrote to a friend some time later: "We were returning from London to Prestwick when our plane about half way along was obliged to come down. It was from a leakage of oil . . . the smoke . . . became quite dense. . . . Fortunately, our pilot was able to land us and to get the oil turned off before an explosion took place. The incident was kept a secret at the time because it was an American plane. . . ."[85]

While he had been in London, Robertson had discussed a number of non-conference matters with various officials. Early on he had told the Dominions Office that the British should not raise with the Prime Minister the difficulties they were having over reductions in Canadian financial and material aid.[86] That was the advice of a man who knew his Prime Minister well, even though the British were much concerned that the $887 million Canada had made available for 1944-45 did not seem likely to cover their needs. It was good advice because Robertson remembered the difficult time there had been in the Cabinet War Committee to get even that much. His own memorandum to the War Committee had argued that Canada had to continue its Mutual Aid programme "because it is impossible to discontinue production in Canada of supplies for export ... without causing grave dislocation. ..." Moreover, he went on, ending aid would do nothing to ease the budgetary position, "as we should have to finance the same amount of domestic production" in any case. Alternatives to giving the goods away—selling on credit or giving the British a loan—were certain to be disapproved of in the United States.[87] Despite his arguments and those of others, two ministers in the War Committee had objected to additional Mutual Aid, and there was serious concern about the political implications of continued high taxes in Canada.[88]

The British did not take Robertson's advice, and on 16 May, the Chancellor of the Exchequer, Sir John Anderson, raised the question with Mackenzie King, only to be met by King's refusal to treat the matter in the absence of his Minister of Finance. Worse, Anderson had talked as if further aid was an obligation upon Canada—"it had become a sort of duty to meet a request of the kind," an angry Prime Minister noted. "There was not a word of thanks for what we had done. ..."[89]

The British had messed up matters, but Robertson was still trying to accommodate them. In talks with Anderson's officials, he seemed, according to the British record, to "under[stand] broad political implications of [the] position. He said that Canadian Government might find very great difficulties in increasing Appropriation to make a gift for us." But when the Treasury suggested that military expenses borne on behalf of Canada by Britain since the beginning of the war—air force training and the payment of costs and expenses for stores and equipment that *in toto* might reach $500 or 600 million—could be paid by Canada, Robertson "expressed purely personal opinion that this solution was worth exploring and proposed to discuss [the] matter with [Clifford] Clark immediately on his return." Robertson knew that, after Anderson's blunder, it was far better for an initiative to appear to come from Canada.[90]

Why was Robertson so helpful? His first reason was that it was only proper that Canada, enriched by the war, should pay all the costs of her military forces; the second was that he held the view that the struggle was a common one in which each partner should do its utmost; the third was that Canada had few options, and the only result of a tight-fisted policy would be unemployment; finally, he was acutely aware of the difficulties a strapped Britain would face in the peace, difficulties that might force the British into efforts to reduce their imports from the dollar countries. Indeed, at precisely this time, Keynes was suggesting switching purchases from Canada to the United States. The economist said that "I hope we shall have the strength of mind immediately the war, or even the first phase of it, is over, to cancel purchases of food-stuffs in Canada, if all our reserves have been previously used up....The Canadians will then, I opine, think again."[91]

On top of commercial policy, Robertson was fully aware of this possibility, and was as good as his word in talking with Clark on his return to Ottawa. After discussions between Clark and Keynes at the Bretton Woods Conference in July[92] and after a visit to Ottawa by Keynes at the beginning of August,[93] Canada agreed to cover all the costs of its forces in Britain, just as the British had desired.[94] The reason, as expressed in a paper by Robert Bryce, was that Canada wanted to leave Britain enough financial resources to get through the transitional period between war and peace. "We certainly want the U.K. to be in a position to buy food from Canada during this transition period," Bryce argued.[95]

The difficulty with this plan, as Robertson told Malcolm MacDonald, was that there continued to be sharp criticism within the cabinet of further aid. "One thing that these critics have in mind is political expediency in Canada. They urge that with a general election in the offing and the Government none too popular," MacDonald reported, "taxation should if possible be reduced ... there has been strong pressure against doing anything more which amounts to a gift." Robertson had warned that "the situation is really difficult."[96] The difficulties were overcome, but only by stressing to King and his colleagues that, without further aid, there was scant prospect of postwar trade with Britain. "They are now in a very desperate position," King noted, revealing the efforts Robertson and others had made, "and if we are to get the markets in Britain which we shall wish to have and need to have later on, we should have to assist at this time in meeting the situation...."[97]

The British had substantial success with their implicit threats to stop Canadian imports. They succeeded again with explicit threats in November 1944 when Keynes was again in Ottawa to negotiate for Mutual Aid in Stage II, the period between victory over Germany and the end of the war with Japan, expected to be about one year. Keynes wanted $1,200 million, and he won the fight by telling a group of officials and ministers that "if Canada was unable to provide aid to the U.K. . . . to something approaching 1,200 million dollars, the U.K. Government would have to review their programs thoroughly and see what they can reduce or do without." The Canadians got the message, considered its implications on domestic employment and, after further difficult cabinet discussions, coughed up the money.[98]

Meanwhile Robertson and his friends were trying to look at the longer-term picture against the background of these British threats and other warnings about the future of multilateral trade. The key document was a long paper by the Governor of the Bank of Canada, Graham Towers, "A Proposal for Averting a Breakdown in International Trade Relationships," and the decisive meeting was one that brought five ministers together with the key economic policy mandarins, including Robertson, on 18 January 1945.[99] Towers argued that, since Britain's trade had dwindled and its productive capacity had been battered, it could hardly join in a multilateral world unless it was helped by its friends. Such assistance was in Canada's interest, he argued, for it would keep up employment and help Canada's export industries. What he was looking to was a credit of $1.2 billion at 2 per cent interest to help Britain through the first three years of peace.

Towers's proposals were thoroughly canvassed at the meeting, all the officials essentially supporting them. Robertson's contribution was to suggest that the only alternative to a scheme such as that proposed was closer trade relations with the United States, something certain to have a major impact on Canada's Commonwealth link. Those, he said, "who are strong for the maintenance of the British Commonwealth have to put their weight behind the competitive solution to trade problems." That was the right line for a meeting chaired by J.L. Ilsley, the Minister of Finance, a good loyal Nova Scotian, and an Imperialist at heart. The result was a decision to send telegrams to London along the line of Towers's memo.[100]

Although the telegrams were drafted by Clark, Towers and W.A. Mackintosh, the Special Assistant to the Deputy Minister of Finance, Robertson had the critical job of selling the result to King. " . . . I had a talk with Robertson," the Prime Minister wrote on 13 February, "who outlined the whole problem of future trade relations with Britain and which it seemed to me . . . made perfectly clear the possibility of Britain to save her own position lending herself to a series of restraints in trade which might raise the most serious problems within the Empire that have come up thus far. Something that might drive Canada into a position of annexation with the States through inability to get any markets in Britain. He has drafted a series of telegrams which set out the position clearly and which we went over carefully together." [101]

The telegrams went out on 23 February, offering a loan and suggesting discussions. In return, Canada hoped and trusted that Britain could avoid restrictive and discriminatory trade policies. It was perhaps the grandest gesture ever made by Canada, "a quite exceptional largeness of economic imagination," or so Douglas Le Pan described it. [102]

The British naturally were pleased, and Robertson gave the High Commission a full description of Canada's motives; [103] similarly, the plan was conveyed to American officials by Robertson on a visit to Washington on 10 March and by King to Roosevelt. [104] Finally, under pressure from MacDonald, Robertson and Clark agreed to despatch a delegation to London to discuss the proposals, a team ultimately headed by Mackintosh (acting Deputy Minister of Finance) after Clark became desperately ill, and including Towers and Hector McKinnon. [105]

Those meetings, splendidly described by Douglas Le Pan in his memoirs, took place at Cambridge in May 1945. The immediate result for Canada was British agreement to a policy of non-discrimination against Canadian imports. In effect, goods from Canada would be treated the same as goods from within the sterling area. [106] That was a substantial gain, even if the agreement later broke down. [107]

The Canadian loan negotiations did not begin until the new year, after the conclusion of Keynes's transactions with Washington for another loan to Britain. That bargaining had been tough, so tough that Keynes's fragile health broke and he died soon after. The Canadians, or so the High Commission reported to London, "consider the [American] terms not only harsh in themselves but out of keeping with the real fundamentals and spirit of the case when looked at from the broadest viewpoint." [108]

If the British expected an easy ride in Ottawa as a result of that view, they would be disappointed. The Anglo-Canadian negotiations were difficult in the extreme with the ministers taking a tough line. The officials, much to King's disgust, were soft on the British, and in this instance the cabinet got its way. The Canadian terms were the same as those exacted by Washington.[109] No detailed record of Robertson's position exists, but there is every reason to believe that he shared the officials' view and that he hoped for a loan on generous terms. Certainly the Economic Division in his Department took that view.[110]

IV

One of Robertson's most important tasks during the war was to fit Canada into the structure created by the United States and Britain to coordinate their war efforts. On 26 January 1942, the two nations announced the creation of three Combined Boards to deal with raw materials, the assignment of munitions, and shipping, in addition to the Combined Chiefs of Staff who were to direct military strategy. Later a Combined Food Board and a Combined Production and Resources Board were established.[111]

How was Canada to operate within this structure established by the fiat of Roosevelt and Churchill? How was Canada to get representation sufficient to enable it to preserve its sovereignty, exercise its due share of power, and secure the supplies it needed to arm and equip the Canadian forces and to produce the war material that was now going to almost every Allied nation? And how was Canada to get this representation without impeding the supreme goal, victory over the Axis?

That was a neat dilemma, and one that exercised Robertson and his colleagues throughout 1942 and much of 1943. In seeking to resolve it, Robertson, Wrong and Pearson effectively rewrote the Liberal government's definition of Canadian nationalism. In 1939, nationalism to Mackenzie King had been almost akin to isolationism, to a policy of no commitments and to pledges that Parliament would decide, later. But in the course of fighting to secure a place commensurate with Canada's new power, the Department of External Affairs made nationalism equal involvement. In effect, nationalism now marched hand in hand with internationalism. Astonishingly, Robertson brought Mackenzie King along with him in this, the Prime Minister agreeing that Canada's power and capacity in 1942 merited a place with the Great Powers on some of the Combined Boards. Canada had come of age.

The touchstone of this process was the functional principle. In 1938 in a paper on the Munich débâcle, Loring Christie had written that "It was found that function was different from status; that in the conduct of foreign affairs and in defence matters, of the issues of peace and war—the most vital, decisive field of all—the functional and real responsibility had to be left to the Government of Great Britain." [112] That had been true in 1938. But by 1942, when Robertson sent the first word of the Combined Boards to the Prime Minister, he was already able to say with some confidence that, even if Canada was not a member of the Boards, no one could commit the nation without consent. And Canada's ability to produce food, raw materials and war material was already such that he could affirm that the Great Powers "will have to consult Canada whenever Canadian cooperation is required." What was necessary now was to work out the ways in which that cooperation could be sought. [113]

Hume Wrong, stationed in Washington as Minister-Counsellor at the Legation, also examined the new set-up. "The principal question causing me concern," he wrote to Robertson, "is the nature of the Canadian representation which should be sought and the status with respect to their British and U.S. colleagues which should be claimed for Canadian representatives on any of the combined organizations." There were twenty-six governments at war with the Axis, he wrote, and ten or eleven had a reasonable claim to participation on the basis of their contribution. Such a polyglot crew could coordinate nothing. "How far, then, is Canada entitled to go in pressing a claim to participate in inter-Allied bodies which are designed to co-ordinate the war effort? It is easy to state the general principle, but remarkably difficult to apply it," Wrong wrote. "The principle, I think, is that each member of the grand alliance should have a voice in the conduct of the war proportionate to its contribution to the general war effort. A subsidiary principle is that the influence of various countries should be greatest in connection with those matters with which they are most directly concerned." [114]

Robertson agreed with that formulation, and over the course of the next year and a half, the idea of functionalism would be developed and honed, as Canada fought vigorously and sometimes toughly for a place on the Combined Boards and in the key committees of the United Nations Relief and Rehabilitation Administration (UNRRA), the great agency through which aid was to be channeled to a devastated world. On 18 January 1943, a year after Wrong's first stab at the principle, Robertson wrote to the Prime Minister about functionalism:

While experience between the wars has shown the great practical difficulties of applying to membership in international bodies the legal concept of the equality of states, we are confident that no workable international system can be based on the concentration of influence and authority wholly in bodies composed of a few great powers to the exclusion of all the rest. It is not always the largest powers that have the greatest contribution to make to the work of these bodies or the greatest stake in their success. In international economic organizations such as the Relief Administration representation on such bodies can often be determined on a functional basis and in our view this principle should be applied wherever it is feasible. [115]

Robertson's formulation found its way into the Prime Minister's address to the House of Commons on 9 July 1943, the first public pronouncement of this Canadian principle. [116]

Compare the principle with any Canadian policy statement before the outbreak of war in 1939 and it is difficult to believe that the same country is involved. In fact, by 1943, Canada was in a vastly different state than four years earlier. The country was richer, immeasurably more powerful, confident and armed to the teeth both with righteousness and the weapons of war. And if many Canadians had not yet realized the dimensions of the change, Robertson had, and he and his colleagues were bargaining with great skill to secure a place for Canada at the conference tables. To a substantial extent, it was the struggle over the Combined Boards and UNRRA that precipitated the change in mind, attitude and policy.

The initial questions at issue concerned the Munitions Assignment Board, where both the British and Americans fobbed off Canada with promises that were never kept. All that Robertson and his colleagues could get was a place on the Combined Production and Resources Board, created in June 1942, and destined not to amount to much. Still, to be on that Board was recognition of a kind.

More serious was the Combined Food Board (CFB), also created in June 1942. Initially, Britain and the United States had omitted Canada from this Board too, something that infuriated Robertson. Canada was going to protest, he told Moffat, "given the fact that she considers herself the largest holder of surplus exportable food in the world. Canada had about three hours advance notice from England of the constitution of this Board before the matter was in the papers." [117]

Canada formally demanded membership on the Combined Food Board on 14 July 1942, a demand justified by the unanswerable claim that "Next to the United States, Canada is by far the most important contributor of foodstuffs to the common pool of the United Nations." [118] For more than a year, that argument was pressed, with Canada telling the British, at a meeting on 27 July, that "Canada would have to be brought into consultation if her full co-operation was desired...." [119] Robertson was at the heart of this fight, one that mobilized the full weight of the bureaucracy.

On 29 July, for example, Robertson emerged from a War Committee meeting to talk with Sir Frederick Leith-Ross of the Treasury, who was in Ottawa to try to persuade Canada to accept second-best on the CFB and on UNRRA. Robertson had told the British official that the War Committee was adamant[120] and that a "spirit of dictatorship" seemed to inspire the proposals to deny Canada her place in the sun. Canada, he said, "did not claim to be represented on the Shipping Board or on the Chiefs of Staff Committees; but she did feel that as regards munitions and food and post-war relief, she had a right to a place on the Board of Directors. Mr. Robertson admitted that prestige came into the question, but Canadian vital interests were affected and prestige could not be distinguished from the psychological leadership required of public opinion."[121]

Unfortunately, this was a case where the cabinet initially talked toughly and then caved in. Although the government pressed its case skilfully, the British stayed firm, and King and his cabinet gave way at a meeting in Ottawa on 16 September. Robertson was off on his first vacation of the war and missed the meeting. He could not have been pleased with the result, but he undoubtedly knew that he could not have reversed the cabinet's decision.[122]

Because the role of the CFB expanded, Robertson soon told R.H. Brand, the British Ministry of Food's man in North America, that Canada was going to reopen its case for membership "and that the British and United States Governments should be asked to meet it." The CFB, Robertson said, was now dealing with commodities produced in volume in Canada, not just those in short supply of which Canada was a consumer. Moreover, "Canada was participating fully in nearly all the subcommittees of the Board and was the only country to do so. The Board was in effect operating on a tripartite basis except at the top level." Brand's rejoinder was the typical British one: if Canada were added to the CFB, other countries would seek a place. That argument drove Canadians wild, leading them to suggest that when other countries produced the goods that Canada did, then, and only then, would they be entitled to a place. Robertson suggested "that as shortages grew greater and the necessity for restricting consumption increased, it became more important to bring about a comparable equality of restrictions, especially in the producing countries, especially as between Canada and the United States....As the Canadian public were asked to tighten their belts,"

Robertson said, neatly covering his iron fist with silken words, "they would want to know that their own Government had participated directly in the decisions." Brand, or so the Canadian minute of this talk stated, "appeared to appreciate the force of this argument" and his opposition to Canadian membership on the CFB slackened.[123] On 13 April 1943, Robertson formally conveyed to the High Commissioner the Canadian request for a seat.[124]

The British huffed and puffed[125] but their position was weakening, and the Americans too seemed convinced that a reorganization of the CFB was essential.[126] In October, therefore, representation was offered and accepted, a major victory for Canadian diplomacy.[127]

While this struggle for representation was being fought, Robertson was simultaneously directing another, this time for a place on the chief committee of UNRRA. The need for a major relief effort after victory was won had been recognized at least since August 1941, and the plans for UNRRA had been formally put forward in June 1942. Canada had accepted them in principle but reserved the right to raise the question of Canadian representation later. The Canadian aim, based on the country's "probable post-war position as a major supplier of needed foodstuffs,"[128] was a seat on UNRRA's executive committee, the directing body.

The British position was the standard one. Others would seek a seat if Canada got one and, furthermore, the Americans would be unhappy to see the British side overweighed with Canadian representation.[129] London simply never learned, but soon the British were beginning to reverse their field, in part because of concern that this stand might kill the chances for additional gifts of Canadian dollars and supplies.[130] By the beginning of 1943, the United Kingdom was supporting a proposal to expand the executive committee to seven members, one of whom would be Canadian. On 4 January, Robertson told the Prime Minister that this idea seemed acceptable in Washington and Chungking (the wartime capital of China), but not in Moscow.[131] That information was incorrect, and on the 18th Robertson had to tell King that only the British were supporting an expansion of the committee. The Americans, he added, had suggested that one way around the problem "might be for Canada and the United Kingdom to be represented by two members with but one vote or alternatively that a committee of supplying countries might be set up." Those were unacceptable suggestions, Robertson maintained, adding that "I think it important that we should enter an immediate warning against our acceptance of the Four Power pattern for post-war organization. This is the first occasion on which the question has come up in specific form. I would not restrict our objection to economic international organizations alone."[132] A further note on 3 February added that "so far as Canada was concerned we believed that it would be very difficult after the war for us to play our expected part unless we could satisfy Parliament and the public that we had a fair share in the direction of the Organization."[133] That was as tough as Canada talked at any time in the war, and the same tone was evident in a memorandum handed the American government on 9 February.[134]

The hard line produced results. On 26 February 1943, Pearson telephoned from Washington with word that the British and Americans were considering a situation in which Canada, as chairman of the supplies committee of UNRRA, sat on the executive committee whenever supplies were being discussed. "It was represented," Robertson said, "that, in practice, this would be tantamount to membership." Wrong, he added in a note for the file, had suggested saying that the chairman of the supplies committee would be *ex officio* a member of the executive. Robertson had agreed and told Pearson so, but "making it clear that this was a personal opinion which had not been confirmed by the Cabinet."[135] Just as well he put in that proviso, for on 3 March the War Committee decided "strongly and unanimously" to hold out for full membership.[136] For "your guidance," Robertson told Pearson, "it is felt here that this is a test case, on the satisfactory solution of which other and perhaps more important issues will depend. If we cannot go into the Central Committee by the front door we are unwilling to use a side or back entrance."[137]

Again hard talk paid dividends. This time the British suggested that perhaps Canada could replace them on the executive. That did not please Robertson: "The idea that Canada might represent the whole Commonwealth (even though this not be formalized in any way) savors of outworn constitutional doctrine. Doubtless in the United States and elsewhere the argument would be made in some quarters that we were merely a spokesman for the United Kingdom....I should favour having both Canada and the United Kingdom on the Central Committee and not either Canada or the United Kingdom."[138]

That was good stuff, one of Robertson's pithiest memoranda. But once again the government retreated in the end. On 31 March, Anthony Eden, the British Foreign Secretary, came to Ottawa for talks on UNRRA. On the first day he largely converted King and the War Committee to the Great Power position,[139] and Robertson and company had to scramble to save anything. The Under-Secretary saw Eden on 1 April and heard the Foreign Secretary suggest an exchange of letters between Canada and the

United States (on behalf of the Great Powers) "confirming our understanding that any arrangement arrived at with regard to the position of the Central and Supplies Committees of the Relief Organization would not be a precedent fixing the Canadian relationship to other postwar agencies which might be established . . . I was rather skeptical of the value of this," Robertson wrote King, "arguing that the actual outcome . . . would be a de facto precedent which would be invoked regardless of any formal reservation of the position. . . ." He added that "the root of the present difficulties lay in the way the Combined Boards had been shaped as agencies of the United Kingdom and United States rather than of the United Nations. Our relationship with the Combined Boards had not been very satisfactory and we wanted to see the post war organizations get off to a good start." That, Robertson maintained, could only be done if the people of Canada believed their government was a full partner.[140]

But Canada was not to be a full partner in UNRRA's executive committee. On 7 April, with Robertson's concurrence, the War Committee accepted the chairmanship of the supplies committee and representation on the executive when supplies were being considered. "The whole business is very involved," King wrote, "and is one of the cases where it is clearly impossible for a lesser power to really do other than be largely governed by the views of the greater powers. . . ."[141] King was correct, but there was no doubt that his backtracking had cut the legs out from under External Affairs' case, which had been carefully built up over the entire field of postwar organization. Part of the pain, perhaps, was eased by Canada's elevation to the executive in mid-1945.[142]

Thus the functional principle had essentially been tried and found wanting during the war. Canada had argued a good case well, but for political reasons she usually backed down when the matter reached a sticking point. That political weakness, however realistic it was, made Robertson's task very difficult. The road to being a middle power was not an easy one.

V

Nor would it be easy as Canada set out to win itself a place in the new postwar world organization. All agreed that another war had to be prevented. But how? What was to take the place of the League of Nations? What arrangements were necessary to administer the defeated

Axis powers, when and if they were defeated? And what role was Canada to play?

Those questions first began to concern the Department of External Affairs seriously in the spring of 1943.[143] The war was far from won, but the tide had clearly turned, and victory seemed probable if not yet inevitable. In June 1943, therefore, London asked for Canadian views on the problems concerned with the cessation of hostilities, the means of implementing armistices, and the best ways of coordinating civil and military authorities after victory.[144] Those were important questions and the Cabinet War Committee authorized their study on 15 July.

As a result, one week later an *ad hoc* committee that consisted of Norman Robertson, Hume Wrong, Arnold Heeney, two of the Chiefs of Staff and a representative of the third, met on the Under-Secretary's initiative to consider the Canadian response. Robertson, as usual, demonstrated that his concern was for the long view, and he looked beyond the demilitarization of the Axis to "the biggest problem . . . economic relief and rehabilitation." He pointed out that at the armistice "Canadian soldiers would have been away from home longer than the soldiers of any other United Nation," an obvious political consideration that was certain to affect the actions of the Canadian government and its willingness to play a role in the occupation of Germany. But, above all, Robertson offered his colleagues good advice on the ways to sell their recommendations to the politicians:

Mr. Robertson suggested that in placing the proposals before the War Committee they should be put in perspective by pointing out that this was the first instalment in the plans for post-war world order and that a refusal by Canada to take part would mean a reversion to isolationism. He suggested that a note to this effect should be circulated to members of the War Committee along with the proposals. Robertson also asked whether the 'functional principle' advocated by the Canadian Government did not mean that Canada should not demand a place on the Steering Committee of the United Nations Commission for Europe, which, according to the proposals [received from the UK], was to be composed of representatives of the United Kingdom, the Soviet Union, the United States and France 'if she recovers her greatness.' If this were so, Canada might prove that the principle works both ways by pointing out that she does not expect membership on the Steering Committee.[145]

That was extraordinarily clever. By mid-1943 Robertson had become supremely skilled at playing the political games necessary to secure the support of the Prime Minister and the War Committee. He knew, as the authors of a study of "post-hostilities planning in Canada" point out, "when and on what matters he should approach King alone, or by-pass the Prime Minister and go directly to the Cabinet War Committee. . . ."[146] And he knew how best to phrase matters to ensure support. Most important, as the man responsible for coordinating and directing Canadian foreign policy, he was fully aware of the uses to which this British request could be put in pressing the case for the functional principle.[147] Thus, on 28 July, the War Committee approved the draft reply to London as submitted.[148]

Another product of the *ad hoc* committee was a "working group" on post-hostilities problems, chaired by Hume Wrong and with representatives from External Affairs, the military, and the Privy Council Office. Neither Robertson nor Wrong had much faith in the political planning skills of the military, and it was obviously important that any decisions and recommendations on such sensitive questions as organizing for the peace should be acceptable to the officers of the Department of External Affairs, the men who had to attempt to implement them in the world arena.[149] Wrong's presence was an indication of the potential importance of the subject and of the trust Robertson placed in his closest colleague, a trust that was further demonstrated by Robertson's giving him full control of all questions concerning the formation of a new world organization.

The Post-Hostilities Planning working group functioned to the end of the war, the first inter-departmental "planning" body in Ottawa.[150] Its role changed on occasion, and its mandate was extended to cover such subjects as the postwar defence relationship with the United States and the Commonwealth, the place of Newfoundland, and the advantages and disadvantages to Canada of regional or universal world security organization. It was essentially Hume Wrong's committee, but in January 1944 an Advisory Committee on Post-Hostilities Planning was created, with Robertson as chairman, and this body played a supervisory role.[151]

Planning went on elsewhere than in the Post-Hostilities committees. In the Department, Wrong began spending an increasing amount of his time on postwar subjects from 1943 on, and that broad subject was also coming to occupy the Prime Minister more and more. Wrong was an activist, Mackenzie King was not, and Robertson was probably somewhere in between the two in his qualified penchant for Canadian activity. He was well placed to mediate, to sell Wrong's ideas to King, and to urge King's caution on his colleague. Wrong and Robertson had no disagreements on what Canada's aims should be in a new world organization, but Robertson was definitely better at divining the Prime Minister's mood, at getting along and going along, and at helping King to accept the advice of his diplomatic experts.[152]

What were those aims? There was little disagreement on them. All wanted a new world organization in which Canada, although a member of the Commonwealth and a North American nation, was an independent country in its own right. Moreover, while not a great power, Canada was a middle power of some stature, one that had made a very large contribution to the war effort. In some areas, the production of food and raw materials, for example, Canada was far more powerful than Britain, and that specialized strength should be recognized in any bodies established to deal with those questions. But to say those things—and Robertson, Wrong and Mackenzie King did so, time and again—was vastly different from securing them.

The difficulty was to find a workable method of distinguishing degrees of power. The Great Powers stood out (although even here the inclusion of China was difficult to justify), but how did one devise a workable system to differentiate between Canada and Haiti? As Robertson wrote to Pearson in March 1943: "we are not very happy about the current arrangements for organizing the war effort and planning the peace and would welcome their improvement, but do not feel able to advocate as yet any general plan for the better organization of the United Nations. . . ."[153]* The farthest Canada could go, as King told Parliament in July 1943 in his statement of the functional principle, was to say that "authority in international affairs must not be concentrated exclusively in the largest powers. . . .Some compromise must be found between the theoretical equality of states and the practical necessity of limiting representation on international bodies to a workable number. That compromise can be discovered, especially in economic matters, by the adoption of the functional principle of representation."[154] Those remarks, of course, sounded much like Robertson and Wrong. But as Wrong, acting in Robertson's place while the Under-Secretary was in England in May 1944, told Pearson: "we are refraining from any attempt to draw up Canadian schemes for the organization of world security and are confining ourselves largely to the study of proposals which reach us from other countries. . . ."[155] That was sensible, a fair assessment of Canada's weight.

---

*In the area of international monetary policy, however, there was no such difficulty. The Americans and British produced separate plans, and Canada responded by producing and publicizing a third plan, one embodying features of the other two but with new wrinkles.

(Cont'd)

What worried Robertson was that some of these proposals were so
unrealistic. The British, or more properly Winston Churchill alone,
favoured a regional organization. Mackenzie King's address to the Prime
Ministers' meeting in May 1944, one drafted by John Holmes and revised
by Robertson, attempted to shoot down that trial balloon. "We should not
forget," King said, "that a major lesson of this war is the truth that the
seas do not divide and that the peace and prosperity of the world are
indivisible. It would not be wise to encourage the peoples of the world to
return to their illusions about their ability to live in continental
isolation."[156] Churchill withdrew his paper after this, but the issue was not
yet dead. Robertson had to strike it on the head again at a meeting at the
Foreign Office on 17 May. Sir Alexander Cadogan, Permanent Under-
Secretary at the Foreign Office, presided as Robertson systematically
riddled the regional scheme. The British paper before the meeting,
Robertson said, "seemed to be a repetition in all its essentials of the Prime
Minister's own paper which he had withdrawn. . . .From the Canadian
point of view it was open to the same objections. . . ." In the Canadian
view, "the British Commonwealth could not be regarded as a single great
Power, and hence the Dominions could not be represented by the United
Kingdom. . . .Canada was not in favour of the division of the world into
regional Power groups." Robertson then elaborated at length on the
Canadian position, but did say soothingly that no doubt Britain's position
would be fortified "by the fact that she would have had prior
consultations with the Dominions and secured their agreement on the
main lines of policy. . . ." Cadogan tried to reply, but Robertson went on:
"the regional scheme would encourage isolationism in the United States.
Canada's interests would not fit into a regional form of organization, nor
would Canada be willing to represent the Commonwealth in that
[American] region." Cadogan had had enough, and he agreed that he
personally was not in sympathy with Churchill's view.[157] As he wrote in
his diary that night: "meeting with Dominion officials on World
Organisation. Quite useful, I think. But all this is going to be very
difficult. . . ."[158] So it was for all concerned, but Churchill's plan was a
goner.

This scheme was largely produced by Louis Rasminsky of the Foreign Exchange Control
Board, but he had been helped by a group of senior officials, including Robertson.
Robertson was instrumental in presenting the scheme to King and in securing its
publication. (See, on this, Bank of Canada Archives, Rasminsky Papers, docs. in PWCP
files; King Papers, Memos for Prime Minister, 29 May, 10-11 Jun. 43, ff. C184622,
C212600-01.) This subject will be dealt with at length in my forthcoming study of the
Civil Service "mandarins."

Other problems became clear while the Great Powers were meeting at Dumbarton Oaks, near Washington, in September 1944. The Big Four wanted to set out their ideas in isolation, away from the distractions and demands of the lesser states, and that fact itself bothered Ottawa. More important to Robertson and Wrong were the substantive questions. First there was the way in which non-permanent members of the Security Council of the world body were to be chosen. The Canadian government, London was informed, "feel that it would be unfortunate if the statement approved at Dumbarton Oaks were only to provide that there should be probably six members elected by the Assembly. . . ." The Latin Americans could form up to half the members of the new organization, Ottawa warned, and they could claim half the Council seats. That was not desirable, particularly since Canada believed that "non-permanent membership should in some way be related to a dispassionate appraisal of the probable effective contribution of states to the maintenance of security." There were other points, but none so important as those in which Robertson and Wrong tried to establish Canada's claim to near-Great Power status in its eligibility for Security Council membership.[159] Their reason was simple. "The central Canadian difficulty," Wrong wrote on 14 September, "will arise from the imposition of permanent and indefinite obligations which might, in the extreme case, require Canada, by order of a Council on which Canada was not represented, to impose heavy burdens on the Canadian people."[160] That could not be, for Robertson was fully aware of just how shaky was Mackenzie King's conversion to collective security and how easily the Prime Minister could revert to a form of his prewar isolationism.

When the Dumbarton Oaks meeting concluded, there was little joy in the East Block. Canada's major desire—some reference to having the non-permanent members of the Security Council resemble Canada in their attributes—had been scuppered by American and Soviet opposition, and all Canada could do was to register its protest.[161] Robertson and Wrong talked to Malcolm MacDonald to reiterate the position, and the High Commissioner's report stressed the "extremely grave view" they took of "the inadequate consideration shown to secondary powers in the present proposals and of the reception which was likely to be accorded to them. . . ." The two Canadians "perhaps not altogether seriously . . . went so far as to suggest that the secondary powers might all refuse to join . . . taking the view that the present plan meant four-power dictatorship. . . ." MacDonald added that "this question was tied up in the Canadian minds with the treatment of secondary powers throughout the war...."[162] The High Commissioner, sympathetic to Canada and his close friends, probably shared that view; the Dominions Office did not. "This is one of the most remarkable examples of muddled thinking I ever came across," Viscount Cranborne, the Secretary of State for Dominion Affairs, minuted on the file.[163]

Robertson had no more success in persuading the Americans. On 5 November he went to the American Embassy to meet Charles Bohlen, the Chief of the Division of Eastern European Affairs in the State Department. Again he reiterated the Canadian case, implying that it might be better to have no organization at all than one in which all the lesser states would be uncomfortable.[164] The upshot was Robertson's request to the Prime Minister on 13 December for Canada to communicate directly and in a formal way with the Great Powers.[165] After approval by the War Committee, and after much drafting and redrafting, the memorandum to Washington, London, Moscow and Chungking was ready early in 1945. It restated the by now familiar Canadian refrain, adding one new note: a suggestion that only members of the Security Council be initially bound by council decisions until endorsed by two-thirds of the General Assembly's members. In the Canadian view, that would ensure that only those countries that had effective military forces would seek election to the Council. The Canadian concern was with the problems that would arise if Canada was forced by Security Council action to commit military force to the United Nations without having had any say in the decision.[166] It was all too much like the old Empire and its way of going to war; it smacked as well of the League's Covenant and its abortive attempts at sanctions; and to a man like Mackenzie King, those were not happy memories. Canada seemed to object to those clauses of the Dumbarton Oaks text that Mackenzie King, because of the past, could not accept.

Ottawa received some support from other middle powers,[167] but when first Wrong and then Robertson went to Washington to talk with State Department officials, they got nowhere. A British official noted bluntly that "the Canadians did not find much sympathy at the State Department...."[168] and Wrong told the Prime Minister that "our memorandum had not been very seriously considered in the State Department."[169]

Still the process went on, and by this time Robertson and the Prime Minister had begun to consider who should form the Canadian delegation to the United Nations Conference on International Organization that was to be held in April 1945 in San Francisco. "He spoke of Wrong going with me," King noted in his diary on 22 February. "I said I would of course want himself as well. It is characteristically modest of him to suggest Wrong." The two then briefly discussed whether Opposition politicians should be included, the means of travel (both preferred the train), and the possibility "that I might be asked to preside at the Conference. My reaction," King noted, "at once was on no account would I wish this."[170] Later, Robertson sent a detailed memorandum, suggesting names, arguing on the need for a "woman in public life" and "a senior French Canadian official among the advisers." Robertson's suggestions included Wrong, Pearson, Dana Wilgress, the Ambassador in Moscow, Rasminsky from the FECB, Tommy Stone, Charles Ritchie, R.A. MacKay and some junior officers from the Department.[171] It was good advice, and with one or two exceptions, King took it all.

Through March and April, Robertson marshalled his officers in the Department to prepare for San Francisco. There was a week-long flurry over the Americans' expressed desire for three votes in the General Assembly, publicized as the way to counter the British Commonwealth's six votes. That suggestion infuriated Robertson, who spoke strongly about it to Atherton, the American Ambassador.[172] In the end, Washington withdrew the suggestion. There was the need to prepare positions and to get the Prime Minister's approval of them.[173] And there were endless meetings to thrash out policy.[174] The Canadian positions were clear, and essentially unaltered since 1943.

That worried the British. As the Deputy High Commissioner in Ottawa wrote: "unless the United Kingdom Delegation can show themselves sympathetic to Canada's point of view our relations may become very strained in the course of the conference and ... the resultant long term damage may be serious."[175] But London tended to be wary of advice from the High Commission. Far tougher were the views of an official in Washington. Canada was using "high-pressure salesmanship" in its efforts to get its way, he said, but if Britain accepted the Canadian arguments, the Canadians could be very useful in return. If the United Kingdom could not go along, however, the delegation should be "very wary of the manoeuvres of the Canadian delegation, which will use every expedient ... to put their wishes across at the Conference."[176] That was almost a compliment.

The Ottawa contingent set off for San Francisco on 19 April, and arrived there on the morning of the 22nd. "The confusion reigning here is complete," General Maurice Pope wrote in his diary. "We have rooms in the St. Francis Hotel, but no office space nor office equipment....We have had to move some of our staff to a hotel across the street in order to provide ourselves with offices, but we have no typewriters or anything else. . . .Hume Wrong immediately exploded like a bunch of crackers."[177] Pope also talked about the attitudes of his colleagues. Some, "fortunately very few," he said, "are filled with the idea that we are about to participate in a great plan for the regeneration of the world." Another suffered from "bloody-minded Pacifism," saying that he was "prepared to fight Russia should she prove to be recalcitrant" in setting up the United Nations.[178]

The full delegation met first on 23 April with the Prime Minister presiding. His instructions were that the Canadians "would be best advised to withhold suggestions for amendment and positive comment for the time being until there was an opportunity to see how the conference developed and to ascertain what measures would be necessary."[179] The meeting also approved the assignments to committees. Robertson was on three: the Coordination Committee that was to put together the UN's Charter and assist the conference executive, and two technical committees, one on the preamble, purposes and principles of the Charter, the other on membership, amendments and the secretariat.[180] In addition, the Under-Secretary accompanied the Prime Minister to meetings of the Steering and Executive Committees, and he regularly sat through the "rather dreary" plenary sessions.[181]

Fortunately, there was time to meet old friends and to throw an occasional cocktail party. Robertson and Wrong shared a suite in the hotel and on 26 April they gave a party and then dined with Elisabeth de Miribel, an able Free French representative who had served in Canada in 1942.[182] Later in the conference, the ebullient Charles Ritchie saw an advertisement for what appeared to be a luxury hotel near the city, and persuaded Wrong, Robertson, Jean Désy, and a senior member of the French delegation to go there for a weekend. "In our room," Ritchie wrote, "we found an exhausted maid slapping at some dirty pillows as she replaced them in position. 'This is the fifth time I have made up this bed today,' she observed. 'Are you two *men* sharing this room?'. . . .Norman seemingly not in the least disconcerted sank with a sigh into the only available chair and addressed himself to the evening paper." The others, Ritchie adds, were less philosophical, accusing him of luring them into a brothel. Various adventures followed, and the party returned to San Francisco the next morning, the Canadians assuring the French Ambassador that the whole affair could be blamed on Ritchie's "innate folly and vicious proclivities." Robertson, Ritchie added, had been relatively undisturbed by the raucous nightlife in the hotel corridors "and slept peaceably with his deaf ear uppermost."[183]

Robertson's major role at the conference was in the Coordination Committee, where the task was to assemble the reports submitted by various committees and to weld them into a polished and precise Charter. It was an area of interest that he had hitherto left to Wrong, but he enjoyed this kind of important editing and, at San Francisco, as Escott Reid remembers, "he became really excited as he became more and more involved....He became one of the two or three leading members...so much the brains of the committee. We drafted a preamble, not the one which Smuts [of South Africa] had drafted. Norman was sent by the committee to try to sell it to Smuts. He came back with his tail between his legs...but the fact that he was chosen shows the confidence the committee, and especially the Russians, had in him."[184]

The work was tiring and Robertson became ill on 30 April and, as King noted on 9 May, "quite exhausted."[185] Worse yet was the difference in outlook between the politicians and their advisers. King noted one instance when the subject was the admission of Argentina, then a Fascist-leaning state, to the United Nations. King voted with the British and Americans to admit, fearing that to do otherwise would hurt Canada in Latin American eyes. "It was difficult, too, to know what it was best to do as both Robertson and Wrong took a different position toward the end of the morning to that which they had taken on the way to the Conference; also as this morning, Coldwell [the CCF leader who was one of the Opposition politicians in the delegation] seemed to [wish] to take a different attitude because of Argentine's past record."[186] It was all troublesome, and some felt that Robertson played a crucial role in keeping the officials generally moving in tandem with the political delegates.[187]

Moreover, since King and the politicians soon had to leave for home to campaign in the general election set for 11 June, Robertson knew that he was sure to end up running the delegation. He had the task of reining in the more forward spirits—essentially that meant sitting on Escott Reid— and on occasion he simply told his colleagues that Mackenzie King had left certain instructions that had to be followed.[188] There was also the growing worry over the Soviet Union's attitudes at the conference, and while the Canadians fought vigorously for their positions, they always tried to bear in mind Robertson's dictum that the goal was to get and keep Russia in the United Nations, not to drive her out.[189] Once, after receiving a long series of reports from his officials about their committees' progress,

Robertson said, "I wish to God somebody would come back into this room and not start his report by saying 'those Goddamned Russians.' " [190]

Robertson's role was to coordinate and direct, and Jack Hickerson from the Department of State told the Ambassador in Ottawa that "Hume Wrong and Mike Pearson did most of the speaking for the Canadian Delegation. Norman made no speeches whatever but acted as Field Marshal." As Field Marshal, he ran the delegation smoothly. "You probably saw the Newsweek comment," Hickerson added, "that for smooth, efficient performance the Canadian Delegation probably ranked first at the Conference." That remark's source was the American delegation, although the Canadians did not know this. "I kidded Norman about it and asked him how many copies of Newsweek he had to buy as his part of the deal." [191] Planted or not, that was still praise and one indication that, when he worked at it, Robertson could be first-rate as the organizer of a small group.

The Canadian delegation's aims at San Francisco were much as they had been throughout the drawn-out consultation and negotiation since 1943. Eight pages of amendments dealt with every aspect of the Charter, but the most important concentrated on the composition of the Security Council and on "Determination of Threats to the Peace or Acts of Aggression and Action with respect thereto." On the first, Canada proposed adding a sentence directing the General Assembly to "ensure that due weight be given to the contribution of members to the maintenance of international peace and security and the performance of their obligations to The United Nations." On the second, Canada proposed a new paragraph that would oblige the Security Council to invite any non-member of the Council to sit as a member at meetings discussing the use of the military force that country had agreed to make available to the Security Council. In other words, as Maurice Pope put it, "It is impossible for us to grant to a Council on which we may not be represented the right to order us about without our having participated in the decision." [192]

The delegation lobbied vigorously and fought hard for its position on the use of military forces, and won its case, Article 44 of the Charter being the monument to Canada's efforts. "It was a victory," James Eayrs wrote, "but a victory of status rather than substance. For not to this day has the Security Council been able to take any military action on behalf of the United Nations." [193] True enough, but Canada's long view was directed toward preventing any situation in which French Canadians, in particular, could claim that Canada was being manipulated by the UN in a similar way to that in which the Dominion had once been directed by Britain. The delegation's effort met that concern and was wholly justified; it was also correct.[194]

On their other main point, the Canadians had a qualified success, winning the inclusion of a phrase in Article 23 that "due regard" was to be paid in electing non-permanent members of the Council "to the contribution of Members of the United Nations to the maintenance of international peace and security and to the other purposes of the Organization...." Another victory, but unfortunately Canada lost to Australia in the first Council elections.[195]

On other matters, on all of which Canada had strong views, Robertson's policy was straightforward. In a telegram sent to Ottawa on 10 June, he noted that the Australians, Herbert Evatt in particular, were being obnoxious, attacking the British for their position in support of a Great Power veto in the Security Council and using strong language to do so.* "It seems clear to us," Robertson said, "that, in this year of grace, there cannot be a World Organization established, with Russia a member, unless it provides for voting rights in the Security Council substantially as set forth in the Great Power memorandum....The effective choice appears, therefore, to be between such an Organization and an Organization from which the Soviet Union ... [is] excluded. Our view is that it is better to take the Organization that we can get and, having come to that decision, to refrain from further efforts to pry apart the difficult unity which the Great Powers have attained. This means foregoing the luxury of making any more perfectionist speeches...."[196] That was an exemplary summing up of the Canadian position; it was also a good self-analysis of Robertson's own beliefs on the way a country like Canada had to behave in a Great Power world.

Canada's self-denying ordinance may have helped get the UN started. But it was also probably responsible for the gloom that many members of the delegation felt at the result. Escott Reid remembered a gathering in Robertson's room at the conclusion of the conference where all present bemoaned the Charter's deficiencies. Robertson had urged them not to talk that way in public since the sole result would be to destroy the

---

*Pearson said at San Francisco "that the British Commonwealth delegates were obviously just demonstrating that degree of unity on all issues which had led to the criticism in certain quarters that the votes given to them were so many extra votes given to the United Kingdom." (PRO, Dominions Office Records, D.O. 35/1884, Cockram to Stephenson, 16 Jun. 45.) Robertson later described Evatt as "inevattable ... a vital and able embodiment of how not to win friends." (Mrs. A.D.P. Heeney Papers, Heeney to wife, 8 Aug. 46.)

public's faith in the new organization.[197] Whether that was good advice or not is moot, but it certainly suggested that Robertson had few illusions left about the UN. Certainly there was little ground for optimism, for the clouds of mistrust and suspicion were gathering apace and the San Francisco meeting had done nothing to dispel them.

One additional incident deserves recounting. The question of who was to become the first Secretary-General of the United Nations preoccupied the representatives of the Great Powers from the conclusion of the San Francisco meetings until January 1946. There were a number of discussions, particularly at the London meeting of the Executive Committee of the UN Preparatory Commission in September 1945. The Department of State's candidate, or so Dean Acheson said on 22 September, was Norman Robertson. That was flattering, but other considerations were at work and, within a few weeks, Washington had decided that it was not proper to "push any Canadian" because the UN headquarters was likely to be in the United States and to have a North American Secretary-General as well was too much. Nonetheless, the State Department still believed that Robertson was "one of the most able men available."[198] On 8 October, Edward Stettinius, Jr., the American representative at the Preparatory Commission, told an informal meeting of Great Power representatives that Lester Pearson and Robertson were at the top of his list of five preferred candidates for the post.[199] Stettinius also mentioned the two Canadians in a conversation with Prime Minister King in London on 12 October. "It would be a great loss to Canada to lose either of them," King wrote, "but I would not stand in their way though I doubted if Robertson himself would be interested."[200]

That was certainly true. Given Robertson's disinterest in speech-making, his self-effacing approach to publicity, and his preference for exercising influence in the backrooms, it was most unlikely that he would have considered taking the post. On the other hand, Pearson was most certainly interested in the challenge, and although he was properly modest in public, his private correspondence indicated how closely he followed the question.[201]

Both Canadians continued to receive the close scrutiny of the Great Powers. Philip Noel-Baker, Minister of State in the British Labour government, seemed keen on Pearson,[202] and the State Department closely examined which of the two Canadians was most in American interests. Robertson, the European Division of the Department noted on 24 October, had "been of incalculable assistance" to the United States since 1941. "His thinking is North American; he is friendly to the United

States . . . fair and open-minded" on all subjects, and he was the leader of the group in the Department with which Washington had been "particularly successful in reaching constructive solutions."

In the Americans' view, Pearson was a superb conference man and chairman. The European Division argued that if Robertson were shifted from Ottawa, that might be disadvantageous for Washington; Pearson, however, could be replaced in Washington at the Embassy. On balance, therefore, State favoured Pearson over Robertson. Jack Hickerson, however, disagreed, seeing Robertson as having more character and ability than Pearson and believing that he would be "the better S.G."[203]

The private soundings continued into the new year and gradually it became clear that no North American would be acceptable to the Soviet Union. As late as 5 January, the State Department still included the two Canadians on its short list, and there seemed no doubt that if there was an Anglo-American consensus candidate, it was Pearson.[204] In the end, however, Trygve Lie of Norway was selected.

Louis Rasminsky, a member of the Canadian delegation to the first UN General Assembly, wrote to Pearson to "offer my warmest congratulations on not having been elected. The job would be a thankless and heartbreaking one."[205] That was surely so, and it would have been far harder temperamentally for Robertson to do the job than for Pearson. His escape was fortunate.

CHAPTER VI

Moral Questions:
The Japanese Evacuation and Gouzenko

I F MOST OF Norman Robertson's time during the war was occupied with questions of alliance warfare, occasionally other issues impinged upon him. Sometimes these matters posed particularly difficult problems for someone with a humane conscience, and sometimes Robertson suffered acutely as he grappled with them. The expulsion of the Japanese Canadians from the British Columbia coast in 1942 was one such question, particularly difficult because Robertson had been born in Vancouver and his family and boyhood friends still lived there. His liberalism, on balance, survived that test, but it had harder going on the Gouzenko affair, when Robertson had the key responsibility for formulating the Canadian response to the crisis caused by the defection in September 1945 of a Soviet Embassy cipher clerk with documents that proved the existence of a spy network in Canada.

Norman Robertson was a humane man, but he had special responsibilities to the state he served, and he put those before his own conscience. It is easy to criticize his choices and his actions; it is less easy, however, to determine how else he might have acted.

I

When Japan attacked the American, British and Dutch territories in the Pacific in December 1941, Canada found itself at war on yet another front. But because 22,000 Japanese (either citizens by birth or naturalization, or landed immigrants) lived in British Columbia, the locus of action initially shifted to that province, where for decades there had existed a deep-seated hostility to the Japanese, a compound of racial paranoia, fear of the designs of the Japanese Empire, and resentment of economic competition from hard-working, skilful Japanese fishermen and market gardeners.[1] Politicians had manipulated these concerns regularly, and the Japanese 'threat' was a regular whipping boy in local, provincial and federal elections. It was a wretched situation.

The problem for Norman Robertson, who saw his Department drawn into the struggle to determine the fate of the British Columbia Japanese, was made worse by the fact that his father in Vancouver did not seem entirely immune to the anti-Japanese contagion,[2] and by the strongly sympathetic attitude to the Japanese Canadians of Hugh Keenleyside and H.F. Angus, two British Columbians in his Department.[3] Robertson himself had not the slightest sympathy with the British Columbia hysteria, but this was an issue on which the politicians carried the play, one in which his capacity to ameliorate affairs was limited.

Studies of preparatory action in the event of war with Japan had been underway in Ottawa at least since 1938[4] and, under pressure from provincial politicians—and from aroused public opinion, the government had named a Special Committee on Orientals in British Columbia on 1 October 1940. Its report, released in December of that year, called for vigilance to prevent sabotage,* an end to anti-Japanese propaganda, the voluntary reregistration of all Japanese (a previous registration having been completed under the National Resources Mobilization Act of 1940), and exemption of Japanese from call-up for home defence military service under the NRMA.[5] The government carried out those recommendations it could,[6] and the planning for action in case of war continued. In July 1941, a special committee of officials, including L.B. Pearson, Keenleyside, and Angus, recommended after two meetings that in case of war with Japan, Japanese Canadians should be treated no better and no worse than other enemy aliens in 1939 and 1940. "In some individual cases internment may be necessary, but it is anticipated that the bulk of the Japanese population in Canada can continue its normal activities," the committee report recommended.[7] That position, shared by Robertson, was held by External Affairs for as long as possible.

But the attempt to follow a moderate policy was not easy. On 9 December, two days after Pearl Harbor, Robertson acceded to a request

---

* Angus wrote in October 1940 that "There may be unreliable elements among the Japanese here. . . . At first they (in all good faith, I think) distributed a good deal of pro-Japanese, anti-Chinese propaganda. Now they say, 'We are not responsible for what Japan may do.' I tell them that they have unfortunately made people feel that they are identified with Japan by the action in distributing propaganda, and that it is very difficult to find a way of removing this impression." (PAC, J.W. Dafoe Papers, Angus to Dafoe, 15 Oct. 40.)

from the province for the seizure of Japanese-owned and -operated fishing boats. And as he told King, he and Pierrepont Moffat agreed on the need for both Canada and the United States to pursue as nearly similar policies as possible towards their Japanese populations.[8] Early the next month, the Under-Secretary attended a "Conference on Japanese Problems in British Columbia," held in Ottawa on 8-9 January, at which officials from the federal bureaucracy met with representatives from the Pacific province. Although reports from the military and naval commanders on the coast favoured the internment and removal of the Japanese,[9] neither the representatives of the Chiefs of Staff nor the RCMP agreed. Indeed, the officials, whatever their department, called for a limited policy that included formation of a Civilian Corps of Canadian Japanese for public projects and the enlistment of Japanese in the armed forces, and they urged against the removal of Japanese nationals and Japanese British subjects beyond the Rockies. "The acceptance of this proposal," the meeting's report said of the suggestion of deportation, "would be a contradiction of Canadian and Allied professions of justice and humanity. Officers of the Department of External Affairs informed the Conference that in their opinion action of the kind proposed would almost certainly result in cruel retaliation by the Japanese authorities against Canadians now in their power...." But the British Columbia representatives refused to accept this reasoning and angrily dissented from the report.[10]*

The provincial concerns were forcefully presented to the Prime Minister by Ian Mackenzie, Minister of Pensions and National Health, the province's representative in the cabinet, and the key figure in the subsequent events. 'I personally have no doubt whatsoever as to what the opinion is in British Columbia," Mackenzie said, "the opinion of British Columbia is with the minority report."[11] Of that there could be no doubt; nor was there much room for doubting Mackenzie's last words: unless

---

* Robertson's father wrote from B.C. to say that the province's representatives had been offended by the attitudes of Angus and Keenleyside at the meetings. (PAC, Robertson Papers, vol. 2, Personal Correspondence,Lemuel Robertson to NAR, 17 Feb. 42.) Angus was soon being attacked "most unfairly" by A.W. Neill, MP, and Robertson was defending his official. (PAC, W.L.M. King Papers. ff. C249430-5.) Escott Reid told General Maurice Pope that at the conference, "I felt dirty all over.... I said once to Norman [Robertson] that it was one of the rare occasions in my life when I had felt the physical presence of evil. He was exasperated by that remark. ... I don't think he was as revolted by the Canadian Government bending to political pressure ... as ... Pope, Keenleyside and I were." (Department of External Affairs, Escott Reid interview, 21 Jul. 77.)

immediate actions were taken, "our white people may resort to unwise tactics in Vancouver."[12] A note by the B.C. minister indicated that Mackenzie King, a man who had made his early reputation by working to limit Japanese immigration to Canada,[13] was against military service for the Japanese, for a civilian corps, and in favour of evacuation to the interior of all able-bodied male Japanese nationals.[14] That policy was announced on 14 January,[15] with one concession to the representations made by External Affairs: King's statement declared that "all enemy aliens (of whatever origin)" were to be moved out of the protected area on the Pacific Coast. The policy, while racist at root, at least did not seem to be directed exclusively at the Japanese.

Mackenzie's defeat of the moderates was not yet complete. As the Minister told Bruce Hutchison of the *Vancouver Sun*: "The government always intended to move all male Japs. Will compel nationals and invite all others. If they don't accept, will be compelled. . . ."[16] That was probably correct, and Robertson and the Department of External Affairs could do little more than to fight a delaying action against an intransigent Mackenzie and a vicious British Columbia public opinion.

On 20 January, for instance, Robertson urged the Prime Minister to keep the federal government, and not the province, in charge of the evacuated Japanese. "It seems to us important that the schemes for using these two classes of labour"—the Canadian Japanese who might enrol in the Civilian Labour Corps and the Japanese nationals to be moved out of the protected areas—"should be kept quite distinct and separate, and that both should be under the supervision of the Dominion Government." Enemy aliens had to be under federal control, he said, because Canada was responsible for their treatment and that fact might be important in determining how Japan treated the Canadian nationals in its hands. "The primary reason for the Dominion taking direct responsibility for organizing Canadian Japanese," he went on, "is that their enlistment in a Civilian Labour Corps will be on a voluntary basis, and their response is likely to be much greater if the Corps is a Dominion body. . . ."[17] But as Keenleyside pointed out on 26 January, the opinion of the B.C. Members of Parliament was that all Japanese, whether Canadian citizens or Japanese nationals, should be treated alike and forced out of the protected areas unless they could secure RCMP permits to remain.[18] Certainly that was Mackenzie's aim,[19] but he was shrewd enough to go slowly, and on 27 January he agreed, as Keenleyside informed Robertson, that "if in the event it developed that the Canadian nationals did not enlist in large numbers, the whole situation would have to be reviewed and the question of the application of compulsion considered."[20] At that same meeting, Mackenzie accepted an earlier protest by Robertson against the minister's choice for the head of the Civilian Corps. "I am somewhat worried by your suggestion that Lieutenant Colonel [MacGregor] Mackintosh [*sic*, MacIntosh] should be appointed...," Robertson had complained. "As you know, Colonel Mackintosh has been ... the most outspoken opponent of the Japanese in British Columbia during the last ten years. Moreover, he has definitely committed himself ... in support of the view that all persons of Japanese racial origin now in Canada should be deported to Japan."[21] Mackenzie had wanted the one man as head of the Corps who would render enlistment impossible, and so make evacuation from the Coast inevitable. He then tried to cut the allowances to be paid to dependents of those serving in the Corps, a tactic that provoked another remonstrance from Robertson. "This would seem a picayune sort of economy which would prejudice and possibly defeat the purposes the Government had in mind.... It may be that the Corps will not be the final answer to the problem presented by the Japanese Canadians," he went on, but it was the government's policy to make the voluntary enlistment scheme work as a way of removing substantial numbers of Canadian Japanese from the protected area, and "it seems a pity to wreck its chances of success...."[22] That was not the kind of letter a civil servant ordinarily sent a minister.

But inevitably Mackenzie was victorious in the end. On 24 February 1942, the government decided that all Japanese, whatever their citizenship, would be removed from the coast. Singapore, the supposedly impregnable fortress, had just fallen, and public opinion in British Columbia was near hysteria.[23] Most important, perhaps, the American government had decided on 19 February to give its military commanders power to exclude any and all persons from designated areas, the legal basis for action against Japanese Americans. In the circumstances, any hope of moderation in Canada was gone.[24]

Once the policy had been decided, Robertson as a civil servant knew that further resistance was futile. His political masters had determined their course and the onus of decision was on their heads. Angered by the decisions, as were his colleagues, his options were limited to resignation, a pointless gesture in his view, one that did no one any good, least of all the Japanese Canadians, and one that no one chose, or to remaining in the service of the government and attempting to ease the policy where and when he could. He chose the second course, and his task, as he saw it, was to carry out the government's policy as efficiently and humanely as possible. This view showed clearly in a paper he sent to King after the decision to deport the Japanese had been made. It was important, Robertson declared, for "steps to be taken quickly to translate this general policy into action":

In present circumstances, it cannot be expected that the transfer of persons of Japanese origin from the coast to the interior of British Columbia or to other parts of Canada will be effected by individual initiative on the part of the persons who have been asked to move . . . it would be cruel and ineffective to stand on a negative policy of deporting persons of Japanese origin from the protected areas and allowing them to fend for themselves.

It seems to me that this movement has to be organized and controlled from beginning to end. The individuals to be moved have to be told when they are to leave, where they are to go and arrangements will have to be made for the maintenance of them and their families. I am afraid we will, for the present, have to postpone plans for finding immediate useful employment for persons of Japanese origin transferred from coastal areas. This objective must be kept in mind, however. . . . The first task . . . is to get them away from the coastal areas quickly.

There was good sense in that. Robertson then went on to suggest that, as an earnest "of the seriousness of the Government's plans," a large number of Japanese nationals of military age should be removed immediately from the protected area. "The easiest way to remove them quickly is by internment orders under Section 25(8) of the Defence of Canada Regulations," he went on, in an apparent excess of zeal. "An immediate step of this kind would, I think, be much more reassuring to the local population than reliance on minor and irritating discriminations against one class of British subject such as the curfew, automobile license, trade license restrictions, etc., which the British Columbia members [of Parliament] have asked for."[25]

But if Robertson may have been going too far in his efforts to "reassure" the British Columbia population,[26] he had not lost sight of his goal. When, for example, a draft letter addressed to the chairman of the British Columbia Security Commission, the body established to deal with the evacuation and control of the Japanese, was prepared to seek his views on the post-war settlement of the Japanese question, Robertson had shrewd delaying advice. "He thinks," Keenleyside wrote to Angus, "that if we were to ask for the advice of the Commission just now it is probable that the reply would be that arrangements should be made in the postwar period for the repatriation of all persons of Japanese origin." It was better, in Robertson's view, to wait for the bitterness to recede.[27] A few months later, he told the Prime Minister that "I would not like to see our universities outside the Protected Areas exclude students on racial or national grounds."[28]

The question of the Japanese tended to recede from the public view as 1942 turned into 1943. In August 1943 Robertson prepared a memo for King before the first Quebec Conference, in the vain hope that the Prime Minister could seize the opportunity to talk with President Roosevelt about "how he views the postwar position of persons of Japanese race in the United States." Robertson said that Canadian policy "has been largely influenced by what we understood the policy of the United States to be."

We are likely . . . to be faced, at the close of the war, with the problem of some 25,000 residents of Canada of Japanese origin, less than a third of whom are Japanese nationals. . . . The communities into which the Japanese moved accepted them with more or less grace, on the understanding that their placement was an emergency wartime measure. The communities from which the Japanese were evacuated are confident that they have gone for good and will probably resist their return.

That was certainly true. But what should be done with the peace?

My own preliminary feeling is that we should

(1) afford every facility, including free transportation and permission to transfer funds and furniture, for the voluntary repatriation from Canada of all persons of Japanese race, regardless of nationality, who wish to return to Japan;

(2) deport Japanese nationals whose behaviour during wartime made their internment necessary;

(3) revoke the naturalization certificates of naturalized British subjects of Japanese origin and cancel the national status of natural born British subjects of Japanese origin who either had to be interned under the Defence of Canada Regulations or put themselves under the protection of the Protecting Power for Japanese Interests. Such persons would then become liable to the deportation. . . .

(4) permit the residual population of Japanese racial origin who would be predominantly British subjects and Canadian nationals to reside in Canada where they should not be subject to any special or peculiar disabilities with respect to place of residence, employment, civil obligations or educational opportunities; and

(5) stop immigration for permanent settlement.

Those ideas, Robertson said, "outlined the main elements of a possible policy." He cautioned, however, that if the Americans contemplated a more drastic position, public opinion was certain to force the Canadian government to go further.[29]

For 1943, Robertson's was not an illiberal position. As an adviser, he had suggested to the Prime Minister a policy that in his judgment had a chance of being acceptable to the government and to the public. It was no ideal position, and it was not one Robertson could have felt pleased about. For example, he was consciously singling out those Japanese who had had to be interned and suggesting them for deportation to Japan. Their removal then might make it possible for the vast majority to remain and to live anywhere in Canada without discrimination. The Prime Minister, however, was not willing to go so far, for he accepted all of Robertson's points except the crucial fourth one.

The time to declare the postwar policy was coming closer. In January 1944, Robertson called a meeting to consider lifting travel restrictions on the Japanese. He told the officials present that "two years ago it had been necessary to make drastic regulations which did in effect discriminate against Canadians of Japanese origin ... but that now the original danger had disappeared [and] ... it would not be desirable if at all avoidable to re-assert the principle of discrimination." He said in addition that he did not object to restrictions on Japanese nationals or, "because of peculiar conditions there," to restrictions on the travel of Japanese, in British Columbia. But in the country as a whole, "it would be desirable to have only such restrictions as the question of security made strictly necessary and to have them imposed in some manner other than by a general disability of a group of persons because of their racial origin." The matter was taken under consideration, but that was yet another indication of Robertson's acute discomfort at the racialist nature of Canadian policy.[30]

Robertson carried his ideas to a further stage in an important paper for the Prime Minister in March 1944. After recapitulating his recommendations of August 1943, he noted that, on the whole, Canadian policy "has not been unduly harsh and can be defended as reasonable in the circumstances." Nevertheless, he went on,

... many of the restrictions that have been placed on persons of Japanese race work hardship upon them. The people involved are in the great majority of cases British subjects and Canadian nationals who personally are guilty of no offence other than that of having Japanese ancestry. I think it would be very desirable if we could remove as far as possible the aspects of racial discrimination that are involved. In order to do this, however, it is necessary I think to deal strictly, and perhaps more strictly than the individual cases would in themselves justify, with any and all cases in which there is adequate reason to believe that the person involved had endeavoured to assist the Japanese war effort or hinder ours, or has manifested disloyalty toward this country or greater sympathy for Japan.

In effect, Robertson was refining his 1943 suggestions and again proposing severe punishment of the guilty so that the innocent could live freely in Canada. To this end, he proposed the segregation of the disloyal and undesirable, a group to be defined as those who had been interned, those who had declared loyalty to Japan or sought repatriation, and those who had failed to comply with the laws of Canada or had given indication that their sympathies lay with Japan. A tribunal should be established to deal with these cases, with a right of appeal for British subjects to the Minister of Justice. Those segregated were to be deported if they were Japanese nationals, and stripped of British status and deported if they were British subjects. Further, any Japanese who expressed a desire to return to Japan should be given every assistance to do so.

If the above principles should be found feasible for adoption and segregation were instituted, it would, I think, be possible to relax some restrictions on innocent Japanese. It would probably not be possible to allow their return during the war to the protected area of British Columbia. However, if this restriction were maintained, but at the same time loyal Japanese were allowed to buy land elsewhere in Canada, it might encourage them to 'take root' in other provinces. Such a dispersion would facilitate a post-war settlement on a reasonably just basis by helping to meet the otherwise adamant stand of British Columbia in the face of a probable return of almost all Japanese to that province.

The Prime Minister agreed with everything Robertson had suggested, except the right of Japanese to buy land. That, he scribbled on the memorandum, required consideration in the Cabinet War Committee. Robertson added, finally, that, preferably, German and Italian aliens should be treated on the same basis.[31]

Robertson's proposals subsequently went before an interdepartmental committee in April 1944,[32] and then were put in the form of a memorandum to the War Committee on 18 April.[33] The policy was duly approved on 19 April, including a provision that the commissioner to be appointed to review the cases of the Japanese whose loyalty was doubtful should also scrutinize the cases of other enemy aliens or of persons of enemy alien origin and descent.[34] Robertson's paper also formed the basis of Mackenzie King's speech in the House of Commons on 4 August 1944, a speech that was greeted literally with applause by civil servants in the gallery of the House as a victory of the moderates over the hardliners.[35]

Robertson continued to pursue his policy of making it possible for the vast majority of Japanese to remain in Canada, and to be accepted, by urging the Prime Minister to permit their enlistment in the armed forces. "There are obvious objections to training them in British Columbia," he said, "but I see no serious practical difficulty to training them in company or platoon units at Eastern camps. For that matter, I do not think the odd Japanese Canadian soldier would present a serious problem in an ordinary mixed unit. . . ."[36] In November he suggested names and terms of reference for the commission to investigate Japanese loyalty. He argued strongly for generous terms to be offered those Japanese who were voluntarily leaving for Japan[37] and, when the policy was ready for release, he told King he thought it probable "that a fairly large number of Japanese persons who have been loyal and who would prefer to remain in this country will voluntarily seek repatriation, partly through discouragement and partly because of fear that they may never again be offered as favourable terms for repatriation." But on the whole, he said, the plans seem "reasonably fair in terms of what is politically feasible at the moment."[38]

Robertson's policy had been consistent throughout. His intent had been to moderate the hostility to the Japanese, to work within the government for a more humane policy, and in the final analysis to sacrifice those "disloyal" Japanese for the sake of the greater number who could remain in Canada without disabilities. As he said to King in December 1945, the government policy—really what he had proposed in April 1944—"represented a compromise between a very vocal demand for the total expulsion of all persons of Japanese racial origin, regardless of conduct or loyalty, and the less articulate feeling in the country that flagrant racial discrimination was one of the things the war was being fought against." Again in this memorandum, Robertson urged that the same treatment should be afforded to other enemy aliens or naturalized Canadians of enemy alien origin.[39]

Robertson's policy was not as liberal and fair as one might have wished. Nonetheless, it must be recognized that the "less articulate" opinion in favour of moderation was at times almost completely inaudible in the country at large, in the House of Commons, and in the cabinet.[40]

Robertson abhorred the racism in his home province, and he was appalled by its virulence in such men as Ian Mackenzie. But men like Mackenzie had a power that he did not, on a political issue such as this, and represented the aroused public opinion of the Pacific coast and in the rest of Canada. There was a war on, and the Japanese had behaved with appalling brutality to captured Canadian and Allied soldiers. In those conditions, there was only so much that a moderate could do. Robertson's decision deliberately to focus on the "disloyal" as an emotional outlet upon which the House of Commons could concentrate its attention was, or so Gordon Robertson, working in the Under-Secretary's office on Japanese policy, remembered it, carefully calculated to buy time in which passions could cool and to save the vast majority. That tactic worked.

Robertson's critics, and they include Keenleyside and Angus, suggest that Robertson did not feel strongly on the question of the Japanese or consider it a matter of principle. Angus considered him a "passive liberal," and Keenleyside, while agreeing that Robertson's heart was in the right place on this issue, nonetheless believed it shocking that Robertson could advocate deportation of essentially innocent Japanese and appalling that he did not fight for the principle at stake.[41] There is force in these arguments, and Keenleyside and Angus, who both battled vigorously for principle, are entitled to the respect of their countrymen. But on a practical level they are probably incorrect in their strictures against Robertson. Robertson apparently felt as keenly as his colleagues, but he was a better tactician, and he had a clearer realization than Keenleyside or Angus that the politicians were set on action and, given public opinion from 1941 to 1944, had to be. Keenleyside's efforts were honourable and admirable, but possibly counterproductive; Robertson's, on the other hand, largely worked and helped to save much more than might have been expected in the early months of 1942.

But can the policy be defended as reasonable and not unduly harsh, as Robertson had told King? It cannot. The policy was a disgrace to a liberal democracy, one that was compounded after the war by the judicial theft of Japanese property.[42] And as A.E. Ritchie, one of Robertson's close colleagues, recollected it, Robertson on one occasion told Howard Green, the Secretary of State for External Affairs from 1958 to 1963 and one of the more vociferous anti-Japanese spokesmen during the war, that "we have a lot to account for, Howard, we British Columbians."[43] That comment suggested that Norman Robertson too was not very proud of his role in retrospect.

II

After his work on the problem of alien enemies in 1939 and 1940, Norman Robertson was fully aware that ideology could be a powerful motive force. But in 1939, aside from a few home-grown Fascists, the only segments of the population infected with Nazi and Fascist ideas were German and Italian immigrants, peculiarly susceptible to the blandishments and pressures of home. Few native Canadians succumbed, and fewer still were apparently willing to spy for the Axis. The problem was quantifiable and it could be handled with despatch, if not without difficulty.

But Communism was a different story, and the Gouzenko affair of 1945-46 demonstrated that Canadians of whatever origin could be persuaded to spy for the Soviet Union.* Worse still for Norman Robertson, who believed that to work in the public service was a sacred trust, the Gouzenko case demonstrated that even civil servants could become conduits of information to a foreign power. The implications of this for Robertson and the government were far-reaching.

Not that Robertson had lacked experience with espionage and counter-intelligence during the war. But he and his colleagues had operated on the assumption that Canadians were united in opposing Nazism, and he was probably more casual about security than he should have been. On one occasion, for example, he and Arnold Heeney were eating lunch at the Chateau Laurier cafeteria and discussing a policy question. They were overheard, and later that day the RCMP called Robertson's office to report that someone from External Affairs and someone from the Privy Council Office had been reported to have breached security. As Robertson later told a colleague, he had disguised his voice to the caller and said "the matter will be investigated."[44]

Certainly no one in the Department of External Affairs, Robertson least of all, feared that the Soviet Union was running a spy network in Canada.

---

* A brief note on sources for this section and subsequent sections treating security and intelligence questions: despite promises, I was not given access to the security files of the Department of External Affairs, one solitary dossier aside. The regular files of the Department contain little on policy-making in this area, particularly for the Gouzenko case. The transcript of the Gouzenko Royal Commission is not yet available at the Public Archives of Canada, and there are almost no supporting documents there. The main Privy Council Office file is missing, as is the King Diary for the last part of 1945. There are RCMP files, but I was advised by Chief Supt. James on 15 February 1979 that these contain no policy material. This section, admittedly, is based on very shaky documentation.

Indeed, until the Nazi attack on Russia in June 1941, few in Ottawa considered the Communist state at all, other than to lump it generally with other more or less hostile countries. Robertson's initial views on the Nazi invasion of Russia were expressed in a conversation with Pierrepont Moffat on 23 June. His worries were mainly directed at the reactions of Ukrainian Canadians, "some of whom might see in the new situation an opportunity for furthering their ambitions for an autonomous Ukrainian State; and the Finns, among whom there were more actual Communists than in any other racial group in Canada." Robertson and Moffat both agreed that "Russia could not be expected to put up much of a military fight," a common enough belief at the time.[45]

But Russia hung on through that grim summer of 1941, and by mid-September Robertson was beginning to wonder if Canada should establish closer relations with Moscow. "He, Robertson, was trying to find out what Mr. King proposed to do," Moffat wrote. "Personally, he was still inclined to pussyfoot. He felt Canada should do more for Russia, but could do it most effectively in a concealed manner, such as by letting the Joint Metals Board allocate a thousand tons at a time of aluminum for shipment to the U.S.S.R. This would get the aluminum to Russia without running the risk of so stirring the anti-Communist aluminum workers at Arvida [Quebec] that total production might be reduced." The Soviets had not asked for the opening of diplomatic relations, Robertson said.[46]

With Japan's entry into the war, Canada soon moved to take the lead in establishing a link with the Soviet Union. On 11 December 1941, Robertson wrote to the Prime Minister to say that "we all have now an urgent interest in Russia coming into the war against Japan, and any action of ours which could help in any degree to bring this about would, I think, receive pretty unanimous approval...."[47] Two weeks later Robertson suggested that rather than exchange consuls, as proposed by Moscow, Canada should seek to exchange ministers.[48] The cabinet accepted that proposal, and in December 1942 the assembled deputy ministers in the civil service paid tribute to Dana Wilgress, Robertson's trade negotiation partner from the 1930s and the Deputy Minister of Trade and Commerce, who was soon en route to the Soviet Union as Canada's first minister.[49] For the next three years Wilgress was one of the best Allied observers of Russia.

Robertson's major concern at this time was that Russia should survive and continue the struggle against Hitler, and to achieve this, he was even prepared to accept Moscow's prewar territorial acquisitions, or so Moffat reported. "He said that, of course, the Polish frontiers would be reserved, that nobody worried about Finland, and that Estonia, Latvia and Lithuania was a small price to pay to convince Russia of Britain's trust and earnestness." The Russians, Robertson said, kept demanding supplies without providing enough information to justify sending them. If the British and Canadian attitude to Russia's frontiers "can re-establish a relationship of mutual trust with Russia, it may mean a great saving of supplies for the common good."[50]

If Robertson sounded a naïf, he was not alone. But there was an incident in 1944 involving one of External Affairs' temporary wartime officers that suggested he could be hard-boiled and even intolerant to suspected Communists. The incident concerned Harry Ferns, a British-trained scholar with high academic qualifications, who had worked in the Prime Minister's Office and in the Department of External Affairs. The quarrelsome Ferns was rather rough-hewn and sometimes loud in his expressions of left-wing sentiments, and this, some thought, occasionally showed in his work.[51] He was summoned to see the Under-Secretary on 6 November and confronted with his indiscretions, most of which, according to his own account, he rebutted skilfully. Then Robertson altered his attack:

... Mr. Robertson asked me if I was familiar with the novels of Arthur Koestler. I said that I had read *Darkness at Noon* but apart from this I was unfamiliar with his work. Mr. Robertson suggested that I should read *Arrival and Departure* which deals in a very penetrating way with the problems of a disaffected red. I said that I did not see the relevance of this in as much as I am not a disaffected red. I said that by temperament I am catholic, and that I was only happy when my day to day work was in some way related to the larger democratic hopes of society.... Mr. Robertson remarked that a Civil Servant inevitably worked within narrow limits.[52]

Ferns could read the writing on the wall, and he knew that he was not going to be made a permanent member of the Department. His resignation followed within the month.

Robertson had always had difficulty in handling personnel questions, and it may be that he simply felt that Ferns had to go. Nonetheless, it is striking that in 1944 he used the approach he did. He was no longer the man he had been in the 1920s, and he had moved far from the attitudes and ideals that motivated him then.

Of course, by 1944 the Soviet Union had begun its obstructive tactics and was demonstrating its intention to hold on to, or to control, the Eastern European territories the Red Army had liberated. By early 1945 as well, with Wilgress absent from his post, very critical despatches on Soviet policy had begun to come from Moscow above the signature of Arnold Smith, a young wartime recruit to the Department.[53] The Russians in Ottawa were openly sniffing after atomic information, and at a party to celebrate the Japanese request for surrender terms on 14 August 1945, "Robertson said that Russia had already proposed to Canada to include uranium in lend-lease business."[54] Still, no one suspected that the Soviet Embassy in Ottawa was engaged in anything other than the normal diplomatic duties that fell to any mission.[55] An opinion poll in the spring of 1945 found that 46 percent of those sampled were confident of Canada's ability to get on with the Russians after the war, and that 34 percent were not.[56] The Russians, in so far as most Canadians were concerned, were the people who had contributed most to the victory over Hitler. They were good allies but there was little genuine trust.*

Matters altered irrevocably on 6 September 1945. Mackenzie King's account captured the moment:

Robertson and Wrong came to see me this morning . . . both looking very serious. Robertson said to me that a most terrible thing had happened. It was like a bomb on top of everything else and one could not say how serious it might be or to what it might lead. He then told me that this morning, just half an hour or so earlier, a man had turned up with his wife, at the office of the Minister of Justice. He asked to see the Minister. He said he was from the Russian Embassy. . . .

He went on to say that he had in his possession documents that he had taken from the Embassy and was prepared to give to the govt. They would be seen to disclose that Russia had her spies and secret service people in Canada and in the U.S. and were practising a species of espionage . . . he had enough evidence there to prove that instead of being friends, the Russians were really enemies.

Robertson and Wrong wondered what action to take. The Prime

---

* Robertson had one encounter with Pavlov, "the really tough guy at the Russian Embassy," that stuck in two observers' memories. The scene was a dining club for External Affairs' officers and Ottawa diplomats, to which the Russian had been invited. Pavlov "quite arrogantly began to give a little lesson on Marxism to Norman in a rather boorish fashion and Norman just took him apart and punctured him completely—The rest of us stopped talking and watched the performance. . . . Norman just with that quizzical smile of his carrying on a superb piece of dialogue." (Department of External Affairs, F.H. Soward interview, 14 Sep. 78.) Another account, dated 18 Feb. 45 by Charles Ritchie, said Pavlov (who "looks like Harpo Marx but with fanatical eyes and a false mouth") was "out to épater le bourgeois and succeeded." Robertson "was good with him—ironic, sceptical, but he brushed aside argument." (*The Siren Years* (Toronto, 1974), pp.185-86.)

Minister was sceptical about the story and concerned lest the Russians think that Canada had performed an unfriendly act. Robertson then asked if the information might not be so important to Canada, Britain and the United States that it should be seized "no matter how it was obtained." King opposed this, noting that "Robertson looked completely distraught; was so over-powered he could hardly collect his thoughts."

Igor Gouzenko, a cipher clerk at the Embassy, was thus left to wander around Ottawa seeking help with increasing desperation. Word of his movements kept filtering back to Robertson who, distraught or not, kept suggesting to the Prime Minister that the Embassy official could not be allowed to commit suicide as he was now threatening and that Canada could be a party to murder "if we allowed him to fall into the hands of the Embassy...."[57] At this juncture, fortunately, Sir William Stephenson, the head of British Security Coordination in New York and a friend of Robertson's as a result of their cooperation during the war, happened to be at the Seigniory Club in Montebello, Quebec. He was summoned to Ottawa that evening, and urged Robertson to "take him."[58]

Stephenson's advice reinforced Robertson's own inclinations. The next day, after Gouzenko's apartment had been ransacked by Soviet Embassy officials, the cipher clerk was given the opportunity of making a statement to the RCMP and the government now became officially seized of the case. The documents he had brought with him were being translated as quickly as possible, and that afternoon, 7 September, Robertson told the Prime Minister "that everything was much worse than we would have believed.... They disclose an espionage system on a large scale ... things came right into our country to a degree we could not have believed possible. He then told me that they went into our own Dept. of External Affairs, that in the cypher room there was an agent of the Russians who had seen and knew all our cyphers.... The same was true at Earnscliffe [the British High Commission] M. MacDonald's despatches were all seen, read and known. In our Research Laboratories ... where we had been working on the atomic bomb there is a scientist who is a Russian agent. In the Research Laboratories in Montreal ... there is an English scientist who is ... acting as a Russian agent." Robertson went on to say that

he had never been suspicious in his life. He felt now there was something that was real which had to be faced. What he felt most of all was that the people who were helping in this kind of thing were people supposed to be of the highest types of character. He doubted in some cases if it was at all for money. There was a sort of idealism of the Russian revolution which sought to get human rights for the masses of the people and this became a religion with some persons and they were prepared to do anything to further that movement . . . democracy in Russia is not understood by our people. It is really a Russian imperialism—an autocracy of the most desperate and wicked kind, but they are using the language of idealism and words and symbols which while being used and understood by us in one way have a different meaning to them. . . . [59]

If Robertson had been naïve before, he was so no longer.

He quickly notified MacDonald of the situation in his Chancery* and with the cooperation of Stephenson in New York, a special communications system was set up to link London, New York and Ottawa, one that bypassed suspects. [60] Similarly, the Americans were advised and Dr. C. J. Mackenzie of the National Research Council was informed of the spies in the laboratories. [61] Within days, the British had provided two trained intelligence experts, Peter Dwyer and Roger Hollis, to assist with the case [62] (since the RCMP had no such expertise), and, as they were identified, a close watch was kept on all those named in the Gouzenko documents.

What the Russians knew at this point is uncertain. On the 7th they had sent a note to the Department of External Affairs saying that Gouzenko had failed to report for work on 6 September and that after investigation it was found that he had stolen some Embassy money. The Russians' note called for "urgent measures to seek and arrest I. Gusenko and to hand him over for deportation as a capital criminal. . . ." [63] How was this to be handled? Robertson's solution was simple: he handed the matter to Laurent Beaudry, the Assistant Under-Secretary in charge of the Diplomatic Division, who was completely in the dark. With total honesty, Beaudry wrote meaningless replies for Robertson's signature, and indeed a file was set up in the Department full of correspondence between the Russians, the RCMP and the Department, all relating to the ostensible search for the missing clerk. [64]

One immediate problem was Allan Nunn May, a British atomic scientist working in Canada, and one of the people implicated in the

---

* MacDonald had given a garden party on 7 September at his residence. The Soviet Ambassador attended and asked if any little birds had whispered secrets lately, a reference to MacDonald's bird watching, or so the High Commissioner thought. His rejoinder was to ask if the Russian had caught any fish lately, actually a reference to the Ambassador's piscatorial diversions. "Too bad!," MacDonald said after the Russian shook his head. "You look as if you'd been out fishing all night. The fish can't have been biting." MacDonald learned later that day what was afoot and realized how his words had sounded. (M. MacDonald, *People and Places* (London, 1969), pp.182-83; MacDonald interview, 7 Jun. 78.)

Gouzenko documents. Nunn May was to return to Britain soon, and Robertson and Malcolm MacDonald feared that he might be able to pass his information on atomic research in North America to the Soviet Union. What could be done? Robertson's answer, as recorded by Mackenzie King, was "the passing of a special O[rder]. in C[ouncil]. very secretly which would re-enact certain clauses of the Defence of Canada regulations, so far as May was personally concerned, which would enable us to have him watched by the police and if necessary arrest him; also to see that he did not get away with papers, etc." King agreed, and the order was duly signed and locked away in Arnold Heeney's vault.[65]

A secret order of this sort was probably unprecedented. But Robertson believed it was justified by the current situation. The Soviet Union, his information had it, had seized the Kurile Islands off Japan, and both the Under-Secretary and the Prime Minister believed—on 10 September, 1945!—that if "there was another war it will come against America by way of Canada from Russia." Nunn May was scheduled to leave that weekend with papers concerning the establishment of a nuclear plant in England of which he was to be head. He had been asked, King recorded Robertson as telling him, "to give the Russians full particulars of the localities where they will be established. . . ." And courtesy of Gouzenko, the government had full details on where Nunn May was to pass his information to his contact in London.[66] In the circumstances, Robertson had no qualms about using the full power of the state to check subversion.

The impact of this affair on Robertson was very strong. As he had told King, he had been an unsuspicious man, who had assumed that the civil service as a whole took the same attitude to its work that he did. But espionage had gone on in the civil service and outside it, and this deeply shocked him, probably more so than that the Russians should have been gathering secrets. Still, he was fully aware of the need to keep the Gouzenko case quiet for fear that it would disrupt the delicate negotiations underway among the Great Powers on the manifold problems of the peace, and not least those of atomic energy. For Robertson, worn down as he was by his responsibilities, the Gouzenko case was an unwelcome added burden of incalculable weight, and he became very secretive at this stage, able to confide only in Wrong and MacDonald. It was a difficult period, and his wife attributed the loss of his good humour and the increase in the number of his deep sighs to Gouzenko and related security questions. Dealing with people's lives troubled him greatly.[67]

Worse, he knew so many of those named in the Gouzenko papers. One individual, a squadron leader in the RCAF, was the associate secretary of the Ottawa branch of the Canadian Institute of International Affairs, to which every mandarin in Ottawa belonged, as well as most of the senior officers of External Affairs and Finance. Two others were the authors of pamphlets prepared for servicemen in October and November 1945; one of those men occupied a fairly senior position in the Wartime Information Board with which Robertson had close links.[68] The spy net stretched widely, and Ottawa was still a small enough town that Robertson must have felt very uneasy as he contemplated the lists of suspects.

Later in September, at a meeting attended by the Prime Minister, the decision was made that King should go to Washington and London to convey his information on the case directly to President Truman and Prime Minister Attlee. The informal directing group was present for that decision: Robertson and Wrong, Malcolm MacDonald and his deputy, Stephen Holmes, and Charles Rivett-Carnac of the RCMP. The same men, with occasional additions from the Department of External Affairs or from the British secret service, met frequently to discuss the "Corby Case," so-called because the growing files were kept in a Corby's whiskey case by Robertson's private secretary.[69] That MacDonald was present was a recognition of the high regard in which he was held, as much as it was an awareness that there were suspects in the High Commission. Few others knew of the case; even J.W. Pickersgill, head of the Prime Minister's Office, was unaware of it.[70]

Robertson accompanied King to Washington and London. In Washington on 30 September and 1 October, King, Robertson and Pearson discussed the affair; Robertson and Pearson briefed Dean Acheson,[71] the Under-Secretary of State and a close friend of Pearson's at the time; and King saw Truman. The key event was the Canadian decision not to proceed at once with arrests, a course being urged by the British, who were anxious to get Nunn May out of circulation. "Robertson talked this over with me," King noted on 1 October, "and I agreed with him this was not the course to pursue. We must move very slowly and cautiously. We were not ready in Canada to take proceedings and our leading advisers up to the present say it would be very difficult to get a conviction on material we have considering its source." King and Robertson agreed that the proper course was to have any action agreed upon by Attlee, Truman, and the Prime Minister.[72] In effect, that was the course followed.

King and Robertson arrived in England aboard the *Queen Mary* on 7 October. Discussions there were full, Robertson coming away with the conclusion that the British were not thinking further than the simple arrest of the spies.[73] On this trip, King decided that the best thing to do was to set up a Royal Commission to investigate the whole Gouzenko affair, exactly the course that the President of the Canadian Bar Association recommended when the government sought his independent opinion.[74]

King observed in his diary that he found Robertson very cautious about the whole affair, but "quite rightly so. There cannot be too much caution." Nonetheless, King recorded that Robertson wanted the police to search the premises of those suspected, and it seems clear that in this instance caution was in the eye of the beholder. Robertson also urged King to inform the cabinet—at this point only Louis St. Laurent, the Minister of Justice, knew of the spy ring—but King demurred: "I would have to take the decisions myself. They would have to trust me as they have in the past. . . ."[75]

The Canadians were soon back in Washington for discussions with Attlee and Truman. The major focus of the talks was on atomic energy policy,* but at some point between 10 and 16 November, the procedures to be followed in the Corby case were agreed among the three countries. Certainty about these procedures is difficult because the main documents are missing; but there is an undated memorandum that sets out a draft agreement "on procedure for dealing with the 'Corby' case." The parties agreed that, while Soviet behaviour of the sort revealed by Gouzenko could not be tolerated, "it should be dealt with, nevertheless, so as to disturb as little as possible the continuance of normal diplomatic relations with the U.S.S.R.." There was also an agreement to use the case to expose "the uses to which the Soviet Government puts local Communist elements," but nothing was to be done to suggest that action was being taken for "ideological reasons." Coordinated action by the police of the three countries was scheduled to take place in the week of 25 November.[76]

But there were delays at the Americans' request,[77] and no move against those implicated in Canada came until February 1946. Even then, action was forced only by a leak in Washington. Robertson told the Prime

---

* Nothing has been said here of Robertson's important role in atomic energy policy, in part because of the complexity of the subject, but primarily because much has been written about it. The best source is Brian Villa's "Canada and Atomic Collaboration: 1941-43," a paper presented to a conference sponsored by the Canadian Committee on the History of the Second World War, Ottawa, November 1979. Professor Villa is at work on a monograph on the subject of Canada and atomic development. See also his suggestive article, "The Atomic Bomb and the Normandy Invasion," *Perspectives in American History*, XI (1977-78), 463ff.

Minister that "this business has become known to too many people," but King added that "this may be all for the best, as it gives us a special reason for starting immediately with our investigation." The decision to name a Royal Commission of two Supreme Court justices was quickly made, the cabinet was informed at last on 5 February, and the Royal Commission began its work on 6 February in secrecy.[78] No public announcement was made until 15 February.[79]

That morning the first arrests were made. Robertson had learned that the RCMP had intended to make the arrests at 3:00 a.m. but as Pickersgill, who had learned of the Gouzenko case only on 14 February, recalls, "he refused to agree to this. He said we are not going to behave like the Soviets."[80]

The arrests were made under the terms of an Order in Council passed on 6 October 1945, on the recommendation of the Minister of Justice.[81] That order, passed in the expectation that the British might act to arrest Nunn May and force Canada to act, gave the government authority to arrest the suspects and to detain them without the necessity of formal charges.[82] No one, neither St. Laurent nor King nor Robertson, was happy with that procedure, but as the Prime Minister wrote, "this whole matter is so serious that I think there will be disposition by Parliament to agree that the right course in the circumstances has been taken as the evidence is so strong."[83]

The public response in Canada and around the world to the sensational announcement of the Gouzenko case was dramatic,[84] and there was a perceptible shift in opinion that the polls soon reflected. On the evening of the announcement, as Sir Wilfred Eady, a British Treasury official, in Ottawa to negotiate the Canadian loan to England, wrote to Lord Keynes, "Norman Robertson, Clark and Towers came to dinner . . . and Norman was quite grave on the consequences of finding that public servants could have a split loyalty to their country and to C[ommunist]. P[arty]."[85]

By this point, the Royal Commission was well underway with its work, and Robertson was following its transcribed evidence very closely. He was also worrying over the possible actions the Soviet government might take in retaliation against the Canadian Embassy in Moscow,[86] and he must have been surprised when the Russians partially admitted guilt. In a statement given to the Canadian chargé, the Soviet government agreed that there had been illegal actions. "This is most unusual," the chargé reported, "and indicates that they must feel unable to refute completely evidence which will be made public by our Royal Commission."[87]

There were successes in handling the matters raised by Gouzenko's defection, but there were serious problems, too. One was that the Royal Commission hearings produced much unsubstantiated gossip. Someone knew someone who knew someone else who may have done something. Even Mackenzie King recorded in his diary on 20 February that, after reading the transcripts, he was concerned about Jewish influence in Canada, about John Grierson of the Wartime Information Board, about Alex Skelton of the Reconstruction Department, and about O.D. Skelton, dead for five years. Even Lay, his own valet, became a suspected Red in King's Commission-inspired paranoia.[88] That aspect—and King was not the only one to behave in this way—concerned Robertson.[89]

Another problem was that, aside from the evidence provided by Gouzenko and from that voluntarily supplied in confessions, there was almost nothing that would stand up in a court of law against the accused.[90] None of the Soviet spymasters could be questioned, and this was, perhaps, behind Robertson's concern that the Commission should confine its findings only to the guilt or innocence of Canadians. King disagreed, telling the government's counsel before the Commission that "unless this was accompanied by something that would disclose that our own people had been drawn into the net by the Russians, which explained their actions, the Commission would only be lending emphasis to what Russia was seeking . . . namely, that Canadians were the guilty persons and not the Russians. . . ."[91] King was right and he won his point.

Most serious perhaps was the substantial public outcry at the way the arrests had been carried out, at the authority used to justify action, and at the keeping of prisoners in solitary confinement with neither access to counsel nor right of *habeas corpus*. From Norman Robertson's point of view, these harsh measures were made necessary by the circumstances of the case, by the need to ensure that no warning reached those not yet jailed, and to prevent those arrested from getting Communist party orders not to talk.[92] So long as the suspects were held in solitary confinement, one External Affairs officer closely involved with the Royal Commission recalled, the government had successes in securing confessions. But once visitors were permitted, the suspects stopped talking.[93]

Quite properly, those considerations meant little to outraged civil libertarians. Robertson's father complained bitterly to his son;[94] there were denunciations by the Opposition in the House,[95] and there were petitions to the government from academics and others.[96] Robertson was never unaware of the concerns expressed, but in this case he was convinced that the end—the security of the state—justified the arbitrary means used.[97]

The Royal Commission issued a series of interim reports,[98] on 2, 14 and 29 March, and the final report emerged in the summer of 1946.[99] There could be no doubt that the evidence gathered by the Royal Commission substantiated the government's claim that the Soviet Union had operated a spy ring from behind the Embassy walls. There could be no doubt that several Canadians were guilty of spying for the Soviet Union, and most, it seemed clear, had been motivated by ideological conviction.[100]

Similarly, there could be no doubt that the revelations from the Gouzenko affair fed the building Western belief that the Soviet Union had changed from friend and ally into enemy. At a press conference at the East Block on 21 February, Robertson had been asked if the Russians were still allies. His reply—"Certainly"[101]—did not hide the reality, and the Gouzenko affair affected Winston Churchill in the preparation of his famous "iron curtain" speech at Fulton, Missouri.[102] The Cold War was in creation, and the Canadian government's actions against a Soviet spy ring had accelerated its coming.[103] "At the moment," the American chargé in Ottawa, Lewis Clark, reported on 7 March 1946, "the Canadians are like the brave little boy who has talked back to the bully and is wondering what is going to happen to him."[104] There was a good deal of truth in that, but it is clear that Robertson was less concerned with that aspect than that Britain, the United States and other allies should draw the proper conclusions about Soviet and domestic Communist activities. Not that Robertson wanted the subsequent trials of those named by the Royal Commission to turn into an inquest on Soviet policy. Far from it.[105] His aim, as he told the Prime Minister in June, was to "start to straighten out and re-establish, on an honest footing, our diplomatic relations with the Soviet Union,"[106] and in fact he had even wanted to give Soviet Embassy officials key sections of the Royal Commission Report in advance of its public release, so they could begin cleaning house quietly. Mackenzie King wisely had refused this suggestion.[107] But Robertson was deeply concerned that the Report receive the fullest consideration abroad, and he even became involved in details of its distribution.[108]

Despite Robertson's revulsion over the betrayal of trust by civil servants, he had no spirit of revenge in him. In August 1948, while he was posted in London at the High Commission, Robertson wrote Pearson to urge that the government consider clemency for Kathleen Wilsher, the convicted spy from Malcolm MacDonald's office. "I was, as you know, pretty closely concerned in the spy investigation, and although there was no doubt of Wilsher's guilt," he said, "I never felt that she was a vicious traitor. . . . Her confession seemed to be candid and complete. . . ." Eric Adams, the Bank of Canada employee to whom she had passed her information, had also been acquitted by the courts. Pearson was sympathetic, but the cabinet refused to consider clemency.[109] Earlier, Robertson had made an effort to intervene on behalf of John Grierson, whose name had been raised in testimony before the Royal Commission and who had been called to testify. "I am myself morally certain that he knew nothing whatever of his sometime secretary's connection with the Soviet spy ring," he wrote Pearson, "and I should be sorry to think that he felt he was suffering from it. Innocence and omniscience don't easily go together," Robertson said shrewdly of the brilliant Briton who had developed the National Film Board into a great organization, "and John finds it very hard to accept the fact that his secretary never told him she was sleeping with Fred Rose," the Labour-Progressive Party Member of Parliament from Montreal, who was deeply involved in the spying.[110]

Of great importance, too, was the effect of the Gouzenko disclosures on the intelligence-gathering role that Canada assumed. During the war, at Robertson's request, the National Research Council had established the Examination Unit, a cryptographic group whose initial task was to intercept and decode messages to and from the Vichy legation in Ottawa.[111] Vichy was suspected of propaganda activities in Quebec, and the interception of the legation's messages seemed the only way to ascertain what, if any, information was being passed from Canada to France.[112]

The major figures from External Affairs who took part in the Unit's work and in other intelligence questions were Pearson (until his posting to Washington in mid-1942), T.A. Stone, and George Glazebrook. Robertson was kept informed, but essentially, Glazebrook remembered, he had little to do directly with intelligence gathering.[113] The Prime Minister similarly kept his distance, not wanting to know, so he could not answer if asked, and he was more than willing to have the Under-Secretary assume the responsibility. The method of operation then was that Stone and Glazebrook saw Robertson to seek his permission to do some particular job. Robertson offered his comments, almost always helpful, and assented or refused. Nothing was written down. Intelligence, said Glazebrook, "is handled like no other subject. It's purely personal and almost entirely oral."[114]

By February 1945 the Examination Unit's future was in some doubt. On 19 February, Robertson and Glazebrook met Dr. Mackenzie of the

National Research Council "re the future of the Examination Unit. We had a very general discussion," Mackenzie noted, "and probably will cut down the size of this commitment later on."[115] The Gouzenko affair intervened to alter that intent, and in December 1945 Robertson, Wrong, Glazebrook, General Charles Foulkes and Mackenzie discussed the Unit again. "It was agreed to carry on,"[116] Mackenzie noted in his diary. The Chiefs of Staff Committee soon concurred, and one hundred high-speed monitoring positions (and almost 500 servicemen) were allocated to this work.[117] It was obvious that Robertson must have received the Prime Minister's permission to proceed; it was also certain that the decision to continue intercepting embassy wireless traffic was primarily directed at the Soviet Union.[118]

The Gouzenko case also had a considerable effect on the development of government security procedures. Robertson played a key role in their design, proposing a set-up fairly close to the British model, in contradistinction to the Canadian military's penchant for an elaborate American system.[119] Robertson's proposals, offered early in the spring of 1946 after consultation with George Glazebrook and G.G. Crean of his Department's security and intelligence section, were that security questions be separated from intelligence, and that an interdepartmental committee of an advisory nature be set up under the control of the Privy Council Office. Robertson looked to the appointment of departmental security officers "who would be responsible to their Minister" for measures recommended by the Security Panel, his suggested interdepartmental committee.[120] The intent clearly was to keep security questions close by the Department of External Affairs and as far away from National Defence as possible. The suggestion of Privy Council Office control did that.

Robertson's proposals were accepted by the government, and by the late summer of 1946, for the first time, efforts were beginning to be made to organize security procedures. A book setting out security policies was being readied for departmental use, and the Security Panel had begun to wrestle with the difficult problem of "vetting" personnel: considering "security measures which would be practical to prevent the infiltration into positions of trust under the government of persons likely to commit acts such as those in the [Royal Commission] Report."[121] The Security Panel soon recommended that the RCMP investigate the "antecedents of applicants for government employment to determine their suitability from a security point of view,"[122] and on 16 January 1947, the cabinet approved the Panel's recommendations.[123]

Thus the Gouzenko affair had forced Norman Robertson and the government he served far away from the attitudes of the innocent days before September 1945. Security now was a crucial matter, and ideological convictions could be deemed reason enough to bar someone from government work. Robertson could not have been very happy with such a state of affairs, but after Gouzenko, he had no doubts of its necessity.

CHAPTER VII
Administering External Affairs

As UNDER-SECRETARY OF State for External Affairs, Norman Robertson had to initiate and coordinate the work of his Department. This meant that, while he often did not have the time to direct personally the work of his officers on matters of particular interest to himself, nonetheless he had the responsibility for all that was produced. His task was to facilitate the work, to harmonize it with government policy and if necessary to sell it to other departments through interdepartmental committees, and to present it to the political executive. Some aspects of this role he did very well indeed; others were less successful.

He was well aware that administration was not his forte. Some, perhaps all, of his colleagues realized this as well. But as Under-Secretary, it was something he could not avoid, and administrative and personnel questions bedevilled him and absorbed more of his time and energy than he could afford. Regrettably, the results for the expended effort were less than they should have been.

I

The Department of External Affairs had never been well administered. So long as the Prime Minister was also the Secretary of State for External Affairs, so long as Dr. Skelton continued to allow administrative questions to take second place, so long did the Department remain rather slapdash in its methods. Robertson himself was well aware of this, but administrative questions had only rarely concerned him in the 1930s.

In 1936, however, just after he had returned from a trade negotiation trip to England, Robertson had written Lester Pearson an abject note of apology for "our new low in inept and pusillanimous instructions" on a subject being handled by the High Commission in London. "It is a personal apology," he added, for he had just drafted the instructions himself, "half a day late into the bargain," and he knew how the High Commission was going to react to them. There was nothing he could do about the content of those instructions since that was the doing of Skelton and King. Nor was there much he could have done about the delay, for the blame there, he said, lay with the other departments that had an interest in the matter. All he could suggest to Pearson was that Canada House "help to clear up the general mess" by collating "the various unanswered despatches" and presenting the Department "with an ultimatum on the subject."[1]

The blame for that muddle, and a hundred more, lay with the Prime Minister and the Under-Secretary. King was too busy to devote much time to the mundane affairs of the Department, and requests and queries sometimes sat on his desk for months without response. Still, it was Skelton who took the rap for the state of the Department, and certainly there were critics galore to denounce him for his administrative incompetence, his inability to delegate, and the "normal haphazard way" he allowed his Department to operate.[2] For all its able officers, unquestionably the best group of civil servants in the entire bureaucracy, External Affairs was no model of efficiency.

The war compounded all the problems. In 1940, there were only 44 officers and 328 staff to handle a hugely increased workload at home and overseas.[3] The next year, Pearson pointed out that the East Block staff had had a net gain of four senior officers since the beginning of the war, but two, Robertson and Hugh Keenleyside, were less available for routine work; and a net gain of four juniors, three of whom were very junior indeed.[4] Moreover, the work had grown, as a few simple statistics demonstrated. In 1939, the High Commission in London sent 84 bags and 1,660 telegrams to Ottawa; in 1940, it forwarded 246 bags and 2,464 cables. In the same years the cypher section in the Department handled 388,899 and 1,008,605 "telegraphic groups."[5]

Hardest to bear was the Treasury Board ruling that the Department did not qualify for the benefits conferred on "a unit engaged exclusively in war work," a measure that hurt External Affairs in the scramble for scarce accommodation and supplies, and that largely left salaries, promotions and reclassifications of positions frozen.[6] Inevitably the Department lost some of its better clerical staff, and inevitably the result was delay, a factor that had been complicated by Skelton's insistence on overseeing everything and by his refusal to streamline the organization of the Department into functional divisions. T.A. Stone, working in the East Block since he had rejoined the Department in September 1939, told Vincent Massey, the High Commissioner in London, that "As I dig into the files ... I discover each day some delayed action which must be a cause of embarrassment to you over there. It is not that we are not working at this end—there are just not enough of us to get the jobs done and the jobs are not well enough organized among those of us who are here."[7]

The problems were exacerbated by the increasing pressure to create new legations abroad. The war had forced the closing of missions in Paris, The Hague, Brussels, and Geneva. But the war led to the need for a consul in Greenland, for representatives to the Allied governments-in-exile in London, for some recognition of the growing political and economic importance of South America, and for increased staff in London and Washington.[8] Furthermore, other countries were pressing to send missions to Canada: Norway, Sweden, Yugoslavia, China, Mexico and others.[9] Proposals of that sort were embarrassing, because Canada did not wish to receive missions without reciprocating, and that seemed impossible without a major increase in the External Affairs complement. But there were few senior officers to head missions, difficulties in bringing in outsiders as ministers, and even in providing enough first, second and third secretaries.[10]

This was the situation when power passed to Norman Robertson in January 1941. The most urgent need was to restructure the operating elements of the Department and to move away from what Keenleyside described as organization on a "personal basis. When an Officer has returned or has been appointed to the Department, the tendency has been to look around for unassigned work or work in which little interest was being taken and transfer it to the new arrival. The result," Keenleyside said in a draft paper on Departmental reorganization that he prepared in March 1941, "has been that the division of duties has lacked form, specification, clarity and continuity."[11] Keenleyside's proposal attempted to substitute rationality for this hit-and-miss system, putting officers into divisions with responsibility for functions or for different parts of the world, and creating assistant under-secretaries to direct the work and report to the Under-Secretary.

Keenleyside's plan was a good one, and Robertson was not averse to proceeding in the suggested direction. But there was no push behind his desire to reorganize and, as Keenleyside noted in his diary, after going along with the proposal at first, Robertson now seemed anxious and distracted, unable to make decisions or discuss organizational matters. He was fagged out, Keenleyside said, and the strain under which Robertson was working made things difficult for everyone.[12]

L. B. Pearson, on his return to Ottawa in May 1941, reached roughly similar conclusions, although he was more willing than Keenleyside to place the blame for delayed reorganization where it belonged:

[the Department] is a hive of unorganized activity—the senior men are so busy that they haven't time ... to delegate the work to juniors who are, in consequence, not busy enough. Robertson has fallen right into the shoes of Dr. Skelton in more ways than one; I mean he is being asked by the Prime Minister to do far more than any one man can do effectively, and, therefore, other things— with which the Prime Minister is not immediately concerned—are not being done at all. I find, however, that a very real and sincere attempt is being made to reorganize the Department. ... I am not sanguine, however, that this scheme will achieve the decentralisation essential for the speedy and effective conduct of departmental work. There are two obstacles which, I am afraid, will prove insuperable. First, the Prime Minister's insistence on dealing with one person and one person only, the Under-Secretary, on every matter, great and small. Secondly, the necessity under the present system of getting the Prime Minister's approval for practically every step—diplomatic, administrative or political— which the Department desires to take. When the Prime Minister's approval has to be secured before a telephone extension can be installed and when the channel for securing that approval must always ... be the Under-Secretary, you will appreciate that any effective reform of Departmental organization and methods is difficult, if not impossible.[13]

But by July 1941 Robertson had at last, and after much difficulty, persuaded Mackenzie King to go ahead with Keenleyside's suggested organization,[14] and on the 12th letters were despatched to explain the new structure, to take effect on 5 August.[15] The Department was to have four divisions, each headed by an assistant under-secretary or the equivalent: Diplomatic and Commercial Division under Laurent Beaudry; Legal Division under John Read; Commonwealth and European Division under Pearson; and American and Far East Division under Keenleyside.[16] (Later, in June 1942, an Economic Section was established, with three officers.)[17] If the organization sounded grandiose, the numbers involved quickly brought it into perspective: there were five officers in three divisions and four in the other, and only a few loose fish were unassigned. But at least the reorganization had been accomplished;[18] there was an attempt to give the divisions some responsibility, and efforts were made to obviate the necessity of having every piece of paper come before the Under-Secretary. And in the eventual placing of, first, Saul Rae, a young officer with a University of London PhD and impressive expertise in the new science of public opinion sampling, and after him, of Gordon Robertson, one of the ablest young recruits, in Robertson's office as special assistant to the Under-Secretary, there was an attempt to channel, if not interrupt, the flow of visitors and paper.[19] It was almost enough to justify Grant Dexter's comment in the *Winnipeg Free Press*: "the department takes definite form as a foreign office ... the youngsters are now achieving the place which, from the beginning, Dr. Skelton had marked out for them."[20]

But if the fundamental organizational structure had been set, there were still problems, as a long memorandum from Pearson to Robertson made clear in October 1941. There were difficulties with some of the temporary third secretaries, there was a need for wartime emergency appointments to help handle the work—men such as H.F. Angus from the University of British Columbia, already on staff in the Department, and George Glazebrook from the University of Toronto's history department. Women officers could be brought in for the first time to do much of the work now done by third secretaries, and there was a desperate need for a senior administrative officer from outside the service. "I can think of no more important single step to increase Departmental efficiency," Pearson said, noting that "the fundamental weakness of our departmental organization is shown by the fact that I have to write you about matters like this. There should be some one to relieve you of this side of the work....Personally," he added, "I don't see how you are going to show the Prime Minister how to win the war and make the peace if you have to spend two hours each day talking about the cost of ... table linen or the salary of the newest stenographer."[21] Pearson's suggestions were largely accepted, he wrote to London, but there were still the difficulties with the Prime Minister. "Glazebrook had agreed to come, the University has agreed, Norman R. has agreed, but, it's the old story, the P.M. hasn't yet had time to consider the matter."[22]

It was always that way. As the minister, King was as responsible for the operation of his department, as was Howe for the Department of Munitions and Supply. In theory. But, in practice, King was too busy overseeing the operation of the war, the cabinet, and the Liberal party to pay much attention to the problems of External Affairs. In effect, then, Robertson became a quasi-minister, filling a near ministerial role in his relations with the Prime Minister, different from other ministers only in that he lacked a political base.[23] This forced him into acting almost ministerially toward the Department, and it probably explains some of Robertson's caution, as well as his insistence that (except for Hume Wrong), he should be the sole channel of communication between the Department and King.[24]

The relationship with King was difficult and often uneasy, mainly because the Prime Minister did not, and could not, take the time to discuss Departmental matters. Pierrepont Moffat recorded in August 1942 that "Robertson after waiting the better part of two months was at last being given his 'so-called' annual afternoon at Kingsmere with the Prime Minister to thrash out various problems connected with the Department...."[25] That was simply not good enough, and this difficulty explains much about the state of Departmental administration, the delayed appointments, and the unhappiness over petty matters.

On the other hand, when King had some particularly demeaning chore for Robertson, he wanted it done immediately. In April 1941, to cite a single case, the Prime Minister was preparing to go to Washington for important talks with President Roosevelt about Canada's declining holdings of American dollar exchange. Busy as he was, King still had time for petty details, as a Department of State memorandum records:

Mr. Robertson said that Mr. King felt that it would be necessary for him to travel in his private car....Mr. Robertson said that he had tried to dissuade the Prime Minister pointing out that there would certainly be some criticism because of the amount of foreign exchange which the Canadian Government would have to provide in order to pay for this. He said that Mr. King felt that it was essential however that he travel in the private car and that he therefore would appreciate it if Mr. Moffat would find out for him how much the charges would amount to. In the course of the conversation Mr. Robertson took occasion to refer to the fact that the Prime Minister was accepting an invitation from the President....

... Obviously Mr. Robertson's inquiry is a delicate way of asking us to pay for the transportation of his private car in the United States. He of course knew how much it would cost....[26]

Reluctantly, the Americans paid. But how degrading for Robertson to have to go through that charade for $1,200!

Another major obstacle to progress was Agnes McCloskey, the effective administrative head of the Department, even though she was technically an accountant. McCloskey had been in the Department since 1909, she had had great influence with Skelton, and she played a major role in determining personnel and pay policy. Charles Ritchie called her "our female Talleyrand," and Pearson noted in April 1942 that her "sun shows no sign of setting." McCloskey could still "block any proposal to abandon peacetime methods of recruitment," and she forced Pearson to spend too much time on administrative work. "It's the same with Norman—it's pathetic to see him involved in some trifling detail concerning a stenographer's overtime—because the redoubtable Agnes—who won't give up an ounce of her power—shares her petty problems with the head of the Department, who feels himself unable to take the necessary steps by restoring the McCloskey to her rightful duties as an accountant and nothing else."[27]

It was all too true, and there was little doubt that Robertson could not cope with McCloskey (or female employees in general, despite the bachelor George Glazebrook's advice that all he needed was a Kleenex and a cigarette to survive). Indeed, he was no administrator at all. One British observer said he operated in a "most muddled way"; a colleague called him a terrible organizer.[28] Worse, word of the administrative problems was leaking out and had come to the attention of Dexter of the *Winnipeg Free Press*. In a letter to Winnipeg, Dexter said that "The department seems to have slipped badly the past few months. I've tried to find out what is amiss....The explanation seems to be that the department lacks decision. Norman cannot make up his mind."[29]

There was some truth in that. By choice, Robertson had turned himself into a deliberate, cautious man, from whom decisions ordinarily flowed very slowly. "The temperament of the natural Civil Servant," says Compton Mackenzie in his *The Red Tapeworm*, "is not one that lends itself to adventure,"[30] and Robertson was suspicious of the facility with which someone like Escott Reid, for example, produced innumerable ideas and long, detailed memoranda. Those lay for months in one of his overflowing "in" baskets or were put in the heap of files that spilled over the top of his desk.[31] Those heaped dossiers—Robertson called them his "visible filing system"—were full of the problems he hated, full of personnel wrangles, full of intractable diplomatic questions that defied ready response.[32] His philosophy allowed for this, however, and while he knew where everything was, he was convinced that many problems, given enough time, simply disappeared, while others were ameliorated by creative delay. That was often correct, but it did not seem decisive, and certainly no one looking into Robertson's office could believe that its condition reflected an organized man. Part of the problem, of course, was that he was spread too thinly, serving on too many committees, doing too much.[33] On one occasion when he asked H.F. Angus to handle a job "you could do as well as I,", Angus replied that "if I couldn't I would shoot myself as I'd be giving it my full attention and you'd be tackling it on the fringes of yours."[34]

Robertson also could not bring himself to work with the press and had little patience for the representational role that his office demanded. There was no rule on speechmaking, he told somebody in the Prime Minister's Office in December 1941. "I find this responsibility most easily discharged by simply refusing to make any speeches to any group on any subject."[35] In his fixed and unchanging view, a civil servant had to stay out of the limelight, and he took a great joy in a photograph that appeared in a Quebec newspaper during the Quebec Conference of 1944, identifying him only as "un fonctionnaire inconnu." That was the role he sought for himself, and clearly he preferred the practice of diplomacy in quiet, as far away as possible from journalists and the public. But when he had to deal with newspapermen, he was sometimes maladroit. On 30 October 1942, for example, he actually wired a number of important dailies and asked them not to speculate on diplomatic appointments. George Ferguson of the *Winnipeg Free Press*, an old friend, calmly replied that the best way to avoid speculation was to make appointments promptly.[36] Austin Cross, an Ottawa Press Gallery member, was blunter, telling Robertson that the press was not "a lot of ninnies who must come to heel every time you ask us. Had you played ball with the press, this would never have happened. . . .I think you ought to review your whole position. . . .It has been exasperating, unfair and unsatisfactory." Furthermore, Cross went on, Robertson's press conferences, infrequent as they were, "resulted in a lot of nothings. Mike Pearson had the right idea, but of course he was sent away [to Washington in May 1942]. But the boys here all had a good word to say about him and his methods, which you might well emulate if you can which I doubt."[37] Robertson knew that he could not match Pearson's bonhomie and charm, and his press conferences were a bore.[38] The difficulty was that it was King who could not make up his mind about appointments and that, with a few exceptions—Grant Dexter, Blair Fraser, Ken Wilson—Robertson considered newsmen to be both uninformed and often untrustworthy.[39] There were never many leaks from Norman Robertson.

By the end of 1942, therefore, his policy problems and administrative incapacity had combined to convince Robertson that he was in the wrong job. He had tentatively tried to suggest this to Mackenzie King during a long walk in November, one that, King noted, had settled many problems. "The worst remains to be settled, namely, a much too great pressure on Robertson himself, inadequate staff in his office as well as in mine. Gave him authority to use some of the money provided by Parliament for entertaining guests, when persons here on diplomatic missions, whom it is necessary for him to see." King added, almost certainly missing the point of the appeal that Robertson mutely had made to him, that "It is really shameful the burden we have been throwing on our staffs . . . far beyond their capacity to bear."[40] King had heard little of what Robertson was saying, so the next month he drafted a letter to send to the Prime Minister. "I have come to the conclusion that [the Under-Secretary's] job is not one which I am cut out to do satisfactorily," he wrote. "It is in large and growing measure, an administrative post, requiring qualities of temperament and character which I, unfortunately, lack." He had thought of putting Hume Wrong in charge of administrative matters, but that, he had decided, was both unfair and unworkable. "I believe I can be a more useful member of the public service in an advisory than in an executive capacity. In that role I think I could continue to be of help to you and to my successor."[41] What finally provoked this draft is unclear; similarly, there is no evidence to suggest the reasons why Robertson in the end did not send it.

Significantly, however, some of the Department's officers were increasingly fed up at this juncture, although not primarily with Robertson. He was revered by most of his officers, despite the administrative chaos around him, and disliked by none. But there was much rage over Robertson's continued inability to counter the tyranny exercised by Agnes McCloskey on personnel matters.[42] At last, in desperation (or so one officer remembers), a delegation called on Robertson early in 1943 to demand action. The Under-Secretary was placatory, but he did tell the group that his resignation was in his desk drawer.[43] Still, this must have impelled him to action, for within a short time, he had finally promoted McCloskey up and out of the Department, sending her as consul to the Consulate-General in New York City on 8 April. The news was greeted with cheers. In Washington, Pearson noted in his diary that "For anyone who has had to pry expense accounts out of her, the significance of this move will be obvious. In the Legation, it overshadowed all the war news; even the advance of the 8th Army had to take second place." To handle administration, Robertson brought in W. Donald Matthews from the Foreign Exchange Control Board on 19 April.[44] A Toronto lawyer and broker, Matthews proved very effective.

Unfortunately, and despite Matthews's good work, the problems continued to pile up. Robertson's executive assistants—John Holmes, George Ignatieff, Jean Chapdelaine and John Starnes followed Saul Rae and Gordon Robertson in the post—tried to form a "Reserve line of defence against visitors" and calls, but too often the trenches were breached.[45] Robertson's personal files were handled by Marjorie McKenzie,* the Department's principal clerk, and Sybil Rump, his private secretary, gave first-class assistance, but the work continued to outpace the workers.[46]

Thus in December 1943, Hugh Keenleyside became enraged by the way in which what he saw as Robertson's administrative incompetence had adversely affected a bargaining session with the United States on the fisheries. With a weak case, the Americans had got full support from Washington, while Canada, despite the strength of its position, received no help from the East Block. Robertson, he wrote in a white heat, was the worst administrator he had ever seen. He did not keep appointments, he had no time to discuss questions adequately, he failed to return telephone calls promptly despite promises to do so, and he was unable to make decisions or to get King to do so.[47]** Robertson's feeble justification would have been that he had too little assistance to do the work that had to be done, and by late 1943, as wartime conferences proliferated, many of his best people were away for long periods. "Norman R. was muttering over the telephone yesterday," Pearson wrote to Vincent Massey, "that it was time some of his globe trotters came back to Ottawa and helped bear the really terrific burden there."[48]

One who had returned to Ottawa was Hume Wrong. He was far more adept at administration than the Under-Secretary, and took much of the load off Robertson's shoulders, as well as assuming more than his full share

*When Miss McKenzie died in 1957, Robertson wrote to George Glazebrook about "her jealous custody of the most secret papers long before security was our watchword. Security in those days simply meant that Miss McKenzie looked after whatever had to be kept secret." He added that one set of files comprised "the most secret telegrams exchanged between Ottawa and London from the days of Munich on, which Miss McKenzie grouped under the general heading 'Appeasement' and her file on 'Appeasement Part 3' began with the declaration of war on September 3, 1939." (Mrs. N. A. Robertson Papers, Robertson to George Glazebrook, 19 Dec. 57.)

**Another example: "Your letter [dated 2 July] . . . I have just recovered from the depths of one of Norman's baskets. After I had read it and your memorandum, I passed both to Norman and Hume 'to see and return'. Eventually it ended up at Norman's house and only after great searching was it turned up by Jetty and delivered to me last Saturday." (PAC, A.D.P. Heeney Papers, vol. 1, Clerk of Privy Council file, Heeney to Sir Shuldham Redfern, 22 Oct. 45.)

of policy questions. So well did they work together and so impressed did Robertson become with Wrong's ability, that in July 1944 he had him made Associate Under-Secretary, and in November of that year tried to persuade the Prime Minister to make Wrong Under-Secretary, while he took second spot for a few years. King recorded: "He has a difficult problem there as Wrong is senior in many ways. I do not think, however, that this change can possibly be made."[49] A few years earlier, King would have blocked such a move simply on the grounds that he found Wrong impossible to work with, but even that was no longer true. King later told Wrong in complete honesty "how important he was and confidence the govt. had in him, . . . "[50] and in December 1944 he agreed to Robertson's request that Wrong should be paid the same salary as the Under-Secretary.[51]

With Robertson's blessing, Wrong began to look at methods of dealing with the growth of the Department and its almost exponential rate of increase in workload.* By late 1943, for example, there were fourteen new missions open abroad, and more still were certain to be needed after the liberation of Europe. (In January 1945, there were twenty foreign posts.) In addition, twenty nations had representatives in Ottawa, an increase from five before the war.[52] That meant more work and a need for more senior personnel, and the Department still had very few officers. A memo by Wrong noted that, in 1939, the Department's business in Ottawa had been handled by about a dozen officers. "The comparable figure today is about thirty," he said. Of that number, eight were third secretaries (most temporary) and nine special assistants, largely from the universities.** Indeed, the total officer strength in Canada and abroad was only about fifty, again including a dozen or so third secretaries who had not been made permanent. Clearly a rapid expansion of numbers was essential if the Department was to cope. In Wrong's view, at least 115

---

*One concern was to make more efficient the representation of Canada abroad for commercial purposes, something that was difficult because of the weakness of the Trade and Commerce Department in general and its Commercial Intelligence Service and trade commissioners in particular. The result, after study by an interdepartmental committee in 1943, was proposals for coordination and administrative reform and not, as some hoped, for External Affairs to swallow the CIS. (Docs. on Department of External Affairs, file 2446-A-40; King Papers, Memo for Prime Minister, 25 Mar. 42.)

**These were Robertson's "embodied Territorials", as he called them (June Wrong Rogers Papers (Ottawa), Angus to Wrong, 22 Jan. 53); many were historians. "I found a historian in almost every room working away like mad on contemporary affairs," wrote George Brown of the University of Toronto to a friend in the army. "I told them it was the officers were necessary and "Obviously, we have reached a stage where long-term planning and the development of new methods is absolutely essential."[53]

Wrong's paper made an irrefutable case, and in spring 1944 the decision was made to recruit 32 new Foreign Service Officers, all from the armed forces, by 31 December 1945.[54] On Robertson's initiative, recruiting teams were sent overseas to interview and select personnel, and the men were demobilized and enrolled in the Service as quickly as possible.[55] This was, F.H. Soward recalled, "one of the most far-seeing things the Department did in my day...."[56] At the same time, the Department tried to persuade some of the wartime temporaries to stay on. The Department, wrote R.G. Riddell, a wartime officer who had been a History professor at the University of Toronto, "is preparing a list of temporary people whom they wish to have appointed permanently." That was appealing to Riddell, a very able man, and he added: "The chance to be in on the Mezzanine if not the Ground Floor of this expanding Department at the present moment... looks pretty good."[57] But because of Civil Service Commission regulations,[58] there were difficulties in getting such appointments approved, and in March 1945, with his position still in limbo and facing the necessity of telling his university of his plans, Riddell finally saw Robertson. "When I had finished," Riddell wrote, Robertson said the "matter may settle itself automatically." That was little help for Riddell, who did not appreciate Robertson's "creative delay" and he soon found himself in a position "in which I'll be rather badly squeezed."[59] But in fact, Robertson resolved matters and Riddell stayed. So, too, did John Holmes, George Magann and W.D. Matthews, and although academics such as Glazebrook and R.A. MacKay left at the war's end, they were soon back in the Department full-time. The quality of the officers who joined in Robertson's time was very high indeed, and if Skelton properly gets credit for his recruiting successes, so too should Robertson.

The new men had to be properly trained and paid, and as the war went on, Robertson tried to cover both aspects. In December 1943, he established a committee to review the scale of allowances, long a sore point.[60] He waged a battle against the Department of Finance's efforts to tax diplomats serving abroad, arguing to some effect that their allowances

historians' Babylonian captivity." (University of Toronto Library, G.W. Brown Papers, box 23, Brown to Stacey, 3 Feb. 44. See also F.H. Soward, "Inside a Canadian Triangle: the university, the C.I.I.A. and the Department of External Affairs...," *International Journal*, XXXIII (Winter, 1977-78). There is a list of the "territorials" in PAC, External Affairs Records, vol. 678, file 136, "Members of the Staff...," n.d.)

were already so low that they could barely do their job.[61] From 1944 onwards, the "University of the East Block," a lecture series for new officers, helped integrate new and old. Robertson, for example, had the new men to his home on 20 December 1945 and spoke on "International Trade and Commercial Relations."[62]

There was also, from 24 January 1945, a new Department organization that attempted to finetune the 1941 model. Under Robertson and Wrong as Under-Secretary and Associate, there would now be eight divisions: Diplomatic, under Beaudry; Economic, under Angus; Information, under T.W.L. MacDermot; First Political (responsible for international organization), under Charles Ritchie after his return from England; Second Political, under George Glazebrook (and responsible for Commonwealth, European, Middle Eastern and African affairs, and security and intelligence matters); Third Political, under R.M. Macdonnell (responsible for America, South America, and the Far East); Legal, under Read; and Special Division under Robertson's old UBC friend Alfred Rive (responsible, *inter alia*, for prisoners of war). The political divisions reported to Wrong, the others to Robertson; Matthews, as Chief Administrative Officer, reported directly to Robertson.[63]

That seemed a good paper structure, and one that reflected some of the new realities—the need for public information, for example. But in some ways (and particularly because Matthews was ill for much of 1946) little changed. Charles Ritchie wrote to London that he knew the traditional line was that he should be too busy to write. "But my case is somewhat different—I have been completely disorganized since I arrived—trying to find out what my work is to be, to get settled down in an office, to get a Secretary, to get a Liquor Permit, to get some overshoes and above all to get a roof over my head."[64] Some of those problems were out of Robertson's control, but only some, and soon Ritchie would be caught up in the work and swamped like the others.[65] One effort, one useful effort, to ensure that Division heads got a complete picture was the idea of weekly heads of division meetings. The intent was more to share information than discuss policy, and soon the sessions had become known as Robertson's "prayer meetings."[66]

Thus by 1946, Robertson had overseen the beginnings of a well-organized Department. There was a far better administrative element than when he took office in 1941; there was a divisional organization and a realistic sharing of duties; and there was better administration of missions abroad. But the improvements were only relative, and the rapid growth had left the Department gasping in its efforts to keep pace.

Pearson had the task of making such changes as seemed necessary when he took over in the fall of 1946,[67] but in fact External Affairs was never truly efficient until Arnold Heeney took over as Under-Secretary in 1949 and the period of rapid expansion ended. Then at last the trains ran on time.

II

Norman Robertson's position as Under-Secretary was a permanent one, or as permanent as he wished it to be. Skelton had held the post from his appointment to his death, and, if he had wanted it, it was Robertson's for his working life. But was this the best way to run the Department of External Affairs? And could his health stand the strain after the years of war?

Those were the questions that must have been running through his mind from late 1944 on. The diplomatic service had grown rapidly, and the nation's quantum jump in influence and power had been incredible. External Affairs represented Canada abroad, and the service had both shaped this new prestige and benefited from it. The capstone was perhaps Pearson's appointment as Ambassador in Washington in late 1944, the first time a senior post abroad had been filled from the long-time officials of the Department.[68] From Robertson's point of view, the key factor was that, in Hume Wrong and Pearson, there were two men eminently qualified to be Under-Secretary. Wrong, he believed and told the Prime Minister, was the ablest man in the Department, and Pearson too was a star: "His judgment is good, he is a hard worker, and one of the best liked men I know."[69] He could have no qualms about leaving External Affairs in either man's care, and from November 1944, at least, he was apparently thinking of the prospect of a posting abroad.[70]

That prospect did not become a real one until February 1946 when Vincent Massey indicated his desire to return to Canada after his decade-long stint at the High Commission in London.[71] The premier position in the service was soon to be vacant, and Robertson could have it if he wanted. Such was Mackenzie King's immediate response: "Robertson is entitled to the preference if he wishes it. It would be hard to refuse him."[72] Certainly by this stage Robertson was worn out, his health becoming precarious. The Gouzenko affair had preoccupied him for months, and there was no sign in February 1946 of any immediate let-up there. The problems of peacemaking had replaced the problems of war and were proving just as intractable. And the workload continued to grow. In May 1946, for example, King noted Robertson's relief that the Canadian party for the Prime Ministers' meetings in London was to include J.W. Pickersgill and James Gibson as well as himself. "The truth is," King noted with an uncharacteristic concern for his officials, "Robertson himself has become completely swamped."[73] And Pickersgill, worried about his friend's condition, told Mackenzie King: "you are not going to have Norman Robertson here very much longer because he is so tired out that his health is going to break down unless he has an easier job."[74]

Undoubtedly this worried King. But if he was concerned about Robertson's health, the Prime Minister also worried about his own, about whether he should try any longer to hang on as Secretary of State for External Affairs and as Prime Minister, as well as about the difficulties of finding another Under-Secretary, one with whom he could work as easily and effectively as he had with Robertson. The two men finally talked about Departmental matters in London on 12 June:

... I had a talk with Robertson alone about E.A. Told him I thought Pearson would be the best man for London unless he wished to go there himself. He said that would raise the question of Wrong's going to Washington and he did not feel equal to managing without Wrong. He himself would like to go to some small place like Switzerland or Dublin. I told him that would be quite wrong; in his present position he would have to take one of the larger posts if he left Ottawa but would not find that difficult seeing that the main problem was to have to do so many different things and not concentrate on any one. He would find Washington quite simple but would be nearer to Ottawa. I said that would leave Wrong in charge in Ottawa.[75]

The Prime Minister was certainly correct in his assessment of the relative ease of handling even such a very large diplomatic establishment as Washington or London, in comparison to the East Block task. Perhaps Wilgress could take London? King suggested.[76] Robertson pondered this for a few days and then cast doubt on it. Dana Wilgress, who had done so well in Moscow, was better on paper than in conversation, a drawback in London, where the need was "to have the general Canadian position in relation to the United Kingdom, the rest of the Commonwealth and the United States more clearly understood in policy making circles than it is now."[77] Intentionally or not, Robertson was painting a role for the new High Commissioner that he was best able to fill, even though his memo suggested Wrong or Pearson for the post.

At the same time, Robertson sent the Prime Minister a careful memorandum on the Department's need for a minister of its own. There was an unusually high proportion of senior officials in External Affairs, questions of recruitment, promotion and transfer were delicate and important, and the number of administrative decisions involving the securing and furnishing of suitable offices abroad for the expanding foreign service was sure to increase. That last type of problem, one on which King always felt vulnerable to Opposition harassment in the House of Commons, was something King detested. On the other hand, "considerations of general policy argue pretty strongly for continuing to combine the posts of Prime Minister and Secretary of State for External Affairs." The central Commonwealth link was the exchange of views between Prime Ministers, "and major policy questions would continue to be handled this way, regardless of whether we had a separate Departmental Minister." Clearly the Prime Minister had to supervise "very closely" the general conduct of external relations, even if he were assisted by a separate minister. The solution, Robertson suggested, might be to appoint "one of the abler, younger men" to the post, giving him much of the administrative work and a certain amount of attendance at conferences, while still allowing the Prime Minister to meet his special responsibilities.[78]

That was a clever tack, one that let Robertson advance the goal he sought of a separate minister, while simultaneously indicating that he was in no way pressing King to step aside. But neither issue was resolved, and when the Prime Minister returned to Ottawa at the end of June, he talked with Pearson about his future. The Ambassador to the United States, King wrote, was "quite prepared ... to do whatever I may think best, either to stay at Washington, come to Ottawa, go to London, or elsewhere. He admits that, for him, London would represent the highest post of all and he would greatly welcome going there." That was certainly true.[79] Pearson added, or so King recorded, that "He is greatly concerned ... about Robertson. He realizes that he is very tired and a little at a loss to know what decision to make respecting himself."[80] In effect, Pearson was putting in his claim for the London post.

On 5 July, King and Robertson talked again about the postings and King was surprised to discover that Robertson was "disappointed" over the results of the Prime Minister's talk with Pearson.

I asked what had occasioned his disappointment. He said that he himself would have liked London. I said immediately to him that I had from the beginning told him that whatever post he wanted, he could have, mentioning London specifically.

King wrote in his diary that he thought Pearson and Robertson had been discussing this matter between themselves, that Robertson had indicated to Pearson that, "while he would have liked London for some reasons, he would not care for public appearances and public speaking which would be expected in London, but even more he would not like to give up the great position which he now held for something that would not equal in influence what it amounts to." King's comment was characteristically shrewd, for that desire for influence had always been Robertson's goal. Not position, not power, but influence. Both King and Robertson knew that in London, however important that post could become once it was freed from the dead hand of Vincent Massey, Robertson would never be able to exercise his talents as influentially as in Ottawa.

The discussion, as recorded by King, continued:

I said to him I had a distinct understanding with Pearson that there was no commitment. If in any way, Robertson preferred London, he should have it. Robertson said, yes, Pearson told me you had said that and that was how he felt. I then said to him would he say definitely he wanted London, and he would have it. He fell back again in a chair [one can hear the great sigh that must have accompanied this movement] and mentioned Dublin or Geneva; if he could be there for 2 or 3 years. I said that to me would be an indignity so far as he was concerned; also to the office, his position and Canada. These were trivial posts and he had a great position which should be maintained. I knew how he felt; that was due to fatigue; like the rest of us, he would like something easy for a while.

King added, apparently in an attempt to persuade Robertson to stay in Ottawa, that he was certain to find that "the power he had exercised had passed into other hands" if he went to London. "He would begin perhaps to regret that he had given up the most influential post in the service of the country (excepting possibly that of the Deputy Minister of Finance)." But King was not unfair: "I said it was for him to say if he wanted London and that would then be decided." King urged the Under-Secretary not to decide while he was tired. "I would not press him in making up his mind but to be assured that whatever he wanted, whatever he wished was what I most wished, and also that I would feel perfect confidence of his handling of situations in London. I notice he is very tired," King wrote, "and that there is no doubt he has very decidedly lost his grip on [the] administrative end of departmental affairs."[81]

King had seemed unusually considerate and generous, a sure indication of his high regard for Robertson. For his part, Robertson must have been gratified by this, particularly as he was demonstrating an unusual degree of indecisiveness.

But King's consideration for his Under-Secretary ran out overnight, and "first thing this morning" on 6 July, the Prime Minister was on the telephone in a much less conciliatory frame of mind. " ... I had been immensely surprised at his reference yesterday to feeling a sense of disappointment about London. I had gathered wholly from what he had told me that he did not want at this particular time to go to London. He had kept talking of other places and I thought from his manner and what he said, he really wished to hold on to the position he has here and which is one which carries with it a sense of power and has in it, largest possibilities that any man could have who is interested in directing world affairs." King was no mean psychologist, and he understood Robertson's ambivalence as well as the need to press for a decision. "He said he would think the matter over during the end of the week," King noted. "I told him that so far as I was concerned, not to think of me for a moment. . . .He must make the decision; not leave it to me to choose what would be best for him but rather for him to decide himself what he believes would be best." Later that day, King learned from Pickersgill, through Arnold Heeney, that Robertson really did want London. "That his only reason for not saying so was he did not want to appear to be asking for anything himself or to be embarrassing me."[82]

Forced to choose, inevitably Robertson had decided on London.[83]* The perils of the representational role could be surmounted in some way, and however heavy the duties, by comparison with Ottawa the work could only be the rest cure he needed. Moreover, there were the "perks" that went with a major post abroad: allowances, chauffeured limousines, domestic help. Those were not unimportant to the Robertsons, who had never had a chance to enjoy them and who had lived on a modest scale since their marriage. Once the game of musical chairs had been played out, and after Wrong was definitely for Washington, Pearson for Ottawa, and Robertson for London, one friend of all three remembered Robertson saying to Pearson that it was "time for you to share the spoils."[84]

Perhaps it was, but Pearson worried that as Under-Secretary, "I will be on a very tough spot. After all, you & Hume," he wrote to Robertson, "have taken a beating, but there have at least been the two of you. I

Robertson wrote to King on 8 July 1946 to say "I feel I should like to go to London," adding that for "some time I have felt that the war years and their extension into peace have taken more out of me than holidays have been able to put back." (PAC, King Papers, loose letter.)

would have no one like either of you to help. I would be new and I would
have the P.M. in his declining difficult months."[85] That was true, and it
must have worried the conscientious Robertson.

He was relieved, therefore, when in August at the abortive Paris peace
conference, Mackenzie King decided to abandon his External Affairs
portfolio completely. What concerned him were the costs of housing the
embassies abroad, the difficulty in getting Parliament to provide the
monies needed, and the danger of having the Embassy bureaucrats trying
to control policy,[86] and those reasons were really a tribute to Robertson's
careful memorandum of June. But the post was not to go to a junior
minister; instead, King offered it to Louis St. Laurent, the Minister of
Justice, perhaps the ablest man in the administration, and his personal
choice as successor. St. Laurent accepted on 3 September, and the next
day, the same day that the switch in posts among Wrong, Pearson and
Robertson was announced, King made public his decision. Robertson, he
noted in his diary, "was visibly surprised. . . .He said to me that he was
sorry to be severing associations in the Dept. of E.A. but he knew what the
burden had been and thought it would be best for me in the end. He then
said that I had really brought Canada into the world arena in the 20 years
I had been at the head of the Dept.; had created all its missions. It was a
wonderful record."[87] So it was, but it was one that had been shaped by
others too, and not least by Norman Robertson.

III

Robertson had worked as closely with Mackenzie King during the war
years as anyone else. He had seen the Prime Minister in defeat and in
triumph, on state occasions and in the privacy of his office, and he knew
the man as well as anyone could know that extraordinary political being.

Mackenzie King's pettiness has become part of Canada's folklore, his
personal stinginess and his penchant for spiritualism something of a
national joke. Less well known is King's courtesy and kindness, something
that on occasion was demonstrated to Robertson. For example, in the
midst of a cross-country speaking tour as part of a recruiting drive in the
summer of 1941, an exercise that King found particularly wearing, the
Prime Minister nonetheless took time in Vancouver to see Robertson's
parents. Lemuel Robertson wrote to his son in a positive glow:

He could not have been more appreciative of you. He said he missed Dr. Skelton so much but not in the administration of the office—rather nicely put. Then he said that we might rest assured that Canada's External policy was safe in your hands—a nice way of telling us not to be afraid that the duties of your post were too heavy for you. And then at parting told us that you had a wonderful future waiting. All told it was the great hour in our lives and we went home as few old folks are privileged to do. [88]

Mackenzie King was even more generous in February 1946, right in the middle of the Gouzenko spy case and its public uproar. On the 18th he entertained Robertson and Heeney, their wives and their parents at Laurier House. The "details of menu and seating were planned as for a state occasion," Arnold Heeney wrote, and King was very warm in praise of both men. "I spoke of what it meant to have Norman Robertson and Arnold Heeney associated with myself," King wrote after the evening, "and spoke of the gift which in this respect their parents had given to the government and country." [89] The parents loved it, but Heeney wrote that the wives took a less lofty view; "indeed they had obvious difficulty in concealing their amusement during the purpler passages, remembering, as they did, the numerous occasions upon which King had shown little consideration for our private lives." Nonetheless, as Heeney acknowledged, King was genuine in his praise. [90]

But on balance, at the close of his direct working relationship with him, Robertson took a dim view of King the man. According to Charles Ritchie, his colleague and close friend, Robertson "despised" him. [91] Douglas Le Pan, another good friend and colleague, remembered being with Robertson at a cottage on Georgian Bay the day King passed away in the summer of 1950. " ... I turned to Norman," Le Pan wrote, "and made the kind of anodyne remark about the late Prime Minister that the circumstances seemed to require. I will never forget his reply. He said quite simply, 'I never saw a touch of greatness in him.' " [92] But what had he meant by greatness? Jetty Robertson was convinced that her husband believed that King lacked a world view, the long foresight that someone— Winston Churchill, say—had had. [93] Others might feel that to be too charitable an interpretation, one that neglected Robertson's dislike of and resentment at King's pettiness and flawed human qualities. But whatever he meant, there is no doubt that his was a devastating and striking comment on the man for whom he had worked so long.

If Robertson despised King and saw no greatness in him, nonetheless after King's death he tried to serve the man as he had in life. King's will named Robertson one of four literary executors, the others being J.W. Pickersgill, Fred McGregor, King's one-time secretary and his assistant at the time of his death, and W. Kaye Lamb, the Dominion Archivist. The will indicated that the executors had agreed to serve, and provided $500 a year payment for each of them.[94] Most important, the will directed the literary executors to "destroy all of my diaries except those parts which I have indicated are and shall be available for publication or use."[95]

Unfortunately, King had not indicated the sections of his Record that he wanted to preserve, and the executors in consequence wrestled with their consciences and their difficult task for years. Robertson was, as he wrote to Lamb in 1953, "inclined to a strict and narrow construction of Mr. King's testamentary disposition about his diaries,"[96] and he was reluctant even to let Professor R. MacGregor Dawson, the authorized biographer, see them. Yet although Robertson eventually won a promise from his colleagues to destroy the spiritualism diaries,[97] bit by bit he caved in; but not before Dawson had in desperation appealed to Violet Markham, King's old friend, for help. Markham could be "quite a help in broadening Norman Robertson's view of the use to be made of the diary. He is, as you know, one of the literary executors, and the stickiest one ... for narrowing down the use to which the diary may be put. . . ."[98] In the end, after appeals by his colleagues and probably by Violet Markham, Robertson allowed Dawson's manuscript to go forward for publication, contenting himself merely with pointing out errors and offering advice on publishers.[99] Indeed in November 1954, Robertson actually found himself urging the other literary executors to let Sir John Wheeler-Bennett see the diary in his research for the biography of George VI. "I do find it difficult to maintain the completely discouraging line that we have taken up," he wrote Fred McGregor.[100]

So, slowly, the resistance crumbled.[101] The executors eventually agreed to preserve the diaries and later to open them to all researchers. Given the uses to which King's diaries have been put, given the annual excerpts sensationalized and distorted in the press, Norman Robertson, had he lived longer than he did, would have regretted his weakness in agreeing to preserve them.

Norman Robertson's role during the war had been an extraordinary one. He had presided over the change in Canada from a timid Dominion to a sometimes aggressive and nationalistic middle power. He had made the Department of External Affairs into a key ministry and into a foreign service of world class, able and willing to put Canada's case with skill and force in London, Washington, Moscow, Chungking and in a score of additional capitals. He (and his colleagues Hume Wrong and Lester

Pearson) was not anti-British or anti-American, despite his occasional sharp differences with those countries. He was an assured and confident Canadian, but one who knew the British and the Americans well and who recognized that the two countries, however friendly they might be to Canada or sympathetic to Canadian aims, had their own interests to pursue. In other words, Norman Robertson saw his country as an equal, albeit smaller, of the two great powers; just as important, he considered himself every bit the equal of the men with whom he had to deal from Britain and the United States and indeed other countries. And he was.

The war had given Robertson an opportunity to demonstrate this, and although he had his bad moments and his private hesitations and doubts, he had exercised that influence he so coveted with great skill and success and much to the advantage of his nation. Nothing afterwards was ever so satisfying for him; everything in the future was in some way anti-climactic. Only forty-two years old in 1946, Norman Robertson had already completed his most important work.

CHAPTER VIII

High Commissioner in London
1946-49

ORMAN ROBERTSON'S POSTING to London in the fall of 1946 brought him to England in an exciting period. The Labour government of Clement Attlee was determined to remodel and create anew whole sectors of British society and life and, despite a disastrous financial climate, was turning to its work with a will. Robertson was an interested, sympathetic observer of the government's efforts, although his work tended to force him to deal more closely with the commercial, financial and defence relations between Canada and Britain.

Although London was still the premier diplomatic post in the Canadian service, Robertson was no longer at the centre as he had been for the past five years. Ottawa kept him informed and consulted him far more than it did other representatives abroad (with the possible exception of Hume Wrong in Washington), but the loss of influence was pronounced. Despite the cables and frequent visits to Ottawa, Robertson could not overcome the distance that separated him from the Department.

Moreover, there could be no doubt that External Affairs was being led in a different fashion than it had been under Robertson. As the Secretary of State for External Affairs, Louis St. Laurent was finding his way carefully for the first few months, but he was vastly different from Mackenzie King. The new minister was courteous and pleasant, willing to trust his officials, and not bound quite so much by the hoary shibboleths and extreme caution that at its worst had characterized the *ancien régime*.

As Under-Secretary, Lester Pearson too was different from Robertson. He was a temperamental activist, a near utopian, with far greater faith in the United Nations than Robertson had. He wanted to forge ahead, to establish once and for all that the negativism that had characterized Canadian policy in the 1930s was dead and buried. Pearson was no cautious functionalist in the style of Robertson and Wrong; he had assessed the scene, determined that Canada had more power and prestige because of the war, and decided to take every advantage of the circumstances. Europe was in ruins, Germany and Japan were removed from the chessboard of the nations for the foreseeable future, and only Canada and the United States had come out of the war with their power enhanced. This was Pearson's opportunity, and he seized it eagerly. So long as Mackenzie King remained Prime Minister, he had to be careful, but with a new minister he had more leeway, and he took it.

Pearson also received able assistance from Escott Reid, a man who complemented his strengths and reinforced his weaknesses. Reid was forty-one, a Rhodes Scholar and a first-rate political scientist, an enthusiast who crusaded with astonishing energy and eloquence for the causes in which he believed, and those causes ranged (at different periods) from neutrality to the United Nations to the North Atlantic Treaty, from an end to arms sales to a campaign for simplified, basic English. All were approached with equal zeal and a visionary fervour that exhausted those around him. For much of this crucial postwar period, Reid was not the nominal number two,[1] but there seemed little doubt that he often had much influence on Pearson. The Under-Secretary was aware of his colleague's foibles,[2] but Reid did more work better than any three other men, and Pearson made him Assistant Under-Secretary and, after he became Minister in 1948, acting Under-Secretary.

The Department was vastly different than it had been under King and Robertson. The careful functionalism that had shaped much of Canada's policy was gone. In its place was an enthusiasm and an activism that was markedly different.[3] And Pearson at last was in the position he had sought in 1941; he intended to direct External Affairs on his own. Robertson's advice was sought, he was kept informed, but he was also held at a distance from the direction of affairs by geography and possibly by Pearson's wish. External Affairs was Mike Pearson's now, and he was determined that it should remain so.

This should not be overstressed, for relations remained close, and Robertson was never shut out of policy-making the way Vincent Massey, disliked by King and thoroughly mistrusted by him, had been while he was in London. But neither was Robertson involved as much as he might have liked and hoped. His loss of influence must have been deeply felt, and his agonizing through the summer of 1946 about taking the High Commissionership could not have prepared him for the shock that the loss brought.

I

When Robertson and his family came to England in the fall of 1946, they found a country that was at once exhilarated and exhausted. The war had taken a terrible toll, and the British economy was staggering. But if conditions were bad and getting worse, there was nonetheless a widespread feeling that Labour was moving ahead with sense and purpose, that the old and unworthy Britain was being replaced by a land that was truly fit for heroes.

Robertson felt this excitement immediately and the atmosphere of London in 1946 rekindled some of his enthusiasm for socialism and social reform that had largely lain dormant since the 1920s.[4] Best of all was that he had friends at the top levels of government and the civil service, men who valued his judgment and sought his advice, and not only on strictly Anglo-Canadian problems. Abroad he could never have the influence that had been his in Ottawa; but he could have some.

His High Commission was located in Canada House, a great, grey building on Trafalgar Square. The offices, particularly Robertson's own, were huge, and the operation inherited from Vincent Massey was in good working order. Robertson's deputy was Frederic Hudd, "an extraordinary creature from a different era," or so some remembered him.[5] Hudd had come up from the Trade Commissioners' service, but his duties at Canada House seemed limited to advising on ceremonial, to being a sometime-link with the Palace, and to easing the way for the High Commissioner with the Canadian community in London.[6] He did not attempt to interfere with the real business of the mission, and if Robertson was absent, the effective chain of command passed through John Holmes, once one of Robertson's wartime executive assistants, or through Douglas Le Pan, the scholar of English literature, who had become the Canada House economic expert under Massey and who continued in that role with his successor. Both Holmes and Le Pan were able and congenial colleagues, with wide circles of friends and acquaintances in the Foreign and Dominion Offices, in the Treasury, and, in Le Pan's case, in the cultural community.[7]

Postings brought changes in the staff as Robertson's term wore on, and J.H. Warren, Jules Léger, A.E. Ritchie, Max Wershof and others served with him.[8] It was a happy post and, while Robertson was never an organizational expert, Canada House ran well thanks largely to the work of John Sigvaldson as administrative officer.[9] The lines were clear, the responsibilities well-defined, and the officers knew what their work entailed. Wershof, for example, was a legal expert, but Robertson asked him to become thoroughly acquainted with the operations of the National Health Service.[10] Throughout Robertson's term, Le Pan, Warren and Ritchie, a very talented trio indeed, watched over economic questions, the chief business of the High Commission, and bore in mind Robertson's dictum that their despatches should always be at least at the level of the *Economist*, the great British weekly.[11]

Those despatches would come before the High Commissioner for approval. On one occasion, Jake Warren remembers, a paper of his on British urban planning came back from Robertson with only one correction—the closing quotation had been wrongly attributed.[12] Telegrams were usually read over on the spot and initialled or retained until the drafting officer could be called in to discuss the points at issue. If alterations were made, Le Pan said, Robertson almost always cleared the point with the original drafter. But because the officers were so able, because their connections were so widespread, and because they knew what their responsibilities were, there was remarkably little editing required. The officers thought and wrote in Robertson's style. Just about all the High Commissioner had to do was to tone down the occasional harsh reference, particularly when attitudes and opinions were attributed to members of the British cabinet. The Canadian ministry, Robertson said, also had its personalities.[13]*

Robertson also did a substantial amount of writing himself. His private secretary, Eleanor Fleming, had come to the High Commission from British Security Coordination in New York City, where she had been Sir William Stephenson's secretary, and that was a good enough recommendation for Robertson. He paced up and down the great High Commissioner's office while dictating or, occasionally, stood by the window, his foot on a chair, peering out at Trafalgar Square's people and pigeons, an ever-present cigarette in his hand. When he paced, his soft voice became indistinct and Miss Fleming had to follow him around the room. He was, she remembered, a kind man, but one who operated on a different plateau from ordinary mortals, and she was initially terrified of him. Occasionally,

---

* Robertson was generally delighted with his officers and when, in July 1947, he had to forward written assessments to Ottawa, he wrote that his comments read "like a very respectable citation list for the Birthday Honours! Perhaps I could have said more succinctly that all my geese are swans. However, the plain fact is that the Canadian External Affairs Service is very well served by the group of men I have working with me in Canada House . . . [an] exceptionally competent, cheerful and hardworking crew." (PAC, Department of External Affairs Records, vol. 661, NAR to T.W.L. MacDermot, 3 Jul. 47.)

"Our boy is a bug-catcher," Lemuel Robertson wrote of his only son's illness-prone childhood. Norman Robertson with his parents about 1908. (Robertson family)

"The boy's precocity was quickly spotted." Norman Robertson, age twelve. (Robertson family)

The Oxford undergraduate. (Robertson family)

"I felt very rotten at close—quite ill in fact...." Robertson
(fourth from right) did not find rowing "Torpids" easy at
Oxford, but he stuck it out. (Robertson family)

Robertson and his father in Scotland in 1925. The family arrived "right in the middle of schools in June 1925," a distraction that may have contributed to Robertson's second. (Robertson family)

Norman Robertson about the time of his marriage in 1928. (Robertson family)

"I think he is a man of great industry," Robertson wrote of R.B. Bennett, Prime Minister from 1930 to 1935, "honest and with a rather ingenuous faith in his own star." (PAC, PA-52387)

"A rumpled man, casual in his dress, casual in his administrative habits." Dr. O.D. Skelton recuperating in Florida in December 1937, about the time he persuaded Mackenzie King to release Robertson from the Prime Minister's Office. (PAC, C71513)

The East Block, Ottawa. Robertson worked here for all his years in Ottawa.
(Robertson family)

CANADIAN PACIFIC ⁵/ₛ DUCHESS OF RICHMOND.

In the 1930s Canada developed an expert team of trade
negotiators. Hector McKinnon, Dana Wilgress,
Robertson, and Hugh Scully, on their way to England.
(Author's photo)

Norman Robertson at the peak of his influence during the
Second World War. (Robertson family)

The Cabinet War Committee, Robertson said, was "the real policy-making component of the Cabinet." The members of the Committee in 1944 were, l. to r.: back row, N.A. Robertson, Hon. C.D. Howe, Hon. J.E. Michaud, Hon. Angus Macdonald, Hon. L.S. St. Laurent, A.D.P. Heeney; front row, Hon. C.G. Power, Hon. T.A. Crerar, Rt. Hon. W.L. Mackenzie King, Hon. J.L. Ralston, Hon. J.L. Ilsley.
(Robertson family)

Robertson, Mackenzie King, Brooke Claxton, and Arnold Heeney seen in a boring moment at the Paris Peace Conference in 1946. (PAC, C31312)

"The war (and Mackenzie King) had given Robertson his opportunity...." Mackenzie King gave this signed photograph to the Robertsons in 1947.
(Robertson family)

Hume Wrong, when he was Ambassador
to the USA. "The ablest man in the Service,"
Robertson called him. (PAC, C45196)

J.W. Pickersgill "found his niche" in the
Prime Minister's Office and never returned
to the Department of External Affairs after
1937. Pickersgill and Robertson snapped
during an Atlantic crossing in 1946.
(J.W. Pickersgill)

L.B. Pearson, speaking at the San Francisco Conference of
1945. "Affable and charming as he was, Pearson ordinarily
hid his substantial ambition." (PAC, C18532)

Arnold Heeney, seen here in 1952, had made
the Privy Council Office "the smoothest
functioning arm of the Ottawa bureaucracy."
(PAC, PA-121697)

Graham Towers, Governor of the Bank of
Canada from 1934 to 1954, and one of the
most powerful men in Ottawa during that
period. (PAC, PA-114896)

The Canadian delegation at the San Francisco Conference of 1945, with King and St. Laurent in front, and Hume Wrong and an extremely supercilious-looking Robertson behind. At San Francisco, Robertson's "role was to coordinate and direct"; he won plaudits for his work. (PAC, C22720)

Louis St. Laurent, Prime Minister 1948-57, with whom Robertson worked closely as Clerk of the Privy Council. St. Laurent was a "gentleman, a man of first-class intelligence and one with a lawyer's knack for striking at the root of a problem.... but still a bit aloof." (PAC, PA-57931)

"Representational work was part of the job." The High Commissioner and Mrs. Robertson greeting some Canadian visitors at an exhibition in London in 1948. (Robertson family)

Mackenzie King, just retired as Prime Minister, greets Robertson on his return from London to be Clerk of the Privy Council in 1949. That post, Robertson quickly decided, "is a mistake. There is nothing for me to do." (Robertson family)

Jetty, Norman, Judith and Alix Robertson in Ottawa about 1952.
Robertson is wearing the buffalo robe for which he was famous.
(Robertson family)

The Suez débâcle disrupted Canada's relations
with Britain, and "Robertson himself was in a
sense a casualty of the crisis." His farewell
party at the High Commission in 1957 brought
together many friends, including Mr. and Mrs.
Sydney Pierce, next to the Robertsons,
L.B. Pearson, second from the right,
and Frederick Hudd. (Robertson family)

The High Commissioner, 1956.
(Gaby of Montreal and Robertson family)

Robertson presenting his credentials as Ambassador to President Eisenhower in 1957. The President, Robertson said, seemed "friendly, vigorous and in first-rate shape." (Robertson family)

"A marriage and life together of singular happiness." Norman and Jetty Robertson about 1957. (Robertson family)

Norman Robertson in 1958, aged fifty-four, had "grown old in the service of his country." (Robertson family)

Robertson "could putter around at the Gatineau farm on weekends...." With his dogs at the farm in 1959. (Robertson family)

R.B. Bryce, Clerk of the Privy Council when Robertson was Under-Secretary the second time, was "the man of discretion who could keep a secret and keep the wheels of government turning." (PAC, PA114897)

Basil Robinson talking with Jetty Robertson at a party in
1957. Prime Minister Diefenbaker "came to trust Robinson
implicitly, the only External Affairs officer he did...."
(Robertson family)

Howard Green, shown here with Prime Minister Diefenbaker and Governor General
Vincent Massey when he became Secretary of State for External Affairs in 1959,
"had no particular qualifications in international affairs..." but "Green could change
and learn...." (PAC, PA114895)

he could be cutting. Once she had ended a discussion by saying, "Of course, I could be wrong, sir." "Not you, Miss Fleming."[14] But Robertson knew that he had a gem in the efficient and organized Fleming, and the paper moved as rapidly as was possible through his office. Despite her best efforts, however, his desk was the usual heap of files, and creative delay, while still the intent, sometimes became just plain delay.[15]

Robertson also began to coordinate the many departmental representatives in London. Agriculture, Trade and Commerce, National Defence, Veterans Affairs and others—all had their people in Britain, and Robertson was nominally responsible for them. Occasionally, as when J.G. Gardiner, the Minister of Agriculture, was on the rampage, it was hard to keep up with the negotiations that one department might have underway with the British, and sometimes one economic hand did not know what the other was about. But in general there was some success at coordination, and Robertson began the practice, for example, of holding weekly meetings with the service liaison officers to exchange information and to give them reports on developments in Ottawa, as conveyed to him in the minutes of the Cabinet Defence Committee.[16] In addition, he detailed Le Pan to keep the Trade and Commerce representatives informed and R.A.D. Ford to link up with the scientific and military staffs.[17] External Affairs' poets had to be versatile men.

If the office functioned well, there was rather more difficulty domestically. As High Commissioner, Vincent Massey had lived in the Dorchester Hotel, something that worked well enough for the Masseys, whose children had grown and departed. But Robertson, the first professional diplomat to be High Commissioner and no rich man, faced problems. The Robertsons had their two daughters with them—Alix, a teenager, and Judith, just five years old—and while Alix was sent to the Sherborne School for Girls, Judith was at home. Then, there had to be a suitable house for the required entertaining (and for the family dogs), and that entailed ample rooms, kitchens and staff. This was, of course, expected of the High Commissioner, and Robertson's salary of $12,000 was supplemented by allowances of $28,000 a year, much the highest given to any Canadian representative abroad.[18]

But the difficulty was finding a suitable house in London after the blitz, particularly since those who might have rented their homes were barred from most trips abroad because of tight foreign exchange controls. The result was that the Robertsons lived in three houses during their two-and-a-half-year stay. The first was in Albert Place, Kensington, the second in Gloucester Square, Paddington, and the last in Chapel Street, Mayfair.

None of these houses was perfect—the Chapel Street one, even if it had been owned by a lord, was a mess—and the Robertsons spent endless hours with the Department of External Affairs' architect to find a permanent High Commissioner's residence. Although Jetty Robertson preferred a large house on Kensington Palace Row, in the end the government chose a blitzed ruin on Upper Brook Street near Grosvenor Square in the belief that it was cheaper to renovate the ruin than to buy the expensive. It wasn't, and before it was restored (not in time for the Robertsons to live in it), the costs had risen to $280,000, with an additional $76,000 for furnishings, figures that provoked much tut-tutting in Ottawa. [19]

There were additional problems. The winter of 1946-47 was the worst of the century, and to London's other miseries were added morning and afternoon power cuts. The Robertson house was electrically heated (and not very warm, even when the power functioned), and everyone froze during the day. Strict rationing was still in place, and after each move Jetty Robertson had to try to strike up a friendly relationship with a new butcher in order to get good meat. Diplomats received extra ration coupons, but the food did not go far, and there was no riotous entertaining. Indeed, so tight was the economy that the Robertsons hesitated to visit friends. For example, when Rhodes House invited them to Oxford to meet Canadian Rhodes Scholars, Robertson had to "seriously stipulate that when we come we stay at an hotel from which we can visit our friends without taxing their staff and rations." [20]

As that suggested, staff was a problem, too. The High Commissioner's residence needed a cook, a butler, and a maid, as well as a nanny for Judith, and, while the Robertsons occasionally had all four, there were times when there was no cook and no help at all. [21] Despite all the problems, it was a happy time, with official lunches, many small dinner parties and much entertaining of visitors, ministers and officials. [22]

That representational work was part of the job, and the Robertsons handled the entertainment graciously; but as might have been expected, the High Commissioner fell down on speech-making. His first address, one that could not be avoided, was to the Canada Club on 20 November. "As you can imagine," he wrote to Pearson,

I was pretty miserable at the prospect of making a speech, and was very worried about facing such an audience on such an occasion; nevertheless, I couldn't bring myself to the point of actually sitting down and doing some work on it. I finally got a reserve text ready on the afternoon of the appointed evening, but did not give an advance copy to the press, because I still hoped that I might be able to stand up and say a few simple things without reading a prepared text. In the event, I spent the first three or four minutes I was on my feet acknowledging [various telegrams and introductions] ... and then plunged in panic into the text. ... I skipped the paragraphs which are struck out [in the text sent to Pearson—unfortunately including all the wry lines], galloped through the remainder, and sat down![23]

Despite his agonizing, it had been a good speech. Others, such as an address to the closing session of the Preparatory Committee on Trade and Employment, could also not be avoided, and when Pearson wrote in praise of Robertson's remarks on that occasion, the High Commissioner wrote on the letter, "Mr. Le Pan—you'd better take this curtain call," an indication that he had started farming out speech-writing.[24]

Fortunately, speeches do not a High Commissioner make, and Robertson was extremely successful, despite his inability to proffer platitudes on short notice. Much of his business was conducted at lunches or dinners or over the bridge table, and his conversation, his range and his wisdom were at their best in those settings. His bridge companions regularly included Roger Makins of the Foreign Office, Lewis Clark of the American Embassy (and recently transferred from Ottawa) and Lord Addison, the Secretary of State for Dominion Affairs on Robertson's arrival in London; on one occasion, as well, when Prime Minister Attlee was in hospital, Robertson played regularly with him there.[25] There were close ties away from the table with men like J.A.C. Osborne of the Bank of England, an old Ottawa friend, with Norman Brook, the Secretary to the Cabinet, with Roger Makins, and with Frank Lee of the Board of Trade, all key figures in the civil service establishment, and with the author Elizabeth Bowen, a good friend of Charles Ritchie's and hence, by direct transference, of his friends in the Department.[26] Additional friends and acquaintances abounded, with officials of the Foreign Office, the Dominions Office (which after July 1947 was called the Commonwealth Relations Office), and at the Palace predominant.[27]

Occasionally too there were honours that seemed genuine rather than the many that were simply *ex officio*. In June 1948, for example, Robertson was awarded an honorary LLD by Cambridge University on the occasion of the installation of Field Marshal Jan Smuts as Chancellor of the University. Smuts, a Cambridge double first from before the Boer War, had put Robertson up for the degree, and that clearly pleased him, even if his old friend Jack Clyne seized the occasion to twit him unmercifully. The Montreal *Gazette*, Clyne wrote, had reported on Robertson's " 'shyness' which masks your intellectual abilities. Personally

I never noticed either quality." Robertson's reply was benign, noting only that it "was quite an experience to bring up the rear of a very distinguished procession...."[28]

It was in many ways an enjoyable period, a break from the pressures of Ottawa, a chance to ease the strain of the war. "My own memories of life in London," Robertson wrote in 1966, "are probably the happiest I have had,"[29] and that said it all.

But if one intention of the London posting had been to give Norman Robertson a rest cure, away from the stress of the Under-Secretary's role, matters did not entirely work out that way. While High Commissioner, he had a succession of serious ailments that sapped his strength and left him at less than full capacity for some periods of the rest of his life.

Certainly Mackenzie King had been distressed by Robertson's apparent ill-health for some time. During the war he had occasionally noted how tired his Under-Secretary was, and in August 1946 in Paris he had become concerned when Robertson took sick. "I confess I feel a little alarmed about his condition," King wrote. "It might develop into some chest trouble if he is not very careful. I did not like the evidence of the cough which I saw while talking with him."[30] That symptom was likely a result of Robertson's chain-smoking, but while that habit eventually killed him, it was not tobacco that imperilled Robertson in 1947.

The High Commissioner, wrote Frederic Hudd from London in June, "had complained for some time of what appeared to be a rheumatic condition of the leg...." But at the end of May, after a country weekend with the Roger Makinses, the condition grew more acute and, after talking with Jetty Robertson, Hudd called in a doctor who diagnosed a thrombosis. "In addition," Hudd added, "he has obviously not been a well man for some time, displaying rather more than his normal, (and sometimes misleading), signs of fatigue. The sigh has not been altogether an instrument of policy!"[31] The doctors ordered complete rest.

Two weeks later, Hudd was able to report more fully on the patient. "The condition in the leg is minor and merely a symptom of a general condition of ill-health due to years of neglect, as a result of which the patient is so ill-conditioned that he would have no resistance whatever to an attack of illness, and unless he takes the three months' period of rest and detachment prescribed, he will not be out of danger." The X-rays and examinations had turned up no damage to heart or lungs, but a continuing low-grade fever did point to Robertson's deaf ear, that relic of childhood infection, as a source of trouble. Treatment or an operation was necessary, Hudd said. Finally, Robertson's sedentary life and his failure to take exercise had made many of his muscles "so flabby as to be practically useless." Still, the doctors believed that his condition gave no cause for anxiety, "if the patient carries out instructions, which he has promised to do."[32]

That promise was not kept, however, and Robertson turned out to be a difficult patient. On 4 July, Hudd telegraphed Ottawa "rather in despair about this whole situation as, in spite of warnings and exhortations he continues telephone conversations with his secretary or hands drafts to visiting friends." The High Commissioner was in the countryside, staying at a house on the South Downs loaned by Lady Reading ("right out of the blue," Robertson wrote, " & in such an amiably insistent way that it was impossible to decline it."[33]) But, as Hudd went on, he was there with "dog and offspring both of whom are an obvious source of annoyance and worry. He is behaving as though he were a convalescent, which he is not."[34] Hudd was also snobbishly worried that the doctors in charge, a Department of Veterans Affairs medical officer and his surgeon friend, were unknown to "prominent Canadians in London."[35] A further difficulty in the Deputy High Commissioner's rather misguided view was that Jetty, though worried about her husband, did not seem "really seized of how serious it might become without strict obedience to medical orders." (In fact, neither the doctors nor Hudd ever spoke to her about her husband's condition and she was well aware of his need for calm and rest.)[36]

A salutary fright seemed necessary, and it was administered to the patient when, as Robertson wrote to Arnold Heeney, "a brief relapse" and a painful bout of bursitis "put my arm out of action for a few days," followed by a medical decision to operate on the ear condition. "I don't look forward to the prospect—but saw no way of wriggling out of it once I got into medical hands. . . . The timetable is quite dismaying—two weeks in hospital here and then another month close enough to London for weekly dressing. . . ." But, characteristically, Robertson insisted on making "the odd appointment this morning. Canada House's consternation at the thought that I might be seen sneaking out of the F.O. and the Treasury was hard to contain. In the end I crumbled and let them reverse the arrangements—so I am staying home in Gloucester Square and the various mountains are coming to Mahomet for a little final advice as to how to run the affairs of the world for the next fortnight."[37]

The operation, despite Robertson's dread of it, was a success, and Pearson, who had been in touch with Robertson's parents, now wired them that he had heard that "Infection of the ear was found to be much more extensive than expected, which shows importance of operation having been decided upon to clear up condition which would inevitably have become worse." The best estimate was that he would be fit to return to duty by 1 November.[38] To ensure this, Pearson instructed Canada House, as he told the patient, "not to send you any material of any kind which will take your mind off your physical ailments." Pearson added, "Is there any chance that it will mean that I can now walk on either side of you?"[39] (It didn't.) Robertson himself was relieved at the outcome, and as he told one visitor, "judging by the dry washing of hands and licking of chops that went on in his room afterwards," he gathered that the operation had been necessary.[40] The Department listed Robertson as being on leave of absence.[41]

The convalescence proceeded smoothly. Robertson received visitors in his nursing home, "his head still completely enveloped in bandages,"[42] and dabbled at work. Pearson wrote that he had heard Robertson was recovering, though "completely ignoring the advice of your friends not to interest yourself in the state of the world."[43] But in fact, with Dana Wilgress as acting High Commissioner and with Le Pan and Holmes handling much of the day-to-day work, Canada House was in safe hands.[44] By the end of September, after a rest in France and a return to Canada for a visit, he was once again ready to work.[45]

That was no permanent condition, however, and little more than a year later, while he was in Paris as chairman of the United Nations' Berlin Currency Committee, Robertson suffered an apparent phlebitis attack that frightened his friends, if not him. The illness struck in the evening, when the only available doctor was a unilingual Parisian gynaecologist on his way to a formal ball. This apparition in tails pronounced Robertson near death and prescribed a period of bed rest and an end to smoking, drinking and committees. This was all translated by John Holmes, and after the order had been conveyed, Robertson instructed his friend to ask "if he'd settle for an amputation."[46]

In fact, the patient obeyed orders for only one day and then returned to his usual chain-smoking, martinis and committees.[47] And as his wife remembers, he also went out and purchased an expensive five-volume, leather-bound set of the works of Rabelais. "If I'm going to die," he said, "I might as well get something I want."[48] He didn't die, but his London doctors put him on a regimen of massage and, as Hudd said, "removed the smoking and drinking ban. They have done this for psychological rather than medical reasons, as they think the deprivation tends to depress the patient and that on balance it is wiser to allow him to indulge, leaving moderation to his discretion. . . ."[49]

Discretion was never the better part of valour in so far as Robertson's health was concerned. His fatalistic attitude about himself and his complete absorption in his work tended to make him uncaring about his health. Although he was only forty-four years old, Robertson's physical condition was that of an older man. Continuous neglect had taken its toll.

II

Great democracies, Max Beloff has written, "are not deflected from their national policies by personal friendships. Individuals might help to dissipate genuine ignorance or genuine misunderstandings . . . make relations easier . . . [or] break through jungles of red tape that might have strangled lesser men. . . . But the great issues were decided as a result of factors outside their control."[50]

It is important to dispel ignorance and to ease misunderstandings, to put the facts before the decision-makers. That was Norman Robertson's task in London, and on no matter between October 1946 and February 1949 did he work more assiduously than on commercial and financial relations between Britain and Canada. Moreover, as British financial power waned and as the United States and Canada stepped forward to help keep the British and Western European economies functioning, Robertson was perfectly placed to ensure that the North Atlantic triangle remained intact as long as possible and that Canadian interests were not shunted aside.

In his memoirs, Hugh Dalton, the first Chancellor of the Exchequer in the Attlee government, referred to 1946 as the *Annus Mirabilis* and 1947 as the *Annus Horrendus*.[51] Robertson's despatches reflected those titles, as he traced the fluctuating nature of Canada's fiscal and commercial relations with Britain.

In one long despatch (undoubtedly drafted by Douglas Le Pan) after a conversation with R.W.B. Clarke of the Treasury at the beginning of 1947, Robertson reported that the British "had been more than satisfied" by their 1946 balance of payments position. Their global deficit was likely to be under £500 million rather than the estimated £750 million, and even their dollar holdings were "reasonably satisfactory." More surprising still, Robertson noted, Clarke believed that London's rate of drawing on the American and Canadian loans was proceeding as expected. What had happened? Clarke was asked. The British export drive had succeeded and exports were running at 120 percent of the prewar figure; imports were down to about 70 percent of the 1938 level, an alteration dictated more by scarcities than by intent; many British purchases had been made before American price levels began their steep rise in 1946; and, finally, Britain had managed to get substantial sums in dollars and gold from Western European countries that had come through the war, despite physical devastation, with their financial reserves in better condition than Britain's.

If that was hopeful, the makings of *Annus Horrendus* were already apparent. The Treasury expected a serious deficit of American dollars to develop, one of "worrying proportions far in excess of anything that had been allowed for when the size of the United States and Canadian loans were being determined." The causes of this were the inflation in the United States (which effectively lowered the value of the American loan), the world scarcity of cereal grains, the British need to import more food than before the war, and the slower than expected European recovery. The dreadful winter of 1946-47 also had an effect.

That was a good analysis, and one that proved all too true. Robertson concluded his report by noting the Treasury's assurances that it did not see a crisis around the corner but, he said, "I can hardly exaggerate the problem of the dollar deficit. It is a time-bomb ticking away in the heart of Whitehall, and awareness that it may yet blow up the Government and ruin this country's hope of recovery affects the consideration of almost every other major problem."[52]

In fact, the British difficulties were alarmingly similar to Canada's. Britain, Graham Towers said, "has been running a heavy deficit with the dollar area at the same time as it has been providing supplies on credit to various Western European countries", and that was a problem "we can readily understand because it is in some respects similar to our own." Canada had come out of the war with large holdings of American dollars, holdings that were now being drained away to pay for imports from the United States. At the same time Canada had large trade surpluses with European countries that could not pay in convertible currency, and the situation was worsened by the almost $2 billion in loans and credits that Canada had made to Britain and Europe to keep up trade, to foster employment at home, and to help aid Europe's recovery.

Britain's problems were, perhaps, greater. Certainly they were larger in absolute terms. In February 1947 the British had begun to deal with their foreign exchange problem by reducing the proportion of their exports going to countries that could not pay for them in hard currencies and by increasing their export share to Canada and the United States. Those were useful efforts, Towers said, because Canada could use the British goods, particularly if they helped reduce dependence on American sources that only aggravated Canada's own loss of dollars.[53]

Both countries had their difficulties, and in late April Sir Wilfred Eady of the Treasury was preparing to visit Ottawa and Washington to discuss common concerns. Before his departure, he called on Robertson, to whom he "emphasized that he had no proposals to put forward. What he hoped for was an examination of the dollar position, so that Canadian, United States and United Kingdom authorities would be looking at identical sets of facts." Eady was also clearly alarmed about the prospect of making sterling freely convertible into dollars and other currencies in mid-July 1947, as Britain was obliged to do under the terms of its loan agreement with the United States. Another factor disturbing the Treasury official was that Britain's supply of dollars was disappearing, that the Canadian and American loans would be spent by the summer of 1948, all of that total of $5 billions having returned across the Atlantic to pay for Canadian and American goods. Robertson concluded that Eady had full confidence in Britain's ability to regain its equilibrium: "in two years the worst would be over . . . in five years a stable equilibrium could be established."[54]

That was not a bad forecast. But in Ottawa, Eady told Clifford Clark, the Deputy Minister of Finance, and his colleagues rather more than he had put to Robertson. The British had concluded that their financial situation required a cutback of imports; moreover, they believed that this had to be done on a discriminatory basis, favouring the war-shattered countries and some parts of the sterling area and restricting the flow of imports from, among others, Canada. This was a marked shift in British planning, and one that cut close to the heart of the rationale behind the Canadian $1.25 billion loan in 1946.

According to a report Clark sent Robertson, the reductions did "not involve very serious cuts in their imports from Canada during the next year, but might involve fairly substantial cuts thereafter in bacon, meat, cheese, eggs and other foodstuffs as existing contracts expire." There might also be reductions in some manufactured exports, but London did not plan cuts in purchases of grains, metals, and pulp and paper. For their part, Clark and company had told Eady of Canada's financial problems and had informed him that they sprang "in large part through the magnitude of the credit which she has extended to the U.K. and the rapid rate it has been drawn upon." They warned Eady that it was possible "we should probably find it necessary to request his Government to make no further use of the Canadian credit during 1947 and to meet their requirements until end of year entirely by payments to us of convertible sterling or U.S. dollars."

Every country was short of American dollars, the fundamental economic problem of the reconstruction era. "We stated," Clark said to Robertson, "that we believed the Canadian Government would be prepared to make separate but similar representations to the U.S. on the prospects for an acute dollar shortage which could only be met by prompt and large scale action of the U.S. itself in making dollars available to those countries other than U.K. and Canada that were so desperately short of foreign exchange." The British, Clark added, were not sanguine on this score.[55]

At this point, just as matters entered the critical phase in the separate Canadian and British attempts to conserve dollars, just as the United States slowly began to move toward a very large aid scheme for Britain and Europe, Robertson fell ill and was effectively removed from the stage until the beginning of November 1947.

Even on his sickbed, however, the High Commissioner remained concerned with the problems and choices the dollar crisis was forcing on Canada. For several months, he had been watching the European efforts to move toward economic cooperation, a "good" thing, but one that might put Canada's trade into difficulties.[56] He was concerned with the International Trade Organization discussions at Geneva, and he was trying to think of additional ways by which Canada could earn more American exchange.[57]

All those worries came together in a long and remarkable despatch that Robertson, defying his doctors' orders and the High Commission's importunings, sent to Pearson on 19 June. He began by looking at the efforts to create a Western European Customs Union and suggested that the effects of such a development on Canadian trade "would not be very serious." He expected some substitution of one market for another, but did not fear significant net effect on the volume of Canadian exports. Additionally, such a Union might underwrite "our general political and economic interest in [Europe's] stability and prosperity." And, he added, Canada might say publicly "that the United Kingdom can play its full part in European economic cooperation and still be a member of the Commonwealth in good standing, just as Canada combines Commonwealth membership with the fact that it is also an 'American country'. . . ."

Then Robertson turned to the meat of his telegram:

At a time when Canada and the United States are being asked to take a benevolent interest in the effort of European countries to put their economic affairs on a more orderly continental basis, we might consider whether the prescription for Europe has not an application nearer home. I have felt that the current pressure on the Canadian dollar position might squeeze our economy in either of two ways. I.e., it could, for trading purposes, push us into an impoverished sterling area, held together by policies of discrimination against United States exports and not much more; or, conceivably it could result in a much closer continental integration of our economy with that of the United States. Of these polar extremes, I much prefer the second, and wanted to come home to talk to you about it before the Government committed itself to the first and orthodox course. However, it now looks as if we shall have a few months' grace. . . .

The consideration now being given to the possibilities of European regional economic cooperation make me wonder whether we should not more or less simultaneously be thinking of a real reciprocity agreement with the United States, which would strengthen our dollar position in the short run, and, in the long run, ensure us against too great a dependence, relative to the United States, on the European market. It might be possible to work out a scheme for a graduated approach to reciprocal free trade in a good many commodities on a continental basis, with the steps selected and their depth determined largely by the requirements of our dollar position, perhaps on an understanding that in five years' time we would match the tariff removals that the United States would undertake to accomplish in two. All this is very speculative and only half thought out, but I do feel very strongly that the political and economic consequences of a purely 'defensive' discriminatory policy against United States imports would be so disastrous, both for Canada and the world generally, that we should explore exhaustively every alternative to such a course.[58]

It was an impressive telegram, one whose prophecies very nearly came true in the next year. It is striking that Robertson had reverted to the trade negotiator he had been in the 1930s, still striving for the perfect agreement with the United States. Equally interesting, Robertson foresaw no threats to Canada's political sovereignty in a reciprocity arrangement with the Americans. Why? It cannot be that this subject did not concern him, for we have seen his wartime actions to counter American incursions. We know, too, that Robertson was a nationalist, one confident of Canada's strength. The only reasonable explanation of the omissions from his telegram is that he was so convinced that Canada could resist absorptive pressures from the south, even under a régime of free trade, that the need to comment on this scarcely crossed his mind.[59]

For the moment, Robertson's ideas were too visionary, and Ottawa, engrossed in the struggle to avert an exchange crisis, and with many of its key economic and trade experts in Geneva, did nothing.[60] In London, Dana Wilgress, the chief negotiator at Geneva, became acting High Commissioner while Robertson was ill, and all the while world economic collapse drew nearer. The only break in the gloom was the June address by the US Secretary of State, George C. Marshall, in which he held out the prospect of enormous aid to Europe. But as Le Pan wrote to the Department, on 17 July, "the day before Mr. Robertson went into the London Clinic for his operation," he had been visited by Hector McNeill, Minister of State in the Foreign Office. From him, Robertson had been led to believe "that the United Kingdom authorities were full of concern and blank uncertainty about the prospects of the Marshall offer. They wished to do everything they could to make it a success, and yet they hardly knew what steps would be most effective." That essentially summed up the mood, and the British, after several bitter experiences in the past, feared the response of Congress. If there was delay, McNeill feared, it was going to be impossible to get financial help before Britain had to impose crippling import restrictions.[61]

It was all too true. By the end of July, after it had made sterling convertible in accordance with the American loan terms, and after further disastrous economic figures, Britain moved on several fronts to try to maintain its precarious position. Soon convertibility was rescinded, restrictions were slapped on imports, and efforts were made to renegotiate the terms under which Britain paid for Canadian exports. The next several months were harrowing and acrimonious for Anglo-Canadian relations, and Robertson, to his anguish, was effectively out of action.[62]

In one letter that Pearson sent the convalescent High Commissioner, the Under-Secretary indicated that the line Robertson had suggested in June was close to that in Ottawa in September. "I realize," Pearson wrote, "that in the present crisis there is an increasing tendency to fall back on the 'Empire' and to plug the idea that now is the time for all good Britishers to come to the help of the Mother Country...." That was understandable, he went on, but

you can take it from me that, in spite of very real sympathy for the United Kingdom in her present predicament, in spite of a genuine desire to help, and in spite of the developing economic difficulties with the U.S. this tactic will produce no useful results in Canada. We are not so impatient with the U.S.A. as all that but, in any event, if we are forced to choose some closer economic and financial alignment, and I hope we won't be, it will have to be with Washington rather than with London. Surely the British have enough sense to realize that and surely they have enough sense, therefore, not to put Canada in any position where such a choice would have to be made. [63]

Elements of exasperation were creeping in on both sides. One British official wrote to Ernest Bevin, the Foreign Secretary, on 13 September that Canada "can no longer count on us to help them out" financially, an extraordinary interpretation of a situation where the question at issue was how much of the Canadian loan Britain was to be able to draw on. [64] Incomprehension was growing, and the need was evident for someone to say, as Robertson had on another occasion to a British official who was waving the bloody shirt of loyalty and race, "Do you think we could switch from the language of anthropology to that of political science?" [65]

By late September, even if he was not yet officially on duty, Robertson was up and about in London, re-establishing contacts with his British friends and beginning to fire off telegrams. One subject that concerned him, naturally enough, was the Marshall Plan, still in its genesis. Would Canada get any direct benefits from the American scheme? Robertson thought so, as he told Pearson on 24 September, because inflationary pressures in the United States were almost certain to make the Truman Administration anxious to spread the burden of purchases in a tight market over a number of countries. These "off-shore purchases" eventually were accepted in the United States for just that reason, but not without great efforts from the Canadians. [66]

In October Robertson was in Ottawa, continuing his recuperation, and getting and giving briefings. On 3 October he dined with Mackenzie King at Kingsmere, [67] and on the 21st he was at cabinet to hear Hector McKinnon and John Deutsch inform the ministers of the outcome of the Geneva tariff negotiations. "They have really achieved a marvellous result," the Prime Minister bubbled over the General Agreement on Tariffs and Trade (GATT) that lowered duties on a vast array of imports and won Canada substantial concessions around the world. [68] At the end of the month, Robertson went to Washington to stay for a day with Hume Wrong, the Ambassador, incidentally suggesting ways in which Canada could use the Permanent Joint Board on Defence to help secure more dollars. [69] Within a day or two, he was back in London, certified fit for duty.

The flood of telegrams and reports began immediately: on the possibility of a devaluation of the pound, [70] on the resignation of Hugh Dalton as Chancellor of the Exchequer and his replacement by Sir Stafford Cripps, [71] and on complaints that Ottawa was not keeping

Canada House informed of changes in the Canadian import restrictions that had been announced on 17 November, ironically at the same time as the GATT agreements.[72] Robertson was back on the job.

Just in time, too. In late November and December 1947, Britain and Canada engaged in perhaps their most difficult postwar negotiation. The issue was food supplies and the prices London would pay. Although the talks were held in Ottawa, Robertson played an important part from his post in London.

Sir Percivale Leisching, Permanent Under-Secretary to the Minister of Food, represented Britain at the discussions and, as Pearson told Robertson, he argued initially that Britain's financial position was such that purchases of beef, eggs and bacon had to be stopped completely and orders for a wide range of other Canadian products be reduced. This posed major difficulties for Canada. J.G. Gardiner, the rambunctious and opinionated Minister of Agriculture, argued that Canada needed a balanced agricultural programme, and that either every food product went to Britain at the negotiated contract price or none went. Graham Towers, concerned over Canada's balance of payments problems, told the British not to count on getting much from the remaining Canadian credits of 1946.[73] And again acrimony and recrimination filled the air.

What was to be done? Almost alone of those concerned, Robertson did not take an apocalyptic view. "I should not be worried about the immediate cancellation of the beef contract," he wired Pearson. There had never been much chance of securing a permanent peacetime market, and in any case Canada had been able to deliver only a fraction of the quantity it had promised to try to send. "Restoration of our cattle export trade to the United States" was far more important. Similarly, there was little hope of creating a market for Canadian eggs in Britain. "I have never been able to see how it would be economical to ship fresh eggs from British Columbia and Southern Alberta by refrigerator ship through the Panama Canal in successful competition with English, Danish, Dutch and Polish eggs. . . ." Again, Robertson argued, the American market was a better place for any Canadian surplus.[74]

Robertson's calmness was impossible to find in Ottawa, where Jimmy Gardiner was on the rampage. The British had to be made to swallow large quantities of beef, bacon, eggs and cheese, and the Canadian government, despite its dollar problems, offered to permit London to draw $10 million a month from the Canadian loan for the first three months of 1948 as a sugar coating.[75] Again Robertson tried to put the long view, arguing that the current negotiations "provide a real opportunity for correcting in agreement with the United Kingdom what I have always regarded as an over-concentration of our agricultural production on the specific requirements of the United Kingdom market." That suggestion was probably the right one, but it was not given much weight in Ottawa, where the Canadian negotiators focussed on the needs of the politicians and farmers.

While the bargaining continued, Robertson strove to keep Pearson informed on things in London. On 8 December, he telegraphed Pearson his assessment of Sir Stafford Cripps's position. He had been working to build a close relationship with Cripps, and was helped by his own long friendship with Graham Spry,* Saskatchewan's Agent-General in London and Cripps's wartime private secretary.[76] The first fruits of these efforts were his assessment that Cripps knew "in his bones that this country cannot get through the next two years without very substantial American aid. At the same time he cannot budget on its being available by any given date in any given quantity and in a form the Government could welcome."[77] The next day Robertson reported that he had learned that the Treasury "is in fact counting on Marshall aid reaching it in September 1948."[78] That was of immediate relevance to the negotiations. He also mobilized his and his staff's contacts in an effort to determine how firm the British position was. Le Pan, for example, was shown many of the messages between Leisching and London, messages that made clear that the British negotiator had already exceeded his instructions in offering American dollars in payment for Canadian food.[79]

But despite all efforts, the talks were near collapse,[80] and Robertson saw Cripps in one last attempt to keep them going. "I think the Government here are as concerned as we are about the implications and consequences of a failure of the current negotiations," Robertson reported on 13 December, "and would be prepared to take some pretty serious risks with their remaining reserves to avert a breakdown of Canadian-United Kingdom supply and credit arrangements during the period that must

---

* Cripps knew Robertson even before Spry's arrival in London, and had introduced him in warm terms to a Canadian Chamber of Commerce meeting in April 1947. (Nuffield College, Oxford University, Cripps Papers, /249, address, 25 Apr. 47.) Later, on 10 November 1948, Cripps spoke of the High Commissioner in terms that suggested Robertson's success in establishing a link: "so essential and valuable a part of our London Commonwealth circle that it would be a work of supererogation if I were to dilate upon his great qualities. . . . I find him very helpful and cooperative and a mine of wisdom and suggestion whenever there are difficult problems to solve." (*Ibid.*, /47, Canada Club dinner.) Some Canadians have suggested that Robertson's influence with Cripps even extended to areas of British domestic policy, but no firm evidence of this has been found.

elapse before Marshall assistance can begin to become effective."[81] That telegram made a strong impact, persuading Mackenzie King "that the British were as anxious as we were not to break off completely the contracts between Britain and Canada ... and were prepared to make an effort to review the situation."[82]

The result was compromise and an agreement. Canada allowed Britain access to $15 million in credits for each of the first three months of 1948; Britain agreed to provide an additional $100 million in American dollars; the contracts were maintained and, in particular, Britain continued to get Canadian wheat at a price below world levels.[83] But as Robertson pointed out, there was the anomaly that the contracts were for one year, while financing had been arranged only for three months.

I myself have always deprecated any disposition on our side to charge the United Kingdom with bad faith in asking for the revision or even extinction of some of the contracts. Such a charge would lead directly to counter recriminations that we had failed to meet our obligations through short-falls in deliveries under some of the contracts; and, in any case, mutual recriminations would get us nowhere. On the other hand, I accept it as inevitable that in some quarters in Canada at least there should be anger at the United Kingdom's wish to cancel a number of contracts. For better or for worse, their long-term needs had been made the basis of our agricultural policy, and an attempt to escape from their commitments would be bound to provoke some bitterness.

Anglo-Canadian relations were no bed of roses, but Robertson, for one, seemed to feel that much of the blame lay in wrong decisions in Ottawa.[84]

One hurdle had been overcome; but there were many more. On 22 January 1948, Robertson entertained Cripps and many of his key officials at dinner and, as he reported the next day: "As soon as Cripps joined the company, he plunged into an urgent exposition of his concern." What was to happen in March when the interim financing arrangements agreed at Ottawa expired?

He and his advisers had been casting about desperately for some device which could provide a way around the impasse. They had not been able to light on any new ideas and he himself now felt sure that there *were* none, that there were no keys to unlock this intractable problem, at least so long as it was considered in isolation. The only creative approach, he thought, lay in changing the terms of the problem. ... He thought now that it would have to be transposed and considered as a problem affecting Canada, the United Kingdom *and* the United States.

What Cripps wanted, he eventually said, was an approach to Washington by Canada and Britain for "an informal commitment on the part of the Administration regarding the use to be made of Marshall aid for financing the United Kingdom's purchases in Canada, which would allow the United Kingdom to take some large risks before the Marshall Plan came into effect, perhaps in September. Such an informal commitment would involve an agreement with the Administration as to how much of the Marshall aid earmarked for the United Kingdom could be used in Canada," Robertson continued, noting that Cripps expected such a commitment retroactively to cover the British deficit with Canada from the end of March. In his own view, the High Commissioner added, such an approach, aimed at "the only quarter from which aid can possibly come in time," seemed "sensible."[85] A few days later, after he had heard further disquieting news about Britain's financial plight, Robertson again urged Ottawa to follow Cripps's line.[86] Unfortunately, neither Pearson nor St. Laurent, his minister, were "very much enamoured" of the suggested joint approach,[87] and the Interdepartmental Committee on External Trade Policy, the key officials' grouping, agreed.[88] Instead, Robertson was summoned back to Canada for consultations.[89]

Before he left for home, Robertson attended a dinner on 10 February given by Sir John Woods, Permanent Under-Secretary of the Board of Trade, designed to bring Robertson completely up-to-date on the British position. As Cripps made clear, that position was deteriorating quickly. "The fact was," the Chancellor bleakly stated, "that the rate at which their reserves were being exhausted was now again on the increase and the consequences of that development were obviously of extreme gravity." Cripps also feared the worst for the long-term, even with Marshall aid, for he did not expect the Americans to cover the dollar deficits of other members of the sterling bloc. Thus, he worried, when the Marshall Plan ended, Britain might be left in a worse position than she was at present. The implications of this, the Chancellor said, were that Britain had to increase its imports from the sterling countries and its dependent colonies in order to reduce dependence on dollar imports. The effect of such a policy on Canada was clear—fewer exports to Britain.

As he reported to Ottawa, Robertson took the occasion to make "some cautionary remarks." The Americans were beginning to recognize their responsibility as a creditor country, and a "hemispheric solution such as Cripps had sketched would be bound to have a damping effect on this hopeful secular movement of opinion and might also tend to dry up the springs of American generosity which fed the Marshall Plan." Then, he added, "I also put in a gentle warning that too vigorous a hemispheric policy such as Cripps had described would probably force us into a parallel hemispheric grouping with the United States and might destroy the special trading relations which had existed for so long between the United Kingdom and ourselves."*

What was the message Cripps wanted Robertson to carry to Ottawa? "I was anxious to be quite clear," Robertson noted, "what sort of timetable and target the United Kingdom authorities were hoping for, and I obtained a number of useful clarifications."[90] What Cripps wanted was for the United States to pay the cost of the Canadian wheat and other foods that Britain was contracted to take from Canada, a step that helped the British dollar problem—and one that helped Canada too by providing her with a vast sum in American dollars. Few in Ottawa believed this would be feasible.[91]

Norman Robertson returned to Ottawa on 13 February after a long flight that required stops in Iceland, Greenland, Goose Bay, and Sydney.[92] On the 16th he sat in at two meetings of the Interdepartmental Committee on External Trade Policy, explaining the British plight and urging his friends to go as far as they could in seeking assurances from the United States that the Marshall Plan retroactively covered goods shipped after 1 April. "It would be an extremely serious matter for both Canada and the United Kingdom", the committee minutes record him as saying, "if after March 31st the United Kingdom found itself unable to finance the Canadian food contracts."[93] After a cabinet committee approved, a long telegram was subsequently drafted (and amended by Robertson) for despatch to Hume Wrong in Washington. That was where the decisions had to be made.[94]

Unfortunately, the news from the American capital was not promising. Notwithstanding Wrong's best efforts, the Americans tried to press Canada to give more aid to Europe despite the shaky state of the Canadian reserves, and they seemed unwilling to let Marshall Plan funds cover British purchases in Canada for the period between 1 April and the

---

* These remarks were directly in line with those Robertson had been passing to Ottawa since June 1947. What he apparently did not know was that negotiations were underway, in extraordinary conditions of secrecy, on a customs union between Canada and the United States. Those negotiations had developed out of the efforts to discover ways to increase Canadian dollar holdings in late 1947, and were a conscious attempt to reinforce strength, and to maximize North American trade in the face of a world recovery that was proceeding with agonizing slowness. So intense was the secrecy that even Lester Pearson did not learn of the negotiations until mid-March 1948. (See on this Robert Cuff and J.L. Granatstein, *American Dollars-Canadian Prosperity* (Toronto, 1978), Chapter III.)

date the Plan was to go into effect.[95] This, Robertson complained from London, "seemed to invalidate the major assumptions on which our recent discussions of United Kingdom-Canadian relations rested."[96] Indeed it did, and Robertson soon reported that the British officials to whom he conveyed the glum news "were pretty shaken by what appeared to be the implications. . . ."[97] But a few days later the British were calmer, "inclined to doubt whether in the event the situation would be so black" as the Americans had suggested to Wrong.[98]

Robertson added in his account of this series of conversations that he had said nothing about the American attempt "to shake us down for a further contribution" to European recovery, over and above that represented by the $100 million the government believed it could make available in 1948 (as well as the contribution represented by the low wheat prices in the British contract). But when one of the Treasury officials asked if the Americans had suggested if Canada could do any more, "I replied in general terms that I had now heard that the State Department's expectations were pitched somewhat higher than our own estimate of what we would be able to contribute." Such questions were never asked without information, as became clear when the British indicated that their American sources had expressed the view that Canada should give Britain a free hand in drawing on the $240 million remaining of the Canadian loan.[99] The American efforts to "shake down" Canada were continuing, and the British too were becoming more importunate.

More pressure followed when the British began urging Canada to release enough of the credit to cover purchases in April. Robertson had "outlined forcibly" to the Treasury the reasons why this was unlikely, pointing out the still parlous condition of Canadian dollar reserves. But as he informed Ottawa on 16 March, he now believed that the situation had materially altered. "The change of government in Czechoslovakia," the Communist coup and the murder of Jan Masaryk, had "emphasized the gravity of the political dangers within which these financial problems must be considered. They have also produced a much higher temperature in the United States" and that might see the Marshall Plan pass Congress more quickly than had been expected. In this new state of affairs, Robertson said, "I feel strongly that it would be a mistake for us to urge too far our unwillingness to advance even a comparatively small amount of further credit. At a time when the United States is in a temper to grant aid to western Europe on such a large scale and when determined efforts are being made on this side of the Atlantic to make a western association a reality, I think that we have much to lose by an excess of financial caution." He accepted the need to restore Canadian reserves, but on the other hand, "I believe that there are circumstances in which prudential calculations can be carried too far and that this is one of them." This was the time, he concluded, "for us to share in this additional but comparatively modest way in the risks involved in attempting to safeguard western Europe from further encroachments and infiltration."[100]

Ambassadors abroad often tend to become advocates for the policies and needs of the country in which they serve. To some extent, Robertson was such a proponent, and he was evidently more sympathetic to British needs than his colleagues in the East Block, although not so much that he could not contemplate coldly the prospect of linking up economically with the United States in the event that served Canadian interests. But with this telegram, Robertson had cast his arguments in a broad fashion, relating them to the Soviet rape of Czechoslovakia and the end of Masaryk-style democracy there, linking them to the nascent efforts to create a North Atlantic alliance, and shaping them in a fashion that should have appealed to political circles in Ottawa.

His arguments did make an impact,[101] and by 25 March Canada had agreed to permit the British to draw $3.5 million a week of the Canadian credit until Congress passed the Marshall Plan.[102] In fact, the gesture to London turned out to be just that; a frightened House and Senate, alarmed by events in Europe and by telegrams from Germany that raised the threat of a war with the Soviet Union, passed the European Recovery Program on 3 April. The Economic Cooperation Act allocated $5.3 billion in aid for twelve months beginning on 1 April 1948. The Economic Cooperation Administration (ECA), the agency charged with running the Marshall Plan, came into operation on 9 April, and within a few days had agreed to cover the costs of Canadian wheat destined for Britain.[103]

This was extraordinarily good fortune, an ideal (if far from permanent) resolution of hitherto insoluble problems for Britain and Canada. The food continued to cross the ocean, much to the delight of Jimmy Gardiner's Prairie constituents; the weak Canadian dollar reserves were strengthened by infusions of American dollars; the British public saw its rations maintained; and the hard-pressed Attlee government got an economic breathing spell. Robertson had played his part in this happy result, but there could be little doubt that the real architects of the Marshall Plan were in the Kremlin. Soviet policy and actions, however they might have been misinterpreted and used in Washington, had led the Congress to approve on 3 April forms of aid that it might otherwise have rejected or delayed.

Unfortunately, however, the British economy continued its lurching and staggering course, and, despite further close consultations with Cripps, further Anglo-Canadian meetings in Ottawa, and the creation of a United Kingdom-Canada Continuing Committee on Trade and Economic Affairs, Britain's economic weakness still posed a threat to fundamental Canadian trade interests. For all the long-term good it had done, Canada might never have offered the huge loan of 1946. Britain's troubles were not going to disappear, and Robertson soon had additional opportunities to deal with London's crises.

III

While the commercial and financial relations of the North Atlantic Triangle dominated Robertson's mind, his post in London necessarily involved him in an extremely wide range of other activities and problems. The Labour government (which Robertson had anticipated might be isolationist and of whose personnel he was not initially sanguine)[104] still seemed surprisingly Empire-conscious,[105] and this forced him to wage some of those old battles against centralization, battles that were always won yet always had to be refought time and again. Robertson was probably more sympathetic to the Commonwealth link than many in the Canadian government's service,[106] but he was acutely aware of what Lord Keynes shortly before his death privately assessed as Britain's "sticky . . . self-pity" and unwillingness "to accept peacefully and wisely the fact that her position and her resources are not what they once were."[107] To be the representative of a rising nation in a declining one was no easy task.

Almost the first issue that faced the High Commissioner on his arrival in London in the fall of 1946 made that clear. The problem was Imperial defence, a hoary chestnut indeed, and one that was raised at the first High Commissioners' meeting Robertson attended on 7 November. The Australian representative, J.A. Beasley, pitched his remarks in the context of a complaint that Australia was ready to go further in the direction of defence cooperation than was Britain. The British minutes (not circulated to the High Commissioners) indicate that Robertson had said "that in Ottawa they were impressed by the opposite considerations . . . to those voiced by Mr. Beasley." Ottawa, he went on, had been disturbed by the tenor of discussion in London and in the Houses of Parliament, and he was afraid that this was "liable to provoke negative statements defining the position, which might have the effect ultimately of retarding progress." Arguing in a typical fashion for him, Robertson noted that cooperation was already a practical reality, "and in his view it would be a mistake to try to formulate the arrangements." [108]

Those remarks were eminently sensible, and Robertson's view ultimately prevailed, but not before inspired press reports caused some difficulties in Canada. Robertson subsequently called on officials in the Dominions Office and the cabinet secretariat to press the case for silence. The officials agreed, but stated that they could not control what Opposition figures or retired civil servants said. [109] Robertson was not unsympathetic, but he ventured the opinion that

. . . there was in his view a reasonable prospect that there would now be sufficient interest in Canada, as there had not been in the past, to ensure the maintenance of a proper defence organisation and preparations, and he hoped that the liaison arrangements for exchange of information would be sufficiently effective to ensure that Canadian plans would be such as to enable effective cooperation to take place if the emergency ever arose. He reiterated his view that to say too much in public about these liaison arrangements would only be embarrassing from the point of view of the prospect of such cooperation. [110]

Robertson's report to Ottawa went over the same ground but added more of his own views:

I said that in my private opinion, continued harping on the 'Imperial' aspects of defence policy in this country tended to defeat its own purposes, at least so far as cooperation in defence matters between Canada and the United Kingdom was concerned. In the course of the next few months our Government would probably have to face more difficult decisions on questions of defence policy than it had ever had to do in peace time, and that consideration of these major questions arising out of our North American position could only be made more difficult by the ever-lasting public emphasis in this country on the Imperial aspects of defence which were not central or even really relevant to the problems of defence policy with which our Government was confronted. [111]

That was pretty blunt speaking by Robertson, but he knew that his were the views both of the Department and the Prime Minister. For British officials, used to the exquisite soporifics of Vincent Massey, that meeting with Robertson must have come as a bit of a shock. Subsequent exchanges between King and Attlee made clear that Robertson spoke for his government.[112]

The High Commissioner's references to the difficult decisions on defence that faced the King government had to do with American pressure to establish defence installations in the Canadian Arctic.[113] Robertson had had something to do with the beginnings of this issue, but in London he was effectively removed from the development of policy. So, too, should have been the British government, but since London had heard of the American plans, the matter was discussed in the Chiefs of Staff Committee and by Ernest Bevin, the Foreign Secretary, with Louis St. Laurent. At the Committee, Prime Minister Attlee had "said he thought our advice in view of the political complications to the Canadian Government would be for them to proceed slowly. The American request ... would involve serious difficulties over Canadian sovereignty. ..."[114] That stated the obvious. Bevin offered similar arguments to St. Laurent.[115] The American requests would be artfully stalled and ultimately negated, primarily through Pearson's efforts, but what is significant about this incident is that Attlee sounded like Churchill, and Bevin could have been Eden. In late 1946, despite all the changes that the war had caused, despite billion dollar gifts and the loan of 1946, Britain's leaders still seemed duty-bound to seek the right to act *in loco parentis* to Canada.

But in early 1947, Robertson was beginning to think that opinion in London was changing. The Conservative Opposition still seemed to expect a ritual obeisance to consultation with the Dominions on all important matters of foreign policy, but in practice, Robertson ruminated in a message to Ottawa, genuine consultation was unusual. "The fact of the matter is, I think, that the realities of Commonwealth foreign policy are gradually becoming apparent to the people of this country. The British people have become accustomed to reading of the active and independent roles played by Australia, South Africa and Canada in United Nations conferences, and in the Paris Peace Conference. They may welcome or regret such independent activities," he said, "but they have come to take them very much for granted." In Robertson's view, this was no longer "a problem which should worry us very seriously" and he believed the Attlee government's position on consultation was "correct."[116]

In fact, about this time the Secretary of State for Dominion Affairs proposed regular and more formal High Commissioners' meetings, something that upset Mackenzie King and Ottawa, but that did not worry Robertson too much. As he reported, the pressure of work was certain to cause the arrangement to collapse "from natural causes," a shrewd and correct assessment. The idea came up again in November 1947, but on at least one occasion the British hinted that little of importance would be said, thanks to the inhibiting presence of the Indian and Pakistani High Commissioners. Robertson, the British said, could get more information privately, since they "hesitated on security grounds to discuss some questions as freely as might otherwise be possible." The meetings continued, but such utility as they had once had diminished greatly.[117] Britain, Canada and the Commonwealth, too, were much different than a few years before.

But if matters of Anglo-Canadian interest were becoming easier to separate from Commonwealth concerns, Canada was having no more success than it had had during the war in seeing its views taken seriously by Britain in her capacity as a great power dealing with the other great powers. The best instance of this was Canada's lamentably unsuccessful effort to be heard in the making of the European settlement. The great powers, now constituted in their postwar guise as the Council of Foreign Ministers, had effectively presented the world with completed drafts of peace treaties for the German satellites before other governments had the chance even to express their views, something that Robertson characterized to a meeting of High Commissioners on 7 January 1947 as a "fiasco."[118]

But how could Canada and other smaller states help draft the treaty for Germany, one area in which Canada believed it had real interests, without seeing the process collapse under the weight of representations from twenty-two nations, all interested in offering their two cents' worth? That was a question that exercised Robertson, and he told the High Commissioners that here his government "was not so fertile in ideas."[119] In fact, although Robertson essentially disagreed with the policy that Pearson was pressing on St. Laurent, the decision in Ottawa was to seek some way in which Canada could present its views to special deputies named by the Council of Foreign Ministers to hear representations and, as well, to have those views discussed by the deputies. Robertson told the East Block that such an approach was unworkable. Everyone recognized the reasonable nature of the Canadian case, he said, but no one had yet worked out a way to implement it. In his view, it was a mistake "to see Canada ask formally and publicly for more than it is likely to get." Nonetheless, Ottawa instructed Robertson to present the Canadian case to the deputies on 25 January 1947, one indication of the new direction in Ottawa. But as Robertson had warned, the deputies offered no response, nor did they reply to further initiatives presented under instructions by Robertson.[120] In the High Commissioner's view: "In all the circumstances, including the state of the world today, I should be inclined to take a good deal less than half a loaf rather than no bread at all."[121] But in the end, there was no bread; neither was there a peace treaty with Germany, for the Council of Foreign Ministers broke up in disharmony.[122]

Robertson's appraisal of the realities had been more correct than Ottawa's mild utopianism, but he took little satisfaction from this. The rejection of Canadian suggestions on peace with Germany, a country to whose defeat Canada had contributed mightily, was the surest indication yet that the postwar world was the same as the wartime one. There was scant gratitude among nations.

In some respects, the Commonwealth was much the same as it had been, too, or at least it was so long as Mackenzie King remained Prime Minister. King continued to be wary of the British, and there were still enough efforts at centralization to give him reason. Similarly, as when External Affairs tried to proffer helpful advice on the ways Britain could keep India in the Commonwealth once she got her independence, the Prime Minister thought the Departmental proposals embodied "an unnecessary, and possibly dangerous, interference in matters which were of no special concern to the Canadian Government; that," as Pearson told Robertson, "it seemed to approve a doctrine of participation in Imperial affairs which he had opposed all his life, and which might be exploited by people in London for undesirable purposes."[123]

Certainly King remained opposed to participation in Imperial affairs, and Robertson knew his master's mind as well as anyone. Thus in September 1947 when he was recuperating in Paris, Robertson sent a message to Pearson to express his concern that the British were planning too extensively for the meeting of Prime Ministers that was to take place at the same time as the wedding of Princess Elizabeth in November. The agenda was brief, but the press build-up was likely to be huge and, Robertson said, "Our friends in the Antipodes are lavish with the large words which sound well in communiqués and even if they accept the limited agenda ... they can be counted upon to make it public that, for their part, they would have been glad to have taken the occasion of this meeting to discuss questions of immigration, defence and commercial policies." Canada, Robertson said, would be blamed for the exclusion of these items from the agenda. In such circumstances, perhaps Mackenzie King's visit to London should be simply for the Royal Wedding and strictly informal conversations. [124] In fact that was King's desire, and the British had to lower their sights. The Dominions Secretary wrote to Attlee to say he hoped Britain could "persuade [King] to take part in a purely informal and friendly discussion of the major issues, in which he will not be called upon to commit himself in any way." [125]

So King's visit to London was for the wedding, a gala affair that brightened the gloomy fall of 1947 and one that demonstrated that a Labour government could stage circuses with all the skills of any Tory régime. The chief political event of importance was an extraordinary briefing on the building world crisis by Foreign Secretary Bevin, one that seemed to see war ahead in the near future. [126] The Defence Minister, A.V. Alexander, amplified this in private conversation with King and Robertson, and the two Canadians left the meeting agreeing, as King wrote, that "it was the most serious situation that we could possibly have imagined and indeed was altogether beyond anything I had hitherto thought possible . . . within three weeks, there may be another world war." [127] But when Robertson began to check Bevin's account against other sources, the picture seemed brighter. "First," he wrote to Pearson, "no similar warning about the seriousness of the immediate situation has been suggested through Service channels to our Liaison Officers here." Nor was there any sign of British or American preparations to meet the contingency foreseen by the British ministers. "For what they are worth, these supplementary impressions that I have reported do suggest that there are grounds for taking a rather more hopeful view of the prospect of peace this winter than the Prime Minister and I took away from the meeting at Downing Street." [128]

A more formal and full-fledged Prime Ministers' Meeting took place in the autumn of 1948, Mackenzie King's last visit abroad as Prime Minister. King had begun his trip in Paris, at the United Nations meeting there, with Robertson in attendance. Evidently the Prime Minister was at his very worst, fussing, complaining and criticizing, and driving those near him to distraction. [129] Gordon Robertson, now on the Prime Minister's Office staff, wrote to Jack Pickersgill in Ottawa that the "first week here was one of the worst I want to put in. Basically, I think the reason is that the P.M. felt he had to make a good speech to the United Nations—that he should give a 'message'—but the horrible truth was that he had no message to give. He liked nothing that was prepared for him . . . and the mood became pretty poisonous. However, after days of struggle by Norman, Gerry Riddell, [General A.G.L.] McNaughton, sundry others and myself something got put into shape. . . ." He added that "Norman and Jules [Léger from the High Commission staff] are invaluable, despite the Prime Minister's considered view that 'none of the people around me are worth their weight in mud.' "[130] Norman Robertson was not one to complain; he limited himself to sending Pickersgill a sardonic "Having a wonderful time. Wish you were here" postcard.[131]

In London, Mackenzie King fell seriously ill with heart strain, and on the advice of Lord Moran, Churchill's physician, was obliged to miss the Prime Ministers' Meetings. Robertson was summoned to the bedside and told the news. "I could see that this was a heavy blow to him," King wrote. "His thoughts were of who should come over" to represent the government.[132] In the end, St. Laurent came, but not before Robertson attended as the Canadian representative for several days. [133]* The results of the meetings were both an increase and a decrease in Commonwealth membership. The way was paved for India, Pakistan and Ceylon to be admitted, and at its own wish the Irish Republic left.[134] Robertson shared the interest and concerns of his Prime Minister and colleagues over these questions, but there was, it seemed clear, an indefinable sense that somehow the Commonwealth now mattered less. In part this was a reflection of Britain's weakened power; in part it was the new status and independence of the Dominions; in part it was a feeling that with the admission of the non-white nations the club had altered; and in part it was because of the new power relationships in the world.

For Canada this new power balance was most noticeable in the long process that culminated in the negotiation and signature of the North Atlantic Treaty in spring 1949. The conversations took place in Washington, and Hume Wrong did most of the work; Robertson was again removed from the scene. This was not the result of any deliberate policy; far from it. Pearson and Escott Reid made a conscientious effort to keep Robertson informed at every stage of the process, and the High Commissioner received far more material than did any other Canadian representative abroad.[135] Nonetheless, his influence on the creation of NATO was relatively slight.

But it was not non-existent. In late April 1948, after the conclusion of the talks in Washington between Britain, Canada and the United States

---

* In addition, the Robertsons attended the dinner given by the King at Buckingham Palace for the Prime Ministers and their wives. This didn't bother Robertson, but his wife was terrified to discover that she was placed between Winston Churchill, then Leader of the Opposition, and Pandit Nehru. Fortunately, Ernest Bevin, across the table, and Churchill sang music-hall songs for most of the evening. (Mrs. N.A. Robertson interview, 25 Feb. 80).

that launched the process that led to NATO, Robertson, according to Reid, "the most profound thinker in the Canadian foreign service," set out the reasons why he believed a North Atlantic Treaty vital to Canada:

Ever since we have been in a position to shape our own policy abroad, we have had to wrestle with the antinomies created by our position as a North American country and as a member of the Commonwealth, by our special relationship with the United Kingdom and at the same time, although in a lesser degree, with other countries in western Europe as well. A situation in which our special relationship with the United Kingdom can be identified with our special relationships with other countries in western Europe and in which the United States will be providing a firm basis, both economically and probably militarily, for the link across the North Atlantic, seems to me such a providential solution for so many of our problems that I feel we should go to great lengths and even incur considerable risks in order to consolidate our good fortune and ensure our proper place in this new partnership. [136]

Robertson was not insensitive to the dangers posed by the Soviet Union, [137] but as that message suggested, his major interest in the proposed alliance was with the economic and political problems it might help to resolve. If the negotiations were handled correctly, he seemed to be saying, Canada could solve its long-standing commercial difficulties or at least ease them greatly. A North Atlantic arrangement could give Canada access to markets that were now fragile, it could solidify links with western Europe, it could even help to ease the problems of sharing a continent with the Americans. In other words, as Reid said later, Robertson definitely saw "the usefulness of the Alliance as an instrument of Canadian economic foreign policy." [138]

Robertson's longstanding concern that Canada might find itself caught in a squeeze between Britain (or a European economic community that included Britain) and the United States had led him to suggest what ultimately became the great Canadian crusade for Article 2 of the North Atlantic Treaty. His reasoning was clear: how could the nations unite for defence if they were to engage in trade wars among themselves? [139] Because of this, as Reid explained in his excellent history of the negotiation of the Treaty, Robertson strongly supported the Canadian suggestion that the pact include a clause indicating the parties' agreement "to make every effort in common to eliminate conflict in their economic policies and to develop to the full the great possibilities of trade between them." Robertson suggested adding the word "international" before "economic policies," and he considered that such a sentence in the Treaty "might not only prepare the way for another triangular attack on the trade and dollar problem but perhaps in the meantime make it easier for the United States to keep our interests in mind in determining E.C.A., and particularly off-shore, purchasing policies."[140] In other words, the difficulties in late 1948 and early 1949 that Canada was running into in having the Economic Cooperation Association finance wheat sales to Britain, provided yet another reason for having an economic clause in the Treaty.

The negotiation of Article 2 was as difficult as any part of the Treaty, and Wrong, who had never believed it to be either necessary or desirable, exhausted himself in the effort to secure even a watered-down version. Robertson did what he could in Britain, and as he reported to Ottawa on 16 February 1949, the Foreign Office had told the British representative at the negotiations to support "our desire to have an economic clause included in the treaty. I think it is clear that they decided to do so because they wanted to meet our wishes and not because they had any special interest themselves in having such a provision in the treaty."[141] In the end the Treaty did include a clause binding the signatories to "seek to eliminate conflict in their international economic policies and . . . encourage economic collaboration between any or all of them." That was a victory for Robertson's conception of the world, but regrettably not one that had great practical import.

There was at least one additional reason for Robertson's enthusiasm for the Treaty.[142] He remembered the war all too well, all the humiliations Canada had suffered as it tried to win just representation for itself in Allied decision-making. A North Atlantic Treaty, he believed, meant "that in another war the organs of the alliance could be created by the alliance as a whole and could derive their authority from the alliance."[143] That would give Canada some share from the outset, and here Robertson was certainly correct, although he could not have foreseen the way the United States came to dominate NATO.

So Norman Robertson's was apparently the original idea that led to Article 2, an important contribution and one that derived from his twenty-year connection with the development of commercial policy. That was something, but he must have railed at the fate that had sidelined him in London at a time the world was being restructured in Washington.

Vital events were occurring in Europe, too, and Robertson became directly involved in the Berlin blockade of 1948-49. That crisis was a product of the failure of the Big Four powers to reach agreement on a

German settlement, and followed directly on the British, American and French decision to undertake a major reform of currency throughout their occupation zones. In response, the Russians declared that, by so acting, the Allies had forfeited their right to participate in the occupation and administration of Berlin, located deep within the Russian zone. A blockade of the former capital followed, ostensibly to protect the old currency that was still valid in the Eastern zone, and after the failure of attempts by the Big Four to create a Berlin currency, the Russians introduced a currency reform of their own and tightened the blockade.

Robertson was in London throughout this initial period of tension, fending off press reports that Britain had formally requested the Canadian government to contribute to the airlift which the Allies were mounting to supply West Berlin with necessities and to maintain the Allied presence in the city. Robertson had initially favoured the despatch of transport aircraft and the Department agreed, but the cabinet chose not to participate in the operation. [144]

But in September 1948 Robertson was in Paris at the United Nations meetings when the Berlin crisis came before the Security Council. "I am not very happy about the reference to the United Nations," he wrote to Pearson in Ottawa, "but relieved that so far it is to the Security Council rather than to the Assembly. I think it is desirable that the question be kept there for quite a long time. Certainly no effort should be made to force it onto the floor of this General Assembly. The reference to the Security Council," he went on, "of a situation in which four of the five great powers are directly involved will clearly throw a much heavier relative strain and responsibility on the non-permanent members of the Council than any business with which the Council has had to cope heretofore." [145]

Just how heavy a responsibility soon became clear. Canada had been elected to the Council in 1948, and after the failure of attempts to resolve the Berlin crisis, the President of the Security Council on 6 October invited the governments of the members not directly involved (Canada, Argentina, Belgium, China, Colombia and Syria) each to nominate a financial or economic expert to recommend ways to reach an agreement on trade and financial arrangements for Berlin. [146] The Berlin Currency Committee was wholly unofficial, but, at the request of the US, Norman Robertson was named Canada's representative. At the first meeting of the committee, his colleagues chose him as chairman. [147]

The committee worked under intense pressure, meeting in Paris twenty-eight times between 30 November and 28 December and, after its life was extended, for forty-two more meetings between 14 January 1949 and 11 February.[148] Robertson was properly sceptical that currency was at the heart of the matter, but as John Holmes remembers, he believed that once countries reached the point where they were prepared to agree on a technical formula, everyone could save face.[149]

The difficulty was in arriving at that technical agreement. The committee had at its service a number of able experts from the United Nations secretariat, including Nicholas Kaldor of Britain and Walter Rostow of the United States, but while the experts were fertile in advice, neither they nor the committee could readily crack the nut of Great Power intransigence. The committee did, however, on 22 December, produce a draft proposal for the settlement of the crisis and in the new year those proposals were discussed and criticized by representatives of the Great Powers. For Robertson, clearly doing the West's work on the committee, the most embarrassing moment came in mid-January when the Soviet Union essentially accepted the draft recommendations as the basis for an agreement, while the United States, apparently fearing that any compromise weakened the will to resist, rejected them. At that point, Lord Kaldor recalled, Robertson's usefulness ended,[150] and although the committee plodded on for another month, there was little chance of success. If only the committee "either died or succeeded," Jetty Robertson worried over her husband, "but it just goes on amongst great difficulties."[151] On 11 February, it reported to the President of the Security Council that it had reached the conclusion that the Great Powers "are so far apart that further work ... does not appear useful."[152]

A futile effort, one that left a bad taste in Robertson's mouth and led him to pronounce himself "increasingly puzzled and disturbed at the U.S. attitude. ..."[153] But perhaps the committee had helped marginally to cool a difficult situation, and it may have moved the Russians and Americans towards a willingness to reduce the antagonism. Certainly the blockade was lifted on 12 May 1949.[154]

IV

The feeling that events had passed him by grew stronger as Robertson's term in London continued. As early as October 1947, he had told Mackenzie King that "while he liked London, he would be happier within another year in being back in Ottawa."[155] That was repeated in February 1948 when, as King recorded, Robertson "did not hesitate to make clear to me his preference to be back in Canada and to hold the position here that he had before." King believed this to be a good thing: "I really think Robertson's judgment is sounder than Pearson's on these international affairs, and that he would be better at the head of the Dept. here. Is less fond of speaking or of travelling or of participating in the U.N., etc. Less likely to get the govt. into trouble." [156]

It was highly unusual for Robertson to indicate his interests in a post for himself; it would have been extraordinary if he had done anything to secure it, and he did not. Thus, in September 1948, when Pearson went into the cabinet as Secretary of State for External Affairs, he had Robertson's blessing and support, [157] and there was no move by him to return to Ottawa as Under-Secretary. Some in Ottawa, notably in the American Embassy, seemed to feel that was a possibility, [158] and King raised the subject with Robertson in Paris. The High Commissioner, King wrote, had said "that he would like and is quite prepared—while he is prepared to do whatever is suggested of him—would welcome . . . going back to Ottawa, and that at once rather than a year hence."

But the Prime Minister's successor, Louis St. Laurent, had already been picked by a Liberal convention, and although King remained at the head of the government in a rather extraordinary state of affairs while he went abroad to Paris and London, his influence clearly was drawing to an end. There was an inkling of this when he noted that St. Laurent and Pearson might prefer Jean Désy or Pierre Dupuy as Under-Secretary until the elections, presumably as an indication that French Canadians could rise to senior bureaucratic positions. "My own view is that if Robertson is to return to Ottawa," King said, "he should return at once and be of help to the govt. there. What is needed is someone to guide them on a variety of policies rather than only on E.A. He himself sees that necessity." [159]

But nothing happened, and King was soon in retirement. Louis St. Laurent was fully in charge, reliant on Pearson for advice on foreign policy and on Jack Pickersgill to run his office and provide counsel on a multiplicity of political and policy questions. Pickersgill has since recalled his concern that the Prime Minister relied on him too much and his view that there should have been another source of advice close at hand. [160] At the same time, with the position of Under-Secretary vacant and with Escott Reid filling the post on an acting basis (Désy and Dupuy having declined the honour and the work), there was both the opportunity and the necessity to juggle a number of senior posts.

Of the participants in that diplomatic minuet, only Pickersgill survives today. His recollection is that St. Laurent began to consider bringing back

Robertson to Ottawa after his return from the 1948 Commonwealth Conference. "You don't suppose that there would be any possibilities of having Robertson come back to Ottawa?" he asked Pickersgill. The aide said he thought there might be. [161]

But in what role? He could be Under-Secretary, if Pearson wanted that; he could conceivably even fill the post of Deputy Under-Secretary or Ambassador on duty in the Department, positions that Pearson and Robertson had earlier discussed. [162] But it seemed clear that Pearson preferred his friendly rival not to be in his Department. In part this was good sense. Pearson knew that as Minister he could not and would not be able to administer the Department. But if that was so, Robertson was no administrator and, in any case, Robertson had his own strong views on policy and operational style. Pearson also believed—and here Pickersgill's testimony is certain—that it was unwise to reverse the superior-subordinate role. And finally, the suspicion exists that Pearson believed Robertson to have a better intellect than his own, something that might take some of the gloss off his performance. [163] In the circumstances, Robertson was out, and from early December 1948 onwards, Pearson's eye was on Arnold Heeney, the Secretary to the Cabinet. [164]

Heeney was extremely able, a marvel of organizational expertise. But he lacked the original mind that was Robertson's greatest trait, and he did not have his foreign policy experience. Possibly that was in his favour in Pearson's eyes, for he was much less likely than Robertson to try to impose his own sense of policy on the work of the Department. Another possibility was Hume Wrong, the Ambassador in the United States, senior to both Pearson and Robertson in years of service. In 1941, Wrong had been disappointed at being passed over for the Under-Secretary's post, but by 1948 his ambitions had cooled, he was "loath to leave Washington" for personal and family reasons, so soon after his appointment there, and he was concerned about his health. Wrong had only one eye—"it *is* a good eye," he said, "but it's getting a bit elderly & feels the strain more than it used to do." [165]

So matters remained in flux into the new year. Pickersgill wrote to Robertson on 7 January 1949 that "Hume Wrong is here today, pleading his indispensability in Washington. My guess is he will be unsuccessful, and that Arnold will move. This is conditional, of course, upon Bob Bryce [of the Finance Department] being Arnold's successor. I shall be glad when all this is over," Pickersgill added feelingly. "Personally, I wish you were coming back to the East Block. . . ." [166] Certainly that sounded as if Robertson was to remain in London.

But within two days the position had changed. In a thirteen-page, hand-written letter, Pickersgill gave Robertson word of the proposals, stating that he was speaking for the Prime Minister.

I assume you probably know that the two alternatives under consideration have been
1.   Wrong to External & Wilgress to Washington
2.   Heeney to External & Bryce to Privy Council.

The P.M. first inclined to alternative no. 1 but Hume's reluctance to move combined with the [Dean] Acheson appointment [as Secretary of State in the Truman administration—he and Wrong were close friends] swung the balance towards no. 2. It looked yesterday morning as though it was settled that way, but everyone (except me) had reckoned without [Finance Minister Douglas] Abbott and particularly without Clark [both of whom objected to losing Bryce from the Department of Finance]. . . . I do not think this opposition would have weighed so heavily had the P.M. not discussed the whole matter with W.L.M. K[ing]. last night. . . . Mr. King was very emphatic in his view that the P.M. should have you returned to Ottawa—that you would be more use than anyone else to the P.M. and the govt. . . .*

Pickersgill told his friend that he had become convinced that morning that St. Laurent "really would like to have you here, but was very dubious about the fairness of making any proposal to you." Pickersgill had had to put the question bluntly to the Prime Minister: "You *personally* would really like to have Norman here as your adviser, wouldn't you?" His reply, Robertson was told, was "I would much rather have Norman than anyone else in the public service." Pickersgill then asked the Prime

---

* Mackenzie King's account is in his diary. 8 Jan. 49: "I strongly advised St. Laurent to bring Norman Robertson back. He has Heeney in mind for Ex. Affairs. On score he is a very good organizer. He has no real judgment or knowledge of Ex. Affairs, Govt. being too much run by Claxton & Pearson, not enough on domestic policies." 18 Jan. 49: King called the Prime Minister about the proposed changes. "I think these changes are a mistake. Robertson should certainly be here but in External Affairs—He alone is qualified to deal with world problems. Arnold has neither the knowledge or the judgment nor the Liberal point of view. He will create jealousies etc. Gordon Robertson has not the mental agility to do the [Privy] Council work. & R. should not have to do the clerical kind of work expected there." But two days later, King changed his mind, realizing that Robertson was to be deputy to the Prime Minister. "Had he gone to External Affairs, he would have been Pearson's deputy. I had strongly pressed St. Laurent to have Robertson come to be a strength & support to him. I now see how that may be more effectively brought about by his being in the Privy Council, hearing *all* discussions there. Economic as well as international. He can be free of clerical routine & do thinking for 'the lot of them.' " (PAC, King Diaries.)

Minister if he had ever thought of "appointing Arnold to External and bringing you back as his own Deputy. This was obviously an entirely new idea to him, and a most attractive one." St. Laurent worried that Robertson might not care for the mechanical and administrative side of the Privy Council Office and Cabinet Secretary roles, but Pickersgill assured the Prime Minister (and Robertson) that the Office was well organized, that "practically all of that could be done by subordinates, and that, in the position, you should be free to advise the P.M. on the whole range of policy." That attracted St. Laurent mightily, but he did tell Pickersgill that Robertson should have a completely free choice between the Under-Secretaryship and the Privy Council Office posts.

Pickersgill went over some of the arrangements that could be made, including the posting of Dana Wilgress to London as High Commissioner, and dealt with the timing of a possible changeover. But then he added one "final thing. The conditions of work with the present P.M., the degree of personal consideration, the complete frankness and unqualified confidence are as satisfying as they are novel."[167] The contrast with Mackenzie King was clear.

The same mail brought Robertson a letter from Heeney, conveying his blessing on the proposal and urging Robertson to take the Privy Council Office post. Heeney had two main reasons for this: Robertson was badly needed in Ottawa both by ministers and the senior officials and, second, he could be employed as an adviser on policy "for which you are suited as no one else in the service." Heeney was aware that Robertson might prefer to return as Under-Secretary, but as a man who always had his own plans for his career, Heeney was frank enough to bare his ambitions for the post.[168]

What aspects of the arguments advanced by Pickersgill and Heeney weighed heaviest on Robertson we do not know. Probably his preference was to return to the Department of External Affairs, but he must have been aware of the difficulties this would pose for Pearson and himself.* As well, he did not want to disappoint Heeney, his old and good friend. Certainly it was flattering to have the Prime Minister express a desire for his advice, and offering advice was what he was best at. That seems to have tipped the balance, and within a few days he had telephoned

---

* Pearson wrote on 22 January 1949 to express his congratulations at Robertson's new post. Agreement, he said, had practically been reached on having Heeney stay in the Privy Council Office and Wrong return to Ottawa "when the Prime Minister thought the matter over again and decided that an even better arrangement would be for you to become, as

(Cont'd)

Pickersgill his acceptance of the Privy Council Office. The order-in-council naming him to that post was signed on 19 January. At a salary of $15,000, Norman Robertson was to become Clerk of the Privy Council and Secretary to the Cabinet with effect from March 1949.[169]

Robertson had built up unmatched links with the senior levels of the Whitehall establishment and with several of the ministers in the Attlee government. His ability to provide suggestions and his knack for producing useful compromises was highly valued; these traits helped guarantee him access, that most precious of commodities for an ambassador. At a farewell party, J.H. Warren, one of Canada House's young and able third secretaries, saw Ernest Bevin take Robertson's hand in both of his own and say, "We'll miss thee, Norman."[170] The British did miss him.

There was a small crisis when news of the appointment leaked out;[171] there were some problems in working out the precise date of the return, complicated by a Liberal by-election loss in Quebec and the probability of a general election soon, and some behind the scenes efforts by Jetty Robertson to have the return put off until 1 April rather than early March;[172] and Pickersgill had to reassure Lemuel Robertson in Vancouver that this was not a demotion for his son.[173] As well, there were difficulties in arranging for a house in Ottawa[174] and successful pleas for Robertson to speed his return. Heeney was the key man here, arguing that difficulties in External Affairs demanded his own presence there as soon as possible. On receiving this plea, Robertson offered to sail on 2 March, leaving the family to follow two weeks later. "In some ways I would myself prefer this, because the fag end of a spent job is rather dusty," he said. "However, I would not feel free to exercise this preference unless you think in Ottawa that my returning a fortnight earlier than planned would really help. . . ."[175] Ottawa did, and Robertson departed for Canada on 2 March, leaving his wife behind with the children and all those "dusty" details. "At times," Robertson wrote to his wife from the ship, "I have qualms of conscience about once more leaving you to tidy up & complete the moving. I hope it hasn't been too much of a chore. . . ."[176]

Norman Robertson arrived in Ottawa on 10 March and was sworn in

---

he put it, 'his Deputy Prime Minister' and for Arnold to move into External Affairs." Pearson thought this an admirable arrangement, one that would let Robertson "develop those peculiar talents of yours to the utmost!" (PAC, Pearson Papers, N1, vol. 13, 22 Jan. 49.) St. Laurent also wrote warmly and expressed pleasure at having Robertson's counsel and assistance to draw on. (PAC, Robertson Papers, vol. 2, Personal Correspondence file, 3 Feb. 49.)

as Secretary to the Cabinet on 15 March 1949.[177] Sometime earlier, Mackenzie King had told Jetty Robertson that her husband was more than an External Affairs man—"he was a Government man—very helpful for policies generally."[178] The government man was to have his opportunity.

CHAPTER IX

Secretary to the Cabinet

J ETTY ROBERTSON AND Judith arrived in Canada two weeks after the
new Secretary to the Cabinet had reached Ottawa. Norman
Robertson was waiting to greet them, and almost the first thing
he said to his wife was that "the new job is a mistake. There is
nothing for me to do."[1]

Nothing for him to do? That seemed difficult to believe, and yet in a
curious way it was almost so. The position of Clerk of the Privy Council
and Secretary to the Cabinet, while it might have been designed to fit
someone of Robertson's unique talents, combined routine chores and the
opportunity for proffering advice to the Prime Minister and the cabinet.
But the difficulty was that Louis St. Laurent and Norman Robertson were
similar in too many ways. Both were diffident, both were men who
responded better than they initiated, and in the circumstances the
relationship between them never reached the level of intimacy, trust and
cooperation that had bound Robertson (however uncomfortably) to
Mackenzie King.

I

The modern Privy Council Office and Cabinet Secretariat was a creation
of the war. Before 1940, the Clerk of the Privy Council and a tiny staff
had concerned themselves with the mechanics of formal executive action,
processing and then passing on orders in council. There were no records
of cabinet decisions, no agendas, no minutes. As Arnold Heeney later
wrote, the wonder was that "such a regime could function at all."[2] The
retirement of E.J. Lemaire as Clerk in March 1940, and the press of
business brought on by the war, opened the way to change, and Arnold

246

Heeney, since 1938 the Principal Secretary to the Prime Minister, was appointed Clerk of the Privy Council and Secretary to the Cabinet to modernize the system.

Heeney's work since September 1939 had engaged him almost completely in the work of the Cabinet War Committee, the directing body of government, and when Dr. Skelton, the Under-Secretary of State for External Affairs, realized the necessity for a Cabinet Secretariat and conceived the idea of putting it in the Privy Council Office, where it could serve the Prime Minister and his Ministers, Heeney was the logical choice to run the new unit. Over time, and often with only grudging acceptance from Mackenzie King, Heeney introduced the systematization without which Canada's war could scarcely have been run or won. "In essence," Heeney wrote, all he did was to introduce "simple clear-cut rules for the systematic disposition of business—the form and matter of introducing items for the agenda, provision for adequate notice of proposals calling for decision, the preparation and circulation of papers, the maintenance of suitable records of discussion and the formulation of agreed conclusions, arrangements for follow-up to ensure that decisions were given effect promptly by the responsible Ministers and their departments." In addition, Heeney effectively created, organized and kept track of a plethora of committees.[3] It was a revolution in the conduct of the Canadian government and, when the Cabinet War Committee ceased to operate after V-E Day, the procedures Heeney had devised were essentially transferred to the full cabinet.[4]

Heeney's role was more than that of secretary and paper-pusher. From the outset, the Secretary to the Cabinet was in close, almost daily, contact with the Under-Secretary of State for External Affairs and the Chiefs of Staff Committee. "It was also natural," Heeney wrote, "that the Secretary should be employed by the Prime Minister to consult with colleagues on matters of Government policy not yet at the stage for Cabinet consideration. Frequently too the Secretary and members of his staff would prepare memoranda on subjects of major interest for the Prime Minister's own guidance, either on direction or on the Secretary's own initiative."[5] Clearly the Secretary to the Cabinet had great potential power. Heeney's talents were in organization and administration and not in the formulation of policy,[6] and he made his Secretariat the smoothest functioning arm of the Ottawa bureaucracy.

Yet for all its importance, the Privy Council Office and Cabinet Secretariat was tiny, usually no more than nine or ten officers.[7] "We are a very small but separate department of government," Heeney told the

National War College in Washington in 1948. "The personnel . . . consists of a very small number of permanent officers who have no other departmental allegiance, and at least two or three times as many who are seconded for a tour of two or three years from other departments. . . . Each of the Services," he continued, "is represented in the Cabinet Secretariat. There are also representatives from Defence Research and from most of the departments of government which have important matters of policy coming up for decision. . . ."[8] In addition, Heeney's staff served as secretaries on cabinet committees and as secretaries (and occasionally as chairmen) of interdepartmental committees—roles of substantial importance and power.[9]

Thus the Secretary to the Cabinet exercised considerable influence in the running of government. Did a matter go to the full cabinet or to a cabinet committee? Had the question been cleared properly and fully with all interested departments? Is the cabinet paper on the subject adequate for the task? Where will the item be placed on the agenda? When? Will all the interested ministers be present? How will the cabinet conclusion be worded?[10] The Secretary to the Cabinet, a journalist noted, with only some exaggeration,

. . . is, in a sense, the Cabinet's toll gate. Extend the idea by saying that tribute of some kind must be exacted before [he] says 'enter.' That payment is in ideas. If the idea in [his] judgment is not good enough, then the matter does not get before the Cabinet. Without bothering about further imagery, just picture the position the Clerk of the Privy Council holds. He could at least stave off things he did not like for a long time. Items agreeable to him would obviously move to council table with accelerated despatch.[11]

The position could be a vital one.

This was the post that now was Robertson's. Heeney had tried to prepare his friend for the task by sending him useful briefing memoranda before he left England. The nature of the job, Heeney said, "can be suited to the incumbent as very few can in the service; the duties of the Clerkship are not onerous and have in fact been performed . . . by the Assistant Clerk and his staff since I took over. . . ." He added that "the mechanical and procedural part of the Secretary's function can be performed by assistants—agenda, minutes and all the rest of it; you would, of course, have responsibility for this and it is in my view important that the progress made in arrangements for the despatch of business should not be lost." All that, he said, well aware of Robertson's distaste for the mechanics of administration, could be handled by the Office staff. Heeney added that "your taking over here would make this position in fact what it has been in theory viz. that of the first of the principal officers of the service. . . ."[12]

Heeney also reorganized the Cabinet Secretariat just before he left it, "to put into commission the principal routine duties which I have performed as Secretary to the Cabinet" and to "relieve you for the tasks for which your presence here is primarily required," — to provide advice to Prime Minister St. Laurent. What he had done, he told Robertson, was to assign departmental responsibilities to the four senior officers on his staff: Evan Gill, Paul Pelletier, Gordon Robertson, and W.E.D. Halliday. "The four senior members of the Secretariat will be responsible for Cabinet and Committee work in the areas assigned to them," Heeney's memo noted, "will have immediate supervision of the staffs in their respective sections," and would assist Robertson at cabinet meetings and by acting as secretaries of cabinet committees and, in exceptional cases, of senior interdepartmental committees. Halliday would be responsible for the preparation of agenda and documentation for cabinet, for committees, and for cabinet conclusions. The formal Privy Council work would remain with A.M. Hill, the Assistant Clerk, who, Heeney said, "performs admirably."[13] Robertson could have Sybil Rump from External Affairs as his personal secretary, who, Heeney wrote, "told me yesterday that she would be very happy to accept transfer . . . to work directly under you. . . ." Robertson could not have asked for a better staff with which to begin in the Privy Council Office and Cabinet Secretariat, and Gordon Robertson, in particular, proved invaluable.[14]

Over time Robertson tinkered with the structure he had inherited from Heeney. On 1 March 1950, the files of his office and the Prime Minister's Office were consolidated into a single unit with two subdivisions: cabinet files and the Prime Minister's personal files.[15] There was a proposal to amalgamate the Prime Minister's Office newspaper clipping staff of seven with that of the Department of External Affairs,[16] and there was an attempt to reduce the vast amount of filing by returning to the Department all External Affairs telegrams not explicitly linked to cabinet records.[17] Most important, in 1950, the Chiefs of Staff Committee Secretariat, linked with the Cabinet Secretariat since 1944, was physically separated and combined with the Joint Staff Secretariat under the Minister of National Defence.[18]*

---

* Charles Ritchie described the subsequent renovations of the East Block to a friend: "The vulgarization of the East Block by the minions of Public Works goes on apace and I for one regret the cobwebs and dun-coloured walls of the classic epoch. . . . The corridors

(Cont'd)

Still, Robertson's position as Secretary to the Cabinet simply did not work out. As we have seen, he did not take long to realize this and in July 1949, just three months after his return to Ottawa, Robertson wrote to Heeney to express his concerns:

On the day I left Ottawa [for a secret trip to England to discuss the British financial crisis], I had a word with Mike and the Prime Minister about my own position. I told them that I felt it wasn't working out very well, and though I recognized that these last three or four months were not in any sense a representative period, yet my misgivings about the arrangement went deeper than that, and would still be valid even when there was a good deal more work to do at our end of the East Block.

St. Laurent's first election had taken place on 27 June, and that contest had reduced the number of cabinet meetings and kept ministers on the hustings; it had also slowed the operations of government and put the Prime Minister more in need of political advice than of counsel on policy.

Robertson continued in his letter to Heeney:

As you probably know, I have worried a good deal about these arrangements, and have tried to think of some way in which they might be made to work out in the way that you and Jack [Pickersgill] and the Prime Minister had in mind. I have, however, reluctantly come to the conclusion that the best way to clear up an unsatisfactory situation is to move me somewhere else for two or three years. I haven't any very strong personal preferences in the matter. . . .

Robertson then suggested he might go to Switzerland, Yugoslavia or even to the Vatican as Ambassador. He had thought for some time that there was a good case for opening a mission in Vatican City "and that initially it should be filled by a protestant (l.c.). I should have to refurbish my Presbyterianism for the purpose, but perhaps I could qualify." [19]

Robertson must have been persuaded not to press his plans. But it is striking that he had within three months reached the conclusion that he was in the wrong place. In 1942, after just a short time as Under-Secretary, he had prepared but not sent a letter of resignation to Mackenzie King, and seven years later he had done the same. Why?

The crucial point in 1949 was the relationship with the Prime Minister. St. Laurent was a man of first-class intelligence and one with a lawyer's knack for striking at the root of a problem. He was courteous, considerate

---

carpeted with a hideous green and red linoleum are further adorned by circular scarlet spitoons at discreet intervals. The effect is that of a fourth class commercial hotel. On the other hand the main entrance hall has been transformed by the installation of elaborate oak panelling into the likeness of a Presbyterian church." (Bishop's University, T.W.L. MacDermot Papers, file 54, Ritchie to MacDermot, 14 May 52.)

of his staff, but still a bit aloof. When he wanted information, he wanted it quickly and succinctly, and he preferred to have options laid out with recommended courses of action. But that was not Robertson's style. His mind worked quickly, but his normally cautious instincts had been reinforced by his years with King. Problems had to be handled carefully, checked and rechecked, and solutions probed for flaws again and again before irrevocable action. There had to be time for reflection. Furthermore, Robertson was not a self-starter and never had been. He needed someone to get him underway on a problem, someone like Mackenzie King, who telephoned him at any hour with a series of impossible demands to which Robertson responded with superhuman efforts. St. Laurent himself responded rather than initiated and did not seem able to operate in a way that meshed with Robertson's. The result was that both men sat in their offices waiting for the other to take the initiative. They were like "two canons bowing in the choir," or so Jetty Robertson told Marcel Cadieux, much bowing, much respect, but little rapport.[20] Even Robertson's splendid conversational skills were wasted on the Prime Minister, who was and remained all business.

Another factor in Robertson's disquiet was Pickersgill. As head of the Prime Minister's Office, Pickersgill tended to have a monoply on political advice, and the Prime Minister gradually came to look on his invaluable aide almost as a son. Pickersgill was aware of this, and indeed that was one reason he had suggested Robertson return to Ottawa, so that St. Laurent had ready access to an alternate source of advice. Pickersgill had promised his friend access, influence and power, but through no fault of his own he could not deliver. St. Laurent simply preferred to work with Pickersgill and, as Pickersgill later wrote: "I was too often the intermediary between St. Laurent and Robertson, and they never developed the easy direct relationship I had hoped for."[21] Pickersgill is not universally admired in Ottawa, but none suggest that he connived at Robertson's isolation, and the relationship between the two friends continued as before.

Pearson was yet another problem for Robertson. The Secretary of State for External Affairs had a very close relationship with the Prime Minister, who encouraged him and supported him in cabinet. In the circumstances, Pearson was the channel of advice on foreign policy questions, and thus, even in his prime area of expertise, Robertson found himself frustrated. The relationship with the minister was friendly but slightly distant, and the degree of tension that had existed between the two men since 1941 was in no way dissipated. In fact, Douglas Le Pan, back in Ottawa after his stint in London and a Guggenheim fellowship, frequently found himself playing the role of go-between.[22] The absence of a close working relationship with the head of his old Department, and the consequent feeling that he was being shut out of the making of foreign policy, left Robertson unhappy. When this was combined with his inability to get close to the Prime Minister, the result was an intense dissatisfaction.

But if Robertson was unhappy, his time in the Privy Council Office was not a tragic one. He made a considerable impact on all levels of government except the top one, he was consulted freely by ministers, and he had his usual good relations with his colleagues among the mandarins. The press still buzzed around, seeking information and getting little,* and there were pleasant Saturday afternoons at the Rideau Club and summer weekends at the Five Lakes Fishing Club with talk and bridge and friends.[23] The Robertsons also bought a farmhouse near Ste.-Cécile-de-Masham in the Gatineau, sharing the costs fifty-fifty with C.M. Drury, the Deputy Minister of National Defence, and his wife. The Drurys had found the place, a rather inefficient dairy farm without plumbing and with heat provided only by a wood stove, but Jetty Robertson liked it because it was far enough from Ottawa to make it difficult for her husband—who still could not drive a car—to go into the office on weekends. And Robertson loved it because he could walk through the trees with his dog and putter away at clearing the property's back lot.[24] He loved the Gatineau, as he loved Ottawa, and he fitted in to his old haunts as if he had never been away.

Being Secretary to the Cabinet, then, was no tragedy, but it was still a difficult period. His wit, friends remember, began to develop a cutting edge that had been lacking before, and the stress of his position (complicated perhaps by the illness of his mother, still in Vancouver, in the spring of 1950)[25] affected him. He should have been at the centre, providing the advice that his capacious mind could, exercising his influence to serve the Prime Minister and his government. And yet,

---

* Peter Dempson of the Toronto *Telegram* tried to reach Robertson on one story, leaving messages for days without a response. "Finally one evening, I began ringing his home every hour"; he finally connected at 11 p.m. He put his question, and Robertson replied: "Oh, I don't want to say anything about it. I've never given it much thought. Anyway, I've just come from a party and don't feel like commenting on it right now." Could Dempson call him in the morning? "I'm a pretty busy man. I don't know whether I'll have time to talk to you tomorrow." (Peter Dempson, *Assignment Ottawa* (Toronto, 1968), p. 35.) That account may have been embellished in retrospect, but it does capture the tenor of Robertson's relationship with the press.

although he was at the heart of the machinery, somehow it hadn't worked out. It was again anti-climax, again a marked change from the heady days of the war.[26]

II

Robertson's work in the Privy Council Office ranged over all aspects of government policy. His expertise was greatest on questions of international economic policy, where he was without question the government's leading specialist. But his experience and interests were broad: he had been involved with wheat policy since the early 1930s; with questions arising out of immigration from before the Second World War; with the St. Lawrence Seaway since the early 1940s; and, because of his key role in the Economic Advisory Committee, with questions of social policy and the domestic economy. In other words, Robertson was a "compleat" civil servant, one with a finger in every pie.[27]

One such pie was unemployment policy. The great skill with which reconstruction had been managed after the war had resulted in a smooth integration of demobilized servicemen and women into the economy, and the unemployment rates had stayed under control. But by 1949, with a dangerous recession in the United States and with growing difficulties in Canadian export markets, trouble seemed to lie just ahead for Canada. A memorandum on the "Economic Outlook for 1950," prepared in October 1949 for the Cabinet Committee on Economic Policy, foresaw serious weakening in the economy in late 1949 "and possibly more serious deterioration in 1950." To counter the trend, "useful projects" of a national nature were recommended, such as the Trans-Canada Highway, housing construction, and additional federal projects in distressed areas.[28] In total, as the Interdepartmental Committee on External Trade Policy (despite its name, the senior committee on domestic economic policy) was told, public investment projects of $3 billion were in various stages of preparation.[29]

Whether those projects could be taken off the shelf, and whether they would be sufficient to deal with the economic situation, was not yet certain. But in December 1949, a new Interdepartmental Committee on Social Security was created,[30] with Robertson in the chair and a membership that included Graham Towers, Clifford Clark, two of his senior officials, Robert Bryce and K.W. Taylor, as well as Alex Skelton of Trade and Commerce. At the committee's first meeting, just before the new year, Robertson responded cautiously to suggestions for alterations in the Unemployment Insurance Compensation programme. The past calendar year had been the plan's first real test, and the need for changes could not yet be assessed. He reminded his colleagues that there was to be a Dominion-Provincial Conference in 1950, at which the question of fields of jurisdiction was sure to be important; and since the Dominion had presented its proposals to the Dominion-Provincial Conference in 1945—proposals that had not met with acceptance—the impression had developed across the country that Ottawa was responsible for assistance to the unemployed. [31]

But if Robertson sounded too circumspect here, at a meeting of the committee the next day he took a bolder line, urging his colleagues to inform the Cabinet Committee on Economic Policy of broader considerations. "It seemed . . . questionable whether the actuarial basis of the Unemployment Insurance scheme, which was related to the 10 per cent. level of unemployment over the period 1921 to 1931, was realistic in the present situation," he suggested. "It seemed to involve an attempt to insure against a scale of risk that it was politically impossible to countenance." But if that was so, and "If it was not politically possible to have unemployment exceed 7 per cent., the difference between that and 10 per cent. was room for manoeuvre in extending coverage, in increasing the period of benefit or in adjusting the rate of contribution." He also reminded the committee that, since the passage of the Unemployment Insurance Act in 1940, a host of new dynamic features had been added to the economy, including family allowances, increased old age pensions, agricultural floor prices and the like. [32]

But the unemployment rolls were lengthening, increasing at a higher rate than Ottawa had predicted. Robertson informed the Prime Minister in January 1950 that there were now 345,000 unemployed or 7 percent of the labour force, an increase of 70,000 since the previous month. [33] Next month the news was worse, and the rate reached 7.4 percent, a rise that Robertson suggested did not tell the whole story. The figures for unplaced applicants for work, he told St. Laurent, did not represent the full extent of unemployment, which might be as high as 440,000 or 12 percent of wage and salaried workers and 9 percent of the total labour force. [34] By this time Robertson had begun to question the data provided by the Department of Labour, which, he said, created an incorrect impression, being based on the total civilian labour force that included such groups as agricultural labourers and unpaid family workers. [35] Was there even adequate data on which to compare the current situation with past unemployment? Robertson thought not, a criticism of the Labour Department, which he found inadequate in other ways as well.[36] He told the interdepartmental committee that there had to be a detailed study and analysis of experience under the Act and its place in maintaining income and employment levels.[37]

With the spring, the rate of increase in unemployment began to slow. In April 1951, unplaced applicants were at 424,000; in May, 220,400; in June, 183,100; and in July, 132,000.[38] The problem had proved temporary, and the renewed stimulus brought to the economy by resource development, the Korean War and increased rearmament expenditures apparently did the trick.

The fiscal strain caused by rearmament could interfere with social security measures, too. In November 1950, when the Interdepartmental Committee on Social Security was looking at the question of revising the old age pension scheme in preparation for the Dominion-Provincial meeting the next month, Clifford Clark was unhappy about any alterations to the old pension plan and its means test. In a "semi-war economy," he suggested, further measures of social security might best be postponed. But Robertson, aware of the resentment over the means test and of the work of a parliamentary committee that had studied the pension scheme, told the committee that it was "its business to present alternative Old Age Security plans to Cabinet and also to advise as to the desirability of implementing any improved scheme despite the strain placed on our economy by increased defence expenditures."[39]

At the next meeting, Robertson explained his views. Because of increasing life expectancy, he said, seventy was no longer realistic as the minimum age for old age security purposes. A better scheme might be to make seventy-five the minimum, but with a means test for those from sixty-five to seventy-five years. Costs, he suggested, might be shared on a 50/50 basis with the provinces, with Ottawa assuming responsibility for universal pensions without a means test for all over seventy-five. That idea became the basis of a committee submission to the cabinet,[40] and the scheme that emerged from the December Dominion-Provincial Conference and from Parliament was only marginally different. Those above seventy would receive a pension of $40 a month, while a means test was demanded of those between sixty-five and seventy.[41]

The next summer, Robertson became concerned with the rapid rise in prices, the issue that had replaced unemployment as the government's major domestic concern. In the United States, price controls had been imposed to counter the inflationary impact of rearmament, but the St.

Laurent government refused to adopt the American tactic.[42] The result was that the cost of living rose rapidly, the index increasing (with 1939 equal to 100) from 161.6 in 1949 to 167.3 in 1950 and 185.4 in 1951. That was more than ten percent inflation in 1951.[43]

As chairman of the Interdepartmental Committee on External Trade Policy, Robertson directed that body in its search for suggestions or modifications in policy that could be recommended to the government. In August 1951, in particular, the committee spent much time hashing over the figures, and Robertson concluded one meeting with an impressive summary:

The Chairman said that the consensus of the meeting appeared to be that the probability as to future developments made it desirable for the government to try to avoid having to move into any direct measures of price control. At the same time, it seemed apparent that the present indirect restrictions should be maintained and that probable pressure to provide protection against outside competition should be resisted. Tariffs should not be put up and, while there would be difficulty in doing anything, consideration might be given to the desirability of trying to accelerate the competitive effect on prices by temporary suspensions of specific import duties. It might be desirable to consider whether the standards relating to food imports could not be revised in some cases to provide more uniformity as between Canada and the United States. A further matter that might be looked into was the relationship between combines investigations and provincial provisions with respect to price maintenance. Apparently the Combines Investigation Commissioner did not intervene in cases where price maintenance was carried on under permissive provincial legislation.

With regard to the effect of defence expenditure on the inflationary pressures, it seemed important to distinguish between the direct effect of such expenditures themselves and the effect of collateral private spending that arose from the anticipation of shortages resulting from defence requirements. It was important to limit in any way possible the inflationary effect of the latter, but it was equally important to see that there was no slacking in the former.[44]

An interesting comment, revealing of Robertson's frame of mind. The defence effort had to be maintained regardless of its impact on the cost of living,[45] the tariff should not be raised, and the government should continue its employment of fiscal measures as a weapon against inflation.

Interesting too was Robertson's reference to price maintenance or, as it was usually known, resale price maintenance, a practice that saw manufacturers refuse to sell their goods to a retailer who sold at less than the manufacturers' fixed price. According to Pickersgill, Robertson persuaded the Prime Minister to move to prohibit this practice by law, despite the absence of strong public support for such a measure. Robertson probably favoured this "as a form of inoculation" against the temptation of price controls, and the practice had also been considered and condemned by a House of Commons special inquiry. Few expected any major resistance to an end to resale price maintenance, but Robertson may have believed that the government had to be seen to be doing something to counter rising prices, something more than higher taxes and fiscal measures to counter inflation.[46] The result was a knockdown political fight, as the Conservative Opposition launched a filibuster, and St. Laurent threatened to impose closure to end debate. In a testy House of Commons, the bill curbing price maintenance passed finally on 28 December 1951.[47]

Other domestic questions occupied Robertson, too. In the winter of 1950, he had visited Newfoundland to discuss the problems of the fishery with officials of Canada's newest province. The saltcod trade was in grave difficulty, there was a substantial carry-over from 1949 despite a large government gift to UNICEF and, as Robertson told the Interdepartmental Committee on External Trade Policy: "the Newfoundland fishermen did not know whether they could dispose of their catch at all or, if so, whether the price would be in a range to make their operations worth while. With this situation complicated by the transfer payments that had been provided since Confederation in the form of family allowances and unemployment assistance benefits," he went on, "the interest in taking the steps and incurring the costs involved in going fishing during the present season was pretty marginal. A serious social and economic situation could easily result." But there were difficulties in intervening to ease the Newfoundland position, as the Deputy Minister of Fisheries pointed out, and Ottawa proved unable or unwilling to do much.[48] Robertson had also discussed the island's heavy unemployment—more than 19 percent in April 1950—and had come away from his visit convinced "that expenditures on railway improvement might be the most value-giving outlays the government could make both in providing employment and in creating assets of continuing worth to the province."[49] There was some success in getting action on these matters.

Two years later, Robertson played a major role in the foot-and-mouth disease crisis that threatened to destroy the Canadian export market for Canadian cattle. As Gordon Robertson remembers, the Secretary to the Cabinet was at least as important in developing the government's policy as anyone in the Department of Agriculture.[50] The disease was discovered in the West in February and March 1952, and the government moved quickly to stop exports to the United States, to slaughter diseased animals, and to provide compensation for farmers who had seen their herds decimated.[51] The difficulty was that the disease threatened the whole beef export industry, and Robertson turned his mind to ways to avoid this political and financial disaster. At the Interdepartmental Committee on Export Trade Policy on 10 March 1952, he suggested that, since Canada could no longer export its beef to the United States, "it might be possible to arrange a three-way deal between Canada, the United Kingdom and Australia, under which Australian meat normally marketed in the United Kingdom would be diverted to the United States and replaced with Canadian meat in the United Kingdom."[52] Since British standards were lower than those in the United States, Canadian beef could still be exported to the United Kingdom, and Robertson's proposal was a truly ingenious one that would keep Canada's markets open in the United States. Two weeks later, the committee decided to send a delegation to Britain to work out such an arrangement, and the deal was struck.[53] Robertson's idea had helped cushion the impact of the disease, but the effects on exports were nonetheless severe.[54]

III

Norman Robertson's work at the Privy Council Office and Cabinet Secretariat required him to participate in a wide range of activities. But as might have been expected, his greatest influence was in Canadian commercial policy, where he continued his efforts to re-establish Canada's trade with an increasingly desperate Britain and to build a sound and equitable commercial relationship with the United States. Indeed, for the period from June to September 1949, he was on the road almost continuously, shuttling between Ottawa, London and Washington. Robertson was recognized as the government's senior expert in commercial subjects; in addition, as the Prime Minister's deputy, he was chairman of the Interdepartmental Committee on External Trade Policy (ICETP), the matching officials' committee to the Cabinet Committee on Economic Policy, chaired by the Prime Minister.[55] His greatest impact on the course of Canada's international economic policies was exercised through this committee.*

Almost the first issue that greeted Robertson on his return to Canada in

---

* A British MP noted the way officials' committees meshed with ministerial ones. "What happens," he said, "is that having to serve on many cabinet and other committees, anyone other than a top-grade and experienced minister tends to use the brief he has been given.

(Cont'd)

March 1949 was the question of a new trade agreement with the United States. The free trade proposals of 1947-48 had died, but with an election approaching in Canada and with the possibility of further import restrictions against Canadian goods in the British market, the St. Laurent government was interested in letting the voters know that it was seeking new trade links with the United States.[56] At cabinet on 14 March, the ministers decided to approach Washington formally with a request that negotiations be begun and, as important, to seek American consent for an early announcement of the negotiations, possibly in the forthcoming budget.[57] When the budget was brought down a week later, Douglas Abbott, the Minister of Finance, included just such a reference, although full approval had not yet been secured. The cabinet, Ambassador Wrong was informed, had decided an announcement was necessary.[58]

But as Robertson and his colleagues soon learned, there was little chance of progress before the election on 27 June. The new Reciprocal Trade Agreements Act had not yet passed Congress, and the House and Senate were embroiled in a number of other matters that made early passage unlikely.[59] After an ICETP meeting on 27 May, Robertson reported to the Prime Minister that the Act might pass in two weeks and that the United States might be prepared to negotiate. "It was felt to be important," the committee's minutes noted, "that there should be no speculation or public comment of any sort on the possibility of an agreement until the Senate had completed action on the Bill."[60] After Robertson had talked with St. Laurent and canvassed others, however, the decision that there was too little time to conclude an agreement before 27 June was obvious. The most that should be done, St. Laurent instructed, was a note to the Secretary of State in Washington declaring Canada's desire at a later date to open negotiations and, St. Laurent added, he himself might refer to that note in the course of the campaign.[61] The issue drifted away, forgotten in the course of the election and in the crisis over the British financial situation.

The first hints of difficulties in London began to be heard towards the end of May 1949. A telegram from Dana Wilgress, Robertson's successor at Canada House, informed Ottawa that the British were interested in relaxing their restrictions against soft currency exports but in maintaining

And before every ministerial committee, an equivalent official committee meets and goes over the points, so that the whole thing can go through without a hitch to an agreed conclusion provided none of the ministers wishes to interject a personal note." (Quoted in J.B. Christoph, "Higher Civil Servants and the Politics of Consensualism in Great Britain," in M. Dogan, ed., *The Mandarins of Western Europe* (New York, 1975), p. 42.)

them against goods from Canada and other hard currency nations. There were complications here, Robertson informed the Prime Minister, because of a clause in both the Canadian and American loan agreements of 1946.[62] The matter was important enough for Robertson to call an informal meeting of the key deputy ministers concerned and, despite the imminence of the election, ministerial decisions were deemed necessary.[63] The Americans seemed unlikely to go along with the British request, and Canada might have followed suit; but before any decision could be made, the crisis was on the British.

St. Laurent received a personal message from Attlee on Saturday, 18 June, informing him that the British were in the midst of a run on their reserves, something attributed to the business recession in the United States and the resulting decline in British sales there.[64] Attlee suggested a meeting of Commonwealth finance ministers to consider possible remedies. St. Laurent replied the next day, telling the British Prime Minister that he could not hold a cabinet meeting to consider the proposal with the election only a week off. But, he said, Norman Robertson would fly to London immediately, "to explain fully the various considerations which appear to us to be so important from the Canadian standpoint."[65]

Robertson secretly left Ottawa by Trans-Canada Airlines on the night of the 19th and arrived in London on Monday evening, 20 June.[66] In a series of telegrams back to Ottawa, he reported fully on the mood in the British capital and on the suggested Commonwealth meeting. In addition, and of most concern to Ottawa, he discussed fully the British proposal to relax import restrictions in a way that discriminated against Canada.

To officials of the Treasury, the Board of Trade, the Foreign Office, and the Commonwealth Relations Office, and to Sir Stafford Cripps, Robertson stressed the need for secrecy, pointing out that it "would be most undesirable to have any publicity given to the proposed Commonwealth meeting within the next week, before Canadian ministers could have replied to the invitation or at least considered it." The election and the possible effect on it of the British crisis must also have worried Robertson. He also objected strenuously to the way the British message had placed all the blame for Britain's difficulties on the American recession. Some members of the Commonwealth, Robertson said, were prepared to seize all too eagerly on that as the explanation for their problems. And if the American downturn was to be discussed with a view to doing something about it, "it seemed doubtful that a gathering of Commonwealth countries was the most appropriate group. . . . We thought that many in the United States might see a parallel between such discussions and those which took place in Ottawa in 1932, and that their reaction might be the same now as then. Some in the United States," he went on, might "even see a resemblance between the North Atlantic discussions on the containment of Russia and the proposed Commonwealth discussions which might be regarded as aimed at 'containing' the United States economically." That was pretty straight and sensible talk, and Robertson could hark back to the Ottawa Agreements of 1932 with full awareness that almost twenty years of effort had so far not fully eliminated the harm done by those preferential arrangements.

Robertson went on to urge the British to do everything possible to retain American cooperation, "on which so much depends," and suggested that they should discuss their situation with Secretary of State Dean Acheson. "In general," he said, "it seemed to me that in the circumstances Canada should probably not participate in a meeting of Commonwealth representatives if the discussion . . . was to be concentrated on the United States recession. . . . If the intention was to discuss merely emergency measures . . . designed to prevent the exhaustion of the sterling area's gold and dollar reserves, it seemed to me that such a meeting of sterling area countries might be appropriate. . . ." In such a case, however, Robertson doubted the necessity for Canada to participate. Canada had decided that its economic future lay with the United States, a decision that was never clearer than in Robertson's arguments in London.

The British responded, however, by stressing their desire to keep the Americans informed.[67] And Cripps told his friend of his desire for "confidential discussions at the highest level among the United States, the United Kingdom and Canada." The Chancellor also "argued most earnestly for Canadian participation in the proposed Commonwealth talks. He thought that the presence of Canada would serve as a restraining influence on those representatives who might be inclined merely to pillory the United States and to urge reductions in dollar imports as the solution," an interesting argument in the light of the phrasing of Attlee's telegram to St. Laurent, which had blamed the Americans for Britain's ills.[68]

In his discussion of the proposal on import restrictions, Robertson "intimated that although the Canadian Cabinet had not yet discussed the matter, we should probably be able to reconcile ourselves to the application of the proposed relaxations" to Western Europe. "The extension of such treatment to include all sterling area Commonwealth countries, but not Canada or the United States, was quite another matter." The British understood and assured the Secretary to the Cabinet that they "would like of course to extend the same treatment to Canada if balance of payments difficulties did not stand in the way." But they did, and the British were markedly unwilling to accept or even to understand the Canadian position. Robertson's efforts to persuade Harold Wilson, President of the Board of Trade, were no more successful than with his officials. [69]

Robertson continued to make the rounds of Whitehall and Downing Street on 22 June, talking with the Prime Minister, the Foreign Secretary, the President of the Board of Trade again, and with the Secretary of State for Commonwealth Relations. The most interesting point was Ernest Bevin's suggestion, already conveyed to Washington, that a joint British-American committee with Canadian participation be established to keep the crisis under study. Robertson spoke again to Attlee of "the disturbing similarity between the approach proposed this time and the one followed in 1932-33. Robertson thought that an attempt should be made to learn from past mistakes and that refuge should not be taken in recriminations against the United States." [70]

His visit, it seems certain, had helped press the British into consulting more closely with the Americans than was their original intent. He had helped dissuade Cripps and his officials from launching an all-out assault on the United States and its recession as the cause of all ills, and he had probably ameliorated some of the restrictionist fervour against dollar imports. [71] Whether or not he had a firm invitation for Canada to participate in tripartite talks before the Commonwealth finance ministers' meeting was unclear, and remained so for some days after his return, but in the event passage was booked on a "Queen" for a group of Canadian officials, including Robertson, on 30 June. [72] In the end, Canada was invited. As the American Ambassador in London wired to Washington: "We suggest that Canada sit in, first because unless we are able to prevent the development of an unfortunate U.K. policy Canada will be compelled to decide whether to go with the U.K. or the U.S.—a question which, however resolved, would have adverse effects everywhere—and second because Canada by sitting in would find it easier to attend the meeting of Commonwealth finance ministers called for July 11 and there to play more effectively the part of *amicus curiae*." [73] Canada was in the middle, playing its role as an intermediary. Robertson's visit had been very useful.

After less than a week in Ottawa, he was on his way back to the United Kingdom, this time by sea. By 7 July, he, Clifford Clark, Louis Rasminsky of the Bank of Canada, and M.W. Mackenzie, the Deputy Minister of

Trade and Commerce, were meeting their counterparts—the extraordinarily high-powered nature of the Canadian delegation an indication of concern. That night Robertson arranged a dinner at the Dorchester Hotel for his team, for Wilgress and A.E. Ritchie from Canada House, and for eight British officials, including the Ambassador in Washington, the High Commissioner in Ottawa, and the Secretary to the Cabinet.

Robertson began the discussion by suggesting that it was essential "for political as well as economic reasons, to carry the U.S. and Canada along in any course which might be followed in the present situation. Officials and Ministers in Ottawa," he said, "had been disturbed at the emphasis in the original message ... on the U.S. recession as the cause of the difficulties. Apart from his doubts on the validity of this diagnosis, he was concerned at the consequences which the adoption of this approach to the problem would have on cooperation with the United States." Sir Oliver Franks, the very able British Ambassador in Washington, then indicated what he saw as the objectives of the tripartite talks, the main one being the necessity of satisfying Canada and the United States "that the repugnant measures which the Sterling Area was likely to adopt (and some of the practices already being employed) were matters of 'necessity' and not of 'policy'." Franks and his colleagues vigorously argued that it was not their intent to build up a bloc separate from the dollar area, but on the other hand they were equally firm in indicating that they intended to proceed with measures to check the drain on British reserves. The outcome of the talks, Franks indicated, was to be only an agreed public statement and an announcement of intent to meet again.[74]

The tripartite discussions began the next day and ended on 9 July. The Chancellor of the Exchequer pointed out Britain's need to save some $500 million by reducing imports in 1949-50, cuts that hit Canadian exports. In addition, the British asked that Canada encourage the import of British and sterling area goods, that Canada give Britain greater access to the remaining credits from the 1946 loan, that there be an immediate decision to allow London the freedom to relax its restrictions against soft currency countries, and that both Canada and the United States accept a host of additional measures. The press release reaffirmed the countries' objective of a multilateral trading system and, the communiqué said, "No suggestion was made that sterling should be devalued," an idea that was already being canvassed widely as a remedy to the British difficulties.[75]

Robertson and his colleagues met the British again on 11 July, this time under the aegis of the Anglo-Canadian Continuing Committee on Trade and Economic Affairs. There was to be a renewed round of tripartite talks in Washington in early September, and the British promised to discuss their trade restrictions with Canada before implementing them. When a Treasury official noted that Britain wanted to be able to draw on the Canadian credit, however, Clark was quick to demur. The present rate of draw was difficult enough and no increased rate could be justified. Clark "emphasized the relationship between anything which Canada might be able to do . . . and the action which the U.K. might take to reduce costs [and thus increase its exports] and generally to provide evidence that there was some hope of the U.K. returning to multilateral trading."[76]

Then followed the Commonwealth finance ministers' conference, with Douglas Abbott leading the Canadian team. "Canada made it clear from the outset," Clifford Clark's account noted, "that she was by history and force of economic circumstances, a member of the dollar area rather than the sterling area, and that she could not therefore be considered as giving approval in any sense to the decisions of the others to restrict dollar imports." Abbott had admitted that "when a hemorrhage was in process it might be appropriate temporarily to apply a tourniquet to stop the flow of blood, but emphasized that the greatest care was necessary to avoid allowing the tourniquet to become a substitute for other positive measures designed to avoid the loss of the limb." Abbott and the Canadians argued that the cause of the difficulties was not the American recession but the high cost level in the sterling area, an implicit call for devaluation.[77] The result of the Commonwealth meeting was largely a decision to defer action until after the tripartite Washington meeting, and that too was something of a Canadian victory.

By 20 July, the Canadians were getting ready to leave England, and telegrams ordering a vast body of studies in preparation for Washington had been sent. Those studies were wide-ranging, covering, among other things, the competitive position of British industry, the internal financial situation of Britain and the sterling countries, the sterling bloc oil and rubber position, and the problem of monetary reserves. To produce them, practically the entire resources of the Departments of Finance and of Trade and Commerce, as well as the Bank of Canada, had to be employed,[78] and as chairman of the ICETP, Robertson played a major role in coordination.[79]

At the same time, he and his colleagues tried to ensure that the agenda at Washington was as complete as possible. There had been discussions in London about this,[80] and at the ICETP meeting on 2 August, a few days after Robertson's return from England, Arnold Heeney suggested that he should go to Washington for talks with officials there. "Heeney felt personally that there would be more likelihood of getting our views adequately represented at a senior level in Washington if the Chairman could go down on the basis of speaking for all the Canadian departments concerned." The Canadians wanted the British to place less emphasis in their proposed agenda on what the Americans should do and the Americans less emphasis on what the British should do. To attempt that was Robertson's task.[81]

Accompanied by A.F.W. Plumptre of the Economic Division of the Department of External Affairs, Robertson went to Washington in the first week of August for meetings with representatives from the State Department, the Treasury, and the Economic Cooperation Administration. He urged the Americans to tilt the agenda they had proposed rather more in the direction of the "responsibility of creditors" and away from the "duties of debtors," and found his listeners receptive. The Americans, he discovered, were becoming more interested in the question of a devaluation of sterling, with ECA and Treasury officials feeling that unless this occurred, all other action would be useless. Robertson in his turn emphasized the "primary need for maintaining 'boom' conditions in the United States. This," he said, "has a direct effect in obtaining imports. It also makes possible tariff reductions and other adjustments." But as he well knew, "if the United States is to go forward on the desired path, it will have to be for domestic reasons and not merely to facilitate imports from the United Kingdom."[82]

The Washington meetings were to take place on 27 August for officials and on 7 September for ministers. As late as 23 August, matters were in flux, and no one was precisely certain of the questions that might have to be considered. On Heeney's suggestion, and with Robertson's and the ICETP's concurrence, the Prime Minister and the ministers going to Washington were asked for "a general authorization . . . to consider any matters that might appear to be helpful in any way, on the understanding that such discussion would be without commitment of the government."[83] That authorization presumably granted, Robertson and his colleagues were in the American capital by the 27th.

The American preparations for the talks had included character sketches of the key Canadians present. Robertson was portrayed in these secret notes as an "outstanding Canadian economist" and as "one of the closest advisers of Prime Minister St. Laurent," something he must have wished was so. "He is a man of liberal outlook and is said to be devoid of class or racial prejudice. Straightforward and honest, he inspires his associates with confidence in his judgment," the assessment continued.

"His tact and judgment make him an excellent presiding officer." The conclusion was that Robertson was "in fact, thought to be more sympathetic in general to American view-points than to British," an arguable point, but one that was probably correct.[84]

At Washington, Robertson was a member of the Combined Official Group, the central committee of officials looking at questions of "high political delicacy," and one that spawned a number of technical sub-committees and the ministerial agenda.[85] The other members, British and American, spent much time rehashing the record and fixing blame, but not Robertson. His interest, as always, was in solutions, and at one of the committee sessions he suggested that "in the field of import regulation, consideration might be given to the use of fiscal measures (tariffs and taxes). These had been outlawed by G.A.T.T. and I.T.O. Nevertheless, they might prove a useful 'halfway house' between, on the one hand, 'quantitative restrictions' which are permitted by G.A.T.T. and I.T.O. under certain circumstances and, on the other hand, complete nondiscrimination. Fiscal measures," Robertson suggested, "had the great advantage of allowing the price system to work, although cushioning its effect." In other words, he was seeking a way for the British to avoid discriminatory restrictions on imports while still satisfying their fiscal needs. The Americans tacitly accepted his suggestion, a Canadian report noted, but the British took "quite a fright" at the idea;[86] indeed in the absence of clear instructions from London, the British officials claimed to feel "completely ineffective."[87]

Nonetheless, the officials had paved the way for their ministers, and from 7 to 12 September Robertson stayed in Washington with the Canadian delegation, now headed by Abbott and Pearson.[88] The major result of the talks, although for years no one dared directly attribute it to the Washington meetings,[89] was the sudden and drastic devaluation of the pound sterling from $4 US to $2.80, a chop of thirty percent. In the circumstances, could Canada keep the dollar at its current level or must it devalue? And if so, by how much? Abbott had decided on a 9.1 percent devaluation, but C.D. Howe, the Minister of Trade and Commerce, objected vehemently, fearing that devaluation would raise the price of capital goods from the United States. Abbott, who was prepared to resign if the cabinet did not support him, made a strong case for devaluation, and the cabinet decided to go along.[90] But the United States might have resented devaluation, particularly when it was applied on top of the still existing import restrictions from November 1947. Thus on 17 September, Robertson and Pearson returned to Washington "in part to sound out

American attitude and had found it to be sympathetic."[91] The dollar was devalued to approximately 90¢ US, to keep down the price of Canadian goods in the sterling area, to make Canadian goods more attractive in the American market, and to help restore the balance between North America and the rest of the world.[92]

The tripartite meeting also took additional steps to achieve that same end. The North Americans agreed to reduce barriers to the entry of sterling area goods into their countries, and special studies were launched of a number of subjects—the stockpiling of tin and rubber, for example— that seemed likely to bolster British dollar earnings. Of particular interest to Canada was the American decision to begin again to pay for Canadian wheat destined for the British market. This was expected to produce an additional $175 million in American dollars for Canada's balance of payments, and it eased Britain's difficulties by the same amount.[93]

The decisions at Washington, embodied in a communiqué that Robertson had a large hand in preparing,[94] and supported by a process of consultation established there,[95] went a substantial distance to restoring the equilibrium in the economy of the North Atlantic triangle. The process was not truly successful, however, until the Korean War confirmed the continuation of the boom that had begun in the fall of 1949 in the United States.[96] But if matters had been eased, there was still no shortage of problems between Canada and Britain.

In November 1949, for example, St. Laurent sent a stiff message to Attlee objecting to the "false picture" Britons had received of the financial relationship between Canada and the United Kingdom. "Such statements have suggested that the chief cause of the United Kingdom's exchange difficulties is the necessity of paying dollars for imports from Canada. You do not need to be reminded, I know," St. Laurent said, "that this is a serious misinterpretation of the facts."[97]

But the misunderstandings were not all on one side, for at almost the same time Robertson was protesting to the Prime Minister about public remarks of J.G. Gardiner, the Minister of Agriculture and the *bête noire* of the civil service. Gardiner had told a public meeting in Saskatchewan (and subsequently his cabinet colleagues) that it was "dangerous doctrine" to suggest that increased British sales in Canada were necessary if Canada was to keep her markets for food in Britain. That statement, Robertson said, "could be taken as a negation of the basic policy agreed on at Washington to make every effort toward an increase in United Kingdom exports to dollar markets. It could also weaken the efforts the government will be making to hold the line against demands for protection against

U.K. imports." Worse yet, Robertson went on, in this extraordinary memorandum denouncing one of the Prime Minister's senior colleagues, Gardiner had implied that the government was unanimous in favouring food contracts with Britain and in supporting an increase in bacon production. There had to be discussions with the provinces about the agricultural programme for the coming year, and "It would be particularly undesirable if Mr. Gardiner were to indicate...that the government concurred in his suggestion that bacon production should be increased. It might similarly be embarrassing if the impression were given that the government were unanimously behind the policy of continuation of concentration on the U.K. market for Canadian food products and of carrying on our sales on the basis of contracts similar to those that have prevailed thus far."[98]

That was a gallant effort to shut up Gardiner, but it was no more successful than earlier ones. The next month the British were complaining about the minister's statements. "The suggestion that there was a conscious effort being made by the United Kingdom Government," the High Commissioner in Ottawa complained, "to stop imports from Canada without an explanation of the dollar difficulties...could only create a misunderstanding."[99]

The difficulties were many and continuous, the arguments sometimes fierce,[100] but the sense of crisis that had dislocated the normal commercial relations between Canada and Britain was largely ended, although there was another reserves problem in 1951-52.[101] Robertson had done his part to ease matters, but in fact the real cause was that Britain was simply less important economically to Canada after 1949. As recently as 1936, Canada had sent 42 percent of its exports to Britain and only 36 percent to the United States. But by 1949, exports were 23 and 50 percent respectively, and the Economic Cooperation Administration was paying for a hefty proportion of the goods going to Britain. The simple fact was that Canada's economy was tied to the United States, and although some in the government worried about this, the trend was strengthened and confirmed.[102] In effect, Canada had entered a bilateral trading relationship with the United States, and Robertson's dreams of multilateralism had gone aglimmering into a haze of prosperity and boom brought on by the Cold War and rearmament.

IV

The beginning of the Korean War on 25 June 1950 opened a difficult period for the St. Laurent government. There were calls for action against Communism at home and abroad, there were demands for compulsory military service, and there were the high costs of rearmament. As Secretary to the Cabinet, Robertson was occupied in all these matters, although to some extent, on pure questions of foreign policy, his involvement could be only that permitted by Pearson and Heeney.

Robertson played some part in determining the character of Canadian participation in the war in Korea. For a month after the start of the war, the Canadian response was limited—three destroyers were sent to the area and an RCAF transport squadron shuttled supplies from North America to Japan. But the war was going badly for the South Koreans and the Americans who were doing the fighting, and both the United States and the Secretary-General of the United Nations wanted a greater contribution from Canada.

As a result, on 29 July the cabinet instructed Robertson and Lester Pearson to fly to Washington to examine the situation at first-hand. A few days earlier, while its members were returning by train to Ottawa after Mackenzie King's funeral in Toronto, the cabinet had discussed contributing ground forces to the UN war effort and had reached no definite decision. Now the American position was to be plumbed.[103] The most important discussion was with Acheson, the Secretary of State, on the evening of the 29th. Acheson went over the American position, telling the two Canadians that Korea was only a phase "and not, in the long run, the most important phase, of the general conflict between the free and the Communist worlds." In such circumstances, the Secretary of State argued, apparently to the general agreement of Robertson and Pearson, the need now was "for strengthening as rapidly as possible the forces of the free world to meet aggression elsewhere and to act as an effective deterrent against a general attack." The "naked aggression of the Communists against Korea," Acheson said, had made general rearmament easier to achieve.

On the need for a Canadian contribution to the war, Acheson argued that one would be "of great immediate help and of even greater political value," and he offered the American view that everything possible had to be done to emphasize the UN character of the operation. Pearson and Robertson discovered, however, that the American Joint Chiefs of Staff were running the war (or at least as much as General Douglas MacArthur permitted them to run). [104]

The two then went to New York on 31 July to see the UN Secretary-General, Trygve Lie, and Robertson prepared a long memorandum of the conversation. Lie had stressed that Soviet aggression could be contained only by adequate force in the hands of free nations "and repeatedly spoke of the necessity of them all building up their armed forces as a matter of the highest urgency. 'Otherwise, in 10 or 15 years we would all be slaves.' " The Secretary-General said that he had begun exploring the idea of UN-raised troops for Korean service and for other duties. "It could be the nucleus of a permanent force, available for police and preventive duties, and might, in part, be stationed in Western Europe, where it could be a net addition to the effective forces of the North Atlantic countries." The talk with Lie, with his extraordinary view of the role of the UN, nonetheless "convinced us," Robertson wrote, "that he is determined to do his part to make the United Nations action in Korea effective and successful. . . . He has no doubts about the rightness of the action taken by the United Nations in this crisis and he is willing and anxious to follow it through to a good conclusion. [105]

If Lie was determined, so too were Robertson and Pearson. On 7 August, after hearing Pearson's report on the talks, the cabinet decided to raise a brigade group "to be trained and specially equipped . . . for use in carrying out Canada's obligations under the United Nations Charter or the North Atlantic Pact." The troops would be used in Korea if they could be most effectively employed there when they were ready for service. The thrust of that decision followed closely Acheson's arguments to Robertson and Pearson. [106]

Well before the brigade was ready for service, however, the UN forces had recovered the initiative, thanks to MacArthur's brilliant Inchon landing, and the North Koreans reeled northwards, completely routed. What was the UN now to do—pursue the enemy into North Korea or halt at the 38th parallel, the task of freeing South Korea over? At the UN, Pearson supported the latter view, bolstered in this position by telegrams from Ottawa. On 28 September, Escott Reid told the minister that he and Robertson had discussed "the dangers implicit in the assumption that the objectives of the United Nations military action in Korea should now be changed from repelling aggression to achieving the unification of Korea. We consider," Reid went on, expressing his and Robertson's view,

that the broad military and strategic implications and risks of this proposed change in objectives should be weighed very carefully. . . . The United Nations and the Western powers have achieved a signal military success in Korea on a narrow margin. Should United Nations forces now cross the 38th parallel and undertake to occupy North Korea they face at best the prospect of maintaining large occupation forces on the Chinese and Soviet borders, and there would be a good deal of pressure to have our Special Force included in those occupation forces. Moreover occupation of North Korea would involve a continuing risk of clash with the Russians. . . .[107]

That was good advice and impressive prophecy, and Pearson tried to prevent the UN advance northward. But his efforts failed and, within two months, the Chinese had entered the war, forcing a retreat on the UN forces that was not checked until the 38th parallel had been recrossed again from the other direction. Korea turned into a long slugging match, and the Canadian brigade was obliged to serve there.

Robertson also became involved in an *ad hoc* Committee on Government Information Services, established at the Prime Minister's request "to counter Communist propaganda outside Canada."[108] He told the first meeting of this high level committee (its members including Heeney, Pickersgill, Bryce, Charles Ritchie of External Affairs, and C.M. Drury, the Deputy Minister of National Defence) that it should consider not only ways to counter Communist propaganda abroad but in Canada too. Should there be a NATO conference on ideological warfare as some had suggested? Robertson doubted the usefulness of this—"any attempt to define and approve a single policy on an international basis in a formal conference would probably not only be abortive but might also prejudice seriously the cause of democracy." That was certainly true, and Robertson added that the effectiveness of any campaign would be reduced when it became known it was the product of "quasi-Cominform policy directives."[109]

At later meetings, Robertson urged the preparation of ideologically oriented films by the National Film Board, suggesting that, if they worked with Canadian audiences, they could be given overseas distribution. He also proposed that the CBC should broadcast over shortwave to Canadian troops in Europe, and he believed European audiences might find that type of programming more interesting than broadcasts beamed directly at them. In addition, he felt that the BBC could be persuaded through diplomatic channels to use more Canadian material, something that might also encourage immigration to Canada.[110] The Cold War clearly had altered the perceptions of the government; it had also changed Norman Robertson.

Robertson was involved in more than propaganda. As Secretary to the Cabinet, he automatically became chairman of the Security Panel that he had been responsible for establishing in 1946. In 1949, matters were somewhat further advanced than they had been at the time of the Gouzenko revelations. Top-secret and secret material was now stored in safes or locked filing cabinets, security considerations were examined when offices were sited, and a booklet on security had been distributed throughout the civil service.[111] Furthermore, a series of cabinet directives on security questions had been promulgated, the product of extensive discussion in the Security Panel and in cabinet. One directive, issued in March 1948 on security investigations of government employees, noted that "the establishment of precise and rigid standards for determining the 'loyalty' of government employees, along the lines adopted in the United States, is open to serious objection on grounds of principle...."[112] A supplement, issued the next month, pointed out that Communists or Fascists "should not be employed by the government in positions of trust or upon work of confidential character."[113]

These directives were in effect when Robertson returned to Canada in 1949. But the mood in the country was becoming less tolerant as the Cold War continued. One National Defence study noted that the "hard core" of the Communist element in Canada could be estimated to be 35 or 40 percent of the membership of Communist organizations, "or about 6,000 fully indoctrinated militants willing to follow the orders of the Kremlin." In the event of a general war, plans were in hand to arrest and intern "All known prominent Communist functionaries," and to outlaw the party and its satellite bodies. Such action was expected to reduce Communists to covert activities and to prevent strikes or an insurrection. "Sabotage, however, may be expected on a rather wide scale."[114]

Robertson's influence seems first to have been exerted on immigration questions.* In February 1947, the Security Panel had looked at the problems of screening European immigrants and, aghast at the difficulties, had proposed checking closely only those from Eastern Europe. The cabinet had agreed, and by August 1949, as Robertson told the ministers, of 60,000 displaced persons considered for entry, 1,000 had been refused admission on security grounds. But under present conditions, Robertson went on, it was almost impossible to do screening on prospective

---

* There is no doubt of Robertson's general views on immigration. He favoured it, and he favoured its liberalization. But as always he was aware of the problems. In March 1947, for example, when the government contemplated an announcement of a liberal policy, Robertson pointed out from Canada House that there was little shipping free. People

(Cont'd)

immigrants from Eastern Europe, the Far East and Israel. Should security clearance still be a prerequisite for entry? Or should those prospective immigrants be allowed in without screening?[115] Robertson reminded the cabinet that entry could be refused on security grounds, if applicants were known or suspected Communists, former members of the Nazi party, other Fascist parties, or revolutionary organizations, collaborators, or users of false names or fictitious documents.[116] The cabinet apparently decided that screening had to be maintained, and a new directive emerged, one that stressed the importance of ensuring that those denied entry on security grounds should not learn that this was the reason they were barred.[117] Presumably that had not been Robertson's intention.

But if there was concern over security, there had been little hysteria in Canada of the kind that was developing in the United States. The first signs of a change in this attitude became apparent in February 1950, when George Drew, the leader of the Conservative Party, returned to a theme he had tentatively essayed a year earlier.[118] Drew assailed the

---

might ask why "if Canada is prepared to welcome settlers . . . does it not attempt to implement this new attitude by making immigration possible?" (PAC, External Affairs Records, vol. 2119, file A.R. 444/1, tel., NAR to Pearson 25 Mar. 47.) The next year he was pressing for a genuine liberalization of regulations, to permit larger numbers of displaced persons to come to Canada, and objecting to the "terms of indenture" Canada had required of Polish soldiers permitted entry. "I also had some doubts about the usefulness of the very elaborate screening on the basis of war service which we devised chiefly for domestic political reasons. Our various screens are made with many different types of mesh, and probably it was the finest through which the . . . Poles had to pass." (*Ibid.*, vol. 2105, file A.R. 405/1/4/27, Pearson to NAR, 17 Jan. 48 and NAR to Pearson, 26 Jan. 48.)

As Secretary to the Cabinet, Robertson tried to liberalize policy where he could, arguing against the veiled racism of the government. In April 1949 a recommendation came to cabinet removing Syrians, Lebanese and Armenians from the "persons of Asiatic race" excluded from Canada. "The present Order in Council barring persons of Asiatic race is open to serious objection," he wrote the Prime Minister, "but this does not seem to me the way to amend it. To single out the Syrians, Armenians and Lebanese is bound to point up the question of Turks and Palestinians, and might easily re-open the whole delicate question of the status of Indians. . . ." The cabinet dropped the amendment and agreed to deal with individual cases by order in council. Two years later, Robertson resisted the suggestion of the Deputy Minister of Labour to handle the problem of Italian immigrants who left farms for the cities before their year of agreed service with deportations. In his view, it would be much more acceptable to say that no dependent would be allowed in until the year was served. (Privy Council Office, Records, PARC Box 287375, file I-50-3, NAR to Prime Minister, 29 Apr. 49 and Memo to Cabinet, 27 Sep. 49; *ibid.*, PARC box 287285, file I-50-5, NAR to MacNamara, 5 Sep. 51). And in 1950, he was instrumental in securing support for loans to immigrants (Department of External Affairs, file 50092-40, ICETP Minutes, 13 Jun. 50. See also J.W. Holmes, *The Shaping of Peace: Canada and the Search for World Order 1943-57*, Vol. I (Toronto, 1979), 94ff.)

government for failing to take sufficient action to safeguard Canadian institutions from Red infiltration. His case in point was the National Film Board, a body that he charged had been refused the right to make films for the Department of National Defence because of doubt about the loyalty of some of its employees. Drew argued—correctly—that the government had quietly undertaken its own housecleaning of the NFB. Indeed, Robertson and Pickersgill had played a major role in this, and Robert Winters, the Minister of Reconstruction and minister responsible for the Film Board, had consulted Robertson closely on the best way to deal with the problem. But as a report, issued in late March, made clear, the problem was not very serious. Screening of the Board's employees had been largely concluded and only three employees had been "separated" from the Board as a result.[119] Drew nonetheless persisted with his attacks and in May proposed legislation to make Communist activities punishable under the Criminal Code. The Prime Minister, to his great credit, rejected Drew's position in a good, liberal speech.[120]

But the government had clearly been alarmed by Drew's attacks, and about the same time a memorandum prepared in the Privy Council Office, possibly by Robertson, noted the increasing risks of subversive and espionage activities and suggested that more attention be given to protecting the country from such disruptive efforts. The body responsible for internal security was, of course, the RCMP, and it seems clear that few of Robertson's concerns about the Mounties had eased since 1946. Late in 1949, he considered the possibility of establishing an organization like MI-5, the British counter-intelligence group, but by March 1950, he had dismissed the thought. It took years to build a new agency, and the RCMP had the trained personnel and the files.[121] He also considered borrowing an officer from MI-5 and putting him in charge, but the effect of that on the RCMP was uncertain.[122] The concerns did not disappear, however, and in summer 1950 both Pearson and Robertson raised them with Sir William Stephenson. "Your problem," Stephenson wrote Robertson, "is one of co-ordination. It appears to me that there are several good cooks without a master chef to control the final brew. . . ."[123]

In the end, the RCMP emerged unaltered, although the force greatly increased its security checks in the government. In the last quarter of 1948, for example, the RCMP had conducted 3,878 field investigations and 1,587 record checks in the civil service, producing 213 adverse reports on individuals, most of which concerned character flaws and not security considerations. In the second quarter of 1951, by contrast, there had been 1,488 field investigations and 27,492 record checks.[124] There was also worry over sensitive areas of industry. Communist efforts among merchant seamen, for instance, clearly concerned Robertson, who favoured sacking Communists in shipping companies. Characteristically, however, he pointed out the need for an appeal procedure to be available to those fired on security grounds. [125]

That type of Robertsonian concern was evident again in October 1950, when a recommendation went to cabinet from the Department of External Affairs suggesting that passports be withheld from known Communists. Robertson disagreed and said, as he wrote to the Prime Minister that, "I think the alternative suggestion of working out reciprocal arrangements with countries of destination . . . to see that we do not give travel documents to persons they would not wish to receive, is worth serious exploration before we start withholding passports from any given class of people." [126] The cabinet deferred its decision, an interdepartmental committee studied the question and objected to the measure as an " 'iron curtain' of our own," and on 24 January, the cabinet decided to take other steps instead. [127] That was a small victory for reason.

There was no victory in the case of Herbert Norman, the External Affairs officer and distinguished scholar of Japan, who was recalled from his post in Japan in the fall of 1950. Norman had been a Communist at Cambridge in the 1930s but had broken his ties with the party after joining the Department at the outbreak of war in 1939. The RCMP had labelled him clean, but in 1950 the force passed derogatory information about Norman to the Federal Bureau of Investigation, and soon telegrams began to fly between Ottawa and Washington. Norman was recalled, investigated and reinvestigated, and finally, despite being cleared, shunted off to less sensitive duties. Eventually his name was raised publicly by an American Senate investigative committee in 1951 and again in 1957, smears that led directly to his suicide in Cairo where he was Ambassador. [128]

Of Robertson's role as chairman of the Security Panel in the recall of Norman and in the subsequent investigations, there are no available records. Certainly there seems little doubt that Robertson was concerned that Norman may have been subverted, a not unreasonable fear in an era marked by the case of Klaus Fuchs in the United Kingdom and by the defection of British diplomats Burgess and Maclean. [129] But there is equally no doubt that, after the searching interrogations of Norman, Robertson became convinced of his innocence. [130] And after Norman's death in Cairo on 4 April 1957, Robertson wrote movingly to Pearson from Rome, where he was on holiday:

Two or three things I feel I should report: the arrangements in Rome for Herbert Norman's cremation and burial were decent and seemly. . . . The Protestant cemetery at Tentaccio is a beautiful and memorable place. There was no service, no ceremony. . . . [The groundskeeper] had found a spot beneath a big cypress—a yard from where Shelley and Trelawney lie and he had a small camellia bush ready to plant above.

. . . The other thing I want to say is that Herbert Norman had no better or braver friend than you have been. You did and said everything that could have been done and said and said them promptly and unequivocally. I meant to write him from London when the Jenner [Senate Committee] attack was renewed telling him how good & how indispensable a job I thought he was doing in Cairo—but I didn't do it. [131]

Norman's death by hounding upset Robertson deeply, [132] a reminder, as if he had needed one, how difficult security decisions were.

Robertson had never had any doubts on that score, and he showed extreme care, after the initial RCMP gaffe in sending information to the FBI, before he permitted any despatches of similar material to the Americans. In August 1951, for example, the FBI asked for copies of a petition sent to Mackenzie King on behalf of one of those implicated in the Gouzenko documents. It had been sent openly, not designated confidential, and the signatories had been listed in a House of Commons Sessional Paper in 1947. One of the signers was being considered for a sensitive government post, but why in the circumstances the FBI wanted the original document copied is unclear. Robertson agreed that the copy could go south, adding that he, for one, did not accept "an inference from signing this appeal to the political unreliability of the signers." He added that "What we should have done was to have acknowledged the letter & sent each of the signatories a copy of the Royal Commission. Apart from Einstein who signs all appeals on principle the list contains half a dozen of the leading U.S. mathematicians." [133] It was typical that Robertson knew that, and typical too that he personally passed on the request for information. After the Norman case, apparently, all such requests came to him. Unfortunately, the barn door had been locked too late to save Herbert Norman.

The Cold War, the Korean war, and the NATO build-up of forces in Europe continued apace, all putting different pressures on the government. One demand, building in intensity from 1948, was for a more rational system of military recruitment in the event of another war—for conscription, in other words. Robertson remembered the crises of 1942 and 1944, the way the King government had sunk into paralysis as it wrestled with the issue. He, and others, were determined that next time there had to be a better way of handling the problem of military service.

And problem it was. Vincent Massey for one had noted the small size of the Canadian military, adding that this "does little to help us maintain a position of reasonable dignity in joint discussion between ourselves and Washington" on the subject of defence. The Canadian Legion passed resolutions for conscription, and General H.D.G. Crerar, wartime commander of the First Canadian Army, made speeches in favour of compulsory military service. In addition, there were after 1950 the beginnings of criticism from allies of Canada's voluntary system, and the coming of the Korean War in June 1950 made the issue politically important. [134]

The issue was first discussed in cabinet around the time that St. Laurent announced the decision to raise a brigade for UN or NATO service. Brooke Claxton, the Minister of National Defence, noted in his unpublished memoirs that "as I expected [I was] put on the spot about the manpower problem. 'Can the Cabinet be given positive assurances that we could raise the men we needed to support the initial forces and maintain them at full strength in the field by ordinary voluntary means?' " Claxton told his colleagues that he believed the job could be done with volunteers. [135] But no one was entirely certain.

From Washington, Hume Wrong wrote Robertson on 11 September 1950: "You asked me when I saw you in Ottawa a week or so ago whether I thought there was likely to be criticism in the United States of our manpower policy for the armed forces." Wrong had initially thought this unlikely, but he had changed his mind since his return to the Embassy. He now thought Canada should pursue urgently the idea of stationing an air component and a brigade in Europe as part of NATO, and he added, "It may turn out that the political atmosphere will be fairly propitious early next year for the re-institution of national registration in Canada." [136]

Wrong was correct in part, for on 1 February 1951, the Prime Minister told the House of Commons that the question of conscription "is not a matter which can or should be decided on sentimental grounds. It is one which should be decided on its merits, and strictly on its merits." [137] And there are some indications that the cabinet had already decided to introduce conscription immediately on the outbreak of a major war. [138] But if there was to be compulsory service, preparations had to be put in hand and, as Wrong had indicated, a national registration taken.

Preparing for this registration was Robertson's task, and from the end of December 1950 the Privy Council Office staff, and particularly Gordon Robertson, devoted substantial time to the question. As one paper passed to the Secretary to the Cabinet made clear, there was little unanimity on the desirability of registration. The Deputy Minister of Labour did not believe it necessary yet, while the RCMP thought such a step "would help them greatly in handling security. They consider that an over-all registration . . . would help in tracing and keeping track of people, in identifying individuals through making cards compulsory with a certain amount of physical description on them, in checking on aliens, and in keeping track of immigrants until their position is established." Perhaps those RCMP reasons lay behind Gordon Robertson's conclusion that "it would appear that a national registration would not be necessary. . . ."[139]

Nonetheless, the preparations went on. On 1 February 1951, the cabinet passed P.C. 567, establishing a National Advisory Council on Manpower to advise the Minister of Labour "on matters related to the most effective utilization . . . of the present and potential man and woman working force of Canada."[140] And on 20-21 February, the Advisory Council held its first meeting in Ottawa. Chaired by Robertson and Arthur MacNamara, the Deputy Minister of Labour, the Council brought together representatives of business, labour, farm and women's organizations, veterans' groups, and an array of Ottawa officials. The Council was intended as a body to help the government diffuse the responsibility for measures that might be unpopular, and Milton Gregg, the Minister of Labour, made clear that the Prime Minister had decided to "take such compulsory steps as are necessary" to get men for the armed forces to serve anywhere in the world. One of those steps was a national registration, and the chairmen shepherded through a divided Council agreement that "steps of a preparatory nature should be undertaken . . . which would reduce to a minimum any delay that might occur if and when a national registration becomes necessary. . . ."[141]

After the Council meeting, Robertson sent a long memo to the Prime Minister with his recommendations on how to proceed. In the War Book, the government's compilation of plans for an emergency, a national registration was to be undertaken by the Department of Labour. But, said Robertson,

I do not think this would be an adequate or safe disposition of so delicate a problem. Apart from the political elements in the question, national registration is of importance for purposes other than the civil and military use of manpower and it is important that it should not be regarded as simply a manpower or labour question. One of the principal reasons for registration would be as a precaution against the needs of a really serious crisis of war, high among which would be security and plans for rationing. Plans have also to be seen in relation to the census procedures. For such reasons preparatory work should, I think, be coordinated and scrutinized by an interdepartmental committee. It would also be desirable to have a ... small Cabinet group to which questions could be submitted from time to time.

In fact, Robertson continued, there were a whole range of questions requiring action; he listed internal security, security screening of merchant seamen and others in essential employment, censorship, civil defence, protection of vital points, the dispersal of government offices from Ottawa for defence reasons, and general emergency plans. To better coordinate matters, the various committees at work on these questions should report to a single cabinet committee.[142]

The recommended committees were set up, and work proceeded on the registration plans. One paper sent to Robertson noted that, from the standpoint of civilian manpower and from that of national planning for the use of available manpower, a registration on a national scale had little purpose. Nor was it particularly useful for military purposes, where a registration by age-groups was more economical and more efficient.[143] But Robertson, who seems to have made up his mind that registration was necessary, was not deterred. In a memo to MacNamara, he asked that alternative courses of action be prepared for cabinet: no decision on a registration now, with the risk that the international situation might suddenly worsen; a national registration to take place soon; a registration of men from 17 to 25 years only; a registration of men from 17 to 40 years as the first stage of a full registration; and the institution of a progressive general registration.[144] The choice of alternatives made obvious Robertson's view.

He made this clear again to the cabinet committee on 16 April. When one minister suggested that it was unthinkable to have registration of age-groups in advance of a decision to institute compulsory military service, Robertson argued that "in any war that might occur in present circumstances the security problem would be much more serious than in the last war." For example, he said, there was little point in registering enemy aliens when Communists could be found among the native-born. Then he entered dangerous ground. "In connection with the use of finger printing to provide positive identification for security, it had been felt that one advantage in starting a progressive registration on a voluntary basis was that finger printing would thus become an accepted and accustomed practice without arousing opposition." A further advantage, he went on, in having registration underway on the basis that it was to proceed to a general registration was that it would tend to create a general climate of compliance with the measures that might become necessary in a war emergency. There would be a feeling that the ground was being laid for a controlled and selective use of manpower on an enforceable basis. There would not be the feeling that things would be hit or miss or that evasion would be relatively simple. This might be quite important in gaining acceptance for measures that might prove necessary. [145]

Initially, Robertson's arguments seemed to have overcome some of the ministerial qualms, and Claxton, the Defence minister, suggested a few days later that all the preparatory work be done, followed by a registration of limited groups, and followed by a national registration when war became inevitable. [146] But officials too were reconsidering matters, and MacNamara told Robertson that, for the purposes of a military draft, he preferred to use the birth and death registries, supplemented by family allowance records, a suggestion whose political dynamite was immediately apparent to the Cabinet Secretary. [147]

Thus matters began to drift from Robertson's point of view. On 2 May the cabinet committee reported that it believed registration unnecessary at this time, and the ministers limited themselves to the suggestion of a trial registration or a registration of persons on a selective basis determined by their employment. Robertson noted on a draft that "I think that this is fine," a sign that he had been persuaded that registration at present was not politically acceptable to ministers who remembered the war's events too clearly to set out on a potentially dangerous course unless they had no choice.

Thus, when the National Advisory Council on Manpower met for its second meeting on 18-19 May 1951, Brooke Claxton told the members that the government had decided against registration now and decided to hold one only if the risk of war increased. Even then, Claxton added, its value was mainly for security purposes. [148] A few months later, the cabinet reaffirmed its decision, although it did decide to permit preparatory work to go on. Paper was ordered, cards were prepared, and planning went on, but little more was done. [149]

This was a story of unfulfilled, and perhaps misplaced, initiatives. Robertson's role was disturbing, and he was clearly prepared to countenance rather drastic measures in a democratic society because of his fear of war, his knowledge of subversive activities, and his concern that if war came, manpower matters had to be handled more expeditiously and with less regard for political consequences than had been the case in the Second World War. Perhaps he was correct, but the politicians did not agree, and his efforts were to no avail.

IV

Robertson's time as Clerk of the Privy Council and Secretary to the Cabinet had not been a success. He had realized quickly that he had made a mistake in returning to Ottawa, but had hung on, his unhappiness evident to his close friends and colleagues. By late 1951, Pickersgill had talked to the Prime Minister about his friend, telling St. Laurent that he had the impression that Robertson would prefer to return to London. St. Laurent was willing—"if that is what he wants to do we'll just arrange it. . . ."[150]

As always, other appointments were involved, and possibly other choices. Heeney's list of possible appointments for the Department included Robertson as a potential Ambassador for Rome, The Hague, and Washington, and as a candidate for Under-Secretary.[151] Pearson's preference was to bring Wilgress back from London as Under-Secretary and to send Heeney to Europe as Ambassador to NATO. But Pearson had no objection to Robertson's return to London,[152] and by mid-December 1951 St. Laurent had apparently accepted the Wilgress-Heeney-Robertson shuffle.[153] Soon after, he decided to put Pickersgill in Robertson's place as Secretary to the Cabinet.[154]

But by mid-March, nothing definitive had been said. Not until 15 March 1952 did Pearson finally speak to Robertson about the change, telling him to be ready to take over in London by the end of May or early June.[155] A few days later the cabinet agreed to the changes, and public announcement was made on 18 March.[156] "The whole thing," the Auditor-General, Watson Sellar, noted in his diary, "another 'musical chairs' & makes one wonder what is the morale in the diplomatic service."[157]

At about this time, there were some quiet soundings from London about Robertson as a possible Secretary-General of NATO. The British knew that he was not averse to returning to London, a Canadian Secretary-General was ideal from their viewpoint, and Robertson's qualities made him the first choice. But after polite feelers made by the Foreign Secretary, Anthony Eden, the word from Pearson was that Robertson was not really suitable for the post.[158] In fact, Pearson himself was interested in the position, telling Bruce Hutchison in strictest confidence that the post was "the biggest job in the world at the moment." Whether Pearson discussed the position with Robertson, before pouring cold water on talk of him, is unknown; whether Robertson might have been interested is doubtful; and in the end, Pearson stayed in Ottawa and the position went to Lord Ismay instead.[159]

Thus it was to be Canada House again. "You will both be received in London with bells & confetti," 'Tommy' Lascelles wrote from the Palace. "I always think of you ... as the beau ideal of what a High Commissioner should be," added Frank Lee, still Permanent Secretary at the Board of Trade. The *Times* welcomed his return, calling him the "most distinguished Canadian Civil Servant, with that background of scholarship and respect for academic standards of thought which have so often marked the heads of the profession in England." And Douglas Le Pan said that he trusted the Charing Cross Road booksellers "are preparing themselves for new and massive raids. . . ."[160]

Robertson himself was delighted to be returning. Pickersgill wrote to a friend that "Norman is obviously greatly pleased to be returning to London. It is a great misfortune that he has not really enjoyed these last three years. . . . But I feel everything is going to work out all right now."[161] On 23 May the Robertsons left Ottawa by train, heading for Quebec and their ocean liner. " . . . I was not able to be there," said Wynne Plumptre, "but Beryl [Plumptre] went to the station and tells me that there was a terrific send-off. All of Ottawa was there from the Prime Minister down."[162] That was a good way to return to better things.

CHAPTER X

Suez

THE LONDON TO which the Robertsons returned in the spring of 1952 was very different from what it had been in 1946. The damage from the blitz had been repaired and the shabby dress of the population had been replaced with new clothing. Britain was more prosperous than six years before, the people's health was better, thanks to the National Health Service, and the countryside was as splendid as ever. But the Attlee government had gone, replaced in 1951 by the Conservatives, still led by Winston Churchill. The grand old man was now a spent volcano most of the time, although occasional flashes of fire and volleys of brimstone issued forth. Nothing, however, not even a Churchill at his peak, could have restored Britain to its prewar power, nor could anything make the Commonwealth and Empire again into a cohesive force.

The simple fact, in consequence, was that the post of High Commissioner in London was no longer the pre-eminent one in the service. Washington was now the capital of the world, and most of the important business of the West—and of the Canadian foreign service—took place there.

For Robertson, therefore, the work of Canada House was easier than it had been on his first tour.[1] The press of business was less, the pressures much eased. There was more time to write letters,[2] to read, to walk all over the city, to browse in the bookshops, and to play bridge at the Savile Club, a slightly run-down, oddball and literary club conveniently close to the High Commissioner's residence at 12 Upper Brook Street.[3] There was even time to attend an occasional football match[4] and to entertain friends. For example, when John Hicks, Robertson's Balliol colleague, gave his inaugural lecture in economics at Oxford, Robertson insisted on attending and on throwing a party at Oxford's Randolph Hotel. A grand gesture, made no less so when the time set ran afoul of the licensing laws, leaving all the guests standing without a drink for half an hour.[5]

The Robertsons' residence was greatly different than on their first stint in London. Then they had lived in a variety of rented accommodation; now their home was a pleasant townhouse with space for entertaining, some fine furniture that had been given to the diplomatic service by P.C. Larkin, Mackenzie King's High Commissioner in London in the 1920s, quarters for guests and staff, good if rather underfurnished quarters for the family, and even an elevator.[6] There was no trek from house to house to bedevil the Robertsons (or more particularly, Jetty), and with the new accommodation, entertaining was much easier. At No. 12, wrote Robertson's old friend, John Stevenson, there was "a happy mixture of gracious living and democratic simplicity, flavored with culture. In the generous hospitalities which they dispense, they do not show the partiality for the British aristocracy to which some of their predecessors were addicted, and Canadians of all walks of life, provided they are not snobs or uncivilised Philistines, are always welcomed inside their doors."[7] In fact, Robertson and Canada House's social secretary had to check the visitor's book at Trafalgar Square each day to see who was in town and to determine appropriate entertainment. The representational duties were well done, although Robertson still avoided speeches whenever possible.

Alix, the Robertson's eldest daughter, did not come to London with her parents. She stayed at Queen's University in Kingston to complete her degree in history, graduating in 1953. Then she came to London, found a job and a flat and lived there on her own for some time until she returned to Toronto. Judith, not yet in her teens when the Robertsons returned to London, continued her schooling, democratically being given some share in choosing the boarding school she was to attend. The choice was St. Davids, Englefield Green, where she stayed three years. It was probably just as well she was away for most of the year, for even if the pressures on this posting were less than in the past, both her father and mother were so busy with entertaining and social obligations that it was a rare night when both were home. A difficult life for a child.[8]

At Canada House itself little had changed; some said, too little. The High Commission had "just grow'd, like Topsy," one officer later noted, and there were "a remarkable number of sacred cows—institutions and practices that seemed to be considered untouchable merely because they had been that way for many years." Moreover, the morale of the non-officer staff was not very high "and it was notorious throughout our Foreign Service that London was a poor post for Canadian non-officer staff." Over time Robertson worked to improve Canada House, reorganizing the central registry and making a start at cleaning out the files left from a generation before, but there were still problems about receiving and informing the public and it was always difficult to upset routines that had gone unaltered for years.[9]

Still at Canada House, as the High Commissioner's private secretary, was Eleanor Fleming, efficient and unflappable, a quiet but amused observer of the foibles of her boss. On one occasion, Robertson had to attend a Trafalgar Day ceremony, but when a minor crisis blew up, he left his hat at the Foreign Office. The solution was to borrow Frederic Hudd's much smaller one, a hat that simply could not fit on Robertson's great bald dome. "For God's sake," Miss Fleming exhorted, "don't put the hat on," but unconvinced that her urgings would succeed, she hung out of the Trafalgar Square windows to see if the High Commissioner followed orders. This time, he did.[10]

As the story suggested, Hudd remained as Deputy High Commissioner for much of Robertson's term. Not until 1956 was he replaced by Sydney Pierce, an experienced economics specialist who had served in Munitions and Supply, Trade and Commerce, and External Affairs, latterly as Ambassador to Brazil. Robertson and Pierce were old friends with a shared passion for bridge, and Robertson was pleased to get him after an earlier choice for the Deputy's slot, his friend C.M. Drury, the Deputy Minister of National Defence and co-owner of the farmhouse in the Gatineau, was unable to accept.[11]

Other officers on the staff of Canada House were an able lot, for London, like Washington, still got some of the best officers in the Department.[12] There were at various periods Basil Robinson, Klaus Goldschlag, Louis Couillard, G.G. Crean, Margaret Meagher and Arnold Smith. Smith was an experienced officer who had made a name with his reports from the Soviet Union at the end of the war; he now had excellent contacts in the Foreign Office. Margaret Meagher was one of the still rare female officers in the Department, and Robertson, who ordinarily was uncomfortable working with women, got along well with her and formed a high opinion of her judgment. "She is able, clear-headed and thoroughly competent," he wrote R.B. Bryce, the Secretary to the Cabinet, in 1956, when Meagher was suggested for a post on the Civil Service Commission. "Her judgment is independent and good, and I am told that it is a special recommendation for a woman in the public service when the girls who work for her speak well of her and are in fact very fond of her." She was,

Robertson added, "a woman whom I could see rising to be a head of mission,"[13] but she did not get chosen for the Commission.

As always, Robertson was the effective head of his mission. He set the tone, shaped the style, and carried his share of the work. Pacing the office, wreathed in smoke, he dictated his letters and despatches to Miss Fleming. There were meetings with an endless chain of visitors—Cardinal Léger visited once and, after a talk with Robertson, told his brother, Jules, "that man could be Superior of the Jesuits," and meant it as a compliment[14]— and the regular discussions with officials in Whitehall. Above all, he had access, that priceless commodity for any diplomat. His forte was conversation, his judgment was extraordinarily good, and he had no axes to grind. He was discreet. In other words, Robertson was the perfect man on whom to try out ideas on a multitude of subjects, to offer a second opinion, to advise and to consult. After Suez, for example, at a time when his influence was not at its peak in London, J.W. Pickersgill, by this time the Minister of Citizenship and Immigration in the St. Laurent government, discovered that his friend could still open doors. "I realized ... in a way I had never realized before how Norman had the entrée everywhere. He thought I should see the Queen so I saw the Queen. There were two or three Ministers he thought I should see and I saw them right off, there was no problem of any kind. I could see perfectly well," Pickersgill said, "how influential he was. . . ."[15] That was what made him such a valuable representative for the Canadian government in London. What a pity, therefore, that at the time of Suez he was powerless to prevent the stupidities of British policy from being carried into action.

I

London was, as always, a good vantage-point to observe the progress of relations between the West and the Soviet Union. Progress, perhaps, was not the best word to describe the difficult period of the early 1950s, a time when the Great Powers tested their hydrogen bombs, and relations were difficult, suspicion rife, and disarmament seemed a will o' the wisp impossibility.

At the beginning of 1954, however, the foreign ministers of the Great Powers had met at Berlin and agreed to discuss disarmament. The result was the establishment of a disarmament sub-committee under United Nations auspices, and Canada was given a place on it. After one meeting in New York, the sub-committee continued its operations at Lancaster

House in London, with Robertson as the Canadian delegate, assisted by Geoffrey Murray, a young officer.

Robertson held few illusions about the prospects for success. He knew that both the Russians and Americans were more interested in scoring propaganda points than in genuine disarmament, but he recognized that the subject was so important, the stakes so high, that to begin talking about it had to be a gain for the world. That was difficult enough, and the atmosphere of mistrust and suspicion that hung over the conference table was almost palpable. As Murray remembers, Robertson brought everyone back to Upper Brook Street for lunch one day, and after the meal made sure that all could talk freely. It was typical of Robertson's attempts to facilitate matters, to help bridge the gap between the super-powers and their super-weapons.[16] To achieve something concrete, however, was the difficulty, and Robertson played some part in moving the discussion to the consideration of a graduated programme of disarmament that could cover both conventional and nuclear weapons.

But, as he knew, there was little that Canada, with its strictly limited powers, could do. "So far as my experience goes," he wrote to Pearson in November 1955, "our only opportunity of putting anything in the pot has been in the private, off-the-record discussions between the Western delegations." In his view, therefore, the Western nations had to achieve some unanimity before discussions with the Soviet Union got down to important questions.[17] It was a good try, but disarmament did not progress much further. Perhaps Robertson's later suggestion that a summit meeting be held in the face of "one of these awesome demonstrations of nuclear power in the Pacific or the plains of Siberia" might have got East and West to talk together seriously about peace.[18] There was little doubt that Robertson's apocalyptic views on nuclear weapons, an important factor in the Canadian dispute over the arming of the Bomarc missiles in the early 1960s, had been formed during the futile discussions in the Disarmament sub-committee.

He was concerned with other ways to ease the relations between East and West, and his fertile mind was full of suggestions. In 1954, for example, at a time when the rhetoric of the day on both sides of the Iron Curtain stressed the need to reunite divided Germany, China and Korea, Robertson took a different tack. In a letter to Pearson, the High Commissioner suggested that the Minister should "say something sensible about the dangers of indiscriminate seeking after unification as an end in itself." Without suggesting, Robertson said,

... that you should set yourself up as the Prophet of Partition, I do think it would be worth while to remind people that there are worse fates in the world today than political separation.... The desire and pursuit of the whole is commonly counted a good thing, but I think quite a fair case could be made for diagnosing it as just another of the tendencies toward totalitarianism which are the curse of our time.

The argument could be put in philosophic jargon as a plea for a pluralistic universe against the monomania of our modern Hegelians, whether they be Marxists or not. Alternatively, respect for difference and diversity, emphasis on opportunities for political experiment, distrust of dogma are sound Liberal attitudes which still have an application to problems of foreign policy.

It might be worth reminding some Canadian audience that this new orthodoxy of unification everywhere runs directly counter to the lessons of our own political experience, whether inside Canada or in our relations with the other countries of the Commonwealth.... We used to think self-determination even to the point of secession had a good deal to be said for it.

Formosa was then the current hot-spot and Robertson suggested that there was merit in getting the idea of an independent Formosa "into current political circulation before the field is left completely to the people who either want to annex Formosa to the mainland of China or to annex the mainland of China to Formosa."[19] That was good advice, radical for its day, but it took at least a decade before it was accepted generally.

Yet if that suggestion was far-reaching and concerned a matter of high international policy, most of Robertson's work was with more prosaic matters, most notably questions of commercial policy. In late 1951 and early 1952, the British pound had come under attack and Britain's reserves again fell to a dangerous level.[20] This produced the usual flurry of meetings and plans to overcome the crisis. From the Canadian point of view, the key question was whether or not Britain moved to make sterling convertible, a Canadian goal since the end of the war.[21] The British soon decided to stage a full-scale Commonwealth economic conference in December 1952, preceded by a gathering of officials in September, and Robertson became fully involved in the preparations for both.[22]

In his view, the real anxiety was that the Commonwealth countries might "seek congenial forms of evasive action" rather than face up to the real problems.

When one talks about putting the problems of this conference agenda in their world setting [Robertson told Ottawa on 21 August 1952], one really means putting them in terms of the relationship between North America and the rest of the world, or for the purposes of the London meetings of the relationship between

North America and the Sterling Commonwealth. Our interest and the American interest is to do everything within our power to help the United Kingdom and Europe pay their way in the world. What the United States does is, of course, vastly more important than what we can do. Nevertheless, what we do is important both from its direct substantive effect on the dollar imbalance and from the impetus and support which our action can give to appropriate American action. . . . On the positive side, I think we should be ready, within the G.A.T.T. framework, to go on reducing or removing tariffs on imports from the United Kingdom, and where necessary lessening customs administrative obstacles. . . .[23]

Robertson also worried, as he told R.A. Butler, Churchill's Chancellor of the Exchequer, over the "light-hearted way in which [the UK] government had proposed a Commonwealth conference to consider questions on which, with all the good will in the world, it would be difficult to make substantial progress. . . ." Butler's "only but not inadequate reply," Robertson reported, was "you're telling me," one indication that there were differences in the cabinet on economic policy.[24]

But despite the differences, the conference went on. Robertson headed the delegation to the September meetings and presented the Canadian position paper on 22 September.[25] The conclusion, reached in much secrecy, was that sterling be made convertible for non-residents of the sterling area, although payments of sterling to those outside the bloc continued to be controlled. In addition, and much to the pleasure of the Canadian government, there was to be a progressive reduction of quantitative restrictions on imports into the sterling area.[26] That sounded promising.[27] But, although those decisions were essentially reaffirmed at the full-scale conference in December, little ultimate progress resulted.[28] Convertibility was shelved for the time being—and remained so throughout the whole of Robertson's term in London.[29] It was disappointing that however much effort was made to create the kind of free-trading world that Canada had sought since the war, major advances never seemed to occur. Canada's only market of assured strength lay to the south, and the importance of the British market to Canadian exporters continued to decline.[30]

Yet not for want of effort from Robertson. Could the British be persuaded to purchase Canadian canned fruit? Would they take some wheat at a higher price and leave the bulk of their purchases to be made on the open market? Could the difficulties affecting the pulp and paper industry not be turned to advantage in the British market? Trade promotion indeed occupied a good deal of his time. So, too, did the search for information on a wide variety of topics, including the Central African Federation and its prospects, and the British government's attitude to the control of the new transatlantic cable which, Ottawa feared, would see the United States in effective charge of Atlantic communications.[31] There were questions of atomic policy,[32] and there were discussions, often with Pearson and visiting Canadian ministers, with British officials and cabinet members.[33]

NATO and its future was a persistent worry, something that concerned all the Foreign Service after Pearson was named in March 1956 to a three-man committee—the Three Wise Men—to consider the Alliance's course. In discussions in Ottawa and London, Robertson added his mite to the flood of paper and trickle of ideas going to the Minister. In 1953, for example, he had suggested that NATO should stockpile wheat against the threat of war. The idea was a sensible one, saving shipping space vitally needed for other purposes in the event of hostilities; it was also an insurance policy for the Europeans and, of course, a useful way of disposing of surplus Canadian stocks.[34] Three years later Robertson was still pushing the scheme, although there had been no success in selling it to NATO.[35] He also stressed the need to improve communications across the Atlantic, a practical way of strengthening the alliance, and his primary interest, as always, lay in the fostering of economic and commercial ties.[36] But the British were cool to any such efforts through NATO and were pressing their own proposals, ones that Robertson and Ottawa found extremely impractical. "Judging by our talk this morning at the official level," Robertson told Pearson in June 1956, "you probably should not count on deriving very much inspiration on any economic aspects of your assignment from your discussions with the U.K."[37] The Wise Men would propose and tinker, but nothing profound resulted.

One of Robertson's chores was to deal with the Palace. In the normal course of his duties as High Commissioner, he had certain formal contacts with George VI and, after his death, with Elizabeth II. There was no personal relationship—Massey was the last High Commissioner to seek that—but there was attendance at formal dinners, garden parties and the like and, for example, before every royal tour there was the obligatory dinner at Upper Brook Street, and before his departure for home, a weekend at Windsor Castle.

These duties were greatly multiplied by the Coronation of Elizabeth II on 2 June 1953, an event that presented the High Commission with difficult problems of etiquette and ceremonial punctilio. For example, was

Prime Minister St. Laurent obliged to wear court dress with white knee breeches at Westminster Abbey? It seemed he might and, as Robertson wrote to Pickersgill, "it looked for an hour or so as if the whole fabric of the Commonwealth was in some jeopardy," but sanity prevailed in the end. It was just as well it did, for St. Laurent was adamant in his refusal to countenance court dress. Robertson had a personal interest in the matter too, for as High Commissioner it was his duty to carry the Standard of Canada in the procession in the Abbey, and in 1937 Vincent Massey had happily worn the "scarlet cloak lined with white fur, a blue tunic trimmed with gold, a cape, breeches and white stockings" of the standard-carrier. Fortunately, the Prime Minister's ukase against such foolishness covered him as well. As it was, Robertson had more than enough difficulty learning to move his rather awkward and uncoordinated frame in step with the others in the procession.[38]

There were as well all the difficulties of allocating seats along the route of the procession—Canada House apparently was allocated more than 9,000 places—to the hordes of applicants. A Coronation Section was created at Canada House to deal with this and other matters and close liaison established with the Coronation Executive Committee in Ottawa.[39]

When the Coronation itself neared, the pace of life increased markedly, with a flood of invitations directed to the Robertsons. In addition to engagements at the Palace and those sponsored by the British government, there were, among others, a luncheon given by the Corporation of the City of London at the Guildhall, a Gala Performance at the Royal Opera House of Benjamin Britten's *Gloriana*, a review of the fleet at Spithead, a march-past of Commonwealth ex-servicemen and -women at Hyde Park, and a British Empire Coronation Ball at the Hurlingham Club.[40] Above all, the Prime Minister, his family and his party were in London for the festivities, and although the St. Laurents stayed at the Dorchester Hotel, Robertson had to be available at all times. The Prime Minister was not an easy guest to entertain, particularly since he was worried about the election he knew he had to call as soon as he returned to Canada, and the Robertsons fretted about how best to entertain him. Jetty Robertson thought small dinners were more comfortable, but the High Commissioner was adamant that things had to be done properly and that all the appropriate guests had to be invited. Propriety won.[41]

After the Coronation, dealings with the Palace returned to normal. There was the usual difficulty with royal tours in 1953, when the invitation to the Duchess of Kent to open the Canadian National Exhibition at Toronto had to be cancelled because it coincided with the general election.[42] Robertson thought that was foolish. As he later told Pearson, the idea that royal tours interfered with politics was superstition. "Oysters can, I am told, be eaten quite safely in months without 'r'. I should think that a fortnight's grace before and after polling day ought to be safe enough margin to keep a Royal visit well out of politics."[43]

There was even some concern about a new title for Prince Philip, the Duke of Edinburgh. The Prime Minister of Australia, Robertson informed Ottawa in the summer of 1956, apparently preferred "The Prince" as a suitable title, a choice that led Robertson to report that he had heard that "Machiavelli had thought of the title first...." His impression was that the British cabinet were inclined to "leave well enough alone," but he added a personal "gossipy footnote" to Pearson:

I gather that the Mountbattens have been officiously busy in promoting the idea of the new title, from which I gather that the Duke himself has not been unaware of the Menzies initiative. . . .

They are an able, thrusting family with remarkable personal qualities. . . . I don't remember if I ever told you at the time of Prince Philip's marriage there were some questions as to whether the new Royal line would go into history as 'Mountbatten' or 'Windsor'. In the event 'Windsor' won, but the episode seems to me not unrelated to the present pushing for a new and more important title.[44]

In the end, Machiavelli kept "The Prince" and Philip the Duke of Edinburgh.

Such questions took time, and although not intrinsically important, they obviously concerned many important people. For Robertson, a pragmatic Canadian monarchist, but one without any deep and abiding love for the idea of monarchy, such questions could not have been among those he liked to handle.

Two deaths shook Robertson during his tour in London, those of Clifford Clark and Hume Wrong. Clark, the Deputy Minister of Finance, had been a friend and both men had worked continuously and warmly since 1932 when the financial expert had been brought from Queen's University to help with the preparations for the Ottawa Conference. During the war, Robertson had served on Clark's Economic Advisory Committee, and the two, with Graham Towers, had largely shaped the direction of Canadian economic and commercial policy for more than a decade. Clark's last years had been difficult, and the consensus on policy that had been the striking feature of the 1940s was at last beginning to break down. Nonetheless, his death on 27 December 1952 left a vacuum that would never be filled in quite the same way. He had been, as the *Globe and Mail* described him, "one of the greatest economic planners,"[45] and Robertson and many of his colleagues in the civil service contributed willingly and substantially to the Skelton-Clark Memorial Foundation that Principal W.A. Mackintosh established at Queen's University in 1953.[46]

The death of Hume Wrong on 24 January 1954 hit Robertson harder. He had many friends in the Department, but Hume Wrong alone among Robertson's contemporaries was at once close friend, trusted colleague and intellectual equal. The relationship that had grown up between the two during the war, when they had cooperated closely for almost five years, carrying an enormous burden with near-perfect agreement, had been particularly warm, and although subsequent postings kept them apart, that closeness was never breached. In many ways, Wrong was the ablest diplomat the Canadian service had produced. As a technician, he had no equal; as a writer and formulator of ideas, he was without peer; as an intellect he was every bit Robertson's match. Precise, sometimes cool, Wrong could not be replaced.

Wrong had been appointed Under-Secretary on 1 August 1953, a belated capstone to his career.[47] He had desperately wanted the post in 1941 when King's eye had lit on Robertson; he could probably have had it in 1949 if he had wished, but had stayed in Washington at the Prime Minister's request because of his close friendship with Dean Acheson, the new Secretary of State. In 1953, when he was already ill and when he did not really want the post, it had simply been assumed that he was to get it. "I am not very happy about going back to Ottawa," Wrong had written to Escott Reid. "Perhaps if I stage a sit-down strike in the Under-Secretary's office, my tenure there will be brief."[48] The arrangement with the Minister was that Wrong would take a long three months' leave before assuming his duties (a furlough that allowed him to visit London and stay with the Robertsons), but he had no sooner got to his desk in the late fall than his health broke down. His blood pressure soared, he suffered violent nosebleeds, and there was a haemorrhage behind his one good eye. "I suppose it was a fool thing his consenting to take on this job," his wife wrote to Wrong's sister, but "It was hard to refuse, particularly as our dr. in Washington said that on medical grounds he could not say that he shouldn't do it. Heaven knows, Hume never wanted to take it. . . ."[49]

A few days after Wrong's death, Pearson wrote movingly to Robertson about their friend. It was a terrific blow "because of our very old and close friendship. I was, of course, counting on him greatly to help me in my work, and I shall miss his wise counsel and assistance, but that is a small matter compared with the loss of such a long and good friend." Pearson added that "There was no burial service yesterday, merely the church service, but in the Spring Hume may be buried in the little cemetery on the hill near Wakefield [in the Gatineau Hills]. . . . It seems to be a good choice because they had so many happy times in that district, and he loved the hills and lakes and trees there."[50] Robertson and Pearson eventually were buried in the same cemetery.

Wrong's death left the Under-Secretary's post vacant, and indeed it left the Department in something of a fix for a replacement. There was no desperation, for R.A. MacKay, one of the academics brought in during the war, could do the work of acting Under-Secretary in an admirable fashion, but there were difficulties in selecting a permanent head. Apparently, at this point Robertson offered to return to Ottawa and take the post if Pearson thought that would help. T.W.L. MacDermot, the High Commissioner to South Africa, had been told that by Robertson. "But Mike had turned him down," Grant Dexter of the *Winnipeg Free Press* wrote privately after talking with MacDermot. Dexter then pursued the question with his friend Jack Pickersgill, by this time Secretary of State in the St. Laurent government. " . . . Jack said that it was quite true that Norman had volunteered to come back. Mike had so reported to the Cabinet. He added that Mike did not want Norman. Mike had the same feeling toward Norman as he had to Hume. He felt inferior and feared being cramped and dominated. . . . What I did not realize," Dexter ruminated, "is that Mike has a sense of inferiority and allows it to interfere with his judgment of men. Obviously if Norman could be had, he was the only man for the job."[51] Perhaps, but Pearson did not think so. As he wrote to Arnold Heeney: "Neither you nor Norman nor Dana Wilgress should, of course, be disturbed in the jobs you are doing, even if it were desirable, which I do not think it is, to bring a previous incumbent back to fill the position."[52]

But if not Robertson, Heeney or Wilgress, then who? Pearson asked Robertson for his views, and drew a longer letter than Robertson was wont to produce. First, Robertson began by admitting that there was "no hope of ever quite filling Hume's place," but above all he believed it was important not to go outside the Department for a successor. "I think it would be bad for the position of the Department vis-à-vis other departments of government in Ottawa, and in the country generally, which rightly or wrongly has given our Department a good deal of confidence and pride, to have a new department head brought in from outside." More important, such an appointment would have a "pretty discouraging effect on the confidence and morale of the very good younger team whom you have been bringing along in these last years." Nonetheless, Robertson canvassed the names of some outsiders that Pearson had suggested. Mitchell Sharp, the Assistant Deputy Minister in Trade and Commerce, he thought lacked the "range, displacement, and perhaps the personality." George Davidson, the Deputy Minister of National Health and Welfare since its establishment as a department in 1944, suffered from similar liabilities, Robertson said. "With the single exception of Bob Bryce, I cannot think of anybody now in another government department in Ottawa who could bring to External Affairs the kind of top-level reinforcement in executive and intellectual capacity that would offset the very real drawbacks of an appointment from outside the Service."

Inside the Department, then, Robertson assessed the candidates. Charles Ritchie, he said, was eminently qualified to take over, "has grown in grace and wisdom with the responsibilities put upon him, and I would be very happy about the Department with Charles as Under-Secretary." On the other hand, after four years in Ottawa, Ritchie was entitled to an embassy, particularly in light of the "really great discrepancy that still remains between the terms of employment abroad and employment at home." MacKay was good and able, and if the choice was between him and a more speculative appointment, then MacKay should be the choice. Tommy Stone, he felt, was a better number two, and T.C. Davis, the very able Ambassador in Germany, he thought an outside possibility.[53]

Pearson soon replied that he had considered Robertson's points, that he had decided against Sharp, and that he had "dismissed from my own mind" Ritchie and Davidson, for, among others, the reasons you indicate...." In short, Pearson said, "my choice inside our service has more or less narrowed down to Jules Léger or Bert MacKay...."[54] Either one was satisfactory to Robertson, who responded with his views on the two. MacKay, he said, lacked the flair and range of Léger, but he would have the confidence and support of the Department and "I would not be worried if he were confirmed as Under-Secretary...." As for Léger, who had just taken up post as Ambassador to Mexico: "I have tried to imagine how such an appointment would appeal to Jules, who is a wise and sensitive person." Robertson was concerned that Léger might worry about his brother being Cardinal and about bringing his wife back to Ottawa after only a few months abroad. But about Léger's suitability he had no doubts. "I think he would fill [the post] admirably and with real distinction. He is wise, generous, with a real feeling for scholarship and a sense of responsibility on which everybody could relay [sic]. My only doubt, which I have found it hard to resolve, is whether he should be asked to take on now responsibilities which in the ordinary course would come to him in six or seven years' time."[55] Robertson might have added that Léger would be the first francophone Under-Secretary in the Department's still-brief history, a political asset to the government and an indication that the Department now had French-speaking officers who could carry a full share of the work. Pearson, who had consulted others about the choice, eventually made Léger his man, and the new Under-Secretary did his job well until 1958 when Robertson returned to his old post.[56]

II

Robertson's term as High Commissioner had been placid and remarkably free of crises from 1952 to the middle of 1956. But it did not end that way. The Suez affair, a slowly building series of events that culminated in the abortive Anglo-French effort to "separate" Egypt and Israel and to protect the Suez Canal, shattered any illusions that might have remained of British power. It destroyed Anthony Eden's prime ministership; it destroyed relations between Washington, London and Paris for a time; it negated the political and propaganda effects of the Soviet invasion of Hungary in October 1956 and the brutal suppression of dissent there; and it gave Lester Pearson the opportunity to exercise all his superb tactical skills at the United Nations in the Canadian efforts to resolve the crisis and to win an amply justified Nobel Peace Prize. But the Suez crisis spoiled Robertson's term in London and made him, the bearer of the bad news from Ottawa, if not persona non grata with London, at least a High Commissioner who had stayed on long enough.

The crisis in the Middle East had been at the low boil for years, certainly since the Israeli war of independence of 1948 that had left the new state in possession of territory that Palestinians and their Arab supporters considered to be Arab. The matter was complicated by the emergence of Colonel Nasser at the head of Egypt's revolution. An attractive leader, Nasser was full of resentment at the West, the imperialists and the Israelis, and not at all averse to taking aid from the Soviet Union, then making every effort to extend its influence in the region. The French, still engaged in a desperate effort to hold on to their

North African colonies, had their interests in the area, too, and their own reasons to fear Nasser's pan-Arabism. The area was ripe for trouble.

From London, Robertson had reported intermittently on developments in the Middle East as they were seen from the British capital. In late 1955, he had told Ottawa of a conversation with a Commonwealth Relations Office official who had seemed mildly anti-Israeli, certain that there could be no peace in the Middle East until Israel made territorial concessions. The real problem, Robertson quoted the official as saying, was whether "they can be dissuaded from an apocalyptic tendency to prefer extinction to concession."[57] Two months later, the High Commissioner added that the British and Americans were now close together in their positions on the Middle East, agreed on the methods to be tried to resolve the Arab-Israeli conflicts and almost committed to helping Nasser finance the vast expenditures necessary to build the Aswan Dam on the Nile.[58]

That cooperative attitude to the Aswan project, however, had been the Anglo-American response to a Soviet offer of aid, not a gesture of benevolence towards Nasser. This concerned Robertson, who wired Ottawa in March 1956: "I feel affairs in the Middle East have developed to a point at which there is little prospect of stabilizing the situation without some degree of Soviet cooperation. They have demonstrated that they have the power to upset that area, and we should try to make them take some responsibility for keeping order in it." In his view, the only way to move the Russians from "their present wrecking line" was to bring the Middle-East problem to the United Nations.[59]

That might have been good advice, but it was pointless so long as John Foster Dulles coordinated and directed American foreign policy. As Pearson noted in his memoirs, Dulles "had begun to think of Egypt as a threat to his policy of containment of Soviet Russia, rather than as a people struggling to be free from British imperialism."[60] The result was that, although Nasser announced his acceptance of the Anglo-American loan offer on 17 July, the Secretary of State pulled the United States out of the scheme two days later. The British followed suit, the loan offer became null and void, and Nasser's rage became intense. On 26 July, he nationalized the Suez Canal, declaring his intention to use the Canal tolls to help pay for the Dam. The crisis had begun, catching London and Washington by surprise, for neither capital had anticipated the Egyptian reaction.

In London and Paris, in particular, the response to Nasser was very sharp. Despite her unending financial problems, Britain had not yet completely realized that her power had waned, and Suez was still seen as the lifeline of an Empire that was already in total dissolution, the link from the home islands to the Gulf, to India, and to Australasia. Paris was also increasingly fearful of Nasser's disruptive talents, and the anger in France was pronounced. Summoned to two meetings of High Commissioners at the Commonwealth Relations Office on 27 July, Robertson had done his best to urge caution on the British and to suggest that they make use of the United Nations, hoping, as he told Pearson, that they would not "gather too many spears" to their bosom. [61]

That was again good advice but, because Nasser had begun to appear as a Hitler to Eden and 1956 to seem like 1936 or 1938, it was not followed. Robertson's reports on the British attitude led his Minister, Pearson, to set out the Canadian position in a telegram to London on 28 July;

[The situation] has broad implications of a potentially explosive character. We believe that you have adopted a prudent line in urging upon the United Kingdom the wisdom of proceeding in a manner designed to obtain the greatest amount of international support.

. . . I am deeply concerned at the implications of some parts of Eden's message [to St. Laurent of 28 July in which he urged the internationalization of the Canal and a firm stand]; especially as I doubt very much whether he will receive strong support from Washington in the firm line which he proposes to follow. . . . Surely the U.K. Government will not do anything which would commit them to strong action against Egypt until they know that the U.S. will back them. I am also worried [at Eden's internationalization proposal, since] with the Russians dissenting and supporting Egypt, the U.K. do not think that this can be done, as they profess to hope, 'by political pressure' alone. There remains force—which they visualize as a last resort. But is it not clear that to be effective enough force would have to be used to destroy the Nasser Government and take over Egypt? Any effort to use force, in fact, would in all likelihood result in an appeal by Egypt to the U.N. That would be bringing the U.N. into the matter with a vengeance, and by the wrong party.

I'm glad that you have stressed the importance of bringing the U.N. into the question. This may not be practicable but it certainly shouldn't be dismissed without the most careful consideration. [62]

Those were Robertson's marching orders, and he carried them repeatedly to British officials.

In one conversation, Robertson had argued to a British official and old friend that "the last resort" of force could not be reconciled with Britain's obligations under the Charter of the UN. Surely economic pressure was better, although Robertson admitted that that probably was not sufficient. What then should London do? the official asked. The best that Robertson could suggest, admitting the inherent difficulties, was that Britain should seek UN sanction for any pressure it might eventually apply. He believed that Nasser would get sustantial support from what was not yet called the "third world," and he feared a catastrophe if British action led to the breakup or disruption of the UN, something that he could already visualize.[63] Robertson was looking ahead and, if he had no suggestions for a resolution of the problem, he could certainly foresee the coming difficulties. Given London's mood and the non-comprehension there of the position of the newly independent states, he was right to be gloomy.

Compounding evidence came quickly when, on 3 August, Canadian military sources in London passed the word that "it is not a question of whether military action will be taken but rather a matter of how and when." A plan for an assault on the Canal had been approved by the Chiefs of Staff the day before and that plan was en route to the Eden cabinet.[64] The information went to Ottawa, and although the usual processes of diplomacy were underway with meetings, conferences and plans, that advice of British contingency planning increased Robertson's despair.

That was in no way lessened by a message from Pearson on 6 August that "Our main worry is that the United Kingdom and the French have gone too far in committing themselves to the use of force" if the diplomatic route did not produce a satisfactory resolution.

If the political pressure fails [Pearson went on], then the British and French seem committed to the use of force for which they might have little legal justification.... But here I think they will be entirely on their own ... the consequences would be far-reaching for the Commonwealth, for Anglo-American cooperation, and for peace in the Middle East generally....

It is clear that every possible effort must be made to prevent a chain of developments which would result in Anglo-French military force being exerted against Egypt in a way which would split the Commonwealth, weaken the Anglo-American alliance, and have general consequences which would benefit nobody but Moscow.[65]

Pearson was extraordinarily prophetic, and Robertson again took every possible opportunity to stress the Minister's points to British officials and ministers. He asked Lord Home, the Secretary of State for Commonwealth Relations, if it was the British intention "to proceed with an attempt to humiliate and replace Nasser." The reply—"the possibility can't be washed out"—was not designed to ease Robertson's and Canada's worries, nor was Home's own question. "If we have to use force, would we have the approval of Canada?" Robertson's answer was blunt: "In my opinion, no." Later he told Sir Ivone Kirkpatrick, the Permanent Under-Secretary at the Foreign Office, that while "We sympathize with your predicament" and while "we even support your concern that the canal operations should be insulated against the political whims of any one nation," nonetheless "we cannot support, nor even approve, any resort to force."[66] The British should have been in no doubts about the Canadian attitude.

While the British and French continued to ready their military forces and the diplomatic palavering went on, the Robertsons left for France and a holiday, one made less pleasant than usual by his concern over the Middle East situation. By 4 September, he could stand it no more and was back at Canada House where he had talks with Krishna Menon, the Indian gadfly and confidant of Nehru, about means to a settlement.[67] Conversations with some British ministers also suggested that a political settlement was now more likely than war.[68] But in fact, as Terence Robertson demonstrated so irrefutably, the situation was changing in a radical and dangerous way. The French had determined to concert planning with Israel, and the British, acquiescing in and aware of the conspiracy, went along.[69] The secrecy was intense, and the matter was confused further for observers when the Suez question became the subject of heated and extensive debate in the UN Security Council.

No one outside of the few in the know in London, Paris and Jerusalem anticipated what took place. On 29 October, the Israelis launched their armoured forces against Egypt, and the next day Britain and France issued an ultimatum to both Egypt and Israel to draw back from the Suez Canal. As planned, the Israelis accepted; as expected, the Egyptians refused; and the Anglo-French air forces soon began to bomb selected targets in the Canal Zone.

Robertson had been informed of the British ultimatum of 30 October just one hour before its issue to the belligerents. No one on his staff, with the solitary exception of Margaret Meagher, had expected the British to threaten a resort to force at this time,[70] and Robertson was horrified. Eleanor Fleming still remembers his response: he walked over to the window of his office above Trafalgar Square, stared out and said "Jesus Christ." It was, she said, the only time she heard him swear.[71] Well he might. As he told Pearson the next day over the telephone (newly installed cables made telephone use easier and fortunately so, for sunspots were interfering with radio communications at the time), "he had had no information whatsoever about the decision just taken by the British and French to send an ultimatum . . . the members of his staff who had just returned from canvassing the Foreign Office and the C.R.O. had not had the slightest intimation. . . ."[72] Pearson's response was to urge Robertson "to express to the United Kingdom Government our feeling of bewilderment and dismay at the decisions which they have taken . . . decisions which came as a complete surprise to us and which had not been hinted at in any previous discussion." The Americans were in an apoplectic rage at the British-French-Israeli actions, particularly since the Soviet Union, up to its ears in the destruction of the fragile flowering of Hungarian democracy, had been on the run and now would be freed of much of the moral obloquy of the world. That such a step had been taken without consultation, Pearson said, "makes cooperation extraordinarily difficult."[73]

Robertson continued his efforts to determine the British course all that terrible 30 October. He was unable to see any key officials, their doors being firmly shut and their telephones off the hook to calls from Canada House, but one underling who had access only to the public information thought "the government would try to prevent any major fighting taking place, but he did not know whether or not they were contemplating sending forces to the area. . . ."[74] At last at 6 p.m., Home, a loyal backer of Eden's policy,[75] met the High Commissioners. The sole object of the ultimatum, he lied, "was to prevent the fighting spreading and to protect the lives and property of peaceful users of the canal . . . the U.K. feel that the initiative which the French and themselves have taken is in accordance with the purposes of the U.N.. . . ."[76]

That was specious nonsense, and Eden sent more of the same to St. Laurent in a prime minister-to-prime minister message. Britain had acted, Eden said, because the Middle East was boiling over, and he feared Israeli action against Jordan, an eventuality that might have forced Britain to intervene against Israel and with Egypt as an ally. That seemed a nightmare to Eden, who said Britain could not allow a war between Egypt and Israel to block the Suez Canal; that he and the French would feel bound if war broke out to request a ceasefire and withdrawal from the Canal. In the event of a refusal, the two European powers were prepared to take any military action necessary to compel each party to conform. Eden added that he knew he could look for Canadian understanding and expressed the hope that he might receive Ottawa's support.[77] There was scant prospect of that, for Ottawa was beginning to receive reports of the connivance between the Israelis and France,[78] and St. Laurent and Pearson knew that Eden's message was replete with falsehoods. The Prime Minister's reply, much toned down from the white heat that went into the first draft,[79] let the British know what they should have learned months earlier from Robertson's repeated statements to them—they could not count on Canadian support for their aggression. Without more information, St. Laurent told Eden, "we cannot come to the conclusion that the penetration of [Israel's] troops into Egypt was justified or that the probable resistance of the Egyptians necessitated the decision of the U.K. and France to post forces in the canal zone." Canadians, he added, "will endeavour to shape our course in conformity with what we regard as our obligations under the Charter of and our membership in the United Nations."[80] That was a chilling message for Eden, who had probably expected Canada to do her duty by saying ready, aye ready. London, an officer of the British High Commission told External Affairs, was "aghast" at the tone of the message.[81] The consequences of Eden's folly were already becoming apparent.

What is sure, however, is that although St. Laurent, Pearson and Robertson were appalled at what Paris and London had done, their immediate concern was not to punish the miscreants but to salvage the situation, to get the war stopped, and to restore the links between London and Washington, so sadly disrupted by the British action in the closing days of President Eisenhower's campaign for re-election. That kind of approach was abundantly evident in Pearson's actions at the UN, so fully and ably covered in his memoirs, and in Robertson's messages from Canada House.

On 1 November, for example, Robertson suggested to Pearson that it might be useful "trying to assemble a meeting of Commonwealth Prime Ministers as a cover for a reversal of U.K. policies. Neither membership in the U.N. nor in the North Atlantic alliance has in fact restrained the U.K. and France from going it alone, and so far the Govt's pretty solid majority support in Parliament does not appear to be deeply shaken. There remains," he said, "the unassessed effect of U.K. actions on the Commonwealth relationship. One might have thought that this consideration would have weighed more heavily with an English Conservative Cabinet than it appears to have done." Nonetheless, Robertson added, if Eden and Company were aware of "their appalling isolation and were seeking ways of recovering support and balance," they might be prepared "to defer to a consensus of Commonwealth opinion, even though pride and bloody-mindedness are likely to prevent [them] accepting the same advice from the U.N." or from NATO.[82] That was a good idea, but events at the UN moved too fast for it to be used.

That same day Robertson reported on meetings with Home and Kirkpatrick. To Home, "I found it difficult to say anything which did not sound an explicit endorsement of every criticism the Opposition had made of Govt policy . . . [and told him] I had found it difficult to explain to my Govt the reasonableness of the policies his Govt had been advocating and acting on since Nasser's seizure of the Canal. I was afraid that some of the foundations of the relationship between Commonwealth countries had been severely shaken."[83] That was tough talk from the representative of the senior Dominion. With Kirkpatrick, Robertson tried out Pearson's idea of proposing a ceasefire, to be followed by a major diplomatic conference on the problems of the Middle East. He told the Permanent Under-Secretary that "as part of this approach it would be essential to set up an adequate U.N. military force to separate the Egyptians from the Israelis" pending a settlement. Kirkpatrick, not the ablest senior official in the history of the Foreign Office, gave Robertson advance notice of Eden's address to Parliament that afternoon in which he opened the door to such a force. Kirkpatrick added that if there were to be such a UN presence, "it would have to be a substantial and properly supported international force" and "not just a notional force thought up as a diplomatic gimmick to meet this evening's diplomatic requirements." He was also concerned about what he saw as the Canadian attempt to rush Britain into a ceasefire.[84]

At the same time, Robertson's officers were gathering information for him. Arnold Smith spoke privately with a friend at the Foreign Office, who told him that the "bitterness about the Canadian attitude on Suez was as great as that against the Americans." Canada had been softer than the United States before the crisis, even agreeing to sell wheat to the Egyptians at a time when Britain had urged her not to do so. Smith was also told that Eden was in "a highly emotional state," worried and uncertain, something of which Canadian officials had long been aware.[85] And finally, Smith was told that the British view was that the course at Suez had been in effect forced on Britain. "For years the Americans and you have been urging us to follow a more European type of policy . . . now you have got it." Britain, the official said, had acted "on the rebound . . . foiled in her desire to marry the woman she loved . . . [Britain] found the only thing left was to visit the whore-house." The United States was the "woman she loved" and France the brothel.[86] Clearly Eden was not the only Briton who had been unstrung by the crisis.

By 3 November, Pearson had raised the idea of a UN military presence at the General Assembly and he could tell Robertson over the telephone that "We're going to go ahead with a resolution calling for the creation of a United Nations force. You should tell the government there that there's absolutely no hope of Assembly approval if landings take place before the vote. If they are sincere about handing over to a United Nations force, they've got to play their part in helping to establish it."[87] Robertson carried this message to the Foreign Office, and he won from Kirkpatrick the guarantee that no landings in Egypt would take place before the evening of 4 November.[88] The result was that at 2 a.m. on 4 November the General Assembly agreed to Pearson's motion, carried without a dissenting vote, to establish "an emergency international United Nations force to secure and supervise the cessation of hostilities." The UN had added "peacekeeping" to its functions.[89]

On the night of the 4th, however, the British and French began their belated assault on the Canal Zone, sending in paratroops and marines, although Egypt and Israel had almost ceased hostilities by that point.[90] Eden explained his government's actions to St. Laurent: Britain had decided that the operation to separate the combatants and to ensure the safety of the Canal must proceed as planned. It had been a difficult, indeed an agonizing decision to take, Eden said, but he was sure that it was right. Britain welcomed the Canadian initiative to create an emergency force, but that was going to take some time. This made it imperative for Britain and France to take a grip of the situation and to create conditions under which the UN force could relieve the Anglo-French armies of their responsibility.[91] The reasoning, if imaginative, was as tortuous as in Eden's first telegram to St. Laurent, and the Canadian response was tougher still. "I think we have a sympathetic understanding of your and France's position but we still regret you found it necessary to follow the course you are taking. Of course the motives and the known character of the actors do make a difference, but it is unfortunate that the events in the Middle East have cloaked with a smoke screen the renewed brutal international crimes of the Soviets." That was as tough a message as had ever gone from Ottawa to London and it must have smarted.[92] Eden replied the next day with a confused message that painted the intervention at Suez as a lifesaver for both Israel and the Arabs, that suggested Britain had weighed the moral considerations with scrupulous care and had considered the Commonwealth above and before everything else. The British Prime Minister added that he hoped Canada saw what London had had to do as paving the way for the UN force to become a reality.[93] In one sense at least, if not that intended by Eden, the last sentence was true.

The frigid blasts from Ottawa and other capitals, not least from Moscow, which was brandishing its missiles in defence of peace while its tanks crawled through the rubble of Budapest, had their effect. On 6 November,[94] officials of the Prime Minister's office told Robertson at the House of Commons that Britain and France were now ready to accept a ceasefire. "They wanted me to say to the Prime Minister and you," Robertson told Pearson, "that they are very grateful for Canada's steadying influence in the Councils of the U.N." Eden wanted the UN force to be set up as soon as possible and immediate efforts to begin clearing the Canal of the blockships Nasser had sunk in it, an effective tactic that negated any military gains the Anglo-French invasion might have produced.[95]

Still the ceasefire was progress, a tribute to Canadian diplomacy. There was praise too from Opposition quarters in London. On 7 November Robertson received a letter from Philip Noel-Baker, a minister in Attlee's government and one with whom the High Commissioner had worked closely on his first tour in London. "I wanted to tell you," Noel-Baker wrote, "that [Hugh] Gaitskell [the leader of the Labour Party] and I both feel very strongly that Canada, having rendered an immense service throughout the Suez crisis, and having proposed the solution of the international force, should now make that solution appear realistic in the eyes of Eden and his friends, of the people and of the Russians, by contributing a contingent at least a brigade strong. . . ."[96] That was well-meaning advice (if more than a little unrealistic in Canadian military terms), and Robertson certainly agreed, at least in so far as he wanted Canada to contribute to the Emergency Force. "I want you to know," Pearson told him, "that we share your feeling that it is of paramount importance now to get a U.N. Force, even of token strength, into the area. . . ." And he graciously added that "I want you to know also how greatly I have been assisted in recent days by the messages from Canada House. . . . I cannot thank you enough."[97]

The remainder of the crisis, from Robertson's point of view, was essentially clearing up. The High Commissioner was too far away from New York where the work of creating the UN force was in hand, and he was largely uninvolved in the difficulties Pearson had in persuading the Egyptians that Canadian troops, although regrettably dressed much like British Tommies and more regrettably still named "The Queen's Own Rifles," were not after all British. From London, Robertson could only suggest possible ways round the problems. "Quite apart from the graver implications if Nasser is remaining obdurate on this point," he wired to Pearson on the 14th, "you will appreciate that the U.K. would find it difficult to understand a U.N. acquiescence in such obduracy from Nasser, after the U.K. and French Govts and the Israeli Govt bowed to U.N. pressure."[98] A compromise arranged by General E.L.M. Burns, the commander of UNEF (as the force was now becoming known) resolved that problem. Burns, a Canadian seconded to UN service, decided that he needed logistical support more than infantry, and Nasser was persuaded that Canadians in trucks and ordnance depots would be less galling than in infantry units.[99]

Other suggestions, some of which did not prove practical, flowed in a steady stream from Robertson to Ottawa. Could a UN resolution not authorize the Secretary-General to call on any UN member to provide supplies and equipment for UNEF? That way British and French stocks in the Canal Zone and in Cyprus could be used.[100] Could a system not be devised to allow General Burns to let contracts for clearing the Canal of its blockships, a device that might let skilled British contractors participate?[101] Would it not ease matters greatly if the Israelis, who in London at least were making noises about their willingness to assist in the settlement of the Palestinian refugee question, "were now ready to make an important new contribution. . . ."? Sympathy, Robertson said, "can work wonders now that it is aroused but . . . may not be sustained for long."[102] Could a UNEF navy be established? A destroyer on patrol in the Gulf of Aqaba could help to prevent any renewed interference with peaceful traffic, Egyptian sovereignty was in no way affected, and so Egyptian consent was unnecessary.[103] And, after the Israelis became stubborn and refused to allow UNEF to be stationed on their side of the border with Egypt, Robertson could be tart. "To ask the Secretary General to make arrangements with Israel invites a prolongation of the bargaining process which in my judgment Israel has already carried to the tolerable limit. When one remembers that after all, less than four months ago, it was the deliberate and calculated political decision of the Government of Israel which precipitated the present crisis. . . ."[104] The crisis, like most crises, did not disappear once it had been ameliorated.

Robertson and his officers were also still trying to put together the story on the way Eden's government had fallen into the Suez mess. There were suggestions—and more than suggestions—that Secretary Dulles had agreed to the removal of Nasser two months before the opening of hostilities.[105] There were clear indications too that Eden had gone to pieces under the stress of the crisis, and the British Prime Minister had indeed left for Jamaica for three weeks recuperation on 23 November; nonetheless, both Robertson and Pearson were shocked at the frankness with which Eden's colleagues discussed his flaws. R.A. Butler's comments to Robertson and him, Pearson wrote, "were so frank that they should not be put down even in a personal report."[106] Butler hoped for the succession, but he did not get it when Eden, ill and discredited, resigned on 9 January 1957. Harold Macmillan, who had been fully involved in the Suez planning, became Prime Minister.[107]

Robertson himself was convinced that London's action at Suez could be explained only as "the politics of the menopause."[108] Eden and his colleagues had acted in a hot flash of rage, and they had had cause to regret their actions almost immediately. Curiously, others were seeking sexual images to explain Suez, too. Nye Bevan, the Welsh firebrand, gave an off-the-record speech on 3 December that Robertson attended. He pointed out "that Casanova had boasted most of his power of conquest when he was too old to carry it through." "All in all," Robertson commented, "Bevan's speech struck me as more impressive than most of the oratory heard lately in these parts."[109]

The High Commissioner's most important analysis came in a long telegram on 13 December 1956. The very failure of the Anglo-French intervention, he said, "may in itself tend through frustration to strengthen some of the underlying attitudes which contributed to the Anglo-French decision to intervene by force...." There was great dissatisfaction in London with the Americans, with NATO and with the UN. The British believed that Washington was indifferent and unreliable, that it cared not a whit for vital European interests in the Middle East. Robertson added that Eden was encouraging every effort to make the United States into the scapegoat. As for the UN, the British had begun to question whether an institution with a built-in double standard could serve their interests. "The institutions of the U.N., and particularly the General Assembly," he said, "unquestionably do involve a double standard in more than one way. First, the force of recommendations is largely moral, and therefore inevitably more effective in democracies where public opinion is decisive, than in totalitarian societies...." Moreover, the Afro-Asians followed a double standard on race issues. The result, Robertson concluded, was that many British officials now believed that the UN "has been a gravely damaging factor, 'if not, indeed, a disaster', for Western Europe."[110] As for NATO, Robertson reported the Foreign Office view that some French ministers were thinking about emasculating or breaking up the alliance during 1957 to free them from the irksome restraints imposed by the United States. The British view, he added, was that NATO tied up British troops and freed Germany to concentrate on competing with British goods without carrying its own weight in defence. Complicating the picture further were the spats between the British and French, arguing over who did or did not do what during the crisis. It was a bleak picture, a portrait of the Western alliance in disarray. The only comfort Robertson could offer was that "the recent enforced contemplation of the abyss and the very costliness of the errors may prove salutary for future judgment."[111]

That was scant comfort indeed, although Prime Minister Macmillan soon quickly began to clear the wreckage and to restore relations with the United States and Canada. With the mood in London so apocalyptic, it could not be surprising that Robertson himself was in a sense a casualty of the crisis. His mission in London had been to keep Canada and Britain close, and there was no doubt that, through no fault of his own, he had failed. Relations between London and Ottawa had been temporarily interrupted,[112] and although some officials and politicians in London professed gratitude for Canada's efforts to save England from its folly, few meant it. Robertson had warned the British time and again before the intervention, and he had spoken frankly and bluntly to them during it. He had carried messages from his Prime Minister, sizzling inside their crested envelopes, and in consequence his usefulness in London was over. Too many ministers—Selwyn Lloyd at the Foreign Office was one—and too many officials, most notably in the Commonwealth Relations Office, thought of Robertson as having let down the side. It was, as one long-time friend, Michael Adeane, said from his vantage-point at Buckingham Palace, a "sad end."[113]

A sad end, too, to Britain's (little-deserved) reputation for wisdom in dealing with the non-white world. Robertson had dealt with British officials for as long as any man, in good times and in bad, and he wrote to a colleague in the summer of 1957 of his "loss of confidence in British judgment and good sense, which derives from the whole handling of the Suez problem." People, he said, again reverting to a familiar image, "are fairly quick to diagnose the problems of adolescence in politics. They are not yet quite ready to recognize the symptoms of the menopause."[114]

III

Robertson must have realized that the crisis had damaged his position in London. Before the Anglo-French intervention, in September 1956, Prime Minister St. Laurent had sent him an extraordinary personal letter. "I was told yesterday," St. Laurent began, "that you and Jetty would like to come back to Canada before very long. I was surprised," he went on,

and I know that Mike will not find it easy to get someone to replace you in London but I do want you to know that it can be arranged and that we have several quite important posts that you might find interesting. Of course, the one in which I would best like to see you would be the Privy Council Office and I know we could arrange something that would be quite satisfactory to Bob [Bryce, the Secretary to the Cabinet since 1953] but, before long, we will have to find someone to replace General McNaughton on the International Joint Commission as well as on the Permanent Joint Defence Committee [*sic*].

We are also thinking very seriously of creating our Canada Council and, of course, we want that to be headed up by someone of real prestige.

The Prime Minister added that only he and his secretary knew of this letter, that Jules Léger, the Under-Secretary, had not been informed, and that he awaited "your answer as to whether or not there is anything in this story that you and Jetty would like to come back." Robertson was assured "that if your answer is negative, I would treat it as absolutely confidential and, should it happen to be affirmative, I would like to be able to mention, not that I have been in correspondence with you but that I do know that you would be available for something here."[115]

An extraordinary letter indeed. First it exhibited the personal concern and courtesy that endeared St. Laurent to all who worked with him; then it showed the high regard in which he held Robertson, something that had apparently survived despite the limited success of the years in the Privy Council Office. Most important, perhaps, the letter suggested that someone had been carrying tales to Ottawa of a dissatisfaction with London that Robertson simply did not feel in September 1956.

How to answer such a letter? For a few weeks Robertson did nothing, but he apparently did discuss the matter with Pearson, who in turn talked with the Prime Minister. "I had a very good talk with the Prime Minister last night," Pearson told Robertson on 3 October in an "High Commissioner's Eyes Only" teletype. "He understands your position perfectly and would be quite happy if you continued in London. He, however, received the impression last June that you were both somewhat tired and would be glad of a return to Ottawa, so he wanted you to know that if that was still your wish it could be arranged, and he thought, in a way satisfactory to you." Pearson added that "I explained to him that you were a little worried about what kind of a reply you should send to his letter and he assured me that you need not worry and, indeed, that no reply was now necessary."[116]

Less than a month before the Suez crisis, therefore, it seemed that Robertson's term was far from finished. But on 6 December, after the worst of the crisis had passed and after Robertson's position had become, if not untenable, at least uncomfortable, Léger wrote to him to suggest that he should succeed Arnold Heeney as Ambassador in Washington. "En toute franchise et honnêteté," the Under-Secretary wrote (in French so that he could be "plus subtile et convainçante" than in English), "il n'y a que vous qui soyez équipé pour remplir ce poste,"[117] That letter was followed up with a telephone call and by a chat with Pearson, who passed through London on a trip that was designed to help mend the rents in the fabric of alliance unity. "Our talk was inconclusive," Robertson told Léger. "He asked me if I was willing to have my name put up to the Prime Minister. I said I was. . . ." The subject was not raised again by the Minister, and knowing Pearson as well as he did, Robertson clearly knew that nothing was firm. "The position so far as I am concerned," he said, "is that I am quite ready and happy to do what I can in Washington."[118] Suez had changed his mind about staying on at Canada House.

The change of posts was soon decided and announced, an event that moved the *Times* on 16 March 1957 to an editorial of commendation and farewell. "It is some consolation," the Thunderer observed, "to know that as Canadian Ambassador in Washington MR. ROBERTSON will be ideally placed to help forward the healing work which still needs to be done among the three great English-speaking powers of the Atlantic." That was true. So was the *Times*'s conclusion: "Every High Commissioner passes through bitter days, but one thing is certain. The troubles last autumn would have been much greater but for the high quality and steadfastness" of Robertson and his Commonwealth colleagues in in London.[119]

The Americans, or at least those who prepared confidential assessments of negotiators, ambassadors and politicians for briefing books, shared the *Times*'s high opinion. An appraisal in fall 1958 noted that Robertson was "an outstanding economist and diplomat and one of Canada's ablest and most experienced public servants." He was an "imaginative as well as profound thinker on world issues . . . [a] trusted adviser of heads of government in both Canada and the United Kingdom. He is extraordinarily well informed on American affairs. . . ." The brief, probably drafted in the Treasury Department, added that in London, "Robertson, who is well-disposed toward the United States, skillfully pursued North American objectives without prejudicing Canada's ties with the British Commonwealth."[120]

That was very flattering, even if tending to overstate Robertson's attachment to the United States and its policies. More percipient, perhaps, was the letter of appointment prepared for Robertson in the Department at Ottawa, a statement of the current condition of relations between the two countries. Prepared by the American Division, the letter referred to the inevitability that "opportunities for irritations to occur would increase" and stressed the anger felt in Canada over the chain of events that had led to Ambassador Herbert Norman's suicide in Cairo in the spring of 1957. Clearly "a reassessment must now be made of relations between the two countries which have changed since the end of the war and perhaps since the advent of the Republican Administration [in January 1953]. If the old procedures are outmoded, what shall take their place?"[121] What indeed?

After a brief holiday in Rome, the Robertsons left for Washington on 8 May 1957 after five years in London.[122] The work had been satisfying and challenging, but Britain was no longer as important to Canada as it had once been, something that the Suez crisis had made irrefutably clear. Robertson had performed a difficult task well; the blame for the failure of his mission was in no way his.

IV

The Robertsons arrived in Washington in mid-May. The Chancery of the Canadian Embassy was the heart of their new empire, a large, handsome building full of rich wood, marble and sweeping staircases. Since 1947, the Ambassadorial residence had been a red brick Georgian mansion overlooking Rock Creek Park, largely furnished and equipped by the Hume Wrongs, its first occupants.[123]

The house came complete with a staff of four live-in servants: a butler, cook, parlourmaid and a housemaid, as well as a two-day-a-week laundress and a part-time gardener. There was also a chauffeur. Ordinarily, only the butler and chauffeur were paid from government funds. The house was well furnished, complete with paintings "of varying quality but generally agreeable," Arnold Heeney said later, all provided from Ottawa. The wine cellar in the house could contain up to 2,000 bottles, although the Heeneys had not replenished the stocks as their term drew to a close. [124]

It was all very pleasant, more like a family home than Upper Brook Street had been; the family dogs quickly took over the house, as always happened. Although both Robertsons still had some friends in Washington from their Brookings days and from later years (James Reston, Walter Lippman and Felix Frankfurter), the rigorous formal entertaining that went with the Ambassador's job, and the demands of "society," which seemed worse than in London, tended to overshadow personal links. There were the formal "dos" at the Embassy—a Queen's Canadian birthday party that drew one thousand guests, an annual party for the Chancery staff and spouses, a Christmas children's party, a party for the officers of the Canadian Joint Staff and the Department of Defence Production's Washington office, and one for the annual visit to Washington by the National Defence College, Kingston. Then there were the small dinners and luncheons at the residence, usually bringing together from eight to twenty-two carefully chosen and complementary guests. Those dinners took place two or three times a week, and on nights when the Robertsons were spared, they were almost certain to be dining out or attending a cocktail party somewhere. [125] A strong constitution and a good liver were necessities in Washington. [126]

The pace could be gruelling. A few years earlier, Hume Wrong had expressed his feelings about his life in private notes to his sister:

23 April 1948: this week has been hellish and next week looks worse, since C.D. Howe arrives tomorrow for a round of discussions. . . . We had 58 members of the National Capital Planning Committee from Ottawa last Monday and they consumed almost two cases of hard liquor in an hour!
17 November 1948: This place is bedlam just now—conference after conference and delegation after delegation arriving. . . .
5 February 1949: I wish more Canadians would stay at home. We had three substantial delegations from Ottawa here at the same time last week. [127]

The pace had not slowed between 1948 and 1957.

Robertson also had to attend to the other necessities of his new post. The first requirements were the formal calls on all Heads of Mission in Washington who were, in due course, expected to return the visits. Since there were at least a hundred embassies, legations and missions in the capital, that was a staggering chore. [128] More important, but no less wearing, were the calls on American officials. Robertson's staff had prepared a list of those on whom calls were obligatory; it included the President, the Secretary of State, the Chief Justice, the principal officers of Congress, and twenty-two senior officials of the Departments of State, Treasury, Defense, Agriculture and Commerce, as well as of the White House Executive Office. "It might be sufficient to allow about half an hour for your talk with each one of them" A.E. Ritchie and Saul Rae, the two ministers on the Embassy staff, noted. The calls "might begin on Monday afternoon or Tuesday morning and might continue at whatever times can be arranged through the rest of the week with some of your formal and ceremonial calls interspersed."[129]

Many of these visits were for the sake of politeness and custom alone, but most were designed to introduce Robertson to the officials with whom he would have to work, men such as the Director of the Office of British Commonwealth Affairs, the Assistant Secretary of State for Economic Affairs or for International Organization Affairs. And as Robertson well knew, "the great weight of Washington-Ottawa business has, but for short interludes—Pierrepont Moffat's term in Ottawa was one of them— fallen on our Washington Embassy. From what I hear of the new American Ambassador to Ottawa," he had written Arnold Heeney on his appointment to Washington in 1953, "we can expect that most of the real work will have to be done by your Mission."[130] Regrettably, that was usually the case. Canada ordinarily sent its best to Washington, an indication of the importance attached to Canadian-American relations in Ottawa. To Canada, however, all too often the Americans despatched superannuated politicians and undistinguished career officers. Fortunately, perhaps, in 1957-58 this was not the case, for the Ambassador in Ottawa was Livingston Merchant, an able and senior diplomat whose previous post had been Under-Secretary of State for Political Affairs.[131] The Americans, as much as the Canadians, were aware of the growing problems, "pretty well over everything,"[132] and they felt the need for an able representative in Ottawa. There were plenty of difficulties.

The first that directly confronted Robertson was the *contretemps* with the Americans over differing methods of handling security information. Herbert Norman's suicide in Cairo had been a direct consequence of the unscrupulous use of information (originally supplied by Canada in part) by a Senate Internal Security sub-committee, and feelings were high in Canada as a result.[133] Robertson personally was incensed by the matter, appalled at the tendency of American legislators to lash out at suspected

Communists. His reaction, one American official said later, was like watching the husband next door attack his wife with an axe. [134]

On 17 May, the new Ambassador presented his official letters of credence to President Eisenhower, who seemed "friendly, vigorous and in first rate shape." The President, Robertson reported to Ottawa, plunged directly into the Norman case:

> He said we knew how his administration felt about it. At the same time we should know better perhaps than any other people how American institutions worked. Their Govt set-up was different from ours. Sometimes and in some situations it worked pretty well and at other times and in other situations it did not work so well. He didn't claim their set-up was better than ours but it was the one that he had to try and make work, and other countries should recognize that. He did not refer specifically to our note on security procedures [notes were sent on 18 March and 10 April 1957] which is still awaiting a reply but I felt from the earnestness with which he was trying to expound his general argument about the importance of restraint, forbearance and unremitting efforts to understand each other's special preoccupations and ways of doing things, that he was deeply concerned about the differences between Canadian and American approaches to security problems. At the same time I had the feeling that he was trying to make me understand why it would not be possible for him to give us the explicit assurances on security procedures that our note had requested. [135]

Robertson had got the message. A week later, after a chance to see the American draft reply to Ottawa's protests, he reported that it was "about the best we can get now and it is probably as good as we would be likely to receive even if it were to be delayed for some time." For anything more, the President would have to do battle with Congress on both security and human rights grounds, and that could not realistically be expected. [136] All that could be done was to press the United States government to do everything in its power to ensure that Canadian-supplied material was not passed to any committee over which the Executive branch had no control. On 13 August 1957, finally, the State Department delivered a note to Robertson that stated that the safeguards sought by Canada were already in effect in so far as it was in the power of the Administration to devise them. [137] That was not wholly satisfactory, but nothing more could be secured. [138]

Robertson did do one thing more on his own initiative. He quickly made up his mind to call on every Senator from states bordering on Canada and to put the Canadian concerns about the Norman case directly to them. Saul Rae accompanied the Ambassador on these visits, which had some effect. Rae remembers visiting Senator Green of Rhode

Island, then a vigorous nonagenarian, who confused Norman Robertson with Herbert Norman initially, but who, when matters were sorted out, agreed to support the Canadian position. [139]

Nonetheless, these was some substantial disillusionment for Robertson in this whole affair, a concern that the American Congress was essentially uncontrollable. Perhaps that led him to object to the establishment of a Canada-US Interparliamentary group when the idea was raised late in July 1957. A legislator in the United States, he argued with Ottawa, "is in a rather different position from a parliamentarian in Canada.... I question whether in fact you could count on the U.S.A. Congress fielding really good ... members." Further, "U.S.A. members would expect to use it as an instrument for bringing their views to bear on the Canadian Govt and Parliament. Would we really be wise to open up this avenue ... ? Our main dealings must continue to be with the Executive element whom we must be able to hold firmly accountable in connection with problems that arise between us." [140] That fight was lost, and in 1959 a Canadian-American Interparliamentary Group was established. Fortunately, perhaps, it proved anodyne. [141]

The protests from Ottawa about the Norman case had been sent by Pearson; the American reply of August, however, was delivered to the government of John Diefenbaker. After twenty-two years of uninterrupted Liberal rule, the Canadian people had finally determined on a new régime in June. Norman Robertson was as surprised at the turn of events as everyone else, and although he was usually seen by outsiders (and by many in the new government, too) as close to the Liberals and to Pearson in particular, [142] he was certainly prepared to give the new administration its chance. Jack Pickersgill, who came to Washington on a personal visit soon after the election, remembered making some disparaging remarks about Diefenbaker to Robertson. His friend's reply was almost sharp: "I must realize that he was the Prime Minister and that he was bound to take a different attitude from that he took in opposition and that I should give him a chance...." Robertson added that he thought Diefenbaker "will take a strongly Canadian position ...," and that was a good thing. [143]

Robertson had his first chance to see the new government in action at a meeting he attended in Ottawa on 22 June, the day after Diefenbaker's administration had been sworn in. The meeting had been called to review Canadian trade and economic policies prior to the Prime Minister's attendance at the Commonwealth Prime Ministers' Conference scheduled for the end of the month. [144] When Diefenbaker, on his return from London, began to speak about switching 15 percent of Canada's trade from the United States to the United Kingdom, Robertson knew well how unrealistic this was. [145]

There were further signs of unreality. When John Foster Dulles came to Ottawa at the end of July for talks with Diefenbaker (his own Secretary of State for External Affairs until 13 September 1957), Robertson waited in vain for the customary detailed memorandum of the conversation, a piece of information that he needed in order to know how to deal with the Administration. On 1 August, John Holmes, the Assistant Under-Secretary, finally sent him a note based on what he had learned from the American Ambassador, who had been present at the Dulles-Diefenbaker talks. "The new administration as you know," Holmes apologized, "is not very familiar with the usual habits of diplomacy.... No official was present at any of the talks and we cannot therefore make a first-hand report. In answer to my enquiries the Prime Minister has told me something of his discussions ... but I don't think he quite understands the necessity of our keeping a record and passing it on to you. I have no doubt," Holmes said, "that he will come to realize these aspects of diplomacy but I think it best, particularly in my position, not to force the pace.... I do not want to suggest that he has shown an inclination to conceal things from us. He is just unaware of the usual practices." Holmes added that the Prime Minister "is also very willing to accept advice provided the advice is clearly and succinctly stated." [146] That all sounded slightly ominous, and Robertson's feelings of foreboding must have increased when, in October 1957, Diefenbaker came to Washington and refused to permit Robertson to accompany him on his visit to Eisenhower. [147]

Another indication of trouble to come was the way the North American Air Defence Agreement was signed in Ottawa by the new government. The idea of an agreement had been a live issue since February 1956, something actively desired by the air forces in both Canada and the United States, [148] and the Liberal government might well have signed had the election not intervened, although there were serious reservations in the Department of External Affairs about some aspects of it. [149] Nonetheless, the decision to agree to the integration of the two air defences came on 24 July in the very early days of the Diefenbaker administration and even before a Cabinet Defence Committee had been formed. To make matters worse, the decision had been made by the Prime Minister and the Minister of National Defence, General George Pearkes, acting alone. Apparently no other ministers knew of the decision, and seemingly only the Chairman of the Chiefs of Staff Committee, General

Charles Foulkes, and the Secretary to the Cabinet, R.B. Bryce, were aware that a decision was imminent.[150] Jules Léger, the Under-Secretary of State for External Affairs, was informed on the day the decision was taken,[151] but he did not seem to realize that this was final and did not pass it on to his officers. Thus his Department did not learn of the decision until 31 July—from the American Ambassador.[152] The Department, with Diefenbaker as its Minister, was in a difficult position, and it chose to fight not on the extraordinary way the decision had been made, but on the need to secure a formal intergovernmental agreement to cover NORAD. Orderly practice, the lack of peacetime precedent for such an air defence agreement, the belief that a formal arrangement would make it easier to defend NORAD in Parliament, and a conviction that this would help Canada push the United States into giving adequate consultation to its partner—all those were among the reasons advanced by the Department, and in due course the government agreed.[153]

At this point Robertson entered the picture. His previous participation seems to have been limited to offering a few comments on the press release that had announced NORAD's interim establishment on 1 August.[154] But in November, while the formal agreement was being negotiated, Robertson talked with the Assistant Secretary for European Affairs at the State Department, who indicated that his government was "considering whether it would be helpful ... for the U.S.A. and Canada to offer to make our continental defence arrangements a N.A.T.O. command. I said that I could see a number of advantages from a Canadian point of view," Robertson reported, "in working out a closer formal relationship ... but I thought it very important that the U.S.A. did not raise this question in N.A.T.O. until its implications could be fully explored ... and agreement reached...."[155] Although General Foulkes, the Chairman of the Chiefs of Staff Committee, argued that this was already the case (and Mr. Diefenbaker in his memoirs took the same position),[156] Robertson for one was not convinced.[157] There was no documentation on NORAD except for the agreed press release of 1 August, and that was surely "an unusual situation."[158] Robertson wanted the development of "appropriate links between the new command and the N.A.T.O. military structure ...,"[159] and clearly was seeking some way of counterbalancing the disparate strengths of the two air forces and the two nations in the NORAD scheme. He also argued — in prose so prolix someone else must have drafted it — that NORAD'S terms of reference, still under negotiation, should include a paragraph to bring out "the interim basis on which initial planning arrangements have been made between the [US and

Canadian] commanders in collaborating on the steps necessary in connection with its establishment prior to the final approval by Govts of the terms of reference." [160]

Robertson soon became involved in negotiating those terms of reference, [161] concluded on 12 May 1958 with NORAD's formal establishment, and he became increasingly disturbed at signs that the military and intelligence communities in the United States were getting testy over what they saw as Canadian obduracy in the negotiations. In fact, difficulties were becoming apparent elsewhere too, since the Diefenbaker government had already developed its tendency to dither over decisions. In March 1958, Robertson reported on "the unfortunate reaction which seems to be taking place in quite a few quarters here, especially in the Department of the Air Force, to what is understood to be the Canadian attitude regarding electronic procurement conditions and regarding early permission for the entry of U.S. personnel into Canada for planning and preliminary work. ..." Robertson was as aware as anyone of the need for Canada to be cautious in its dealings with Washington, but as Ambassador his job was to facilitate relations, something he could not do in the face of "a very rigid position taken by Canadian officials. ... I am concerned," he said, "at the likelihood that this experience may be bringing about a change in mood on the part of officials concerned with U.S.-Canadian defence relations which could have very serious effects on cooperation in many matters. ..." [162] There were explanations from Ottawa and complaints that the Americans never provided advance information of their requests, [163] but the simple fact was that the difficulties were beginning to interfere with Robertson's other tasks. [164]

One of those tasks that Robertson must have known was futile was to persuade the Americans to buy the CF-105 Arrow and the Argus anti-submarine aircraft, a near-impossible undertaking, even if relations had been as smooth as silk. As usual, he approached the problem of the Arrow from a fresh perspective. For example, when a telegram in November 1957 from the High Commission in London suggested that the British were beginning to believe that NATO fighter production should be concentrated in one country, possibly France, Robertson suggested that Canada could make the Arrow programme "a real test case of the meaning of a co-ordinated production programme within the context of continental defence. It may be" he said, "that we should look at it in the wider N.A.T.O. context," possibly seeking to make the Arrow the "standard fast interceptor" for years ahead. If Ottawa thought that suggestion useful, it had to move quickly before Britain and France stole a march. [165] That was a clever ploy, but Ottawa wouldn't and didn't.

Robertson's direct attempts to sell the Arrow and Argus to the United States got no further. In November 1957, he had to ask Ottawa to give him "at least some general background on the economic aspects of the CF-105 project . . . how much the development costs for this aircraft are likely to total . . . the kind of unit cost. . . ." [166] That month and the next he talked with the Secretaries of Defense and the Air Force about the merits of the two aircraft, trying to bring out, as he informed Ottawa, "the general economic and political reasons why both countries have a real interest at this time in rationalizing their defence production programmes in continental if not in N.A.T.O. terms." The Americans were friendly, but the Secretary of the Air Force expressed doubts about taking an aircraft that his people had not helped design. "Effective integration and specialization in defence production should begin at a much earlier stage. . . ." [167] Shortly thereafter, the Secretary of the Navy turned down the Argus on the grounds that it did not meet the USN's "high performance standards." [168]

There were some signs of desperation, therefore, when Robertson met the Secretary of the Air Force on 30 January 1958. The Arrow, Robertson said, had been built to meet the American evaluation of the bomber threat, but he himself was wondering if it made sense to put such a major portion of Canadian resources into a weapons system that would be almost obsolescent by the time it became operational. The American offered little comfort, saying that his experts had looked at the Arrow, but believed that their own F-101B and F-106 were in the same class while the F-108 was more advanced. Possibly the United States could purchase Arrows and give them to the RCAF? "The Ambassador commented," the note of the meeting recorded, "that this would pose certain problems against the background of Canada having remained aloof from Lend Lease and from the acceptance of aid from the U.S. or any other country." The Secretary did say that the United States would be happy to see more Arrows operational in Canada than the government was planning, and one of the Secretary's aides wondered if a swap of aircraft of some sort could not be worked out. [169]

The efforts to sell the aircraft continued throughout August 1958, when General Pearkes came to Washington, again seeking word of American intentions. The Minister was left with no illusions about the prospect of a sale after seeing the Secretary of Defense, and it was clear that Pearkes himself had doubts about the aircraft's cost. [170] The Arrow was dead; all that remained was to minimize the political risks of the decision to cancel work on the fighter. To its cost, the Diefenbaker government did not succeed in that task.[171]

Robertson was involved in a vast array of other Canadian-American questions. The Columbia River and its development was one,[172] the crisis in Lebanon in the summer of 1958 another.[173] There was also his continuing concern about disarmament, expressed to a "Meeting of Consultation between Representatives of the Canadian and United States Governments" on 20 September 1958. Robertson referred to the American proposal of the previous year for trials of inspection techniques with the Russians. Might it not be useful, he asked, to begin with joint Canadian-American studies on a technical and military level to examine the practical problems of overflight and inspection systems? For example, trial runs could be done on the American industrial complex and over some appropriate zone in the Arctic. If those worked, other Western nations could be involved.[174]

A few months earlier, Robertson had attended a briefing at the Pentagon on Communist breaches of the Korean armistice. "I was fully satisfied," he informed Ottawa, "that the North Korean and/or 'Chinese Peoples Volunteers' had begun to welsh on their armistice undertakings not to import new and additional equipment. . . ." But should the United States make this public and begin a build-up in South Korea? What he found worrying, he said, "is the conjunction in time of this new move in Korea with the President's determination to seek at least a preliminary disarmament agreement with the U.S.S.R."[175] That was a typical Robertsonian coupling of disparate subjects; certainly no one in Ottawa had made the connection before.[176]

There was little opportunity to make further suggestions from Washington, for in August 1958 Robertson was told he was to come back to Ottawa to become Under-Secretary once more. The Secretary of State for External Affairs since September 1957 had been Sidney Smith, unsure of himself in the diplomatic field (and with ample reason), who apparently had received Jules Léger's suggestion of Robertson as his successor with enthusiasm.[177] Léger had told Smith, "if not Robertson, I don't know who else"; but once that name had been suggested, Smith began to insist on Robertson.[178] The Prime Minister was less enthusiastic about Robertson, a man he considered a Grit and a "Pearsonality,"[179] and he agonized over the choice. On 20 May 1958, Diefenbaker discussed the position with Robertson,[180] and in June Robertson went to the UN with Smith, a trip that apparently did nothing to diminish the Minister's enthusiasm.[181] In the end, the hesitant but not reluctant Diefenbaker agreed to Robertson's appointment, and in August cabinet approved it. [182]

Robertson had hardly had the time to make any impact on Washington. He had not particularly enjoyed his posting there—he was known to have said that the only places worth living in were London and Ottawa—and he was uncomfortable with the relics of Dulles's hardline policies. Nonetheless his departure received apparently sincere tributes from the press, [183] and Mr. Justice Felix Frankfurter wrote to Arnold Heeney to bemoan his departure: "Who am I to fathom the mysterious ways of Canadian statesmanship that whisked Norman North before he hardly got settled in our midst...." [184] By October, all the farewell calls had been paid, [185] A.E. Ritchie was installed as chargé *ad interim*, and Robertson had returned to Ottawa, where he would try to "fathom the mysteries of Canadian statesmanship" for the next six years.

CHAPTER XI

The Nuclear Crisis

ORMAN ROBERTSON WAS delighted to return to Ottawa in the fall of 1958. It was not so much the job of Under-Secretary that attracted him—that, he could see, was going to be difficult—as to return to the city in which he felt most comfortable. He had been away for six years and, as he reflected to a friend, it had been seventeen years, just the cycle of the locust, since he had first been made a deputy minister. Now he was one again.[1] He had changed a great deal in that time, grown old in the service of his country, although he was still only fifty-four years old. But he was aged beyond his years, his health starting to give way under the strain of chainsmoking and his relentless sedentary life. He could putter around at the Gatineau farm on weekends, occasionally clearing brush, walking the hills in his awkward stoop-shouldered way or even snowshoeing, but his only real relaxation was to sit in front of a fire in a big, comfortable armchair with a good book of history, philosophy or biography or to talk with friends over dinner and drinks. He enjoyed his family and was genuinely close to his wife, Jetty, but Alix had gone away, married to Richard Houston, a Toronto lawyer, and Judith was going to high school. He was as happy as he was ever likely to be, but remained a man who worried and one whose work took precedence over everything else.

One small worry for him on his return to Ottawa was that he had unaccountably agreed to deliver a series of three lectures at Acadia University in Wolfville, Nova Scotia at the end of November 1958. The President of Acadia, Watson Kirkconnell, had pressed him to speak on "Aspects of the Commonwealth," and had even offered a handsome honorarium and the promise of publication as inducements. But by mid-November, settling into his new job and suffering from the endemic condition of being unable to get his speeches down on paper, Robertson

322

had clearly begun to regret accepting. No, he wrote Kirkconnell, he really did not want the talks to be broadcast either nationally or locally. He won that issue, but he did have to go to Wolfville to speak, carrying with him the rough drafts of three rather traditional but pleasantly wry talks. Apparently the lectures were a success, or so Kirkconnell's letters suggest. But in March 1959, after four months of trying to revise them for publication, Robertson returned his honorarium of $1,125, less $75 for out of pocket expenses. Because he had been unable to put the lectures into shape as he had promised, Robertson said, he did not feel he could keep the fee. That was the quintessential Norman Robertson.[2]

I

The Ottawa to which he returned in October 1958 was very different from the capital he had left in 1952. The government of John Diefenbaker was in power, revelling in the largest majority ever accorded a Canadian government. The civil service had swollen, increased by more than 50 percent;[3] there were new power relationships, new bureaucracies with their own interests to serve, and the whole operation had become too rigid and too stratified for complex issues to be settled over lunch at the Chateau Laurier.

The old mandarinate, the key group of which Robertson had been such an integral part, had also altered. Graham Towers had retired from the Bank of Canada, Deutsch from the Department of Finance, and Sharp from Trade and Commerce. Hume Wrong, Alex Skelton and Clifford Clark were dead. Some of the old crew remained in the service, men such as Plumptre, Rasminsky, Escott Reid and Bob Bryce, but Ottawa was certainly different.

Worse yet, the atmosphere was rife with the suspicion the new government had brought with it in 1957—and with which some in the civil service had received it. Surely, the Tories seemed to have thought, surely those civil servants who had spent their whole working lives under Liberal governments had to have become infected with the Grits' political attitudes. Whether they were or not, the Prime Minister and some of his ministers, most notably Gordon Churchill, the Minister of Trade and Commerce, acted as if they were, and the results were unpleasant.[4] The atmosphere of doubt in the service had been heightened when the Prime Minister made use of a classified economic forecast in the House of Commons, brandishing the secret report as a weapon to smite the

Liberals. The problems were increased by the presence of Lester Pearson as Leader of the Opposition. Pearson's friends of longstanding were senior civil servants scattered throughout the key departments of government, a fact that increased the Tories' suspicions and simultaneously made life difficult for the mandarins. Did they dare to see the Pearsons socially? Some carried on as before, damning the consequences, but others, including Norman Robertson, believed their department to be in particular danger and tried to limit contacts so as to keep themselves and their staffs as free of suspicion as possible. The strains produced were severe, at work and at home.

In this situation, fortunately, the decisive position of Clerk of the Privy Council and Secretary to the Cabinet was in good hands. Robert Bryce had become Clerk after Jack Pickersgill had entered the St. Laurent cabinet in 1953, and although he too was initially viewed with suspicion by Prime Minister Diefenbaker, Bryce quickly established himself as an invaluable adjunct to the administration. He was the source of information and advice, the repository of ideas, the man of discretion who could keep a secret and keep the wheels of government turning. In a way, Bryce became the buffer between a mistrustful government and its mistrustful civil servants, a man who reassured each side of the good faith of the other, a man who could ameliorate some of the harsher effects of Tory suspicions. And although John Diefenbaker mentioned Bryce only twice in passing in his three volumes of memoirs, he was fully aware of the value the Secretary to the Cabinet had for his government. Bryce, Diefenbaker recalled a few months before his death, had done his utmost to keep the civil service loyally working for his government. "I couldn't have carried on without him."[5]

Neither could Norman Robertson. The Prime Minister considered the Under-Secretary of State for External Affairs to be an enemy, yet another in a Department that was riddled with them,[6] and he later said squarely that he considered him a Liberal, too close to the Opposition to be trusted.[7] That attitude showed. On one occasion, Jetty Robertson remembers, her husband returned home to say, "I almost resigned today." The Prime Minister, acting as Secretary of State for External Affairs in the ten-week interim between the death of Sidney Smith and the appointment of Howard Green, had come into Robertson's office to ask for a report, adding gratuitously that he wanted Robertson to do it "just as well as you would have done it for Pearson."[8] That was the wrong approach to take with Robertson, a man whose loyalty to the government he served was total, whatever his (increasingly dark) opinion of the Prime

Minister and his policies.[9] At the same time, as some recollected, Diefenbaker knew what a storehouse of ideas and information he had in Robertson and was troubled at his inability to unlock it; the Under-Secretary similarly was frustrated that he could not break through Diefenbaker's wall of suspicion to offer the help that he could give and that the Prime Minister needed.[10] In its own way, the total failure of communication was more severe but not dissimilar to that between Robertson and St. Laurent from 1949 to 1952. The result was that, as a skilful bureaucrat, Robertson had to discover other ways to bring his influence to bear. The crucial channel was Bryce. The two were old friends and colleagues, men who liked, admired and respected each other, and who met for lunch at least once a week and saw each other at meetings two, three, or four times more.[11] In addition, because their offices were both located on the second floor of the East Block, just a moment apart, they could drop in on each other, and did, regularly.[12] Ideas, requests, information on events and individuals—all could be conveyed to Bryce, who had the Prime Minister's ear and confidence as Robertson did not. The two men worked closely together, each serving as the other's safety valve, and although they diverged sharply on such issues as the nuclear arms question, their personal ties remained firm.[13]

Another channel of access to the Prime Minister was Basil Robinson, an External Affairs officer who had attended the University of British Columbia and Oxford, and who had served with Robertson in London for a time on his second posting. Robinson had been attached to the Prime Minister's Office in 1957 at a time when Diefenbaker had yet to name a Secretary of State for External Affairs and was holding that position himself. After Sidney Smith was appointed, Robinson served as liaison between Smith and the Prime Minister for a period, but when Ross Campbell, another Department officer, became special assistant to the Minister, Robinson worked full-time in the Prime Minister's Office.

His was an excruciating, delicate task. After an initial period of suspicion, the Prime Minister came to trust Robinson implicitly, the only External Affairs officer he did,* and he maintained that attitude to his death.[14] The two formed a confidential relationship that covered the whole range of the government's foreign policy, but Robinson, after all,

---

* Arnold Heeney wrote in his diary that this was "a period of malaise and discouragement for the senior officers of the dept. The P.M.'s relations with E.A. are not good; he apparently has little confidence in the dept., is even suspicious of their 'loyalty' (or so the E.A. officers think). The consequence is demoralizing—to produce, it seems to me, the very attitude that the P.M. may fear or suspect viz. that 'they are all Pearson men'." (PAC, A.D.P. Heeney Papers, vol. 2, Diary, 4 Feb. 62.)

was in the PMO to represent his Department, and had to tell Robertson what was on the Prime Minister's mind as well as to interpret Robertson to Diefenbaker. At the end of each day Robinson would drop in to the Under-Secretary's office, talk over the problems and draw such strength and guidance as he could from Robertson's sympathy for his position.

Robinson's difficulties were considerable. Memoranda and papers from the Department of External Affairs came up through the Under-Secretary to the Minister (first being seen by Campbell, who often added a note with his own views). Most decisions were made by the Minister. But many had to go to the Prime Minister, and these papers came into Robinson's hands. At his own insistence, Robinson dealt directly with Diefenbaker on these important or delicate questions, seeing him before and after question period in the House and ordinarily once more, usually at the end of working hours in his office or often at Sussex Drive. The Prime Minister liked to give immediate answers, and oral responses were the norm, something that required Robinson to make very sure he got matters straight. Occasionally, the Prime Minister asked his views and when, despite his caution, Robinson had to reply, he was conscientious about telling Robertson what he had said. If possible, he talked over the subject with Robertson first to ensure that the views he expressed were those of the Department.

There was unlimited room for misunderstanding here. But Robinson did his near-impossible task with great skill, holding the trust and confidence of both his masters until July 1962 when he was posted to Washington as Minister. Still, his presence in the PMO and his close relationship with Diefenbaker inevitably diminished Robertson's role, much as Campbell's in the Secretary of State for External Affairs' Office did. That it diminished it as little as it did was a tribute to Robinson's scrupulousness in representing the views of his Department to the Prime Minister and vice versa.[15]

Robertson's influence was also diminished, particularly by comparison with his first term in office from 1941 to 1946, by the simple presence of a Secretary of State for External Affairs. Mackenzie King had been his own Minister, and to be deputy to the Prime Minister carried with it a prestige and influence that Robertson had used with great effect. But in 1958, there was in Sidney Smith a separate Minister, and inevitably this greatly altered the relationship between Under-Secretary and Prime Minister. The change would have been apparent even if Robertson and Diefenbaker had been soulmates.[16]

The Prime Minister had named Smith as Secretary of State for

External Affairs in September 1957. Smith had been President of the University of Toronto since 1945, and had been President of the University of Manitoba for a decade before that. A lawyer, he had served in the Great War, had good Tory connections, and indeed had been touted as a potential Tory leader at the party conventions in 1938 and 1942.[17] But as an article in *Saturday Night* pointed out after his appointment was announced, "his views on international affairs are not widely known and he has no special academic qualifications on the subject."[18] It soon became apparent that Smith had few qualifications of any kind for the job; his post at the University had turned him into a gladhanding Rotarian, and there was nothing left. The Prime Minister, too, soon appeared to realize that he had made a mistake, and relations with Smith deteriorated, particularly once Diefenbaker realized that Smith was being propped up by advice from Robertson.[19] That advice was needed, and although some in the Department believed that in his last few months in the post Smith was at last getting the hang of the work,[20] his term was an unmitigated failure. Douglas Le Pan, one of Robertson's Assistant Under-Secretaries, remembered that he and Robertson had gone to see the Minister on a Sunday to discuss a pressing matter. But Smith, just back from a South American junket, could talk only about the way in which the Latins had feted him, and the conversation never got to the purpose of the visit. It was, Le Pan said, impossible to interrupt the flow of words and superficial bonhomie. As they returned home, Robertson said only, "Oh, God, isn't this awful."[21] Smith's death in office in March 1959 ended his brief career in the government.[22]

Howard Green succeeded Smith, taking office after a ten-week interim. Green was a British Columbian, one who had known Robertson's family for years; his wife had been at university with Robertson, and he had long admired the Under-Secretary.[23] But like Smith, Green had no particular qualifications in international affairs, and his views, as expressed in his long career in Parliament, were cliché-ridden with Tory catchphrases of support for the Empire and suspicion of the United States. And yet Green could change and learn, and his growing interest in questions of disarmament, while probably fostered by Robertson, was both sincere and destined to have a major impact on the Diefenbaker government. Most important, perhaps, Green quickly became an admirer of the officers of his Department. He occasionally chatted with junior officers,[24] and some who impressed him were accelerated into important positions. Green became as well a defender of External Affairs to his Prime Minister.[25]

Nonetheless, Green posed problems for Robertson. He liked the man personally and called him by his first name; he even had Green and his wife out to the Gatineau farm for occasional Sundays. But for all his good will, Green was simply not knowledgeable about whole areas of foreign policy and was, to boot, sometimes naive, susceptible to the flattery of foreign representatives and apt to return it with a suggestion of foreign aid. Robertson appreciated Green's interest in the Department and his rock-hard integrity, but on balance he found it an uphill chore to cope with him, to educate him on the basics, to say nothing of the subtleties.[26]

The Department itself was also very much changed. When Robertson had been Under-Secretary during the war, the officer strength had been small, never more than fifty or sixty, and the total staff had not reached 500 until 1944. By 1959, however, there were 177 officers in Ottawa and 225 abroad with 1,500 administrative staff. All those figures would continue to grow, too, so that in 1963, his last full year as Under-Secretary, there were 465 officers and 1,694 staff. External Affairs was not large by comparison with some Ottawa departments, but for Robertson, who had begun in 1929 with a group that could be listed in full on one sheet of paper, the growth must have seemed spectacular.[27]

As personnel increased, so did the budget. In 1912, just after the Department's creation, the annual operating cost had been less than $25,000. In 1940, it was $750,000. But in 1962, so reported the Glassco Commission on the Organization of Government, the Department budget was $20.5 million, although only one officer, Robertson, earned more than $22,000 and only eight were paid more than $15,000. In addition, the Department spent more than $93 million in 1962, most of that sum on foreign aid.[28] That was small potatoes, but it was a marked change from the recent past.

The Glassco Commission also noted that External Affairs continued to hold its place as one of the key departments in Ottawa. A report for the Royal Commission, however, found that the Department had an "unfortunate reputation administratively" with other departments, something that Robertson did not rectify,[29] and it found that External Affairs was still viewed with that mixture of envy and doubt that had long been a characteristic Ottawa response to it. The report also noted that an attitude existed within the Department "that it is difficult to make an impact unless one is a member of a select few who are in the inner circle," although this was counterbalanced by the pride all the officers had in the Department's reputation and that of its senior officials.[30]

There was some truth in that comment, although there was substantial movement into and out of the senior posts. When Robertson came back to Ottawa in 1958, for example, the Deputy Under-Secretary was R.M. Macdonnell and the Assistant Under-Secretaries were Marcel Cadieux, John Holmes, Douglas Le Pan and W.D. Matthews. Within six months or so, Macdonnell had gone to the International Civil Aviation Organization, Matthews had died, Le Pan had returned to academic life at Queen's University, and Holmes was soon to depart to join the Canadian Institute of International Affairs.[31] Change could occur, but it could never be quick enough for the young thrusters in the Divisions.

Those Divisions too had expanded from the organization designed by Hume Wrong almost fifteen years before. In 1958 there were twenty divisions and four independent units. The Divisions dealt with the various geographical areas (American, Commonwealth, European, etc.), with subjects (Consular, Historical, Legal, etc.) and with administrative questions (Establishments and Organization, Personnel, Supplies and Properties, etc.). The independent units were the Financial Adviser, the Inspection Service, the Political Coordination Section, and the Press Office. All the Divisions, except for Defence Liaison (2), which handled security and intelligence questions, and Protocol, reported to the Deputy Under-Secretary or one of the Assistant Under-Secretaries. The two exceptions reported directly to Robertson.[32]

Robertson saw the Assistant Under-Secretaries daily at his morning "prayer meetings". Those gatherings were "one of the real privileges in Ottawa," one official told a journalist in 1964. "They are never organized, just half a dozen people sitting around, kicking some subject about. Then Norman will heave a big sigh and come out with some idea, and you'd wonder later, 'why didn't I think of that?'"[33] Unlike Pearson, who had held similar meetings when he was Under-Secretary, Robertson did not preside over a seminar like a university professor, and he had no compunctions about remaining silent on certain issues.[34]

He could not remain silent when he had to appear before the House of Commons Standing Committee on External Affairs as it pored over the Departmental estimates. There had been almost no parliamentary scrutiny of the Department during the 1941 to 1946 period, and such as there was had been handled by Wrong. But, beginning in 1959, Robertson spent at least two days each year answering the queries of Members of Parliament. Some, like Paul Martin, tried to probe policy areas and even to mousetrap Robertson into revelations,[35] but most of the questioning revolved around mundane matters of personnel, embassy housing, salaries and the like. It was not onerous, but it was not the kind of work that Robertson enjoyed.[36]

Nor did he enjoy dealing with postings and other personnel questions, although he conscientiously devoted much time to them. The Under-Secretary received a regular flood of letters from his officers abroad with their requests and complaints, all of which absorbed his time and energy.[37] And on occasion he had to try to protect his officers from their folly. One senior ambassador in ill-health returned to Ottawa and made the mistake of telling the Prime Minister in no uncertain terms at a lavish and liquid party that he had made a bad appointment to the Paris Embassy. Diefenbaker was taken aback, and George Hees, the Minister of Transport, intervened. "You can't talk to the Prime Minister that way." The rash rejoinder was, "You can't talk to an Ambassador that way." The gala occasion turned into farce, and only with difficulty was Robertson able to persuade the Prime Minister to allow the ambassador to retire on grounds of ill-health.[38]

Personnel questions were sometimes enmeshed with security and intelligence, an area of long-standing interest and concern to Robertson. His general approach, George Glazebrook remembered of his years of working with Robertson on security questions, "was to be fair but never to take risks in anything to do with security. He wouldn't delegate the supervision of D[efence] L[iaison] 2. He was very firm about that . . . he thought the decisions that had to be made were often the kind that had to do with personalities . . . he wasn't going to pass it to anybody else, nor did he want anybody else to make that decision." As Glazebrook said: "He would never allow a man to be done in if it could possibly be avoided and he never would take what he considered a risk to the national interest."[39]

There were bound to be conflicts between the national interest and the individual, and those Robertson unfailingly resolved in favour of the state. John Starnes, deeply involved with security questions in this period, remembered that this was a particularly difficult time for the Department with a number of personnel security problems, some of which had resulted from the aggressive activities of various foreign intelligence agencies. Such questions ripped Robertson apart, Starnes said, and if he had to decide to place the national interest first, invariably he tried to do his best to protect the privacy of the individual. And because Howard Green had such a fundamentalist view of sin and sex, Robertson tried as much as possible to keep such questions away from the Minister.[40]

At times, however, Robertson's security-consciousness went too far. In October 1963, for example, the Canadian Association of University

Teachers' complaints about RCMP surveillance on university campuses across the country were considered by the Security Panel, the committee of officials that handled questions of policy. Robertson spoke at length about the complaints:

> While it was obvious that the worries expressed by the university people were in part uninformed, their real concern was to preserve the university as a place where all the issues were open to discussion without interference from established authority. The real difficulty lay in the fact that, particularly during the 1930s, attitudes of enquiry and protest about some of the more unpleasant facts of history ... had become a breeding ground for later conspiracy of a very serious order. He gave as examples some of the cases ... Burgess, McLean [sic], Philby.[41]

In Robertson's view, RCMP surveillance was essential to the national interest.

The intelligence side also concerned Robertson. He took the material provided by Canada's allies very seriously and spent long hours digesting it. And he continued to give thought to the best form of organization for Canadian intelligence.

In the fall of 1958, for example, just before he left Washington for Ottawa, Robertson wrote at length on the proposals for reorganization of the intelligence establishment that had been suggested by General Charles Foulkes, Chairman of the Chiefs of Staff Committee. "My own feeling," he said, "is that the intelligence structure in Ottawa has grown up on an empirical basis over the years, and that with the sets of new problems which now confront us ... a careful review of the existing structure, and of various possible ways of making it more responsive to current needs, is fully justified. ..." In his view, there were three problems to consider in any reorganization. First was the need to raise the status and broaden the scope of intelligence in the government, something that could best be achieved, he thought, by creating a "National Intelligence Body." Second, he wondered if a new administrative apparatus was necessary to achieve this. Robertson doubted if it was. "It is my impression that the coordination of intelligence through the creation of a new agency here [in Washington] has caused almost as many difficulties as it has solved. It is only recently, after ten years of operation that C.I.A. has approached the performance of its statutory role. ..." A central agency like the CIA, he added, worked better in the United States than in Canada, where it was difficult to envisage the effective operation of an executive agency under the Cabinet Secretariat without responsibility to a particular department. A better solution would be an interdepartmental committee chaired "by that Department having most concern with the consequences of intelligence operations, and with responsibility for relations with other governments, particularly those with whom our interests are most closely linked." The third problem, where the responsibility for coordinating intelligence should rest, Robertson had already answered. Clearly it should be the responsibility of External Affairs, but in the long run the Department's ability to keep its guiding position depended on the contribution it was prepared to make in personnel, expertise and intelligence.[42]

Back in Ottawa, Robertson continued his efforts to move in the direction he had outlined. In a letter to Foulkes in November 1959, written after weeks of patient negotiation by Defence Liaison(2) Division, Robertson again stressed the importance of the link between his Department and intelligence. Unless the director-general of any new organization was from External Affairs, he argued, his Department could not accept the responsibility for liaison with the intelligence services of friendly powers or the direction of efforts to collect intelligence abroad. Furthermore, it would be difficult for the director-general to function under the Cabinet Secretariat without responsibility to a Department. In his view, a National Intelligence Policy Committee should be set up with its members being the half-dozen deputy ministers most interested in intelligence. That committee would meet once or twice a year to establish a framework within which the principal intelligence-gathering operations could work.[43] Later, Robertson recommended that the committee should be called the Intelligence Policy Committee.[44] This reorganization took place in May 1960 when the new committee came into operation with the Under-Secretary of State for External Affairs as chairman and the Chairman of the Chiefs of Staff Committee as vice-chairman. The new committee, its term of reference indicated, was to maintain general control and policy direction of intelligence-gathering, as well as determining the objectives, priorities and resources necessary to achieve this.[45] The Intelligence Policy Committee's creation was a bureaucratic victory for Robertson and the Department of External Affairs.

II

As Under-Secretary, Robertson was concerned with the whole gamut of Canadian foreign policy. But in the greatly expanded Department of the late 1950s and early 1960s, there were usually capable officers heading the Divisions, and no Under-Secretary could possibly keep watch over the entire range of policy questions. The complexities of 1958, to say nothing of the volume of paper, made the practices of 1941 an impossibility, and most of the memoranda bearing Robertson's signature or initials were drafted elsewhere. His influence within the Department was exercised at the prayer meetings or in private conversations with the head of a Division or possibly with a more junior officer handling a specific matter, and all too often Robertson's influence on particular issues cannot now be traced.

Certainly he was interested in disarmament, a subject on which Howard Green shared his enthusiasm. Years later, Green remembered that when he and his Under-Secretary went to NATO meetings, the hat racks would be filled with gold-braid encrusted officers' caps. "There'd be enough gold braid on these hats to redecorate the Quai d'Orsay! And there would be Norman's old black hat and my old black hat. We used to feel that at least the dove of peace had two hats at the meeting anyway."[46] On disarmament, Robertson and Green thought of themselves always as on the side of the angels.

Robertson gave his blessing to the appointment of General E.L.M. Burns as Adviser to the Government on Disarmament in 1959,[47] and himself brought much experience to the subject. Canada, he told his Minister in November 1959, "has come to be regarded as a normal participant in disarmament negotiations . . . ," adding that "we tended to consider that we had a certain 'representative' quality and that we should be the medium through which the views of the lesser powers might be heard. . . ." But as he knew, there were really only two parties at the disarmament talks, and the circumstances required Canada to spend more time negotiating with the United States, its ally, than with the Soviet Union.[48] Robertson nonetheless approved the initiatives that emerged through General Burns's work, he accepted and supported the nine principles that the government made the foundation of the Canadian position in the negotiations that began in January 1960,[49] and he had the ultimate responsibility for harmonizing positions with the Department of National Defence. Sometimes that was hard to manage, particularly in the light of Robertson's views on nuclear weapons. In September 1960, for example, Air Marshal Frank Miller, Foulkes's successor as Chairman of the Chiefs of Staff Committee, prevailed on Bryce to talk with Robertson about disarmament and to "find out what is going on." External Affairs, Miller complained, was not interested in nuclear weapons, while National Defence was pressing for them. Miller said he did not want Burns, something of a maverick, to drift into an illogical position, to ignore NATO, and to operate in a vacuum.[50] The tension between the two departments over the role of nuclear weaponry in Canadian defence was beginning to grow, and the position on disarmament was just one of the topics on which there was some disagreement.

Not so the United Nations forces formed for the Congo in the summer of 1960, when the Belgians gave their long-time colony independence and then watched horrified as the new state collapsed into anarchy. Although there was initial reluctance about sending Canadian troops to black Africa, largely for fear that they would be seen as coercing the Congolese,[51] Robertson nonetheless helped push a reluctant cabinet into a commitment of signallers when the UN proved unable to find them elsewhere. "In a very short time," he wrote to Green, "the United Nations Force may find itself in a serious administrative difficulty . . . the need for rapidly developing an administrative tail is self evident" and the importance of the Secretary-General's request for troops from Canada could not be overemphasized.[52] Indeed, Robertson even spoke strongly to the Soviet Ambassador about his country's behaving "irresponsibly and not giving full support to the United Nations effort to re-establish order" in the Congo.[53] He made no headway, however, and could not stop the Russians from protesting that "Canada is known to be a member of the N.A.T.O. bloc, as well as Belgium, which has committed aggression against the independent republic of the Congo." Canadians in the Congo, the Russians claimed, would be there only to assist in aggression.[54] There were problems aplenty with the Congo operation, attacks on Canadian soldiers, difficulties with the command of the multinational force, threats and counterthreats, but Robertson felt that UN peacekeeping was one of the duties Canada owed the world; indeed, he even asked the UN Division to report directly to him for a time so that he could pay closer attention to the problems.[55] You had to pay your dues.

Dues still had to be paid to Britain and the Commonwealth, too. In 1960 and 1961 the question of South Africa had to be faced, an episode that ended with the departure of the new republic from the Commonwealth. That issue was particularly difficult for Robertson. He had no sympathy with the apartheid policies enforced by the Boer nationalists, and events such as the Sharpeville massacre of 1960 revolted him. But he recognized the complexities of the South African problem, and believed that Canada, without any salient experience in the area and with its own racial policies not without blemish, was not in a strong position to prescribe solutions.[56] Worse, the bureaucracy was divided, with George

Glazebrook and the Commonwealth Division strongly supporting the continuation of a South African presence in the Commonwealth, while Bryce, the Secretary to the Cabinet, opposed this forcefully. Indeed, Bryce's role in the officials' discussions in England in the spring and summer of 1960 had been critical in leading the British to recognize that South Africa had to go.[57] Compounding matters was the Prime Minister's exclusion of Robertson from some of the discussions at the Prime Ministers' conference of 1960. It was "gut-wrenching" to see, Basil Robinson recalled, and although it was the Prime Minister's undoubted right to select his own advisers, that exclusion nonetheless hurt.[58]

Robertson also had to help coordinate the government's response to the British desire to join the Common Market. His own views were straightforward: Canada had little reason to attach much weight to the retention of its preferences in the British market.[59] But that was not the view of the Diefenbaker government, which vigorously resisted the British move to Europe.[60] "The Canadian views," Robertson reported to his Minister after a heated meeting in London in September 1960, "were put forward in strong terms and were vigorously supported by some delegations ... the discussions undoubtedly gave U.K. ministers some food for thought."[61] But at the same time, he could pass along almost without comment the trade statistics that traced the inexorable decline in the importance of the British market to Canada.[62] Perhaps none was needed. Still, he did produce the arguments the government case required, telling Green before the visit to Ottawa of one British minister in July 1961 that, "From a Canadian point of view the continuation of the status quo clearly has advantages over United Kingdom accession to the Common Market. This course would leave unimpaired our position in the United Kingdom market and our political relationship with the United Kingdom. At the same time," he added, "we would remain free to vary our own trade and financial policies within our existing international commitments."[63] The British tried to accommodate the protests from Canada and other Dominions and colonies but, as Robertson summarized the situation for his Minister on 2 January 1962: "Nothing in the course of the negotiations so far seems to call for a reassessment of our view that Britain will find it virtually impossible to maintain satisfactory terms of access for Canadian exports to the British market."[64] In the end, after Diefenbaker used the Commonwealth Prime Ministers' meeting of September 1962 for one last effort to disrupt the British plans, General de Gaulle and France did the job and kept Britain out of Europe—for the present.

III

Important as all these questions were, they paled into insignificance beside the central issues of Canadian-American relations. Nuclear weapons, Cuba, the relationship between Diefenbaker and President John F. Kennedy—those were the key issues with which the Under-Secretary of State for External Affairs had to contend.

Of Norman Robertson's general views on nuclear weapons throughout the mid- and late 1950s, there is little doubt. As much as any man, he recognized that the development of the multi-megaton hydrogen bomb raised the possibility of an end to human existence, and he brought some passion, tempered with political realism, to the discussions over disarmament that dragged on throughout the decade. And yet there was little sign for most of the period that Robertson, troubled and ambivalent as he was on the subject, had taken a position for or against the equipment of Canadian forces with nuclear weapons for air defence, for anti-submarine warfare or for use by the NATO brigade and air division.

Indeed, there was initially little sign that anyone opposed the acceptance of nuclear weapons, although there was much discussion on the best way to bring them to Canada without political difficulty. In September 1957, for example, while Robertson was still in the Washington Embassy, Jules Léger, the Under-Secretary, told a "meeting of consultation" between American and Canadian officials that it would be easier to deal with the question of stockpiling nuclear warheads in Canada if the question could be resolved as part of the broader Alliance problem.[65] Robertson made the same point in November the next year, after Diefenbaker had given a public indication that Canada was likely to take Bomarc anti-aircraft missiles,[66] and the Under-Secretary had countered American objections to the alliance-oriented approach by pointing out that only a general reference to the NATO procedures would be necessary, certainly nothing that implied a direct parallel in method of operation. He added that Canada in general found it easier to make special arrangements with the United States under the NATO umbrella, a recurring Canadian theme and one that reflected the imbalance of the bilateral Canadian-American relationship. When the Americans then asked what Canada's position was on the storage of strategic and defensive nuclear weapons at Goose Bay, Labrador, an RCAF base partially leased to the United States Air Force, Robertson referred to some difficulty with the strategic weapons. But, he said, the problem could be deferred pending the satisfactory resolution of the whole nuclear question.[67] Certainly, at this point Robertson did not sound like one who was outraged by the siting of nuclear weapons in Canada; instead, his position was pragmatic, concerned with the resolvable difficulties and the best ways of handling them.

That same attitude was evident in Paris in December 1958, when Robertson attended a gathering of Canadian heads of missions there and the first meeting of the newly established Canada-United States Committee on Joint Defence.[68] Robertson discoursed to the assembled ambassadors on Canadian-American economic relations and defence. The notes for his remarks spoke of the American need for Canadian cooperation and good will to achieve the high degree of integration in continental air defence that the Americans believed essential, and, he added, "it is in our interest to preserve that goodwill and extend that co-operation." That was true, and Robertson carried on to talk about the governing factors in the bilateral defence relationship, a list that included the faith of the two governments in deterrence, the need for American help in the defence of Canada, and the US need for Canadian cooperation in defending itself. The objectives of North American defence, he said, "are to contribute to the overall deterrent. In particular, continental air defence must provide a level of defence sufficient to permit the United States Strategic Air Command to carry out its assigned tasks and to give the population of North America a reasonable chance for survival."[69] A reasonable chance for survival. That phrase must have stuck in Robertson's craw, for what it meant was that the Soviet Union and its bombers had to be obliterated in a nuclear holocaust if North America was to survive.

Nevertheless, there was still no overt sign of opposition from Robertson to the trend of policy. The Canada-United States Committee on Joint Defence briefings, prepared by Robertson's Department and National Defence, clearly looked to the Canadian acquisition of nuclear weapons. The main External Affairs paper, however, made the point that "It is in Canada's best interests to adhere to the principle of limiting the spread of nuclear weapons at the independent disposal of national governments." To that end, therefore, Canada should not seek concessions on custody and control of the weapons from the United States that might encourage the more "nationalist" members of NATO. Similarly, the acquisition of nuclear weapons "will have to be related to the Government's stated position on disarmament," something that could be eased around by presenting the need for the weapons "as a deplorable necessity in the face of present Soviet intransigence." Finally, the Department's paper recognized that Parliament had to be told something soon, probably at the first session of 1959, about Canadian policy. It was therefore a matter of urgency to settle matters with Washington. The position recommended was that the Americans control the warheads until their release for use was authorized by the President and that the question of control of use of the weapons be dealt with in public statements under a formula reflecting the joint responsibility of the two governments.[70] Again it was clear that Canada was moving toward taking the weapons and that Robertson seemingly accepted this.

But at some point after Robertson's return from Paris, his position began to alter. He learned, for one thing, that the Bomarc missiles that Canada was going to acquire, according to the Prime Minister's announcement of 20 February 1959, were high-yield weapons that produced substantial fallout.[71] He discovered that the Americans (whose refusal to purchase the Arrow interceptor had helped lead the government to cancel its production, a decision also announced by the Prime Minister on 20 February) now were pressing Canada to get an air defence interceptor for the 1960s in addition to the Bomarcs.[72] The United States was also making signs that it wanted Canada to permit SAC bombers to be stationed at airfields in northern Canada, airfields that in theory were only for refuelling of the bomber force.[73] At the same time, the American General, Lauris Norstad, the Supreme Commander of NATO forces, was beginning to urge Canada to secure F-104 fighter-bombers and to use them in a nuclear strike role in Europe.[74]

All these pressures must have weighed heavily on Robertson's mind, and at a meeting in March 1959, when he had been briefed by Bryce and others who had just returned from visits to SAC and NORAD headquarters, Robertson unburdened himself:

In concluding this part of the discussion, which had evoked the geni [sic] of destruction, Mr. Robertson said that the whole philosophy of deterrence had been developed at a time when conditions were vastly different from those existing today. It was a sad comment on our generation to envisage the possibility of global suicide. Our minds should be turned instead to the tremendous political effort that needed to be undertaken to avoid the awesome consequences of nuclear warfare.[75]

Robertson's position seemed to be changing rapidly now, his long-standing doubts becoming more serious, and in June 1959, he sent the Prime Minister, via Basil Robinson, a copy of an article in the British magazine *The Spectator* of 1 May. The author, Christopher Hollis, argued that the H-bomb had changed the nature of war. Even if the West were the nominal victors, "there is no chance that the pattern of our own national life with which we entered the war will still survive when we emerge from it," Hollis reasoned. He then went on to argue in favour of unilateral nuclear disarmament and a Western build-up of conventional strength. It was not in Russia's interest to blot out the West, Hollis said, because Marxist theory told it that inevitable victory was certain; why destroy what you would take in any case? Furthermore, unilateral nuclear disarmament would only strengthen the West in the battle for the allegiance of the uncommitted nations. Hollis admitted that a lunatic in the Kremlin could destroy the world, if the Soviet Union found itself losing a conventional or ideological war. "All that can be said on that is that the Communists can equally destroy the Western world whether the Western world possesses the bomb or whether it does not." A great power, Hollis concluded, strengthened itself, rather than the reverse, if it divested itself of weapons it could not dare to use. The memorandum that Robinson attached to the article told Diefenbaker that "Mr. Robertson wishes you to know that his personal views coincide with those of the author of the article."[76]

Coincidentally, just two days later Howard Green became Secretary of State for External Affairs, bringing a belief in disarmament, a moral revulsion against nuclear arms, and an abiding suspicion of most things American to his new post. In a memorandum to the Minister on 12 June, Robertson talked about the French government's refusal to allow the storage of nuclear weapons on its territory unless France controlled them. That conflicted with Canadian policy, for "although we plan to equip Canadian forces with modern weapons we consider it expedient that the ownership and custody ... should remain with the United States." Robertson urged Green to press for a NATO review of nuclear policy. "Such a review would be of special interest to Canada since we are, as you know, on the threshold of equipping Canadian forces with nuclear weapons." Beside that statement, Howard Green scrawled a large question mark.[77] Robertson had found a Minister who shared his doubts about atomic weapons, and the long struggle to reverse Canadian nuclear arms policy was soon underway.

There were some inklings of this in the affair of "Exercise Sky Hawk" in August-September 1959. In the summer of that year, Arnold Heeney, the Ambassador in Washington, had told Diefenbaker and Green that relations with the United States were so good that he believed "there had been a conscious U.S. decision at a high level to meet us whenever possible."[78] Whether that was true or not, Canadian reciprocity was not forthcoming. Sky Hawk was an air defence exercise scheduled for one day in September; it required the grounding of all civil air traffic. But in Robertson's Department, the view quickly took form that the exercise was a mistake. The Canadian public was sure to misunderstand the reasons for it, the Department reasoned, and more important still, following so fast on the heels of Soviet Premier Khruschev's visit to the United States, it would be misunderstood by the Soviet Union. "Totally inappropriate and provocative now," Howard Green noted. "Reserve right to consider proposal further."[79]

The exercise had been planned for months, and the Americans were furious at the last-minute Canadian objections. Their Ambassador called on the Prime Minister, the telegrams of remonstrance flowed north from Heeney, and the Secretary to the Cabinet stressed how unfortunate it might be if the public learned of the difficulty.[80] But the Prime Minister, supported by Green and Robertson, was adamant. Diefenbaker told Basil Robinson that, while the blame in terms of consultation and procedure lay on the Canadian side, he was determined "not to have Canada 'put on the tail of the United States' in a scheme of such questionable wisdom."[81]

A small issue, perhaps, but one that "left its mark in the minds of the Americans concerned," or so Heeney reported.[82] Still, Robertson recommended to the Minister that the exercise be allowed to proceed next year. "I am inclined to believe that failure to do so could have serious repercussions on relations between Canada and the United States. The present integrated state of our air defences..., the role played by N.O.R.A.D. in the protection of the West's principal strategic retaliatory force and the general support the Canadian government gives to the strategy of deterren[ce] would make a negative decision on our part difficult to understand by the United States." But, Robertson advised, every precaution had to be taken to ensure that the Russians knew what was involved; in addition, the military had to be able to demonstrate its need for an exercise on so large a scale.[83] In the circumstances that was the proper advice, for Robertson's task was to retain good relations with Washington if at all possible.

The Under-Secretary returned to the Sky Hawk question at the 1959 meeting of the Canada-United States Ministerial Committee on Joint Defence at Camp David, Maryland, in November. When the Americans (whose briefing notes observed that Robertson "is known to favor a 'soft' approach in the solution of East-West problems") very politely remonstrated with the Canadians about the September fiasco, Robertson said "it was sometimes difficult, no matter what one's intentions might be, to ensure that the political effects of a particular action were desirable. Intentions and political effects were not necessarily synonymous...."[84]

All that was so, but it was becoming increasingly difficult, even for Norman Robertson, to sort out intentions and effects on the nuclear issue. In memoranda prepared for Green before the Joint Defence Committee meetings, his own wavering—and that of his Department—was becoming apparent. In one paper, he argued fervently that "a global nuclear war could destroy society as we know it upon the planet," a truism but one no less heartfelt for that. Worse, he said, "When one looks at the siting of particular air defence weapons, can one say that the plan is really continental? ... is it not likely that much of the defence action that is possible would take place over the settled areas of Canada?" And then there was the problem posed by the "steady increase of [American] facilities on Canadian territory, which may seem necessary if tension continues, [but which] cannot but appear as a steady diminution of Canadian sovereignty no matter how necessary."[85] On the other hand, Robertson told the Minister that the "adverse political effects in international terms" of a Canadian decision to let the Americans store nuclear weapons at Goose Bay were probably controllable, while a refusal "would have serious repercussions on Canada-United States relationships, and would lessen our ability to influence United States policy on important issues...." To delay further had to increase misunderstanding, and hence Robertson, troubled and unsure about his course, recommended that the government grant storage facilities to the United States, a suggestion not immediately accepted.[86] A few months later, he told the Minister that Liberal Party complaints about the handling of the nuclear issue were unjustified. The Leader of the Opposition had argued that to have warheads for the Bomarcs in Canada under American control weakened Canada's sovereignty, an argument that Robertson himself had touched on, but now the Under-Secretary suggested that the key point was the joint control and that launchings were to be made by Canadians. Furthermore, he said, to press the case for sovereignty too far could lead to a situation in which Turkey, for example, could control the nuclear weapons on its soil.[87] The complicated political and moral questions were blurring, not just for Robertson but for all involved in the nuclear question.

By June 1960, matters had progressed no nearer to resolution, and there was a host of questions awaiting decision. Howard Green told his colleagues that month that there were five aspects to the question:

(a)   The United States has sought permission for the storage at Goose Bay and Harmon Air Force Base [one of the bases leased to the US by the UK in 1940] of nuclear air-to-air defensive weapons for use by United States interceptor aircraft under N.O.R.A.D. control.

(b)   The United States has sought permission for the storage of nuclear anti-submarine weapons at the United States Naval Base at Argentia [Newfoundland, another leased base]. . . .

(c)   The United States has sought permission for the use of existing storage facilities at Goose Bay for the storage of nuclear warheads for the Strategic Air Command.

(d)   The possible acquisition of nuclear warheads for Canadian use in Canada, especially for BOMARCs.

(e)   The possible acquisition of nuclear weapons for Canadian use in Europe for the CF-104 and for the Honest John [a 762mm rocket, in effect a surface-to-surface missile for use by the brigade in NATO].

Only the first point was near settlement. The others were at various stages of consideration or discussion, and the question of acquiring nuclear weapons for Canadian use in Canada or in NATO had yet to be decided in principle by the cabinet.[88]

Discussions with the United States went on through the summer of 1960. The Ministerial Committee on Joint Defence met at the Seigniory Club in Montebello, Quebec in July and some headway was made,[89] but there was no doubt that positions were growing more rigid and that public opposition to nuclear weapons, mixed with and almost indistinguishable from anti-Americanism, was building. Arnold Heeney came up from Washington at the end of August 1960 to talk with the Prime Minister about the situation:

Mr. Diefenbaker [he wrote in his diary] then went on to speak of what he characterized as 'anti-Americanism' in Canada. Since we had last met, the state of Canadian opinion in this respect had deteriorated seriously. In his judgement, anti-American sentiment was now worse than at any time in his lifetime or mine. The P.M. characterized popular criticism of the U.S. as growing into an 'avalanche'. This was causing him the greatest concern. He would like the President [Eisenhower] to know about this situation. . . .

Heeney expressed his surprise, telling the Prime Minister that he had had no idea matters had reached such a state.

The most serious issues, in my opinion, [Heeney said] arose in relation to joint defence where the U.S. were currently worried about our cooperation. For example, they were puzzled by our hesitancy to go along with them in such matters as nuclear storage. (Here the P.M. interrupted, comparing the Liberal policy of *no* nuclear weapons for Canadian forces and purely Canadian control with the government's concept of 'joint control'. . . .)

That day and the next, Heeney heard more of the same from Diefenbaker, who even showed him some of the mail he had received, and carefully annotated, on defence and other questions of Canadian-American concern.[90] Shortly afterwards, Heeney talked with Howard Green and recorded his Minister's worry "at the idea of any nuclear devices being located on Canadian soil." In Heeney's view, "this instinctive repulsion from nuclear involvement of any kind is at the base of Mr. Green's own negative attitude on all defence matters, especially where the U.S., the great nuclear power is involved."[91] That was certainly true, as was Heeney's later assessment of the way Green and Robertson tended to reinforce each other's views:

. . . H. G. himself, though he continues to have the loyalty even affection of those who work with him, and who supports the dept. stoutly, is sadly miscast in his office. Nevertheless, his own attitudes and prejudices, in a curious way, combine with NAR's cosmic anxieties, particularly in our defence relationships, external and domestic, to produce a negative force of great importance.[92]

That negative force was working to keep nuclear weapons out of Canada.

The suspicions Robertson and Green had about the United States were reinforced by the American policy towards Cuba. Fidel Castro had overthrown the Batista government and then had gone "bad." Through 1959 and 1960 the signs that Castro was a Communist grew clearer, and American attitudes hardened perceptibly, as did the pressures on Canada to toughen its policy to the new government.

In July 1960, the Ministerial Committee on Joint Defence considered the Cuban situation, first at a private meeting of ministers called at American request, and then in the committee sessions. Robertson attended the private meeting, made notes and said nothing, but he and Green were upset by what they heard. The Secretary of the Treasury, delivering a typically hardline American briefing, indicated that his government believed Cuba was "already under Communist domination," and the United States, he said, was moving to economic sanctions, including the blocking of all Cuban funds in the United States. The

Secretary wanted Canada to follow suit, and the Secretary of Defense chimed in to add that this "would be a real test of the meaning and solidarity of the Alliance," a hint that the United States might be unforgiving of those who did not go along with it. Such pressures, quickly and steadily applied, had to bring home to Cubans what their government was costing them.

Green responded to the American presentation by noting that "this was a grave and disturbing communication with very serious implications for Canada. . . ." For his part, "he was very doubtful of the wisdom of attempting to deal with the Cuban situation by external economic pressure," and he feared that Latin American countries would not go along with the American position. The discussion ended there, with the American ministers making clear that they intended economic measures "strong enough to make the Cuban people wish to get rid of Castro. They hoped to avoid the use of armed force," Robertson noted in his memorandum of the discussion, although clearly he had reached the conclusion that the Americans were planning military action.[93]

At the committee sessions, the question of Cuba came up again. Livingston Merchant, the Under-Secretary of State for Political Affairs and a once and future Ambassador in Ottawa, spoke of the opposition to Castro and about the inevitable hardships that Cuba would suffer because of the American reduction of sugar imports. Robertson then intervened:

Mr. Robertson referred to the impression which had been made by the great tolerance and patience shown by the United States up until recently, despite the provocations of Castro. . . . He regretted that it had not apparently been thought possible to continue to display such restraint . . . he asked if reliance must be placed on opposition to Castro developing around expatriate Cubans. He thought it would have been better if such opposition had been allowed to develop internally. There were numerous signs of disillusionment among prominent Cubans who had originally supported Castro. While such people might not reflect current attitudes of the population generally, their criticism or even desertion of the régime could in time have produced profound and widespread effects on opinion within Cuba. Speaking personally, he was inclined to question the wisdom of cutting the sugar quota. He found it hard to accept the argument that the United States would have been risking its future sugar supplies if it had continued to rely on Cuban sources. In any case, was it politically wise to take such action at this stage instead of letting the process of disenchantment with Castro run its course? Such action by the United States gave Castro a ready-made opportunity to blame the United States for Cuba's troubles and to identify Cuban nationalism with Communism to our detriment.[94]

Thus Robertson and Green made no bones about the unwisdom of the American policy, and there was further uneasiness when Cuba became an issue in the Presidential election, with Senator Kennedy, the Democratic candidate, talking toughly, even as the outgoing Eisenhower administration tightened further its economic controls on the Caribbean island.[95] The American tendency to go off half-cocked, or so it seemed to the East Block, was worrying.

None of this made anyone feel easier about the nuclear question, which continued to bedevil the government and the bureaucracy. The Prime Minister for one had gone on record in the House of Commons on 20 February 1959 as seemingly favouring the equipment of the Canadian forces with nuclear weapons,[96] and R.B. Bryce certainly believed that Diefenbaker supported the principle. He himself did, as did the Department of National Defence, which was becoming increasingly unhappy about the delays.[97] But External Affairs was divided. The Defence Liaison (1) Division favoured taking the weapons; but the key men, Green and Robertson, were opposed, with Green more rigid on the question than the Under-Secretary; nonetheless, they bolstered each other's resolve and Robertson supplied the Minister out of duty and conviction with tactics and strategy.[98] The goal was to capture the Prime Minister and to convert him from an advocate into an opponent of nuclear weapons, and neither man doubted that public opinion was helping in this task.

Meanwhile, the wheels of government continued to turn. On 30 November 1960, Bryce brought Robertson and Air Marshal Miller together to discuss the situation. The result, or so Bryce set it out in a memorandum he wrote that afternoon, was that a paper be prepared "to lead up to the following recommendations, which I think was the course we agreed upon this morning." Those recommendations were, first, that the government should proceed with the necessary negotiations to permit the Canadian forces to acquire *when and if needed* [Bryce's emphasis] those nuclear weapons it has already announced Canadian forces will be equipped to use; simultaneously, physical preparations for nuclear weapons and training could continue. At the same time, the negotiations for the storage of nuclear weapons for US forces at Goose Bay and Harmon would proceed without delay. But, and this was a concession to Robertson as were the words "when and if needed," Canadian action in holding or using nuclear weapons was to be subject to progress on disarmament or arms control.[99]

But if that had been agreed by the three, there seemed to be some differences in interpretation. On 5 December, Robertson sent Green a draft memorandum for the Cabinet Defence Committee, prepared by the Department of National Defence and calling for negotiations with the United States to be pressed forward.[100] His own comments accompanied the draft, and he laid out his views very clearly:

At a time when Western Governments generally, and Canada in particular, have been urging in the United Nations that every effort should be made to get disarmament discussions going again, . . . it would be inconsistent and hypocritical for us at the same time to adopt policies which can only have the effect of compounding the nuclear problem.

The Prime Minister, in his recent speech to the Canadian Club [of Ottawa on 24 November 1960] stated that 'we have taken the stand that no decision will be required while progress toward disarmament continues. To do otherwise would be inconsistent.' The proposals contained in the D.N.D. memorandum, in my judgment, are diametrically opposed to this statement of policy.

Robertson went over questions of NATO policy and the prospects that the new Kennedy administration might seek *détente* with the Soviet Union. Then he turned to the question of nuclear weapons for Canada:

Negotiation of agreements for acquisition of nuclear weapons, even on a contingent basis, carries with it an implication of ultimate intention to obtain the weapons. It is therefore contrary to the policy enunciated by the Prime Minister, as referred to above.

Inevitably, it would become known that such negotiations were in progress. To argue that the Government's policy remains what it had been for the past 18 months would not be tenable in the light of subsequent developments. It would be regarded by public opinion as inconsistent. . . .

Robertson now seemed to have reversed his earlier position in favour of concluding arrangements with the Americans for storage of nuclear weapons at Goose Bay and Harmon. Conclusion of such an agreement, he told Green, "would have great symbolic importance because it would be the first agreement authorizing the storage of nuclear weapons on Canadian soil and would be generally interpreted as the prelude to completion of arrangements for the acquisition of weapons for the Canadian forces. In any case," he warned his receptive Minister, "it would make it more difficult for the Government to justify its policy of deferring a decision on this latter issue."[101] Clearly nothing had been resolved at the meeting with Bryce and Miller, and the division between External Affairs and National Defence was wider than ever.

The struggle within the Canadian government and bureaucracy soon became more complicated, when the Kennedy administration, taking power in Washington in January 1961, brought different and tougher tactics to Canadian-American relations. Diefenbaker and Eisenhower had got on well together, and the Prime Minister and the new President initially had a good meeting when Diefenbaker flew to Washington for a one-day visit on 20 February 1961. The two men talked together and, as Livingston Merchant remembered, they "got along extremely well . . . ,"[102] while Basil Robinson told Robertson the next day that the Prime Minister's "first close impression of President Kennedy . . . was a most favourable one. . . ."[103]

The two leaders had talked about the nuclear problem and, as Robinson reported,

The Prime Minister said that he had spoken along the following lines to the President:

a) Negotiations toward agreements on Goose, Harmon and Argentia should proceed. With regard to Goose and Harmon, Canada insisted 'there should be joint control and custody, and joint decision on use.' With regard to Argentia, Canada would have joint control and joint custody but the question of use would be determined by N.A.T.O.;

b) Canada does not intend to follow a 'bird watching' policy, i.e., a policy limited to identification. Any such policy of limited participation in N.O.R.A.D. would make Canada less, not more, independent than we are now. . . .

c) The Canadian authorities would carry on discussion so that terms might be arrived at as to nuclear weapons for the BOMARC and for interceptor aircraft, but the above terms (i.e., under (a) above, as to control, custody and use) were conditions precedent;

d) While disarmament was being pressed forward, no agreements would be signed but all the preliminaries in negotiation as mentioned above would be completed so that there would be no holdup should the need arise;

e) In answer to a subsequent question by Mr. Rusk [Kennedy's Secretary of State] the Prime Minister stated that 'we do not intend to enter into any of these arrangements or agreements piecemeal—the whole thing is a package.'[104]

Apparently Diefenbaker's "package" proposal was a new tack, possibly even one thought up on the spur of the moment. The Secretary of State for External Affairs did not learn of the proposal until Bryce wrote to him on 2 March, and the officers of Defence Liaison (1), handling the detailed External Affairs' work on the nuclear question, heard of it later still.[105]

From Green's and Robertson's point of view, however, this change of course by the Prime Minister was all to the good. Their tactics, as Ottawa prepared to receive President Kennedy in mid-May, were to build on Diefenbaker's concerns about the Americans' nuclear policy and to stall the issue as long as possible. Indeed, this had been underway for some time. Green delayed replies to queries from the Minister of National Defence, Douglas Harkness,[106] and Robertson was extremely fertile in suggesting go-slow tactics.[107] Finally on 3 May 1961, after many delays, Green and Harkness met to try to sort out the situation and reach a common front to present to the visiting Americans. They agreed that an External Affairs paper on the proposed general agreement on nuclear weapons should be made the basis of a submission to the cabinet and should go to Diefenbaker before Kennedy's arrival. But that was all they agreed, for Harkness refused to accept several of Green's points. Green maintained that a decision to enter negotiations could not be considered a decision to accept nuclear weapons, but only as a wish to be in a position to do so if necessary. Continuing, Green held that only after a master agreement had been negotiated would the government consider the question of taking the nuclear weapons, and that decision had to be based on progress on disarmament and on controlling nuclear proliferation.[108] That was no progress at all.

To some extent, the Green and Robertson case was strengthened with the Prime Minister by the Kennedy visit. Fresh from the humiliating rout of his American-sponsored invasion of Cuba, and with indications of Canadian disapproval and of warnings that he should not expect sympathy for the use of force against Castro,[109] the cold-warring Kennedy was in a testy mood. The President had also been briefed that Diefenbaker showed "a disappointing indecisiveness on important issues, such as the defense program, as well as a lack of political courage and undue sensitivity to public opinion,"[110] and in consequence he probably tried to push too hard.[111] In particular, a briefing memorandum, lost by someone on the President's staff and found by the Canadians, fed Diefenbaker's new hostility to the American. Arnold Heeney, who saw Diefenbaker some time later, wrote in his diary that

What distressed me most was the P.M.'s reference to a *paper* which had been left, by inadvertence, in his office after his talk with the Pres. in Ap [*sic.*, May]. He had mentioned this to me on the 'phone to Washn some time before but had not identified it. On this occasion he told me that it had been signed by Walt Rostow. . . . It was 'instructions' for the Pres. as to the points to be made in conversation with the P.M. There were four or five objectives to which, Diefenbaker told me, Canada was to be 'pushed,' among which was membership in the O.A.S., acceptance by Canada of nuclear arms—and others. The P.M. said he had not so far made use of this paper but 'when the proper time came' he would not hesitate to do so; mentioned it was being kept safely.[112]

In all likelihood the memorandum in question was anodyne; but from the Prime Minister's viewpoint, harassed and troubled by a sea of insurmountable problems and with the nuclear question becoming increasingly difficult to resolve, the American pressures must have seemed too much to bear. And given Diefenbaker's readiness to harbour and nurture slights, the grudge against Kennedy could only grow, and this in turn, while complicating the relations between the two countries, made Diefenbaker less and less ready to consider taking the nuclear warheads from the United States.

Thus, although at times (particularly during the Berlin crisis of fall 1961) it seemed likely that the decision to begin negotiations on the basic agreement on nuclear arms was close, matters continued to drift.[113] In October 1961, for example, Harkness tried to get the question onto the cabinet's agenda, but Robertson advised his Minister that support from uncommitted nations at the UN for a Canadian resolution on nuclear testing and fallout might be prejudiced "if word leaked out—which it might well do—that we were about to open negotiations with the United States on nuclear weapons."[114]

The government, therefore, had not advanced matters significantly from the position in 1959. Indeed over three years the situation had possibly even regressed for, as Diefenbaker told Basil Robinson on 27 February 1962, he was now thinking of the ways to maintain Canada's potential defence capability, which, he said, "in terms of North American defence means to have available Voodoos [CF-101 interceptors used by RCAF squadrons on Canada] and Bomarcs so that if nuclear war starts, nuclear warheads could readily be placed at the disposal of Canadian forces." That, as Robinson explained, seemed to imply that warheads or parts could be supplied by the Americans on one hour's notice.[115] But if that sounded a new note, Diefenbaker was far more hawkish in a conversation with the American Ambassador, Livingston Merchant, on 8 March 1962. At that point, as one of President Kennedy's aides later learned, "the Prime Minister said confidentially that he expected 'to proceed forthwith on negotiations looking at least to initialling texts as finally agreed.' At that time the Prime Minister seemed more confident than previously of his ability to carry through and to the Ambassador's surprise, in light of the Prime Minister's customary sensitivity to any evidence of adverse public comment, he discounted the significance of pacifist or quasi-pacifist organizations in Canada."[116]

Evidently the Prime Minister himself suffered from confusion on the course to be followed, on the policy that he could best sell to increasingly sceptical voters. For Canada was into an election in the spring of 1962 as Diefenbaker fought against the Liberals, the New Democrats, and a resurgent Social Credit party in Quebec, to say nothing of unemployment, a run on the dollar that forced the government into devaluation in the midst of the election campaign, and unfavourable opinion polls. Plans to bolster the dollar were prepared (and announced six days after the election),[117] but the Opposition could not be countered so readily. In his increasing desperation during the campaign, the Prime Minister's latent anti-Americanism surfaced and he made some unwise comments to the press, even indicating that the Kennedy administration wanted his government defeated because it didn't take orders. Those comments drew protests from the Embassy in Ottawa and offended Norman Robertson, among others.[118]

When the government survived the election with a minority in the House of Commons (116 Conservative to 100 Liberal, 30 Social Credit and 19 NDP), Robertson, it seems, began to contemplate resigning. He had little or no admiration for Diefenbaker as an individual or as a national leader; the Prime Minister's suspicion of the Department of External Affairs seemed occasionally paranoiac in its intensity; and the indecisiveness that, to be fair, had given Robertson his opportunity on the nuclear question was slowing the machinery of government to a crawl. However strongly he may have felt on the nuclear question, Robertson did not see that so much as an American threat to Canada as a world problem. It was Diefenbaker's anti-Americanism and the mindless quality of it that troubled him, as well as the government's reckless squandering of Canadian influence abroad. "Prestige," Michael Howard later wrote, "remains the coin of the realm of international politics...,"[119] and Robertson was appalled by the way the coinage had been debased. Thus in mid-June 1962 he tried to discover what his pension might be if he left the service. The results of his enquiries could not have satisfied him—an annuity of $11,430, with the possibility of a retirement gratuity and accrued leave, was not much after thirty-three years service—and the idea was abandoned.[120] What was significant was that Robertson, concerned above all to protect his Department against the Prime Minister's suspicion, and feeling deeply about nuclear weapons, had even contemplated resignation.

The decision to stay made, Robertson returned to the nuclear problem after the election. Early in June, he told one of his senior officials, he had asked Air Marshall Miller for information on the armament system of the CF-104s, the aircraft being provided for the RCAF Air Division with NATO. Could the aircraft use conventional weapons? If not, what changes were necessary to let it do so? If NATO had to contain a Soviet attack without nuclear weapons, could the CF-104s, be employed? [121] Those were good questions, but Robertson received no answers, the Chairman of the Chiefs of Staff Committee probably fearing to put more ammunition in the hands of his opponent. By early October, with the arrival of the CF-104s imminent in Europe, Robertson told Green that the Minister of National Defence wanted to open negotiations on the general agreement immediately. The Under-Secretary pointed out that the general agreement did not provide for warheads for the weapons, and was a necessary step before the negotiation of subsequent agreements for the warheads could begin. If it was the intention of the government to have a peacetime agreement on nuclear weapons with the United States, he went on, the draft general agreement provided a reasonable basis on which to open negotiations. But if, as the Prime Minister had said, the government planned to accept nuclear weapons only in an emergency, then the existing draft was not a suitable point of departure. "Indeed to use the draft with only war time acquisition in mind would give the United States Government renewed cause to question Canadian good faith in opening negotiations." Robertson's solution was an interdepartmental working group to thrash out the details, a tactic that was certain to prolong the process. [122]

But if Robertson seemed to be proposing more stalling tactics, a week later, with the public now aware of the arrival of CF-104s in Europe, he warned Green that this was going to step up the pressure on the government at least to make a statement on the nuclear warheads question. Once the cabinet had reached its decision on the matter of transacting the general agreement with the United States, then possibly a separate arrangement might be negotiated for the CF-104s. "If we begin with negotiations for weapons for the Air Division this might be represented as a response to a N.A.T.O. approach," he said to Green, "and you might consider that this would be more acceptable to Parliament and the country." [123]

At this juncture, with Robertson seemingly prepared to bow to the inevitable and to accept the idea of nuclear arms for the NATO Air Division, the Cuban missile crisis altered perceptions. The first full word of the developing crisis came from two Canadian intelligence officers who had been in Washington for a meeting where they had picked up word of what was coming. They called Robertson and Bryce from the American capital and, on their return to Ottawa on Sunday, 21 October 1962, briefed them. [124] The next day, Livingston Merchant flew in to brief Diefenbaker, [125] and that night President Kennedy went on television to accuse the Soviet Union of a "clandestine reckless and provocative threat to world peace" by bringing offensive missiles into Cuba. Kennedy imposed a naval blockade to quarantine the island. The world moved close to war.

That night in Parliament, Prime Minister Diefenbaker suggested that the people of the world wanted "a full and complete understanding of what is taking place in Cuba" and suggested that neutral members of the UN Disarmament Committee constitute themselves a fact-finding commission to provide an "objective answer." There is no confusion about the origins of this suggestion—it was Robertson's—but there is some about the motives behind it. Ross Campbell, one of Robertson's Assistant Under-Secretaries at this point, believed that Robertson proposed the idea because he shared Diefenbaker's suspicions of the Americans. [126] But A.E. Ritchie, another Assistant Under-Secretary and one who was closer to Robertson, remembered that Robertson thought he would be unable to get Diefenbaker to support the Kennedy stance immediately and, therefore, came up with the idea of an investigation, a device that might compel Canada to support the United States if the missiles were in fact in Cuba, as Robertson had no doubt they were. [127] But what almost all agree on was that Robertson was impressed by the gravity of the situation, impressed with the air reconnaissance photographs Merchant had brought with him, and was ready to accept the integrity of the American position. [128]

The Prime Minister's refusal to order the Canadian forces in NORAD to an immediate alert, in support of the United States, proved particularly harmful to relations with Washington.* The Bomarcs were unarmed at

---

* R.B. Bryce jotted down a message from Basil Robinson at the Washington Embassy: "Basil said in W[ashington] 1) Norad failed in alert 2) U.S. requested & were refused right to put warheads at their bases [in Canada] 3) U.S. request & refused right to put U.S. fighter planes on Cdn bases—E[xternal] A[ffairs] have no trace of 2) or 3)." This remains unexplained. (PAC, R.B. Bryce Papers, Telephone Notes, 2 Nov. 62.)

the one site at North Bay where the weapons had been put in place and the CF-101s had no nuclear weapons, but worse, for two days Diefenbaker authorized no alert. (In fact, however, the Minister of National Defence, on his own, apparently put the Canadian component of NORAD at war stations.)[129] The Americans were furious, but Robertson apparently supported the cabinet and his Minister in their initial reluctance to follow the American lead. "The information given to the Canadian Government of the United States intentions vis-à-vis Cuba does not seem to have constituted consultation as provided in these [NORAD] arrangements, as we had understood them," he told Howard Green. "In fact it seems that the United States took a deliberate decision not to consult any of its allies in order to achieve maximum surprise and impact on the Soviet Union. The question arises for Canada whether the existence of NORAD presupposes special obligations which entitle Canada to special treatment over and above that accorded the other allies of the United States."[130] In Robertson's view, Canada was.

By 26 October, the crisis had eased, the blockade of Cuba had been lifted, and the missiles were soon removed from the island. The crisis had been fomented by Khrushchev, Robertson estimated, "to stir things up" and possibly as an attempt to reduce the strategic superiority of the United States. If he had got away with putting the missiles in Cuba, Khrushchev would have been in a good position to deal with the Americans; if not, he could count on a *quid pro quo* for removing them."[131] That was a shrewd assessment.

But if the world crisis was over, the Canadian crisis was just about to begin. "Many Canadians," wrote one academic observer, "had the uncomfortable feeling that when the chips were down the response of the Canadian government had been hesitant, uncertain, and inglorious."[132] That was certainly true, and under the pressure of public opinion on 30 October the Diefenbaker cabinet finally agreed to open negotiations with the United States on the master agreement.[133] The cabinet's mandate was that negotiations be undertaken to produce agreements under which "Nuclear warheads would be held in storage for and made available to the Canadian forces in Europe under N.A.T.O. command for use in CF-104 aircraft and the Honest John rockets; and Nuclear warheads would be held on bases in the United States to be moved to Canada to be available to the R.C.A.F. for use in Bomarc missiles and interceptor aircraft, on request by the Canadian government when war appears imminent. . . ." The negotiations were to be conducted by a troika of Green, Harkness and Gordon Churchill, the Minister of Trade and

Commerce.[134] The government, it seems, had definitely decided to choose a "missing piece" approach, a system under which Canada received a key component of the nuclear weapons only after the onset of an emergency.[135] The Diefenbaker administration wanted its cake and to eat it too.

Although American studies indicated that the missing pieces could be airlifted to Canadian bases within one hour,[136] and although at a meeting of ministers of the two countries in Paris on 14 December 1962, no objections were raised to this scheme, nevertheless in mid-January the Americans indicated that the operational problems could not be overcome. Instead they suggested that the missing pieces (which parts these might be was still under discussion) be stored in Canada under either American or Canadian control, a proposal that Robertson for one considered unacceptable.[137] That was the state of affairs when, at the beginning of the new year, General Norstad, the retiring NATO commander, said bluntly to a press conference in Ottawa that Canada had committed itself to a nuclear role.[138] A few days later on 12 January, Liberal Leader Pearson announced that he was unilaterally reversing his party's policy of opposition to nuclear weapons for the Canadian forces. Once Canada had fulfilled its commitments and taken the weapons, Pearson pledged, then a Liberal government would "negotiate Canada into more appropriate roles, ones which would not require ... nuclear weapons."[139] The heat was increasing, and Diefenbaker compounded his difficulties with an extraordinarily fuzzy speech to Parliament on 25 January, a speech that drew a sharp rejoinder from the US Department of State five days later: "the Canadian Government has not as yet proposed any arrangement sufficiently practical to contribute effectively to North American defense."[140]

That statement, according to McGeorge Bundy, one of Kennedy's senior aides, had been released without the President's knowledge. It was, Bundy apologized, "a case of stupidity and the stupidity was mine."[141] Perhaps, but the American statement, intentionally or otherwise, created the crisis that led to the fall of the government. As Bryce scribbled in his diary just before a meeting with Robertson to discuss the American press release, "pretty damaging statement to say the least—will appear to involve the U.S. in Canada's domestic [affairs]—"[142] So it did, but as the American Ambassador telegraphed from Ottawa on 2 February, after widespread resentment at the American "intrusion," there was now a "strong swing ... in direction recognition facts this overridingly important matter had to be brought into open and the United States had long been patient and forbearing. . . . Major political cartoonists concentrating their ridicule on Prime Minister Diefenbaker. . . ."[143] There seemed to be no regret there, and we might fairly conclude that the Americans toppled the dying Diefenbaker government.

The events of the next few days are already legend. The resignations from the cabinet; the revolt against Diefenbaker, squelched by caucus; the abortive bargaining for Social Credit support in the House of Commons; and finally, on 5 February, the defeat of Diefenbaker on a motion of non-confidence denouncing his government's confusion and incompetence.[144] The defeat left the nuclear question unresolved.

Some indication of Robertson's attitude to the Prime Minister at this point can be gleaned from a note of a conversation that one of Governor General Georges Vanier's aides made on 6 February, the day after the defeat in the House. Vanier clearly was concerned about his course if the Prime Minister sought to make major appointments between dissolution and the election, soon scheduled for 8 April 1963. "If he were advising the Government," Robertson told Michael Pitfield, the aide, "he would advise them not to make any appointments with security of tenure; but if he were advising the G.G. he would advice [*sic*] that the P.M. be warned, but the recommendations in the end result be approved." Robertson, who doted on constitutional questions and matters of protocol, added that the role of "the G.G. when a politician tried to fix responsibility upon the Crown, was to return the responsibility to the politician and this especially when the very mandate of the Government itself was being placed before the people. . . . He was of the opinion," Pitfield wrote, "that a formal warning on record from a Canadian-born, Canadian-appointed G.G. was a tremendously powerful defence." The aide said as well that both Robertson and Bryce, to whom he had also spoken, "are agitated lest some action be taken which would embarrass the Crown and put you in a position of having to act quickly without the benefit of prior consultation."[145]

The election campaign did nothing to disabuse Robertson of his concerns about Diefenbaker's possible actions. The Prime Minister staged a magnificent one-man battle against the odds, but *in extremis* resorted to what a Kennedy aide called "snide comments, insinuations, innuendoes or other anti-U.S. overtones."[146] Toward the end of the campaign, in fact, Diefenbaker or his staff leaked the story of the lost memorandum from May 1961 and also tried to suggest, apparently on the basis of a forged letter, that the American Ambassador, Walton Butterworth, had written a congratulatory letter to Pearson for his nuclear weapons policy.[147] It was a dirty campaign, and Robertson was greatly relieved when the government was defeated on 8 April.

To what extent, if any, was Robertson responsible for the Diefenbaker government's disarray on the nuclear question? That is a fair question, given the influence Robertson had on his Minister and the influence Green had on the Prime Minister. From late 1959 on, the Under-Secretary had campaigned and manoeuvered against nuclear weapons; he had argued his case as forcefully as he could to his Minister, and Green had shared his views; both men did what they could to try to turn Canada away from a defence policy based on nuclear weapons. But was there anything improper in this or in the tactics of delay employed? Certainly not. Robertson's primary loyalty was to his Minister, his task to supply Green with arguments; and if the Prime Minister had not been congenitally unable to make decisions, unable to resolve the nuclear question one way or the other, unable to choose between Green and Harkness and the public opinion ranged behind them, the issue in all likelihood would not have toppled his government. The blame for the Tory defeat in the House of Commons in February 1963 rests with John G. Diefenbaker.

Still, in a curious way, Robertson had taken a position on the nuclear issue that smacked of his youth. There was more than a touch of moralism and radicalism in his opposition to the weapons, and there was a substantial element of Machiavellianism in the way he had brilliantly orchestrated the delaying tactics of himself and his Minister. Then, too, as a practitioner *par excellence* of quiet diplomacy, Robertson, while never helping the public opponents of nuclear weapons, had calmly watched them interfere with and shape Canadian foreign policy—and indeed thoroughly disrupt Canadian-American relations. Robertson's position, sound and ethical as it may have been, marked a significant change in his approach to policy questions.

It was his last major campaign, but it ended badly for him when the Pearson government accepted the nuclear weapons that Diefenbaker in the end had spurned.

IV

There can be no doubt that Norman Robertson was delighted by the election results. Pearson was an old friend, and so were Mitchell Sharp,

C.M. Drury and Walter Gordon, all senior members of the Liberal team. Paul Martin, the probable Secretary of State for External Affairs, while not a close friend, was at least an acquaintance of long standing. And the presence of a strong contingent of ministers from Quebec, too, pleased Robertson, who had become increasingly alarmed about tensions in Quebec and between Quebec City and Ottawa.

And, yet for a variety of reasons, Robertson failed to hit it off as well as he had expected and hoped with the new Prime Minister. There are some indications that he met privately with Pearson before the Liberal government took power on 22 April,[148] but when Pearson called all the Deputy Ministers together for a meeting, Robertson unaccountably failed to turn up. The Under-Secretary felt very sheepish about his gaffe—he had been the only absent deputy—and Pearson must have seen the omission as a deliberate slur.[149]

The result was a wariness between the two, but in truth that was a long-standing condition. Pearson did not consult Robertson very often— no Prime Minister after King often consulted the Under-Secretary directly—and that hurt (although Robertson did his best not to show it). Moreover, Pearson, with substantial justification, believed that he had his finger on more of the variables than the Under-Secretary could or did. Further, Paul Martin was Robertson's Minister, and Martin was jealous of his prerogatives and concerned that he be seen as the spokesman for his Department to the public and the Prime Minister.[150]

Robertson had no problems with Paul Martin in the months they worked together. Martin was the boss, to be sure, but he was clearly dazzled by Robertson's range, by his ability to discourse at length and with fluency on the telegrams and the issues. The two worked together closely and well, and there was little Robertson sought that he did not receive.[151]

Except on nuclear weapons. Robertson understood that the new government had committed itself to taking the weapons that had been one of the major issues in the election. And while he still did not, and never would, agree with this position, he recognized how futile it could only be to rail against it, and took some solace from Pearson's promise to negotiate Canada out of the nuclear role in the future.[152] At least Pearson's government had a clear policy, one that appeased the United States. Indeed, the first gestures to Ottawa from the Kennedy administration were placatory,[153] and Robertson told Martin the day after he had taken office that the United States, to avoid appearance of "pushing," wanted the Pearson government to initiate the process of discussing nuclear weapons policy.[154] The matter was on the way to resolution, speeded by the instant rapport established between Pearson and Kennedy when they met at Hyannis Port, Mass. on 10 and 11 May.[155]* The agreement providing Canada with nuclear weapons was made public by Prime Minister Pearson on 16 August 1963. The question was settled; from Robertson's point of view the only worthwhile result of it all was that relations with the United States returned to normal on a wide range of problems.

But if Robertson had expected relations with the Department of National Defence to improve under the Pearson government, he was quickly disabused of that notion. The tension continued and possibly grew worse, with the generals, air marshals and admirals passing their dislike of the "striped pants boys" on to Paul Hellyer, the new Minister.[156] For example, in June 1963, the United States Department of Defense announced plans for the dispersal of interceptor aircraft to a number of civilian airports and military bases in the United States. Robertson informed his Minister of these plans and, as a courtesy, prepared answers for Hellyer if, in the event, questions came up in Parliament about Canada's relationship to this step.[157] Hellyer's response, however, was sharp: "May I say that I was quite unimpressed with the answers to questions suggested in the memorandum. I do not think I should have to speak untruths in reply to questions."[158] Robertson was genuinely puzzled, reiterating to Martin that the proposed answers were completely consistent with the facts.[159] A small matter to be sure, but one that indicated that relations between the Departments continued to be troublesome.

A few months later another incident confirmed this. Hellyer visited Secretary of Defense Robert McNamara in Washington on 11 October 1963 and refused to permit an External Affairs officer from the Embassy to accompany him. That disturbed the State Department, which, having its own difficulties with McNamara's band, feared that in consequence it

---

* The Hyannis Port meeting should have buried the question of whether the secret memo found by the Canadians in 1961 had referred to Diefenbaker as an "S.O.B.", a claim used in the election. In the course of after-dinner conversation, the subject arose and Pearson indicated that Basil Robinson, then Minister in Washington, would know what if anything had been on the memo. "Mr. Robinson was asked whether he had seen it, to which he replied affirmatively, and stated that there was no handwritten comment on it. Both assertions he made unambiguously." (Kennedy Library, Kennedy Papers, POF, Box 113, Canada Security 1963 file, Memo by W.W. Butterworth, 10 May 63.) But Professor P.V. Lyon, who has studied this matter with care and in detail, considers the question still open. (Letter to author, 29 Oct. 80.)

might have no one at the meeting as well. Robertson, consulted about the rebuff, had decided not to appeal to the Prime Minister, a decision with which Basil Robinson concurred. It was better, he wrote to his ambassador, Charles Ritchie, "to take the risks of being left in the dark than to tear open still further the gap in confidence between the two Departments and Ministers."[160] Fortunately for External Affairs, perhaps, Hellyer's focus soon turned to unifying the armed forces, a subject that provided him with enough enemies to occupy him full-time.

Paul Martin too had ambitious plans, but he had the full support of Robertson in carrying them out. Martin's intent was to make his Department a truly bilingual institution, one that reflected the reality of Canada, and Robertson, aware of the coming difficulties with Quebec and somewhat guilty about the lack of serious attention he had paid this problem in the past, wanted to move ahead as quickly as possible.

In fact, the Department was already the best in the civil service "in providing an appropriate balance between French and non-French-speaking officers," or so the Royal Commission on Government Organization reported in 1963.[161] Although that was so, the situation nonetheless was far from satisfactory. In 1959 only 21.8 percent of foreign service officers were French Canadian; in 1962, 21.6 percent; in 1964, 19.8 percent.[162] Worse, despite efforts to remedy the problem, recruiting did not bridge the gap, particularly as the Quebec civil service during the Quiet Revolution had become an exciting place to work for *Québécois*. Between 1946 and 1964, only 80 of 368 entries into the Department were francophones, and between 1959 and 1963, the years in which Robertson had effective control, only 18 of 93.[163]

There had been some successes. Robertson initiated the provision of 75 hours tuition in French to anglophone entries (at a cost of $1,100 each), and in 1963, for the first time, six incoming "probationaries" were sent to the Université Laval French summer course. Those steps helped, but the Glassco Commission found that the Department still had "172 officers incompetent in French," 256 with a "reasonable" or reading knowledge, and, Robertson estimated, perhaps a hundred capable of doing their work in both languages. Of that group, at least three-quarters were French Canadians,[164] and Robertson himself, while capable of reading French and understanding conversation, could hardly be said to be fluent in it.

Robertson supported the Glassco Commission's recommendations on bilingualism in the civil service. As he wrote to his Minister in May 1963, a senior officials' committee had prepared recommendations that

included the establishment of a secretariat to give attention to bilingualism in the public service; a statement of language equality; a directive
requiring all departments to deal with documents in both languages
without translation; language training; and pay incentives for the
bilingual. There were "no simple or early solutions," Robertson said, but
"I believe it is a matter of real importance that initial steps should be taken
without delay." He urged Martin to press those views on the Prime
Minister, and the Minister did. [165]

In July Robertson returned to the issue, telling his Minister that it was
vital that "the Cabinet Committee on bilingualism should begin to operate
and be seen to operate tout de suite." He also expressed his concern that
the provinces—and he meant Quebec—might develop the means to
handle their own external relations, and "If this happens the repercussions
nationally and internationally will be very grave." One way around this,
he suggested, might be to expand Canadian representation in Francophone Africa, but that took money to recruit and train French-speaking
officers. Politically, Robertson said, "it is essential that we should do
proportionately in relation to France and her former colonies what we are
doing in relation to Commonwealth countries" on matters of aid and
cultural affairs. Furthermore, "biculturalism must be reflected somehow in
our relations with France. We must engage in a dialogue with Paris," he
said; the Prime Minister should pay an early visit there, the selection of the
next Ambassador should be carefully weighed, and no opportunity
should be lost to associate the government with French "manifestations"
in Canada. [166]

By September 1963, Robertson had pushed the Department even
further ahead. He had pressed the Treasury Board for more money for
language training and was moving forward with efforts to make the two
languages true working languages in the Department. "The objective we
should pursue," he wrote, "is the possibility of producing work in either
language at the author's choice. . . . A conversation, interview, debate or
discussion in French should also be reportable in French." [167]

The steps he took in his last term as Under-Secretary, encouraged and
pressed by Paul Martin, effectively remodelled the Department of
External Affairs. And yet in his last years Robertson came to believe that
this was too little, too late. Too many of the best young Canadians had
been directed toward international affairs, too few to domestic questions,
he believed. That concerned him, and he worried that he himself had
never paid enough attention to the problems that beset relations between
French and English Canada. [168] That was certainly true. In fact, discerning

and intelligent as he was, Norman Robertson had never really tried to understand Quebec; he had always assumed incorrectly that the province's interests were strictly domestic ones that could be resolved in Ottawa, and he had somehow failed to think deeply about the major problem of the nation to whose service he had devoted his life. Norman Robertson suffered from the same blindness about French Canada that afflicted so many English Canadians.

V

By the time the Pearson team took office in April 1963, Robertson had been Under-Secretary for four-and-a-half years. The salary of $22,000 was comfortable (it was soon raised to $27,000),[169] and he even had enough money to give Balliol College $1,000 for its special appeal in 1964.[170] But the salary was scant compensation for the exhausting nature of the work, a strain on his physique and a terrible pressure on his nerves. Robertson was worn out and, relieved of the necessity to be on guard against Diefenbaker's depredations, he felt oddly let down as well. But he was only fifty-nine, a long way from retirement, and he knew that he could not remain much longer as Under-Secretary. It could only be bad for him and, equally important, bad for the Department with its able, younger officers hankering for a crack at the top job. But where could he go? At various times, he and his wife had talked about postings, and again and again he kept coming back to Ireland as one place he might enjoy. The Embassy there was small, the residence comfortable, the work light, but he had no answer when Jetty told him he would quickly become frustrated and bored.* Perhaps South Africa held more of a challenge and even the possibility of persuading the Boers of the error of their ways on race. There was little chance of that, and Jetty stopped him in his tracks by asking what he would do if the South Africans refused to talk to him. The simple fact was that Robertson could not make up his mind where he wanted to go or what he wanted to do.[171]

---

* In May 1964, after Robertson had been named Canada's chief negotiator to the GATT Kennedy Round tariff negotiations, Marcel Cadieux, the Under-Secretary of State for External Affairs, asked the Irish chargé in Ottawa if his country would accept Robertson as Ambassador. "This would be on the understanding that Mr. Robertson would retain as a primary task that of Chief Canadian Negotiator ...," Cadieux said, adding that Robertson was personally interested in the post. The chargé was agreeable and was certain his government would be, but the appointment nonetheless fell through. (Department of External Affairs, John Starnes Papers, Cadieux memo for file, 5 May 64.)

The Minister soon raised the question. By every account, including his own, Martin was not trying to get rid of Robertson, for whom he had the highest regard; but the Minister knew that the Under-Secretary had to move on. Robertson told Martin, as he had told his wife, that Ireland interested him, but Martin refused to believe that he was serious and, he recalled, said that he thought Robertson really wanted to return to London. The Under-Secretary indicated that that posting was acceptable and Martin, again by his own account, promptly called the Prime Minister and took Robertson with him to Sussex Drive.

But it was not to be. Pearson refused to consider naming Robertson High Commissioner for a third tour. Although Robertson was hurt by his old friend's firm refusal, at bottom he knew that Pearson was right.[172] For political and party reasons, the High Commission went to Lionel Chevrier, who assumed his duties at Canada House on 1 February 1964.[173]

By that date certainly, Robertson was in no condition to carry a heavy load. His chainsmoking had finally taken its toll, and late in January 1964, after coughing blood into his handkerchiefs for some time, after pain and difficulty in breathing, Robertson finally was persuaded to see a doctor. The diagnosis was cancer, and in the space of a few days he was hospitalized, operated on, and left with only one lung. His friends were appalled, although few were surprised;[174] further service as Under-Secretary was now impossible.

Before his illness, Robertson had told Martin that he thought Marcel Cadieux should be his successor. In his view, Cadieux was able, experienced in the ways Ottawa operated, a man of sound judgment, generally conservative views, and with the depth of culture that Robertson himself had and looked for in his officers. Equally important, Cadieux was a French Canadian, and Robertson firmly believed that a francophone should be Under-Secretary at that point in Canadian history.

But apparently Paul Martin was not initially convinced that Cadieux was the man for the post. Immediately after his operation, therefore, and while he was still confined to bed, Robertson began to do his utmost to ensure that Cadieux got the job. Jetty became his surrogate, and after she had consulted Gordon Robertson, the Secretary to the Cabinet since the summer of 1963 and an old friend, on how best to proceed, she went directly to the Prime Minister. "Whatever Norman wants," Pearson told her, and Jetty then carried that message to the Secretary of State for External Affairs. Martin hemmed and hawed, but Jetty Robertson reminded him that "the Prime Minister said it would be whatever Norman wanted." That apparently swung the issue, and Cadieux was named acting Under-Secretary and then confirmed in his own right on 7 May 1964.[175]

The skill with which Robertson had stage-managed events from his sick bed must have impressed Pearson, for on 21 February, well before Robertson's recovery, he announced that he had been named chairman of a special committee to deal with the Canadian preparations for the Kennedy Round of GATT negotiations. In fact Robertson was to be the chief negotiator, the man in charge of an interdepartmental group of officials charged with preparing the Canadian tactics and carrying them out.[176] It seemed an ideal appointment, one that put Robertson again in direct contact with the subject that had been his *métier* since the mid-1930s.

CHAPTER XII
Last Years

AFTER THE LUNG cancer and his radical surgery, Norman Robertson was too weak to resume work. Instead, he and Jetty went to South Carolina for recuperation, making use of Snee Farm near Charleston, put at their disposal by Tommy Stone, now retired from the Department. It was pleasant and warm, a good place to rest and to begin to contemplate the problems of the Kennedy Round.

Those were certain to be many. The Kennedy Round of the General Agreement on Tariffs and Trade negotiations, decided upon at the GATT meetings in May 1963 were so named because they stemmed in substantial part from the initiative of President Kennedy in seeking and securing from Congress the Trade Expansion Act of 1962. That Act, for the first time, gave the President the power to reduce tariffs over a five-year period by fifty percent and to eliminate completely tariffs that were at or below five percent.[1] There seemed to be a unique opportunity to lower duties generally among the great trading states, and GATT leapt to its opportunity.

But as Robertson was well aware, the Canadian situation was becoming increasingly difficult.[2] First, Canada was an exporter of raw materials and an importer of finished products with a huge trade deficit with the United States—$1,116,000,000 in 1962.[3] That weakened Canadian bargaining power in trade negotiations that were to focus primarily on manufactured goods. Second, there were serious differences between the Minister of Trade and Commerce, Mitchell Sharp, and the Minister of Finance, Walter Gordon, on trade policy and a host of issues, and indeed Robertson had been named chief negotiator at Geneva precisely because both he and his Department were seen as "neutrals" in the struggle.[4] The Sharp and Trade and Commerce view was that of the traditional free traders: Canada had to expand its trade and set its sights on large-scale production for world markets. Gordon and his Department, on the other hand, were far more protectionist and continued to stress cautiously that Canada had to get concessions from its trading partners for any tariff reductions it granted, and the impact of tariff changes on the various sectors of the economy and on the balance of payments had to be carefully assessed.[5] Moreover, as Robertson knew, the Canadian government had taken a very tough, and very unpopular, position at the GATT meetings of May 1963, Mitchell Sharp arguing that Canada could not accept equal linear tariff cuts, a system proposed by the United States that looked to all GATT members reducing their tariffs by half over a five-year period. Such a scheme was impossible for Canada because of the economic structure of the country, because of its dependence on the export of raw materials and on the import of manufactured goods, and not least because of the weak condition of the secondary manufacturing structure. The Canadian view had been expressed well by Maurice Schwarzmann, one of Sharp's senior officials, in an address in Washington late in 1963: "Since we import about ten times more manufactured goods than we export, a linear cut in the Canadian tariffs to match a similar linear cut in the tariffs of our major trading partners would clearly be out of balance in terms of compensating benefits received and given by Canada, as well as being out of all proportion in terms of the degree of adjustment that would be required in Canadian industry as compared with the mass production industries of the U.S. and Europe."[6] Nonetheless, as Canadian ministers continued to stress, Canada was not asking for a free ride and was ready to "pay in full" for concessions it received.[7]

But because the United States and the Common Market countries had already reached agreement on the linear cuts when the Canadian position was heard, the most strenuous efforts had been necessary to achieve the special status sought. But those had succeeded, and GATT had recognized in May 1963 that Canada was a special case, a country to which across-the-board tariff cuts could not yield a "fair balance of advantage." Thus Canada was to participate in the Kennedy Round on a basis ensuring reciprocity of benefits, but one not precluding across-the-board cuts where appropriate.[8] The Common Market went along "with deep resentment," or so the historian of the Kennedy Round observed;[9] and the Americans too were unhappy, one economic adviser to the President bemoaning the "recrudescence of Canadian nationalism" at

Geneva in May 1963 and the attitude of "narrow and short-run self-interest" that characterized it.[10] It was no easy task that faced Robertson, particularly since his views had always been those of a free trader at heart and especially since the Finance Department's view predominated, for some time at least.

That was the situation early in February 1964, when Robertson was in hospital and when the government decided that he should chair the Canadian Tariffs and Trade Committee as well as lead the negotiating team in Geneva. His old friend and colleague from the trade negotiations of the 1930s, Hector McKinnon, became the vice-chairman, and the committee had the task of preparing a detailed assessment of the benefits Canada sought, consulting with industry, and formulating the responses to requests made of Canada.[11] On 27 February, a press release, issued in Robertson's name, invited interested parties to present briefs to the committee and, if they wished, to supplement them with testimony before the committee. Canadian industry was to receive every opportunity to make its views known, and the committee actively sought the advice of exporters and importers on their problems, their dealings abroad, and their difficulties with the non-tariff barriers that many countries used to get around their pious protestations of low tariff virtue.[12]

While Robertson recovered in South Carolina, the committee began its work under McKinnon's guidance. The task was far more complicated than had been true in the 1930s, when industry had made no formal representations to government. By late April, the committee had already received some 200 briefs (of an eventual total of 450) and had held a dozen or so hearings with many more scheduled for the weeks ahead.[13] Moreover, the government team had grown like Topsy. In the 1930s, Trade and Commerce, Finance and External Affairs had handled the job. In 1964, however, those departments had been joined at the negotiating table by Mines and Technical Surveys, National Revenue, Agriculture, and Industry, and the question of the number of officers each department was to provide was a matter for endless discussion. In the end, Finance and Trade and Commerce settled for three each, External Affairs got two, and the others one each.[14] In addition, when the negotiators left for Geneva, the Tariffs and Trade Committee remained in operation in Ottawa and a cabinet committee, chaired by the Prime Minister, kept close watch on the progress of the bargaining.[15] It was all a far cry from those long-ago days in Washington when Robertson made up policy as he went along. There was one positive change in all this, however. In 1938, no arrangements existed for spouses and children; but in 1964, care was taken to post officers and their families to Geneva in time for the beginning of school and in ample time for them to find accommodation.[16]

Robertson learned all this from D.S. McPhail, an economics specialist from his Department who kept him informed in South Carolina with regular shipments of documents and telegrams.[17] And when he returned to work at last in April 1964, taking an office in the Trade and Commerce building on Wellington Street, Robertson quickly plunged into the task of working out the bargaining position. There were discussions at the ministerial level with the Americans at the end of April. There were bargaining sessions between Finance and Trade and Commerce, refereed by the neutral chairman. And there was a flying trip to Geneva on 2 May to work out the complicated procedures for the talks.[18] Jetty Robertson used that visit to find accommodation, a large flat on the ground floor of a beautiful "hotel particulier" built in 1723 and overlooking a square in the Old City.[19]

The result of the discussions was a decision, again accepted with reluctance in Geneva, that Canada's offer of tariff reductions "shall be subject to confrontation and justification of exception lists." In other words, although Canada was in a special position, its offer had to pass through a procedure similar to that of most of the Kennedy Round participants, one that required confrontation and justification for commodities excluded from the tariff cuts.[20] The procedure, as Robertson told Paul Martin early in August, was that "preliminary negotiations will be concluded" in the fall. "In November the deposit of exceptions lists by countries making linear tariff cuts and of offer lists by other participating countries, including Canada, will take place. Thereafter intensive negotiations will commence and are likely to continue into 1966."[21]

By September all the Canadian team was in place in Geneva, except for the chief negotiator, who had fallen victim to new medical difficulties that twice delayed his departure from Canada. The problem was in Robertson's throat, a difficulty in swallowing. It could be relieved by what he described "as a rather modest operation (or perhaps I should say exercise) described as a dilatation of the oesophagus." It was a frightening feeling, one that recurred at Christmas 1964, necessitating a trip to Guy's Hospital in London from Geneva.[22] And as Robertson wrote to Marcel Cadieux after that episode, he still could not eat properly. There was no apparent physical reason for this, "but thus far I have not been able to develop any appetite or enjoyment of eating. I am taking enough to keep me going and supplementing it with some kind of prescribed infants' food which prevents my losing more weight. . . ." Worst of all was the lack of energy. "This may be understandable in terms of the shock and physical weakness following a major operation plus the psychological shift from an active and always interesting post to a much quieter assignment in which there are, I fear, always plausible reasons of public policy for postponing decisions which I shirk facing." Perhaps, he added, he was suffering from the "medieval vice of accidie. I think the 18th century clinicians attributed the same symptoms to spleen. Perhaps I can work out of it."[23] Unfortunately he could not, and his health continued its steady deterioration.

But the time in Geneva was not all gloomy and marred by his illness. The Robertsons purchased a Triumph sportscar and both loved the little machine. With Jetty at the wheel—her husband had still not learned to drive—they disappeared for weekends into France, and at Easter for a longer stay in Provence, visiting friends and meeting colleagues such as Charles Ritchie and George Ignatieff.

And there were books. The Geneva post was not very demanding, and there was ample time to write off to the bookstores of London or Ottawa for the titles he wanted. In 1965, for example, Robertson's eclectic purchases included A.J.P. Taylor on *English History, 1914-1945*, Janet Smith's biography of John Buchan, Harry Johnson on *International Trade and Economic Growth*, Thomson's *Life in a Noble Household 1641-1700*, Wise and Ross's book on the Central Intelligence Agency, *The Invisible Government*, Shonfeld on *Modern Capitalism*, and Young, *Eros Denied*. There were also subscriptions to *Le Monde*, the Manchester *Guardian* and *Foreign Affairs*, and the catalogues of the used booksellers were studied with care in a variety of fields.[24] Robertson's ill-health complicated his daily life, but it affected his mind not at all. He remained as he always had been, interested and alert, whimsical in his humour, invariably (sometimes infuriatingly) correct on points of fact across an enormous range of subjects. If he knew that he was getting no better, and he did, he was able to push that thought and its consequences out of the forefront of his mind.

The work at Geneva continued, troubled by the difficulties Lester Pearson's minority government faced at home. In mid-November 1964, for example, just before Canada was to table its offer at Geneva, the government decided to change front and to decline to present a package at Geneva. Deeply troubled by this, Robertson decided to call the Prime Minister. According to D.S. McPhail, the Department of External Affairs representative in Geneva with the Tariff Mission, Robertson had put his case to Pearson calmly and clearly. He had been asked to go to Geneva with a position that had been carefully worked out and accepted by the government. Now ministers wished to renege on that position, a significant alteration and one, if carried out, that left him with little reason to remain in Geneva. The choice of words was careful, but there could be no doubt that Robertson proposed to resign if his instructions were to be changed at the last moment. After Pearson consulted the ministers involved, however, Robertson's position was reaffirmed, and with only a few minor modifications, the Canadian offer was duly tabled on 16 November 1964.[25]

That offer called for the establishment of a general ceiling on Canada's tariff rates, together with a series of tariff reductions by broad categories. The ceiling was fixed at a moderate level, one that involved significant reductions in a large number of important tariff items. For a limited number of particularly sensitive items, Canada proposed a lowering of duties, but not to the general ceiling. For items already below the ceiling, selective reductions were proposed. In addition Canada offered cuts of fifty percent on a group of semi-fabricated materials, the removal of duties on almost all industrial materials, free entry on most tropical and semi-tropical products (a gesture to the less developed countries), a fifty percent cut on fish (where adequate reciprocity was offered), and reductions of fifty percent on many agricultural products and the elimination of duties on others. That offer, Canada told her trading partners, was predicated on certain assumptions: that the main industrial countries would in turn offer linear cuts of fifty percent on all industrial items of actual or potential interest to Canada; that agricultural items of interest to Canada not be excluded from tariff reductions; that, where bound margins of preference existed, agreement could be reached with the countries to which bindings had been accorded; and, finally, that other developed countries took similar action on tropical and semi-tropical products and thus compensated Canadian suppliers for their loss of preference.[26]

The offers submitted, the process of confrontation and justification began and continued through to the middle of February 1965. Although the expectation had been that a parallel examination of Canada's list would take place, this did not happen.[27] The time was filled with bilateral discussions, and Robertson became involved in a series of meetings with the Americans, including Governor Herter and Ambassador Blumenthal, that ran interminably. In all, 88 meetings were held with the United States negotiators before the conclusion of the Kennedy Round,[28] as the two nations struggled to maximize the benefits each received. In 1964, almost

70 percent of Canada's imports came from and 54 percent of its exports went to the United States, and because Canada exported raw materials and imported finished goods, the trade structure between the two countries created and reinforced an imbalance in duty payments. The tariff normally was highest on manufactures, and Canadian duties on American products were in the 17 to 25 percent range, while the average American duty on imports from Canada was only 3.4 percent. In essence that was the reason Canada could not accept linear cuts. Those could lead only to large tariff cuts on price-sensitive imports of manufactured goods, while Canadian exports, basically price-insensitive, could receive very modest cuts in absolute terms. The result was a difficult negotiation for both countries, each offering a series of specific requests and concessions.[29]

A similar pattern was followed with each of the other countries with which Canada had substantial trade and in particular with countries with which Canada had contractual preferential arrangements. In April 1965, Robertson's team prepared an individual *aide-mémoire* for each country and, as Robertson reported to Ottawa: "We are not seeking acquiescence in the proposed removal of preferential margins in the Canadian tariff. Instead we are pointing out that it is premature to reach firm conclusions on the probable impact of the Kennedy Round, and suggest simply that there should be continuous consultation on these problems."[30] The process was time-consuming, annoyingly complex and, in Robertson's view, the Canadian government's position, tied to the receipt of concessions for each and every one offered, was nowhere near as forthcoming as it should have been. The Americans, he believed, were well-prepared and broad-minded in their approach, unlike the niggling, cautious Canadian position, and it is clear that Robertson became very disappointed that the opportunity to further multilateral trade offered by the Kennedy Round did not seem likely to be seized.[31]

There were some signs of this when Robertson went to Paris for a Heads of Mission meeting on 7 and 8 May 1965, presided over by Paul Martin, the Secretary of State for External Affairs. Robertson led the discussion on the second day of the Kennedy Round's "Prospects and Implications," and began by saying that the talks had been "very slow in getting underway." It had been six months since the industrial offers had been tabled in November "and yet even in that sector Canada was not at grips with any of its trading partners, nor were they really at grips with each other." The cause, he said, was a tendency to shadow-box, as well as the simple fact that "Canada did not seem to be very high on other countries' negotiating lists." There had been remarkably few inquiries of the Canadian delegation, and this, he suggested, was because "recovery in Europe has made our relative position weaker now than ten years ago. The evolution of other countries, such as Japan, also had a bearing on our relative position." The result, in Robertson's view, was that what came out of the Canadian-American negotiations was certain to be of most importance for Canada.[32]

Somehow that limited prospect held little appeal for Robertson. He told his wife he was "so bored" with the negotiations, fed up with it all and with his health problems and the limitations they placed on his ability to see his colleagues and friends on social occasions. Jetty conveyed that feeling one afternoon to a visiting Marcel Cadieux, and the Under-Secretary began to search for something else Robertson might do.[33]

The Kennedy Round lasted until the middle of 1967 with the Canadian team directed by Robertson's good friend, Sydney Pierce. The results were made public late in June when the Minister of Trade and Commerce, Robert Winters, told the country that Canada had won concessions on more than $3 billion of its trade. "It may be," he said, uttering a pious hope, "that the Kennedy round will be regarded in the future as a crucial turning point in the transformation of Canada from a resource-based economy to one of the most advanced industrial trading nations of the world." Canada's concessions covered almost $2.5 billion worth of imports, almost $2 billion of that from the United States. In return, the Americans offered Canada concessions on a similar amount in exports, eliminating duties on lumber and paper, on some classes of fish, agricultural and other products. Other American rates were substantially reduced.[34]

I

Once Robertson's unhappiness in Geneva had been quietly communicated to Cadieux, the wheels began to turn. Carleton University in Ottawa had received a donation of $400,000 from Senator Norman Paterson, a wealthy grain shipper and investor, whose Liberal connections with C.D. Howe had resulted in his elevation to the Red Chamber in 1940, and the University and its President, Davidson Dunton, wanted someone eminent as the first head of the Paterson School of International Affairs. Dunton had worked with Robertson during the war, and had presumably talked with Cadieux and with R.A. MacKay, another of Robertson's long-time colleagues in the Department of External Affairs and Visiting Professor of Political Science at Carleton since his retirement in 1961. There seemed general agreement that Robertson was the man.

"The School," Dunton wrote to Geneva on 4 May 1965, "will promote research and publication in the field of international affairs," and the Director of the School would be assisted by a committee of university officers and faculty. The teaching programme was to include courses already offered in a number of departments, but the plan was for an "inter-disciplinary seminar, in which each year some aspect of international affairs will be examined from the points of view of the different disciplines." As Director, Robertson was to preside over this seminar. "The chief work of the Director," Dunton went on, "would be to co-ordinate the teaching program of the School, and to stimulate and advise about matters of research and publication.... He would probably supervise the theses of some students . . . [and] have chief responsibility for the admission of students." Despite this, Dunton promised that administrative demands would be small—Robertson's reputation in this area was legend—and he offered a salary of $19,000 a year with the prospect that the appointment could continue after the normal retirement age of sixty-five.[35] It was a good offer, and although Robertson's wife reminded him that he had not enjoyed teaching when he last tried it in 1934, he accepted.[36] The chance to escape Geneva and the trade negotiations, the opportunity of returning to his beloved Ottawa, was too good to pass up.

"The framework is one in which I ought to be able to fit in quite satisfactorily," Robertson wrote to Dunton. "I have joked in the past about going back to University now and then to make some extra money to enable one to carry on as a civil servant. The joke had a point," he said, overestimating the general level of university salaries which in the mid-1960s were appallingly low, "but I do not want to over-prove it in practice. To my mind a salary of $17,000 would be entirely acceptable. The difference between that figure and the salary suggested could be earmarked for books, periodicals and papers for the School, and I would be quite happy."[37] That was a splendid gesture, and a characteristic one.

That was that, and Robertson's lifetime of government service had drawn to a close. The announcement of his departure from government service came in September 1965 with the effective date of retirement at 1 January 1966.[38] But at Cadieux's request, and with his Minister's blessing,[39] Robertson was offered a consultancy as a "Senior Adviser" on a contract basis at $5,000 a year. The Under-Secretary had done this because he feared Robertson did not have long to live and he wanted to help him build up some capital for Jetty, because he wanted to keep him occupied with the work he loved, and most of all, perhaps, because he wanted Robertson's advice.[40] That was a parting gift from the Department of External Affairs, a way of supplementing Robertson's pension of almost $16,000 a year and his university salary.[41] Administratively inefficient to the end, however, Robertson negated Cadieux's gesture by failing to return the signed contract to the Department, and almost two years passed before Cadieux discovered that Robertson had never been paid and rectified matters.[42] The Under-Secretary soon was sending Robertson difficult files for his consideration, and the two friends began to meet for lunch and talk about policy at the Rideau Club on a regular basis.[43]

There were other chores too. Robertson lectured to the Senior Course on Government Administration for civil servants, and he became a member of the Advisory Group of the National Defence College at Kingston.[44] In 1966 he was invited by the Ontario government to serve on the Committee on the Healing Arts, an offer he refused.[45] In the same year, when the Pearson government was caught up in a storm over security procedures, and when the Prime Minister began to consider establishing a Royal Commission on Security, Pearson telephoned and invited Robertson to visit him at Sussex Drive. Security had always fascinated and obsessed Robertson, and he wanted a position on the Commission. But he had never asked for anything for himself, and he was not about to start now. Pearson fenced with him and dangled the position in front of his nose, waiting for Robertson to say that he wanted it. That was very much in Pearson's style, one of the more unattractive characteristics of a most charming man; but Robertson was too stubborn and proud to give in. The post went to Maxwell Mackenzie instead.[46]

There were some honours. In July 1967 Robertson was made a Companion of the Order of Canada, the highest award in the gift of the nation. To his surprise, Robertson was pleased by this. "Candour compels me to admit that in the days when I had something to do with advising on government policy in these matters," he wrote to one who had congratulated him, "I was one of the hard core who thought that we were getting along quite nicely in Canada without innovations and revivals of this kind. However," he said, "I find myself flattered by the company I keep."[47] A number of friends, notably Arnold Heeney, Louis Rasminsky, Dr. C.J. Mackenzie and Fraser Bruce, also nominated Robertson for the Royal Bank's Centennial Award, but that honour and its large cash prize went elsewhere.[48]

All this was secondary to Robertson's work at Carleton, which was not a success. He was conscientious in travelling south to Carleton's bleak campus, but his reputation, his massive brow, and his somewhat austere and forbidding appearance tended to frighten off those students who might have consulted him. In the interdisciplinary seminar, one participant recalled, he was cautious and conservative in expression, rigorously refusing to put life into the discussion by drawing on his own experiences. Not surprisingly, what little contribution Robertson made was historical in nature, and certainly he had little patience with or interest in the kinds of conceptualization that political scientists liked or the arcane techniques that were beginning to proliferate in that discipline in the 1960s. In his view, the key virtue in foreign policy was and should be caution. [49]

Robertson had little more success in running the School. According to one faculty member, he did not deal effectively with the programme, and he failed to raise money or to keep Senator Paterson happy. [50] That anyone should have expected Robertson to be a fundraiser or to stroke an old, rich man revealed that miscalculations had been made by the University. Clearly the Carleton post was no success, and although some students did learn from him and at least one faculty member benefited from his comments on a manuscript, [51] Robertson seemed too intimidating to be approachable. On one occasion, for instance, just after his appointment had been announced, Robertson was introduced to a visiting senior scholar and a harsh critic of Canadian foreign policy. His first words to the visitor were to thank him for sending some of his papers to him. "I've read them. They're empty." That was cruel and harsh; it was also wrong. [52] No, Carleton did not work out, although almost certainly it was Robertson's increasing ill-health, his troubles with eating and his dwindling weight that caused the problems.

Probably it was his awareness of the lack of success he was having at the University that made Robertson receptive when he was asked by his old Department in the late summer of 1967 to undertake a review of Canadian foreign policy. That policy was under attack by academics and by certain segments of the press, and the Department of External Affairs regularly found itself portrayed as a "lackey" of the United States and as the American errand boy in Vietnam, where Canadians still served on the International Control Commission established at Geneva in 1954. That criticism bothered the Prime Minister, who was himself troubled by the efforts of his Secretary of State for External Affairs to press Canada into a mediatory role in Vietnam and by the denunciations of policy coming from such men as Walter Gordon, the former Minister of Finance and, in

1967, the President of the Privy Council.[53] At the same time, the Under-Secretary of State for External Affairs, Marcel Cadieux, who took a conservative line on policy, was worried that any review of policy might by definition seem a criticism of his stewardship of the Department, and he was insistent that only a review by a professional diplomat could be acceptable to him. Paul Martin, of course, was aware of the differences between Pearson and himself, and he generally shared Cadieux's view. Thus to all sides, Robertson seemed an acceptable and indeed indispensable figure.

But Robertson was ill, and it seemed certain that he would need help to do the review. Geoffrey Murray, an able officer, just back from service in the United Kingdom, and one with whom Robertson had worked while High Commissioner and Under-Secretary, was available and acceptable to both Robertson and Cadieux. So too at a later period was Geoffrey Pearson, the Prime Minister's son and an officer in the Department for fifteen years, and he was added to the team, initially on a part-time basis.[54]

Murray began by visiting Robertson to discuss the approach. Robertson gave him a list of subjects to be studied—it included defence questions, Vietnam and China, Canada and Europe, the Commonwealth, and aid—and suggested the names of some who should be consulted. "He believes," Murray noted, "the Under-Secretary should set up [the Report team] quietly," a reflection of Robertson's awareness of the way Cadieux viewed the exercise.[55] That same concern was reflected in a memorandum Murray sent to the few senior officers aware of the review: " . . . I have emphasized the role of Heads of Divisions. You are aware of the reasons why this project should proceed quietly and in strict confidence. It should not excite widespread speculation and gossip within the Department and above all should not attract outside attention."[56]

By October 1967, then, Murray had taken Robertson's sketchy outline and produced a draft schema of the review. It was Robertson's and Murray's intention that the timeframe should extend back a maximum of five years, with a concentration on the events of the last two years. Their aim was to examine the main lines of policy, to look at Canada-United States and Canada-France questions, at defence, and at the foreign policy implications of French-English relations in Canada. Further, Murray wrote, the review would proceed in the following way: first, by determining what the policy was and how it was presented; second, by searching for the considerations that led to the policy; third, the validity of the policy in the light of the international environment; and finally, the options that were open when the policy was adopted, or that had opened since.[57] It was at this point that Pearson was brought in, Murray asking him to draft half the chapters in the review. "I believe in the end you and I will wish to collaborate in preparing drafts for Mr. N.A. Robertson, which hopefully can be used to get a three-way consensus."[58]

Obviously the work was not going to be done by Robertson, although his role had importance. Given an attic office in the East Block (the place he had begun his career in 1929), Robertson received Murray there frequently. He read Murray's outline and approved it, and offered advice and suggestions, taking the opportunity to press his long-held views on certain policy matters.[59] But it was really the "Murray Report," and that was how Marcel Cadieux referred to it more than a decade later.[60]

By the end of 1967, just as the drafting of chapters was getting into gear, Robertson's health broke down completely. His weight had continued its inexorable decline, and Jetty, terribly worried for her husband's health and life, had begun to think that he should go to Toronto for examinations. Reluctantly Robertson agreed, and for some weeks he was away from Ottawa; but the Toronto doctors did little to alter his inability to eat or hold food down and little to check his loss of weight. Robertson looked increasingly frail, and his strength was ebbing fast.[61]

By March 1968, a complete draft of the review was ready, and Murray carried it to Toronto General Hospital for Robertson to read. Murray remembers Mrs. Robertson's unhappiness at the intrusion of business, but Robertson, he said, had shooed his wife from the room and offered him a drink. His mind was alert, Murray added, and Robertson worried that the review might have some political implications.[62] In December 1967, Pearson had announced his impending retirement, and the Liberal Party in that winter of 1968 was in the midst of a scramble for the succession. Apparently Robertson feared that Paul Martin, one of the candidates, might try to use the report in his campaign, and that prospect disturbed him enough that he delayed delivery of the report until 5 April, the day before the vote on the leadership at the convention and too late for it to be a factor. On 6 April, Pierre Trudeau, once one of Robertson's officers in the Privy Council Office and possibly Robertson's personal choice for the position of Prime Minister, was selected as leader.[63]

The report, simply labelled a "Foreign Policy Review" and classified secret, ran to more than 200 pages. "I concentrated on those areas of policy which have been the subject of particular criticism by some observers of Canadian policy . . . ," Robertson said in the introduction, adding the hope that "the review will lead to a continuous process of planning and review. . . ." In the main, the report was a defence of present policies. Quiet diplomacy was defended, the "integrity" of American aims in Vietnam recognized, and a "fundamental agreement with the United States on the essentials of the Western strategic position in the prevailing international situation" declared. The critics of Canadian foreign policy, their views set out fully and fairly thanks to Geoffrey Pearson's work,[64] were also assailed for their "emotional and at times ill-informed rhetoric." In many respects, the report sounded more like Norman Robertson, cold warrior, than the critic of defence policy Robertson had been a few years earlier.

But not in all respects. In places, Robertson's insights showed through:

The chief restraints on Canadian foreign policy are the lack of a clear sense of national identity and the need to preserve tolerably friendly relations with the U.S.A.. . . .

The confrontation [in Europe between East and West], and thus the existence of N.A.T.O., is no bad thing if it helps to prevent war. If N.A.T.O. were to disappear the effects in Germany would be unpredictable and possibly very dangerous. N.A.T.O. would not collapse if Canada were to leave but it would be weakened. . . . Canada has a particular interest in arrangements such as N.A.T.O. which enable her to deal with the United States on the basis of equality and with the support of others. For this reason alone it would seem wise not to discredit our military contribution to the alliance to the point where equality becomes too obvious a fiction. . . .

[Canada cannot] depend on peacekeeping as a normal task. . . .

[There are] no solid grounds for believing that Canada has a special role to play in the 'third world', except insofar as we can satisfy special needs—cultural bridge-building. . . .

There was, the review said, little possibility for independent freewheeling by Canada in the face of the "essential need to maintain mutual confidence and respect in our relations with the United States with all the dilemmas which that relationship poses for us." Earlier, Robertson had noted that maintaining "credit" in Washington was certainly most desirable, "but if we cannot draw on it to any good purpose, we may wish to reconsider the line of credit in question." Thus, for Robertson, Canada's American dilemma remained the central one.

Most startling, perhaps, was his reappraisal of the Commonwealth. This paragraph, written in Robertson's own hand on the draft of the review,[65] was in the first person, the only section of the report (other than the introduction) that was:

I am inclined to take a bleak view of the future of the Commonwealth relationship and feel strongly that Canada should discourage hopes and suggestions from any quarter that it will take up Commonwealth roles and responsibilities that the United Kingdom is compelled to relinquish whether in the field of defence, development, subsidized communications or tariff preferences. This last area in particular needs early and critical scrutiny because there are already suggestions that the Commonwealth countries in Asia and the Caribbean are looking to Canada to maintain a system of Commonwealth preferences which the U.K. is fast shuffling off. Generally, I regard the Commonwealth, as distinct from relationships between the U.K. and the older dominions, as a transitional arrangement of positive but limited value which should not be expected to continue indefinitely.

That was an unexpected comment from Robertson, hitherto a devotee of the Commonwealth link, but when he went on to call the relationship "superficial" and to point out that members had closer relations with foreign states than with their "partners"—something that was obviously so—his reasoning was clear. "We see no long term reason for trying to revitalize the Association," the review noted, pointing out that the Commonwealth offered little by way of a counterweight to American influences, that its multiracial basis was founded only on aid, and that aid could be channeled through other organizations if necessary, and that it was extremely unlikely that Commonwealth meetings would ever again reach the level of confidence and frankness that had prevailed a decade earlier. For better or worse, the review's message seemed to be that Canada was locked into a world where the struggle between the United States and the Soviet Union dominated the stage. The only arena in which Canada could effectively influence the Americans, the only possible counterweight to the United States, lay in NATO. Norman Robertson could not have been particularly happy to reach that conclusion, but he did not blink from it. [66]

Few, however, received the review, and fewer still considered it closely. When the Under-Secretary forwarded it to the Minister, he noted that "it is not a departmental paper in the usual sense" but one that reflected the government's intentions "that insofar as possible an objective review should be made of current Canadian policies. . . ." [67]

But within days there was a new Prime Minister in Trudeau and a new Secretary of State for External Affairs in Mitchell Sharp, and although Cadieux passed the report to Sharp, telling him of its origins and stating that it made no recommendations but only suggested modifications or revisions subject to detailed Departmental consideration, [68] the report received little consideration. Copies eventually were distributed to most heads of posts abroad, but the new régime was determined to cut itself loose from the shackles of the past, and Robertson's review disappeared.[69] In a press conference on 23 April 1968, just after the dissolution of Parliament, the new Prime Minister promised a "severe re-assessment" of foreign policy,[70] and indeed another long review soon began. But because Geoffrey Murray was closely involved in that second review, and because the new government, after flirting with neutralism, gradually reached conclusions markedly similar to that of the old on foreign policy, in the long run such change in policy as occurred was only incremental.[71]

II

After his return to Ottawa in the spring of 1968, Norman Robertson was very weak. Nonetheless, he insisted on going to Carleton University each day and Jetty drove him to the campus where he passed the hours reading student papers or talking with faculty. In the afternoon, he regularly went by taxi to the Rideau Club to play a rubber of bridge and to talk, and then he returned home to try to eat and to read.

By the summer, there were new medical problems. In the humid heat of Ottawa, Robertson had difficulty in breathing, and soon he lost his voice as well. In his very weakened condition he had no strength left to fight, and on 16 July he died quietly and without pain.

Ill as he had been, and Robertson as a convinced realist must have known that he was close to death, there had been no last-minute rush to religion. Norman Robertson remained what he had been since his youth—a convinced sceptic about religion, one with a total absence of belief in the prospect of an afterlife. He was as firm in his faith as any churchman.

Nonetheless, Robertson was buried from Christ Church Anglican Cathedral. This was the family's decision, in consultation with Arnold Heeney, Robertson's close friend of almost half a century, and Dick Houston, Alix's husband and Robertson's son-in-law. In addition, Jetty Robertson knew that her husband would have wanted some ceremony at which friends could say farewell. It could be either Anglican or Roman Catholic, she said with her tongue just a bit in her cheek,[72] and Heeney and Houston, both firm Anglicans, naturally chose their preferred alternative.

The service at the Cathedral was brief—no more than fifteen or twenty minutes and, as Robertson would have wanted, almost non-denominational in character. The Apostle's Creed, for example, was omitted and there was no eulogy. At the graveside in the little cemetery at Wakefield in the Gatineau Hills, the same cemetery where Hume Wrong was buried and where Mike Pearson would be laid to rest, the service was only five minutes. Norman Robertson was buried as he wished, with grace and brevity, and in the presence of his family and friends. The honorary pallbearers were Douglas Le Pan, Sydney Pierce, A.E. Ritchie, W.A. Mackintosh, C.J. Mackenzie, Arnold Heeney, John Holmes, Alfred Rive, Geoffrey Pearson, Scott Macdonald, Louis Rasminsky, and Jack Pickersgill.[73]

The press offered many assessments of Robertson's role and influence, something that might have troubled that *éminence grise*. The *Times* of London called him a "Canadian diplomat of world rank," adding that "Everyone who met him . . . gained a heightened respect for Canada, for the profession of diplomacy, and for Norman Robertson himself."[74] The *Ottawa Journal* said that "His mind was regarded by many as the finest in Canada,"[75] and Maurice Pope, Robertson's old colleague from the war and postwar days, noted in the *Journal* that Robertson's "knowledge of men and things knew no limitations."[76] Prime Minister Pierre Trudeau called him "the perfect civil servant"[77] and Lester Pearson wrote that his old colleague never ceased "to amaze with his fund of knowledge, and, more important, to impress with the calm good judgment he always showed in the application of that knowledge to the particular matter under consideration, whether it was the technical relationship between the currencies of East and West Berlin or the influence of Jean-Paul Sartre on college teaching in Quebec."[78] Hundreds of letters came to Jetty from Canadian embassies, from friends at home, in the United States and in the United Kingdom, all attesting to the influence Robertson had had on affairs and on the lives of his friends and associates.[79]

But of all the tributes, the one that Norman Robertson would most have appreciated, probably because he could have disagreed with its author about the conclusion, was that by his old Balliol friend, Denis Brogan. Writing in the *Spectator*, Brogan reminisced about the days in Oxford forty-five years before and about his subsequent meetings with Robertson, and ended by noting that Norman Robertson

was a man of great kindness and would go to very great lengths to help friends. . . . He had a uniform—a black hat and black coat—which he never seemed to change. No one less like diplomats of the type of M Couve de Murville and Sir Alec Cadogan could possibly be imagined. Canada and the Western world has lost a great public servant. In other words he was a Balliol man. He thought there was

> *nothing worth the wear of winning*
> *But laughter and the love of friends.*[80]

CHAPTER XIII ·

Conclusions

N ORMAN ROBERTSON WAS "a kind of Paul Bunyan of the public
service," his friend and colleague John Holmes wrote of him,
"and the legend will not be much exaggerated."[1] There is a
great deal to that view, for Robertson served his country at the
highest levels for a quarter of a century. He accomplished much at home
and abroad: in trade policy, in the war, in shaping and strengthening the
postwar alliances, and in standing against nuclear weapons in the 1960s.
But most important perhaps, Robertson left the government service, and
in particular the Department of External Affairs, a legacy of great value.
Intelligence, honest advice, a shrewdness in tactics and in the formulation
of policy advice, the necessity for caution in judgments—all those
characteristics he brought to his own work and passed on to his
subordinates as essential traits.

There was something else, too. Norman Robertson had the courage to
fight for causes in which he believed. In his youth, his cause had been
social justice, and he had marched at the side of the workers in the
General Strike of 1926. In the 1930s and 1940s, the cause was the freeing
of world trade from the shackles of protectionism and preferences, and he
had worked and negotiated with skill towards this goal and for the
interests of his country. During the war and after, his cause was the
victory of the democracies and the creation of Canada as an independent
nation and a valuable ally. In the 1960s, his great cause was the struggle
against nuclear war, the most important fight of all.

The causes were the right ones, no doubt of that. Yet for all his efforts,
Norman Robertson's name is unlikely to be emblazoned on the battle
flags as a hero of the struggles. The reason is simple. He fought for his
causes, he waged his battles, away from the glare of publicity. As a civil
servant, as one who owed loyal service to the government of the day, he

had to operate within a more constrained framework than those outside. He could exercise his substantial influence on the making of policy, he could attempt to persuade and convert the doubtful, but once the government had determined its direction, he had no choice, except the ultimate one of resignation, but to carry out that policy.

He was a careful man by inclination and by temperament, but he had to be, because the issues with which he was concerned were so important. An error or miscalculation could have tremendous impact on the country and its people, and mistakes had to be avoided. And yet he was not averse to using whatever means came to hand to help achieve his goals. If Mackenzie King fuzzily believed in the virtues of freer trade or that he was the author of the functionalist theory, if Howard Green stood foursquare in favour of disarmament and against atomic weapons, that could be employed. A civil servant had to take whatever material was at hand and to employ it in the furtherance of his country's cause. Robertson did this; he played by the rules as they existed, and he achieved much of benefit.

But sometimes it was very difficult to believe that anyone was benefiting from the actions of the government. Robertson opposed the internment and deportation of Japanese Canadians during the Second World War and worked to ameliorate the policy; but yet he went along with it. He was appalled at the revelations of Igor Gouzenko, shattered that public servants could violate their oaths and spy for a foreign power. Those two unhappy affairs unquestionably calcified Robertson's spirit, making him a bit more cynical about government, much less trusting about people. Security came to matter very much to him, and he could be a hard man ever after, hard in the defence of the state and the system he served.

He was a servant of that state, and his task was to advance its power and interests. He did this well, and his goal was always to have Canada act as independently as possible. This he strove for in trade negotiations, in the hard battling during the war over Combined Boards and the functional principle, and in his resistance to British policy at the time of Suez and to American policy to Cuba and nuclear weapons. But there can be little doubt that Robertson recognized that Canada on its own was prey to all manner of enemies, and he accepted the necessity of allying with stronger nations. His training, his broad culture and his civilized nature led him naturally enough to support Canada's links with Britain, Europe and with the United States, and he viewed his country as every bit the equal of the other members of the alliance. To him, Canada was no victim of British or American conspiracies. He was too confident in his own abilities and in his country's capacities to believe that. His nationalism was strong but not defensive, and he knew that, while there were certain to be battles with London or Washington on important questions, the grudges and resentments that occasionally developed could not be allowed to persist.

Nonetheless, after the war, the power of the United States grew faster than he or his colleagues could have expected, its influence burgeoned, and wisdom in the Congress or the White House did not always keep pace. That caused terrible difficulties for Canada—smaller, weaker, and essentially defenceless against the full weight of American power, money and culture. Robertson and his friends, however, were so confident of their ability to deal successfully with the United States, a confidence born out of the experience of the war and postwar years, that they probably overestimated the ability of their compatriots to resist Americanization. They assumed that because they had done so well, Canada as a whole could meet and best the American challenge. The growth of American economic control, the spread of television, magazines and consumer goods, however, could not be managed so easily.

Nor could the American pressures on Canada to take nuclear weapons. Robertson had never had any doubts about the horror explicit in such weapons, but he had seemingly accepted that Canada was to take them until 1959. Then his doubts, his thoroughgoing scepticism, returned, and he found himself forced to take sides and ultimately choosing to resist a nuclear role for his country. He opposed the weapons with the force of his mind and every ounce of bureaucratic skill that he had acquired in more than thirty years of public service; with Howard Green he delayed the process for three or four years. That was an achievement, but Robertson had always balanced his opposition to atomic weapons with the necessity to retain more or less friendly relations with the United States. His world view, his realism, demanded that.

Perhaps that world view made him less sensitive than he should have been to some Canadian realities. Norman Robertson was the quintessential "Ottawa man" (in Christina Newman's telling phrase) of his generation. The capital was his favourite place, its inhabitants his chosen friends. He had been trained by Skelton, and moulded by Clark, Towers and the other mandarins into their common image. He was male, middle-class, well-educated at home and abroad; he was frugal, shy of the limelight, and cautious; and he believed that the federal government had to have and should fully exercise just as much power and authority as possible. Above all, he was a unilingual English Canadian, and although he was close to men such as Georges Vanier, Jules Léger and Marcel Cadieux, he somehow failed to grasp the bilingual and bicultural reality of Canada until the 1960s. He was not alone in this, of course, nor the worst sinner, and he belatedly tried as best he could to make amends by fostering the use of French in his Department and by encouraging the expansion of Canadian links with French-speaking nations. But it was not enough. Norman Robertson had a world view, yes; but for most of his life in Ottawa his own view of his country was flawed, and one of the great fears of his last years was that his nation might split apart under the pressure of domestic strains.

Thus Norman Robertson, civil servant. He had great achievements, great success; he made errors, and he missed things. He was, after all, only a man. What those who knew and loved him remember most clearly, aside from his gentleness and friendship, was the force and range of his mind. "From a memory fantastically stocked," John Holmes wrote, "he could filter and assemble all the relevant precedents and considerations. His policy recommendations might be safe or daring; they were never trite, never just the dogma of the moment. There might be no decision at all, because he knew how often the wise thing to do was nothing." He could pull together disparate fragments of information, arrange them, discover how they were interrelated, and reach a judgment that none of those around him could see; but once reached, it was immediately obvious to all. The power of that mind, the force of its concentration, was very great indeed.

Norman Robertson was one of the men who made modern Canada. With a handful of other mandarins, he created for the Canadian public service the ethos of duty, high competence and intelligence that animated it in its heyday, and with Hume Wrong and Lester Pearson, he made the Department of External Affairs into the pre-eminent ministry of that service and into one of the ablest foreign offices anywhere. He was, John Holmes said, "the greatest mandarin of them all,"[2] a civil servant who served his country and Canadians well.

References

Chapter I

1. Mrs. N.A. Robertson Papers (Ottawa), N.A. Robertson [NAR] to mother, 30 Sep. 23.
2. *Ibid.*, letters, 2, 8, 9, 10, 26 Oct. 23; Brian Heeney Papers (Peterborough), A.D.P. Heeney Draft Memoirs, 66-67.
3. The birth certificate is on file at Balliol College, Oxford.
4. The family history can be found in "A Talk Given by Professor Lemuel F. Robertson to a Group of Members of the Faculty of the U.B.C.," n.d. [1943], copy in Ms. Judith Robertson's possession, Toronto, and in "Granny's book," transcribed recollections of Floretta Robertson, also in Ms. Robertson's possession.
5. "Makers of the University—Lemuel Robertson," *U.B.C. Alumni Chronicle*, (Spring 1955), 18; Hugh MacLennan, ed., *McGill, The Story of a University* (London, 1960), p. 93.
6. *Ibid.*, p. 93; H.T. Logan, *Tuum Est: A History of the University of British Columbia* (Vancouver, 1958), pp. 18, 19; F.H. Soward, "The Early History of the University of British Columbia," mss., (1930), 27n.
7. University of British Columbia [UBC] Archives, Special Collections Div., McGill University College Records, *passim*; Logan, p. 25.
8. Barbara Robertson Morton, untitled memoir of Lemmy Robertson, in Ms. Robertson's possession.
9. Public Archives of Canada [PAC], W.L.M. King Diary, 18 Feb. 46.
10. Howard Green interview, 1 May 78; H.L. Keenleyside interview, 4 May 78; Dr. Margaret Ormsby conversation, 9 March 78; Heeney Papers, Draft Memoirs, p. 31. For an example of Lemmy's campus political skills, see UBC Archives, Special Collections Division, Angus Family Papers, box 1, folder 1 and 2, H.F. Angus Autobiography, 196.
11. Barbara Robertson Morton interview, 16 Nov. 78. The book, with a

notation by Norman's mother, is still in the possession of Mrs. Norman Robertson.

12. McGill University College Records, box 6-10, Robertson to George Robinson, 17 Apr. 12. Lemmy had tart views on Stephen Leacock, then teaching economics at McGill: "Leacock is ... given to ... words, smartness, cleverness. Success are his ideals and of course it is infectious. A great proportion of the staff feels to him—Leacock—much as we would—a vaudeville artist in the market standing on his head for the diversions of the public, and drawing to McGill a good deal of not very discriminating applause. He is a cheap authority on everything on earth, and gets advertising out of it all. I meet no one who does not feel that he sold himself at a handsome figure." *Ibid.*, Robertson to Robinson, 24 Feb. 12.

13. Barbara Robertson Morton, "A Childhood of Summers," mss.; Mrs. Mary Robertson Oliver interview, 13 Feb. 78.

14. Mrs. Robertson Papers, NAR to mother, 31 Jul. 15.

15. Dr. Frank Turnbull interview, 3 May 78. Turnbull was NAR's closest friend in high school.

16. Mrs. Robertson Papers, report card.

17. Mrs. Oliver interview. According to his graduation certificate, in Mrs. Robertson's Papers, he nonetheless received an 82% average, despite a 64 in History.

18. Universities in Canada at this time attracted only small numbers. In 1920-21, full-time enrolment in Canada was only 23,418, just 3.2% of youths aged eighteen to twenty-two. M.S. Horn, "Professors in the Public Eye: The League for Social Reconstruction and Canadian Universities," unpub. mss., 6.

19. Mrs. H.F. Angus interview, 29 Apr. 78.

20. Mrs. Oliver interview; Mrs. Morton interview.

21. Dr. Turnbull interview.

22. Mrs. Oliver interview.

23. Roberta Thurlow Morrison conversation, 3 May 78; Mrs. Sallee Murphy Creighton interview, 30 Apr. 78.

24. J.V. Clyne interview, 30 Apr. 78; Mrs. Creighton interview.

25. UBC Archives, M.G. 79, Minute Book of Class of '23, e.g., entries for 5 Oct. 21, 19 Oct. 21, 5 Oct. 22, 18 Oct. 22.

26. As detailed in NAR's letter of application for a Rhodes Scholarship in Balliol College Records, Oxford, Robertson file, NAR to Professor H.T. Logan, 20 Oct. 22.

27. *Ubyssey*, 3 Nov. 21.

28. *Ibid.*, 26 Jan. 22.

29. *Ibid.*, 8 Feb. 23.

30. *Sixth Annual of the U.B.C..*, 1921, p. 42.

31. Mrs. Angus interview. Another member, a year or so later, was Earle Birney, whose memoirs, *Spreading Time*, Vol. I: *1904-1949* (Montreal, 1980), 8ff., refer to his UBC years.

32. UBC Archives, Letters Club, vol. 4, 1921-22; *Ubyssey*, 17 Nov. 21.

33. Balliol College Records, Robertson file, Angus to Rhodes selection committee, 23 Oct. 22.

34. NAR's UBC transcript; *U.B.C. Calendar 1924-5*, p. 251; UBC Archives, "Memoranda of U.B.C. 1916-33," p. 79 [a scrapbook of memorabilia].

35. Letters of reference in Balliol College Records, Robertson file.

36. Clyne interview.

37. *Eighth Annual of the U.B.C.* (1922-3), p. 28. (I am indebted to Mrs. H.F. Angus for the loan of her copy of the Yearbook.) Clyne cheerfully admitted making up the stories of female adoration. Interview.

38. Balliol College Records, Robertson file, Sage to the Master, 10 Dec. 22 and Sage to K.N. Bell, 10 Dec. 22; *ibid.*, NAR to Mr. Bailey, 11 Mar. 23.

39. *Ibid.*, Sir Francis Wylie to Bailey, 16 Jul. 23; Sir John Hicks interview, 15 Jun. 78.

40. Mrs. Robertson Papers, NAR to mother, 19 [?] Sep. 23.

41. *Ibid.*, McMaster to Lemuel Robertson, 25 Sep. 23.

42. *Ibid.*, NAR to mother, 22 Sep. 23.

43. *Ibid.*, n.d.

44. *Ibid.*, NAR to mother, 22 Oct. 23.

45. Vincent Bladen, *Bladen on Bladen* (Toronto, 1978), p. 9.

46. Hicks interview.

47. Peter Quennell, *The Marble Foot: An Autobiography 1905-38* (London, 1976), p. 125.

48. Evelyn Waugh, *A Little Learning* (London, 1964), p. 172. Cf. his *Brideshead Revisited* (Boston, 1945), pp. 21ff.

49. Quennell, pp. 112ff.

50. Queen's University, J.M. Macdonnell Papers, Box 60, unpub. mss., p. F11.

51. *Transatlantic Blues* (New York, 1978), p. 27.

52. *Tempest Tost* (Markham, Ont., 1980), p. 30.

53. Mrs. Robertson Papers, NAR to father, 10 Oct. 23.

54. *Ibid.*, NAR to Mary, 12 Oct. 23.

55. *Ibid.*, NAR to "folks", 15 Oct. 23.

56. *Ibid.*, NAR to mother, 22 Oct. 23.

57. *Ibid.*, NAR to father, 28 Oct. 23.

58. *Ibid.*, 9 Nov. 23.

59. J.M. Minifie, *Expatriate* (Toronto, 1976), p. 8.

60. Mrs. Robertson Papers, NAR to Mary, 27 Nov. 23; NAR to mother, 19 Nov. 23; Graham Spry interview, 17 Feb. 79.

61. Mrs. Robertson Papers, NAR to Barbara, 12 Nov. 23.
62. Elsie Lemon, ed., *The Balliol College Register 1916-67* (Oxford, 1969).
63. Spry interview; A.D.P. Heeney, *The Things that are Caesar's* (Toronto, 1972), p. 19.
64. Mrs. Robertson Papers, NAR to Mary, 4 Jan. 24.
65. *Spectator*, 2 Aug. 68.
66. Mrs. Robertson Papers, NAR to mother, n.d. [Jan. 24].
67. *Ibid.*, NAR to Rive, n.d. [Jan. 24].
68. Alfred Rive, "Graduate Profile—Norman A. Robertson," *U.B.C. Alumni Chronicle* (Autumn, 1956).
69. Mrs. Robertson Papers, NAR to Mary, 13 Feb. 24.
70. *Ibid.*, NAR to mother, 25 Feb. 24.
71. *Ibid.*, NAR to father, 15 Mar. 24.
72. *Ibid.*
73. *Ibid.*, NAR to mother, 25 Feb. 24.
74. *Ibid.*, 6 Apr. 24.
75. *Ibid.*, 9 May 24.
76. *Ibid.*, fragment, n.d.; *ibid.*, NAR to mother, 4 Mar. 25.
77. *Ibid.*, 15 May 24.
78. Hicks interview.
79. *Ibid.*, NAR to mother, 23 Nov. 24.; *Spectator*, 2 Aug. 68.
80. Mrs. Robertson Papers, NAR to mother, 15 Dec. 24.
81. Letters in *ibid.*
82. *Ibid.*, NAR to mother, 17 Mar. 25.
83. Letter, Professor W.P. Morrell to author, 17 Aug. 78.
84. *Spectator*, 2 Aug. 68; Hicks interview. Cf. *The Times*'s obituary of NAR, 18 Jul. 68, which offers yet another explanation for the result.
85. Rhodes House, Oxford, Robertson dossier, Report to Selection Committee, 1923-24.
86. *Ibid.*, Sir Francis Wylie confidential notebook, NAR entry.
87. Mrs. Robertson Papers, NAR to mother, 8 Nov. 25.
88. Brian Heeney Papers, Arnold Heeney to sister, 18 Oct. 25; PAC, A.D.P. Heeney Papers, vol. 8, Diary, 10 Nov. 25; Heeney, *Caesar*, p. 21; Morrell letter; W.P. Morrell, *Memoirs* (Dunedin, N.Z., 1979), p. 45. Morrell said that NAR was "one of the ablest men and wittiest conversationalists I ever met. . . ." (p. 36).
89. Mrs. Robertson Papers, NAR to Vancouver, 18 May 26.
90. Brian Heeney Papers, Draft memoirs, p. 91. J.V. Clyne also supported the government and served as a special constable, but he and NAR would meet for dinner to talk and argue over the day's events. Interview.
91. Hicks interview.
92. *Spectator*, 2 Aug. 68.

93. Mrs. Robertson Papers, NAR to father, 24 Jan. 26.
94. *Ibid.*, 14 Apr. 26.
95. Brookings Institution, (Washington), NAR file, EHW [?] to NAR, 24 Feb. 26.
96. *Ibid.*, NAR's application form, 11 Mar. 26.
97. *Ibid.*, Hamilton to NAR, 31 Mar. 26.
98. *Ibid.*, NAR to Hamilton, 26 Apr. 26.
99. *Ibid.*, Lindsay to Hamilton, 17 Apr. 26; Eastman to Hamilton, 20 Apr. 26.
100. *Ibid.*, Tel., Cassidy to NAR, 7 May 26; reply, 8 May 26; Hamilton to NAR, 15 May 26.
101. *Ibid.*, NAR to Hamilton, 14 Jun. 26.
102. *Ibid.*, Hamilton to NAR, 29 Jun. 26.
103. UBC Archives, UBC Faculty Ledger Sheets 1926-27; *ibid.*, Board of Governors Records, 1926-27.
104. Soward interview, 1 May 78; Angus interview, 29 Apr. 78.
105. See R. Faris, *The Passionate Educators* (Toronto, 1975), pp. 8ff.; J.W. Pickersgill Papers (Ottawa), Brooke Claxton to Ned Corbett, 18 Nov. 54, on the early history of the League, whose members included Arnold Heeney, Frank Scott, and T.W.L. MacDermot.
106. Brookings Institution, NAR file, Hamilton to NAR, 14 Apr. 27.
107. PAC, N.A. Robertson Papers, vol. 3A, Personal Correspondence 1960 file, NAR to W.A. Mackintosh, 9 Feb. 60.
108. Mrs. Robertson Papers, NAR to mother, 15 May 27.
109. *Ibid.*, NAR to father, 21 May 27.
110. Spry interview; PAC, Civil Service Commission, Historical Personnel Records, NAR file, vol. 839, Memo by Coats, 16 Jun. 27; Memo to Secretary, Civil Service Commn., 20 Jun. 27. The salary was $1,920 per year.
111. Mrs. Robertson Papers, NAR to Mary, 1 Aug. 27.
112. *Ibid.*, NAR to mother, 18 Jul. 27.
113. *Ibid.*, 27 Sep. 27.
114. Brookings Institution, folder "Students and Fellows," General Announcement 1927, pp. 4ff.
115. *Ibid.*, Robert G. Moulton, "The History of the Organization of the Brookings Institution," mss., (June 1928), 15.
116. *Ibid.*, Students' card file, NAR entry.
117. Mrs. N.A. Robertson interview, 17 Oct. 78.
118. Mrs. Robertson Papers, NAR to mother, 12 Nov. 27.
119. *Ibid.*, NAR to W.A. Claydon, 25 Nov. 27: "I've been among the philistines now for a trifle more than two months and they are simply

appalling. I loathe them. . . .general illiteracy, xtian kindliness and all-round inadequacy. . . .there is no one here who can talk, walk or play a respectable game of bridge. . . .believe me I mean every word of it."

120. *Ibid.*, NAR to mother, 12 Nov. 27. On the ceremonies, see Vincent Massey, *What's Past is Prologue* (Toronto, 1963), pp. 141-44; and for Robertson's reporting, see *Montreal Star*, 11 Nov. 27, p. 1: "A little corner of Arlington cemetery has been marked out as Canada's own"; *ibid.*, 14 Nov. 27, p. 22: "Canada's friendly invasion . . . the biggest social event of the season."

121. Mrs. Robertson Papers, NAR to mother, 21 May 28.

122. *Ibid.*, 23 Feb. 28.

123. Mrs. Paul Lewinson conversation, 20 Sept. 78.

124. Mrs. Robertson Papers, NAR to Mary, 14 Jun. 28.

125. *Ibid.*, NAR to mother, n.d.

126. Brookings Institution, NAR file, "General Examination of Mr. Norman Robertson, May 12, 1928."

127. *Ibid.*, Hamilton to L. Robertson, 26 Jun. 28; and NAR card file.

128. Mrs. Robertson Papers, NAR to mother, 23 Feb. 28.

129. Brookings Institution, NAR file, NAR to Miss Quill, 15 Oct. 28.

130. Mrs. Robertson Papers, NAR to mother, 21 May 28.

131. PAC, Department of External Affairs Records, [EAR] vol. 786, file 407, Skelton to Chester Martin, 2 May 28.

132. Mrs. Robertson Papers, NAR to mother, 21 May 28.

133. EAR, vol. 787, file 408, Civil Service Positions, list 392, 30 Apr. 28.

134. Historical Personnel Records, NAR file, vol. 839, application form. Other letters were received from Professors Angus and Logan at UBC. Angus suggested that NAR would give an excellent account of himself, but shrewdly observed that "ideas will always interest him more than men, and that with many ideas the interest lapses as soon as they have been exploded." *Ibid.*

135. Mrs. Robertson Papers, NAR to father, n.d. In Montreal, NAR called on his father's friend Andrew McMaster, who promptly wrote King and Skelton on NAR's behalf. "A.R.M., in writing King put it on with a trowel ending with the subtle suggestion that I was *not* the first Canadian who preferred to serve his country rather than teach at Harvard." *Ibid.*, and see King Papers, McMaster to King, 21 Jun. 28, f. 131542.

136. EAR, vol. 787, file 408, Civil Service Positions, list 392.

137. *Ibid.*, List of Names in order of merit . . . , 24 Sep. 31.

138. *Ibid.*, vol. 749, file 469, Skelton to Marler, 13 Mar. 29 and vol. 788, file 409 and vol. 789, file 413 for further detail.

139. Robertson *père* arranged for the Premier of British Columbia to write King. King Papers, MacLean to King, 6 Jun. 28, f.131469.

140. EAR, vol. 789, file 409, Memo, 14 Aug. 28.
141. PAC, W.L. Grant Papers, vol. 9, Skelton file, Skelton to Grant, 13 Jun. 28.
142. EAR, vol. 793, file 454, Skelton to Massey, 4 Aug. 28.
143. Mrs. Robertson Papers, NAR to mother, 28 Aug. 28.
144. *Ibid.*, NAR to Mary, 30 Sep. 28.
145. Harvard University Archives, file UAV 453.288, Tutorial Assignments 1928-29; file UAV 453.288.18, Alphabetical list of tutors 1919-20–1933-34.
146. *Ibid., Official Register of Harvard University, Division of History, Government and Economics*, vol. XXV (26 May 1928), p. 85.
147. PAC, Paul Martin Papers, vol. 184, Diary, 30 Sep., 5 Oct. 28; Martin interview, 16 Jun. 78, and letter to author, 13 Dec. 78.
148. Lower interview, 27 Oct. 78.
149. Mrs. Robertson Papers, NAR to "Papa," 16 Oct. 28. NAR attended a Smith rally in Boston at which Felix Frankfurter spoke. *Ibid.*, NAR to mother, 13 Oct. 28. Paul Martin attended the same rally. Martin Papers, Diary.
150. Hicks interview.
151. Mrs. Robertson interview, 17 Oct. 78.
152. Mrs. Robertson Papers, D. McIntosh to Robertsons, 24 Dec. 28; Bella McIntosh to Robertsons, 26 Dec. 28.
153. *Ibid.*, Jetty to Robertsons, 12 Dec. 28.
154. *Ibid.*, NAR to mother, 11 Jan. 29.
155. *Ibid.*, 21 Jan. 29.
156. *Ibid.*, NAR to parents, 21 Jan. 29.
157. EAR, vol. 793, file 454, Skelton to Massey, 18 Feb. 29.
158. Mrs. Robertson interview, 27 Nov. 78.
159. EAR, vol. 840, file 95, "Material from Dr. Skelton's office," list, n.d.; *ibid.*, vol. 794, file 468, "Tokyo Post," n.d. Arnold Heeney was asked by Marler to go with him to Tokyo, but declined. Heeney, p. 30.
160. Mrs. Robertson Papers, NAR to mother, 27 Mar. 29.
161. *Ibid.*, NAR to Mary, 14 Apr. 29.
162. *Ibid.*, NAR to mother, 20 May 29.
163. His record shows his date of joining as 13 May 1929. EAR, vol. 787, file 408, chart.
164. *Ibid.*, vol. 793, file 454, Skelton to Massey, 16 May 29. See Skelton's comments to House of Commons Select Standing Committee on Industrial and International Relations, 25 Mar. 30, pp. 11ff.
165. EAR, vol. 786, file 407, Skelton to Professor Burton, 5 Jun. 29 and King Papers, Memo, 5 Jul. 29, f. C51418.
166. Historical Personnel Records, NAR file, vol. 839, Memo, 25 Sep. 29.
167. *Ibid.*, Memoranda, 1, 2 Oct. 29. The required character testimonials were

not filed until November and the necessary medical examinations not held until that month as well. Copies are on file in *ibid*. Robertson told the examiners that his hearing was good (although he was deaf in one ear) and that, although he drank wine occasionally, he touched malt spirits not at all.

Chapter II

1. Department of External Affairs [DEA], John Starnes Papers, Wrong to Skelton, 12 Sep. 29. (These documents were collected from a variety of sources by Starnes and are held in the Historical Division, External Affairs.)
2. PAC, Department of External Affairs Records [EAR], vol. 787, file 408, Report to Prime Minister, 8 Aug. 30; Donald Story, "Canada's Covenant: The Bennett Government, the League of Nations and Collective Security, 1930-35," PhD thesis, University of Toronto, 1976, p. 30.
3. EAR, vol. 787, file 408, "Memo on Work of Department . . . ," n.d. For NAR's joining date, see Montreal *Gazette*, 26 Sep. 29.
4. G.A.H. Pearson interview, 10 Jan. 79.
5. Walter Gordon interview, 1 Aug. 78. The Gordons rented the Skelton house after the Doctor's death in January 1941.
6. Queen's University Archives, Grant Dexter Papers, Memo, 16 Sep. 41; G.N. Hillmer, "The Anglo-Canadian Neurosis: The Case of O.D. Skelton," in P. Lyon, ed., *Britain and Canada* (London, 1976), p. 63.
7. Story, 19.
8. Sir Robert Borden Diaries (Toronto), 9, 12 Aug. 30.
9. Copies in PAC, Sir Robert Borden Papers, vol. 275, file 273 and in PAC, N.A. Robertson Papers, vol. 9, file 84.
10. Mrs. N.A. Robertson Papers (Ottawa), NAR to mother, n.d. [30 Aug. 30]; Mrs. N.A. Robertson interview, 7 Jan. 79.
11. Mrs. Robertson Papers, NAR to mother, [30 Aug. 30]; Borden Diary, 18 Aug. 30.
12. *Ibid.*, dates as noted.
13. Henry Borden interview, 7 Dec. 78.
14. There is a hint that Skelton was not entirely happy with Robertson, in a letter from Mrs. Robertson to her mother-in-law: "It is so nice that he and Skelton get on so much easier this year. . . ." Mrs. Robertson Papers, Jetty to Mrs. Robertson, 10 Jun. 31.
15. Borden Diary, 11 Sep. 30.
16. *Canada at Geneva* (Toronto, 1946), p. 88. See also Alex Inglis, ed.,

Documents on Canadian External Relations, IV: *1926-1930* (Ottawa, 1971), 637. [Cited hereafter as *DCER* IV].

17. PAC, R.B. Bennett Papers, Mf. M-1092, Borden to Skelton, 12 Sep. 30, ff.269468-9. Cf. Mrs. Robertson Papers, Mrs. Robertson to L. Robertson, 24 Sep. 30.
18. Bennett Papers, Mf. M-1092, Borden to Bennett, 17 Sep. 30, ff.269450-1.
19. Rasminsky interview, 30 Nov. 78.
20. Lord Balogh interview, 8 Jun. 78.
21. Mme. Vanier interview, 22 Jun. 78. See NAR's very warm note of congratulations to the Vaniers when Georges became Minister to France. PAC, Georges Vanier Papers, vol. 14, NAR to Vanier, 22 Jan. [1939].
22. Bennett Papers, Mf. M-1092, Tel. Geneva to Secretary of State for External Affairs [SSEA], 3 Oct. 30, f.269406.
23. Borden Diary, 9, 10 Nov. 30, 29 Dec. 30.
24. NAR also prepared the Report of the Canadian Delegation for Borden. Robertson Papers, vol. 9, file 78 and Borden Diary, 17 Feb. 31. The two remained friendly until Borden's death. C.J. Mackenzie Diary (Ottawa), 3 Oct. 44; letter, Professor R.C. Brown to author, 6 Apr. 77.
25. EAR, vol. 1567, file 377-1930; Robertson Papers, vol. 9, file 74.
26. *Ibid.*, vol. 10, file 90, Memos, 13 May and 6 Aug. 31.
27. *Ibid.*, file 91, Memo, 29 Jun. 31.
28. Mrs. Robertson Papers, NAR to mother, 26 Feb. 31.
29. PAC, W.L.M. King Papers, Skelton to King, 14 May 31, f.160723.
30. Robertson Papers, vol. 10, file 86, Memo, n.d.
31. Mrs. Robertson Papers, NAR to mother, n.d. [17 May 31]. A much more sympathetic view of Ferguson can be found in Peter Oliver, *G. Howard Ferguson Ontario Tory* (Toronto, 1977).
32. C.F. Wilson, *A Century of Canadian Grain* (Saskatoon, 1978), p. 354; Robertson Papers, vol. 4, file 5, Memo, n.d. [Mar. 31] and additional material in vol. 4, files 2, 3, 5. On Bennett wheat policy, see PAC, R.K. Finlayson Papers, draft memoirs, Chapter VIII.
33. EAR, vol. 1582, file 65-FP, Memorandum on the Agenda . . . ; and file 65, Skelton to Riddell, 19 Aug. 31, and reply, 1 Sep. 31.
34. Queen's University, Norman Rogers Papers, box 1, file 1a-1931, Macdonald to Rogers, 10 Nov. 31. Robertson spoke to the CIIA in Ottawa on his return. PAC, CIIA Records, vol. 6, file Oct.-Dec. 31, mimeo form, 4 Dec. 31.
35. Mrs. C.H.A. Armstrong Papers (Toronto), Hume Wrong to Marga Wrong, 6 Jun. 30.
36. Mrs. Robertson Papers, NAR to father, 2 Mar. 32.
37. H.F. Angus interview, 29 Apr. 78.
38. Mrs. C.H.A. Armstrong Papers, *passim*; L.B. Pearson, *Mike: The Memoirs*

of the Right Honourable Lester B. Pearson, Vol. I: *1897-1948* (Toronto, 1972), 77-78.

39. Churchill College, Cambridge, Burgon Bickersteth Papers, "Special Memorandum Re Ottawa Conference, May 1932."

40. Bennett Papers, Mf. M-986, ff.90668ff.; Rogers Papers, box 1, file la-1932, Macdonald to Rogers, 4 Jan. 32.

41. Mrs. Robertson Papers, NAR to father, 2 Mar. 32. NAR's draft income tax returns for 1933 and 1936 are in Starnes Papers. The Salary Deduction Act remained in force until 1937.

42. Borden Diary, 22 Jan. 32.

43. Mrs. Robertson Papers, NAR to mother, n.d. [Jan. 32].

44. *Ibid.*

45. EAR, vol. 1589, file 159-U, Notes on the Canadian Organization ..., 15 Nov. 32 and Department of External Affairs, State Papers, 10-2-1-1932/1-31. Generally on the Conference, see D.R. Annett, *British Preference in Canadian Commercial Policy* (Toronto, 1948), especially Chapter III; O.J. McDiarmid, *Commercial Policy in the Canadian Economy* (Cambridge, 1946), pp. 279ff.; and, particularly, Ian Drummond, *Imperial Economic Policy 1917-39* (London, 1974), *passim*. There is some useful material in Chapter V of G.N. Hillmer, "Anglo-Canadian Relations, 1926-37," PhD thesis, Cambridge University, 1974.

46. EAR, vol. 1589, file 159-U. See also on the organization and NAR's role, material in *ibid.*, vol. 1591, file 159-AF and vol. 2369; in Robertson Papers, vol. 10, file 103; in PAC, Department of Trade and Commerce Records, vol. 62, file 19915; and in Bennett Papers, Mf. M-998-9 and M-1172.

47. Mrs. Robertson Papers, NAR to father, 2 Mar. 32.

48. Drummond, p. 208-09. Cf. Mrs. C.H.A. Armstrong Papers, Wrong to Marga Wrong, 16 Jul. 32.

49. Mrs. Robertson Papers, NAR to mother, n.d.

50. See Drummond, pp. 275-79; *DCER* V, 46ff.

51. Public Record Office [PRO], Cabinet Records, docs. on Cab. 32/115.

52. PRO, Dominions Office Records, D.O. 121/61, Whiskard to Harding, 22, 27 Jul. 32.

53. Cambridge University Library, Stanley Baldwin Papers, vol. 98, L.S. Amery to Baldwin, 15 Aug. 32.

54. *Ibid.*, A. Lascelles to Baldwin, 21 Nov. 32. In addition, on Bennett's extraordinary behaviour, see Queen's University, Grant Dexter Papers, Dexter to Dafoe, 16 Oct. 32.

55. Drummond, p. 31; Hillmer, Chapter V; Finlayson, draft memoirs, pp. 153ff.

56. O. Mary Hill, *Canada's Salesmen to the World* (Montreal, 1977), pp. 528-29. No source for this is cited. See also Dana Wilgress, *Memoirs* (Toronto, 1967), pp. 94-95; H. Blair Neatby, *William Lyon Mackenzie King*, Vol. III: *The Prism of Unity* (Toronto, 1976), 24ff.

57. See on the results, K.W. Taylor, "Canadian Tariff Policy," in *Canadian Papers 1938* (Toronto, CIIA, 1938), 102; Drummond, "Imperial Preference," in R. Bothwell and G.N. Hillmer, *The In-Between Time* (Toronto, 1975), pp. 56-59.

58. Bennett Papers, Mf. M-1179, ff.116160ff. and Mf. M-1279, f.347007; and James Struthers, "No Fault of their Own: Unemployment and the Canadian Welfare State, 1914-41," PhD thesis, University of Toronto, 1979, 309ff.

59. See on this incident, Story, 227-28; EAR, vol. 1607; Bothwell and Hillmer, pp. 113ff.; Richard Veatch, *Canada and the League of Nations* (Toronto, 1975), pp. 118ff.; York University Archives, W.A. Riddell Papers, Correspondence 1932-34, Riddell to Skelton, 13 Dec. 32 and ff.

60. Bickersteth Papers, "1937": NAR, "much the ablest of the younger men" in External Affairs, "is a keen believer in Canada playing her full part as a member-state of the League."

61. Borden Diary, 23 Mar. 33; PAC, A.G.L. McNaughton Papers, vol. 5, League Disarmament file, postcard; Veatch, p. 123, on Robertson's views.

62. On NAR's cold-bloodedness, F.H. Soward recollects a later discussion where he argued strongly that if Canada did not sell strategic raw materials to Japan, someone else, probably Chile or Peru, would. Who then would be helped? Interview, 1 May 78.

63. Mrs. Robertson interview, 26 Feb. 78.

64. *DCER* V, 277ff.; Finlayson Papers, draft memoirs, pp. 172ff.; and Bennett Papers, Mf. M-1180, f.117615.

65. Mrs. Robertson Papers, NAR to father, n.d. [Jun. 33].

66. Bennett Papers, NAR to Skelton, 16 Jun. 33, f.121244, Mf. M-1183.

67. Mrs. Robertson Papers, NAR to father, n.d. See the minutes of British Commonwealth delegations meetings in Bennett Papers, Mf. M-1181, ff.118412ff., where this question is also raised. See Drummond, pp. 304-07 for a discussion of Empire aspects of the Conference.

68. Mrs. C.H.A. Armstrong Papers, Wrong to sister, 18 Jun. 33. See on the US role, Robert Dallek, *Franklin D. Roosevelt and American Foreign Policy 1932-1945* (New York, 1979), pp. 23ff.

69. Mrs. Robertson Papers, NAR to father, 8 Jul. 33.

70. Wilson, pp. 376-77.

71. EAR, vol. 1650, file 149, vol. 1, sec. 2.

72. *Ibid.*; *DCER* V, 566-67; Wilson, p. 383.

73. *Ibid.*, pp. 384ff.; *DCER* V, 568-70. See Hume Wrong's view in EAR, vol.

1652, file 149, part VII, Wrong to Robertson, 13 Aug. 34 and PAC, Hume Wrong Papers, vol. 1, file 2, Memo, "What has the Good Neighbour Policy Accomplished in the Case of Canada?," 6 Jul. 35.

74. PAC, Civil Service Commission, Historical Personnel Records, vol. 839, NAR file, has material on NAR's request. It was approved because "to be chosen as Visiting Lecturer would be looked upon more as an honour" than "taking a position outside the Service." Memo to Secretary, 22 Jan. 34. There was a delay that upset some Harvard planning. See Harvard University Archives, UAV 434.10.5, file "A-Appointments," W.Y. Elliott to G.G. Wilson, 7 Jul. 33. *The Harvard Catalogue 1933-4*, pp. 60 and 942, lists NAR as "Under-Secretary, Department of External Affairs of Canada."

75. Mrs. Robertson Papers, NAR to mother, Thursday [Fall, 1933].

76. *Ibid. The Times*, 18 Jul. 68, suggested NAR was promised a full professorship within five years at Harvard, but there is no evidence of this.

77. Mrs. Robertson interview, 26 Feb. 78; *The Times*, 18 Jul. 68.

78. EAR, vol. 793, file 454, Skelton to Herridge, 2 Feb. 34. One officer less hurt—the total strength of officers in Ottawa and abroad in 1935 was still only twenty-one. Veatch, p. 23.

79. Mrs. Robertson Papers, NAR to mother, Thursday [Fall, 1933].

80. *Official Register of Harvard University*, XXX (27 Jun. 33), *Division of History, Government and Economics*.

81. Mrs. Robertson Papers, NAR to mother, Thursday [Fall, 1933].

82. *Ibid.*, 11 Apr. 34.

83. Mrs. Barbara Robertson Morton interview, 16 Nov. 78.

84. EAR, vol. 835, file 52, Joint Memorandum, 17 Jul. 34; *ibid.*, Treasury Board minute, P.C. 19/1852, 16 Aug. 34 and Revision of Classification, 27 Aug. 34; Historical Personnel Records, vol. 839, NAR file, Memo to Secretary, 18 Aug. 34. This cumbersome procedure was necessary to circumvent the freeze.

85. EAR, vol. 788, file 408, Memo, External Affairs Staff, 9 Aug. 34.

86. Robertson Papers, vol. 6, file 34, NAR to D'Arcy McGreer, 14 Sep. 36.

87. Historical Personnel Records, vol. 839, NAR file, Salary Service Record, and Skelton to Secretary, 7 Dec. 35; EAR, vol. 786, file 405, Memo, External Affairs Staff Revised, n.d. and *ibid.*, vol. 835, file 53, Secretary, C.S.C. to King, 27 Dec. 35 and *ibid.*, vol. 842, file S-2-E, "Salary Rates," 1 Nov. 36; Mrs. Robertson Papers, NAR to Vancouver, fragment, n.d. [Feb. 36].

88. EAR, vol. 786, file 405, "Division of Duties . . . ," n.d. But see Story, pp. 309-10, which suggests NAR did work on the sanctions crisis of late

1935, and R. Bothwell and J. English, "'Dirty Work at the Cross-roads'...", *Historical Papers 1972*, 277. Certainly NAR believed in collective security and was dismayed by the government's weak response to the crisis. DEA, J.W. Pickersgill interview, 4 Dec. 77.

89. Generally on trade with the US, see EAR, vol. 1658, file 303-A; Trade and Commerce Records, vol. 161-2, file 26699; Bennett Papers, Mf. M-1027, ff.187136ff.; Finlayson Papers, draft memoirs, Chapter VII.

90. See Herbert Feis, "A Year of the Canadian Trade Agreement," *Foreign Affairs*, XV (July 1937), 619ff.; C. Southworth and W.W. Buchanan, *Changes in Trade Restrictions Between Canada and the United States* (Canadian-American Committee, 1960), *passim*; W.B. Kelly, Jr., ed., *Studies in United States Commercial Policy* (Chapel Hill, 1963), pp. 6ff., 63ff.

91. *Foreign Relations of the United States 1933* [*FRUS*], Vol. I (Washington, 1949), 502-3; Bickersteth Papers, "Some Observations on the Present and Political Situation in Canada," 16 Apr. 33.

92. *FRUS 1934*, I, 845. Additional material is in W.D. Herridge Papers (Toronto), file C30. There are indications in Harvard University, William Phillips Papers, Diary, 11 Dec. 33, f.84, that Canada did not seize every opportunity to press matters. But cf. US National Archives, Department of State Records, 611.4231/883, Memorandum of Conversation, 7 Aug. 34.

93. EAR, vol. 811, file 622, Herridge to Skelton, 22 Jan., 23 Feb. 35. Details on US preparations are in US National Archives, Commerce Department Records, Box 156, "Canada Country Committee file," in Box 157, "Basic Data...," in Box 167, "Canada Minutes" and "Schedule 2 Canada" and in two envelopes labelled "Canada." There is a memo detailing the steps the US had to follow in preparing for negotiations, in Herridge Papers, file C30, Minute, 31 Jan. 35.

94. Commerce Department Records, Box 167, Canada envelope #2, Memo, "Most Favored Nation Treatment," n.d.

95. Wilgress, p. 101; *DCER* V, 193.

96. State Department Records, 611.4231/1234, Despatch, 4 Sep. 35; *FRUS 1935*, II, 21-22.

97. EAR, vol. 1659, file 308B, "Trade Negotiations Between United States and Canada," 25 Oct. 35. At these negotiations, Wilgress had responsibility for concessions Canada sought, McKinnon for concessions the US sought, and Robertson, apparently, responsibility only for keeping the Prime Minister informed. Trade and Commerce Records, vol. 1422, file "Canada-United States Trade Agreements 1935 and 1938," pp. 5-6. H.F. Feaver interview, 8 Jan. 79; Scott Macdonald interview, 8 Sep. 78.

98. State Department Records, 611.4231/1273, Despatch, 17 Oct. 35.

99.   King Diary, 24 Oct. 35; *FRUS 1935*, II, 27-30.

100. King Diary, 31 Oct. 35.

101. *Ibid.*

102. US National Archives, Department of State Records, Hickerson files, box 6, "W" file, Hickerson to Wilgress, 19 Nov. 35.

103. Phillips Diary, 8 Nov. 35, ff.1122-23.

104. King Diary, 8 Nov. 35.

105. EAR, vol. 811, file 622; King Diary, 10-11 Nov. 35; *DCER* V, 195; Phillips Diary, 11 Nov. 35, ff.1131-32.

106. King Diary, 11 Nov. 35; Phillips Diary, 15 Nov. 35, f.1140.

107. S. Drabek, "The Tariff Board and the Development of Tariff Policy," MA thesis, Queen's University, 1965, p. 7. See also F.H. Soward, *et al.*, *Canada in World Affairs, The Prewar Years* (Toronto, 1941), pp. 195ff.

108. Mackintosh and Taylor, 103; McDiarmid, pp. 290ff.; Finlayson Papers, draft memoirs, 180-81; Feis, *passim*. For the results of the treaty, see *ibid.* and Wrong Papers, vol. 3, file 15, Despatch, 28 Nov. 36.

109. Mrs. Robertson Papers, fragment, n.d.; King Diary, 11 Feb. 36.

110. For example, Queen's University, Norman Lambert Papers, Diary, 31 May 36.

111. David Sim interview, 2 May 79.

112. Mrs. Robertson Papers, fragment, n.d.; Professor M.A. Ormsby conversation, 9 Mar. 78.

113. Hon. Paul Martin interview, 16 Jun. 78.

114. Churchill College, Cambridge, P.J. Grigg Papers, PJGG 2/7, Floud to Batterbee, 16 Jan. 36. See also PRO, Foreign Office Records, F.O. 372/3096, Despatch from N.E. Archer, 15 Jan. 35.

115. King Diary, 28 Oct. 37.

116. DEA, Pickersgill interview, 3 Dec. 77; King Diary, 9 Oct. 37.

117. *Ibid.*, 28, 29 Oct. 37.

118. *Ibid.*, 1 Nov. 37; Neatby, p. 263.

119. DEA, Pickersgill interview, 3 Dec. 77. See also NAR's comments in Bishop's University, T.W.L. MacDermot Papers, file 70, Diary, 24-25 Jul. 37.

120. J.W. Pickersgill interview, 13 Oct. 78; Walter Turnbull interview, 16 Oct. 78.

121. Pickersgill interview, 13 Oct. 78.

122. Mrs. Robertson Papers, NAR to mother, n.d. [late Nov. 38].

123. Pickersgill interview, 13 Oct. 78; DEA, Pickersgill interview, 3 Dec. 77. Cf. Pearson Papers, N1, vol. 1, Christie to Pearson, 1 Dec. 37; *ibid.*, vol. 2, NAR to Pearson, 2 Dec. 37; King Diary, 9 Dec. 37 and 18 Jan. 38.

Chapter III

1. PAC, W.L.M. King Papers, Memo, "Export of Oats . . . ," 6 Mar 36, ff. C147712ff.

2. PAC, L.B. Pearson Papers, N1, vol. 2, Skelton to Pearson, 4 Jun. 35; PRO, Board of Trade Records, BT 11/612, Vanier to Batterbee, 19 Jun. 36, and Street to Griffiths, 12 Jun. 36. Wrong wrote to Pearson in July to say, "I expect you are having a busy summer, with our trading team in London (a damned good one it is—much better than our suffering country deserves to have). . . ." Pearson Papers, N1, vol. 3, 15 Jul. 36.

3. Board of Trade Records, B.T. 11/609, "Memo of H.M. Senior Trade Commissioner in Canada . . . ," 22 Jun. 36.

4. King Diary, 24 Jun. 36; King Papers, "Questions for Consideration . . . ," July 1936, ff. C146890ff.

5. For example *DCER* VI, 333ff.

6. One break for NAR was to represent Canada at the 8th session of the Wheat Advisory Committee, 21-23 Jul. 36. See King Papers, NAR to SSEA, 4 Aug. 36, ff.193958ff.

7. Board of Trade Records, B.T. 11/609, Memorandum on the Negotiations . . . , Oct. 36.

8. O.M. Hill, *Canada's Salesmen to the World* (Montreal, 1977), p. 548.

9. *Ibid.*, p. 548.

10. See PAC, N.A. Robertson Papers, vol. 7, file 43, "Negotiation of a New Trade Agreement . . . ," n.d.

11. Board of Trade Records, B.T. 11/609, Memorandum on the Negotiations . . . , Oct. 36; King Papers, "Canada-United Kingdom Trade Agreement," n.d., ff. C147095ff.; documents on Robertson Papers, vol. 6, files 30, 36; W.M. Drummond, "Trade and Trade Agreements Between Canada, the United States and Great Britain," *Journal of Farm Economics*, XX (August 1938), 592; Hill, pp. 549-50.

12. Ian Drummond, *Imperial Economic Policy 1917-39* (London, 1974), pp. 384ff., 414ff.

13. King Diary, 11, 15, 16 Dec. 36; *DCER* VI, 343-47; and documents on PRO, Dominions Office Records, D.O. 114/77, pp. 8ff.

14. King Diary, 11 Jan. 37; *DCER* VI, 354ff.

15. Mrs. N.A. Robertson Papers (Ottawa), NAR to mother, n.d.

16. Hill, p. 549.

17. Robertson Papers, vol. 7, file 43, "Negotiation of a New Trade Agreement with the United States," n.d. Cf. PAC, Hume Wrong Papers, vol. 3, folder 15, Despatch, 5 Feb. 37. As an example of the information reaching Ottawa from the US, see *DCER* VI, 566ff.

18. See, for example, Minister Marler's views in Floyd Chalmers Papers (Toronto), Conversations 1937 file, Memo, 12 Apr. 37.

19. King Diary, 18 Jan. 37. PRO, Cabinet Records, Cab. 23/87, cabinet meeting, 20 Jan. 37, pp. 14-15. See Hull's views of King in Cordell Hull, *The Memoirs of Cordell Hull* (New York, 1948), I, 526ff.

20. Robertson Papers, vol. 6, file 38, "Notes on Aspects of the Canada-United Kingdom Trade Agreement Affecting Canadian-American Relations," 3 Mar. 37; copy in King Papers, ff. C147108ff.

21. See *FRUS 1937*, I, 641ff.

22. R.N. Kottman, *Reciprocity and the North Atlantic Triangle, 1932-1938* (Ithaca, 1968), p. 161; James Eayrs, *In Defence of Canada* (Toronto, 1965), II, 41-43, 223-25.

23. Robertson was responding to a letter from Hull to King, copy in Robertson Papers, vol. 7, file 46, 2 Apr. 37. His memo, "Imperial Preferences and the United States," 15 Apr. 37, is in *ibid*. See Skelton's somewhat variant views in EAR, vol. 745, file 167, "U.K.-U.S. Trade Agreement," 15 Apr. 37, in which he argued that it was impossible for Canada to abandon trade advantages in the UK so that Britain could secure trade advantages in the US.

24. Despite Robertson's best efforts. See Robertson Papers, vol. 6, file 35, "United Kingdom-United States Trade Negotiations," 10 May 37: "Such a declaration of policy as Mr. Hull has in mind, would be in accord with the Canadian Government's general policy." Copy in EAR, vol. 746, file 167, dated 14 May 37. See also Chalmers Papers, Chalmers to Hull, 27 Apr. 37; Kottman, pp. 166ff., 180-81. King also had difficulties with his ministers, notably Dunning. King Diary, 26 May 37. See also G.N. Hillmer, "The Pursuit of Peace: Mackenzie King and the 1937 Imperial Conference," in J. English and J. Stubbs, eds., *Mackenzie King: Widening the Debate* (Toronto, 1978), pp. 149ff.

25. Robertson Papers, vol. 6, file 35, "United Kingdom-United States Trade Negotiations," 10 May 37. NAR also prepared on 30 May 37 a detailed memo on the questions at issue between the US, and UK, with their Canadian implications. *Ibid.*, vol. 6, file 38, "Notes on Anglo-American Trade." Copy in King Papers, ff. C147251ff.

26. There are two sets of minutes for this meeting. King Papers, ff. C147244ff., and a printed version in Robertson Papers, vol. 6, file 34, along with a letter from NAR of 3 Jun. 37, suggesting amendments.

27. The King Papers version is the one used here. See also Dominions Office Records, D.O. 35/880, Sterling to Nowell, 17 Aug. 37. British and Canadian ministers met to talk trade on 7 June, with King in attendance, and that offer was not repeated. Robertson Papers, vol. 6, file 34, Note of a Meeting . . . ; King Diary, 7 Jun. 37. NAR also spoke to the American

Ambassador after the 1 June meeting. *FRUS 1937*, II, 34-35. The US requests of the UK are on D.O. 114/93.

28. King Diary, 11 Jun. 37; Cf. *FRUS 1937*, II, 53-54.

29. King Diary, 11 Jun. 37.

30. Harvard University, Pierrepont Moffat Papers, Diary, 20 Jul. 37.

31. King Diary, 26, 28 Jul. 37, copies in King Papers, ff. C147279ff. and in EAR, vol. 746, file 167. See Kottman, p. 183. Part of the difficulty arose from a stupid comment by the British Ambassador in Washington that "Canada would have to be pilloried" to get a US-UK agreement. See Kottman, pp. 191-92 and King Papers, Memo, 9 Jul. 37, f.147284, and Dominions Office Records, D.O. 35/877, Tel., Lindsay to London, 22 Jul. 37 and London to Ottawa, 31 Jul. 37.

32. Moffat Papers, Diary, 3 Aug. 37, and vol. 12, Memo, 6 Aug. 37, and Moffat to Squire, 14 Aug. 37. See also PRO, Foreign Office Records, F.O. 414/274, p. 13.

33. Moffat Papers, Diary, 14 Sep. 37, and vol. 12, Memo, 9 Aug. 37 and Moffat to Dunn, 7 Aug. 37; US National Archives, State Department Records, John Hickerson Papers, Memo, 6 Aug. 37. See also US National Archives, State Department Records, 611.4231/2025, Memo of interview, 7 Aug. 37. But cf. *FRUS 1937*, II, 73, which indicates that the UK continued to blame Canada. See also Dominions Office Records, D.O. 35/877, Lindsay to London, 6 Aug. 37 and Kottman, pp. 190-91. Cabinet Records, Cab. 24/271, Memo, "The U.S.A. Negotiations," 14 Oct. 37 indicates a claim by the President of the Board of Trade that King was present when the offer was made.

34. Moffat Papers, vol. 12, Memo, 6 Aug. 37; State Department Records, 611.4231/2025, Memo of interview, 7 Aug. 37.

35. *FRUS 1937*, II, 160-61 and King Diary, 6 Aug. 37; State Department Records, 611.4231/2025, encl. with Armour to Hickerson, 8 Aug. 37.

36. *FRUS 1937*, II, 162; Hickerson Papers, Memo, 11 Aug. 37; Moffat Papers, Diary, 11-12 Aug. 37; Kottman, pp. 193-94.

37. Hickerson Papers, Memo, 16 Aug. 37; State Department Records, 611.4231/2025, Hull to Bingham, 20 Aug. 37.

38. Hickerson Papers, Moffat memo, 25 Aug. 37; Moffat Papers, Diary, 25 Aug. 37; Robertson Papers, vol. 6, file 34, "Visit to Washington . . . ," 30 Aug. 37.

39. *Ibid.*, vol. 6, file 39, Memorandum for Dr. Skelton, 26 Aug. 37.

40. *Ibid.*; copy in EAR, vol. 746, file 167. Skelton passed on a report of his talks to Floud. Copy in Dominions Office Records, D.O. 35/880, 1 Sep. 37. The American record is in Hickerson Papers, Memo of Conversations . . . , 1 Sep. 37.

41. *Ibid.* See Skelton's conversation with a UK official in Washington on Dominions Office Records, D.O. 35/877, 30 Aug. 37.

42. Hickerson Papers, Hickerson to Armour, 4 Sep. 37.

43. King Diary, 8 Sep. 37.

44. *FRUS 1937*, II, 66ff.; Dominions Office Records, D.O. 35/880, Tel., Mallet to London, 23 Sep. 37.

45. King Papers, Skelton to King, 1 Oct. 37, ff.208821ff.; Robertson Papers, vol. 7, file 40, NAR to Wrong, 5 Oct. 37.

46. EAR, vol. 746, file 167, Memo, 1 Oct. 37. NAR had told a UK official this in London on 18 June 1937. Dominions Office Records, D.O. 35/877, "Note of Conversation. . . ." For a sample of the pressures on ministers, see Mackenzie Papers, vol. 33, folder B-2.

47. Robertson Papers, vol. 7, file 40, Memo, 5 Oct. 37.

48. EAR, vol. 746, file 167, "Commercial Relations with the United States and the United Kingdom," 4 Oct. 37.

49. King Diary, 8 Oct. 37; Robertson Papers, vol. 7, file 40, Memorandum of Conversations with the Prime Minister, 8, 9 Oct. 37.

50. *Ibid.*

51. King Diary, 14 Oct. 37; State Department Records, 611.4231/2047, Armour to Secretary of State, 14 Oct. 37. See also Hume Wrong's account of his talk with Francis Sayre on the question of simultaneous negotiations. Robertson Papers, vol. 7, file 40, Wrong to NAR, 14 Oct. 37. Cf. Sayre's account in State Department Records, 611.4231/2044, 12 Oct. 37 and Hickerson Papers, Memorandum, 13 Oct. 37.

52. Robertson Papers, vol. 7, file 48, Memo for the Prime Minister, 28 Oct. 37. The fullest account of these talks in Washington is in Dominions Office Records, D.O. 35/881, Notes of conversations 20, 23, 24 Oct. 37 between the Canadians and UK representatives. See also documents on D.O. 35/880 and especially Tel., Mallet to London, 26 Oct. 37; King Diary, 28 Oct. 37; Kottman, pp. 201-02.

53. *FRUS 1937*, II, 166-67; Kottman, pp. 208ff. On the US shift, see Dominions Office Records, D.O. 35/881, Minutes on T766/1/64 and D.O. 114/93, pp. 22ff.

54. King Diary, 17 Nov. 37. For the public response, see Dominions Office Records, D.O. 35/881, Holmes to MacDonald, 30 Nov. 37 and 16 Dec. 37.

55. There is a substantial body of material on these harried negotiations. See *FRUS 1937*, II, 166ff.; King Diary, 17-18 Nov. 37; King Papers, ff. C147359ff; Robertson Papers, vol. 7, file 41, Memoranda for Prime Minister 17-18 Nov. 37; State Department Records, 611.4231/2071, Despatch, 19 Nov. 37. This last source makes clear how skilfully

Robertson conveyed King's requests and how well he camouflaged his own views.

56. For example, *DCER* VI, 377ff.
57. Robertson Papers, vol. 7, file 48, Memo for Prime Minister, 14 Mar. 38, copy in External Affairs Records, vol. 1846, file 822. See Kottman's account of Canadian tensions, pp. 243-44.
58. J. Hickerson interview, 6 Apr. 78; Wilgress, p. 108.
59. PAC, Department of Finance Records, vol. 3610, file ITO-26, Wilgress to Deutsch, 14 Oct. 47 refers to this.
60. Robertson Papers, vol. 9, file 68, NAR to Skelton, 10 May 38.
61. EAR, vol. 746, file 167, Memo to Prime Minister, 12 May 38. At this stage the British and Americans were still far apart. Documents on Board of Trade Records, B.T. 11/934 reveal the gulf.
62. King Papers, NAR to Skelton, 25 May 38, ff. C147328ff.
63. Robertson Papers, vol. 4, file 7, NAR to Skelton, 30 May 38.
64. EAR, vol. 746, file 167, Memo for Prime Minister, 8 Jun. 38.
65. Robertson Papers, vol. 8, file 62, NAR to Skelton, 22 Jun. 38.
66. EAR, vol. 746, file 167, NAR to Skelton, 7 Jul. 38.
67. *Ibid.*, Skelton to NAR, 14 Jul. 38, copy on Robertson Papers, vol. 8, file 62.
68. Pearson Papers, N1, vol. 2, NAR to Pearson, "Tuesday," [Jul. 38?].
69. Minutes of the meetings can be found in Dominions Office Records, D.O. 35/881.
70. Cabinet Records, Cab. 24/278, "Memorandum Summarising the Position of the Negotiations," 16 Jul. 38, ff. 193-94; Foreign Office Records, F.O. 371/21502, "Draft Conclusions of the Cabinet Committee on Trade and Agriculture," 21 Jul. 38.
71. Dominions Office Records, D.O. 35/881, "Discussion ... 2nd August, 1938," in which NAR "said that the Canadian Delegation had just received a most uncompromising 'No' to requests for the Modification of margins guaranteed to Australia on oranges, orange juice and prunes."
72. Robertson Papers, vol. 8, file 63, Skelton to NAR, 8 Aug. 38.
73. *Ibid.*, NAR to Skelton, 13 Aug. 38. See also M.R. Megaw, "Australia and the Anglo-American Trade Agreement, 1938," *Journal of Imperial and Commonwealth History*, III (Jan. 1975), 191ff.
74. In July, the Americans threatened to break off; in August the British refused any more concessions. Cabinet Records, Cab. 23/94, "Conclusions of Cabinet Meeting, 28 Jul. 34, ff. 263ff.; Foreign Office Records, F.O. 371/21503, Minute, 31 Aug. 38 and docs. on F.O. 371/21504 refer.
75. Robertson Papers, vol. 8, file 62, Skelton to NAR, 24 Aug. 38.
76. EAR, vol. 745, file 167, Memo for Prime Minister, 12 Sep. 38.
77. King Diary, 14 Sep. 38; Robertson Papers, vol. 8, file 53, NAR to Skelton,

15 Sep. 38; H.B. Neatby, *William Lyon Mackenzie King*, Vol. III: *The Prism of Unity* (Toronto, 1976), 285. At this point British Foreign Office officials were stressing the "paramount political importance" of the US-UK agreement and urging concessions to get it. For example, Foreign Office Records, F.O. 371/21505, Minute, Balfour to Mounsey, 12 Sep. 38.

78. Robertson Papers, vol. 8, file 53, Skelton to NAR, 14 Sep. 38.

79. King Diary, 26 Sep. 38. Neatby, III, 285-86, notes that each region received some benefits in the agreement.

80. King Diary, 27 Sep. 38.

81. Mrs. Robertson Papers, NAR to mother, 29 Sep. 38. Jetty wrote that Robertson was returning to the US "to see that the treaty is not quite pushed in some dark corner with the international situation taking up too much of everybody's mind. . . . Poor Norman . . . looked so worried—had been listening to Hitler too." *Ibid.*, Jetty Robertson to mother-in-law, n.d. In Washington NAR was asked by Skelton to determine if the US would enforce the Neutrality Act against Canada in the event of war. Robertson Papers, vol. 8, file 62, 27 Sep. 38.

82. *Ibid.*, Robertson to Skelton, 29 Sep. 38; F.O. 371/21506, King to Chamberlain, 30 Sep. 38. The UK position on the trade question is best stated in Foreign Office Records, F.O. 371/21505, U.S. Des. 33, 6 Sep. 38, which makes clear that the British thought they were losing out to the US.

83. F.O. 371/21507, Lindsay to London, 8 Oct. 38 and documents on F.O. 371/21506.

84. Skelton and King had been at a holiday resort in Bermuda. See Robertson Papers, vol. 8, file 62, correspondence of 11, 14, 17 Oct. 38 between Skelton and NAR; DEA, John Starnes Papers, Skelton to NAR, 29 Oct. 38.

85. King Diary, 6 Nov. 38.

86. *Ibid.*, 8 Nov. 38. The question of anthracite was the subject of a special appeal from Hull (*FRUS 1938*, II, 174-77) and a refusal by Lindsay (Foreign Office Records, F.O. 371/21508, 25 Oct. 38).

87. King Diary, 8 Nov. 38. Moffat said this was "the big day" in Mr. Hull's career. Moffat Diary, 17 Nov. 38.

88. Texts of remarks at the signing are in Foreign Office Records, F.O. 414/275, ff.62ff.

89. On the agreement, see Hill, pp. 560-61.

90. EAR, vol. 810, file 611, "Mr. Bennett on the Trade Agreement," 22 Nov. 38.

91. Bank of Canada Archives, Graham Towers Papers, Memorandum 227, "The C.M.A. Memorandum on the Trade Agreements," 6 Feb. 39.

92. For example, see PAC, Department of Trade and Commerce Records, vol. 213 for files of criticisms. There is additional detail on criticism in *ibid.*, vol. 1422, "Canada-U.S. Trade Agreements" file, "The Canada-U.S. Trade Agreement of 1938: Negotiation." And see House of Commons *Debates*, 21, 22, 23 Feb. 39 for Parliamentary comment. On the UK response, see King Papers, Massey to King, 25 Nov. 38, ff.217567ff. On the US response, see Kottman, pp. 269ff.
93. Dominions Office Records, D.O. 35/882, Holmes to MacDonald, 24 Nov. 38.
94. House of Commons *Debates*, 14 Feb. 39, p. 899. Robertson prepared a substantial number of papers for the Prime Minister's use in the debates on the agreement. See, e.g., King Papers, ff. C146257ff., C147630ff., C149317ff., and C146509ff.

Chapter IV

1. Mrs. N.A. Robertson Papers (Ottawa), NAR to mother, 24 Jul. 39; and PAC, N.A. Robertson Papers, vol. 2, Personal & Family, father to NAR, 13 Aug. 39. Among other things, NAR was still in charge of economic matters and was dealing with the whole question of raw material and mineral exports to Britain in the event of war. See PAC, EAR, vol. 824, file 706; *DCER* VI, 256ff.
2. Mrs. Robertson Papers, NAR to father, 19 Aug. 39.
3. *Ibid.*, NAR to mother, n.d.
4. Robertson Papers, vol. 12, file 124, Skelton to Jennings, 21 Mar. 36.
5. On NAR's pro-semitism, see *ibid.*, NAR to Wrong, 18 May 36.
6. Material in *ibid.* and letters to NAR from J.S. Woodsworth, 18, 23 Mar. 36. The main RCMP material is in "Weekly Summary, Report on Revolutionary Organizations and Agitators in Canada," at least one copy of which (No. 667) is in *ibid.* See also *DCER* VI, 87, for Canadian policy on Nazi groups in Canada. There was no translation of German material available in the Department, and NAR occasionally took newspapers home for his wife to translate. Mrs. Robertson interview, 13 Aug. 79.
7. For example, see EAR, vol. 1846, file 794 and vol. 1999, file 953.
8. PAC, Ian Mackenzie Papers, vol. 32, file X-52, "First Interim Report...," n.d. and Heeney to Mackenzie, 6 Feb. 39; *ibid.*, Chief of General Staff to Mackenzie, 3 Sep. 38.
9. See Jonathan Wagner, "The Deutscher Bund Canada, 1934-9," *Canadian Historical Review*, LVIII (June 1977), 197-98.

10. Robertson Papers, vol. 12, file 134, Memo, 24 May 39; EAR, vol. 822, file 701, Skelton to Lapointe, 26 May 39.

11. Robertson Papers, vol. 12, file 134, "What can be done . . . ," n.d.

12. EAR, vol. 767, file 320; Robertson Papers, vol. 12, files 133 and 136; Montreal *Gazette*, 30 Jun. 39.

13. EAR, vol. 1964, file 855E, Memo for Dr. Skelton, 28 Aug. 39 and attached letter, S.T. Wood, RCMP, to Lapointe, 26 Aug. 39. Copy in PAC, W.L.M. King Papers, ff. C155898ff. Skelton's views are on *ibid.*, ff. C155896-7.

14. For example, see Robertson Papers, vol. 12, file 137, Rivett-Carnac to NAR, 24 Jan. 39.

15. J.W. Pickersgill interview, 20 Feb. 79.

16. EAR, vol. 1964, file 855E, "Minutes of Committee Meeting . . . ," 31 Aug. 39; *ibid.*, NAR's memo, "Plans for the Detention . . . ," 2 Sep. 39. Copy in King Papers, ff. C154931ff.

17. EAR, vol. 1964, file 855E, NAR to Lapointe, 3 Sep. 39.

18. As quoted in Canadian Civil Liberties Union, *The War and Civil Liberty* (Montreal, 1939[?]). For criticism of the DOCR, see G.M.A. Grube, "Civil Liberties in War Time," *Canadian Forum*, XX (July 1940), 106-07, and other articles in this magazine.

19. EAR, vol. 824, file 713, Memo for Prime Minister, 1 Nov. 41. On the Jehovah's Witnesses, the victims of the most appalling and indefensible breaches of civil liberties in the war, see M.J. Penton, *Jehovah's Witnesses in Canada* (Toronto, 1976), especially Chapter 7, and King Papers, ff.201329ff.

20. See PAC, Department of Justice Records, vols. 964-65.

21. DEA, George Glazebrook interview, 8 Jul. 77.

22. Robertson Papers, vol. 12, file 141, NAR to Tucker, 16 Oct. 39.

23. *Ibid.*, NAR to Woodsworth, 23 Sep. 39.

24. *Ibid.*, MacNeill to NAR, 7 Dec. 39.

25. *Ibid.*, NAR to Bavin, 13 Dec. 39.

26. King Diary, 16 Nov. 39 and 24 Nov. 39.

27. King Papers, "Subversive Activities," 13 Dec. 39, ff. C155901-2.

28. For example, see NAR's comments on the RCMP in King Diary, 30 May 41.

29. *Ibid.*, 3 Jan. 40. See C.G. Power's reaction in *ibid.*, 4 Jan. 40, and his drafted but unsent letter of resignation in Queen's University, C.G. Power Papers, Power to King, 4 Jan. 40. The best published account of war civil liberties is Ramsay Cook, "Canadian Freedom in Wartime 1939-1945," in W.H. Heick and R. Graham, eds., *His Own Man* (Montreal, 1974), pp. 37ff.

30. Robertson Papers, vol. 12, file 145-1, NAR to MacNeill, 2 Feb. 40.

31. PAC, Department of Finance Records, vol. 4663, file 187-EAC-49, Report of Economic Advisory Committee on Relief Policy, 25 Sep. 40.

32. Robertson Papers, vol. 13, file 148, Skelton to Wood, 27 Dec. 40.

33. *Ibid.*, NAR to Skelton, 9 Dec. 40.

34. King Diary, 30 May 41.

35. See, for example, *The Globe and Mail*, 1 Mar. 40; "Civil Liberties," *Canadian Forum*, XIX (December 1939), 269; Phyllis Clarke, "The Right of Asylum Canadian Style," mss. article.

36. Robertson Papers, vol. 12, file 139, Memo, 14 Oct. 39.

37. *Ibid.*, Blair to Skelton, 6 Mar. 40. On Blair's activities and prejudices, see Irving Abella and H. Troper, " 'The Line Must be Drawn Somewhere': Canada and Jewish Refugees, 1933-9," *Canadian Historical Review*, LX (June 1979), 178ff.

38. Robertson Papers, vol. 12, file 139, NAR to Blair, 6 Mar. 40.

39. *Ibid.*, Skelton to Blair, 27 Mar. 40.

40. Clarke mss.

41. EAR, vol. 824, file 713, Memo for Dr. Skelton, 17 Apr. 40.

42. For pressure, see *Financial Post*, 20 Jul. 40.

43. King Diary, 22 May 40.

44. See on this, *inter alia*, John Kolasky, *The Shattered Illusion* (Toronto, 1979), p. 28; I. Avakumovic, *The Communist Party in Canada* (Toronto, 1975), pp. 142ff.; W. Beeching and P. Clarke, eds., *Yours in the Struggle: Reminiscences of Tim Buck* (Toronto, 1977), pp. 289ff.

45. EAR, vol. 822, file 701, Memo for Prime Minister, 21 Mar. 41.

46. For further examples, see Robertson Papers, vol. 13, file 151 and vol. 12, file 145-II.

47. *Ibid.*, vol. 13, file 164, "Statistics of Internment," 3 Jan. 41.

48. EAR, vol. 824, file 813, Memo for Prime Minister, 1 Nov. 41.

49. King Diary, 6 Dec. 41.

50. Queen's University, John Deutsch Papers, file 845, "Exchange Control," mss. article, n.d., n.a.

51. *Ibid.*, [Sydney Turk] "Foreign Exchange Control Board: Genesis and Exodus," mss. article, [1956]; J. Schull, *The Great Scot ... Donald Gordon* (Montreal, 1979) pp. 34ff.

52. Bank of Canada Archives, Graham Towers Papers, Memorandum no. 285, 12 Sep. 39.

53. Bank of Canada Archives, Foreign Exchange Control Board Records, Minute Book, 16 Sep. 39.

54. *Ibid.*, and *passim.*

55. Louis Rasminsky interviews, 30 Nov. 78, 4 May 79.

56. Robertson Papers, vol. 12, file 135, Gordon to NAR, 28 Aug. 39.

57. EAR, vol. 824, file 705, Memo for Dr. Skelton, 1 Sep. 39; R.B. Bryce interview, 28 Nov. 78.

58. EAR, vol. 824, file 705, Memo, 9 Sep. 39.

59. *Ibid.*

60. King Diary, 12 Sep. 39.

61. Department of Finance Records, vol. 4660, file 187-EAC-1, Heeney to Ralston, 12 Sep. 39.

62. Bryce interview, 13 Feb. 79; Department of Finance Records, vol. 4660, file 187-EAC-1, Memo to Mr. Brockington, 20 Jan. 40.

63. See J.L. Granatstein, *Canada's War: The Politics of the Mackenzie King Government, 1939-45* (Toronto, 1975), Chapter II.

64. Department of Finance Records, vol. 4660, file 187-EAC-1, Memo to Mr. Brockington, 20 Jan. 40, provides a useful summary of subjects handled by the EAC.

65. *Ibid.*, file 187-EAC-3, Minutes, 7 Oct. 39.

66. See on this, C.F. Wilson, *A Century of Canadian Grain* (Saskatoon, 1978), pp. 632ff.; Granatstein, pp. 63-64.

67. Presumably this was the reason that Floyd Chalmers of the *Financial Post* called Robertson on 2 September 1939 to enquire about the replacement of Ian Mackenzie as Minister of National Defence. See Floyd Chalmers Papers (Toronto), Memo on Phone Conversation with N.R. . . .

68. Department of Finance Records, vol. 4660, file 187-EAC-3, Minutes, 7, 13 Oct. 39.

69. *Ibid.*, file 187-EAC-1, Memo, "Unfinished Business E.A.C.," n.d.

70. *DCER* VIII, 1206-08.

71. Department of Finance Records, vol. 3551, file B-04a, Memo for Dr. Skelton, 14 Jun. 40; United States National Archives, Department of State Records, Hickerson Files, Memo, 16 Jul. 40. [Cited hereafter as Hickerson Papers.]

72. Harvard University, Pierrepont Moffat Papers, Memo of Conversation, 18 Sep. 40.

73. Department of Finance Records, vol. 4660, file 187-EAC-4, Report of the EAC, 15 Aug. 40.

74. Moffat Papers, Memo of Conversation, 12 Oct. 40.

75. *Ibid.*, 5 Nov. 40.

76. Hickerson Papers, Memo, 6 Nov. 40.

77. Moffat Papers, Memo of Conversation, 8 Nov. 40.

78. Hickerson Papers, Memo of Conversation, 8 Nov. 40.

79. Moffat Papers, Memo, 2 Dec. 40.

80. US National Archives, Department of State Records, 842.50/154 1/2, Memo, "Visit of Norman Robertson to Washington," 18 Nov. 40.

81. Moffat Papers, Memorandum, 2 Dec. 40; PAC, Privy Council Office Records, Cabinet War Committee Records, Minutes, 27 Nov. 40.
82. *Ibid.*
83. House of Commons *Debates*, 2 Dec. 40, p. 556. See also Warren James, *Wartime Economic Cooperation* (Toronto, 1949), pp. 18, 191-92.
84. *DCER* VIII, 305.
85. For NAR and exports to Japan, see DEA, file 592-40, *passim.*
86. On nickel to Japan, see *DCER* VIII, 1202ff., 1235ff.
87. *Ibid.*, 1301-03.
88. *Ibid.*, 1256-57.
89. *Ibid.*, 1306-08.
90. *Ibid.*, 1297-98.
91. *Ibid.*, 1318-19.
92. Moffat Papers, Memo of Conversation, 4 Oct. 40. Copper exports were blocked on 8 Oct. 40 and led to Japanese protests. See *ibid.*, 22 Oct. 40; *DCER* VIII, 1319-20, 1327-28.
93. Undated clipping in King Papers, f. C270487.
94. House of Commons *Debates*, 5 Dec. 40, in King Papers, f. C270488.
95. Ottawa *Citizen*, 5 Dec. 40 in King Papers, f. C270489.
96. House of Commons *Debates*, 6 Dec. 40, in King Papers, ff. C270490-1.
97. Munroe Scott, *McClure: The China Years* (Toronto, 1977), pp. 284ff.
98. King Papers, Memo to Prime Minister, 7 Dec. 40, ff. C270495-6.
99. Text in *ibid.*, f. C270493. Printed in *Toronto Star*, 7 Dec. 40.
100. Author's correspondence with McClure's biographer, Munroe Scott, 4, 9 Oct. 79.
101. Grant Dexter, "Oscar Douglas Skelton," *Queen's Quarterly*, XLVIII, (Spring 1941), 3.
102. King Diary, 28 Jan. 41.
103. Mrs. C.H.A. Armstrong Papers (Toronto), Wrong to Marga Wrong, 2 Feb. 41.
104. State Department Records, 842.00 PR/195, Simmons to Secretary of State, 5 Feb. 41.
105. Dexter, 1. Other obituaries: G.S. Graham, "Skelton of Queen's," *The Queen's Review* (February 1941); "The Finest Gentleman," *Winnipeg Free Press*, [30 Jan. 41?]; G.S. Graham, "Oscar Douglas Skelton," *Canadian Historical Review*, XXII (June 1941), 232ff.; W.A.M[ackintosh]., "O.D. Skelton," *Canadian Journal of Economics and Political Science*, VII (May 1941), 270ff.; *The Times* [of London], 30 Jan. 41.
106. On this, see Hickerson Papers, Moffat to Hickerson, 10 Feb. 41; PRO, Foreign Office Records, F.O. 371/29115, Hankinson to Stephenson, 21 Feb. 41 and atts.
107. King Diary, 22, 23 Apr. 37.

108. See on this, documents on PAC, Civil Service Commission, Historical Personnel Records, vol. 359, Wrong file, correspondence, Apr.-Oct. 40.

109. King Diary, 26 Sep. 42.

110. Hickerson Papers, [Moffat] Memo of Conversation, 13 Feb. 41. When Skelton was ill in 1937, Christie was clearly his replacement, at least in King's mind. See King Diary for Fall 1937, *passim*.

111. Pickersgill interview, 13 Oct. 78.

112. Scott Macdonald interview, 8 Sep. 78.

113. *Ibid.*; Max Wershof interview, 5 Apr. 79.

114. Keenleyside interview, 4 May 78. In the car, King asked Keenleyside if he thought Read or Robertson should be successor. Keenleyside did not answer directly, but did say there were others worthy of consideration.

115. Cabinet War Committee Minutes, 28 Jan. 41; PC 703, 29 Jan. 41.

116. King Diary, 28 Jan. 41.

117. DEA, file 1596-40, Memo, 29 Jan. 41; Escott Reid interview, 14 Oct. 78. The next day King discussed the NAR appointment in the War Committee: "Howe thinks I am right in appointing Robertson as Acting. I pointed out other men in the diplomatic service who would be available for the post. Hume Wrong among the number, but that he would be impossible because of his inability to work with men." King Diary, 29 Jan. 41.

118. Wershof interview.

119. Robertson Papers, vol. 2, Personal and Family file, NAR to parents, Thursday [30 Jan. 41]. There are a number of letters of congratulation in DEA, John Starnes Papers.

120. Pearson Papers, N1, vol. 2, NAR to Pearson, 30 Jan. 41.

121. *Ibid.*

122. Mrs. Armstrong Papers, Wrong to Marga, 2 Feb. 41.

123. PAC, J.W. Dafoe Papers, Dexter to Dafoe, 11 Mar. 41; copy in Queen's University, Grant Dexter Papers.

124. Mrs. Wrong apparently believed that NAR was a sneak who had insinuated himself into King's graces. But once she came to know NAR, she was captivated and indicated rather wryly how wrong she had been. Mrs. June Wrong Rogers interview, 13 Apr. 78.

125. Keenleyside interview, 4 May 78. Dr. Keenleyside read his diary entry on the subject to me.

126. Confidential interviews.

127. Pearson Papers, N8, Diary, 27 Feb. 41.

128. Cited in *ibid.*, 29 Mar. 41.

129. *Ibid.*

130. *Ibid.*, 2 Apr. 41.

131. *Ibid.*

132. *Ibid.*, 3 Apr. 41. Cf. L.B. Pearson, *Mike: The Memoirs of the Right Honourable L.B. Pearson* ... (Toronto, 1972), I, 192ff.
133. Pearson Papers, N1, Pearson to Massey, 27 May 41. Cf. Peter Stursberg, *Lester Pearson and the American Dilemma* (Toronto, 1980), p. 41.
134. King Diary, 19 May 41.
135. J.R. Beal, *The Pearson Phenomenon* (Toronto, 1964), pp. 71-72; B. Thordarson, *Lester Pearson* (Toronto, 1974), p. 37. See the account of Pearson's speech in the *Financial Post*, 5 Jul. 41.
136. King Diary, 5 Apr. 41.
137. *Ibid.*, 24 Jun. 41.
138. Mrs. Robertson interview, 27 Nov. 78. Robertson's salary had been $5,760 when he was made Counsellor; it had risen to $6,000 on 1 April 1941. Historical Personnel Records, vol. 839, Robertson file, "Salary Service Record." See also P.C. 4645, 24 Jun. 41.
139. See Robertson Papers, vol. 1, Congratulations file, and letters on Starnes Papers.
140. *The Globe and Mail*, 26 Jun. 41; Winnipeg *Tribune*, 28 Jul. 41; *Financial Post*, 5 Jul. 41. See also clippings on Starnes Papers.
141. *Ibid.*, Isabel Skelton to NAR, 25 Jun. 41.
142. King Papers, King to NAR, 14 Jul. 41, f.265849.
143. Rhodes House, Oxford, NAR file, Warden to NAR, 25 Jun. 41.

Chapter V

1. PAC, Escott Reid Papers, vol. 5, file 11, NAR to Reid, 30 Dec. 48.
2. Harvard University, Pierrepont Moffat Papers, Memo, 19 Dec. 41.
3. Reid Papers, vol. 5, file 11, NAR to Reid, 30 Dec. 48; DEA, Escott Reid interview, 21 Jul. 77.
4. *Ibid.*
5. PAC, Watson Sellar Papers, Diary, 17 Nov. 43.
6. DEA, Malcolm MacDonald interview, 15 May 78.
7. MacDonald interview, 7 Jun. 78.
8. David Sim interview, 2 May 79; H.F. Feaver interview, 8 Jan. 79. But cf. DEA, George Ignatieff interview, 7 Dec. 77.
9. DEA, Escott Reid interview, 21 Jul. 77.
10. Royal Archives, Windsor, Geo. V, CC 53/1063, King to Athlone, 31 Aug. 42.
11. PAC, N.A. Robertson Papers, vol. 2, Personal Correspondence, Wrong to NAR, 2 Sep. 42.
12. *Ibid.*, NAR to Brogan, 21 Jul. 41.

13. PAC, W.L.M. King Papers, Memo for Prime Minister, 29 May 44, ff. C162873-4.

14. Interview, 5 Apr. 79.

15. J.M.S. Careless interview, 4 Oct. 78.

16. See, for example, *DCER* XII, 1-3.

17. Moffat Papers, Memos, 14 Feb., 5 Mar., 15 Apr. 41.

18. See J.L. Granatstein, *Canada's War: The Politics of the Mackenzie King Government, 1939-45* (Toronto, 1975), Chapter IV.

19. PAC, J.W. Dafoe Papers, Memo by Dexter, 8 Apr. 41.

20. King Papers, Memo for Prime Minister, 12 Mar. 41, ff. C250323ff.

21. The Joint Economic Committees will not be treated here. They were largely handled by H.L. Keenleyside in the Department and ultimately did not work out well. See Granatstein, *Canada's War*, pp. 146-47. For some NAR views, see PAC, Department of Finance Records, vol. 3977, file E-3-2-1, Memo of Conversation with Robertson, 16 Jan. 42; Moffat Papers, Memo, 19 Jan. 42, 6 Mar. 42.

22. King Papers, Memo for Prime Minister, 7 Apr. 41, ff. C287996ff.; Granatstein, *Canada's War*, Chapter IV.

23. King Papers, Memo for Prime Minister, 14 Aug. 41, f. C240194.

24. Moffat Papers, Memo, 16 Sep. 41.

25. *Ibid.*, 25 Sep. 41.

26. King Papers, Memo for Prime Minister, 3 Oct. 41, ff. C250326-7.

27. United States National Archives, Department of State Records, Hickerson Papers, Moffat memo, 8 Oct. 41.

28. *Ibid.*, Hickerson to Moffat, 15 Oct. 41.

29. *Ibid.*, Moffat memo, 27 Oct. 41. The UK War Cabinet was told that the Dominions had been kept continuously informed. PRO, Prime Minister's Office Records, Prem. 4/17/5, Memo, 21 Jan. 42.

30. Much to the concern of the UK. See Cranborne's memo to Churchill, 5 Mar. 41 on *ibid.*, Prem. 4/43/2.

31. One issue not cited in NAR's memo was the Canadian difficulty in getting a military mission accepted by Washington. This struggle began in spring 1941 and ran into heavy weather from the US and UK that lasted until mid-1942. See *Foreign Relations of the United States 1942* [*FRUS*], III, 129 ff; Moffat Papers, memos, 25 Sep., 22 Oct. 41; Department of State Records, 842.20/203, Memo and letters, pp. 1090ff; King Papers, Memos for Prime Minister, 8 Dec. 41, ff. C240069ff. etc.; C.P. Stacey, *Arms, Men and Governments* (Ottawa, 1970), pp. 354ff.; S. Dziuban, *Military Relations between the United States and Canada, 1939-45* (Washington, 1959), pp. 73ff.

32. PAC, Privy Council Office Records, vol. 8, file U-12-8, Memo for Prime Minister, 30 Dec. 41; copy on King Papers, ff. C230956ff.

33. Moffat Papers, Memo, 2 Jan. 42; Prime Minister's Office Records, Prem. 4/17/5, Memo on W.P. (42) 32, 21 Jan. 42.
34. See King Papers, Memo for Prime Minister, 14 Feb. 62, ff. C230962-4.
35. See on this, R.N. Gardner, *Sterling-Dollar Diplomacy* (New York, 1969), pp. 54ff.
36. University of Toronto Library, George Brown Papers, box 23, Personal letters 2, Riddell to Brown, 20 Feb. 43.
37. Moffat Papers, Memo, 6 Aug. 41.
38. Moffat memo on DEA, file 463-40c, 13 Feb. 42.
39. See James Eayrs, *In Defence of Canada* (Toronto, 1972), III, 349. On Canol, see R.J. Diubaldo, "The Canol Project in Canadian-American Relations," *Historical Papers 1977*, 179ff., and DEA, file 4349-40c, Memo, Keenleyside, to NAR, 6 Oct. 42.
40. *Ibid.*, file 52-B(s), Memo for Prime Minister, 30 Mar. 43; copy on King Papers, f. C213745; Privy Council Office Records, Cabinet War Committee Minutes, 31 Mar. 43; King Papers, MacDonald to King, 6 Apr. 43, ff. C213750ff. For King's and External Affairs' views on the US in 1942 and after, see J.L. Granatstein, "Getting on with the Americans . . . ," *Canadian Review of American Studies*, V (Spring 1974), 13ff. See also PAC, L.B. Pearson Papers, N8, Diary, 20-22 Feb. 43; and docs. on DEA, file 4349-40C.
41. *Ibid.*, file 5221-40c, letter to Brigadier Foster, 20 May 43.
42. *Ibid.*, file 463-N-7-40c "Minutes of a Meeting . . . ," 2 Dec. 43.
43. *Ibid.*, Minutes, 31 Jan. 44.
44. Cabinet War Committee Minutes, 17 Feb. 44. See also P.S. Barry, "The Prolific Pipeline . . . ," *Dalhousie Review*, LVII (Summer 1977), 205ff.
45. Cabinet War Committee Minutes, 22 Feb. 44. See also DEA, file 463-N-7-40c, Minutes, 6-7 Mar. 44.
46. See Dziuban, pp. 331ff.
47. Cabinet War Committee Minutes, 8, 10 Mar. 44; documents on DEA, file 5207-40; Dziuban, pp. 320ff.
48. Documents on King Papers, ff. 300422ff.
49. PAC, Maurice Pope Diary, vol. 1, 23 Aug. 43.
50. King Diary, 27 Jan. 44. See also King Papers, NAR to Pearson, 24 Oct. 44, ff. 319624-5 and reply in Pearson Papers, N1, vol. 2, Pearson to NAR, 30 Oct. 44.
51. DEA, file 6000-A-40c, Memo for Prime Minister, 26 Apr. 43.
52. Department of Finance Records, vol. 3592, file L-11-E, Report, 16 Jul. 43; *FRUS 1943*, I, 1100ff.; King Papers, "Post-war International Economic Policy," ff. C222248ff.
53. *FRUS 1943*, I, 1104-5.

54. King Papers, Memo for Prime Minister, 21 Dec. 43, ff. C230358-9. On the UK-US talks that preceded this, see Gardner, Chapter VI.

55. PAC, EAR, vol. 811, file 619, "Commercial Policy," 1st meeting, 4 Jan. 44.

56. *Ibid.*, 4th meeting, 6 Jan. 44.

57. *Ibid.*, 5th meeting.

58. Copy on *ibid*. Printed and final version on DEA, file 6000-40c. A copy went to the British.Prime Minister's Office Records, Prem. 4/18/2. There were also simultaneous talks on cartels and commodities. See Department of Finance Records, vol. 3592, file L-11-D and vol. 3591, file L-11-b. See also State Department Records, 611.4231/3075 1/2, Hickerson note.

59. See King Papers, "Post-War International Economic Policy," n.d., ff. C222252-3.

60. Bank of Canada Archives, Bank of Canada Records, Postwar Commercial Policy file, NAR to Towers, 10 Mar. 44.

61. DEA, file 6000-A-40c, NAR to Pearson, 7 Oct. 44.

62. Department of State Records, 842.00/2-2145, Parsons to Clark, 21 Feb. 45; Joe Garner, *The Commonwealth Office* (London, 1978), Chapter VII; Pearson Papers, N8, Diary 10-11 Mar. 45.

63. *FRUS 1945*, VI, 61ff.; Department of State Records, 842.00/7-2645, Memo, 26 Jul. 45.

64. *Ibid.*, 611.4231/7-1545, Report on Ottawa Trip, 18 Jul. 45; Queen's University, W.A. Mackintosh Papers, file 192, Informal Discussions, 14-15 Jul. 45.

65. *Ibid.*, "Trade and Employment Proposals," n.d.

66. King Papers, Memo for Prime Minister, 24 Apr. 46, f. C230794.

67. *Ibid.*

68. Moffat Papers, Memo, 2 Nov. 42.

69. King Papers, Memo for Prime Minister, 27 Jul. 41, ff. C248276-7.

70. Robert Speaight, *Vanier* (Toronto 1970), pp. 230-31.

71. Moffat Papers, Memo, 8 Sep. 41; King Diary, 11 Aug. 41.

72. For the British view of this, see PRO, Foreign Office Records, F.O. 371/36607, "British Commonwealth Relationship," 15 Mar. 43.

73. *Ibid.*, F.O. 371/36603, "The Post-war Position of the British Commonwealth of Nations," 23 Feb. 43.

74. See documents on *ibid.*, F.O. 371/36607. One UK paper found its way to Canada and was the subject of much comment. See DEA, file 62-A(s).

75. King Papers, Memo for Prime Minister, 14 Oct. 43, ff. C159845-6.

76. DEA, file 6311-40c, Tarr memo, 30 Dec. 43. See also James Eayrs, "Confrontation of the Prophets," *Round Table* (January 1971).

77. Speech quoted in J.L. Granatstein, ed., *Canadian Foreign Policy Since 1945* (Toronto, 1969), pp. 13-14.

78. King Diary, 25 Jan. 44.

79. House of Commons *Debates*, 31 Jan. 42, pp. 41-42. The speech was drafted by Wrong. King Papers, ff. C160273ff.

80. Robertson Papers, vol. 2, Personal Correspondence, Wrong to NAR, 3 May 44, att. *Ottawa Journal*, 1 May 44.

81. John Holmes at NAR Round Table, 18 Feb. 78. See his *The Shaping of Peace: Canada and the Search for World Order 1943-57*, Vol. I (Toronto, 1979), pp. 148ff. On the divisions between Churchill and the Foreign Office, see especially P.A. Reynolds and E.J. Hughes, *The Historian as Diplomat: Charles Kingley Webster and the United Nations 1939-46* (London, 1976), pp. 20, 33, and *passim*.

82. King Papers, Memo for Prime Minister, 15 May 44, f. C223047.

83. King Diary, 15 May 44.

84. Prime Minister's Office Records, Prem. 4/42/5, P.M.M. (44), 12th Mtg., 11 May 44. See also on the meeting generally, King Papers, J4, vols. 322-3 and DEA, file 7-V(s).

85. PAC, Violet Markham Carruthers Papers, vol. 1, King to Carruthers, 13 Apr. 50.

86. PRO, Treasury Records, T160/1376, Waley to Eady, 9 May 44.

87. King Papers, Memo for Prime Minister, 31 Dec. 43, ff. C250975-6.

88. King Diary, 4 Jan. 44; J.L. Granatstein, "Settling the Accounts: Anglo-Canadian War Finance, 1943-5," *Queen's Quarterly*, LXXXII (Summer 1976), 238ff.

89. King Diary, 16 May 44.

90. PRO, Cabinet Records, Cab. 110/45, Tel., D.O. to High Commissioner, Ottawa, 20 May 44; Treasury Records, T160/1376, Eady to Clutter-buck, 19 May 44; Cabinet War Committee Minutes, 14 Jun. 44.

91. Treasury Records, T160/1376, Keynes to Eady, 19 May 44.

92. Cabinet Records, Cab. 110/45, Tel., British Del. to F.O., 3 Jul. 44.

93. DEA, file 154(s), "Notes on a Meeting . . . ," 1 Aug. 44. See also D. Moggridge, ed., *The Collected Writings of John Maynard Keynes*, Vol. XXIV: *Activities 1944-1946. . . .* (London, 1979), *passim* for Canada-UK financial negotiations to 1946.

94. Cabinet Records, Cab. 65/43, W.M. (44)113, 31 Aug. 44; Department of Finance Records, vol. 415, documents on files U-3-8-4 and U-3-11.

95. *Ibid.*, file 101-106-2E, "Memo of Comment on U.K. Proposals . . . ," 6 Aug. 44.

96. Cabinet Records, Cab. 110/45, Tel., Ottawa to D.O., 3 Jul. 44.

97. King Diary, 14 Aug. 44; Department of External Affairs, file 154(s), NAR to Massey, 30 Aug. 44.

98. Granatstein, "Settling the Accounts," 245ff.

99. Towers's paper on DEA, file 154(s); Minutes of meeting on Department of Finance Records, vol. 3437, Trade Policy file.

100. *Ibid.*; see also D.V. Le Pan, *Bright Glass of Memory* (Toronto, 1979), pp. 63ff.; and documents on Bank of Canada Records, Postwar Commercial Policy file.

101. King Diary, 13 Feb. 45.

102. Le Pan, p. 63; tels. on DEA, file 154(s), copies on PRO, Board of Trade Records, B.T. 11/2730.

103. *Ibid.*, Tel., High Commission to D.O., 7 Mar. 45; DEA, file 154(s), Tel. Churchill to King, 4 Mar. 45, and SSDA to SSEA, 21 Mar. 45.

104. Pearson Papers, N8, Diary, 10-11 Mar. 45; Board of Trade Records, B.T. 11/2730, Tel. Washington to F.O., 14 Mar. 45.

105. *Ibid.*, Tel., High Commission to D.O., 30 Mar. 45; Le Pan, p. 74; DEA, file 154(s), NAR to Wrong, 12 Apr. 45.

106. R. Bothwell and J. English, "Canadian Trade Policy in the Age of American Dominance and British Decline," *Canadian Review of American Studies*, VIII (Spring 1977), 58; DEA, file 154(s), Mackintosh to Pierce, 28 Jun. 45 and Mackintosh to NAR, 16 Jul. 45; Bank of Canada Records, Postwar Commercial Policy file, Mackintosh to Towers, 28 Jun. 45.

107. Bothwell and English, 59. See Dominions Office Records, D.O. 35/1220, "Financial Relations with Canada," 30 Aug. 46 and other documents on this file; and DEA, file 6864-40c, M.W. Mackenzie to NAR, 6 Dec. 45 and att.

108. Dominions Office Records, D.O. 35/1219, "Note on Forthcoming ... Negotiations," 15 Dec. 45.

109. Documents on DEA, file 154(s); King Diary, 21-22 Feb. 46.

110. DEA, file 154(s), Pierce to NAR, 7 Feb. 46; State Department Records, 842.00/3-746, Clark to Parsons, 7 Mar. 46; Dominions Office Records, D.O. 35/1220, S. Holmes to Addison, 6 Apr. 46; *DCER* XII, 1387ff.

111. S.M. Rosen, *The Combined Boards of the Second World War* (New York, 1951) refers.

112. PAC, Loring Christie Papers, vol. 26, file 107, "Note on Munich," 1 Nov. 38, ff. 24095-6. See also A.J. Miller, "The Functional Principle in Canada's External Relations," *International Journal*, XXXV (Spring 1980), 313.

113. King Papers, Memo for Prime Minister, 28 Jan. 42, ff. C243537ff.

114. DEA, file 3265-A-40c, Wrong to NAR, 20 Jan. 42. See also Holmes, Chapter 2, for a discussion of functionalism.

115. DEA, file 2295-G-40, Memo, 18 Jan. 43, att. to Memo for Prime Minister, 18 Jan. 43.

116. House of Commons *Debates*, 9 Jul. 43, p. 4558. See also Bodleian Library,

Oxford, Lionel Curtis Papers, Ms Curtis/26, Brooke Claxton to Curtis, 14 Jun. 43.

117. Moffat Papers, Memo, 15 Jun. 42.
118. Dominions Office Records, D.O. 114/112, pp. 8-9; DEA, file 3265-D-40c, draft memo, 14 Jul. 42.
119. Treasury Records, T188/252, unsigned memo, 27 Jul. 42.
120. Cabinet War Committee Minutes, 29 Jul. 42 and Moffat memo on DEA, file, 3265-D-40c, 31 Jul. 42.
121. Treasury Records, T188/252, Memo, Leith-Ross to MacDonald, 20 Jul. 42 and MacDonald to "Leithers," 1 Aug. 52; Foreign Office Records, F.O. 371/31502, minutes and tels.
122. DEA, file 3265-C-40c, Minutes, 16 Sep. 42; Foreign Office Records, F.O. 371/31543, Minutes and tels. for UK preparations.
123. DEA, file 3265-D-40c, "Combined Food Board," 16 Mar. 43. See Cabinet Records, Cab. 109/11, tels. 17, 19 Mar. 43 on Brand's views.
124. Copy on Dominions Office Records, D.O. 35/1221, att. to MacDonald to Attlee, 14 Apr. 43.
125. See memos on *ibid.*
126. Granatstein, *Canada's War*, p. 300; Cabinet Records, Cab. 115/548, Tel., 6 Sep. 43.
127. Documents on Dominions Office Records, D.O. 35/1212; Rosen, pp. 232-33; Stacey, pp. 176-77.
128. DEA, file 2295-G-40c, SSEA to Massey, 6 Jun. 42.
129. King Diary, 30 Jul. 42.
130. Documents on Dominions Office Records, D.O. 35/1014.
131. DEA, file 2295-G-40, Memo for Prime Minister, 4 Jan. 43.
132. *Ibid.*, 18 Jan. 43. The Cabinet War Committee agreed on 21 Jan. 43.
133. DEA, file 2295-G-40, Memo for Prime Minister, 3 Feb. 43.
134. *Ibid.*; *FRUS 1943*, I, 866-67.
135. DEA, file 2295-G-40, Memo, 26 Feb. 43.
136. Cabinet War Committee Minutes, 3 Mar. 43.
137. King Papers, Tel., NAR to Pearson, 4 Mar. 43, f. 301282. See Holmes's account, pp. 36ff.
138. DEA, file 22-D(s), Memo for Prime Minister, 17 Mar. 43. Dean Acheson briefed the British officials on the way to shoot down Canada. US National Archives, State Department Records, Dean Acheson Papers, box 5, file 2, "Canadian Participation . . . Relief and Rehabilitation Administration," 26 Mar. 43. For British views, see Foreign Office Records, F.O. 371/36607, Holmes to Hall, 18 Mar. 43.
139. Cabinet War Committee Minutes, 31 Mar. 43.
140. DEA, file 2295-G-40, Memo for Prime Minister, 2 Apr. 43. Note the amusing switch in Massey's letters to NAR. Massey College, Massey

Papers, unboxed folder, Massey to NAR, 17 Mar., 10 Apr. 43; also NAR to Massey, 10 Apr. 43 on EAR, vol. 2120, file AR 1031/1. See also Pearson Papers, N8, Diary, 26 Mar.-1 Apr. 43.

141. King Diary, 7 Apr. 43.
142. On the working out of UNRRA and Canada's role, see George Woodbridge, *U.N.R.R.A: The History of. . . .* 3 vols. (New York, 1950).
143. DEA, documents on file 22-D(s). See Holmes, Chapter VII, for a good and full account.
144. DEA, file 7-AB(s), Tels., SSDA to SSEA, 19 Jun. 43.
145. *Ibid.*, file 7-AD(s), Minutes, 22 Jul. 43.
146. Don Munton and Don Page, "Planning in the East Block: the Post-Hostilities Problems Committees in Canada, 1943-5," *International Journal*, XXXII (Autumn 1977), 687ff.
147. If this was NAR's ploy, as late as February 1945 Canada was still pressing for a share in the control of defeated Germany and bargaining toughly to get it. See Dominions Office Records, D.O. 114/104, p. 94 and J.F. Hilliker, "No Bread at the Peace Table: Canada and the European Settlement, 1943-7," *Canadian Historical Review*, LXI (March 1980), 69ff.
148. Cabinet War Committee Minutes, 28 Jul. 43 and Documents, Memo, "Cessation of Hostilities . . . ," 26 Jul. 43; DEA, file 7-AB(s), Tel., SSEA to SSDA, 30 Jul. 43.
149. In a study ("Organization of Work on Post-Hostilities Planning") on *ibid.*, file 7-AQ(S), n.d., George Glazebrook noted that the army and RCAF "were not able to supply expert research students who had the required knowledge of both military and political affairs."
150. Munton and Page, 687ff.
151. See *ibid.*; Eayrs, III, *passim*; DEA, files 7-AQ(s), 7-AD(s), and 7-CB(s).
152. DEA, J.W. Pickersgill interview, 3 Dec. 77.
153. DEA, file 22-D(s), Tel., NAR to Pearson, 16 Mar. 43.
154. House of Commons *Debates*, 9 Jul. 43, p. 4558.
155. DEA, file 7-AB(s), Wrong to Pearson, 11 May 44.
156. Quoted in EAR, vol. 1025, file 101C, "Proposals for the Establishment of a General International Organization . . . ," 15 Jan. 45.
157. DEA, file 7-V(s), "Future World Organization," 17 May 44.
158. Entry, 17 May 44 in D. Dilks, ed., *The Diaries of Sir Alexander Cadogan, 1938-45* (London, 1971), p. 629. See also Reynolds and Hughes, pp. 30ff.
159. DEA, file 7-V(s), Tel., SSEA to SSDA, 4 Sep. 44.
160. *Ibid.*, Memo, 14 Sep. 44.
161. King Papers, Memo for Prime Minister, 26 Sep. 44, ff. C235922-3; DEA, file 7-V(s), Tel. SSEA to SSDA, 28 Sep. 44.

162. Dominions Office Records, D.O. 35/1870, Note att. to Garner to Boyd Shannon, 7 Oct. 44.
163. Minute on *ibid.*, 21 Oct. 44. See also *ibid.*, D.O. 114/119, pp. 112-13, for MacDonald's views on the Canadian position, 18 Jan. 45.
164. *FRUS 1944*, I, 933-36.
165. DEA, file 7-V(s), Memo for Prime Minister, 13 Dec. 44.
166. *Ibid.*, SSEA to Massey, 12 Jan. 45; King Papers, ff. C235953ff.
167. *Ibid.*, ff. C235969ff.
168. Dominions Office Records, D.O. 35/1881, Minute by Boyd-Shannon, 27 Feb. 45.
169. DEA, file 7-V(s), Memo, 15 Feb. 45.
170. King Diary, 22 Feb. 45.
171. King Papers, Memo for Prime Minister, 1 Mar. 45, ff. C233760ff.
172. *Ibid.*, Memo, 30 Mar. 45, f. C233942; King Diary, 3 Apr. 45; Dominions Office Records, D.O. 114/119, pp. 103-05.
173. King Papers, Memo for Prime Minister, ff. C235983ff.
174. For example, DEA, file 7-V(s), "Discussion on Social and Economic Aspects ... March 23rd, 1945."
175. Dominions Office Records, D.O. 35/1891, Holmes to Stephenson, 2 Apr. 45.
176. *Ibid.*, att. to Cockram to Stephenson, 20 Mar. 45.
177. Pope Diary, 25 Apr. 45; Bank of Canada Archives, L. Rasminsky Papers, file L.R. 76-17, Rasminsky to Towers, n.d.
178. Pope Diary, 25 Apr. 45.
179. DEA, file 7-V(s), Meeting of Canadian Delegates ... April 24th."
180. Chart in King Papers, f. C234123.
181. DEA, file 7-V(s), Wrong to Read, 29 Apr. 45; King Diary, 30 Apr. 45; *Report on the United Nations Conference on International Organization* (Ottawa, 1945), pp. 13-15.
182. Pope Diary, 26 Apr. 45.
183. C.S.A. Ritchie, *The Siren Years* (Toronto, 1974), pp. 198-200.
184. DEA, Reid interview, 21 Jul. 77; State Department Records, 842.00/7-2645, Atherton memo, 26 Jul. 45; Pearson Papers, N8, Diary, 19 Jun. 45. See generally Ruth Russell, *A History of the United Nations Charter* (Washington, 1958).
185. King Diary, 30 Apr., 9 May 45.
186. *Ibid.*, 30 Apr. 45.
187. DEA, John Holmes interview, 27 Jul. 77.
188. *Ibid.*
189. *Ibid.*
190. *Ibid.*, Reid interview, 21 Jul. 77.
191. Hickerson Papers, Hickerson to Atherton, 4 Aug. 45.

192. Pope Diary, 25 Apr. 45; "Amendments to Dumbarton Oaks Proposals Suggested by Canadian Delegation," May 4, 1945, copy on DEA, file 7-V(s); J.W. Pickersgill, and D.F. Forster, eds., *The Mackenzie King Record*, Vol. II: *1944-45* (Toronto, 1968), 386-87; Reynolds and Hughes, pp. 61-62.
193. Eayrs, III, 160.
194. See on the fight, DEA, file 7-V(s), documents on parts vii-viii; and British Library of Political and Economic Science, Sir Charles Webster Papers, Diaries, April and May 1945; Pope Diary, April-May, 1945; Pearson Papers, N8, Diary, 16, 18 May 45.
195. See Eayrs, III, 166-67.
196. DEA, file 7-V(s), Tel., NAR to Read, 10 Jun. 45; King Papers, f. C235244.
197. DEA, Reid interview, 21 Jul. 77.
198. James Barros, "Pearson or Lie: The Politics of the Secretary-General's Selection, 1946," *Canadian Journal of Political Science*, X (March 1977), 70ff.; D.G. Anglin, "Lester Pearson and the Office of Secretary-General," *International Journal*, XVII (Spring 1962), 145ff.; Reynolds and Hughes, pp. 76ff.
199. Prime Minister's Office Records, Prem. 8/119, "Meeting at Mr. Stettinius' Flat . . . October 8th," 1945.
200. King Diary, 12 Oct. 45; State Department Records, 500.CC(PC)/10-1345, Tel. to Washington, 13 Oct. 45.
201. Pearson Papers, N1, vol. 11, Secretary-General file.
202. Barros, 76.
203. State Department Records, 501.BA/10-2445, Memo to Hiss, 24 Oct. 45.
204. Barros, 86ff. T.M. Campbell and G.C. Herring, *The Diaries of Edward R. Stettinius, Jr., 1943-46* (New York, 1975), pp. 443ff.
205. Rasminsky Papers, file L.R. 76-39, Rasminsky to Pearson, 30 Jan. 46.

Chapter VI

1. See on the background, Patricia Roy, " 'Educating the East': British Columbia and the Oriental Question in the Interwar Years," *B.C. Studies*, no. 18 (Summer 1973), 50-69; W.P. Ward, *White Canada Forever* (Montreal, 1978); Ken Adachi, *The Enemy that Never Was* (Toronto, 1976).
2. PAC, N.A. Robertson Papers, vol. 2, Personal Correspondence, L. Robertson to NAR, 17 Feb. 42.
3. On Angus, see PAC, J.W. Dafoe Papers, Angus to Dafoe, 15 Oct. 40; University of British Columbia Archives, Special Collections, Angus

Family Papers, vol. 1, file 2, Mss. Autobiography, especially pp. 320-21; Vancouver City Archives, Add. Mss. 351, H.F. Angus Collection, file 7, NAR to Angus, 26 Dec. 45. On Keenleyside, see especially PAC, W.L.M. King Papers, J4, vol. 361, file F3849 for his role before 1941.

4. PAC, Ian Mackenzie Papers, vol. 32, file X-52, Committee on Treatment of Aliens and Alien Property, First Interim Report, 9 Feb. 39.

5. *Ibid.*, vol. 32, file X-81, *Special Committee ... Report and Recommendations*; Adachi, pp. 190-91.

6. King Diary, 8 Jan. 41, 26 Sep. 41; Patricia Roy, "The Soldiers Canada Didn't Want ... ," *Canadian Historical Review*, LIX (September 1978), 341ff.; Adachi, pp. 192-93.

7. PAC, Privy Council Office Records, Cabinet War Committee Documents, Report of Special Committee ... , and especially Appendix A., Report of Sub-Committee. . . .

8. King Papers, Memo for Prime Minister, 10 Dec. 41, f.C249381. NAR told the Prime Minister that some thirty Japanese had been interned as threats to security by this time. See also M.A. Pope, *Soldiers and Politicians* (Toronto, 1962), p. 117.

9. Mackenzie Papers, vol. 32, file X-81, extracts from letters by General Alexander, 30 Dec. 41, and Commodore Beech, 27 Dec. 41.

10. Copy of Report on DEA, file 773-B-40c. See also Pope, p. 177 and Adachi, pp. 203-04.

11. Mackenzie Papers, vol. 32, file X-81, Mackenzie to King, 10 Jan. 42.

12. *Ibid.*

13. See R.M. Dawson, *William Lyon Mackenzie King*, Vol. I: *1874-1923* (Toronto, 1958), pp. 146ff.

14. Mackenzie Papers, vol. 32, file X-81 note, n.d. See also *ibid.*, Mackenzie to King, 10 Jan. 42 with Heeney's indication of King's views.

15. Copy on DEA, file 773-B-40c. See the strong memo by J.E. Read on DEA, file 3464-J-40c, 12 Jan. 42.

16. Dafoe Papers, Hutchison to Dafoe, January 1942.

17. King Papers, Memo for Prime Minister, 20 Jan. 42, f. C249389.

18. Mackenzie Papers, vol. 32, file X-81(2), "The Japanese Problem," 26 Jan. 42.

19. See his statement in *Vancouver Province*, 4 Apr. 42.

20. DEA, file 773-B-40c, Memo, 27 Jan. 42.

21. Mackenzie Papers, vol. 32, file X-81(2), NAR to Mackenzie, 23 Jan. 42; DEA, file 773-B-40c, Memo, 27 Jan. 42.

22. Mackenzie Papers, vol. 32, file X-81(2), NAR to Mackenzie, 13 Feb. 42.

23. See *ibid.*, vols. 19, 24, 25 for samples of opinion in British Columbia.

24. See Adachi, p. 216; F. La Violette, *The Canadian Japanese and World War II* (Toronto), 1948, especially Chapters II, III.

25. DEA, file 3464-J-40c. Memo for Prime Minister, n.d.
26. Certainly that concerned him. See Robertson Papers, vol. 2, Personal Correspondence, NAR to L.W. Brockington, 4 Apr. 42.
27. DEA, file 3464-V-40, draft letter, 23 Jun. 42 and Keenleyside to Angus, 27 Jun. 42.
28. King Papers, Memo for Prime Minister, 27 Aug. 42, f. C249465. See on UBC, Elaine Bernard, "A University at War: Japanese Canadians at U.B.C. During World War II," *B.C. Studies*, no. 35, (Autumn 1977), 36ff.
29. DEA, file 104(s), Memo, 20 Aug. 43; copy in US National Archives, State Department Records, Hickerson Papers with attachments indicating that Atherton, the Minister in Ottawa, agreed completely. For an account of life among the hardline Japanese internees, see T.U. Nakano, *Within the Barbed Wire Fence* (Toronto, 1980).
30. DEA, file 104(s), Note for file . . . , 18 Jan. 44. In August 1945 NAR drew King's attention to travel and property acquisition restrictions and said they had no justification now and should be removed if the government intended to encourage the dispersion of loyal Japanese. Privy Council Office Records, PARC box 1002, file P-50-1-B, Memo, McClung to Heeney, 12 Sep. 45.
31. King Papers, Memo for Prime Minister, ff. C249497ff. This memo was drafted by Gordon Robertson and was based on an earlier memo from him to NAR on DEA, file 104(s), 20 Mar. 44.
32. Notes on *ibid.*, 17 Apr. 44.
33. *Ibid.*, and Cabinet War Committee Documents, "Policy with respect to Japanese in Canada."
34. *Ibid.*, Minutes, 19 Apr. 44.
35. House of Commons *Debates*, 4 Aug. 44, p. 5948; R.G. Robertson interview, 1 Dec. 78.
36. King Papers, Memo for Prime Minister, 22 Jun. 44, f. C249504, and subsequent memo, 2 Oct. 44, f. C249547.
37. *Ibid.*, 4 Nov. 44, ff. C249551ff.
38. *Ibid.*, 21 Feb. 45, ff. C249584-5. As of 29 Jun. 45, 8,676 of 15,101 Japanese surveyed in B.C. wanted repatriation. DEA, file 104(s), NAR to MacNamara, 9 Jul. 45.
39. Privy Council Office Records, PARC box 1001, file J-25-1, Memo for Prime Minister, 14 Dec. 45. See also DEA, file 104(s), Memo for Prime Minister, 31 Aug. 45.
40. There was some. See PAC, Cooperative Committee on Japanese Canadians Records, vols. 1, 2.
41. Keenleyside interview, 4 May 78; Angus interview, 29 Apr. 78. In December 1945, Robertson reversed his earlier position of calling for deportations of native-born Japanese suspected (or proven) of disloyalty.

His policy was clearly to go no further than necessary. Privy Council Office Records, PARC box 1001, file J-25-1, Memo for Prime Minister, 14 Dec. 45.

42. The question of property rights and deportations went on for some years. See Adachi, pp. 307ff.
43. Ritchie at NAR Round Table, 18 February 1978. On Green's views, see House of Commons *Debates*, 17 Feb. 38, pp. 556-58 and 29 Jan. 42, pp. 154-56.
44. Geoffrey Andrew interview, 29 Apr. 78.
45. Harvard University, Pierrepont Moffat Papers, Memo, 23 Jun. 41.
46. *Ibid.*, 16 Sep. 41.
47. DEA, John Starnes Papers, Memo for Prime Minister, 11 Dec. 41.
48. *Ibid.*, Memo for Prime Minister, 23 Dec. 41, and "Canadian Representation in the U.S.S.R.," 4 Mar. 42. Cabinet War Committee had approved the consular exchange on 6 Jan. 42.
49. PAC, Watson Sellar Papers, Diary, 2 Dec. 42; C.J. Mackenzie Papers (Ottawa), Diary, 2 Dec. 42.
50. Moffat Papers, Memo, 13 Apr. 42.
51. J.M.S. Careless interview, 4 Oct. 78.
52. "Memorandum of an interview ... Nov. 6, 1944." I am indebted to Dr. Ferns for giving me this memo and for an interview, 12 Jun. 78. Also J.W. Pickersgill Papers (Ottawa), Brown file, Pickersgill to E. Brown, 16 Dec. 44.
53. For example, King Papers, Memo for Prime Minister, 20 Jun. 45, ff. C237899ff.; Arnold Smith interview, 18 Feb. 78.
54. Queen's University, Norman Lambert Papers, Diary, 14 Aug. 45.
55. E.g., King Papers, Memo, Wilgress to NAR, 22 Aug. 45, ff. C231140-2; PAC, EAR, vol. 2078, file AR 5/33, Memo of a Conversation with Soviet Ambassador," 28 Aug. 45. But cf. Massey College, Vincent Massey Papers, Diary, 17 Aug. 45, which indicates Massey found King "pretty naive" about the USSR.
56. PAC, Wartime Information Board Records, vol. 4, WIB Survey 1945 file, WIB Survey 63, 19 May 45.
57. King Diary, 6 Sep. 45. See also John Sawatsky, *Men in the Shadows* (Toronto, 1980), Chapter VI.
58. Malcolm MacDonald interview, 7 Jun. 78.
59. King Diary, 7 Sep. 45.
60. Eleanor Fleming Auston interview, 14 Dec. 78 [Stephenson's secretary during the war; later NAR's secretary in London]; DEA, Glazebrook interview, 12 Jan. 77.
61. C.J. Mackenzie Diary (Ottawa), 10 Sep. 45; Interview, 18 Oct. 78.
62. DEA, MacDonald interview, 15 May 78.

63. DEA, file 8159-40c, Transl. of Note 35.

64. *Ibid.*; DEA, Glazebrook interview, 12 Jan. 77.

65. King Diary, 10 Sep. 45.

66. *Ibid.*

67. DEA, Glazebrook interview, 8 Jul. 77, and Holmes interview, 27 Jul. 77; Mrs. N.A. Robertson interview, 26 Feb. 79.

68. PAC, Charles Clay Papers, vol. 10, files 18, 19; *Canadian Affairs*, vol. 2, October and November, 1945.

69. King Diary, 23 Sep. 45; NAR Round Table, 18 Feb. 78. Cf. DEA, file 50303-40, Memo, 2 Dec. 53.

70. DEA, J.W. Pickersgill interview, 3 Dec. 77.

71. PAC, L.B. Pearson Papers, N1, vol. 3, Pearson to Wrong, 1 Oct. 45.

72. King Diary, 1 Oct. 45. On the legal problem, see "The Canadian Spy Case: Admissibility in Evidence of Stolen Embassy Documents," *University of Chicago Law Review*, XV (Winter 1948), 404ff.

73. King Diary, 8 Oct. 45.

74. *Ibid.*, 10 Oct. 45; King Papers, "Chronology and Commentary," 30 Jan. 47, f. C274026.

75. King Diary, 22 Oct. 45.

76. King Papers, unheaded memo, n.d., ff. C187018ff. and documents on vol. 234, file 2284; Chief Supt. James interview, 15 Feb. 79.

77. King Diary, 5 Feb. 46. See H.M. Hyde, *The Quiet Canadian* (London, 1962), p. 235, and his later book *The Atom Bomb Spies* (London, 1980), Chapters I-II.

78. Paul Martin interview, 16 Jun. 78; King Diary, 4, 5 Feb. 46; Arnold Smith interview, 22 Nov. 78. See also Privy Council Office Records, Cabinet Conclusions, 2, 29 Mar. 46.

79. Copy in King Diary, 15 Feb. 46.

80. DEA, Pickersgill interview, 3 Dec. 77; cf. Dale Thomson, *Louis St. Laurent, Canadian* (Toronto, 1967), p. 182; King Diary, 15 Feb. 46.

81. P.C. 6444; printed in *The Report of the Royal Commission. . . .* (Ottawa, 1946), pp. 649-50.

82. J.W. Pickersgill, *My Years with Louis St. Laurent* (Toronto, 1975), p. 85; A.D.P. Heeney, *The Things that are Caesar's* (Toronto, 1972), p. 85. Nunn May was not arrested until 6 March 1946. Hyde, *The Quiet Canadian*, p. 235.

83. King Diary, 15 Feb. 46; Heeney, p. 85.

84. See *Le Devoir*, 18 Feb. 46; *The Globe and Mail*, 18 Feb. 46; *Winnipeg Free Press*, 21 Feb. 46; *Public Opinion Quarterly* (Summer 1946), 264-65; PAC, Laurent Beaudry Papers, vol. 4, file 60, "Reaction Outside of Canada to the Investigation. . . .", 1 Jun. 46; *ibid.*, vol. 3, file 44, Press Conference in

External Affairs, 21 Feb. 46. See also Sellar Diary, 15 Feb. 46; Mackenzie Diary, 15 Feb. 46.

85. Cambridge University, Marshall Library, Lord Keynes Papers, file L(E), Eady to Keynes, 16 Feb. 46.
86. King Diary, 15 Feb. 46.
87. *DCER* XII, 2042; DEA, file 8531-40c, Tel., Moscow to SSEA, 22 Feb. 46.
88. King Diary, 20 Feb. 46.
89. NAR Round Table, 18 Feb. 78.
90. US National Archives, State Department Records, 842.00/5-2246, Clark to Parsons, 22 May 46.
91. King Diary, 22 Feb. 46.
92. *Ibid.*, 27 Feb. 46; Mrs. Graham Spry interview, 16 Feb. 79.
93. Arnold Smith interview, 22 Nov. 78.
94. Saul Rae interview, 10 Jul. 78.
95. See, for example, John Diefenbaker, *One Canada: The Memoirs of the Rt. Hon. John G. Diefenbaker* (Toronto, 1975), I, 224-26.
96. DEA, file 8531-40c, "Statement on the Procedures . . . ," 3 Apr. 46; and a flood of articles in law journals, in popular and scholarly magazines, and in the press. For the last, see, for example, *The Globe and Mail*, 18, 21 Mar. 46. The Commission's rejoinder is in *Report*, pp. 649ff.
97. Wrong agreed. See Massey Papers, file S.O. R4, Wrong to Massey, 28 Feb. 46.
98. On the interim reports, see State Department Records, 842.00/3-746, Clark to Parsons, 7 Mar. 46. The interim reports were published in the *Report*.
99. Robertson worked on the editing of the *Report*'s galleys. See Robertson Papers, vol. 2, Personal Correspondence, Wrong to NAR, 30 May 46.
100. For a British comment on the *Report*, see PRO, Foreign Office Records, F.O. 371/54705, Clutterbuck to Addison, 22 Aug. 46.
101. Beaudry Papers, vol. 3, file 44, "Press Conference," 21 Feb. 46.
102. Pearson Papers, N1, vol. 13, Pearson to NAR, 4 Mar. 46, and vol. 7, Pearson to King, 4 Mar. 46. On the impact of the Gouzenko case on the US, see Robert Donovan, *Conflict and Crisis* (New York, 1977), pp. 171, 173, 187.
103. See, for example, King Papers, Memo for Prime Minister, 3 Apr. 46, ff. C237959-60 and 7 May 46, ff. C237771-2 for NAR views. See also PAC, Hume Wrong Papers, vol. 4, file 20, "The Possibility of War with the Soviet Union," 28 Jun. 46.
104. State Department Records, 842.00/3-746, Clark to Parsons, 7 Mar. 46. Although relations with the USSR were not broken, there was a distinct period of coolness, and the respective Embassies were for a long period

under chargés, not ambassadors. Canada also pressed for the Russians to withdraw personnel suspected of spying. See *DCER* XII, 2058-60.

105. EAR, vol. 2081, file AR 13/13, Tel., NAR to Wrong, 29 May 46.

106. King Papers, Memo, 26 Jun. 46, f. C274338.

107. *Ibid.*, f. C274339, 10 Jul. 46; King Diary, 12 Jul. 46.

108. EAR, vol. 2081, file AR 13/13, NAR to Pearson, 9 Oct. 46. See also Privy Council Office Records, file 1-40-3 (1946), McClung to Robertson, 17 Jul. 46. The government allowed books to be published that were derived wholly from the *Report*. See, for example, J.B. White, *The Soviet Spy System* (London, 1948).

109. DEA, PSP Special Registry, file 7-1-5-1, NAR to Pearson, 9 Aug. 48; reply, 28 Aug. 48; Memo, Reid to USSEA, 18 Jun. 48. NAR's own copy of the *Report* has a mimeographed sheet tucked in, listing the disposition of the spy cases, with his pen notes on the sentences awarded and results of appeals.

110. Pearson Papers, N1, vol. 13, NAR to Pearson, 27 Dec. 46.

111. C.J. Mackenzie interview, 18 Oct. 78. See also Dominions Office Records, D.O. 35/1004, D. Morton to N. Archer, 22 Nov. 40.

112. Mackenzie Diary, 14 Feb. 42. See also M. Thistle, ed., *The Mackenzie-MacNaughton Wartime Letters* (Toronto, 1975), pp. 81, 103, which dates the creation of the Unit to May-June 1941.

113. DEA, Glazebrook interview; Mackenzie Diary, 1 Dec. 41, 14 Jan. 42, 19 Feb. 45.

114. DEA, Glazebrook interview.

115. Mackenzie Diary, 19 Feb. 45.

116. *Ibid.*, 29 Dec. 45.

117. Privy Council Office Records, PARC Box 287330, file C-30, Memo, Gill to NAR and Heeney, 30 Mar. 46. See also documents on *ibid.*, PARC Box 287417, file I-50-5.

118. DEA, Glazebrook interview; John Starnes interview, 5 Jun. 79.

119. EAR, file 50207-40, Memo, Heeney to NAR, 27 Apr. 46; Confidential interview.

120. DEA, file 50207-40, Memo to Cabinet Defence Committee, 4 May 46; Privy Council Office Records, PARC Box 287423, file C-10-9-1, Memo to Cabinet Defence Committee, 4 May 46.

121. DEA, file 50207-40, Memo, Crean to NAR, 12 Sep. 46, and Memo for Security Panel, 16 Sep. 46. See also *Financial Post*, 6 Apr. 46.

122. DEA, file 50207-40, Memo for Security Panel, 16 Sep. 46.

123. *Ibid.*, 22 Jan. 47.

Chapter VII

1. PAC, L.B. Pearson Papers, N1, vol. 2, NAR to Pearson, 4 Nov. 36.

2. Churchill College, Cambridge, Burgon Bickersteth Papers, "Some Observations on the Present Political Situation in Canada," Apr. 36; PRO, Dominions Office Records, D.O. 121/64, Campbell to Harding, 13 Oct. 38; and D.O. 35/600/6307/9, Campbell to Harding, 9 Feb. 39.

3. *Report of the Royal Commission on Government Organization* (Ottawa, 1963), IV, 103.

4. Pearson Papers, N1, vol. 7, undated memo.

5. *Report of the Secretary of State for External Affairs 1940* (Ottawa, 1941), p. 8; PAC, Treasury Board Records, vol. 555, file 2-7, Memo n.d. [Dec. 1942]. For later figures, see *ibid.*, Memo, Cullen to NAR, 7 Jul. 44.

6. Don Page, "Coping with a War: The Experience of the Canadian Department of External Affairs," a paper presented at a Conference on the Second World War, Ottawa, November 1979, pp. 2-3.

7. Massey College, Vincent Massey Papers, box 688, file P.S. 9, Stone to Massey, 2 Feb. 40.

8. PAC, W.L.M. King Papers, Memo for Prime Minister, 12 Sep. 40, f. C163166.

9. PAC, Laurent Beaudry Papers, vol. 2, file 25, "Outlines . . . ," 12 Jun. 41; Harvard University, Pierrepont Moffat Papers, Memos, 18 Feb., 24 Apr., 28 May 41.

10. Beaudry Papers, vol. 2, file 25, "Proposals re Opening of Foreign Legations . . . ," n.d.; King Papers, Memo for Prime Minister, 7 Apr. 41, ff. C163183ff.; Moffat Papers, Memo, 24 Apr. 41.

11. H.L. Keenleyside Papers (Victoria), Departmental Reorganization Draft. I am grateful to Dr. Keenleyside for giving me this paper and others.

12. Keenleyside Diary. This entry was read to me. Also Keenleyside interview, 4 May 78.

13. Massey Papers, unboxed material, file S.O. Pl, Pearson to Massey, 27 May 41; copy in Pearson Papers, N1, vol. 1. Massey replied with the hope that Pearson's 'sound administrative sense'[!] could create order from chaos. Massey Papers, file S.O. Pl, Massey to Pearson, 25 Jun. 41.

14. *Ibid.*, Pearson to Massey, 4 Jul. 41.

15. Pearson Papers, N1, vol. 7, Letter, 12 Jul. 41; Keenleyside Papers, "Memorandum for Members of the Staff," 3 Aug. 41.

16. See *Winnipeg Free Press*, 12 Aug. 41.

17. DEA, file 1086-40, Wilgress to NAR, 15 Jun. 42.

18. *Report of the Secretary of State for External Affairs 1941* (Ottawa, 1942), p. 5.

19. Saul Rae interview, 19 Jul. 78; Massey Papers, file S.O. Pl, Pearson to Massey, 4 Jul. 41.
20. *Winnipeg Free Press*, 12 Aug. 41.
21. PAC, EAR, vol. 799, file 524, Memo, 6 Oct. 41.
22. Massey Papers, unboxed material, Pearson to Massey, 4 Nov. 41, copy on Pearson Papers, N1, vol. 1. Glazebrook's appointment took effect on 1 Jan. 42. EAR, vol 678, file 136, "Members of the Staff . . . ," n.d.
23. John Holmes interview, 4 Oct. 78.
24. H.F. Angus interview, 29 Apr. 78.
25. Moffat Papers, Memo, 29 Aug. 42.
26. US National Archives, State Department Records, J.D. Hickerson Papers, Memo, 12 Apr. 41.
27. Massey Papers, file S.O. Pl, Pearson to Massey, 1 Apr. 42.
28. Lord Garner interview, 25 May 78; Confidential interview.
29. Queen's University, Grant Dexter Papers, Memo, 16 Jun. 42. Dexter's memo also contained some incorrect information on NAR's relations with King.
30. (London, 1955), p. 15. Mackenzie also said that "some men are born Civil Servants, some achieve Civil Service, and some have Civil Service thrust upon them. . . ." (p. 15)
31. Escott Reid interview, 14 Oct. 78.
32. Rae interview, 19 Jul. 78.
33. King Papers, Memo for Prime Minister, 3 May 43, ff. C167474-6.
34. Angus interview, 29 Apr. 78.
35. EAR, vol. 799, file 526, NAR to Gibson, 24 Dec. 41.
36. DEA, file 11488-B-40, Ferguson to NAR, 2 Nov. 42.
37. *Ibid.*, Cross to NAR, 31 Oct. 42.
38. For example, Beaudry Papers, vol. 3, folder 44, Press conference, 26 Nov. 42.
39. For example, see King Papers, Memo for Prime Minister, 2 Feb. 44, ff. C230349-50.
40. King Diary, 2 Nov. 42.
41. DEA, John Starnes Papers, NAR to King, 13 Dec. 42.
42. Pearson Papers, N8, Diary, 9-13 Jan. 43.
43. Confidential interview.
44. Pearson Papers, N8, Diary, 9 Apr. 43; EAR, vol. 678, file 136, "Members of the Staff . . . Appointed by Order-in-Council," n.d.
45. DEA, John Holmes interview, 27 Jul. 77.
46. *Saturday Night*, 17 Mar. 45, p. 2.
47. Keenleyside Diary, 28 Dec. 43, as read to me. See also *DCER*, IX: *1942-3*, 935 ff.
48. Massey Papers, file S.O. Pl, Pearson to Massey, 29 Oct. 43.

49. King Diary, 25 Nov. 44.
50. *Ibid.*, 13 Nov. 44.
51. *Ibid.*, 17 Dec. 44. Cf. Treasury Board Records, vol. 555, file 2-7, NAR to Smellie, 19 Sep. 44.
52. DEA, file 1086-40, "Memo re Personnel in Diplomatic Ranks," 2 Jan. 45. See also Treasury Board Records, vol. 555, file 2-7, Memorandum, n.d. [December 1943].
53. PAC, Hume Wrong Papers, vol. 4, file 24, "Probable Expansion . . . ," 5 Feb. 43; King Papers, "Statement for Advisory Committee on Personnel," 9 Mar. 43; ff. 3012188. According to *DCER* XII, xvii, the total officer strength in 1942 was 61, in 1943, 69.
54. *Report of the Secretary of State for External Affairs 1945* (Ottawa, 1946), p. 8.
55. See on this, Wrong's testimony before the House of Commons Standing Committee on External Affairs, 4 Jun. 46, pp. 55ff.
56. DEA, F.H. Soward interview, 14 Sep. 78.
57. University of Toronto Library, George Brown Papers, vol. 23, Riddell to Brown, 16 Oct. 44.
58. See Wrong testimony before House of Commons Standing Committee on External Affairs, 4 Jun. 46, pp. 56-57, and Department of External Affairs, file 1086-40, "Memo re Personnel in Diplomatic Ranks," 2 Jan. 45.
59. Brown Papers, Riddell to Brown, 6, 12 Mar. 45.
60. Beaudry Papers, vol. 2, file 29, Memo, 10 Dec. 43. See also Treasury Board Records, vol. 555, file 2-7, NAR to Secretary, Treasury Board, 9 Dec. 42.
61. King Papers, Memos for Prime Minister, 3 Jun. 42, ff. C230505-6 and 4 Feb. 43, ff. C230509-10.
62. Beaudry Papers, vol. 3, file 39.
63. DEA, file 1086-40, "Note for the Information of Officers . . . ," 23 Jan. 45; *ibid.*, "Memo re Personnel in Diplomatic Ranks," 2 Jan. 45; Wrong's testimony to House of Commons Standing Committee on External Affairs, 21 May 46, p. 12.
64. Massey Papers, unboxed material, Ritchie to Massey, 7 Feb. 45.
65. C.S.A. Ritchie, *The Siren Years* (Toronto, 1974), p. 208.
66. Documents on DEA, file 8508-40c; DEA, Soward interview.
67. Pearson Papers, N1, vol. 7, "Organization of Under-Secretary's office." and a series of additional memos from Wrong in October 1946. See also, *ibid.*, vol. 32, Wrong to Pearson, 18 Oct. 46.
68. See King Papers, Memo for Prime Minister, 29 May 44, ff. C162873-4; King Diary, 13 Nov. 44.
69. King Papers, Memo for Prime Minister, 29 May 44, ff. C162873-4.

70. King Diary, 13 Nov. 44.
71. Massey Papers, file S.O. R4, Wrong to Massey, 28 Feb. 46.
72. J.W. Pickersgill and D.F. Forster, eds., *The Mackenzie King Record*, Vol. III: *1945-6* (Toronto, 1970), 177.
73. King Diary, 9 May 46.
74. DEA, Pickersgill interview, 3 Dec. 77.
75. King Diary, 12 Jun. 46. L.B. Pearson, *Mike: The Memoirs of the Right Honourable Lester B. Pearson* (Toronto, 1972), I, 282, indicates that King had promised London to Robertson. This presumably was the occasion.
76. King Dairy, 12 Jun. 46.
77. King Papers, Memo for Prime Minister, 14 Jun. 46, ff. C163335; *DCER* XII, 5-6.
78. King Papers, Memo for Prime Minister, 13 Jun. 46. ff.
79. See Dexter Papers, Memo, 15 Oct. 46. *Mike*, I, 282 indicates that his preference was to stay in Washington.
80. King Diary, 29 Jun. 46. Pearson told Dexter that NAR "had reached such a point of physical exhaustion as to be incapable of doing the job— had been in this condition for the past six months at least." Dexter Papers, Memo, 15 Oct. 46.
81. King Diary, 5 Jul. 46.
82. *Ibid.*, 6 Jul. 46.
83. See on the decision, *ibid.*, 9 Jul. 46; PAC, Georges Vanier Papers, vol. 21, Notes G.P.V. file, pencil notes, n.d.; Dexter Papers, Memo, 15 Oct. 46; PAC, N.A. Robertson Papers, vol. 2, Personal Correspondence, Pearson to NAR, "Thursday" [July 1946].
84. Confidential interview.
85. Robertson Papers, vol. 2, Personal Correspondence, Pearson to NAR, "Thursday" [July 1946].
86. King Diary, 4 Aug. 46.
87. *Ibid.*, 3, 4 Sep. 46.
88. Robertson Papers, vol. 2, Personal Correspondence, Father to NAR, 5 Jul. 41.
89. King Diary, 18 Feb. 46.
90. A.D.P. Heeney, *The Things that are Caesar's* (Toronto, 1972), p. 91.
91. C.S.A. Ritchie interview, 14 Nov. 78.
92. D.V. Le Pan, "The Spare Deputy: A Portrait of Norman Robertson," *International Perspectives*, (July/August 1978), 4.
93. Mrs. N.A. Robertson interview, 17 Oct. 78.
94. Robertson Papers, vol. 3B, King Will file, "Last Will and Testament," Those fees ceased in 1962 at the request of the executors. *Ibid.*, unmarked file.
95. *Ibid.*, Last Will and Testament.

96. *Ibid.*, King Will, part II file, NAR to Lamb, 13 Mar. 53. See also, on the whole question of the King papers and diaries, the excellent piece by Jean Dryden, 'The Mackenzie King Papers: An Archival Odyssey,'' *Archivaria*, No. 6 (Summer 1978), 58.

97. *Ibid.*, 65.

98. PAC, Violet Markham Carruthers Papers, vol. 1, Dawson file, Dawson to Carruthers, 13 Sep. 53; *Ibid.*, 18 Mar. 54.

99. Robertson Papers, vol. 3B, King Will, part II file, NAR to Dawson, 3 Aug. 56, McGregor to NAR, 4 Nov. 53, and NAR to McGregor, 12 May 53.

100. *Ibid.*, NAR to McGregor, 26 Nov. 54.

101. Dryden, 62ff.

Chapter VIII

1. Beaudry was nominally second in command. See PAC, L.B. Pearson Papers, N1, vol. 1, Pearson-NAR correspondence, 10, 26, 27 Feb., 17 Mar. 47.

2. *Ibid.*, vol. 32, Pearson to NAR, 5 Apr. 47.

3. Douglas Le Pan interview, 5 Jul. 79; NAR Round Table transcript, 18 Feb. 79.

4. Mrs. N.A. Robertson interview, 30 Nov. 78.

5. Confidential interview.

6. *Ibid.*

7. On Holmes's contacts, see Pearson Papers, N1, vol. 32, NAR to Pearson 15 Dec. 47.

8. Detail on the staff appointments and some on the officers can be found in PAC, EAR, vol. 661, Personnel London Staff, part IV ff.

9. DEA, J.W. Holmes interview, 27 Jul. 77.

10. Wershof interview, 5 Apr. 79.

11. Warren interview, 15 May 79.

12. *Ibid.*

13. Le Pan interview, 20 Jun. 79.

14. Eleanor Fleming Auston interview, 14 Dec. 78.

15. Le Pan interview, 20 Jun. 79.

16. Privy Council Office, Privy Council Office Records, PARC Box 287326, file D19-1-L, NAR to Col. E.W.T. Gill, 26 Mar. 47; DEA, Washington Embassy Records (Washington, D.C.), file 1-1-1-11-1, Gill to Wrong, 8 Mar. 47.

17. Pearson Papers, N1, vol. 32, NAR to Pearson, 15 Dec. 47.

18. US National Archives, Department of State Records, 701.4200/2-1247, Atherton to Secretary of State, 12 Feb. 47, reporting on a parliamentary

return. See also *Canada in London: An Unofficial Glimpse of Canada's Sixteen High Commissioners 1880-1980* (London, 1980), for anecdotes.

19. Queen's University, T.A. Crerar Papers, vol. 105, Crerar to Dexter, 25 May 50; *The Globe and Mail*, 10 Jun. 48.

20. Rhodes House, Oxford, NAR file, NAR to C.K. Allen, 23 Jan. 47.

21. PAC, W.L.M. King Papers, Diary, 8 Oct. 48.

22. This whole section is based on a long letter from Mrs. Robertson to the author, 26 Oct. 79.

23. Pearson Papers, N1, vol. 13, NAR to Pearson, 22 Nov. 46. See also King Papers, Memo for Prime Minister, 30 Nov. 46, f. 390297; PAC, A.D.P. Heeney Papers, vol. 1, Heeney to NAR, 30 Nov. 46; PAC, Georges Vanier Papers, vol. 16, NAR 1946 folder, Tel., Vanier to Chairman of dinner, 19 Nov. 46 and tel., NAR to Vanier, 21 Nov. 46.

24. PAC, Douglas Le Pan Papers, vol. 1, file 2, NAR to SSEA, 25 Nov. 46 and attached speech; EAR, vol. 2117, file AR 429/311, Pearson to NAR, 4 Dec. 46.

25. Lord Sherfield interview, 2 Jul. 78; letter, A.E. Ritchie to author, 25 Jul. 79.

26. Lord Garner interview, 25 May 78; Judith Robertson interview, 9 Mar. 78; Mrs. Robertson interview, 26 Feb. 78.

27. On the transition from DO to CRO, see Joe Garner, *The Commonwealth Office 1925-68* (London, 1978), pp. 287ff.

28. PAC, N.A. Robertson Papers, vol. 3, Cambridge Degree file, NAR to D'A. McGreer, 7 May 48; *ibid.*, Clyne to NAR, 10 Jun. 48 and reply, 18 Jun. 48. To his mother he wrote that "I'm naturally uneasy & embarrassed by the company I'm to keep ... and feel properly bogus— however it's probably good news for parents—at least." Mrs. Robertson Papers, NAR to mother, 29 May 48.

29. Robertson Papers, vol. 1, Congratulations file, NAR to G. Roberge, 29 Mar. 66.

30. King Diary, 4 Aug. 46.

31. Pearson Papers, N1, vol. 13, Hudd to Pearson, 4 Jun. 47. See also King Diary, 4, 5 Jun. 47.

32. Pearson Papers, N1, vol. 13, Hudd to Pearson, 21 Jun. 47. NAR's illness was announced in the press and resulted in a warm letter from Attlee. Bodleian Library, Oxford University, Attlee Papers, Box 7, file Q-R, Rowan to Attlee, 8 Jun. 47; Attlee to NAR, 8 Jun. 47; NAR to Attlee, 10 Jun. 47. During the war Attlee had become impressed with the civil servants he met in Ottawa. See his *As It Happened* (London, 1954), p. 127.

33. Heeney Papers, vol. 1, NAR to Heeney, 24 Jun. 47.

34. One example of NAR's tendency can be found in Attlee Papers, Box 6,

file K-L, Memo to Attlee, 9 Jun. 47. See also Pearson Papers, N1, vol. 13, Pearson to NAR, 24 Jun. 47.

35. *Ibid.*, Tel., 4 Jul. 47; Le Pan interview, 5 Jul. 79.
36. Pearson Papers, N1, vol. 13, Hudd to Pearson, 8 Jul. 47.; Mrs. Robertson interview, 25 Feb. 80.
37. Heeney Papers, vol. 1, NAR to Heeney, 17 Jul.47.
38. Pearson Papers, N1, vol. 13, Mrs. L. Robertson to Pearson, 8 Jun. 47; tel., Pearson to Mrs. Robertson, 18 Jul. 47.
39. *Ibid.*, vol. 3, Pearson to NAR, 19 Jul. 47.
40. *Ibid.*, vol. 13, Hemsley to Pearson, 26 Jul. 47; PAC, W.H. Measures Papers, vol. 7, Visit to Europe file, Measures to wife, 4 Aug. 47.
41. *Ibid.*, vol. 2, External General file, DEA Postings as at August 1st, 1947.
42. Heeney Papers, vol. 1, N.A.M. Mackenzie to Heeney, 17 Sep. 47.
43. Pearson Papers, vol. 13, Pearson to NAR, 20 Aug. 47.
44. For example, see PRO, Treasury Records, T236/640, minute by C.G.L. Syers, 8 Sep. 47.
45. King Diary, 2 Oct. 47; C.J. Mackenzie Papers (Ottawa), Diary, 23 Oct. 47.
46. NAR Round Table transcript, 18 Feb. 78.
47. *Ibid.*
48. Mrs. Robertson interview, 13 Feb. 79.
49. Pearson Papers, N1, vol. 13, Hudd to Pearson 29 Dec. 48.
50. Max Beloff, "The Special Relationship: An Anglo-American Myth," in M. Gilbert, ed., *A Century of Conflict, 1850-1950* (New York, 1967), p. 169.
51. Hugh Dalton, *High Tide and After: Memoirs 1945-60* (London, 1962). See the account of UK economic problems in G.D.N. Worswick and P.H. Ady, eds., *The British Economy 1945-50* (Oxford, 1952).
52. DEA, file 9388-40c, NAR to SSEA, 8 Jan. 47.
53. *Ibid.*, file 154(s), Memo, 18 Feb. 47.
54. EAR, vol. 2083, file AR 16/14, Memo attached to NAR to Pearson, 29 Apr. 47; copy on Le Pan Papers, vol. 1, file 3.
55. DEA, file 154(s), Clark to NAR, 13 May 47. See also Clark's note to Eady, conveyed by Robertson on 16 May 47. EAR, vol. 2083, file 16/14.
56. See, for example, *ibid.*, Towers to NAR, 28 Dec. 46; and Le Pan to Pearson 5 Jun. 47 on DEA, file 264(s).
57. For example, DEA, file 265(s), Le Pan to Pearson, 10 Jun. 47.
58. EAR, vol. 2079, file 12/1, NAR to Pearson, 19 Jun. 47; copies on DEA, file 264(s) and Le Pan Papers, vol. 1, file 6.
59. For the immediate response in Ottawa to NAR's telegram, see Bank of Canada Archives, Graham Towers Papers, Memo #546, 24 Jun. 47.
60. *Ibid.*
61. EAR, vol. 2083, file 16/14, Le Pan to Pearson, 21 Jul. 47.

62.   See on this period, DEA, documents on file 154(s); on Treasury Records, T236/240; on PAC, Department of Finance Records, vol. 3437, closed file, and vol. 3992, file U-3-8. By September 1947, UK reserves were down to 28% of what they had been in 1938. See R.N. Gardner, *Sterling-Dollar Diplomacy* (New York, 1969), p. 324.

63.   DEA, file 154(s), Pearson to NAR, 8 Sep. 47.

64.   PRO, Foreign Office Records, F.O. 371/62495, Memo to Bevin, 13 Sep. 47.

65.   C.S.A. Ritchie interview, 9 Jun. 71. See also the testy exchanges between Abbott, Bryce and Rasminsky and British officials in tels. on Department of External Affairs, file 154(s) and in British Library of Political and Economic Science, Hugh Dalton Papers, Diary, 18 Sep. 47.

66.   EAR, vol 2079, file 12/1, Tel., NAR to Pearson, 24 Sep. 47.

67.   King Diary, 3 Oct. 47.

68.   *Ibid.*, 21 Oct. 47.

69.   Department of Finance Records, vol. 3438, file "Canadian Ambassador to U.S." "Arrangements in Connection with Washington Talks," n.d.; tel., Wrong to SSEA, 1 Nov. 47. On the whole subject of Canadian-American financial discussions in this period, see Robert Cuff and J.L. Granatstein, *American Dollars-Canadian Prosperity* (Toronto, 1978), Chapters IIff.

70.   DEA, file 154(s), NAR to Pearson, 15 Nov. 47.

71.   Department of Finance Records, vol. 3437, closed file, High Commissioner to SSEA, 15 Nov. 47.

72.   EAR, vol. 2081, file 13/8, Tel., NAR to Pearson, 16 Dec. 47; Cuff and Granatstein, Chapter II.

73.   DEA, file 154(s), Tel., Pearson to NAR, 29 Nov. 47.

74.   EAR, vol. 2100, file 106/4, Tel., NAR to Pearson, 29 Nov. 47.

75.   *Ibid.*, Pearson to NAR, 4 Dec. 47. See Minutes of Cabinet Committee on External Trade Policy, 2 Dec. 47 on DEA, file 154-A-s.

76.   Graham Spry interview, 13 Feb. 79.

77.   EAR, vol. 2084, file 16/14, Tel., NAR to Pearson, 8 Dec. 47.

78.   *Ibid.*, 9 Dec. 49.

79.   DEA, file 154-A-s, NAR to Pearson, 10 Dec. 47.

80.   See, for example, King Diary, 11 Dec. 47.

81.   DEA, file 154-A-s, NAR to Pearson, 13 Dec. 47.

82.   King Diary, 13 Dec. 47.

83.   DEA, file 154-A-s, Pearson to NAR, 14 Dec. 47; PRO, Cabinet Office Records, Cab. 128/10, C.M. 96(47)7, Cabinet minutes, 18 Dec. 47; documents on EAR, vol. 2100, file 106/4; and Robert Spencer, *Canada in World Affairs 1946-9* (Toronto, 1959), p. 204.

84.   Pearson Papers, N1, vol. 13, NAR to Pearson, 27 Dec. 47.

85.   EAR, vol. 2079, file 12/1, NAR to Pearson, 23 Jan. 48.

86. DEA, file 264(s), NAR to Pearson, 27 Jan. 48.

87. *Ibid.*, file 154(s), Pearson to Towers, 29 Jan. 48 and St. Laurent note on memo, 27 Jan. 48.

88. *Ibid.*, Memo for SSEA, 6 Feb. 48; Privy Council Office Records, PARC box 287341, file T-50-1-M (1948), ICETP Minutes, 5 Feb. 48; copy on DEA, file 50092-C-40.

89. *Ibid.*, file 154(s), Memo for SSEA, 6 Feb. 48; State Department Records, 842.00/2-1048, Harrington to Foster, 10 Feb. 48.

90. Department of Finance Records, vol. 3436, UK Exchange file, Memo, 13 Feb. 48; copy on Le Pan Papers, vol. 1, file 5 and in EAR, vol. 2084, file 16/14.

91. Cuff and Granatstein, pp. 91ff.

92. King Diary, 13 Feb. 48.

93. Privy Council Office Records, PARC box 287341, file T-50-1-M, (1948), Minutes, 16 Feb. 48.

94. DEA, file 265(s), Tel., Moran to Wrong, 21 Feb. 48. See *ibid.*, file 50091-C-40, Minutes of Cabinet Committee on External Trade Policy, 17 Feb. 48.

95. *Ibid.*, file 154(s), Tel., Canadian Ambassador to SSEA, 27 Feb. 48.

96. *Ibid.*, tel., NAR to SSEA, 1 Mar. 48; Cuff and Granatstein, p. 96.

97. DEA, file 154(s), NAR to Pearson, 1 Mar. 48 and *ibid.*, file 50091-C-40, Cabinet Committee on External Trade Policy Minutes, 2 Mar. 48.

98. Le Pan Papers, vol. 1, file 7, tel., NAR to Pearson, 4 Mar. 48; Cuff and Granatstein, p. 97.

99. Le Pan Papers, vol. 1, file 7, tel., NAR to Pearson, 4 Mar. 48.

100. DEA, file 154(s), tel., NAR to Pearson, 16 Mar. 48. See *ibid.*, file 50091-C-40 Cabinet Committee on External Trade Policy Minutes, 16 Mar. 48.

101. *Ibid.*, Memo to SSEA, 18 Mar. 48; but cf. EAR, vol. 2079 file 12/1, Towers to Pearson, 24 Mar. 48.

102. DEA, file 264(s), Tel., SSEA to High Commissioner, 25 Mar. 48.

103. Cuff and Granatstein, pp. 100-01.

104. State Department Records, 842.00/7-2645, Atherton Memo, 26 Jul. 45.

105. Marshall Library, Cambridge University, Keynes Papers, file L/E/, Eady to Keynes, 12 Oct.45.

106. Sir Stephen Holmes interview, 15 Jun. 71.

107. Keynes Papers, file L/B/April 1945-46, Keynes to Brand, 29 Jan. 46.

108. PRO, Dominions Office Records, D.O. 121/15, "Note of Discussion on Organization of Defence . . . ," 7 Nov. 46. NAR also had to resist Australian efforts for fortnightly High Commissioners' meetings. See King Papers, Tel., Pearson to NAR, 28 Feb. 47, f. 388939. See also F.H. Soward, "A Survey of Canadian External Policy," Chapter II, pp. 19-20, a classified study prepared for DEA in 1952; PAC, Privy Council Office

Records, PARC Box 287327, documents on file D-19-15; and J.W. Holmes, *The Shaping of Peace: Canada and the Search for World Order 1943-57,* Vol. 1 (Toronto 1979), 154ff.

109.   See S. Roskill, *Hankey Man of Secrets,* Vol. III: *1931-63* (London, 1974), 606-07, for one who caused the problem.

110.   Dominions Office Records, D.O. 35/1748, Memo, 13 Nov. 46. See James Eayrs, *In Defence of Canada,* Vol. III: *Peacemaking and Deterrence* (Toronto, 1972), 223ff. for King's reaction to the tub-thumping from London.

111.   DEA, file 7-CM-1(s), Tel., NAR to Pearson, 13 Nov. 46.

112.   Documents on Dominions Office Records, D.O. 35/1748 and D.O. 121/10c.

113.   See on this Soward, Chapter III, pp. 71ff.; Eayrs, III, 344ff.; *DCER* XII, 1541ff.; and especially J.T. Jockel, "The United States and Canadian Efforts at Continental Air Defense, 1945-47," PhD thesis, Johns Hopkins University, 1978, Chapter III.

114.   Cabinet Records, Cab. 122/629, COS. (46) 165th Mtg., 11 Nov. 46.

115.   *Ibid.,* tel., Bevin to Attlee, 13 Nov. 46.

116.   PAC, Louis St. Laurent Papers, vol. 155, file 100, NAR to SSEA, 19 Feb. 47.

117.   See Soward, Chapter II, pp. 19-21, and Garner, pp. 299-300.

118.   Dominions Office Records, D.O. 121/16, Notes of a Meeting, 7 Jan. 47. Eayrs, III, 195ff.; *DCER* XII, 151ff. for 1946 lead-up to these events.

119.   Dominions Office Records, D.O. 121/16, Notes of a Meeting, 7 Jan. 47.

120.   Based on J.F. Hilliker, "No Bread at the Peace Table: Canada and the European Settlement, 1943-47," *Canadian Historical Review,* LXI (March 1980); Dominions Office Records, D.O. 121/16, Note of a Meeting, 17, 20 Jan. 47; Dexter Papers, Memo, 22 Feb. 47.

121.   Hilliker, "No Bread. . . ."

122.   For detail and for NAR's role in the events that led up to the establishment of the Federal German Republic, see Soward, Chapter V, pp. 28ff. and Holmes, p. 123.

123.   Pearson Papers, N1, vol. 12, Pearson to NAR, 2 Jun. 47.

124.   EAR, vol. 2118, file 430/19, Tel., NAR to Pearson, 9 Sep. 47. See also King Papers, Memo for Prime Minister, 10 Sep. 47, ff. C160335-6 and DEA, file 270(s), Tel., Pearson to NAR, 17 Sep. 47.

125.   Dominions Office Records, D.O. 121/17, Noel-Baker to Attlee, 13 Nov. 47.

126.   Bevin, a great and able man, had occasional difficulties with spoken grammar, something that caused Canada House problems. On one occasion, John Holmes asked NAR if he wanted grammar or accuracy in a report quoting Bevin and was told to settle for accuracy. NAR Round Table transcript, 18 Feb. 78.

127. J.W. Pickersgill and D.F. Forster, eds., *The Mackenzie King Record*, Vol. IV: *1947-8* (Toronto 1970), 111.
128. DEA, file 270(s), NAR to Pearson, 6 Dec. 47.
129. For example, King Diary, 4 Oct. 48.
130. J.W. Pickersgill Papers (Ottawa), Trip to England and Paris 1948 file, R.G. Robertson to Pickersgill, 4 Oct. 48.
131. *Ibid.*, NAR file, n.d. [6 Oct. 48].
132. *King Record.* IV, 402-3.
133. See EAR, vol. 2118, file 430/21 for details. Robertson's reports on the sessions are on DEA, file 50023-40.
134. For Robertson's view of the Irish question, see *ibid.*, file 283(s), D. Johnson to SSEA, 4 Mar. 49; on India, see NAR's tels. in *ibid.*, State Papers, 1-1949/2; Eayrs, III, 235ff.
135. See DEA, file 283(s).
136. Quoted in Escott Reid, *Time of Fear and Hope* (Toronto, 1977), p. 132.
137. For example, EAR, vol. 2119, file 434/19, NAR to Reid, 1 Jun. 48.
138. DEA, Escott Reid interview, 21 Jul. 77.
139. NAR Round Table transcript, 18 Feb. 78.
140. Reid, p. 141.
141. DEA, file 283(s), Tel., 16 Feb. 49. James Eayrs, *In Defence of Canada*, Vol. IV: *Growing up Allied* (Toronto, 1980), pp. 123-24.
142. See Reid, p. 229 for another NAR interjection. NAR was also cautious about building in too grandiose a manner from the outset, preferring that specific agencies be built, as the need for them became apparent. Soward, Chapter III, p. 92.
143. PAC, Hume Wrong Papers, vol. 5, file 29, Reid to NAR, 9 Oct. 48.
144. Documents on DEA, file 11488-B-40; Soward, Chapter V, pp. 35ff.; Eayrs, IV, 41ff.
145. Pearson Papers, N1, vol. 13, NAR to Pearson, 27 Sep. 48.
146. See the brief account in *Canada and the United Nations 1948* (Ottawa, 1949), pp. 42ff., and *1949* (Ottawa, 1950), pp. 37ff.
147. Lord Kaldor interview, 7 Jun. 78.
148. Minutes on DEA, file 7-CA-19-B. During much of this period, Robertson was away from London, leaving the High Commision's work to be handled by his staff. See EAR, vol. 2122, file 1177/1, NAR to Handy, 30 Dec. 48.
149. DEA, Holmes interview, 27 Jul. 77.
150. Kaldor interview; Soward, Chapter V, p. 39.
151. Pickersgill Papers, Questionnaire Privy Council file, Jetty Robertson to Pickersgill, 25 Jan. 49.
152. DEA, file 7-CA-19-A(s), Report of the Technical Committee on Berlin Currency and Trade . . . , 11 Feb. 49.

153. Soward, Chapter V, p. 39.

154. *Canada and the United Nations 1949*, p. 49.

155. King Diary, 3 Oct. 47.

156. *Ibid.*, 20 Feb. 48.

157. *Ibid.*, 10 Sep. 48.

158. State Department Records, 842.002/9-948, Harrington to Snow, 9 Sep. 48; 842.002/9-1048, Harrington to Secretary of State, 10 Sep. 48.

159. King Diary, 20 Sep. 48.

160. J.W. Pickersgill interview, 13 Oct. 78.

161. DEA, Pickersgill interview, 3 Dec. 77.

162. Pearson Papers, N1, vol. 4, Memo for SSEA, 3 Mar. 48 and NAR to Pearson, 24 Feb. 48.

163. Pickersgill interview, 13 Oct. 78.

164. Heeney Papers, vol. 1, Tel., Heeney to Pearson, 6 Dec. 48.

165. Pearson Papers, N1, vol. 17, Wrong to Pearson, 22 Aug. 48.

166. Pickersgill Papers, loose letter, Pickersgill to NAR, 7 Jan. 49. See also Wrong's account in Bishop's University, T.W.L. MacDermot Papers, file 70, 1931-51 Notebook, entry n.d.

167. Robertson Papers, vol. 2, Personal Correspondence, Pickersgill to NAR, 9 Jan. 49. There is a slightly different account in Pickersgill's *My Years with Louis St. Laurent* (Toronto, 1975), p. 64.

168. Robertson Papers, vol. 2, Personal Correspondence, Heeney to NAR, 10 Jan. 49.

169. *Ibid.*, P.C. 261, 19 Jan. 49. See also *The Times* (of London), 20 Jan. 49.

170. Warren interview, 15 May 79.

171. See documents on DEA, file 11488-B-40.

172. Pickersgill Papers, Questionnaire Privy Council file, Mrs. Robertson to Pickersgill, 20 Jan. 49.

173. *Ibid.*, Pickersgill to L. Robertson, 4 Feb. 49 and reply, 10 Feb. 49.

174. *Ibid.*, Jetty Robertson to Pickersgill, 8 Feb. 49 and Robertson Papers, vol. 2, Personal Correspondence, Heeney to NAR, 16 Feb. 49.

175. Heeney Papers, vol. 1, USSEA 1949-52 file, Tel., NAR to Heeney, 24 Feb. 49.

176. Mrs. Robertson Papers, NAR to Jetty, 8 Mar. 49.

177. DEA, file 40-AS-40, S. Rump to H. Measures, 29 Dec. 49. King Diary, 10 Mar. 49. King noted that no cabinet minister met NAR at the station, but only the deputy minister from External Affairs. By this point, King had decided that NAR's appointment to the PCO, instead of External Affairs, was an error.

178. *King Record*, IV, 424.

Chapter IX

1. Mrs. N.A. Robertson interview, 23 Oct. 78. See also PAC, W.L.M. King Papers, Diary, 21 Mar. 49.

2. A.D.P. Heeney, "Mackenzie King and the Cabinet Secretariat," *Canadian Public Administration*, X (September 1967), 367.

3. *Ibid.*, 370-71.

4. See on this, DEA, file 270-40, Memo for Prime Minister, 16 Jun. 45 and King to Ministers, 25 Jul. 45 and attached. A small section in the Privy Council Office was created during the war to keep track of Statutory Orders and Regulations. See Privy Council Office, Privy Council Office Records, PARC Box 1002, file P-50, Submission to Royal Commission on Administrative Classification in the Public Service, 4 Apr. 46.

5. Heeney, "Cabinet Secretariat," 372.

6. J.W. Pickersgill, *My Years with Louis St. Laurent* (Toronto, 1975), p. 64.

7. A.D.P. Heeney, "Cabinet Government in Canada . . .," *Canadian Journal of Economics and Political Science*, XII (August 1946), 296.

8. Privy Council Office Records, PARC Box 287290, file N-10, lecture, 25 Oct. 48; and *ibid.*, PARC Box 1002, file P-50, Halliday to Heeney, 4 Apr. 46.

9. W.E.D. Halliday, "The Executive of the Government of Canada," *Canadian Public Administration*, II (1959), 241; Privy Council Office Records, PARC Box 287285, documents on file I-50-5-M.

10. Donald Gow, "Canadian Federal Administrative and Political Institutions," PhD thesis, Queen's University, 1967, pp. 159ff.

11. Austin Cross, "Oligarchs at Ottawa," *Public Affairs*, (Autumn 1951), 22.

12. PAC, N.A. Robertson papers, vol. 2, Personal Correspondence, Heeney to Robertson, 10 Jan. 49.

13. *Ibid.*, Heeney to Robertson, 16 Feb. 49 and attached memo, 15 Feb. 49. Robertson presumably agreed on the merits of his officers, and tried to get their salaries raised. PAC, Civil Service Commission, Historical Personnel Records, vol. 839, NAR file, Memo to Commission, 21 Jan. 52.

14. Robertson Papers, Heeney to NAR, 16 Feb. 49. For changes in the staff, including the addition of P.-E. Trudeau, see Privy Council Office Records, PARC Box 287294, file P-50, "Draft Telephone list," 16 Dec. 50. The officers then were Messrs. Chipman, Eberts, Gaskell, Halliday, Mackenzie, Pelletier, R.G. Robertson, and Trudeau. The files relating to Trudeau's hiring seem to have been stripped.

15. *Ibid.*, Notice by NAR, 1 Mar. 50.

16. *Ibid.*, PARC Box 287293, file P-35-3, Memo, Martin to Mayrand, 12 Jun. 50.

17. *Ibid.*, PARC Box 287294, file P-50, Memo, Halliday to NAR, 19 Dec. 50 and NAR's note.

18. Halliday, 237. The East Block was also renovated, and Robertson's office was altered so that visitors no longer entered the room from behind his desk. Privy Council Office Records, PARC Box 287334, file P-50, Halliday to NAR, 25 Oct. 49.

19. PAC, A.D.P. Heeney Papers, vol. 1, NAR to Heeney, 12 Jul. 49.

20. N.A. Robertson Round Table, 18 Feb. 78.

21. Pickersgill, p. 64.

22. D.V. Le Pan interview, 5 Jul. 79.

23. Norman Smith interview, 18 Jan. 79.

24. C.M. Drury interview, 4 Apr. 79.

25. Robertson Papers, vol. 2, Personal Correspondence, L. Robertson to NAR, 23 May 50.

26. This whole section has been based on interviews with C.S.A. Ritchie, 14 Nov. 78; Gordon Robertson, 1 Dec. 78; J.W. Pickersgill, 13 Oct. 78; George Ignatieff, 11 Sep. 78; Paul Martin, 15 Jun. 78; Lord Garner, 25 May 78; and at DEA, interviews with Pickersgill, 3 Dec. 77 and Ignatieff, 7 Dec. 77. In addition, the Robertson Round Table was most helpful.

27. Le Pan interview, 5 Jul. 79. Le Pan suggested that this caused some resentment and was seen in some Ottawa civil service quarters as a sign of creeping External Affairs influence.

28. Privy Council Office Records, PARC Box 287323, file E-20, 13 Oct. 50.

29. DEA, file 50092-C-40, ICETP Minutes, 13 Oct. 49. and file 50091-C-40, Cabinet Committee on Economic Policy Minutes, 17 Oct. 49.

30. Privy Council Officer Records, PARC Box 287302, file S-60, Memo for file, 18 Nov. 49 and other documents on file.

31. Bank of Canada Archives, Bank of Canada Records, Social Security file 2B-200, Interdepartmental Committee on Social Security Minutes, 29 Dec. 49.

32. *Ibid.*, 30 Dec. 49.

33. Privy Council Office Records, PARC Box 287311, file U-11, NAR to Prime Minister, 25 Jan. 50.

34. *Ibid.*, 7 Feb. 50.

35. *Ibid.*, PARC Box 287302, file S-60-M, Minutes, 13 Feb. 50; Queen's University, Grant Dexter Papers, Memo, 4 Feb. 50.

36. Robertson Round Table, 18 Feb. 78.

37. Privy Council Office Records, PARC Box 287302, file S-60-M, Minutes, 13, 14 Feb. 50.

38. *Ibid.*, PARC Box 287311, file U-11, Memos, MacNamara to NAR, 2 May 50, 26 Jun. 50, and so on.

39. *Ibid.*, PARC Box 287302, file S-50-M, Minutes, 2 Nov. 50; Dexter Papers, Memos, 12, 17, 18 Oct. 50.

40. Privy Council Office Records, PARC Box 287302, file S-60-M, Minutes, 13, 20 Nov. 50.

41. Pickersgill, pp. 134ff.; Dale Thomson, *Louis St. Laurent, Canadian* (Toronto, 1967), pp. 302-03; R.M. Burns, *The Acceptable Mean; The Tax Rental Agreements, 1941-1962* (Toronto, 1980), pp. 94ff; Dexter Papers, Memo, 1 May 51.

42. *Ibid.*, 23 Jan., 1, 2, 4 May 51.

43. M.C. Urquhart and K. Buckley, eds., *Historical Statistics of Canada* (Toronto, 1965), p. 304.

44. DEA, file 50092-C-40, Minutes, 10 Aug. 51.

45. Defence expenditures rose from $400 million a year before Korea to $2 billion a year by 1952. See J.D. Gibson, "Post-War Economic Development and Policy in Canada," *Canadian Journal of Economics and Political Science*, XX (November 1954), 449; and United States Treasury Department, Treasury Records, Acc. 68-A-5918, Box 87, file Can/9/00, Memo, "Canadian Contribution to the Defense Effort," 22 Jan. 51.

46. Letter, J.W. Pickersgill to author, 25 Jan. 80. See the budget of 10 April 1951 in House of Commons *Debates*, especially pp. 1800ff. for government anti-inflation policy.

47. Pickersgill, pp. 153ff.; Thomson, pp. 321-22.

48. DEA, file 50092-C-40, Minutes, 18 Apr. 50. On the fisheries, see David Alexander, *The Decay of Trade* (Memorial University, 1977) and especially pp. 121-22 for the best account.

49. DEA, file 50092-C-40, Minutes, 18 Apr. 50.

50. Robertson Round Table, 18 Feb. 78.

51. Pickersgill, p. 170.

52. DEA, file 50092-C-40, Minutes, 10 Mar. 52.

53. *Ibid.*, 16, 28 Apr., 12 May 52.

54. Urquhart and Buckley, p. 377, gives the figures.

55. DEA, file 50092-40, Heeney to NAR, 8 Apr. 49; file 50092-C-40, ICETP Minutes, 11 Apr. 49.

56. See PAC, St. Laurent Papers, vol. 175, file "Washington Trip...," Memo, Pearson to St. Laurent, 9 Feb. 49; Dexter Papers, Memo, 9 Feb. 49 and Hutchison memo, February 1949.

57. DEA, file 265-B(s), Cabinet conclusion, 14 Mar. 49; PAC, EAR, vol. 2158, Economic Cooperation Canada-US file, minute by Wrong, 14 Mar. 49.

58. *Ibid.*, minute by Murray, 23 Mar. 49.

59. DEA, file 265-B(s), Memo for SSEA, 16 Mar. 49 and Memo for Plumptre, 20 May 49.

60. *Ibid.*, file 50092-C-40, Minutes, 27 May 49 and file 265-B(s), Tel., Wrong to Heeney, 25 May 49.

61. EAR, vol. 2158, Economic Cooperation file, minute by Wrong, 31 May 49.

62. DEA, file 264(s), NAR to Prime Minster, 8 Jun. 49 and tel., SSEA to High Commissioner, 8 Jun. 49.

63. PAC, L.B. Pearson Papers, N1, vol. 5, Heeney to Pearson, 11 Jun. 49.

64. St. Laurent Papers, vol. 175, External Affairs, Monetary Situation, UK, file, tel., Attlee to St. Laurent, 17 Jun. 49.

65. DEA, file 50010-40, Memo for SSEA, 29 Jun. 49.

66. *Ibid.*, file 264(s), Heeney to Wilgress, 19 Jun. 49.

67. See *Foreign Relations of the United States 1949* [*FRUS*] (Washington, 1975), IV, 784ff.

68. DEA, file 50010-40, NAR to Heeney, 22 Jun. 49.

69. St. Laurent Papers, vol. 234, Tel., NAR to SSEA, 22 Jun. 49.

70. *Ibid.*, Tel., High Commissioner to Heeney, 23 Jun. 49; Privy Council Office Records, PARC Box 287265, file D-13-4, Memo, R.G. Robertson to Prime Minister, 24 Jun. 49.

71. See, on this, Dexter Papers, Freedman memos, n.d. [August and September 1949]. See NAR's account of his talks in PAC, Privy Council Office Records, PARC Box 287342, file U-10-15, Memo "Meetings to discuss U.K. financial developments," 28 Jun. 49, and "Memorandum for the Cabinet," 28 Jun. 49.

72. St. Laurent Papers, vol. 234, Memos, Heeney to SSEA, 29 Jun. 49. Heeney told Pearson that he hoped Robertson would go "because of his special knowledge and experience," adding that if he went, "there is no need for direct representation from this Department," a revealing comment. *Ibid.*

73. *FRUS 1949*, IV, 789.

74. DEA, file 50010-40, "Informal Notes . . . ," 7 Jul. 49.

75. PAC, Privy Council Office Records, PARC Box 287342, file U-10-15, Memo to Cabinet, 13 Jul. 49; St. Laurent Papers, vol. 175, External Affairs Monetary Situation file, tels., Abbott to St. Laurent, 9 Jul. 49; *FRUS 1949*, IV, 799ff.

76. Privy Council Office Records, PARC Box 287342, file V-10-15, "Discussion under the Aegis of the United Kingdom-Canada Continuing Committee . . . ," 11 Jul. 49.

77. PAC, D.V. Le Pan Papers, vol. 1, file 11, Clark to Plumptre, 20 Dec. 49. See also EAR, vol 2118, file A.R. 430/27, "British Commonwealth Finance Ministers' Meetings, July 13-18 1949," 10 Dec. 49; Dexter Papers, Memo, n.d. [August 1949]; PAC, Privy Council Office Records, PARC Box 287342, file U-10-15, Memo to Cabinet, 20 Jul. 49.

78. EAR, vol. 2085, file A.R. 16/31, Tel., Clark to Taylor, 20 Jul. 49.
79. PAC, H.R. Kemp Papers, vol. 20, file 15, J.E. Coyne, *et al.*, to NAR, n.d., and attached papers. I am indebted to Professor John English for drawing this material to my attention. See also DEA, file 50092-C-40, ICETP minutes, 2 Aug. 49.
80. *Ibid.*, file 50011-40, Shannon to Heeney, 27 Jul. 49.
81. *Ibid.*, file 50092-C-40, ICETP Minutes, 2 Aug. 49.
82. *Ibid.*, file 50011-40, SSEA to High Commissioner, 9 Aug. 48 and file 50092-C-40, ICETP Minutes, 9 Aug. 49.
83. *Ibid.*, 23 Aug. 49.
84. US Treasury Records, Accession 67A-1804, Box 34, Miscellaneous file, "Canadian Delegation," n.d.
85. See PAC, Privy Council Office Records, PARC Box 287342, file U-10-15, Tel., Wrong to SSEA, 30 Aug. 49. American, Canadian and British papers are in US Treasury Records, Acc. 67-A-1804, Box 33.
86. Minutes on *ibid.*, Combined Official Documents file; DEA, file 50011-40, Tel., Washington to SSEA, 30 Aug. 49.
87. PAC, Privy Council Office Records, PARC Box 287342, file U-10-15, Tel., Wrong to SSEA, 31 Aug. 49.
88. The only minutes seem to be on EAR, vol. 2160, "Ministerial Talks ...," 14 Sep. 49. See also PAC, Privy Council Office Records, PARC Box 287342, file U-10-15, tels., Washington to SSEA, 9, 12 Sep. 49.
89. See *FRUS 1949*, IV, 847-49; A.F.W. Plumptre, *Three Decades of Decision* (Toronto, 1977), pp. 104ff.
90. *Ibid.*, p. 108; Abbott interview, 11 Jan. 79.
91. PAC, J.F. Parkinson Papers, vol. 2, "Thoughts on Canadian-American Collaboration on Change in Canadian Dollar," n.d. [September 1949].
92. Dexter Papers, Memo, 26 Nov. 49.
93. House of Commons *Debates*, 12 Mar. 51, pp. 1168ff.; Robert Cuff and J.L. Granatstein, *American Dollars—Canadian Prosperity* (Toronto, 1978), pp. 134-35; EAR, vol. 2160, "Wheat and the Tripartite Talks," 6 Sep. 49.
94. *Ibid.*, minute by Wrong, 13 Sep. 49. The communiqué is in *External Affairs* (October 1949), pp. 7ff.
95. See on this, DEA, file 10651-40, minute by Wrong, 25 Nov. 49 and file 50092-C-40, ICETP Minutes, Fall 1949.
96. See *ibid.*, file 50012-40, Le Pan to USSEA, 16 Jan. 50 and attachments and *ibid.*, Towers to Clark, 2 Feb. 51; also *ibid.*, file 50092-C-40, ICETP Minutes, 29 Jun. 50.
97. St. Laurent Papers, vol. 174, St. Laurent to Attlee, 15 Nov. 49.
98. *Ibid.*, vol. 164, Memo for Prime Minister, 16 Nov. 49.
99. *Ibid.*, Pearson to St. Laurent, 12, 15 Dec. 49.
100. As on wheat. See DEA, file 8925-40c and St. Laurent Papers, vol. 278.

101. See documents on DEA, file 50012-40 for the reserves crisis. For a survey of the 1950 financial situation, see *ibid.*, State Papers, 1-1-1950/1A, papers on the Commonwealth Meetings on General Economic and Trade Questions, September 1950.

102. See the exchange between Pearson and Howe in PAC, C.D. Howe Papers, vol. 4, file S4-12. For trade data, see Plumptre, pp. 301ff.

103. L.B. Pearson, *Mike: The Memoirs of the Right Honourable Lester B. Pearson,* Vol. II, *1948-57* (Toronto, 1973), 148-49; F.H. Soward, "A Survey of Canadian External Policy," (DEA, mimeo, n.d.), VI, 61ff.

104. Pearson Papers, N1, vol. 35, Memo for Prime Minister, 1 Aug. 50; printed in part in *Mike* II, 149ff.; see also Robert Cuff and J.L. Granatstein, *Ties that Bind* (Toronto, 1977), pp. 146-47.

105. Pearson Papers, N1, vol. 35, "Discussion with Mr. Trygve Lie . . . July 31, 1950" and *Mike* II, 154ff. The best study of Canada and the Korean War is Denis Stairs, *The Diplomacy of Constraint* (Toronto, 1974), especially Chapter III.

106. *Ibid.*, p. 90. On the cabinet discussion, see Dexter Papers, Memos, 12 Aug. and 25 Oct. 50. On NATO use for the brigade, see DEA, file 50068-B-40, Reid to Heeney, 23 Sep. 50.

107. *Ibid.*, Tel., Reid to Chairman, Candel New York, 28 Sep. 50; Stairs, pp. 115ff; *Mike* II, 158ff.; Soward, VI, 70ff.

108. Privy Council Office Records, PARC Box 287281, file G-76, Pelletier to Pickersgill, 28 Feb. 51

109. *Ibid.*, file G-76-M, Minutes, 1 Mar. 51.

110. *Ibid.*, Minutes, 5, 17, 21 Mar. 51.

111. *Ibid.*, PARC Box 287334, file P50-7, Memo, Halliday to Bryce, 20 Apr. 48 and Gill to NAR, 2 Dec. 49; *ibid.*, PARC Box 287339, file S-100, Cowley to Heeney, 1 Dec. 48.

112. *Ibid.*, PARC Box 287262, file C-20-7, Cabinet Directive No. 4, 5 Mar. 48.

113. *Ibid.*, Cabinet Directive 4A, 6 Apr. 48. See also documents on DEA, file 50207-40; King Papers, "Loyalty of Government Employees," n.d., ff. C229129-30.

114. DEA, file 50028-V-40, Memo, 10 Sep. 49.

115. Privy Council Office Records, PARC Box 287324, file C-20-5, Memo for Cabinet, 22 Aug. 49.

116. *Ibid.*, Memo, 22 Aug. 49.

117. *Ibid.*, PARC Box 287262, file C-20-7, Cabinet Directive No. 14, 28 Oct. 49.

118. House of Commons *Debates*, 21 Feb. 49, pp. 724ff. See also Pearson Papers, N1, vol. 65, Wrong to Pearson, 7 Feb. 50, for a different view.

119. House of Commons *Debates*, 20 Feb. 50, pp. 43ff. and 29 Mar. 50, pp.

1343-44; Pickersgill, p. 147. See *Financial Post*, 19 Nov. 49, for the article that started the NFB issue; John Sawatsky, *Men in the Shadows* (Toronto, 1980) pp. 114-15.

120. House of Commons *Debates*, 2 May 50, pp. 2077ff.

121. PAC, Privy Council Office Records, PARC Box 287341, file U-10, Heeney to NAR, 12 Dec. 49; Privy Council Office Records, PARC Box 287303, file S-100, Memo, 1 Mar. 50.

122. *Ibid.*, Glazebrook to NAR, 2 Mar. 50.

123. *Ibid.*, Stephenson to NAR, 7 Sep. 50; Pearson to Stephenson, 11 Aug. 50.

124. Documents on *ibid.*, file S-100(r).

125. *Ibid.*, PARC Box 287304, file S-100-2-1, Security Panel Minutes, 16 Sep. 50.

126. *Ibid.*, PARC Box 287262, file C22-1, Memo, NAR to Prime Minister, 25 Oct. 50.

127. *Ibid.*, Memo to Cabinet, 23 Jan. 51, NAR to Prime Minister, 23 Jan. 51, and Cabinet minute, 24 Jan. 51.

128. The best account of Norman is in Charles Taylor, *Six Journeys* (Toronto, 1977), pp. 107ff. See also *Winnipeg Free Press*, 24-27 Apr. 57; *U.S. News and World Report*, 26 Apr. 57, pp. 121ff.; Sawatsky, pp. 145ff. For External officers' views, see Bishop's University, T.W.L. MacDermot Papers, file 54, J.W. Holmes to MacDermot, Labour Day, 1957.

129. NAR was deeply concerned with questions of security of atomic secrets. See Privy Council Office Records, PARC Box 287300, file R-100-A; C.J. Mackenzie Papers (Ottawa), Diary, 31 Oct., 9 Nov. 49 and 7 May 52. For comparative purposes, see E.J. Kahn, Jr., *The China Hands* (New York, 1975).

130. Mrs. Mary Oliver interview, 13 Feb. 78. Mrs. Oliver, NAR's sister, was a good friend of the Normans and had clearly talked about the case with NAR.

131. Pearson Papers, N1, vol. 44, NAR to Pearson 9 Apr. 57.

132. Mrs. Eleanor Fleming Auston interview, 14 Dec. 78.

133. St. Laurent Papers, vol. 118, G. Robertson to NAR, n.d., with NAR pen notes.

134. See J.L. Granatstein and J.M. Hitsman, *Broken Promises: A History of Conscription in Canada* (Toronto, 1977), Chapter VII and particularly pp. 250ff.

135. PAC, Claxton Papers, Draft Memoirs, vol. 6, f.1143.

136. Privy Council Office Records, PARC Box 287288, file M-5, Wrong to NAR, 11 Sep. 50.

137. House of Commons *Debates*, 1 Feb. 51, p. 27.

138. Dexter Papers, Memo, 22 Feb. 51.

139. St. Laurent Papers, vol. 236, R.G. Robertson to NAR, 12 Jan. 51.

140. Queen's University, W.A. Mackintosh Papers, Box 4, file III, NACOM Minutes, 20-21 Feb. 51.
141. *Ibid.*; Ottawa *Citizen*, 22 Feb. 51.
142. St. Laurent Papers, vol. 236, Memo for Prime Minister, 27 Feb. 51.
143. Privy Council Office Records, PARC Box 287288, file M-5-1, A.H. Brown to NAR, 2 Apr. 51.
144. *Ibid.*, NAR to MacNamara, 10 Apr. 51.
145. *Ibid.*, PARC Box 287291, file N-27, Cabinet Committee on Emergency Measures, Minutes, 16 Apr. 51.
146. *Ibid.*, PARC Box 287288, file M-5-1, Claxton to NAR, 20 Apr. 51.
147. *Ibid.*, PARC Box 287291, file N-27, MacNamara to NAR, 21 Apr. 51 and memo, R.G. Robertson to Pickersgill, 27 Apr. 51 with NAR's comment.
148. *Ibid.*, PARC Box 287288, file M-5-1-M, Minutes, 18-19 May 51; *The Globe and Mail*, 21 May 51.
149. Privy Council Office Records, PARC Box 287291, file N-27, R.G. Robertson to NAR, 22 Aug. 51.
150. DEA, Pickersgill interview, 3 Dec. 77.
151. Pearson Papers, N1, vol. 32, Memo, 23 Oct. 51.
152. Heeney Papers, vol. 1, "Memo concerning my future employment . . . ," 1 Dec. 51.
153. *Ibid.*, Memo, 15 Dec. 51.
154. Pickersgill, pp. 173-74.
155. Heeney Papers, vol. 1, Memo, 15 Mar. 52. Cf. A.D.P. Heeney, *The Things that are Caesar's* (Toronto, 1972), p. 107.
156. Robertson Papers, vol. 2, Personal Correspondence, P.C. 1603, 18 Mar. 52.
157. PAC, Watson Sellar Diary, 18 Mar. 52.
158. Confidential source.
159. Dexter Papers, Memo, 23 Jan. 52; *Mike* II, 77; Eayrs, IV, 170ff.
160. Robertson Papers, vol. 2, Personal Correspondence, letters, 20, 21, 22 Mar. 52; *The Times*, 20 Mar. 52. Other UK clippings are on Rhodes House, Oxford, NAR file.
161. J.W. Pickersgill Papers (Ottawa), Congratulations re Appointment to PCO file, Pickersgill to J. Chapdelaine, 16 May 52.
162. Le Pan Papers, vol. 2, file 25, Plumptre to L. Couillard, 23 May 52.

Chapter X

1. Robertson's salary in London was $12,000 plus allowances, down from the $15,000 he had received as Secretary to the Cabinet. He was carried

on the books of DEA as an FSO-10, the highest rank. Documents on PAC, Civil Service Commission Records, Historical Personnel Files, vol. 839, NAR file; see also PAC, A.D.P. Heeney Papers, vol. 1, Wilgress to Heeney, 2 Apr. 53; and Bishop's University, T.W.L. MacDermot Papers, file 57 for samples of the instructions for Heads of Mission.

2. Pickersgill wrote NAR to say that, "I have a whole sheaf of letters of yours to reply to. This must be a situation unique in the experience of any of your correspondents." J.W. Pickersgill Papers (Ottawa), NAR file, Pickersgill to NAR, 2 Apr. 53.

3. Sydney Pierce interview, 12 Oct. 78; Graham Spry interview, 17 Feb. 79. PAC, George Drew Papers, vol. 389, contain a list of honorary memberships in clubs that went with the High Commissioner's post. It includes the Atheneum, the Travellers' and a dozen or so others.

4. Brian Heeney Papers (Peterborough), A.D.P. Heeney to parents, 28 Feb. 53.

5. Sir John Hicks interview, 15 Jun. 78.

6. Mrs. N.A. Robertson interview, 8 Jan. 80. See also NAR's testimony to House of Commons Standing Committee on External Affairs, 12 Mar. 59, p. 55, and Drew Papers, vol. 389, Memo, Arnold Smith to Drew, 25 Oct. 57 for a negative view.

7. John Stevenson, "Men of Action," *The Montrealer* (December 1956), 29.

8. Judith Robertson interview, 9 Mar. 78.

9. Drew Papers, vol. 389, Memo, A. Smith to Drew, 25 Oct. 57.

10. Eleanor Fleming Auston interview, 14 Dec. 78.

11. PAC, L.B. Pearson Papers, N1, vol. 32, NAR to Pearson, 8 Mar. 55; C.M. Drury interview, 4 Apr. 79.

12. Drew Papers, vol. 389, Memo, Pierce to Drew, 7 Oct. 57.

13. PAC, Louis St. Laurent Papers, vol. 170, NAR to R.B. Bryce, 3 May 56.

14. Jules Léger interview, 17 Nov. 78.

15. DEA, J.W. Pickersgill interview, 3 Dec. 77.

16. Geoffrey Murray interview, 15 May 79.

17. Pearson Papers, N1, vol. 29, Pearson to MacKay, 28 Nov. 55, citing NAR letter, 21 Nov. 55.

18. PAC, Norman Robertson Papers, vol. 3A, Personal Correspondence, J. Holmes to NAR, 22 May. 58.

19. Pearson Papers, vol. 13, NAR to Pearson, 2 Sep. 54.

20. See telegrams from the UK on DEA, file 50012-40 and, generally, B.S. Keirstead, *Canada in World Affairs 1951-53* (Toronto, 1956), pp. 198ff.

21. Queen's University, J.M. Macdonnell Papers, Memo, J.H. Warren to George Drew, 3 Sep. 57.

22. See tels. on DEA, file 50123-40 after 23 Jul. 52.

23. Pearson Papers, N1, vol. 23, NAR to Pearson, 21 Aug. 52.

24. DEA, file 50123-40, tel., High Commissioner to SSEA, 22 Aug. 52.

25. PAC, D.V. Le Pan Papers, vol. 5, file 77, Minutes, 22 Sep. 52.

26. DEA, file 50123-40, "Report Made to Ministers . . . ," 31 Oct. 52.

27. See *ibid.*, Memo, Couillard to NAR, 14 Nov. 52.

28. See on the Conference, Queen's University, Grant Dexter Papers, Dexter to Hutchison, 21 Dec. 52.

29. Bank of Canada Archives, Louis Rasminsky Papers, Correspondence file, Rasminsky to Towers, 12 Jan. 54.

30. See on this James Eayrs, *Canada in World Affairs 1955-57* (Toronto, 1959), pp. 175ff.

31. Confidential sources.

32. See documents on DEA, file 50219-AF-40 and on St. Laurent Papers, vol. 233.

33. For example, Pearson Papers, N1, vol. 19, Memos, 17 May and 13 Jul. 55.

34. DEA, file 50092-C-40, ICETP Minutes, 3 Dec. 53.

35. *Ibid.*, file 50105-F-40, Sharp to Ritchie, 3 Jul. 56.

36. *Ibid.*, "Discussion at Mr. Pearson's Home . . . 19 May 56," and tel., High Commission to External, 15 Jun. 56.

37. *Ibid.*

38. Documents on PAC, EAR, vol. 2009, file Coron. 1/3; Mrs. Robertson interview, 8 Jan. 80; *Winnipeg Free Press*, 19 Feb. 53.

39. EAR, vol. 2010, file Coron. 3, "Allocation of Seating Accommodation," n.d.

40. Based on material in Mrs. Robertson's possession.

41. Mrs. Robertson interview, 8 Jan. 80.

42. Pearson Papers, N1, vol. 52, NAR to Pearson, 9 Nov. 53.

43. *Ibid.*, NAR to Pearson, 17 Jan. 56.

44. *Ibid.*, 17 Jul. 56. Later the Royal family name was altered to Mountbatten-Windsor.

45. *The Globe and Mail*, 31 Dec. 52.

46. Queen's University, University Records, Principal's Files, Series I, folder 20. NAR's contribution was $500. Contributor's list, 22 Jan. 54. See also Dexter Papers, Hutchison to Dexter, 6 Mar. 53.

47. DEA, file 46-BU-40, P.C. 1953-899, 9 Jun. 53.

48. Mrs. June Wrong Rogers Papers (Ottawa), Wrong to Reid, 10 Jul. 53. See also Heeney Papers, vol. 1, Heeney-Wilgress correspondence from Jan. 53 and after.

49. Mrs. C.H.A. Armstrong Papers (Toronto), Joyce Wrong to Mrs. Armstrong, 16 Nov. 53. Cf. Heeney Papers, vol. 2, chapter XIV file, Note of 25 Jan. 54: "There was something curiously "fatal' about his going to

Ottawa. Almost one m[igh]t. have thought that . . . he foresaw what would happen."

50. Pearson Papers, N1, vol. 17, Pearson to NAR, 27 Jan. 54.

51. Dexter Papers, Memo, 27 May 54.

52. Heeney Papers, vol. 1, Pearson to Heeney, 1 Feb. 54.

53. Pearson Papers, N1, vol. 32, NAR to Pearson, 12 Feb. 54. See on Davis, James Eayrs, *In Defence of Canada*, Vol. IV: *Growing Up Allied* (Toronto, 1980), 331ff. For John Holmes's views, see MacDermot Papers, file 54, letter fragment, n.d.

54. Pearson Papers, N1, Pearson to NAR, 6 Mar. 54.

55. *Ibid.*, NAR to Pearson, 31 Mar. 54.

56. PAC, Watson Sellar Papers, Diary, 1 Jul. 54: "Interesting . . . because it breaks up a clique. . . ."

57. DEA, file 50134-40, tel., High Commissioner to SSEA, 19 Nov. 55.

58. *Ibid.*, 21 Jan. 56.

59. *Ibid.*, tel. NAR to SSEA, 9 Mar. 56.

60. L.B. Pearson, *Mike: The Memoirs of the Right Honourable L.B. Pearson*, Vol. II: *1948-57* (Toronto, 1973), 225.

61. *Ibid.*, 227.

62. *Ibid.*, 227-8; also Dale Thomson, *Louis St. Laurent, Canadian* (Toronto, 1967), pp. 458-59.

63. Confidential source.

64. DEA, file 50134-40, General Charles Foulkes to USSEA, 3 Aug. 56.

65. T. Robertson, *Crisis: The Inside Story of the Suez Conspiracy* (Toronto, 1964), pp. 83-85.

66. Thomson, p. 461. NAR's views were reinforced in Pearson's talks with Selwyn Lloyd, the British Foreign Secretary. *Ibid.*, p. 462.

67. Pearson Papers, N1, vol. 37, tel., Pearson to NAR, 29 Sep. 56.

68. Robertson, *Crisis*, p. 125.

69. *Ibid.*, Chapters VII-VIII. See also P. Calvocoressi, *et al.*, *Suez Ten Years After* (London, 1967), especially Chapter IV; and Elie Kedourie, "The Entanglements of Suez," *The Times Literary Supplement*, 30 Nov. 79, 69-70.

70. Sydney Pierce interview, 12 Oct. 78.

71. Eleanor Fleming Auston interview, 14 Dec. 78.

72. DEA, file 50134-40, SSEA to Washington Embassy, 30 Oct. 56.

73. *Ibid.*, Pearson to NAR, 30 Oct. 56.

74. *Ibid.*, NAR to Pearson, 30 Oct. 56.

75. Joe Garner, *The Commonwealth Office 1925-68* (London, 1978), p. 327.

76. DEA, file 50134-40, NAR to Pearson, 30 Oct. 56.

77. Document on *ibid*.

78. *Ibid.*, tel., DRCS Washington to DRB, 30 Oct. 56.

79. See *Mike* II, 238.
80. *Ibid.*, 238-39.
81. DEA, file 50134-40, Memo, McInnes to USSEA, 2 Nov. 56.
82. Pearson Papers, N1, vol. 39, tel., NAR to Pearson, 1 Nov. 56.
83. *Ibid.*, 1 Nov. 56.
84. *Ibid.*, 1 Nov. 56; Confidential source.
85. For example, see DEA, file 7631-40, Pearson memo, 14 Dec. 51; Heeney Papers, vol. 2, H. Letson to Heeney, 19 Dec. 56.
86. Pearson Papers, N1, vol. 39, Memo, Smith to NAR, 1 Nov. 56, att. to NAR to Pearson, 1 Nov. 56.
87. Robertson, *Crisis*, pp. 202-03.
88. *Ibid.*, p. 209; Thomson, p. 475. But cf. Pearson Papers, N1, vol. 39, Memo to Minister, 3 Nov. 56, which conveys a different impression.
89. The best overall study of peacekeeping is Alan James, *The Politics of Peace-keeping* (London, 1969).
90. See Anthony Nutting, *No End of a Lesson* (London, 1967), pp. 140-41.
91. Document on DEA, file 50134-40.
92. *Mike* II, 225-56; Thomson, pp. 479-80. For Canadian public opinion, see Eayrs, *Canada and World Affairs 1955-7*, pp. 182ff. For Commonwealth attitudes, see Eayrs, *The Commonwealth and Suez* (London, 1964).
93. Document on DEA, file 50134-40.
94. See *ibid.*, NAR to USSEA, 7 Nov. 56 and USSEA to Acting SSEA, 8 Nov. 56.
95. *Ibid.*, tel., NAR to SSEA, 6 Nov. 56. Robertson, *Crisis*, p. 266, and Thomson, p. 481, attribute this message directly to Eden.
96. DEA, file 50134-40, tel., NAR to Léger, 7 Nov. 56.
97. *Ibid.*, Pearson to NAR, 10 Nov. 56.
98. *Ibid.*, NAR to External, 14 Nov. 56. See also the *Globe and Mail* editorials, 14, 17 Nov. 56.
99. Eayrs, *Canada and World Affairs*, pp. 267ff.; E.L.M. Burns, *Between Arab and Israeli* (Toronto, 1962), pp. 186ff.; and A. Taylor, *et al.*, *Peacekeeping: International Challenge and Canadian Response* (Toronto, 1968), pp. 118ff.
100. DEA, file 50134-40, NAR to External, 10 Nov. 56.
101. *Ibid.*, 10 Nov. 56.
102. *Ibid.*, 14 Dec. 56.
103. *Ibid.*, 9 Feb. 57.
104. *Ibid.*, 20 Feb. 57.
105. Pearson Papers, vol. 39, Léger to Pearson, 21 Nov. 56, and att. tel., London to External, 20 Nov. 56.
106. *Ibid.*, Memo for USSEA, 21 Dec. 56 and attached memo, 18 Dec. 56.
107. See *inter alia*, G. Sparrow, *"R.A.B." Story of a Statesman* (London, 1965), Chapters 8, 9.

108. NAR Round Table, 18 Feb. 78.

109. DEA, file 7631-40, NAR to External, 3 Dec. 56.

110. That attitude persisted for some time. See *ibid.*, file 50134-40, NAR to External, 24 Apr. 57.

111. *Ibid.*, NAR to External, 13 Dec. 56.

112. Eayrs, *Commonwealth*, p. 379.

113. This section based on interviews with Lord Adeane, 21 May 78; Lord Garner, 25 May 78; Arnold Smith, 22 Nov. 78; Sydney Pierce, 12 Oct. 78; and Escott Reid, 21 Jul. 77 and 14 Oct. 78. Garner, p. 327, suggests that officials in London were unhappy with their government's actions. No doubt, but many disliked critics even more, or so some Canadians remember it.

114. Robertson Papers, vol. 3A, NAR to J.W. Holmes, n.d. [Jul. 57?].

115. *Ibid.*, St. Laurent to NAR, 6 Sep. 56.

116. *Ibid.*, Tel., Pearson to NAR, 3 Oct. 56.

117. *Ibid.*, Léger to NAR, 6 Dec. 56.

118. *Ibid.*, NAR to Léger, 17 Dec. 56. The salary in Washington was $16,000. Civil Service Commission, Historical Personnel files, vol. 839, NAR file, Notice of Termination of Employment, 28 Nov. 58.

119. *The Times*, 16 Mar. 57.

120. US Treasury Records, Accession 68-A-5918, box 85, file Can/0/20 (1957), "Joint United States-Canadian Committee on Trade and Economic Affairs, October 7-8, 1958."

121. DEA, file 1415-40, "Draft of Portion of Proposed Letter of Appointment . . . ," May 57.

122. Pearson Papers, N1, vol. 13, NAR to Pearson, 3 Apr. 57.

123. "Official Canadian Residence in Washington," a brochure from the Canadian Embassy, Washington; Mrs. June Wrong Rogers interview, 13 Apr. 78.

124. DEA, Canadian Embassy, Washington, Records, (Washington, D.C.), file 27-3-16-1, Memo No. 1 for Mr. Ritchie, 2 Mar. 62. This memorandum was prepared by Heeney for C.S.A. Ritchie, who was taking over as Ambassador in 1962. Its details are correct for 1957 as well.

125. Mrs. A.D.P. Heeney interview, 20 Nov. 78.

126. DEA, Canadian Embassy Records, file 27-3-16-1, Memo No. 2 for Mr. Ritchie, 2 Mar. 62.

127. Mrs. Armstrong Papers, Wrong to sister.

128. DEA, Canadian Embassy Records, file 27-3-16-1, Memo No. 2.

129. *Ibid.*, file 27-3-12, Memo for Ambassador, 16 May 57.

130. Heeney Papers, vol. 1, NAR to Heeney, 18 Jun. 53.

131.   See the list of ministers and ambassadors in R.F. Swanson, *Intergovernmental Perspectives on the Canada-U.S. Relationship* (New York, 1978), pp. 61-63; Eayrs, *Canada and World Affairs*, p. 106; *Mike* III, 169ff.

132.   The phrase was Brooke Claxton's. PAC, Claxton Papers, vol. 84, Claxton to NAR, 19 Feb. 57.

133.   On the reaction, Eayrs, *Canada and World Affairs*, pp. 55-57, 105, 153ff.; and Heeney Papers, vol. 2, Diary, 16 Apr. 57.

134.   Confidential interview, 27 Sep. 78.

135.   Pearson Papers, N1, vol. 65, NAR to Minister and USSEA, 17 May 57, copy on Department of External Affairs, file 1415-40. Cf. Winnipeg *Tribune*, 21 May 57, in which NAR was quoted: "We didn't get to talk about past issues," when he was asked if the Norman case had been discussed.

136.   DEA, file 50303-40, NAR to External, 25 May 57.

137.   Canadian Embassy Records, file 27-3-12, Note, 13 Aug. 57.

138.   Documents on DEA, file 50303-40. A year later the same Senate subcommittee that had attacked Norman smeared R.B. Bryce, the Secretary to the Cabinet. See House of Commons *Debates*, 14 May 58, p. 64.

139.   Saul Rae interview, 10 Jul. 78.

140.   DEA, file 1415-40, tel., NAR to External, 25 Jul. 57, and 26 Jul. 57.

141.   See M.J. Abrams, *The Canada-United States Interparliamentary Group* (Toronto and Ottawa, 1973).

142.   Dean Acheson had urged NAR to press Pearson to run for the Liberal leadership after the election defeat. See Pearson Papers, N1, vol. 29, Acheson to Pearson, 12 Jun. 57.

143.   DEA, J.W. Pickersgill interview, 3 Dec. 77.

144.   *Ibid.*, file 50330-A-40, "Meeting of Ministers of Finance and Trade and Commerce with Officials . . . ", 22 Jun. 57.

145.   That was a sign of Diefenbaker's pro-British sentiment and his Canadian nationalism. See Trevor Lloyd, *Canada and World Affairs, 1957-1959* (Toronto, 1968), pp. 66ff. The Americans were sensitive to this, particularly after the Gordon Commission Report of 1957. See Treasury Records, Accession 68-A-5918, box 5, file Can/0/25, Desp. 656, from Ottawa, 12 Feb. 57.

146.   Robertson Papers, vol. 3A, Holmes to NAR, 1 Aug. 57.

147.   H.B. Robinson interview, 16 May 79 and memo (read to author), Robinson to Prime Minister, 15 Oct. 57. There is no mention of this in J.G. Diefenbaker, *One Canada: Memoirs of the Rt. Hon. John G. Diefenbaker*, Vol. II: *1956-62* (Toronto, 1976).

148.   PAC, Howard Green Papers, vol. 8, Memo for the Minister, 19 Jun. 61 and attachments.

149.   *Ibid.*, attached memo, 12 Jun. 57.

150. DEA, file 50309-40, Bryce to Holmes, 1 Aug. 57. General Foulkes later said publicly that "we stampeded the incoming Government with the N.O.R.A.D. agreement. . . ." Testimony to a House of Commons Special Committee on Defence, cited in R.W. Reford, "Making Defence Policy in Canada," *Behind the Headlines*, XXIII (December 1963), 14.

151. DEA, file 50309-40, Foulkes to Holmes, 7 Aug. 57. This letter suggests that Léger was consulted by Bryce about the possibility of accepting the agreement without Cabinet Defence Committee approval.

152. *Ibid.*, Holmes to Bryce, 31 Jul. 57. The best accounts of this affair are J.T. Jockel, "The United States and Canadian Efforts at Continental Air Defense, 1945-57," PhD thesis, Johns Hopkins University, 1978, pp. 243ff; Jon McLin, *Canada's Changing Defense Policy 1957-63* (Baltimore, 1967), Chapter III. Also see R.H. Roy, *For Most Conspicuous Bravery: A Biography of Major-General George R. Pearkes through Two World Wars* (Vancouver, 1977) pp. 287ff., and Diefenbaker, III, 22 ff.

153. DEA, file 50309-40, Léger to SSEA, 7 Oct. 57 and ff. documents. See Diefenbaker, III, 23-24.

154. DEA, file 50309-40, NAR to External, 1 Aug. 57.

155. *Ibid.*, NAR to External, 6 Nov. 57.

156. *Ibid.*, Foulkes to USSEA, 26 Nov. 57; Diefenbaker, III, 20, 23.

157. Justly so. See McLin, pp. 54ff.; Lloyd, pp. 30ff.

158. DEA, file 50309-30, NAR to External, 13 Dec. 57.

159. *Ibid.*, 8 Jan. 58.

160. *Ibid.*

161. Documents on *ibid.*

162. DEA, Washington Embassy Records, file 3-2-2-10, Tel., NAR to Léger, 7 Mar. 58.

163. *Ibid.*, Léger to Ambassador, 14 Mar. 58.

164. Those signs predated the Diefenbaker government. See Pearson Papers, N1, vol. 65, Heeney to Pearson, 21 Jun. 54 and attachments.

165. DEA, Washington Embassy Records, file 3-2-2-9, NAR to SSEA, 9 Nov. 57.

166. *Ibid.*, NAR to External, 13 Nov. 57.

167. *Ibid.*, NAR to SSEA, 4 Dec. 57 and 22 Nov. 57.

168. *Ibid.*, Gates to NAR, 19 Dec. 57. Cf. McLin, p. 71.

169. DEA, Washington Embassy Records, file 3-2-2-9, "Notes on lunch . . . ," 30 Jan. 58, encl. with NAR to USSEA, 6 Feb. 58.

170. *Ibid.*, file 4-12-6, Memo, N.R. Chappell to D. Golden, 6 Aug. 58; James Dow, *The Arrow* (Toronto, 1979), p. 117; Roy, p. 317.

171. See Dow, pp. 117ff.

172. For example, Robertson Papers, vol. 3A, Léger to NAR, 23 Apr. 58 and attachments; PAC, R.B. Bryce Papers, Notebook, 23 Jan. 58.

173. DEA, file 50162-A-40, Tels., NAR to External, 5, 18 Jun. 58; *ibid.*, J.W. Holmes interview, 27 Jul. 77.
174. DEA, Washington Embassy Records, file 3-2-2-1, Record of the Meeting . . . ," 30 Sep. 57. See also DEA, file 2462-40, NAR to USSEA, 23 Jan. 58; and file 50128-40, NAR to External, 28 May 58.
175. *Ibid.*, file 50396-40, Tel., NAR to Léger, 31 May 57.
176. *Ibid.*, Léger to NAR, 31 May 57. For more on Korea and the difficulties it posed for Canadian-American relations, see *ibid.*, documents from Feb. 58 and ff.
177. Léger interview, 17 Nov. 78.
178. Marcel Cadieux interview, 3 May 79.
179. Rt. Hon. J.G. Diefenbaker interview, 15 Feb. 79.
180. H.B. Robinson interview, 16 May 79.
181. *Ibid.*
182. *Ibid.*; *Washington Post*, 20 Aug. 58. Robertson's successor, A.D.P. Heeney, was not selected until 30 Dec. 58. See Heeney Papers, vol. 1, Confidential memos, 30 Dec. 58 and 8 Jan. 59. The memos indicate that Robertson was pleased by Heeney's choice but had no advance information of it.
183. DEA, file 1415-40, Tel., Washington to External, 20 Aug. 58.
184. Heeney Papers, vol. 1, Frankfurter to Heeney, 8 Mar. 59. See also DEA, John Starnes Papers, for C.D. Howe's reaction, 8 Oct. 58: "We will all feel better with an experienced hand at the helm of our foreign relations."
185. Treasury Records, Accession 68-A-5918, box 87, file Can/9/30, Murphy to Scribner, 28 Oct. 58.

Chapter XI

1. Mrs. George Ignatieff interview, 11 Sep. 78.
2. PAC, N.A. Robertson Papers, vol. 3a, Personal Correspondence 1958-9, Kirkconnell-NAR correspondence, Oct. 58-Mar. 59. The lecture drafts are in *ibid.*, vol. 3.
3. M.C. Urquhart and K.A.H. Buckley, *Historical Statistics of Canada* (Toronto, 1965), p. 621.
4. See Peter Stursberg, *Diefenbaker Leadership Gained, 1956-62* (Toronto, 1975), Chapter IX; John Porter, *The Vertical Mosaic* (Toronto, 1965), pp. 451ff.
5. Rt. Hon. J.G. Diefenbaker interview, 15 Feb. 79.
6. R.B. Bryce interview, 26 Oct. 78; Stursberg, p. 145.
7. Diefenbaker interview.
8. Mrs. N.A. Robertson interviews, 26 Feb. and 23 Oct. 78.
9. One officer who joined the Department of External Affairs in the late 1950s remembered Robertson "pulling all the junior officers together and explaining how it was an honour and a privilege to serve." Sandra Gwyn,

"Ottawa's Incredible Bureaucratic Explosion," *Saturday Night*, (July-August 1975), 27ff.

10. H.B. Robinson interview, 16 May 79; NAR Round Table, 18 Feb. 78.

11. PAC, R.B. Bryce Papers, Notebooks, *passim*.

12. Bryce interview, 10 Jun. 79.

13. Bryce was also in a position to referee the fights between the Departments of National Defence and External Affairs. See Bryce Papers, Telephone notes, Feb. 60.

14. Diefenbaker interview, 15 Feb. 79.

15. Based on interviews with Robinson, 21 Nov. 78 and 16 May 79; Ross Campbell, 6 Jun. 79; Marcel Cadieux, 3 May 79; John Starnes, 5 Jun. 79.

16. R.G. Robertson interview, Dec. 78.

17. See J.L. Granatstein, *The Politics of Survival* (Toronto, 1967), pp. 13-14, 137, 143-44.

18. R.M. Brisbane, "Sidney Smith: From College to Cabinet," *Saturday Night* (28 Sep. 57), 47. For other, more favourable views, see the round-up of editorial opinion in the Toronto *Telegram*, 16 Sep. 57.

19. Cadieux interview, 3 May 79. See also Bishop's University, T.W.L. MacDermot Papers, file 53, G.V. Ferguson to MacDermot, 12 Jun. and 18 Aug. 58.

20. Robinson interview, 21 Nov. 78.

21. D.V. Le Pan interview, 5 Jul. 79.

22. See the cool comments in House of Commons *Debates*, 18 Mar. 59, pp. 2016-17.

23. For example, *ibid.*, 25 Feb. 41, p. 1008; DEA, Howard Green interview, 13-14 Sep. 78; Green interview, 1 May 78.

24. DEA, George Ignatieff interview, 29 Mar. 78.

25. Hon. Paul Martin interview, 16 Jun. 78.

26. Based on interviews with Mrs. Robertson, 26 Feb. 78 and 17 Oct. 78; Cadieux, 3 May 79; Lord Garner, 25 May 78.

27. Figures from Historical Division, DEA.

28. *Report of Royal Commission on Government Organization* (Ottawa, 1963) IV, 103, 108, 130.

29. Robertson's executive assistant regularly cleaned out NAR's file baskets and briefcase. In March 1961, for example, he took out all documents prior to 1 Jan. 61, and provided a seventeen-page list of documents returned to files, including one at least that was dated April 1959. DEA, John Starnes Papers, Memo, R.D. Jackson to NAR, 15 Mar. 61.

30. *Ibid.*, State Papers 41-1961/2, "Organization of Department of External Affairs—Prepared for Glassco Commission by Prof. Maxwell Cohen Nov. 1961." Sir William Hayter, *The Diplomacy of the Great Powers* (New York, 1961), p. 42, noted that: "It may well be that the best diplomacy now is

not to be found among the Great Powers at all but elsewhere, for instance among the Dutch, the Canadians. . . ." He added (p. 61): "the Canadians, who so brilliantly built up from nothing one of the highest-powered Foreign Services in the modern world. . . ."

31. Starnes Papers, Matthews to NAR, 19 Dec. 58; Memo to Minister, 25 Jun. 59. Replacements included A.E. Ritchie, Ross Campbell, Max Wershof, and George Ignatieff. On Matthews's death, see House of Commons Standing Committee on External Affairs, 16 Mar. 59, p. 93.

32. Based on charts and tables in DEA *Annual Reports*. See the useful capsule history in Gilles Lalande, *The Department of External Affairs and Biculturalism* (Ottawa, 1969), pp. 6ff.

33. Undated clipping of story by John Walker of Southam News [Feb.-Mar., 1964].

34. Max Wershof interview, 5 Apr. 79.

35. House of Commons Standing Committee on External Affairs, 12 Mar. 59. pp. 43-44.

36. *Ibid.*, 16 Mar. 59, 30 Mar. and 6 Apr. 60, 9, 10 May 61.

37. Samples on Starnes Papers.

38. Walter Gordon interview, 1 Aug. 78.

39. DEA, George Glazebrook interview, 8 Jul. 77.

40. Starnes interview, 5 Jun. 79; Bryce interview, 13 Feb. 79; Cadieux interview, 3 May 79. Cf. DEA, documents on file 50207-A-40.

41. *Ibid.*, documents on file 10-1-1-1.

42. *Ibid.*, file 50028-BM-40, NAR to Le Pan, 10 Oct. 58.

43. *Ibid.*, NAR to Foulkes, 23 Nov. 59.

44. *Ibid.*, Memo to Minister, 22 Apr. 60.

45. *Ibid.*, Terms of Reference, 5 May 60.

46. *Ibid.*, Green interview, 13-14 Sep. 78.

47. M. Tucker, "Canada's Role in the Disarmament Negotiations 1957-71," PhD dissertation, University of Toronto, 1977, p. 59. Letter, General Burns to author, 21 Apr. 79.

48. DEA, file 50271-K-40, NAR to Minister, 12 Nov. 59.

49. *Ibid.*, NAR to Minister, 21 Jan. 60; Diefenbaker speech, 11 Feb. 60, printed in Arthur Blanchette, *Canadian Foreign Policy 1955-65* (Toronto, 1977), pp. 53ff.; letter, Burns to author, 21 Apr. 79.

50. Bryce Papers, telephone notes, 6 Sep. 60. On disarmament generally, see Burns's book, *A Seat at the Table* (Toronto, 1972) and Peyton Lyon, *Canada in World Affairs, 1961-3* (Toronto, 1968), pp. 223ff; and documents on PAC, Howard Green Papers, vols. 2, 3.

51. DEA, file 6386-C-40, NAR to Minister, 14 Jul. 60 and ff.; Geoffrey Murray interview, 15 May 79.

52. DEA, file 6386-C-40, NAR to Minister, 27 Jul. 60.

53. *Ibid.*, 20 Jul. 60.

54. *Ibid.*, Tel., Permisny to External, 8 Aug. 60. The fullest account of Canada in the Congo is in Alastair Taylor, *et al., Peacekeeping: International Challenge and Canadian Response* (Toronto, 1968), pp. 148ff.

55. Murray interview, 15 May 79. Marcel Cadieux recalled that NAR "carried the Charter in his pocket" and amazed the Legal Division with his detailed knowledge of the instrument he had helped to draft. Interview, 3 May 79.

56. Robinson interview, 16 May 79. Peyton Lyon recalled that, later in the 1960s, Robertson was sympathetic to the white settlers' position in Rhodesia in a Carleton University lecture. Interview, 13 Oct. 78.

57. Bryce interview, 13 Feb. 79. See tels. from Bryce on PAC, George Drew Papers, vol. 390, Commonwealth file.

58. Robinson interview, 16 May 79; MacDermot Papers, file 71, Diary, 14 Jun. 60. See Diefenbaker's account of the South African question in *One Canada: Memoirs of the Rt. Hon. John G. Diefenbaker* (Toronto, 1976), II, 209ff.; Stursberg, 163ff.

59. Starnes Papers, Escott Reid to NAR, 14 Mar. 61. See also NAR's contribution in *Canada and Europe . . . a New Look* (The Fifth Annual Banff Conference on World Affairs, 1967), pp. 166-68.

60. See, for example, Diefenbaker's speech of 7 Dec. 61 in Blanchette, pp. 292ff.

61. DEA, file 8490-B-40, Memo to Minister, 27 Sep. 60.

62. *Ibid.*, 6 Oct. 60. See Harry Johnson, *Canada in a Changing World Economy* (Toronto, 1962), pp. 51ff., and A.J.R. Smith's essay in P. Lyon, ed., *Britain and Canada* (London, 1976) pp. 129ff. and especially the charts, pp. 138-40.

63. Green Papers, vol. 7, Memo for Minister, 12 Jul. 61; see also Drew Papers, vol. 390, Commonwealth file, Green to Drew, 17 Jul. 61 and attachments.

64. Green Papers, vol. 7, 2 Jan. 62. See also Lyon, pp. 430ff., and Peter Newman, *Renegade in Power* (Toronto, 1963), pp. 270ff.

65. DEA, Canadian Embassy, Washington, file 3-2-2-1, Record of Meeting of Consultation, 30 Sep. 57.

66. See R.H. Roy, *For Most Conspicuous Bravery: A Biography of Major-General George R. Pearkes. . . .* (Vancouver, 1977), pp. 324-25.

67. DEA, Canadian Embassy, Washington, file 3-2-2-1, Draft Record of Meeting of Consultation, 19 Nov. 58.

68. For a brief note on the Committee, see R.F. Swanson, *Intergovernmental Perspectives on the Canada-U.S. Relationship* (New York, 1978), pp. 152-53.

69. PAC, D.V. Le Pan Papers, vol. 4, file 60, Heads of Mission Meeting, Paris, 11-12 Dec. 58.

70. *Ibid.*, vol. 4, file 66, Meeting of Canada-US Committee on Joint Defence, Paris, 15 Dec. 58, "Acquisition and Control of Defensive Nuclear Weapons," 6 Dec. 58. See also Green Papers, vol. 8, NAR to Minister, 23 Jan. 63, att. "Statement of Nuclear and Relevant Force Commitments under N.A.T.O. and N.O.R.A.D.," 23 Jan. 63, summarizing the whole nuclear problem.

71. DEA, file 50309-B-40, Memo, Tovell to Tremblay, 21 Jan. 59. On Diefenbaker's statement, see Diefenbaker, III, 47; on the Bomarc generally, see Jon McLin, *Canada's Changing Defense Policy, 1957-63* (Baltimore, 1967), pp. 84ff.

72. The F-101 would eventually be chosen as part of a complicated swap between the two countries. See Green Papers, vol. 8, NAR to Minister, 5 Dec. 60, 9 Jun. 61, 25 Jan. 62; J.F. Kennedy Library, Kennedy Papers, POF, Box 113, Canada Security 1961 file, Memo for President, 17 Feb. 61 and *ibid.*, Canada Security Trip to Ottawa (B) file, "Triangular Position," 12 May 61; Canadian Embassy, Washington, file 3-2-2-9, "Proposed Aircraft Swap Deal," 17 Feb. 61. The F-101s arrived in Canada in July 1961. See also accounts in Diefenbaker, III, 65ff., and R.A. Preston, *Canada in World Affairs 1959-61* (Toronto, 1965), pp. 61-62.

73. DEA, file 50309-40, Memo, "Visit to N.O.R.A.D. and S.A.C. Head-quarters. . . .," 16 Mar. 59.

74. Green Papers, vol. 8, "Statement of Nuclear and Relevant Force Commitments . . . ," 23 Jan. 63.

75. DEA, file 50309-40, Memo, "Visit to N.O.R.A.D. and S.A.C. . . . ," 16 Mar. 59.

76. H.B. Robinson Papers, (Ottawa), Memo to Prime Minister, 2 Jun. 59.

77. DEA, file 50219-AL-2-40, NAR to Minister, 12 Jun. 59.

78. PAC, A.D.P. Heeney Papers, vol. 1, Memoranda for file, 30 Jun. 59.

79. DEA, file 50309-D-40, pen note on Holmes to SSEA, 25 Aug. 59.

80. Documents on *ibid.*

81. *Ibid.*, Memo, Robinson to USSEA, 31 Aug. 59.

82. *Ibid.*, Memo, SSEA to Prime Minister, 10 Sep. 59. See especially Heeney's tel. to Ottawa, 28 Aug. 59 on DEA, Canadian Embassy Washington, file 3-2-2-7, and other documents on this file.

83. DEA, file 50361-40, NAR to Minister, 22 Oct. 59.

84. DEA, Canadian Embassy Washington, file 3-2-6, Canada-US Ministerial Committee on Joint Defence, 8-9 Nov. 59. Some US papers for these meetings are on US Treasury Records, Accession 68-A-5918, box 87, files

Can/9/10 and Can/9/30. The comments on NAR are on *ibid.*, Scope and Objectives Paper.

85. DEA, file 50309-A-40, "Canada-U.S. Defence Q uestions," n.d.

86. *Ibid.*, Memo, NAR to Minister, 23 Oct. 59.

87. *Ibid.*, file 50219-AM-40, Memo, NAR to SSEA, 2 Dec. 59.

88. Green Papers, vol. 3, Memo to Cabinet, 24 Jun. 60, copy on DEA, file 50309-A-40. See Diefenbaker, III, pp. 55-56. On the Honest John, see Green Papers, vol. 8, "Statement of Nuclear and Relevant Force Commitments . . . ," 23 Jan. 63.

89. For example, see *ibid.*, vol. 3, Memo, NAR to Minister, 18 Jul. 60 with attached draft memo to cabinet.

90. Heeney Papers, vol. 1, Memoranda of Conversations, 30, 31 Aug. 60. Heeney passed the Prime Ministerial views to Livingston Merchant, the Under-Secretary of State for Political Affairs. *Ibid.*, Memo of Conversation, 13 Sep. 60. See Arnold Heeney, *The Things That Are Caesar's* (Toronto, 1972), pp. 163-65.

91. Heeney Papers, vol. 2, Memo of Conversation, 23 Sep. 60.

92. *Ibid.*, vol. 2, Diary, 4 Feb. 62.

93. Starnes Papers, NAR Memo, "The Cuban Situation," 13 Jul. 60, and draft with NAR's corrections; letter, Starnes to author, 20 Apr. 80.

94. *Ibid.*, Record of Meeting on 12-13 Jul. 1960. Those views made an impact. See Kennedy Papers, POF, Box 113, Canada Security 1961 Trip to Ottawa (D) file, CIA National Intelligence Estimate 99-61, "Trends in Canadian Foreign Policy," 2 May 61.

95. DEA, file 2444-40, NAR to Minister, 11 Nov. 60; *ibid.*, 25 Oct. 60. See R.W. Reford, *Canada and Three Crises* (Toronto, 1968), pp. 158ff., and Denis Stairs, "Confronting Uncle Sam: Cuba and Korea," in S. Clarkson, ed., *An Independent Foreign Policy for Canada?* (Toronto, 1968) pp. 58ff.

96. House of Commons *Debates*, 20 Feb. 59 and 10 Mar. 59, collected with other statements in DEA, file 50219-AM-40, "Public Statements on Acquisition and Storage of Nuclear Weapons," 4 Nov. 60.

97. Bryce interviews, 13 Feb., 16 May 79. National Defence showed its displeasure in other ways, in one instance cancelling an agreement with the US without telling External Affairs. DEA, Canadian Embassy Washington, file 4-12-6, Barton to Rae, 28 Sep. 60.

98. Based on interviews with Bryce, 13 Feb., 16 May 79; Robinson, 16 May 79; Murray, 15 May 79; Campbell, 6 Jun. 79.

99. DEA, file 50219-AM-40, Bryce to NAR and Miller, 30 Nov. 60.

100. Green Papers, vol. 3, Memo for Minister, 5 Dec. 60 and attached draft.

101. *Ibid.*, Memo for Minister, 5 Dec. 60.

102. Kennedy Library, Oral History Program, Merchant interview, Spring 1965.

103. Robinson Papers, Memo to Under-Secretary, 21 Feb. 61; Heeney, p. 174.

104. Robinson Papers, Memo to Under-Secretary, 21 Feb. 61.

105. Green Papers, vol. 3, Bryce to Green, 2 Mar. 61; Memo, Barton to USSEA, 10 Mar. 61.

106. For example, *ibid.*, Harkness to Green, 1 Mar. 61.

107. For example, DEA, file 50219-AL-2-40, NAR to SSEA, 14 Feb. 61; copy on Green Papers, vol. 3.

108. DEA, file 50219-AM-40, Memo, Ignatieff to NAR, 4 May 61. Those were points NAR had been making to Green for some time. For example, Green Papers, vol. 3, Memo for Minister, 14 Feb. 61.

109. DEA, file 2444-40, "N.A.T.O. Ministerial Meeting; May, 1961; Cuba," 4 May 61; Kennedy Papers, POF, Box 113, Canada Security 1961, Trip to Ottawa (B) file, "The Cuban Situation" 12 May 61. See J. Ghent, "Canada, the United States and the Cuban Missile Crisis," *Pacific Historical Review*, XVIII (May 1979), 161.

110. Kennedy Papers, POF, Box 113, Canada Security 1961 (C) file, Biographical material.

111. Bryce interview, 13 Feb. 79.

112. Heeney Papers, vol. 2, Diary, 18 May. 62; Heeney, pp. 175-76; Lyon, pp. 496-97.

113. See, for example, Kennedy Papers, N.S.F. Canada, Diefenbaker Correspondence, Box 20, Tel., Armstrong to Secretary of State, 20 Sep. 61; and Ottawa *Citizen*, 16 Oct. 61, Charles Lynch column.

114. Green Papers, vol. 3, Memo for Minister, 16 Oct. 61.

115. Robinson Papers, Memo, "Nuclear Weapons Policy," 27 Feb. 62.

116. Kennedy Papers, POF, Box 113, Canada Security 1962 file, Memo for K. O'Donnell, 11 May 62.

117. On the dollar crisis, see Bryce Papers, telephone notes from 1 May 62; DEA, file 8483-40, "Minutes of Ad Hoc Committee on Balance of Payments (Longer Term Measures)," 28 Jun. 62; Kennedy Papers, POF, Box 89a, Treasury files 1962, Memo, Ball and Dillon to President, 17 Jul. 62 and *ibid.*, POF, Box 90, Treasury file 2/63, Memo Fowler to Bundy, 22 Feb. 63 and other documents in Treasury files 10/62, 11-12/62 and 1/63; see also A.F.W. Plumptre, *Three Decades of Decision* (Toronto, 1977), pp. 166ff; Diefenbaker, III, 117ff.; L.B. Pearson, *Mike: The Memoirs of the Right Honourable Lester B. Pearson* (Toronto, 1972), III, 59ff. In PAC, Georges Vanier Papers, vol. 21, "Diefenbaker and Pearson" file, diary 15 Jul. 62 [?] there is a note indicating that NAR told the Governor General of his fear that Diefenbaker might have considered calling a new election on the issue of Pearson's alleged breaking of his word to support the government measures to counter the run on the

163. Gary Caldwell, "The Participation of French Canadians in the Department of External Affairs," MA thesis, Université Laval, 1965, p.11.
164. DEA, file 3-2-1, Memo for Minister, 4 Sep. 63.
165. *Ibid.*, 27 May 63; Martin to Prime Minister, 27 Jul. 63.
166. *Ibid.*, Memo, NAR to Minister, 27 Jul. 63.
167. *Ibid.*, 4 Sep. 63.
168. Sydney Pierce interview, 12 Oct. 78; P. Lyon interview, 13 Oct. 78; NAR Round Table, 18 Feb. 78.
169. Robertson Papers, vol. 1, Biographical file, "Glassco Commission Survey of Senior Officers," 19 Jan. 62; *ibid.*, vol. 3, Personal Correspondence, P.C. 1963-1856, 20 Dec. 63.
170. *Ibid.*, P. Sabourin to D. Rickerd, 13 Apr. 64. In addition, NAR had almost $30,000 in stocks and bonds. *Ibid.*, lists 1959 and 1964.
171. Mrs. Robertson interview, 23 Oct. 78.
172. Martin interview, 16 Jun. 78; Mrs. Robertson interview, 23 Oct. 78.
173. PAC, Pearson Papers, Prime Minister's files, vol. 287, file 861/V57, Tel., Pearson to High Commissioner, 11 Jan. 64.
174. For example, Vanier Papers, vol. 25, Vanier to Mrs. Robertson, 7 Feb. 64, and Vanier to NAR, 22 Feb. 64.
175. Mrs. Robertson interviews, 9 Jun. 79 and 8 Jan. 80; Cadieux interview, 3 May 79; Starnes interview, 17 Feb. 78; MacDermot Papers, file 70, Diary, 5 Jul. 63. Martin recalls events somewhat differently. Interview, 16 Jun. 78.
176. DEA, file 37-7-3, Press Release, 27 Feb. 64.

Chapter XII

1. See W. Diebold, Jr., "The New Situation of International Trade Policy," *International Journal*, XVIII (Autumn 1963), 425ff.
2. See H.C. Eastman, "Some Aspects of Tariff Protection in Canada," *ibid.*, (Summer 1963), pp. 354-55; H.I. Macdonald, "Commonwealth Preferences: Canada's Strength at G.A.T.T.?," *The Business Quarterly*, XXIX (Spring 1964), 36ff.
3. See Bruce Hutchison in *Christian Science Monitor*, 3 May 63.
4. J.H. Warren interview, 15 May 79.
5. *Canadian Annual Review 1964* (Toronto, 1965), pp. 288-89; Gordon's budget speech in House of Commons *Debates*, 16 Mar. 64, pp. 972-73; editorial in *Winnipeg Free Press*, 5 Mar. 66.
6. *Financial Post*, 7 Dec. 63.
7. From draft remarks for the Prime Minister in Paris, January 1964, copy on DEA, file 37-7-3.

8. Documents on *ibid.*
9. E.H. Preeg, *Traders and Diplomats* (Washington, 1970), p. 10. See also K.C. Mackenzie, *Tariff-Making and Trade Policy in the U.S. and Canada* (New York, 1968), p. 58.
10. J.F. Kennedy Library, Walter Heller Papers, Box 39, US Delegations to Joint United States-Canadian Committee file, Memo, P. Thunberg to Heller, 19 Sep. 63.
11. DEA, documents on file 37-7-3, and Memo, Cadieux to SSEA, 12 Feb. 64.
12. *Ibid.*, Press Release, 27 Feb. 64. On non-tariff barriers, a subject of much contention, see documents on *ibid.*
13. *Ibid.*, Memo, D.S. McPhail to NAR, 27 Apr. 64. For business views, see, for example, ed., *Canadian Business*, XXXVII (January 1964), 23.
14. DEA, file 37-7-3, NAR to Martin, 5 Aug. 64.
15. Documents on *ibid.*, and Warren memo, "Kennedy Round: Canadian Delegation . . . ," [20 May 64]; *Financial Times*, 28 Nov. 64.
16. DEA, file 37-7-3, NAR to Martin, 5 Aug. 64, Warren memo [20 May 64].
17. *Ibid.*, McPhail to NAR, 17 Mar. 64.
18. See *External Affairs* (April 1964), 161ff.
19. DEA, file 37-7-3, Memo, 24 Apr. 64; US-Canadian Talks on Kennedy Round Negotiations, 28 Apr. 64; Memo, 2 May 64; Memo, Schwarzmann to NAR, 28 Jul. 64; Mrs. N.A. Robertson interview, 25 Feb. 80. For NAR's condition in May, see Bishop's University, T.W.L. MacDermot Papers, file 65, Diary note, 31 May 64.
20. DEA, file 37-7-3, Tel., External to Geneva, 30 Jun. 64; Sharp's statement, 11 May 64, in A.E. Blanchette, ed., *Canadian Foreign Policy 1955-65* (Toronto, 1977), pp. 380-81.
21. DEA, file 37-7-3, NAR to Martin, 5 Aug. 64.
22. *Ibid.*, Tel., External to Cadieux (Rome), 28 Dec. 64.
23. DEA, John Starnes Papers, NAR to Cadieux, 14 Jan. 65.
24. PAC, N.A. Robertson Papers, Vol. 1, "Books" file.
25. DEA, file 37-7-3, Tel., NAR to External, 16 Nov. 64. Starnes Papers, Starnes's "Notes of conversation with D.S. McPhail about Norman Robertson," 24 Nov. 76.
26. *Ibid.*, "Canadian Draft Offer," 3 Nov. 64.
27. *Ibid.*, "International Trade Developments," 23 Feb. 65.
28. *Ibid.*, NAR to External, 29 Jan. 65; Preeg, p. 90.
29. *Ibid.*, pp. 187-88.
30. DEA, file 37-7-3, NAR to External, 9 Apr. 65.
31. Mrs. Robertson interview, 25 Feb. 80.
32. Starnes Papers, "Meeting of the Heads of Mission, May 7-8, 1965."
33. Mrs. Robertson interview, 25 Feb. 80; Marcel Cadieux interview, 3 May 79.

34. Department of Finance, *Canadian Tariff Concessions Agreed in the Kennedy Round* . . . . (Ottawa, 1967); Government of Canada News Release No. 1, 29 Jun. 67, and attached press kit; *Canadian Annual Review 1967* (Toronto, 1968) pp. 336ff.; *External Affairs* (August 1967), 306ff.

35. Robertson Papers, vol. 3, Personal Correspondence, Dunton to NAR, 4 May 65.

36. Mrs. Robertson interview, 25 Feb. 80.

37. Robertson Papers, vol. 3, NAR to Dunton, 19 May 65, and Dunton to NAR, 4 Jan. 66.

38. *Ibid.*, vol. 1, USSEA to NAR, 15 Nov. 65; *The Globe and Mail*, 2 Sep. 65.

39. PAC, Paul Martin Papers, vol. 225, file 8, Martin to NAR, 9 Sep. 65.

40. Robertson Papers, vol. 3, Cadieux to NAR, 17 Nov. 65; Cadieux interview, 18 Feb. 78.

41. Robertson Papers, vol. 1, USSEA to NAR, 15 Nov. 65.

42. *Ibid.*, vol. 3, contains the contract copy that was not returned.

43. Cadieux interview, 18 Feb. 78.

44. Robertson Papers, vol. 1, Invitations file.

45. *Ibid.*, vol. 1, Congratulations file, Dymond to NAR, 24 May 66.

46. Mrs. Robertson interviews, 23 Oct. 78 and 22 Jan. 79.

47. Robertson Papers, vol. 2, Order of Canada file, NAR to R. Smith, 18 Jul. 67.

48. Bank of Canada Archives, Louis Rasminsky Papers, Robertson file, Picard to Rasminsky, 12 Dec. 66 and Heeney to Rasminsky, 15 Nov. 66.

49. Professor R.B. Byers interview, 15 Jun. 79; Professor Janice Stein interview, 8 Oct. 80.

50. Professor Peyton Lyon interview, 13 Oct. 78.

51. *Ibid.*

52. *Ibid.*; John Starnes interview, 17 Feb. 78.

53. G.A.H. Pearson interview, 8 Jun. 79.

54. *Ibid.*; Geoffrey Murray interview, 15 May 79.

55. DEA, file 20-1-2-1968, Memo, 14 Sep. 67.

56. *Ibid.*, Murray to Robinson, Collins, Langley, 6 Oct. 67.

57. *Ibid.*, Memo, 5 Oct. 67.

58. *Ibid.*, Memo, Murray to Pearson, 6 Oct. 67.

59. Murray interview, 15 May 79.

60. Cadieux interview, 3 May 79.

61. Mrs. Robertson interview, 25 Feb. 80.

62. Murray interview, 15 May 79.

63. David Mansur interview, 30 Oct. 78. Mrs. Robertson doubts this.

64. DEA, file 20-1-2-1968, Memo, G. Pearson to NAR, 8 Dec. 67 and chapter draft, 12 Feb. 68.

65. Murray interview, 15 May 79.

66.   DEA, State Papers, 36-1968/1, "Foreign Policy Review," *passim.*
67.   *Ibid.,* file 20-1-2-1968, Cadieux to SSEA, 5 Apr. 68.
68.   *Ibid.,* 22 Apr. 68. Cf. Antony Westell in *The Globe and Mail,* 19 Apr. 68.
69.   DEA, file 20-1-2-1968, Memo, USSEA to Heads of Post, 9 May 68.
70.   *Canadian Annual Review 1968* (Toronto, 1969), p. 221.
71.   Cadieux interview, 3 May 79; Murray interview, 15 May 79.
72.   Mrs. Robertson interview, 17 Oct. 78.
73.   Based on material in PAC, A.D.P. Heeney Papers, vol. 2.
74.   *The Times,* 18 Jul. 68.
75.   *Ottawa Journal,* 17 Jul. 68.
76.   *Ibid.,* 20 Jul. 68.
77.   *External Affairs* (August 1968), 318.
78.   *Ibid.,* (September 1968), 347.
79.   Mrs. N.A. Robertson Papers.
80.   *Spectator,* 2 Aug. 68.

Chapter XIII

1.   J.W. Holmes, "The Late Norman A. Robertson," *External Affairs* (September 1968),348.
2.   *Ibid.*

Bibliography of Primary Sources

A. Manuscript Sources

CANADA

1. *Private Collections*

   Mrs. C.H.A. Armstrong Papers (Toronto)
   Sir Robert Borden Diaries (Toronto)
   Floyd Chalmers Papers (Toronto)
   Professor George Glazebrook Papers (Toronto)
   Mrs. A.D.P. Heeney Papers (Ottawa)
   Professor Brian Heeney Papers (Peterborough)
   W.D. Herridge Papers (Toronto)
   Dr. C.J. Mackenzie Papers (Ottawa)
   J.W. Pickersgill Papers (Ottawa)
   Mrs. A.F.W. Plumptre Papers (Ottawa)
   Mrs. N.A. Robertson Papers (Ottawa)
   H. Basil Robinson Papers (Ottawa)
   Mrs. June Wrong Rogers Papers (Ottawa)

2. *Massey College, University of Toronto*

   Vincent Massey Papers

3. *University of Toronto Library*

   Professor G.W. Brown Papers
   Professor Harry Cassidy Papers
   History Department Records
   Professor G.M. Wrong Papers

4. *York University Archives*

   Professor Edgar McInnis Papers

469

W.A. Riddell Papers

5. *Queen's University Archives*

T.A. Crerar Papers
J.J. Deutsch Papers
Grant Dexter Papers
Donald Gordon Papers
Norman Lambert Papers
J.M. Macdonnell Papers
W.A. Mackintosh Papers
C.G. Power Papers
Norman Rogers Papers
Alex Skelton Papers
John Stevenson Papers
Lord Tweedsmuir (John Buchan) Papers
University Records

6. *University of British Columbia Archives*

Angus Family Collection
Norman Mackenzie Papers
McGill University College Records
Alan Plaunt Papers
University Records

7. *Bishop's University Archives*

T.W.L. MacDermot Papers

8. *Vancouver City Archives*

Angus Family Collection

9. *Bank of Canada Archives*

Bank of Canada Records
Foreign Exchange Control Board Records
Louis Rasminsky Papers
Graham Towers Papers

10. *Department of External Affairs*

Canadian Embassy, Washington, Files (located in Washington, D.C.)
Department of External Affairs Files
Interview Transcripts
Norman Robertson Round Table Transcript
John Starnes Papers
State Papers

11. *Privy Council Office*

Privy Council Office Records 1949-52

12. *Public Archives of Canada*

Government Records:

Civil Service Commission Historical Personnel Records
Department of External Affairs Records
Department of Finance Records
    Economic Advisory Committee Files
Department of Justice Records
Department of Munitions and Supply Records
Department of Trade and Commerce Records
Privy Council Office Records
    Cabinet War Committee Minutes and Papers
Royal Commission on Administrative Classification Records
Royal Commission on Espionage in Government Service Records
Wartime Prices and Trade Board Records

Private Collections:

Laurent Beaudry Papers
R.B. Bennett Papers
Sir Robert Borden Papers
R.B. Bryce Papers
Canadian Institute of International Affairs Records
Violet Markham Carruthers Papers
Loring Christie Papers
Brooke Claxton Papers
Charles Clay Papers
Cooperative Committee on Japanese Canadians Records
General H.D.G. Crerar Papers
John W. Dafoe Papers
Jean Désy Papers
George Drew Papers
R.G. Finlayson Papers
Howard Green Papers
A.D.P. Heeney Papers
Canon Bertal Heeney Papers
C.D. Howe Papers
Alex Johnston Papers
J.D. Kearney Papers
H.R. Kemp Papers

W.L.M. King Papers and Diaries
K.P. Kirkwood Papers
Douglas Le Pan Papers
R.A. MacKay Papers
Ian Mackenzie Papers
Robert Manion Papers
Paul Martin Papers
General A.G.L. McNaughton Papers
W.H. Measures Papers
Admiral L.W. Murray Papers
J.H. Parkinson Papers
L.B. Pearson Papers
General M.A. Pope Diaries
J.L. Ralston Papers
John Read Papers
Escott Reid Papers
Norman A. Robertson Papers
Louis St. Laurent Papers
Watson Sellar Diaries
O.D. Skelton Papers
H.H. Stevens Papers
Georges Vanier Papers
Hume Wrong Papers

UNITED KINGDOM

13. *Public Record Office*

Board of Trade Records
Cabinet Records
Dominions Office Records
Foreign Office Records
Prime Minister's Office Records
Treasury Records

14. *Churchill College, Cambridge*

Clement Attlee Papers
Burgon Bickersteth Papers
P.J. Grigg Papers
Lord Hankey Papers

15. *Marshall Library, Cambridge University*

Lord Keynes Papers

16. *Cambridge University Library, Cambridge*

    Lord Baldwin Papers

17. *Bodleian Library, Oxford University*

    Lionel Curtis Papers
    Mss. English History

18. *University College, Oxford University*

    Clement Attlee Papers

19. *Nuffield College, Oxford University*

    Sir Stafford Cripps Papers

20. *Balliol College, Oxford University*

    College Records

21. *Rhodes House, Oxford*

    Records

22. *Royal Archives, Windsor*

    Duke of Athlone Correspondence (Geo. V/CC53/1063)

23. *British Library of Political and Economic Science, London*

    Hugh Dalton Papers
    Sir Charles Webster Papers

    UNITED STATES

24. *Brookings Institution, Washington, D.C.*

    Records

25. *United States Treasury Department, Washington, D.C.*

    Records

26. *Library of Congress, Washington, D.C.*

    Herbert Feis Papers
    Felix Frankfurter Papers
    Cordell Hull Papers
    F.B. Sayre Papers
    Laurence Steinhardt Papers

27. *United States National Archives, Washington, D.C.*

    Department of Commerce Records

Department of State Records
  Dean Acheson Papers
  John Hickerson Papers
  International Trade Files
  Policy Planning Staff Files

28. *John F. Kennedy Library, Boston*

Walter Heller Papers
J.F. Kennedy Papers
Oral History Program Interview Transcripts

29. *Princeton University Library, Princeton, N.J.*

Livingston Merchant Papers

30. *Harvard University, Boston*

Pierrepont Moffat Papers
William Phillips Papers
University Records

B. Interviews

UNITED KINGDOM

Lord Adeane
Lord Balogh
Professor H.S. Ferns
Lord Franks
Lord Garner
Lord Gladwyn
Sir John Hicks
Lord Kaldor
Malcolm MacDonald
Paul Martin
Professor Dennis Wrong

FRANCE
Mme. Pauline Vanier

NETHERLANDS

Saul Rae

UNITED STATES

Lewis Clark

John Hickerson
Mrs. Paul Lewinson
J. Graham Parsons
Ms. M.J. Tibbetts

CANADA

Douglas Abbott
Geoffrey Andrew
Professor and Mrs. H.F. Angus
Mrs. C.H.A. Armstrong
Mrs. Eleanor Fleming Auston
J.R. Beattie
Professor James Beveridge
Professor V.W. Bladen
Henry Borden
R.B. Bryce
Professor R.B. Byers
Marcel Cadieux
Ross Campbell
Professor J.M.S. Careless
J.V. Clyne
Mrs. Sallee Creighton
Mrs. J.J. Deutsch
John G. Diefenbaker
C.M. Drury
H.F. Feaver
A.O. Gibbons
J. Douglas Gibson
George Glazebrook
Walter Gordon
Howard Green
Mrs. A.D.P. Heeney
John W. Holmes
George Ignatieff
Supt. J.B. James
H.L. Keenleyside
Douglas Le Pan
Jules Léger
A.R.M. Lower
Professor Peyton Lyon
H. Ian Macdonald
J. Scott Macdonald

Mrs. W.A. Mackintosh
David Mansur
L.C. Marsh
Mrs. Roberta Thurlow Morrison
Mrs. Barbara Robertson Morton
Geoffrey Murray
Mrs. Mary Robertson Oliver
Professor M.A. Ormsby
Geoffrey Pearson
J.W. Pickersgill
Sydney Pierce
Mrs. A.F.W. Plumptre
Louis Rasminsky
Escott Reid
C.S.A. Ritchie
Ms. Judith Robertson
Mrs. N.A. Robertson
R.G. Robertson
H. Basil Robinson
Mrs. June Wrong Rogers
Ms. Pauline Sabourin
Mitchell Sharp
David Sim
Arnold Smith
Norman Smith
F.H. Soward
Mr. and Mrs. Graham Spry
John Starnes
Professor Janice Stein
Dr. Frank Turnbull
Walter Turnbull
J.H. Warren
George Watts
Max Wershof

Index

477